American Odysseys

American Odysseys

A History of Colonial North America

TIMOTHY J. SHANNON
Gettysburg College

DAVID N. GELLMAN
DePauw University

New York Oxford
OXFORD UNIVERSITY PRESS

Oxford University Press is a department of the University of Oxford. It furthers the University's objective of excellence in research, scholarship, and education by publishing worldwide.

Oxford New York
Auckland Cape Town Dar es Salaam Hong Kong Karachi
Kuala Lumpur Madrid Melbourne Mexico City Nairobi
New Delhi Shanghai Taipei Toronto

With offices in
Argentina Austria Brazil Chile Czech Republic France Greece
Guatemala Hungary Italy Japan Poland Portugal Singapore
South Korea Switzerland Thailand Turkey Ukraine Vietnam

For titles covered by Section 112 of the US Higher Education Opportunity Act, please visit www.oup.com/us/he for the latest information about pricing and alternate formats.

Published by Oxford University Press
198 Madison Avenue, New York, NY 10016
www.oup.com

Library of Congress Cataloging-in-Publication Data

Shannon, Timothy J. (Timothy John), 1964–
American odysseys : a history of colonial North America / Timothy J. Shannon, Gettysburg College; David N. Gellman, DePauw University.
pages cm
Includes bibliographical references and index.
ISBN 978-0-19-978182-9 (alk. paper)
1. North America—History. 2. North America—History—Colonial period, ca. 1600–1775. 3. North America—Civilization. 4. America—Discovery and exploration. I. Gellman, David Nathaniel. II. Title.
E45.S53 2014
970—dc23 2013005059

Printing number: 9 8 7 6 5 4 3 2 1

Printed in the United States of America
on acid-free paper

For our students, who constantly renew our enthusiasm for early American history.

CONTENTS

PREFACE

The Wonder and Terror of Early America

In 2006 a prominent national magazine published a cover story ranking the "The 100 Most Influential Americans of All Time." The list made for some interesting reading. As one might expect, the Founding Fathers were well represented in the top ten: George Washington (#2), Thomas Jefferson (#3), Alexander Hamilton (#5), and Benjamin Franklin (#6). James Madison clocked in at #13, and Supreme Court Chief Justice John Marshall had a remarkably strong finish at #7. But deeper into the list, it became more difficult to find Americans who lived before 1800. In fact, if one removed the names of those figures whose lives are typically associated with the American Revolution, then only one name on the list belonged undeniably to the colonial era. At #90, New England minister and theologian Jonathan Edwards found himself sandwiched between Walter Lippman and Lyman Beecher, not exactly the Snap, Crackle, and Pop of American history. In other words, the period between 1492 and 1763, what might arguably be called the first half of American history, accounted for exactly 1 percent of "The 100 Most Influential Americans of All Time."[1]

Modern Americans are quite comfortable in the company of the Revolutionary generation but suffer a collective amnesia about anything that preceded it. We build monuments, memorials, and statues to the likes of Washington, Jefferson, and Franklin and presumptuously claim kinship with them, calling them our "fathers." Politicians and pundits invoke them constantly, as if channeling directly their thoughts and opinions on our contemporary issues. It often seems as though our entire political discourse might be boiled down to "WWFFD?" ("What Would the Founding Fathers Do?"). Meanwhile, poor Jonathan Edwards languishes in high-school American literature textbooks, and among colonial Americans, he's the lucky one.

Put another way: if American history was an evening spent at the movies, the colonial era—the period from Columbus to the coming of the Revolution—would be the cartoon before the main feature: a quick diversion that has no bearing on what follows. The characters who populate our stories of the colonial past are indeed cartoonish: gold-crazy conquistadors, swashbuckling pirates, guileless Indians, dour Pilgrims and intolerant Puritans, even a few witches thrown in for good measure. In our popular culture and schooling, we rarely encounter the peoples of the colonial era as individuals or proudly proclaim them our progenitors. We name our cities, banks, insurance companies, and even our beers after the Founding Fathers, but when was the last time an American entrepreneur emblazoned Jonathan Edwards's name on a consumer product or marketing proposal? We invoke the names of Washington, Jefferson, and Franklin because we like to think that we are like them, that they would recognize us and regard us with parental affection if they walked the earth today. Colonial Americans we dismiss as strangers, as people whose values and lives were the antithesis of our modern ways. The present often ignores the past, but more than mere forgetfulness lies behind our dismissal of the colonial era. By reducing it to a few stock figures in story books and grade-school pageants, we divorce it from the rest of our national past, wiping the slate clean for the Revolutionary generation to begin the world anew.

Of course, the United States of America did not arrive new-in-the-box in 1776. In its population, economy, and political institutions, it was the product of a long process of colonization and adaptation that involved Europeans, Africans, and Native Americans. It would be foolish to begin a study of American race relations in 1776 simply because that was when the United States came into existence, and the same is true of any number of other themes and issues—immigration, democracy, western expansion, and free-market capitalism—commonly used to make sense of American history. In its character and people, the modern American nation has deep roots in the colonial era, even if our own present-mindedness often leads us to ignore them. But we must also avoid the temptation to view the colonial era merely as a long and necessary prelude to the American Revolution. Simply because one event followed another does not mean that the first caused the second. The generations who populated North America before 1763 had no greater grasp of what the future held than we do today. To understand the colonial world in which they lived, we must do our best to see it through their eyes and experiences rather than trying to make them into a nation in embryo. Freeing them from the obligation to be the visionaries of American nationhood enables us to humanize them, to see them as individuals rather than as caricatures, to appreciate the circumstances in which they lived, and to comprehend the choices they made.

American Odysseys is our attempt to tell the story of early America in this way, to convey the strangeness of the colonial world to modern readers but at the same time to illuminate the shared humanity that connects the people of the past with those of the present. It is the common prejudice of every generation to assume that it represents the culmination of history, that all that has gone before has existed only to produce the glories of the present age. Such an assumption makes it easy for us to imagine the inhabitants of early America as poor benighted souls, lacking the intellectual and material sophistication we take for granted, but history is not a straight line traveled between simple and complex, between ignorance and enlightenment. The story of early America is one of starts and stops, of inspired dreams and harsh realities, of human idealism and brutal exploitation. It is a story of people who ventured individually and collectively into the unknown to face trials they could have never anticipated. It is in the spirit of recapturing that uncertainty, that combination of wonder and terror, that we have borrowed the word *odyssey* from ancient mythology for our title.

Within the field of American history, the colonial era presents particular challenges. The subject's chronology and geography are expansive and often undefined, and any attempt to define such limits invariably means leaving out what others might put in. We have decided on an Atlantic approach that we believe better approximates than a continental focus the bounds of the colonial world as its inhabitants conceived of them. The Atlantic Ocean was the major avenue for trade, communication, and migration between the Old World and the New, connecting diverse peoples in ways both strange and intriguing to modern readers accustomed to satellite communications and the Internet. Studying the colonial era in terms of geography, however, can also leave students feeling as if they have been given the pieces of a jigsaw puzzle without any sense of how to put these pieces together. *American Odysseys* solves that problem by taking a thematic approach, covering important topics that shaped the colonial experience across time and in a variety of places. So that students can feel a human connection to each of these topics and themes, each chapter begins with the story of an individual who experienced the wonder and terror of colonization firsthand. Taken together, these figures—servants, slaves, explorers, plantation owners—embody the full array of peoples and cultures that gave the colonial era a trans-Atlantic, multicultural character. Of course, taking a thematic approach to the colonial era has potential pitfalls. Readers need to have a feel for time and place in order to make the interpretive comparisons and judgments that are at the heart of the historian's work. To help in that regard, each chapter in *American Odysseys* features a chronology of events described in that chapter. Maps and images throughout the book help visually orient readers to the stories that comprise this concise yet broad-ranging narrative.

The colonial era may lack the precise chronological and geographical boundaries associated with other periods in American history, but from that imprecision springs much of the creativity generated by studying it. In *American Odysseys*, we have attempted to convey the array of innovative scholarship that historians continue to produce about the colonial era, in a way that will prove engaging and comprehensible for those readers encountering this field for the first time.

ACKNOWLEDGEMENTS

We are obliged to the editors of Oxford University Press for their confidence in the project, as well as their support and professionalism. We would like to thank Bruce

Borland and Peter Coveney for initiating this project a number of years ago, and Brian Wheel for his patience in shepherding it forward to completion. We received perceptive commentary from Nicholas Aieta, Westfield State College; Michael Arguello, Palomar College; Shelby Balik, Metropolitan State College of Denver; Carol Higham, University of North Carolina–Charlotte; and Matt Mulcahy, Loyola College in Maryland. Their suggestions have helped make this a better book. Karen Omer oversaw the final stages of the manuscript's preparation.

Tim Shannon would like to thank his colleagues at Gettysburg College for providing a working environment so conducive to the teacher-scholar model. He would also like to thank Becca Barth in the History Department office and Natalie Hinton and Meghan Kelly in Musselman Library for their assistance. Family and friends have gone above and beyond the usual limits of patience and encouragement as they have listened to him talk about this project. In that respect, Colleen and Caroline, Daniel, and Elizabeth are as usual in a league of their own.

David Gellman would like to thank DePauw University's former Dean of Faculty Kerry Pannell and Vice President for Academic Affairs David Harvey for ensuring that he had the time and flexibility to pursue this opportunity. The Professional Development Fund overseen by the Faculty Development Committee defrayed the cost of acquiring images. Colleagues Anne Harris, Glen Kuecker, and James Ward offered their perceptive insights about portions of the manuscript. John Schlotterbeck shared books and enthusiasms. Rick Provine, Jamie Knapp, Brooke Cox, Mikah Pritchard, and Jin Kim kept the scholarly and technical resources flowing. David owes special thanks to Claire Dunnett, Frank Fennell, and Sheila Z. Willer for their timely visits. Monica provides the encouragement to go for it and the loving support to follow through. The boundless curiosity of Hannah and Ben inspire him to write. Their impressive patience allows him to finish.

Tim Shannon
Gettysburg, February 2013
David Gellman
Greencastle, February 2013

NOTE

1. *Atlantic Monthly* (December 2006), 59–78. We draw inspiration here, in part, from Richard Hofstadter's observation that "what could still be called not so long ago the entire first half of American history—that is, the colonial period down to about the 1760's—has largely been lost to the American imagination." See *The Progressive Historians: Turner, Beard, Parrington* (New York: Random House, 1968), 5.

CHAPTER 1

Three Worlds

In the spring of 1731, a runaway slave being held by the sheriff of Kent County, Delaware, caught the attention of some local colonists. Although the slave did not speak a word of English, his demeanor and actions indicated that he was from circumstances unlike those of any other African these men had encountered before. When given pen and paper, the slave wrote words in Arabic, and when he read them aloud, listeners recognized the words "Allah" and "Mahommed." His refusal to drink from a glass of wine further convinced the locals that he was Muslim, but they could not "imagine of what country he was, or how he got thither." From his "affable carriage, and the easy composure of his countenance," they knew "he was no common slave."

Over the next few days, the mystery man's origins came to light. "An old Negroe man, who lived in that neighbourhood" spoke with the stranger using Wolof, a West African language. Through this translator, the runaway told his jailers that he was Ayuba Suleiman Diallo, son of the ruler of Bondou, a West African country between the Senegal and Gambia rivers. He had two wives and four children back home, and was in line to inherit his father's throne. As he had already exhibited, he was an observant Muslim and was also literate in Arabic. A bit more than a year previously, his father had sent him to "sell two Negroes, and to buy paper, and some other necessaries" from the captain of an English ship anchored in the Gambia River. But Ayuba could not agree on terms with the captain and so crossed the Gambia into Mandingo country to find better prospects. There he was captured by slave traders who sold him to the very ship captain with whom he had unsuccessfully conducted business a few days before. Before he could be redeemed by his father, Ayuba found himself confined to the hold of a slave ship and headed for Annapolis, Maryland, where he was sold to a tobacco planter and put to work in his fields.

The local gentlemen of Kent County were impressed to have an African prince on their hands, but that did not stop them from returning Ayuba to his master. It could not have been a happy reunion, for Ayuba's master had already found him in "no ways suited for business" when it came to growing tobacco. Ayuba remained steadfast in pursuit of his freedom. He wrote a letter in Arabic begging his father to rescue him and entrusted it to a ship captain, who spread word of Ayuba's plight. Some London philanthropists took up his cause and raised the money necessary to purchase his freedom and passage back across the Atlantic. Ayuba arrived in

Figure 1.1 Job Ben Solomon, or Ayuba Suleiman Diallo. This image of Ayuba first appeared in a London periodical, *Gentleman's Magazine*, in 1750. It is based on a portrait painted during his stay in London in 1733. Courtesy of the Manuscript, Archives, and Rare Book Library, Emory University.

England in April 1733, having acquired enough English along the way to converse with his benefactors and become a minor celebrity in London. His hosts translated his name as Job, the son of Solomon the son of Abraham, draping his story in biblical allusions to the Old Testament figures of Abraham the patriarch, Solomon the king, and Job the faithful victim of God's inscrutable will. Ayuba even had an audience with the royal family, appearing in a "rich silk dress, made up after his own country fashion" and receiving gifts valued at £500 (see Figure 1.1). After a few months in England, he traveled back to West Africa onboard a slave ship owned by the Royal African Company. He worked as an agent for the company in the Gambia region and eventually returned to Bondou, where he assumed his place as king, his father having died during his absence.[1]

Ayuba's story was first published in London in 1734, but its content and themes echoed stories popular in Europe since the Middle Ages. Ballads, travel narratives, and saints' lives from the medieval era told similar tales of mistaken identity, captivity in foreign lands, and life-saving intervention by kind strangers. To English readers of the time, Ayuba's odyssey would have called to mind the plight of their own King Richard, who had been held captive while returning from the Third Crusade in the twelfth century, or perhaps the fate of Christian sailors enslaved by Muslim pirates sailing in the Mediterranean. Two elements, however, distinguished Ayuba from those precedents. First, his travels took him across the Atlantic Ocean to America, a place unknown to Europeans and Africans before 1492. Second, the hero of this story was a Muslim set adrift in a Christian world; it turned the standard medieval narrative of captivity and redemption inside out. Ayuba's world, in other words, was one of shrinking distances and changing perspectives. The Atlantic Ocean had become a highway rather than a barrier between Africa, Europe, and America, making people on those continents more capable of

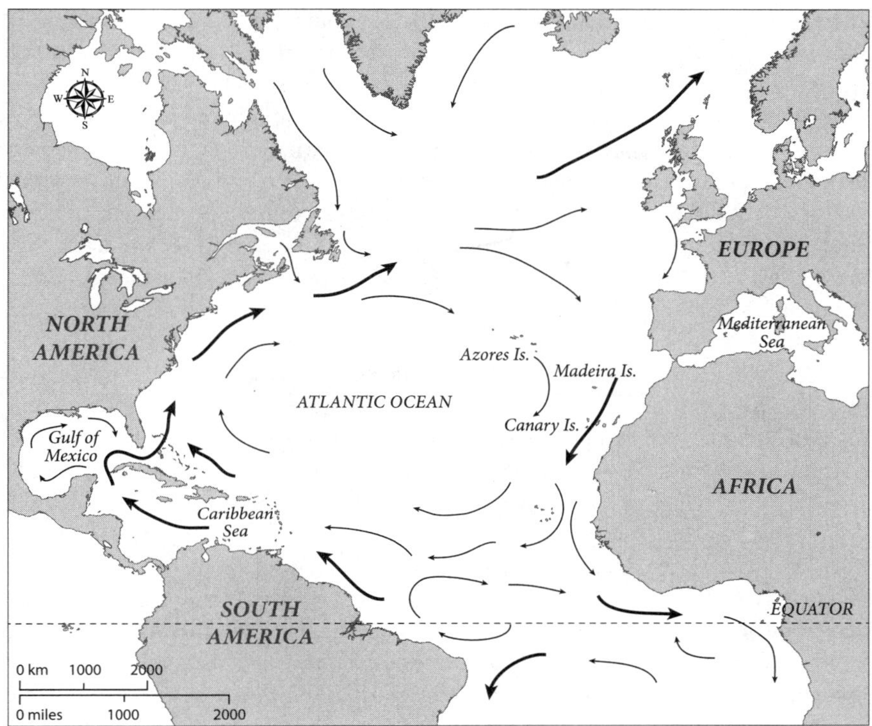

Map 1.1 The Atlantic Ocean.

imagining worlds unlike their own, where humanity exhibited endless variety (see Map 1.1).

Before we can explore the world Ayuba knew in the 1730s, we must first comprehend the ones that provided its foundation: Africa, America, and Europe on the eve of trans-Atlantic exploration and colonization. There is an easy tendency to regard Columbus's famous voyage of 1492 as drawing the curtain on one era and opening it on another, but the transition between the medieval and modern was much slower and more subtle than that. In the case of Europe and Africa, Islam had been playing a vital role for centuries in how these two continents interacted with each other. America was of course shut off from such exchange before Columbus, but the medieval frame of mind would play a significant role in how Europeans approached the native peoples they encountered there. Despite the distance and isolation that separated Africa, America, and Europe before 1492, the societies that inhabited those continents possessed certain common attributes that readily connected their worlds to each other and to Ayuba's. In that shared humanity rests the start of our story.

WEST AFRICA IN THE ISLAMIC WORLD

Bondou, the state from which Ayuba hailed, was part of the Fula kingdom in the Senegambia region of West Africa. As Ayuba's background and education would attest, this part of Africa had a long history of contact and exchange with outsiders from North Africa and other regions bordering the Mediterranean Sea. Ayuba may have been an utter stranger to the colonists who encountered him in Maryland and Delaware, but he came from a cosmopolitan world connected by trade and religion with northern Africa, southern Europe, and the Arabian Peninsula. In the centuries before Columbus, this exchange took place over land, via merchants and traders who traversed the caravan routes of the Sahara Desert. Such long-distance trade led to a diffusion of goods, ideas, and technologies that made West Africa a dynamic and diverse place, already primed for the economic opportunities that would be opened by the arrival of European seafarers in the fifteenth century.

The cultural diversity of West Africa reflected the variety found in its geography and climate. Immediately south of the Sahara, desert gave way to a dry region of scrubby vegetation known as the *sahel* and inhabited by nomadic herdsmen of cattle and camels. Further south, the *sahel* turned into the savanna, grasslands suitable for growing crops and raising livestock. The ease of overland travel on foot or horseback in this region made possible the rise of expansive political kingdoms. Moving closer to the equator, rainfall increased, creating a zone of tropical rainforests in which river transportation was far more efficient than overland travel, and tropical diseases prevented human populations from breeding large animals. South of the equator in central Africa, this pattern reversed itself and rainforests gradually gave way to more temperate grasslands and forest.

North African traders began crossing the Sahara Desert into what they called the Sudan ("the land of the Blacks") in the fourth and fifth centuries, relying on camels brought from the Arabian Peninsula for their transportation. Caravans carried salt, woven cloth, and other goods into sub-Saharan Africa and returned with gold, ivory, and slaves for Mediterranean markets. The rapid spread of Islam across North Africa during the seventh century made religion part of this exchange. Muslim merchants traveled into West Africa and established businesses and centers for scholarship and worship in communities along their trade routes. They brought Arabic literacy, mathematics, medicine, and other advanced learning of their day with them. Their presence was especially strong in the savanna region, between the Senegal and Niger rivers, where populous trading cities like Timbuktu and Gao became crossroads between Mediterranean and African cultures. Great African kingdoms—Ghana, Mali, Songhai, and Jolof—rose and fell in this region between the eighth and fifteenth centuries, their expansion and administration fueled by wealth and knowledge reaped from the trans-Saharan trade (see Map 1.2). Occasionally, African rulers from this region made pilgrimages to Mecca, where the size and wealth of their traveling entourages impressed their Arabian and North African counterparts. This was the world to which Ayuba and his country of Bondou belonged.

The influence of Islam in West African society declined as the savannas turned into rainforests, but long-distance trade still connected equatorial Africa with the Mediterranean world. Along the Guinea Coast, which stretched south of

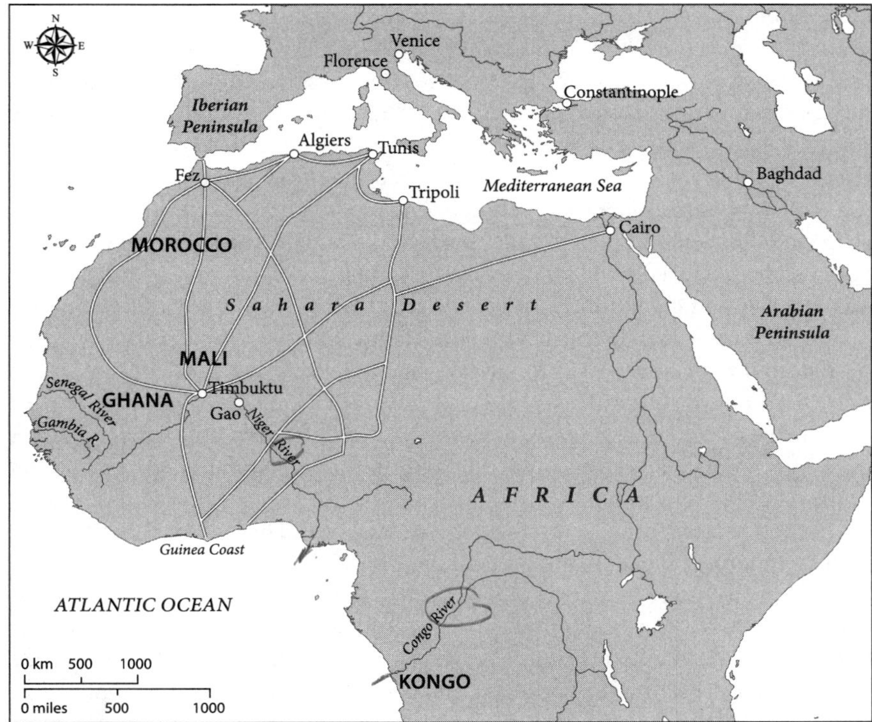

Map. 1.2 Africa in the Islamic World, *c.* 1300.

the Gambia River to the Niger River delta, political states tended to be smaller and more fractured. These "ministates," as one historian has called them, were often the geographic size of a large county or small state in the modern United States.[2] Further south, in the vicinity of the Congo River delta, ministates existed alongside large kingdoms such as the Kongo and Ndongo.

Ultimately, it is misleading to describe West African society in terms of political states and borders. Trade, closely related languages, and habits of culture united people over considerable distances, and African rulers were always more interested in commanding authority over people than land. Dependents, whether they were family members or slaves, could be made to grow the crops that produced wealth; land without workers was worthless. African farmers cultivated a variety of native grains, including millet and sorghum, as well as crops imported from Asia and North Africa, such as rice and cotton. West Africans were also skilled craftsmen who produced pottery, cloth, leather goods, and metal wares of copper, brass, and iron.

Slavery played a significant role in this social and economic system. Whether in the savannas of Senegambia or the equatorial rainforests, African societies relied extensively on slaves to grow crops and produce goods. Slaves also served as soldiers and bureaucrats for powerful rulers and as servants and concubines in the households of the wealthy. Most slaves entered that condition as a result of being taken captive in warfare, although others fell into it as punishment for crimes they had committed or as payment for debts they or their family could not otherwise settle. The exact nature of slavery and the laws and customs that governed it varied from one culture to another, but all recognized the slave as someone cut off from the protective bonds of kinship within the wider community. Slaves were strangers stripped of lineage and family, and thus could be bought and sold with outsiders. Some slaves acquired their freedom and eventual incorporation into their masters' families and communities, most typically by marriage or exemplary service. Slavery in West Africa, in short, was a well-defined but permeable institution. Any person could fall into it as a result of misfortune, but that same person might also climb out. Furthermore, in a world of small communities oriented toward subsistence agriculture, the work of slaves did not differ substantially from that of their free counterparts. A well-educated merchant like Ayuba might have found himself in "no ways suited for [the] business" of cultivating tobacco, but most of his African contemporaries, whether free or slave, would have been all too familiar with earning their bread by the sweat of their brow.

Before the fifteenth century, sub-Saharan Africans and Europeans had contact with each other by way of intermediaries in North Africa. The trans-Saharan trade brought black African slaves into Mediterranean markets, and Muslim merchants and scholars wrote travel narratives describing the peoples they encountered in the Sudan. In fact, most of what medieval Europeans knew about the geography and people of Africa came from Islamic sources, such as the widely translated and reprinted *Geographical History of Africa* first published by the Moroccan diplomat Leo Africanus in Italy in 1550. Muslim scholars were the first to postulate that the black skin color of sub-Saharan Africans was proof of their descent from the Old Testament figure Ham, a son of Noah cursed by his father to have his offspring live as servants to the rest of mankind. While some medieval artwork depicted black Africans in noble settings and poses, such as diplomats visiting the papal court in Rome or as figures in images of the Magi paying homage to the infant Christ, a prejudice also evolved in Europe against black skin color. Long before the voyages of Columbus, medieval Europeans had adopted from Islamic writers the term "blackamoor" to distinguish supposedly less civilized sub-Saharan Africans from the lighter-skinned "Moors" of North Africa.

It is much harder to determine just what sub-Saharan Africans knew about Europeans before Portuguese sailors began showing up along West Africa's coast in the mid-fifteenth century. According to accounts written by the earliest Portuguese sailors to navigate the Gambia River, Africans marveled at their ships and weapons and were surprised by the whiteness of their skin, but they were also ready to trade or fight them. Centuries of encounters with North Africans and Arabians had in some ways primed sub-Saharan Africans for the arrival of Europeans by sea in the fifteenth century. These newcomers would not cause African states to crumble or cultures to disintegrate.

AMERICA BEFORE COLUMBUS

When Ayuba arrived in North America in 1730, the indigenous population of the Chesapeake Bay had already suffered severely from contact with colonizing Europeans. Many had succumbed to diseases brought by the newcomers, while others had been killed in wars with them or had their land wrestled away by plantation owners. There were still Indians living in the Chesapeake in 1730, but their political and territorial autonomy had been broken, and they scrambled to make a living on the margins of a growing colonial economy. Nowhere in Ayuba's narrative does it mention him ever setting eyes on an Indian during his stay in America.

Had Ayuba arrived 150 years earlier, on the eve of England's first attempt to colonize North America, he would have encountered a much different world. The Chesapeake Bay, like much of coastal North America, was home to a large Native American population that practiced a mixture of fishing, hunting, and agriculture. Indigenous peoples lived in towns along the major waterways, spoke a variety of tongues, and formed political ties between their communities that created powerful chiefdoms. In many ways, it was a world that resembled Ayuba's native West Africa, where kinship fixed one's place in a community and trade and warfare shaped one's interaction with outsiders. But such parallels also gloss over significant differences between these two worlds that would play an important role in America's encounter with Europe and Africa.

For a long time, pre-Columbian America (that is, before Columbus initiated European contact and colonization) has been a blank canvas on which artists and scholars have painted pictures rooted more in fantasy than reality. Not long after Columbus's first voyage, images began appearing in Europe that depicted America as a new Garden of Eden, overflowing with natural bounty and people whose nakedness indicated their innocence from sin and corruption. During the Enlightenment, European philosophers speculated about life in the state of nature by drawing comparisons to Native American societies. "Thus in the beginning," John Locke wrote as he theorized about the origins of civil government, "all the world was America."[3] European travelers in North America were fond of noting that the landscape lacked physical evidence of the past; there was no equivalent to Europe's Roman ruins to remind passersby that civilizations had risen and fallen in their footsteps. In such depictions, America was quite literally a land before time, its inhabitants frozen in a perpetual present until Columbus arrived and made history move forward.

Archaeologists have uncovered the pre-Columbian past of America that earlier observers were content to pass over. Working with evidence recovered from sites throughout North America, they have traced the human occupation of the continent to at least ten thousand to thirty-five thousand years ago, although they disagree considerably among themselves about how and when these Paleo-Indians (the first human inhabitants of America) arrived. The standard story describes the Paleo-Indians as hunters from northern Asia who followed game animals across the Bering Land Bridge from Siberia into Alaska about thirteen thousand years ago, a migration made possible by the lowering of the world's ocean levels during the last Ice Age. Once in North America, these nomadic peoples followed an ice-free corridor between glaciers in northwest Canada into more temperate climates, eventually dispersing to populate Central and South America as well. This theory of a single overland migration from Asia is based in large part on an archaeological excavation conducted in Clovis, New Mexico, during the 1930s. Fluted spearheads recovered from this site were most likely made by nomadic hunters of big game, and the subsequent discovery of similar "Clovis points" at other sites indicated a broad diffusion of this technology among the earliest Americans.

In recent years, this consensus on human origins in the Americas has come under fire on a number of fronts. Some contemporary Native American peoples disavow Western science as a means of explaining their origins, preferring instead oral traditions that describe their genesis in worlds above or below the earth. Other scholars find it doubtful that peoples traveling by way of the Bering Land Bridge at the end of the last Ice Age could have moved and reproduced fast enough to account for the antiquity of some archaeological sites in South America. Collectively known as "diffusionists" (although the label does not imply agreement among them), these theorists argue that other migrations may have gone on before, after, or contemporaneously with the Bering migration. Their theories range from the plausible (a sea-borne migration from northern Asia along the western coasts of North and South America) to the unlikely (trans-Pacific trips by Polynesians) to the absurd (ancient Phoenicians crossing the Atlantic to mine copper in the Great Lakes), and so each alternative theory to the Bering migration needs to be judged on its own merits. The most recent theory to gain scholarly support combines archaeological evidence with linguistic and genetic analysis to argue that Paleo-Indians came to America from Siberia in three distinct waves of migration that started fifteen thousand years ago, of which the Clovis people were only one and most likely the last.

The diffusionists may have successfully challenged the old "Clovis first" consensus on human arrival in the Americas, but material artifacts recovered from Clovis-related sites remain our best window into the world of the Paleo-Indians. They were hunter-gatherers who traveled in small bands, made their homes in rock shelters, and manufactured their tools and weapons from stone, bone, and wood. In other words, they were "cavemen" who resembled in their technology and social organization other human societies around the globe approximately twelve thousand years ago. During the Archaic Era (about eleven thousand to three thousand years ago), these first Americans began to domesticate plants, a dramatic development that made possible food surpluses, which in turn led to larger, sedentary populations with greater social and economic specialization. Plant cultivation in the Americas lagged behind that in the Old World, but not remarkably so. In the region of the Middle East known as the Fertile Crescent, crop production emerged *c.* 8500 B.C.E. (i.e., "before the Common Era"); in the Valley of Mexico, it occurred about three thousand years later. Just as the cultivation of grains in the Middle East gave rise to the ancient civilizations of Mesopotamia and Egypt, so too did the cultivation of maize (corn) make Mexico the cradle of civilization for the Western Hemisphere. The Olmec culture, which emerged around 1000 B.C.E., was the first in a series of Mesoamerican civilizations (including also the Maya, Toltec, and Mexica) distinguished by their large urban populations, monumental public architecture, and advanced astronomy and mathematics.

Farming slowly radiated outward from its origins in the Valley of Mexico. Native North American farmers adapted maize, beans, and squash—the staples of Mesoamerican agriculture—to regions as various as the arid Southwest and the stony shores of New England. Generally speaking, the farther north these populations lived, the shorter their growing seasons, and so the less significant the role of farming in their food production. For example, people living near the Great Lakes combined maize cultivation with seasonal moves to hunting and fishing grounds. Rather than being nomadic, they recognized these resource centers as their own and defended them against intrusion by outsiders. In the Southwest and Southeast, where the growing season was longer, populations were less mobile, but produced greater agricultural surpluses, and so they became larger, more sedentary, and more socially stratified. The ancient Pueblo civilization adapted maize cultivation and flourished around 1000 C.E. ("the Common Era"), living in densely populated communities clustered along the Rio Grande in modern New Mexico and Colorado. The irrigation canals and roads built by the ancient peoples of the Southwest testify to their technological and political sophistication, and the elaboration of their spiritual beliefs and practices is evident in the circular *kivas* that served as ceremonial centers for their towns, or pueblos.

In the Southeast, maize cultivation likewise powered a succession of sophisticated civilizations. Collectively known as "mound builders," the Adena (800 B.C.E.–100 C.E.), Hopewell (*c.* 100–500 C.E.), and Mississippian (700–1300 C.E.) peoples flourished as far north as Minnesota, as far west as Oklahoma, and as far east as the Carolinas, but their great artery was the lower Mississippi River and its tributaries (see Map 1.3). Farming the flood plains of this river system, they built towns distinguished by earthen mounds that served as burial chambers and ceremonial centers. The Mississippian city of Cahokia (near modern St. Louis), which flourished *c.* 1100 C.E., featured public plazas and truncated pyramids reminiscent of the great cities of Mesoamerica. Excavations here and at other Mississippian sites reveal evidence of extreme social inequality: elites were buried with elaborate grave goods, but the remains of apparent victims of human sacrifice (most likely killed to accompany their masters into the afterlife) show evidence of malnutrition and short lives spent in hard labor.

The similarities between the Mississippian mound builders and the Mesoamerican civilizations raise the possibility of contact and exchange between the Valley of Mexico and the Mississippi Valley, but there is no scholarly consensus as to how and when this may have occurred. These parallels, however, do speak to a diffusion of technology and ideas in ancient America that accompanied the spread of maize cultivation. As was the case in the Old World, agriculture not only fueled population growth in North America; it was also the driving force behind the rise and

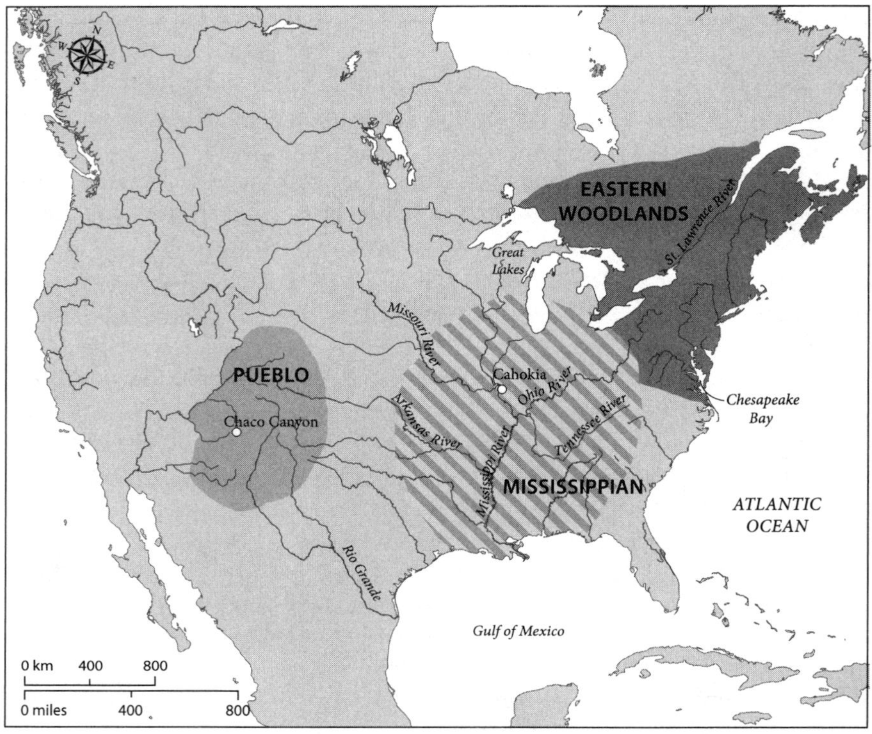

Map. 1.3 Native American Culture Areas.

fall of great civilizations. Growing and storing surplus food gave farming societies the ability to conduct warfare on a grand scale and to enslave conquered populations to work on massive construction projects, such as pyramids, plazas, and canals. The emergence of priest and warrior castes possessed of specialized knowledge and skills made it easier for the elite to assert social and spiritual power over the many. Tribute payment rendered in the form of crops or captives allowed chiefdoms and empires to exploit the resources of regions and populations distant from their own. And when crops failed because of natural disaster or long-term climate change, these civilizations declined as people abandoned urban centers and dispersed to seek security and subsistence elsewhere. By the sixteenth century, Cahokia's population was long gone, but elements of the Mississippian civilization were still evident in the powerful chiefdoms, bountiful cornfields, and town plazas Spanish conquistadors found among the Choctaws, Natchez, and other southern Indian nations.

The Eastern Woodlands, stretching from the northern Atlantic coast to the Great Lakes, were another major zone of Native American cultural development. Maize cultivation came later to this region's peoples, who lived on the fringe of the Mississippian cultural complex, in smaller, more egalitarian communities with less elaborate architecture and social distinctions. Eastern Woodlands peoples were seasonally mobile, gathering at their village sites for planting and harvesting, but dispersing to family hunting and fishing camps for long periods during the year. This mobility was also reflected in their gender roles and division of labor. The village community was dominated by women, who tended the fields, processed animal hides, and cared for children. Adult men spent considerable time away from home, engaged in hunting and conducting trade, warfare, and diplomacy with outsiders. Lineage and kinship determined the most important social relations. Families belonged to clans (usually designated by animal totems, such as the bear, wolf, or turtle clan), and clanship gave an individual claim to hospitality and protection beyond his or her home.

Europeans tended to classify Native Americans into "nations" defined by shared languages and territories, but for most Native Americans, clanship would have been the first and most important definer of identity beyond immediate family. In the Eastern Woodlands, communities governed themselves according to councils of chiefs selected by the elderly women, or matrons, of each clan. Without the wealth or military power exhibited by the elites in Mississippian societies, these chiefs relied on persuasion and consensus-building to sustain their authority. The same structure of clanship also helped organize and sustain political confederacies among Eastern Woodlands peoples. The most famous of these, the Haudenosaunee (known to the English as the Five Nations and to the French as the Iroquois), emerged in the region south of Lake Ontario on the eve of contact with Europeans. The Mohawks, Oneidas, Onondagas, Cayugas, and Senecas formed a union that prevented war among them and facilitated their cooperation in dealing with outsiders. The Grand Council of their confederacy was made up of chiefs selected by the matrons of important lineages in each clan. It met annually to engage in rituals that renewed peace among them and raised up new chiefs in place of deceased ones, thereby perpetuating their union across generations.

There was no single human civilization in North America before 1492. As this brief tour of the Valley of Mexico, the Southwest, the Mississippi Valley, and the Eastern Woodlands indicates, humans in pre-Columbian America produced a variety of civilizations that reflected the physical diversity of the continent they occupied. As in the Eastern Hemisphere, the uneven spread of agriculture had a profound effect on population growth and social development. Where rainfall and growing season allowed, maize cultivation encouraged populations to become more sedentary and stratified. Where people relied more extensively on hunting, fishing, and gathering for their subsistence, they remained more mobile and egalitarian in their political and social orders. When Columbus sailed in 1492, the total human population in the Western Hemisphere probably numbered somewhere between fifty and one hundred million, with anywhere from two to ten million of those living in what would become the modern nations of the United States and Canada. Those populations living north of the Rio Grande spoke approximately 250 distinct languages (which linguists have divided into twelve major groups or "stocks"), another indicator of the remarkable diversity exhibited by Native American societies on the eve of their contact with Europeans.

Pre-Columbian populations in the Americas developed in parallel but isolated circumstances with human societies in the Eastern Hemisphere. Societies on both sides of the Atlantic passed the same landmarks: the domestication of plants, the shift from nomadic to sedentary populations, the development of powerful states. The Maya peoples of Central America had the most accurate calendar of any civilization in the world at their time, and the Incas of Andean South America built a road system and imperial bureaucracy capable of ruling millions of people. Cahokia probably had as many inhabitants in 1100 C.E. as contemporary London or Paris. While such comparisons are useful reminders of the achievements of pre-Columbian Native American societies, they also shroud some very important differences between human societies on opposite sides of the globe.

First, while it is true that Native Americans were productive farmers, they did not domesticate animals to serve as a source of food. They did domesticate dogs for hunting and companionship, and in South America, they used llamas and alpacas for transportation and wool, but humans in pre-Columbian America did not raise animals to eat their meat, drink their milk, or use their manure as fertilizer. None of the major domesticated species found elsewhere in the world—goats, sheep, cattle, pigs, and horses—were indigenous to America. Not only did Native Americans lack this important food source, but the absence of domestic animals also slowed the transition from nomadic hunting and gathering to more sedentary living. On the other hand, the absence of domestic animals in pre-Columbian America may have improved human health. The meat, milk, and manure of livestock have always been vectors of disease transmission from animals to humans. Illnesses such as anthrax and cowpox have adapted from four-legged to two-legged hosts, with devastating consequences ("mad cow disease," which humans can contract from eating beef, is one contemporary reminder of this process).

Second, while Native American civilizations did create sophisticated tools and processes for manufacturing shelter, clothing, and weapons, their metal-working technology did not develop apace with that of the Eastern Hemisphere. Humans in Asia, Africa, and Europe learned to mine and refine ores into metal objects in two great epochs: the Bronze Age, which began six thousand years ago in the Middle East, and the Iron Age, which began three thousand later. Native Americans mined soft metals such as copper, silver, and gold and worked them into decorative and utilitarian objects, but they never manufactured bronze or iron, instead relying on stone, clay, bone, and wood for their tools and weapons. Nor did they apply the wheel to any purpose in farming, milling, or transportation. In the global history of human technology, they remained quite literally in the Stone Age until their contact with Europeans.

America's isolation from the rest of the world after the last Ice Age had a profound impact on the development of human life there. The Pacific and Atlantic oceans prevented the diffusion of new ideas and technologies from the Eastern Hemisphere to the Western. This is not to say that Native Americans remained in a state of suspended animation, waiting for the arrival of more sophisticated peoples to awaken them. The achievements of pre-Columbian populations are testimony to the human ingenuity that powered the rise of civilizations on both sides of the globe. The Mesoamericans built pyramids with engineering skills derived independently from the ancient Egyptians and Romans. Maya astronomers plotted the heavens without instruments or mathematics borrowed from the Islamic World. Working in the arid Southwest, Pueblo farmers made maize a staple of their diet without iron tools to dig their irrigation systems or mill wheels to grind their corn. These accomplishments were undeniably great in their own right, but they are also reminders of the physical and intellectual isolation that set Native Americans apart from the rest of the world before 1492.

THE ORIGINS OF EARLY MODERN EUROPE

Ayuba's odyssey included a stop for several months in England during his trip home. His hosts regarded him as a visiting foreign dignitary and provided him with comfortable lodgings, new clothes, and an audience before the royal family. Although these scenes played out in the 1730s, they had precedent in visits by African princes and diplomats to European courts during the fifteenth century. In Ayuba's own lifetime, England's expanding trade and naval power in the Mediterranean had brought it into closer contact with the Islamic states of North Africa's Barbary Coast. Thus, Ayuba's African background and Muslim faith would have struck English audiences as exotic but not incomprehensible. His tale of wrongful enslavement made him an object of sympathy among London's political and social elites, who considered acts of humanitarianism directed toward suffering strangers a mark of their own refinement and worldliness. These same people, of course, were complicit in the slave trade that had brought Ayuba across the Atlantic in the first place. They invested in merchant companies that sent slave ships to West Africa, and they displayed their wealth by consuming goods produced by enslaved laborers in overseas colonies. In this contradiction rests the key to understanding Europe's encounter with Africa and America. The quest for profit drove Europe's overseas expansion in the early modern era, but equally important were intellectual transformations that made Europeans curious about worlds and peoples beyond their own.

Before the fifteenth century, the Mediterranean Sea was the primary highway for Europe's encounters with the outside world. The Mediterranean connected southern Europe with Asia Minor and North Africa, and its eastern seaports provided a gateway to the Silk Road, an overland route through Central Asia that connected Europe to India and China. Under the rule of the Roman Empire, the Mediterranean had been a conveyor belt of people, goods, and ideas throughout the ancient world, making possible economic and cultural exchange over vast distances. In ancient Britain, the western edge of the Romans' known world, soldiers drank wine imported from Italy, wrote dispatches in Latin, and built temples to a Persian god named Mithras. The political and cultural integration of the Roman world also made possible the rapid expansion of Christianity, a new monotheistic faith that originated in Palestine but spread throughout the empire after it was embraced by Emperor Constantine in the early fourth century. As Rome's power declined in the fifth century, this unity of law, language, and religion disintegrated along with it. Waves of migrations by Germanic tribes—Goths, Vandals, Franks, Angles, Saxons, and others—swept aside Roman civilization north of the Alps, initiating an era of endemic violence and insecurity aptly called the Dark Ages.

In the eastern Mediterranean, the story was different. Constantinople (modern Istanbul, Turkey) inherited Roman law and literacy and became the seat of Christianity in the eastern half of the old empire. In the early seventh century, Islam emerged as another monotheistic faith rooted in the scriptural authority of the Old Testament. From its origins on the Arabian Peninsula, Islam spread rapidly in all directions, making use of the same Mediterranean currents of trade and communication that had helped power the rise of Christianity. Like Christianity, Islam brought to its adherents a sacred text, the Qur'an, and a written language, Arabic, for comprehending it. It also brought a system of law and personal conduct by which the faithful were to order their lives. It was, in other words, a universal creed capable of containing multitudes, regardless of culture, race, or ethnicity. By way of conquest and commerce, Islam spread into India and Central Asia, to Palestine, Syria, and Persia in the Middle East, and along North Africa from Egypt to the Atlantic coast of Morocco. From North Africa, it also expanded into Europe by way of the Iberian Peninsula. Crossing the Straits of Gibraltar, Muslim armies conquered the old Roman province of Hispania (modern Spain and Portugal) and renamed it al-Andalus. The Pyrenees, the mountain range that forms the border between France and Spain, became the dividing line between Christianity and Islam in western Europe for the next several centuries.

In hindsight, the Muslim conquest of al-Andalus was fortuitous for Europe because it provided a lifeline to important cultural and technological achievements happening elsewhere in the world. During the centuries it took the Christian church in Rome to proselytize and convert the barbarian kingdoms to its north, literacy and learning in the Western Christian world hung on by a thread, confined mostly to a professional caste of monks living in isolated monasteries. By comparison, Islamic Spain was a vibrant place, a crossroads that brought together Muslim, Christian, and Jewish peoples to trade and study. Working in Arabic, Latin, Greek, and Hebrew, scholars there translated and circulated the works of the ancient world, while sailors and merchants learned technologies imported from India and China. So-called Arabic numerals came to Europe from India by way of this exchange, as did the abacus and eventually algebra. Paper-making, the magnetic compass, gunpowder, and the printing press were likewise imported to Europe from China over the long course of Islamic domination in the Mediterranean world. The scholars and librarians of the Islamic World helped preserve the legacy of the ancient Greeks and Romans for future generations, but they also advanced learning in the Western world by transmitting throughout the Mediterranean the achievements of Arabia, Asia, and India.

Despite such fertile economic and intellectual exchange, medieval Europe's Christian identity was forged in opposition to Islam. The first recorded use of "Europeans" in the modern sense of the word was made by an eighth-century scribe chronicling the wars between Christian and Islamic forces in al-Andalus. The papacy in Rome, medieval Europe's most sophisticated bureaucracy and richest institution, initiated the Crusades in the late eleventh century to conquer the Holy Land from its Muslim rulers. For two centuries, Christian armies raised under the pope's orders marched and sailed into the eastern Mediterranean, establishing "Crusader kingdoms" that accelerated contact and exchange between the East and West. Ultimately, the Crusaders failed to return Jerusalem to Christendom, but they extended Europe's long-distance trade and fired the popular imagination with tales of far-off lands and unlimited riches. In a manner that anticipated the European arrival in America several centuries later, the Crusades unleashed a mad dash for profits justified in the language of a high-minded spiritual quest. This potent combination of religious militancy and entrepreneurial spirit had remarkable resilience in the face of the human suffering it caused.

The Islamic World system peaked in the early fourteenth century. Hundreds of years in the making, it was disrupted within a few decades by the passage of bubonic plague along its trade routes. From China to Arabia to Europe, the epidemic spread, devastating populations and disrupting old trade networks. The Mongol Empire, which had governed much of Asia in the thirteenth century, shrunk in power and was replaced in China by the isolationist Ming dynasty. In Asia Minor, the Ottoman Turks took advantage of the power vacuum left by the Mongols. They captured Constantinople in 1453, renamed it Istanbul, and carried their wars of conquest into the Balkans, cutting off Europe's access to the Black Sea and overland routes to Asia. Approximately one-third of Europe's population succumbed to the plague, plunging the medieval world into famine, political unrest, and spiritual crisis. The known world was collapsing around the living, promising nothing better than the hope of salvation in the next.

Out of this darkness arose the rebirth in European arts and letters known as the Renaissance. The Renaissance began in the Italian city-states of Florence and Venice, whose leading families were closely connected to Islamic merchants throughout the Mediterranean. Using the wealth acquired from that trade, they became patrons of scholars, painters, sculptors, and architects who drew their inspiration from the ancient Greeks and Romans. The retrieval of classical works on literature, science, philosophy, and history—made possible in part by the libraries of the Islamic World—revived the liberal arts as a system of education still practiced in colleges and universities today. It broke the monopoly that the Church had held on European education for centuries and offered an alternative to Holy Scripture for understanding the natural and metaphysical worlds.

The medieval mind had emphasized the weakness and corruption of the flesh and celebrated the suffering and trials of a life spent in pursuit of spiritual salvation. The Renaissance reversed that equation, elevating humanity and the pleasures of the physical world. Painters and sculptors depicted the body as a thing of beauty rather than a vessel of sin. Those who could afford it reveled in the luxuries of imported fabrics, new foods, and other goods that delighted their senses. Scholars developed the scientific method as a means of studying the natural world and testing the received wisdom of the ancient and Christian philosophers. Humanism, as this spirit of inquiry became known, inspired civic enterprises and political theories aimed at creating just and prosperous societies. It celebrated the human powers of observation and reason as the chief means by which people could comprehend their world and control their own fate. This sense of mastery violated the Christian principle of humility and the ancients' warnings against hubris, but it unlocked remarkable creative energies and imaginative powers. For its adherents, Renaissance humanism transformed the world from a doomed and inhospitable place into an awe-inspiring creation that humans could study and master for their comfort and enjoyment.

The Renaissance also coincided with a period of dynastic consolidation in Europe that produced new nation-states capable of undertaking overseas exploration and colonization. During the medieval era, Europe was a patchwork of kingdoms, principalities, and city-states whose rulers consistently faced challenges to their authority from above and below. The medieval papacy exerted tremendous political as well as spiritual influence over Europe's Christians. Part of that power derived from the Church's wealth as a landholder, but the pope also commanded the loyalty of legions of clergy, monks and nuns, administrators, and soldiers. Church officials collected their own taxes, answered to their own law, and ran their own courts. Monarchs who attempted to tax Church officials or subject them to the king's justice faced retaliation in the form of excommunication and interdict (a suspension of administering sacraments within a particular area), both of which implicitly sanctioned rebellion by the king's subjects. Monarchs also had to deal with their own grasping nobles, who controlled wealth and private armies that often exceeded the crown's own resources.

During the fifteenth century, two dynasties emerged in western Europe that established a new model for royal government. On the Iberian Peninsula, the marriage of Isabella of Castile and Ferdinand of Aragon in 1469 created a joint kingdom that became the core of a unified Spain. Isabella and Ferdinand raised armies to complete the Reconquista, the centuries-long war that Christian forces had been fighting against the Islamic kingdoms of al-Andalus. With the fall of Granada in January 1492, the entirety of Spain was subjected to Christian rule. Isabella and Ferdinand secured their reign against internal enemies by parceling out land grants in the newly conquered lands to loyal supporters and by keeping an unprecedented number of soldiers mobilized in their service. They enforced religious orthodoxy by compelling either conversion or exile from Muslims and Jews who had lived for centuries alongside Christian neighbors in al-Andalus, and they used the Spanish Inquisition to ferret out Christian heretics and Muslim and Jewish *conversos* suspected of practicing their old faiths in secrecy. As they cemented their power at home, Isabella and Ferdinand also turned their attention westward toward the Atlantic. Competing with neighboring Portugal, Spanish sailors mastered the currents and winds that enabled them to navigate the coast of West Africa and the Atlantic islands of Madeira and the Azores. During this same era, the Spanish conquered the Canary Islands, which became an important supply station on their trans-Atlantic voyages to America. Spanish power in the Atlantic was also consolidated by the political union of the Portuguese and Spanish crowns under Philip II and his successors from 1580 to 1640.

Meanwhile, in England, almost a century of dynastic struggle ended on Bosworth Field in 1485, when Henry Tudor defeated King Richard III and seized the throne as Henry VII. Henry elevated his family above the rest of the aristocracy by using the laws that governed treason and inheritance to seize or break up the estates of his political enemies. He also devised prohibitive taxes and fines to discourage powerful lords from maintaining private armies. Henry VIII continued his father's consolidation of power by breaking with the papacy in Rome and seizing all of the Church's lands within his realm. Having secured their power at home, the Tudor monarchs resumed England's centuries' old effort to conquer Ireland. The first English "plantations" in the Atlantic World were established by English colonizers in Ireland, who seized the lands of native Irish whom they either killed or hounded into exile.

During the sixteenth century, Spain and England became great rivals on opposite sides of the Protestant Reformation. The Reformation began in Germany in 1517 when a monk named Martin Luther challenged what he perceived to be corruption and erroneous teachings emanating from the papacy. Luther took issue with many Church doctrines and practices for which he found no scriptural basis, and his protests inspired a movement that spread rapidly among other Christian believers discontent with the worldly and spiritual authority of Rome. Luther rejected the Catholic Church's hierarchy and formalism in favor of personal piety grounded in biblical study and daily devotion. He preached "justification by faith alone," the idea that only personal faith—not sacraments received from priests, favors purchased from the pope, or intercession from saints—could lead a soul to salvation. In Geneva, Switzerland, the theologian John Calvin built on Luther's ideas to formulate the doctrine of predestination, the idea that all human beings, because of their inherent sinfulness, were powerless to affect the fate that an omnipotent and inscrutable God had determined for them.

Lutheranism and Calvinism may at first glance seem to be pessimistic creeds that condemned their believers to hopelessness and anxiety over their spiritual fates, but many Christians found these ideas powerfully liberating. The Protestant Reformation upended the spiritual authority that clergy from local priests to the pope had claimed over their flocks for centuries. God may have been arbitrary in dispensing salvation, but at least His grace was freely given; it could not be purchased from intermediaries nor conjured up by a priestly caste. Because divine dispensation was arbitrary, it was also as likely to be found among the lowly as the high-born, giving all believers a claim to spiritual equality before God that would embolden many to defend freedom of individual conscience against the powers of the state. Luther, Calvin, and other Protestant leaders encouraged the translation of the Bible from ancient Greek and Latin into vernacular languages so that the faithful could read and study scripture for themselves. This elevation of scriptural reading and reflection over other forms of piety gave an enormous boost to literacy and book publishing in Europe that was aided by the advent of the moveable type printing press in the mid-fifteenth century.

Spain, Europe's wealthiest nation in the sixteenth century, led the forces of the Counter-Reformation, a reinvigoration of Catholic orthodoxy and missionary activity meant to turn back the forces unleashed by Luther and Calvin. As Spain pushed into the Atlantic and beyond, missionary activity inspired by the Counter-Reformation became an important justification for its conquest of new lands and foreign peoples. When Henry VIII severed the English Church's ties to the pope in the 1530s, England became the Reformation's bulwark in Europe and vanguard abroad. Early English promoters of colonization made spreading the Protestant faith a national mission and justified their own conquests of indigenous peoples on the grounds that they were delivering these poor souls out of thralldom to Spain and the Catholic Church. Despite the efforts of each side to depict the other as engaged in the devil's work, from the perspective of the indigenous peoples who were on the receiving end of this religious rivalry, the Spanish and English must have looked very similar. The monarchs of both nations insisted on religious uniformity among their subjects and regarded heterodoxy as treasonous. Both nations used religion to justify the slaughter of non-believers who got in the way of God's kingdom on earth. In both cases, too, monarchs relied on private entrepreneurs to raise the capital and men necessary to undertake such conquests. If these enterprises succeeded, the crown happily rewarded the victors with titles

Figure 1.2 Martin Waldseenmuller, *Orbis Typys Universalis* [Nuremberg?, 1513?]. This early-sixteenth-century world map is based on the work of ancient Greek geographer Ptolemy, but it has been updated to reflect the discoveries of Columbus and other explorers, as is evident by the inclusion of Caribbean islands and the South American coast. Courtesy of the John Carter Brown Library at Brown University.

and favors in return for a healthy share of the profits. If they failed, private investors suffered the loss while the crown turned its attention to the next fortune-seekers in line.

Every schoolchild learns that Columbus's voyage in 1492 opened the door to a new age in human history, but it is important to remember that this moment was also a product of Europe's centuries-long encounter with the Islamic World. In planning his voyage, Columbus relied on estimations of the earth's circumference made by the ancient Greek geographer Ptolemy, whose *Geographia* had been preserved by Islamic scholars and transmitted to Italy in the fourteenth century (see Figure 1.2). The ships Columbus sailed made use of navigational technology that came to Europe by way of Mediterranean trade routes, including the magnetic compass, adopted from Muslim sailors in the twelfth century, and the lateen, a triangular sail that when hoisted on a rear (or "mizzen") mast improved the maneuverability of square-rigged vessels in contrary winds. Columbus was undoubtedly a product of the Renaissance, his imagination fired by the humanistic desire to know more about the natural world, but the spirit of the Crusades lived on in him as well. He told Ferdinand and Isabella that they could use the riches he brought back from his voyage to launch a new war against the Muslim occupiers of the Holy Land. That same spirit of militant righteousness and cultural superiority sailed with other European explorers to Africa and America.

SEPARATE WORLDS AND SHARED HUMANITY

What then are the most important lessons to draw from comparing Africa, America, and Europe on the eve of their collision in a new Atlantic World? Differences among them abounded, but so too did similarities rooted in thousands of years of human experience. For the vast majority of people living on these continents at the time of Columbus's first voyage, life was profoundly local. Personal identity derived from lineage and kinship connections that fixed the past and present to a specific spot of ground occupied over generations. Farming was the primary occupation, and most communities numbered in the low hundreds rather than the tens of thousands. The rhythms of work and leisure followed seasonal cycles, as did times of want and plenty. People expressed cultural attributes such as dress, diet, and language in endless variations that reflected the local confines of their worlds.

Significant differences become apparent when the scale shifts from the local to continental. Fired by the spirit, wealth, and knowledge of the Renaissance, Europe was experiencing a technological and intellectual revolution during the fifteen century. Printing presses revolutionized communications and learning. The magnetic compass and innovative ship design made possible oceanic navigation. Gunpowder and firearms were creating new and more lethal types of warfare. Like their European counterparts, sub-Saharan Africans were skilled metalworkers and boatbuilders, but they did not yet possess the means of manufacturing guns or ocean-going vessels. Over thousands of years, Native Americans had developed their own technologies for manufacturing tools and weapons, but all without the benefit of Iron Age methods or materials.

Long-distance trade was another significant difference among these worlds. For Europeans and Africans, it had figured significantly in the creation and consumption of wealth for the elites of society. The major trade routes of the Islamic World, which crisscrossed Central Asia, the Mediterranean, and the Sahara Desert, not only facilitated the movement of goods and people, but also the diffusion of ideas, knowledge, and technology: religious beliefs, mathematical principles, written languages, and the like. In America, cultural diffusion occurred—the spread of maize cultivation out of the Valley of Mexico is perhaps the most significant example—but long-distance trade does not appear to have had nearly the impact on economic production or cultural innovation that it did in Europe or Africa. The archaeological record reveals that Native Americans did exchange exotic objects over great distances, but in small quantities that suggest they were valued chiefly as diplomatic gifts or as prestige goods for the elite. Some Native American cultures—such as the Inca, Maya, and Pueblo—did build road systems for transporting people and crops over great distances, but no intercontinental equivalent of the Silk Road or the Mediterranean's seafaring routes existed in pre-Columbian America.

The future is unknowable, and no person or civilization is ever entirely equipped to meet it. Nevertheless, the clearest legacy that the Islamic World left for Europe and Africa was a growing awareness of and experience with outsiders. Europeans and sub-Saharan Africans had existed for hundreds of years as peripheries of the Islamic World, but they were also inheritors of its learning and wealth. When the trade networks that had kept this world together broke apart after 1300, Europeans in particular emulated the technological know-how and spirit of enterprise that had animated Islamic expansion in earlier centuries. Comparatively speaking, Native Americans were isolated and unprepared for what lay ahead when Columbus set sail. The Atlantic and Pacific oceans had prevented important technological advances in human civilization from reaching the Americas. Human populations in the Western Hemisphere had spent millennia in epidemiological isolation from those in the Eastern, which would leave them vulnerable to diseases carried by Europeans and Africans. Nor had Native American populations participated in the spread of Christianity or Islam, two religions that had helped forge shared identities among peoples of differing cultures and languages across vast distances in Europe, Africa, and Asia.

Ayuba, even though his American odyssey began almost 250 years after Columbus's, is an excellent illustration of this difference between the Old World and the New. He embodied Islam's legacy for sub-Saharan Africa in his literacy, religious beliefs, and commercial orientation; he had been traveling to purchase paper, among other goods, when he was captured by slave traders. During his sojourn in America, he used these cultural inheritances to convince the local colonists of his status. In England, Ayuba's literacy and Muslim faith convinced his benefactors that he was civilized and deserving of their assistance. The past shared between Africa and Europe, a past rooted in the Mediterranean rather than the Atlantic, provided the means by which Ayuba and European contemporaries made sense of each other. No such mutual frame of reference was in place when Native Americans encountered Europeans and Africans in the wake of Columbus.

CHRONOLOGY

c. 33,000 –8000 B.C.E.	Earliest human migrations to the Americas.
c. 8500 B.C.E.	Emergence of agriculture in Fertile Crescent.
c. 5000 B.C.E.	Emergence of agriculture in Valley of Mexico.
c. 1000 B.C.E.	Rise of Olmec civilization in Valley of Mexico.
c. 100–400 C.E.	Christianity spreads throughout Roman Empire.
c. 650–800	Islam spreads from Arabia into North Africa and by way of trans-Saharan trade routes into West Africa.
c. 1100–1250	Crusades fought by European Christians against Muslims in Near East.
c. 1200	Mississippian civilization flourishes in North America.
c. 1350	Timbuktu flourishes as center of Muslim scholarship and trade in African kingdom of Mali. Bubonic plague sweeps through Europe.
c. 1400–1600	European Renaissance.
1453	Fall of Constantinople.
1492	January: fall of Granada, last Muslim kingdom in Iberian Peninsula. August: Christopher Columbus sails on his first trans-Atlantic voyage.
1517	Martin Luther initiates the Protestant Reformation in Europe.
1731–1734	*Ayuba Suleiman Diallo's odyssey from Africa to North America to England and return home.*

NOTES

1. Ayuba's story and excerpts from the narrative of his slavery may be found in Philip D. Curtin, ed., *Africa Remembered: Narratives by West Africans from the Era of the Slave Trade* (Madison: University of Wisconsin Press, 1967), 17–59.
2. See John Thornton, *Africa and Africans in the Making of the Atlantic World, 1400–1800*, 2nd ed. (Cambridge, UK: Cambridge University Press, 1998), 103–106.
3. John Locke, *The Second Treatise of Government* (1690; reprint: Indianapolis: Bobbs-Merrill, 1952), 29.

SUGGESTIONS FOR FURTHER READING

Ayuba's story is featured in James Campbell, *Middle Passages: African American Journeys to Africa, 1787–2005* (New York: Penguin, 2006). For works that examine West Africa in the early modern era, see David Northrup, *Africa's Discovery of Europe, 1450–1850* (New York:

Oxford University Press, 2002), and John Thornton, *Africa and Africans in the Making of the Atlantic World, 1400–1680*, 2nd ed. (Cambridge, UK: Cambridge University Press, 1998). Donald R. Wright, *The World and a Very Small Place in Africa: A History of Globalization in Niumi, The Gambia*, 3rd ed. (Armonk, NY: Sharpe, 2010), offers a clear assessment of the Islamic World's connection to and impact on West Africa.

The development of human societies in North America before European contact is addressed in Charles C. Mann, *1491: New Revelations of the Americas Before Columbus* (New York: Knopf, 2005), and Alice Beck Kehoe, *America Before the European Invasions* (New York: Longman, 2002). For pre-Columbian Latin America, see Brian M. Fagan, *Kingdoms of Gold, Kingdoms of Jade: The Americas Before Columbus* (London: Thames & Hudson, 1991). A concise and provocative article that surveys Indian cultures in North America on the eve of European contact is Neal Salisbury, "The Indians' Old World: Native Americans and the Coming of Europeans," *William and Mary Quarterly*, 3d ser., 53 (1996): 435–458. The scholarship on the earliest migrations to America remains in constant debate. For a pugnacious introduction, see J. M. Adovasio with Jake Page, *The First Americans: In Pursuit of Archaeology's Greatest Mystery* (New York: Random House, 2002). For the standard interpretation, see Jared Diamond, *Guns, Germs, and Steel: The Fates of Human Societies* (New York: Norton, 1999), a book that also does an excellent job of describing the major differences between Old World and New World societies on the eve of Columbus's explorations. For the Mississippian civilization, see Timothy R. Pauketat, *Cahokia: Ancient America's Great City on the Mississippi* (New York: Penguin, 2009).

Of the voluminous literature on Europe in the Age of Discoveries, a few works stand out for their effort to frame early European encounters with Africans and Native Americans in the wider context of the Renaissance. See William D. Phillips, Jr., and Carla Rahn Phillips, *The Worlds of Christopher Columbus* (Cambridge, UK: Cambridge University Press, 1992); Stephen Greenblatt, *Marvelous Possessions: The Wonder of the New World* (Chicago: University of Chicago Press, 1991); and Anthony Grafton, *New Worlds, Ancient Texts: The Power of Tradition and the Shock of Discovery* (Cambridge, MA: Belknap Press of Harvard University Press, 1992). J. H. Elliott, *Spain and Its World, 1500–1700* (New Haven, CT: Yale University Press, 1989), elucidates Spain's rise to world power; Wallace Notestein does the same for England in *The English People on the Eve of Colonization, 1603–1630* (New York: Harper and Row, 1962). On the development of Europe's Christian identity, see Richard Fletcher, *The Barbarian Conversion: From Paganism to Christianity* (New York: Holt, 1997). For the manifold connections between the Islamic World and medieval Europe, see David Levering Lewis, *God's Crucible: Islam and the Making of Europe, 570–1215* (New York: Norton, 2008), and Bernard Lewis, *Cultures in Conflict: Christians, Muslims, and Jews in the Age of Discovery* (New York: Oxford University Press, 1995). Andrew Pettegree, *Europe in the Sixteenth Century* (Malden, MA: Blackwell, 2002), provides a good overview of Europe on the eve of American colonization.

CHAPTER 2

Early Encounters
The Sixteenth Century

The first time the strangers came to Wanchese's and Manteo's country, they did not exhibit any intention of staying. Two ships arrived in 1584, exploring the Outer Banks of what the English would ultimately call North Carolina and trading with the Algonquian peoples they met there. Like many of their neighbors, Wanchese and Manteo were probably drawn to these newcomers by a powerful curiosity about their ships and the exotic goods they brought with them.

An English chronicler of that first voyage to Roanoke and its neighboring islands described the initial encounter with the natives in detail. An unnamed Indian approached a small landing party without any "show of fear or doubt." After speaking "of many things not understood by us," he agreed to accompany them back to their ships, where his hosts gave him "a shirt, a hat and some other things, and made him taste of our wine, and our meat, which he liked very well." The Indian examined the ship with interest and then took his leave, but the visit was not over. After paddling away in his canoe, "he fell to fishing, and in less than half an hour, he had laden his boat as deep as it could swim." He returned to shore and divided his catch into two piles. He signaled to the ships that the fish were his gift to them, and then he "departed out of our sight."

This expedition's subsequent encounters with other natives followed a similar pattern. Wherever the ships stopped, greeting and trading ensued. The English wanted furs and deerskins, which the Indians supplied in return for hatchets, axes, and knives. From these exchanges, the English learned that the Indians had no metal tools except for some nails, spikes, and similar materials they had scavenged from the wreck of a "Christian ship" some twenty years earlier.

When the ships returned to England in late 1584, they carried back something else besides furs: "We brought home also two of the savages, being lusty men, whose names were Wanchese and Manteo."[1] Wanchese came from Roanoke, a large island where the English had done much of their reconnoitering (see Figure 2.1), and Manteo from Croatoan, another island in the Outer Banks to the south of Roanoke. The captains' brief report on the voyage made no mention of the Indians' motives for accompanying the English, but they appear to have gone willingly. They may have been interested in cultivating diplomatic and commercial

Figure 2.1 Theodor de Bry and John White, *A cheiff Lorde of Roanoac* (1590). This image by the German engraver Theodor de Bry is based on a watercolor portrait painted by John White, one of the Roanoke colonists. Depicting its subject from both front and back, it conveys a sense of the physical beauty and noble bearing that White and his contemporaries ascribed to the Indians they encountered. Courtesy of the John Carter Brown Library at Brown University.

ties with the English, but curiosity must have played a role as well. Wanchese and Manteo crossed the ocean to discover a new world.

They were not the first Indians to visit Europe. Columbus had brought natives back with him from his American voyages, and during the sixteenth century others followed in his wake. But those early Indian voyagers were an anonymous and tragic lot. Many had been duped or kidnapped into making the trip and were enslaved by their captors. Homesickness, despondency, and exposure to European illnesses took a devastating toll on their numbers. For almost all of them, the trip to Europe was a one-way ticket. Wanchese and Manteo were different. Neither faced enslavement, and both weathered the trip well enough to return to their homeland.

Wanchese and Manteo did not know it at the time, but the English they met had grand designs for the land they were exploring. Their voyage had been sponsored by Sir Walter Ralegh, who had received approval from Queen Elizabeth I in 1584 to establish a colony in North America. A similar venture led by Ralegh's half-brother Sir Humphrey Gilbert had failed a year earlier in Newfoundland, taking Gilbert and some of the unlucky colonists with it when their ship was lost at sea. Despite such ominous precedents, Ralegh believed he could do better in the more temperate climes of Virginia, a vast region he named in honor of England's virgin (or, at least unmarried) queen. The islands inhabited by Wanchese and Manteo were a safe distance from Spanish settlements in Florida and the Caribbean, but still close enough to provide a base for ships preying on the Spanish treasure fleets returning home from Mexico. After hearing the report of the exploratory expedition he sent in 1584, Ralegh decided that he would locate his new colony on Roanoke.

Wanchese and Manteo figured prominently in his plan. On their arrival in London, Ralegh had them housed comfortably with Thomas Harriot, a friend and fellow participant in the Roanoke venture. Harriot went to work learning the visitors' native language and teaching them English. In the process, he extracted from them as much information as he could about the peoples and environs of Roanoke. As Ralegh pitched his venture to potential investors, Manteo and Wanchese served as its human billboards, living proof of America's exotic allure and the natives' peaceful nature. Both returned home with the expedition that brought the first English colonists to Roanoke in 1585.

After landfall, Wanchese and Manteo parted ways. Wanchese rejoined his people and, despite his experience of immersion in English language and culture, never offered any meaningful assistance to the new arrivals. Manteo, on the other hand, worked as their interpreter, guide, and mediator. When the leaders of the foundering colony decided to pack up and return to England a year later, he went with them, having clearly developed an attachment—whether it was personal, political, or cultural is unclear—to the newcomers. He returned to Roanoke with another group of colonists in 1587, completing his second round-trip Atlantic passage in three years, a remarkable feat considering the mortality rate for Indians on such voyages. Despite the already checkered record of the English at Roanoke, Manteo stuck by them. He interceded on their behalf when his own people, the Croatoans, were poised to attack them, and he converted to Christianity. Eventually, Manteo slipped away from the historical record along with the rest of the "lost colony" of Roanoke. After an interlude of three years, an expedition finally arrived to resupply the colony, but its inhabitants had disappeared. The relief party could only hope that the word "CROATOAN" carved into a stockade wall meant that Manteo had led his English friends to safety among his own people.[2]

In Wanchese's and Manteo's odysseys, we can begin to comprehend the impact that such early encounters had on the course of American colonization. First, there was the overwhelming curiosity that brought strangers together. The European side of this experience is well documented in the journals and letters of early explorers, who time and again blended the practical and fantastic in their descriptions of America. But what of the Indians' discovery of Europeans? Wanchese and Manteo did not keep diaries or submit written reports to their superiors, but they must have told tales of their travels that astonished their kin and neighbors. The actions of the unnamed Indian who dared to board an English ship off the coast of the Outer Banks in 1584 says it all: the desire to encounter the new, to comprehend the strange, and to touch the exotic is a powerful emotion that can draw humans together across gaping cultural and geographic divides.

The experience of that anonymous Indian also reveals how parties on both sides of these encounters tried to process what they witnessed. Humans deal with the shock of the new and the strange by filtering it through what they already know about the world around them. Thus, the English attempted to make this stranger more familiar by giving him gifts of their clothing (the shirt and hat) and by having him "taste of our wine, and our meat." They used their own cultural attributes as the yardstick by which to measure the Indians' civility, noting that they lacked metal tools except for those they salvaged from an earlier "Christian" shipwreck. Their anonymous Indian visitor followed the same approach when he returned the favor of their hospitality by fishing and leaving his catch for them. Maybe he did not like their wine and meat nearly as much as the English thought; maybe the "meat" he tasted was a wormy sea biscuit so disgusting that he decided that what these scruffy-looking strangers needed most was some fresh local seafood. Trading worked the same way. Each side considered itself to be getting the better of the deal when it gave up something it considered cheap and commonplace for something rare and exotic. The natives were no doubt amazed by the newcomers' willingness to exchange hatchets, axes, and knives for the animal pelts so readily available around them.

Finally, after the strangers came together and arrived at some kind of mutual comprehension of each other, each side had to decide how it would deal with the other in the future. Was there reason for this encounter to continue and, if so, on whose terms? Once again, the European participants left a record of the circumstances and motivations that shaped their decisions to trade, war, or conduct missionary work among the native peoples they encountered, but what of the Indians' responses? Wanchese and Manteo exhibited two extremes: disavowing any association with the strangers or joining with them. As other cross-cultural encounters unfolded over the course of the sixteenth century, other native peoples exhibited these reactions, as well as the range of possibilities between them. The choices to resist, accommodate, or identify with the newcomers were always present, but the factors affecting them were as various as the peoples involved.

INDIANS' IMPRESSIONS OF EUROPEANS

Recovering Indians' first impressions of Europeans is not easy. As the stories of Wanchese and Manteo indicate, individuals—even those from similar cultural backgrounds and circumstances—reacted differently to the newcomers, and unlike their European counterparts, they did not leave behind written first-person accounts that help explain those reactions. Indians passed down from one generation to the next stories about their initial encounters with Europeans, but many years passed before such oral traditions found their way into textual sources, after first being filtered through the ears and pens of missionaries, traders, or other recorders.

Consider, for example, one such account recorded by eighteenth-century missionary John Heckewelder from "the mouth of an intelligent Delaware Indian" and first published in 1819. According to Heckewelder's informant, "a great many years ago" some Delawares were fishing along the coast of Manhattan when they saw "something remarkably large floating on the water, and such as they had never seen before." Astonished, they debated whether it was "an uncommonly large fish or animal," or perhaps "a remarkably large house in which the Manitto (the Great and Supreme Being) himself was present, and... coming to visit them." They decided to arrange a great sacrifice and feast for the approaching deity. Women prepared their best food, men put "all the idols or images" in order, and "conjurers" tried to "determine what this phenomenon portended." As the ship drew closer, the Delawares could see that it was "a house full of human beings, of quite a different colour from that of the Indians, and dressed differently from them." They assumed the newcomers' leader, who came ashore with a small retinue of guards and "dressed in a red coat all glittering with gold lace," to be "the Manitto himself."

The brilliantly bedecked stranger drank an "unknown substance" from a small cup and then had the cup refilled and offered it to the Delawares' chief. The chief only sniffed the cup and then passed it on, each successive recipient following his predecessor's example until one brave soul, fearing that the spurned cup might raise the strangers' wrath, "drank up its whole contents." He staggered and fell into a sleep so deep that his companions thought him dead. When the drinker regained consciousness, he declared that the cup's contents delivered to him "the most delicious sensations," and he demanded more. The strangers complied, and soon "the whole assembly" became intoxicated.

Before leaving, the strangers gave presents to the Delawares, outfitting them with "beads, axes, hoes, and stockings such as the white people wear." They promised to come back and stay longer next time, if the Indians provided them with a bit of ground on which to grow their food. The Delawares rejoiced when the ship returned the following year, but the strangers laughed upon seeing how the Indians used their gifts. Instead of fitting the axes and hoes with handles, "they wore them about their breasts as ornaments," and they used the stockings as tobacco pouches. The Indians laughed, too, once the strangers showed them how to use the axes to fell trees, the hoes to cultivate the earth, and the stockings to warm their legs.

The strangers "proposed to stay with them this time" and asked for a plot of land no larger than what might be encompassed by a bull's hide, so that they might plant their own corn. The Delawares granted this request and watched as the newcomers then used a knife to cut a bull hide into a "long rope, not thicker than a child's finger" so that when laid out in a giant circle, it enclosed "a large piece of ground." The Delawares "were surprised at the superior wit of the whites" in cutting up the bull hide, but did not wish to go back on their agreement, and so allowed them the land in question. During the course of succeeding years, the Europeans engrossed more land through similar chicanery, "until the Indians began to believe that they would soon want all their country, which in the end proved true."[3]

In reading this account of the Delawares' first encounters with Europeans, it can be difficult to distinguish between the voice of the Indian telling the story and that of the missionary recording it. When Heckewelder put the story into print, he turned it into a morality play, pitting innocent Indians against grasping Europeans. The Indians are innocent but also suffer a fatal weakness for alcohol, which literally immobilizes them. The Europeans are wiser and more sophisticated, but they are also cunning and greedy. Writing with two centuries' worth of hindsight, Heckewelder offered this oral tradition as a prophecy of the destruction European contact would bring to the Delaware people.

Despite the obvious prejudices in how Europeans recorded such stories, oral traditions still provide a native perspective on early encounters. Europeans liked to think the Indians regarded them as gods, but the spiritual dimensions of their reception were more complicated than that. As Heckewelder indicated, the Delawares associated the Europeans with a great spiritual force, what his Delaware informant referred to as "Manitto." Manitou (as modern scholars spell the term) was a notion of spiritual power shared by many Indian peoples in eastern North America. Missionaries often described manitou as the Indians' supreme deity (note how Heckewelder defined it as the Indians' "Great and Supreme Being"). But this equation of manitou with the Christian idea of a single creator god who ruled over heaven and earth is misleading. Rather than a distant anthropomorphic god residing in some celestial realm, manitou was a pervasive spiritual presence that animated much of the physical world, including animals, bodies of water, wind, and even rocks. It encompassed a wide variety of other spiritual beings and forces connected to specific places, creatures, or objects. Acknowledging and accessing the powers of manitou helped Indians navigate the spiritual and physical worlds. To upset, ignore, or otherwise disturb manitou was to invite personal misfortune and collective disaster.

Understanding the role manitou played in Indian lives helps explain the reception accorded to those early European explorers. The Delawares ascribed great spiritual power to the first Europeans they met. Manitou was evident in the floating house that carried them across the water, in the resplendent fabrics and colors worn by their leader, and in the mood-altering effects of their drink. Had the Delawares treated the new arrivals harshly or denied their gifts, they would have incurred negative spiritual consequences. In Heckewelder's rendition of the story, the Delawares' use of the axes and hoes as bodily ornaments is a comic indication of their technological backwardness, but in the context of the Indians' belief in manitou, it made perfect sense. These objects were other-worldly goods, their spiritual potency evident in the strangeness of their design and materials, not to mention their mysterious origin among strangers who had arrived in a floating house. In the same manner that European Christians believed that saints' medals and other religious amulets could protect them from misfortune, so too did the Delawares try to harness the spiritual power they believed to be inherent in the iron axes and hoes they received from these strangers. Other accounts of early encounters reveal a similar pattern of native peoples ascribing spiritual powers to Europeans and their exotic goods. Columbus, reporting on his first voyage, described how firmly convinced the Indians he encountered in the Caribbean were that "I have come from the sky with these ships and people," and how they bartered with his crew for "bits of broken crockery, fragments of glass or tags of laces," and even "bits of broken hoops from the wine barrels."[4] The acrid smoke and deafening noise from discharged cannon and guns added to the Europeans' other-worldly reputation, and early explorers such as Columbus frequently used such spectacles to awe the natives they met. Clocks, magnetic compasses, and other navigational tools also impressed Indians. Time and again, the Europeans who recorded such encounters cast the Indians as childlike innocents easily enraptured by even the simplest mechanical devices, and in the eyes of such witnesses, the technological sophistication of the Europeans became the most obvious evidence of their cultural superiority. Ralegh's friend Thomas Harriot, who chronicled the experiences of the first Roanoke colony, wrote that "mathematical instruments, sea compasses... wild fireworks, guns, hooks, writing and reading, spring-clocks that seem to go of themselves... so far exceeded their [the Indians'] capacities to comprehend the reason and means [of] how they should be made and done that they thought they were rather the works of gods than of men, or at least they had been given and taught us by the gods."[5]

Harriot's observation was blatantly ethnocentric—that is to say, colored by his belief in the superiority of his own cultural beliefs and customs—but it also got to the heart of the matter. Indians did not interpret mechanical devices and similar wonders as evidence of European superiority in ingenuity or engineering. They did not ask for explanations of the mechanical principles that made these devices work or for tutorials in how to build or use them. Instead, they saw such items as proof of the Europeans' access to spiritual powers and forces that they would like to tap into themselves. A bit of broken hoop from a wine barrel did not make an Indian want to learn how to make wine or barrels, but it did serve as a physical connection to the manitou that enabled Europeans to bring such marvelous things with them across the ocean.

The spiritual power that Indians invested in Europeans during these early encounters was also evident in their insistence that these newcomers assist them in healing the sick. Alvar Nuñez Cabeza de Vaca spent eight years traveling among Indians in southeastern North America after a military expedition in which he was participating collapsed in Florida in 1528. He and three other survivors were among the first Europeans encountered by Indians along the Texas Gulf Coast, who pressed them into service as healers. Cabeza de Vaca and his compatriots "laughed at it, saying that it was a joke and that we did not know how to heal," but the Indians "withheld our food until we did as they had told us." One Indian healer explained that "stones and other things that grow in fields have virtue, and by using a hot stone and passing it over the stomach, he could cure and take away pain." If he could use these objects to cure the sick, the healer told the Spanish strangers, then they could as well, because they were "superior men," who "surely had even greater virtue and power." Faced with starvation if they did not comply, Cabeza de

Vaca and his companions imitated what they had witnessed of the natives' healing practices, adding Christian prayers and the sign of the cross to their recitations and gesticulations. As word of their work spread, neighboring Indian communities sought out their services, and Cabeza de Vaca claimed that his intercession had even helped restore life to an apparently dead man: "This caused great astonishment and consternation, and in all the land, no one talked of anything else. All those who heard this news came to look for us, to have us heal them and sign their children with the cross."[6]

As with Harriot's description of the Indians' reaction to mechanical devices, these passages from Cabeza de Vaca's narrative reveal much about the mental framework through which Indians made sense of Europeans. When his Indian captors pressed him into service as a healer, Cabeza de Vaca considered it evidence of their ignorance and superstition. The Indians' rationale for doing so, however, was evident in the Indian healer's observation that the "virtue" that animated the stones in the field flowed even more powerfully through the marooned Spanish. When Cabeza de Vaca incorporated Christian prayers and gestures into his treatment of the Indians, he unwittingly did exactly what they expected him to do, invoking a spiritual power to which they believed he had special and exclusive access.

The power to heal also implied the power to harm. It did not take long for Indians to notice that strange and devastating maladies accompanied the newcomers, who appeared to be impervious to the same illnesses. In his account from Roanoke, Harriot observed that the natives "did not know whether to think us gods or men . . . because, [in] all the space of their sickness, there was no man of ours known to die or that was specially sick." The Indians believed that Harriot and his fellow colonizers were merely the physical manifestations of invaders who were "invisible and without bodies," and who "did make the people to die . . . by shooting invisible bullets into them."[7] Others accused Harriot and his company of firing the same invisible bullets out of their guns and artillery pieces to kill any Indians who offended them, no matter how far away.

The Indians' "invisible bullets" explanation for the epidemics that accompanied contact with Europeans anticipated modern germ theory by about three hundred years. Diseases to which Europeans, Asians, and Africans had been previously exposed for generations found "virgin soil" in the Americas, and exacted a devastating toll among indigenous peoples there. Epidemics raced through these new host populations faster than any newcomers could colonize them. In the Caribbean and Valley of Mexico, native populations fell by as much as 95 percent within the first century of contact with the Spanish.

Measuring such mortality rates requires first estimating the pre-Columbian population of the Americas. Historians, epidemiologists, and demographers have tried a variety of methods to do so, and not surprisingly, they have come up with widely varying answers. Starting in the early twentieth century, scholars systematically gathered and tallied the earliest population estimates made by European observers as they explored new regions, but such counts were by their nature incomplete and impressionistic, leading to low estimates. Counting methods grew more elaborate as subsequent scholars added multipliers to these totals, to account for Indians who were excluded or overlooked when a missionary tallied the baptisms or burials of converts or a colonial governor estimated the number of warriors in a neighboring Indian nation. With the advent of modern computer modeling, the reconstruction of pre-contact populations became more sophisticated. Demographers applied the concept of "carrying capacity" to pre-Columbian America, basing their estimates on the assumption that a human population in any given region will expand until it reaches the limits of the resources available to support it. Such mathematical models compensate for the lack of textual evidence and have pushed estimates for the population of North America north of the Rio Grande in 1492 up considerably, from the figure of one million commonly accepted in the early twentieth century to the figure of five to ten million commonly accepted today.

Glimpses of the impact that Old World diseases had on Indians come from the accounts of early colonizers such as Harriot. Universally, they express surprise at how quickly Indians contracted and succumbed to maladies described variously as fevers, plagues, and poxes. Smallpox was the deadliest disease to cross the Atlantic, but it was accompanied by measles, chicken pox, the bubonic plague, scarlet fever, and influenza. In the Old World, repeated exposure had built up acquired immunities within host populations to these diseases, many of which were considered childhood afflictions. Among previously unexposed populations, however, these diseases tended to infect adults as well as children and to kill both with alarming efficiency. The overall mortality of smallpox among Native Americans, for example, was probably 30 or 40 percent, akin to the impact that the bubonic plague had in Europe when it first arrived there in the fourteenth century. Repeated epidemics of smallpox and other diseases made it impossible for native populations to recover from one generation to the next. Instead, they endured a demographic collapse. In what eventually became the United States of America, the Indian population reached its nadir of approximately 250,000 during the 1890s, four hundred years after Columbus's first voyage. Sustained population recovery for Native Americans in the United States did not begin until after 1920.

Indians were not genetically weaker than Europeans, but several biological and social factors increased their susceptibility to these new diseases. During their twelve thousand years of isolation from other world populations, their immune systems had developed in response to a different disease environment, fighting illnesses such as tuberculosis and pneumonia that were indigenous to the Western Hemisphere. Indians were also more genetically homogeneous than inhabitants of the Old World, making it possible for some diseases such as measles to adapt more quickly to them as a new host population. In addition to these biological considerations, a host of political and social factors increased the Indians' susceptibility. For those exposed to new diseases as a result of enslavement or warfare with Europeans, malnutrition and physical exhaustion likely weakened their biological resistance. Their immune systems may have also been overwhelmed by concurrent or successive exposure to different pathogens; survivors of a smallpox epidemic may have been too weak to withstand secondary infections or a subsequent outbreak of influenza. Epidemics that killed adults as well as children disrupted social relationships and economic production, causing political chaos and famine that complicated a community's ability to recover. Nursing children, who acquired antibodies from their mothers' milk, were also dangerously exposed when new diseases infected healthy adults.

Many Indians in North America suffered the impact of these new diseases long before colonial populations showed up. In New England, sixteenth-century epidemics among coastal Algonquians, most likely caused by contact with fur traders and fishermen, left the region so depopulated that the Pilgrims built their homes and planted their fields on the sites of towns that had been abandoned by their Indian residents. Thomas Morton, among the first wave of Puritan colonists in New England, described visiting places where the Indians had "died in heaps as they lay in their houses; and the living that were able to shift themselves, would run away and let them die, and let their carcasses lie above the ground without burial."[8] Likewise, the Pilgrim chronicler William Bradford wrote of Indians in the Connecticut River Valley who "dyed most miserably" after Dutch fur traders settled among them: "they fall into a lamentable condition, as they lye on their hard matts, the poxe breaking and mattering, and running one into another, their skin cleaving (by reason therof) to the matts they lye on; when they turne them, a whole side will flea of[f] at once, (as it were), and they will be all of a gore blood, most fearfull to behold; they dye like rotten sheep."[9]

On the other side of the ledger, Europeans did contract some new and deadly diseases in the New World. Historical epidemiologists continue to debate the origins of syphilis, but there is no doubt that a virulent strain of this venereal disease swept through Europe not long after Columbus initiated contact with Indians. Contemporaries believed that the Spanish brought this disease back from America, transmitted it to Italians during a military campaign in Naples, who in turn infected the French, who gave it to everyone else. Yaws, a tropical disease affecting the bones and joints that left many of its victims disfigured, was also of American origin. By far the most debilitating disease Europeans encountered in the Atlantic World was malaria, a mosquito-borne illness common in the tropical and subtropical regions of Africa and the Americas. Combined with malnutrition and overwork, malaria shortened the lifespan of thousands of migrants to just a few years once they arrived in the New World. Still, no diseases of New World origin wrought the same devastation on colonial populations as smallpox and other Old World illnesses did on Indians.

Epidemics rapidly changed the American landscape, emptying it of one kind of human population and opening its doors to others. Transplanted Europeans and Africans settled on former Indian lands, planted new crops in their fields, and helped themselves to the available natural resources. The remnants of Indian populations decimated by newly imported diseases were uprooted by this change. Trying to recover population stability and access to necessary resources, they migrated to new regions and sought allies among other groups that had experienced the same trauma. This breaking apart, moving about, and reconsolidation remade the map of early America. Some Indian nations, such as the Massachusetts, disappeared altogether, leaving only their names on the landscape. Others, such as the Shawnees, moved about in every direction of the compass, seeking new homelands. By the start of the eighteenth century, colonists were dealing with some Indian groups that had not existed a century earlier. They often identified these groups by place names—the Conestogas, the Creeks, the River Indians—because it was more convenient than trying to distinguish the various identities that had amalgamated to form their populations.

Although they may have been initially surprised by Europeans, Indians were not rendered senseless by them. They interpreted the strangers' arrival through their own frame of reference and set to work putting it to their advantage. Turning their backs on these newcomers was not an option, for their manitou was too powerful to be ignored; it was evident in the material goods they brought with them as well as the "invisible bullets" that seemed to go wherever they went. The shock of the new quickly gave way to more practical concerns. Could the strangers heal the illnesses that seemed to follow in their wake? Could the goods they brought with them be incorporated usefully into everyday life and work? Was it possible to knit the newcomers into existing alliances with other outsiders, so that their destructive power might be turned against enemies rather than friends? As sporadic encounters gave way to more regular contact, these were the sorts of questions Indians asked about Europeans.

THE VIEW IN THE MIRROR

Europeans had their own questions. Some had immediate and pragmatic ends: Were the natives friendly or unfriendly, what goods did they offer in trade, could they serve as reliable guides or interpreters in the new land? Other questions reflected the same intellectual challenge that Indians faced when confronted by Europeans: Where did these strangers come from, what do they have in common with us, and how do they fit into our understanding of the natural and spiritual worlds? But unlike Native Americans, Europeans brought with them to the New World a long history of exploration and encounters with peoples and cultures radically different from their own. The Crusades in the eastern Mediterranean, Marco Polo's travels in Central Asia and China, and trade and war with the Islamic kingdoms of North Africa had sharpened Europeans' notions about cultural differences among human societies. Encounters with strangers in distant lands had served as a mirror for medieval Europeans, refining their notion of who they were by forcing them to describe what they were not. Columbus and his followers brought that same mirror with them to the Americas and used it to answer their questions about Indians.

No Europeans crossed the Atlantic without some expectations about what they would find on the other side. Columbus thought he was sailing to the East

Indies and expected to arrive in Cathay, the Chinese kingdom described in the thirteenth century by the famed Italian traveler Marco Polo. To get there, he consulted the work of the ancient Greek geographer Ptolemy. Ancient and medieval authorities also told Columbus what kinds of people and creatures he would find at the far ends of the earth. The Roman scholar Pliny the Elder catalogued the human oddities and strange creatures fabled to live in remote lands—including dog-headed men, cannibals, pygmies, and headless creatures whose faces were in their chests. In the fourteenth century, the widely read travels of Sir John Mandeville, a fictitious English knight, updated Pliny's list. Writing about his first voyage, Columbus reported that "I have not found the human monsters which many people expected," but with matter-of-fact certainty told of a region in Cuba where "the people are born with tails" and of another part of the Indies where the people "eat human flesh."[10] More than a century later, when Sir Walter Ralegh went searching for a city of gold in South America, the monstrous peoples described by Pliny and Mandeville still loomed large in his imagination. Ralegh described two such races that he had heard about from his native guides, the *Ewaipanoma*, who were headless men "reported to have their eyes in their shoulders, and their mouths in the middle of their breasts" and the *Amazones*, warlike women who lived without men except for an annual mating rite.[11]

Only gradually did the accumulated evidence of what explorers like Columbus and Ralegh learned about the Americas displace such fanciful ideas inherited from the classical and medieval worlds. How long this process took is a testament to the power of the human imagination to ignore even the most stubborn realities. Whether it was Columbus's conviction that he had landed in Asia or Ralegh's pursuit of El Dorado, Europeans vested at least as much explanatory power in these fantasies as their Indian counterparts did in their notions of manitou.

Even those Europeans who provided more practical, eyewitness accounts of Indians had to reach back to their intellectual and cultural roots in Europe to make sense of them. Jean de Léry, a participant in a failed French colony in Brazil in the 1550s, was fascinated by the nakedness of the Indians he met there. "The men, women, and children do not hide any parts of their bodies," he wrote in his memoir, "what is more, without any sign of bashfulness or shame, they habitually live and go about their affairs as naked as they come out of their mother's womb." Léry filtered his reaction to the Indians' nakedness through his knowledge of the Old Testament. The story of Adam and Eve taught Europeans to equate nakedness with shame and immodesty. What Léry found most shocking about the Indians' exposure was not the nakedness itself but the apparent naturalness with which they regarded it. Their unwillingness to cover themselves or even blush about their condition before strangers prompted some European travelers to wonder if the New World was a parallel creation to the Old, younger and as yet unspoiled by human sin and suffering. Such questions also prompted Europeans to turn the mirror on themselves. Léry concluded his discussion of the Indians' nakedness by noting that it "is much less alluring than one might expect." In fact, he believed that the "the elaborate attire, paint, wigs, curled hair...and all the infinity of trifles" used by European women to decorate their bodies were "the cause of more ills than the ordinary nakedness of the savage women," which was not intended to arouse or seduce their men.[12]

That willingness to turn their gaze from Indians back onto themselves marked the best efforts by Europeans to recognize their shared humanity with the people they met in the Americas. The French Renaissance writer Michel de Montaigne famously captured this spirit in 1580 when he wrote his essay "Des Cannibales." Reflecting on reports of cannibalism among the natives of Brazil, Montaigne pondered what exactly constituted savagery and concluded that "each man calls barbarism whatever is not his own practice, for indeed it seems we have no other test of truth and reason than the example and pattern of the opinions and customs of the country we live in." Indians, he argued, were superior to Europeans because they "are still very close to their original naturalness" and have yet to be corrupted by the artificial laws and distinctions created by civilization. Montaigne drove his point home by citing contemporary eyewitness accounts of Indian society. Indians were generally stronger and healthier than Europeans and purer in their virtues, valuing nothing higher than "valor against the enemy and love for their wives." Their religion consisted of no doctrines more complicated than the immortality of the soul and just reward or punishment in the afterlife. As for the cannibalism that was supposedly the badge of their savagery, Montaigne found it far more humane than the methods Europeans used to deal with criminals and heretics: "I think there is more barbarity in eating a man alive than in eating him dead, in tearing by tortures and the rack a body still full of feeling, in roasting him bit by bit, having him bitten and mangled by dogs and swine... than in roasting and eating him after he is dead."[13]

Montaigne embodied the spirit of Renaissance humanism in his willingness to think comparatively about the customs and rules by which human societies governed themselves. Two hundred years later, the image of the noble savage remained a powerful rhetorical weapon in the hands of Enlightenment thinkers such as Jean-Jacques Rousseau and Benjamin Franklin, who argued that "savage" Indians enjoyed lives that were more equal, free, and just than those of supposedly civilized Christians.

But did such navel-gazing among writers and philosophers in Europe have much impact on the ground in America? Montaigne never crossed the Atlantic, and his broad-minded opinions about cannibalism might be attributed in part to his lack of firsthand experience with the practice. Nevertheless, the same humanistic spirit that informed Montaigne's work could be found in the reports of those Europeans who got to know Indians firsthand. Harriot's description of the "natures and manners" of the Indians he met at Roanoke was typical in this regard. He did not hesitate to describe them as lacking in the material comforts of life, but he also acknowledged that they were "very ingenious" in their own way and showed an "excellence of wit" in their warfare, hunting, and fishing.[14]

Other writers came to similar conclusions. Indians, like Europeans, lived in small towns, farmed the land, and recognized their own social and political hierarchies. Their dress and bodily ornamentation differed from that of Europeans but served the same purposes of protecting the body and marking social and gender distinctions. Early European observers even attributed the Indians' skin color, often the first noted marker of physical difference, to environmental or cultural factors—such as exposure to the sun or deliberate dyeing—rather than any innate biological difference. Sixteenth-century writers invariably reached the same conclusion when summarizing their impression of Indians: they are a lot like us, only different.

This admirably humanistic attitude was not without its darker side, for similarity was not the same as equality. Europeans presumed that the Indians they encountered would want to be more like them. Even as they sang the praises of their simplicity and virtues, they enumerated the ways in which Indians would have to change in order to meet European standards of civilization. In their reports and journals, early explorers conflated the natural history of the New World with the social maturity of its native inhabitants. Indians, like the land they lived in, were young. Some Europeans believed the Americas to be of more recent vintage than the Old World, and therefore a closer reflection of God's original handiwork in creation. Likewise, Indians were still at civilization's starting line, simpler and more innocent but also technologically backward and heathen. Like the sculptor's clay, they were still waiting for the impression that would give them shape. The most important markers of their progress would be their conversion to Christianity and European methods of farming. The first would save their souls by taming their baser instincts and teaching them to submit to authority. The second would put an end to their indolence and raise them above brute creation.

Christian discipline and instructive labor: these were the gifts Europeans intended to confer on Indians, remaking them in their image. It was never a question of *if* Indians would learn to live like Europeans, but only *how*. Those who cooperated would be sped along the path to civilization through the benevolent guidance of their betters; those who resisted would face greater trial and duress but would be dragged along, too, for the tide of history moved only in one direction. This certainty in the one-way transmission of civilization permeated every early European encounter with Indians. Léry, after praising the Indians' natural nakedness over the artifice of European fashions, wrote without irony about compelling native women to wear clothes "by great strokes of the whip." In like manner, Harriot wrote proudly of leaving no Indian transgression "unpunished or not revenged" while proclaiming in the same sentence that "we sought by all means possible to win them by gentleness."[15] The velvet glove of humanistic tolerance quickly gave way to the iron fist of violent compulsion when it came to imposing European standards on Indian conduct.

The hubris that informed European attitudes about Indians was nowhere more evident than in the willingness of early explorers to kidnap natives and force them to return to Europe. Columbus initiated the practice, bringing Indians to his royal sponsors as evidence of his success in reaching the Indies. An uncounted number of others followed in the sixteenth century, human trophies snatched from the shores of the New World. Wanchese and Manteo arrived in London in 1584 as exotic strangers, but Ralegh and Harriot immediately went to work on changing them. With proper instruction, they were to be rendered familiar, tractable, and reliable. Indians could change, but only to become more useful to the Europeans who presumed to be their new overlords.

THE SPANISH PRECEDENT

The Spanish were the first Europeans to act on the information that Columbus brought back from his voyages, and so in many respects they established the precedents followed by subsequent colonial ventures in the New World. The sheer magnitude of the gold and silver Spain extracted from America during the sixteenth century inspired the envy of other European powers and initiated a competition for empire among them that spread across the globe and lasted for over four hundred years. In this scramble, the eastern seaboard of North America represented a relatively poor and uninteresting slice of the pie. Its native peoples could not rival the Aztecs or Incas in population or wealth, and in terms of natural bounty, North American furs and fish seemed poor substitutes for gold and silver. Nevertheless, Europeans explored eastern North America in hopes that they would find another Mexico or Peru, or at least a quicker route to Asia. In their interactions with the native peoples they met there, they did not hesitate to imitate the Spanish example if they thought it might yield similar results.

In 1501 King Ferdinand and Queen Isabella appointed Nicolás de Ovando governor of Hispaniola (the Caribbean island that is today shared by the nations of Haiti and the Dominican Republic). Ovando replaced Christopher Columbus, whose skills as a navigator had not translated into colonial administration. Impatient with Columbus's shortcomings and anxious to see a return on their investment in his voyages, the monarchs gave specific instructions to Ovando that they hoped would transform their colonial enterprise. He was to treat the natives lovingly, so that they might be converted "without using force" to Christianity, but he was also "to compel them to work in the affairs of our service, paying each one the salary that you feel justly should be paid."[16] Thus did the new governor of Spain's first American colony sail with contradictory goals: treat the Indians well so that they might gain heaven, but exploit their labor so that the Spanish might reap more immediate earthly rewards. When the Indians failed to see the allure of this bargain, the veneer of mutual obligation in Spanish-Indian relations—salvation given in exchange for labor received—quickly gave way to the coercion implicitly condoned in Ovando's instructions.

A variety of legal and historical precedents informed the approach taken by the Spanish in the New World. The Romans had justified the invasion and conquest of foreign lands on the grounds that they were delivering the benefits of civilization—Roman law, literacy, technology, and eventually Christianity—to unlettered barbarians. Shortly after Columbus returned to Europe from his first voyage to America, Pope Alexander VI officially recognized Ferdinand and

Isabella's sovereignty over this new land and charged them with converting its inhabitants. This papal sanction satisfied, at least for the Spanish, the legality of their claim to America, but making that sovereignty a reality required more than a license from Rome.

To accomplish that objective, the Spanish applied lessons learned from their wars against al-Andalus, the Islamic kingdoms established by the Moors on the Iberian Peninsula. During this centuries-long Reconquista, the Spanish wrestled away bits of enemy territory piecemeal, planting loyal Christian subjects in the conquered territory and assimilating defeated foes via enslavement and forced conversion. The leaders of such military expeditions spoke of vanquishing Muslim infidels and extending the borders of Christendom, but they pursued plunder and royal favor just as fervently as the kingdom of heaven. In the century before Columbus's American voyages, Spanish conquistadors brought this same method of conquest and colonization to the Canary Islands in the eastern Atlantic, where they appropriated the land of the native Guanche people and put them to work alongside African slaves on sugar plantations.

The Spanish invasion of the Caribbean followed a similar pattern. Adventurers and their investors raised small armies and struck out in search of native populations that could be plundered for their wealth and labor. If successful, the leaders of such expeditions acquired from royal officials *encomiendas*, or the right to collect labor tribute from the conquered natives, whom they put to work in mines and fields. Foot soldiers in these expeditions—most of whom were young, single men from middle-class backgrounds seeking their fortunes in America—carried away shares of the human and material plunder they found, but with no guarantee of success. As a method of colonization, the *encomienda* system favored private initiative and quick action, whether taken against native peoples or rival countrymen. A gold-rush atmosphere pervaded every new frontier opened by the Spanish: bands of well-armed males rushed from one region to the next, seeking their private jackpots and moving ruthlessly against any who stood in their way. Royal officials and missionaries could barely keep up with them, never mind keep them in check.

From Hispaniola, conquistadors invaded the other large islands in the Caribbean—Puerto Rico, Cuba, and Jamaica—and then the mainland. They brought with them diseases, artillery and steel-edged weapons, horses and dogs, and unsustainable pressures on food supplies that devastated local populations, virtually wiping out within fifty years the Taínos peoples in the Caribbean who had greeted Columbus in 1492. The great chronicler of this free-for-all was Bartolomé de Las Casas, who arrived in Hispaniola in 1502 with Governor Ovando and lived there as an *encomendero* until he joined the Dominican missionary order and became a defender of native rights. His *A Brief Account of the Destruction of the Indies*, first published in Spain in 1542, provided graphic, eyewitness testimony of Spanish brutality toward the Indians. Although Las Casas intended for his book to expose the abuses of the *encomienda* system to the Spanish Crown, it had a much broader impact when it was translated into other languages and circulated throughout Europe. Protestant nationalists and colonial promoters in other countries seized on Las Casas's stories as an opportunity to challenge the moral and political legitimacy of Spain's New World empire; in print and images, they propagated a "black legend" that depicted the Spanish as uniquely depraved and wantonly cruel conquerors of Native Americans.

The rapid and overwhelming impact the Spanish had on the native peoples of the Caribbean was merely prelude to the conquests that followed in Mexico and Peru. When Hernando Cortés landed with a force of five hundred men on the Yucatán Peninsula in 1519, he was not quite sure what to expect. Like many other *encomenderos* in the Caribbean, he had heard reports of a wealthy Indian kingdom on the Mexican mainland, and he and his backers were anxious to get there first; so anxious, in fact, that he sailed without the permission of Cuba's governor, who subsequently sent a much larger army to apprehend him. Cortés defeated the governor's force and then used it to augment his own by promising its soldiers shares in the plunder from his expedition.

Cortés led the first major European foray into the Valley of Mexico, the cradle of civilization for the Americas and its most densely populated region. Beginning with the Olmecs in 1200 B.C., successive civilizations had occupied the Valley of Mexico and Yucatán Peninsula, creating cities with pyramids and plazas, highly stratified social orders, and sophisticated knowledge of astronomy and mathematics. These Mesoamerican societies were ruled by a hereditary nobility who oversaw a religion of sun worship and blood sacrifice of human victims. When the Spanish arrived, the Aztecs were the most recent inheritors of this cultural complex, having migrated into the Valley of Mexico from the north two centuries earlier. Their capital city Tenochtitlan, constructed on an island in Lake Texcoco, was home to about 200,000 people, making it one of the largest cities in the world at that time.

Historians have often depicted the fall of Tenochtitlan and the rest of the Aztec Empire as an epic clash between two personalities: the ruthless and single-minded Cortés versus the indecisive and fatalistic Moctezuma. This tendency might be ascribed to the self-aggrandizing way in which victors tell their tales, but it is worth noting that even native accounts described Moctezuma as "lost in despair, in the deepest gloom and sorrow" as he struggled to deal with these strangers.[17] Some commentators, then and now, attribute Moctezuma's failure to prevent the Spanish from entering Tenochtitlan to his advisers' conviction that Cortés was Quetzalcoatl, a mythic founder-god of the Aztecs who had promised to return and reclaim his throne. Through their adherence to this prophecy, the Aztecs mistook the Spanish for gods and ushered in their own doom. This explanation bears considerable resemblance to other accounts of Indians receiving Europeans as gods and deserves to be read with the same skepticism.

Mesoamericans reacted to the Spanish in much the same manner as Indians who met Europeans elsewhere in the Americas. They were impressed by the newcomers' strange appearance and material goods, but rather than regarding them as gods, they treated the newcomers as spiritually potent humans whose presence offered practical advantages as well as dangers. Before he arrived at Tenochtitlan,

Figure 2.2 **Pictograph of Spaniards on horseback in Cañón de Muerto, Arizona. The use of horses and metal weapons gave Spanish conquistadors a considerable military advantage over Native Americans. Photograph by Helga Teiwes. Courtesy of the Arizona State Museum, University of Arizona, neg. no. 28883.**

Cortés amassed an army of native allies that numbered in the thousands from among the Tlaxcalans, who had managed to remain independent from Aztec subjugation. Aztec messengers and Moctezuma himself received Cortés as an honored guest, extending to him the diplomatic gifts and hospitality that Indians typically used to initiate peaceful relations with strangers. Cortés gained the upper hand by taking the Aztec ruler hostage and locking him away from his people. Horses, firearms, and metal swords gave Spanish soldiers a tactical advantage over Native American warriors (see Figure 2.2), but the most effective weapon they brought with them was the unintentional one of smallpox. This disease did far more to immobilize the population of Tenochtitlan during Cortés's siege than any dithering by Moctezuma or erroneous prophecies by his priests.

A similar story unfolded when Francisco Pizarro, a veteran of the conquest of Panama, led a force of less than two hundred men against the Inca Empire in the Andean highlands of South America. In November 1532 Pizarro's army met a force of some forty thousand warriors commanded by the Incan emperor Atahuallpa at Cajamarca in Peru. Once again, the Spanish commander took the initiative by seizing his counterpart and holding him for ransom. Although vastly outnumbered, Pizarro's small army used their horses, guns, and swords to slaughter thousands of the native warriors and many of Atahuallpa's counselors. As had been the case with the Aztecs, the Incas' highly stratified political order worked against them at this moment of crisis: with Atahuallpa imprisoned and many of his lieutenants dead, military command was immobilized and the army of thousands dispersed. Pizarro held Atahuallpa hostage until the Incas delivered up more than thirteen thousand pounds of gold and twenty-six thousand pounds of silver. After collecting this plunder, Pizarro ordered the emperor killed.

By 1533 two great Native American empires had been toppled by small forces of conquistadors amply assisted by native allies. To contemporary observers, the

Spanish successes in America were startling in their swiftness and dividends. While Las Casas cried out against the sufferings the conquistadors inflicted on the natives, other chroniclers concluded that the dramatic victories of Cortés and Pizarro were evidence of God's favor for the Spanish enterprise. "Who can deny that the use of gunpowder against pagans is the burning of incense to Our Lord?" one such writer proclaimed.[18] Other apologists explained how the Indians were benefiting from the forceful imposition of laws and religion that would raise them out of their barbarism. In the meantime, the Spanish Crown tried to rein in the worst excesses of the conquistadors. The so-called New Laws of 1542 were intended to strengthen royal authority in America and end the de facto enslavement of Indians there by limiting the powers of the *encomenderos*. These reforms represented a victory for Las Casas and likeminded reformers, but they met great resistance in the colonies, where they were either enforced selectively or abandoned altogether.

The aura of Spanish invincibility projected by Cortés and Pizarro masked the much harsher fate that awaited many others who tried to imitate them. The Aztec and Inca empires fell not because they were backward or savage, but because they were the most technologically and politically sophisticated native societies in the Americas. Roads and bridges built by the Incas made it possible for the Spanish to invade Andean highlands that would have been impenetrable otherwise. For the vast majority of people living under Aztec rule, the empire did not so much collapse as change hands. The new Spanish overlords in Mesoamerica inherited a social and political order that already made use of tribute labor and expected farmers in the provinces to produce enough crops to sustain professional classes of civil administrators, priests, and soldiers in urban centers. Mesoamerican cities, some of the most densely populated places in the sixteenth-century world, bore the brunt of the lethal epidemics that accompanied the Spanish invaders. The great Indian empires of the New World fell so quickly because they had risen so high. Their infrastructure, population densities, and political centralization left them fatally exposed to the weaponry and communicable diseases carried by the Spanish.

Elsewhere in the Americas, Spanish encounters with native peoples unfolded differently. In places where populations were smaller or still following semi-sedentary ways of life, conquistadors had a much harder time locating the plunder they desired and asserting control over the Indians they met. Consider, for example, the repeated invasions of southeastern North America, which the Spanish called la Florida. Juan Ponce de León met immediate resistance when he arrived with two hundred men on the southern Gulf Coast of the Florida Peninsula in 1521, and he died from a wound received there not long after his force retreated to Havana. Several years later Pánfilo de Narváez, a veteran of the conquest of Jamaica, landed with a force of three hundred men near Tampa Bay. Hostile natives, bad weather, and sickness spelled the slow doom of this expedition, whose handful of survivors, including Cabeza de Vaca, stumbled across the Gulf Coast until reuniting with Spanish countrymen in northern Mexico eight years later.

Hernando de Soto followed in the same ill-fated footsteps in 1539. Marching north from Tampa Bay into the modern Carolinas and then westward into Tennessee, Alabama, and Mississippi, de Soto's force of six hundred men seized what treasure they could find, but failed to locate any wealth to match that of the Aztecs or Incas. Yet they trudged on, following the vague directions offered by Indians anxious to move them beyond their neighborhood, until they crossed the Mississippi into modern Arkansas. Like most of the men who accompanied him, de Soto did not survive this fruitless search, and the remnant of his force sailed empty-handed into the Gulf of Mexico after three years of wreaking havoc in the lower Mississippi Valley (see Map 2.1).

In other regions, the story was much the same: the quest for gold drove Spanish adventurers to the limits of physical and mental endurance and caused prolonged conflict with native populations. While de Soto was marching through southeastern North America, Francisco Vázquez de Coronado led a similar venture northward from Mexico into the American Southwest. There, he encountered the Pueblo peoples, whose communities he ransacked for food, but was unable to locate the rumored cities of gold that had lured him there in the first place. Unlike many of his fellow conquistadors, Coronado managed to survive his trek, but he

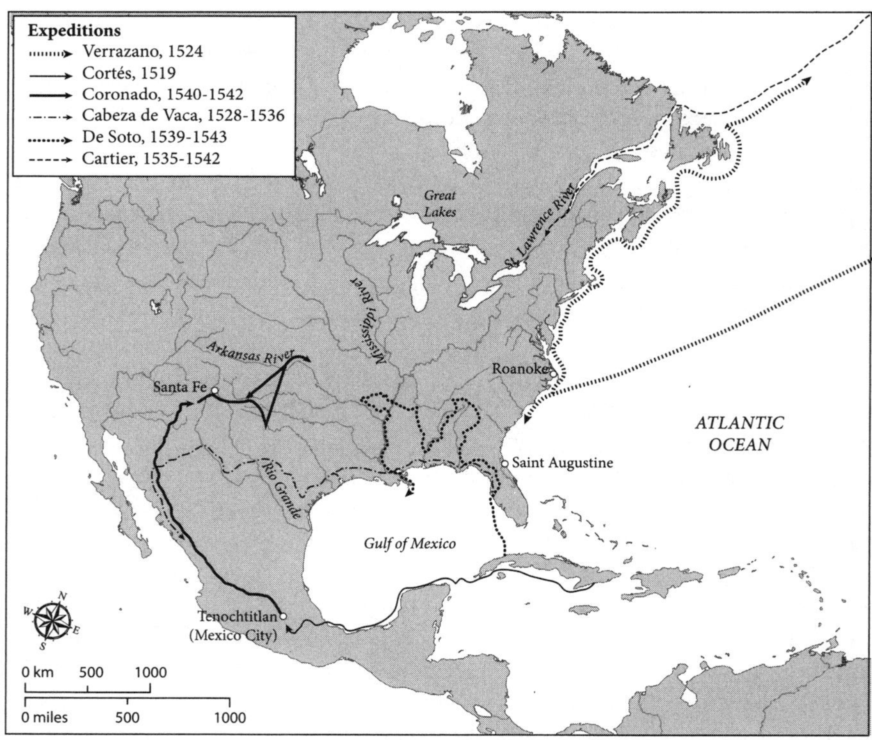

Map 2.1 European Expeditions to North America.

and his backers emerged none the richer for it. In South America, the search for cities of gold prompted the conquistador Lope de Aguirre to seize control of an expedition exploring the Peruvian headwaters of the Amazon River. Aguirre killed his superiors, declared himself the prince of Peru, and led the expedition's remnant on a remarkable journey down the Amazon that paralleled his personal descent into madness. His murderous treatment of Indians and subordinates, including his own daughter, finally led the survivors of the expedition to execute him not long after they reached the Atlantic coast.

The conquests of Cortés and Pizarro gave many Europeans the impression that Native American societies were glimmering with riches, available to those bold enough to seize them. Indeed, long after Aztec and Inca palaces had been pillaged for their movable wealth, the silver mines of Peru and northern Mexico, worked by Indian laborers bound by the *encomienda* system, continued to yield enormous profits for the descendants of the conquistadors. Yet, as the experiences of Narváez, Ponce de León, de Soto, Coronado, and Aguirre indicate, what happened at Tenochtitlan and Cajamarca was the exception to the rule. In most regions of the New World colonized by the Spanish, the conquest of native peoples was uncertain and precarious. In places like la Florida and the American Southwest, Spanish power relied on the slow, unsteady progress of religious missions and military outposts rather than a decisive battle or siege. One lesson offered by the Spanish, if any other European powers chose to take it, was that conquest was a messy and perpetually unfinished business.

RECKONING WITH NORTH AMERICA

For most of the sixteenth century, North America remained an unpromising *terra incognita* in the European scramble for New World wealth. The unsuccessful expeditions of Ponce de León, Narváez, de Soto, and Coronado convinced Spanish conquistadors to focus their energies elsewhere. After Coronado, the Spanish did not return to the Southwest until Juan de Oñate crossed the Rio Grande in 1598 and imposed the *encomienda* system on the Pueblo Indians, establishing the colony of New Mexico. The Spanish built the Atlantic coastal fortress of St. Augustine in 1565 to defend their possession of la Florida against other European powers, but for most of the colonial era it remained an isolated outpost of the Spanish Caribbean. By 1600 any Spanish adventurer seeking his fortune knew better to look for it in the plantations and silver mines of the Caribbean, Mexico, and South America than to chase after cities of gold in the North American interior.

The Portuguese, pioneers in Atlantic navigation in their own right, also colonized the New World but steered clear of North America. The Treaty of Tordesillas in 1494 drew a north-to-south line through the Atlantic, granting the Spanish a monopoly on trade routes west of the line and the Portuguese the same east of the line. Other European nations, of course, ignored this agreement, but it defused a potentially volatile rivalry between the Iberian powers for overseas trade and colonies. While the Spanish were undertaking the conquest of the Americas, the

Portuguese established fortified trading posts in coastal Africa, India, and East Asia, eventually reaching Japan by 1550. Portuguese ships sailing westward from the Indian Ocean entered Atlantic currents that carried them to Brazil, the only part of the Americas that fell within their jurisdiction according to the 1494 treaty line. Initially, they stopped only to take on fresh supplies and cargoes of a dye wood known as brazilwood. By the 1550s, however, investors were turning this way station in Portugal's global trade network into a sugar colony. Portuguese ships carried slaves from West Africa to the northeastern region of Brazil known as Pernambuco (a relatively short trans-Atlantic passage of about three weeks), where landowners put them to work growing sugar, transplanting a method of production the Portuguese were already using in the Madeira Islands in the eastern Atlantic.

Other European powers followed in the Atlantic wake of the Spanish and Portuguese as poachers and interlopers. Gold, silver, sugar, and slaves were tempting targets, and national conflicts rooted in Europe's dynastic rivalries and religious wars provided ready pretexts for acts of aggression on the high seas. As soon as Spanish ships began hauling American gold and silver eastward across the Atlantic, they became prey to an international cast of pirates and privateers (mariners licensed by royal authority to seize enemy ships). French *corsarios* moved from their haunts along the coast of North Africa into the Caribbean, where they raided the Spanish settlements at Havana, Cartagena, and Santo Domingo. English privateers followed suit, raiding and trading with poorly defended outposts of Iberian power along the Atlantic rim. During the 1560s, Plymouth mariner Sir John Hawkins led the first English forays into the African slave trade. Coasting along West Africa, he stole slaves from Portuguese merchants and then carried them to Spanish possessions in the Caribbean. Depending on how happy the Spanish were to see him, Hawkins was greeted either as a smuggler of valuable goods or a pirate who took by force what he could not get by trade. Sir Francis Drake and Sir Walter Ralegh conducted similar raids on Spanish shipping and ports on both sides of the Atlantic, gaining fame and fortune in England as favorites of the queen, but reputations as thieves and desperados among the Spanish.

Religion provided another motive for challenging Iberian hegemony in the Americas. Twice during sixteenth century, French-speaking Protestants known as Huguenots tried to establish New World colonies where they hoped to practice their faith freely and convert local Indians. Europe's Protestant reformers considered such missionary endeavors vital if the native peoples of the Americas were going to be saved from Catholic missionaries sponsored by the Iberian powers. The Huguenots' first colonial venture struggled for five years on the southern coast of Brazil before the Portuguese forcibly evicted the survivors in 1560. Another group of Huguenots who tried to colonize the Carolina coast of North America a few years later were summarily executed by the Spanish, who considered them trespassers on their claim to Florida.

As with other aspects of the colonial enterprise, the English lagged in establishing missions among Indian peoples, but they did not hesitate to use religion in their propaganda attacks against the Spanish. Writing in 1585, the London lawyer Richard Hakluyt the Elder placed "planting religion among those infidels" first on his list of "Inducements" for England to colonize North America.[19] Hakluyt and his cousin Richard Hakluyt the Younger pushed their countrymen to check the expansion of Spain's empire before it was too late. The Hakluyts envied Spain not only for the enormous wealth it was extracting from the New World, but also for the millions of converts it was winning there. If the Protestant Reformation was going to be secured in Europe, then the battle against Catholicism had to be carried to America, where native converts would presumably help turn back the tide of Spanish expansion. In separate publications and reports circulated among councilors to Queen Elizabeth I, the Hakluyts made the case for English colonization abroad, deftly combining appeals to religious duty, economic interests, and international politics. In 1589 Hakluyt the Younger published *The Principall Navigations, Voiages, and Discoveries of the English Nation*, a collection of travelers' accounts and seafaring stories that presented overseas exploration as England's national heritage and destiny, despite the country's obviously late start in the Americas. Meanwhile, the exploits of Ralegh, Drake, and other English privateers on the high seas fanned the spirit of Protestant nationalism evoked by the Hakluyts.

The farther north Europeans sailed from the Caribbean, the more likely they were to spend their time looking for ways to get around North America rather than to colonize it. Vikings sailing from Greenland had tried to colonize Newfoundland in the eleventh century, but the inhospitable climate and hostile natives had caused them to abandon the effort. By the sixteenth century, Europeans had returned to the shores of Newfoundland and eastern Canada, but this time as fishermen. The cod fisheries of Newfoundland and the Labrador coast attracted a multinational array of fishing fleets every year, where they established seasonal camps to process their catch and to trade for furs with local Indians. French navigator Jacques Cartier sailed up the St. Lawrence River, where he encountered the sizable Iroquoian towns of Stadaconé (modern Quebec City) and Hochelaga (modern Montreal) and took samples of local minerals and ores. During the last of these voyages in 1542, the French tried to establish a permanent settlement on the St. Lawrence, but the same problems encountered by the Vikings half a millennium earlier brought a quick end to the enterprise.

A Northwest Passage that would carry ships through North America into the Pacific eluded Cartier and a host of other explorers. Italian navigator Giovanni da Verrazano coasted along North America in 1524 scouting for such a route, but confirmed instead that a sizable landmass blocked passage to China and the East Indies. Cartier's conviction that the St. Lawrence River would carry oceangoing vessels to the Pacific ended when he encountered the Lachine Rapids at Hochelaga. After Cartier's disappointment, the search for the Northwest Passage moved into Arctic waters. English navigator Martin Frobisher made three voyages into the modern Baffin Bay region during the 1570s, carrying back shiploads of ore for analysis by English metallurgists. All the expertise and financial support he secured in London could not turn American dirt and stone into gold and silver. His countrymen Sir Humphrey Gilbert and John Davis followed suit during the 1580s and met similar results.

Like second marriages, the quest for the Northwest Passage was testimony to the triumph of hope over experience. European explorers and cartographers literally tried willing it into existence, placing the as-yet undiscovered route on sixteenth-century maps of North America. Cartier gave the name "Lachine" to the rapids he encountered in the St. Lawrence because he believed China rested not far beyond them. Such dreams could be costly. In 1610 Henry Hudson and his crew wintered in the frozen waters of the vast inland sea of northern Canada, later called Hudson Bay. Convinced that a route to Asia was finally within his reach, Hudson pressed his men to continue their voyage when the ice broke in the spring. Instead, they mutinied and set Hudson, his son, and a few loyal crew members adrift in an open boat. The mutineers headed back to England; Hudson was never heard from again.

The image of Hudson and his hapless companions slowly freezing and starving to death in the Canadian wilderness does not immediately invite comparisons to the exploits of the Spanish conquistadors, but both illuminated the darker side of the human curiosity that drove the European exploration of America. Like the conquistadors, the maritime pursuers of the Northwest Passage were treasure hunters whose obsession and gullibility blinded them to unpleasant realities. Cartier brought back to France tales of Saguenay, a kingdom of gold and silver in the Canadian interior described to him by Indian informants. Verrazano told a similar story of Norumbega, a fabled city of gold in northern New England. Nor did the need for provisions, safety, or reliable directions encourage these explorers to treat the Indians they met as anything other than tools placed at their disposal by divine providence. Cartier, Frobisher, and others kidnapped Indian chiefs, children, and unwitting passersby at will, poisoning intercultural relations for subsequent voyagers and colonists. Eastern North America may not have yielded the same riches or spectacular conquests as Mexico and Peru, but Europeans exhibited the same hubris and avarice there as they did farther south.

HOPE AND FAILURE AT ROANOKE

Wanchese and Manteo came face-to-face with the best and worst of European curiosity about the New World during the English attempt to colonize Roanoke. Their London hosts, Sir Walter Ralegh and Thomas Harriot, embodied the Renaissance spirit of inquiry and cosmopolitanism. Like the two Richard Hakluyts, Ralegh and Harriot were Renaissance men, immersing themselves in the fields of geography, cartography, and ethnography. During the 1580s, they articulated a plan for the English colonization of America that purposefully contrasted their methods and goals with the unbridled pillage and enslavement they attributed to the Spanish. In their version of the story, they expected Indians to be drawn willingly to the English, first as customers in the fur trade and then as converts to Protestant

Christianity. Having secured the cooperation and submission of the natives, the English would turn their colonies into havens for the mother country's poor and unfortunate, who would migrate to America and find prosperity by converting America's natural bounty into "merchantable commodities"—furs, fish, naval stores, pearls, copper, and iron—for export to European markets.

At least, that was the plan. The vision promoted in London by the Hakluyts, Ralegh, and Harriot proved very hard to implement because of the mixture of dreams and experience the English brought with them. In the spring of 1585, a fleet of seven ships carrying six hundred men, about half of them soldiers, sailed from London for the Outer Banks of the Carolina coast. Wanchese and Manteo, who sailed with them, no doubt realized that this expedition had an altogether different purpose than the one they had encountered a year earlier. On landing at Roanoke, the soldiers built a fort while smaller parties conducted reconnaissance among the neighboring Indian towns. Wanchese returned as soon as he could to his fellow Roanoke Indians and discouraged them from assisting the newcomers. Manteo, however, stayed on, working as an interpreter and helping Harriot and the artist John White collect information on the land and its inhabitants. Despite all the talk in London about converting the Indians to Christianity, no missionaries accompanied this expedition. Nor did the farmers or craftsmen needed to create a self-sufficient community. It did, however, bring along a metallurgist, whose skills would be necessary for assessing the gold, silver, and precious stones the English were hoping to find.

The English approach to Roanoke was also shaped by their experience in colonizing Ireland. Long before they applied the word "plantation" to their American colonies, the English used it to refer to the settlement of Protestant subjects on land conquered in the Munster and Ulster regions of Ireland. In the century between 1570 and 1670, more than 100,000 English and Scottish Protestants moved to Ireland, where they wrestled control of the land from the native Irish in a series of bloody wars, rebellions, and reprisals. Ralegh selected two veterans of the Irish campaigns in the 1570s, Ralph Lane and Sir Richard Grenville, to lead the Roanoke colony, and many of the expedition's rank and file came from the Irish service as well. These men approached the Algonquians they met in coastal Carolina with the same guarded suspicion they showed the native Irish; when these English adventurers felt threatened, they responded with the same overwhelming display of force. In one famous incident, an English party burned an Algonquian town in retaliation for a silver cup that went missing during their visit there. When Lane became convinced that a local chief was conspiring against the colony, he led a preemptive attack that ended in the chief's murder and decapitation, a method of terrorizing civilian populations that the English had often used against the Irish.

In the aftermath of such confrontations, the Algonquians decided that the best way to deal with the invaders was to leave them to their own devices. One by one, the inhabitants of nearby towns withdrew into the interior, taking their corn with them. Without the food provided by the local indigenous populations, the English found themselves isolated and starving. In less than a year, the survivors sailed for home. The Roanoke colony had collapsed, a rude and humbling disappointment for the dreams of New World empire launched by colonial promoters in London.

John White led a second group of English colonists to North America in 1587. This expedition had an entirely different character. Rather than young male adventurers drawn from the armies in Ireland, it consisted of fourteen families who planned to cultivate the land and create a self-perpetuating community. This was the famous "Lost Colony" of Roanoke, although "abandoned" is a more appropriate descriptor. White had intended to land them north of the Outer Banks, on the more fertile soil of the Chesapeake Bay, but the commander of the fleet that carried them across the Atlantic refused to take them further than Roanoke because he was anxious to turn his attention to privateering in the Spanish Caribbean. Not long after re-occupying the site of the earlier expedition, White sailed home to recruit more settlers and financial support, but his efforts to resupply the colony were interrupted by the Spanish Armada's attack on England. When White finally returned to Roanoke three years later, the colony was deserted. His search party found "CROATOAN" carved into the abandoned settlement's stockade, a hopeful sign that they had found refuge among Manteo's people. White's pursuit of them, however, went no further because his escort insisted on setting course for the Caribbean.

Ever since, the unknown fate of the "lost colony of Roanoke" has fired imaginations. It is likely that they did move elsewhere, although Croatoan probably would not have been able to support them for too long. They may have moved northward, closer to where White had originally intended to locate the colony. When English adventurers founded Jamestown in 1607, they heard reports from local Indians about fair-skinned people living near the southern reaches of the Chesapeake Bay, but the same informants told them that these were only a remnant of a much larger group that had been killed by hostile neighbors. Captain John Smith sent a detail of men to find these rumored survivors, but they returned empty-handed. In all likelihood, by the time Jamestown was founded, any survivors of the Roanoke colony had dispersed into coastal Algonquian Indian populations by way of captivity and intermarriage.

In 1705 Virginia historian Robert Beverley wrote of the abandoned Roanoke colonists, "So strong was the Desire of Riches, and so eager the Pursuit of a rich Trade, that all Concern for the Lives of their fellow Christians, Kindred, Neighbours, and Country-men, weigh'd nothing in the Comparison."[20] His words provided a fitting epitaph not only for the Lost Colony, but also for all the dashed dreams and human misery that unfolded during the first century of contact between the Old World and the New. Despite their plans to the contrary, the English encounter with the Carolina Algonquians was not all that different from the Spanish encounter with the Aztecs. In both cases, the common humanity that connected Europeans and Indians was no match for the "Desire of Riches" that drove them apart. Europeans, regardless of their national origin, approached the Americas with blueprints for conquest and colonization already in their heads, drawn from their experiences in the Mediterranean and eastern Atlantic. Likewise, Native Americans used their own existing frames of reference for the physical and spiritual worlds to respond to Europeans. Manteo chose to cast his lot with the newcomers, while Wanchese decided it was best to stay away from them. Their successors in the seventeenth century would not have the luxury of Wanchese's option.

CHRONOLOGY

1519–1521	Hernando Cortés leads Spanish conquest of the Aztecs.
1528–1536	Alvar Nuñez Cabeza de Vaca's captivity and sojourn among Indians of the Gulf Coast.
1532–1533	Francisco Pizarro leads Spanish conquest of the Incas.
1534–1542	Jacques Cartier explores St. Lawrence River in search of the Northwest Passage.
1539–1542	Hernando de Soto's expedition in southeastern North America.
1540–1542	Francisco Vázquez de Coronado's expedition in southwestern North America.
1542	Bartolomé de Las Casas publishes *A Brief Account of the Destruction of the Indies.*
1565	Spain establishes St. Augustine to defend its claim to Florida.
1584–1585	*Manteo and Wanchese visit London.*
1585	*Manteo and Wanchese return with first Roanoke colony.*
1587–1590	*Manteo assists second Roanoke colony (the "Lost Colony").*
1611	Henry Hudson abandoned by his mutinous crew in the vast inland sea of northern Canada (later renamed Hudson Bay) while searching for the Northwest Passage.
1819	John Heckewelder publishes Delaware oral tradition of the arrival of the first Europeans in the Hudson River region.

NOTES

1. The report on the first Roanoke expedition by the ship captains Philip Amadas and Arthur Barlowe may be found in Richard Hakluyt, *Voyages and Discoveries: The Principal Navigations, Voyages, Traffiques and Discoveries of the English Nation*, ed. Jack Beeching (New York: Penguin, 1972), 270–275.
2. For the account of the relief expedition's arrival at Roanoke, see "John White's Fifth Voyage, 1590," in Richard Hakluyt, *Voyages to the Virginia Colonies*, ed. A. L. Rowse (London: Century, 1986), 153–168.

3. John Heckewelder, *History, Manners, and Customs of the Indian Nations, Who Once Inhabited Pennsylvania and the Neighboring States* (1818; Bowie, MD: Heritage Books, 1990), 71–75.
4. "Letter of Columbus to Various Persons Describing the Results of his First Voyage and Written on the Return Journey," in Christopher Columbus, *The Four Voyages*, ed. J. M. Cohen (New York: Penguin, 1969), 117–118.
5. See "Hariot's Brief and True Report of the New Found Land of Virginia," in Hakluyt, *Voyages to the Virginia Colonies*, 130.
6. Enrique Pupo-Walker, ed., *Castaways: The Narrative of Alvar Nuñez Cabeza de Vaca*, trans. Frances M. López-Morillas (Berkeley: University of California Press, 1993), 49, 72.
7. "Hariot's Brief and True Report of the New Found Land of Virginia," 132–133.
8. Thomas Morton, *New English Canaan*, ed. Jack Dempsey (1637; Scituate, MA: Digital Scanning, 1999), 19–20.
9. William Bradford, *Of Plymouth Plantation*, ed. Harvey Wish (New York: Capricorn Books, 1962), 176.
10. "Letter of Columbus," 119, 121.
11. Sir Walter Ralegh, *The Discoverie of the Large, Rich, and Bewtiful Empyre of Guiana*, ed. Neil L. Whitehead (Norman: University of Oklahoma Press, 1997), 178–179.
12. Jean de Léry, *History of a Voyage to the Land of Brazil*, ed. and trans. Janet Whately (Berkeley: University of California Press, 1990), 57, 67.
13. Michel de Montaigne, *Selected Essays*, trans. Donald M. Frame (New York: Walter J. Black, 1943), 77, 79–83, 85.
14. "Hariot's Brief and True Report of the New Found Land of Virginia," 127–129.
15. Léry, *History of a Voyage to the Land of Brazil*, 66; and "Hariot's Brief and True Report of the New Found Land of Virginia," 131.
16. "Royal Instructions to Ovando," in *The Spanish Tradition in America*, ed. Charles Gibson (New York: Harper & Row, 1968), 55–56.
17. Miguel Leon-Portilla, ed., *The Broken Spears: The Aztec Account of the Conquest of Mexico* (Boston: Beacon Press, 1992), 29.
18. Gonzalo Fernández de Oviedo, cited in Matthew Restall, *Seven Myths of the Spanish Conquest* (New York: Oxford University Press, 2003), 105.
19. Richard Hakluyt the Elder, "Inducements to the Likeing of the Voyage Intended towards Virginia," in *The Elizabethans' America*, ed. Louis B. Wright (Cambridge, MA: Harvard University Press, 1966), 26.
20. Robert Beverley, *The History of the Present State of Virginia*, ed. Louis B. Wright (1947; Charlottesville: University Press of Virginia, 1968), 25.

SUGGESTIONS FOR FURTHER READING

For the story of Wanchese and Manteo, see Alden T. Vaughan, "Sir Walter Ralegh's Indian Interpreters, 1584–1618," *William and Mary Quarterly*, 3d ser., 59 (2002): 341–376. Vaughan provides a comprehensive account of other colonial-era Indian travelers in *Transatlantic Encounters: American Indians in Britain, 1500–1776* (Cambridge, UK: Cambridge University Press, 2006). Other works that examine Indian reactions to early encounters with Europeans include Daniel K. Richter, *Facing East from Indian Country: A Native History of Early America* (Cambridge, MA: Harvard University Press, 2001), and James Axtell, *Beyond*

1492: Encounters in Colonial North America (New York: Oxford University Press, 1992). The question of whether Indians greeted Europeans as gods is addressed in Evan Haefeli, "On First Contact and Apotheosis: Manitou and Men in North America," *Ethnohistory* 54 (2007): 407–443, and the Indian perspective on gift exchanges in these early encounters is described in Christopher L. Miller and George R. Hamell, "A New Perspective on Indian-White Contact: Cultural Symbols and Colonial Trade," *Journal of American History* 73 (1986): 311–328.

The process by which Indians and Europeans gradually learned to make sense of each other is described in Nancy Shoemaker, *A Strange Likeness: Becoming Red and White in Eighteenth-Century North America* (New York: Oxford University Press, 2004); Colin G. Calloway, *New Worlds for All: Indians, Europeans, and the Remaking of Early America* (Baltimore: Johns Hopkins University Press, 1997); and Karen Ordahl Kupperman, *Indians and English: Facing Off in Early America* (Ithaca, NY: Cornell University Press, 2000). On the pre-Columbian population of North America and the impact that disease transmission had on it, see Noble David Cook, *Born to Die: Disease and New World Conquest, 1492–1650* (Cambridge, UK: Cambridge University Press, 1998); Alfred Crosby, *Ecological Imperialism: The Biological Expansion of Europe, 900–1900* (Cambridge, UK: Cambridge University Press, 1986); John D. Daniels, "The Indian Population of North America in 1492," *William and Mary Quarterly*, 3d ser., 49 (1992): 298–320; and David S. Jones, "Virgin Soils Revisited," *William and Mary Quarterly*, 3d ser., 60 (2003): 703–742. Works that examine the impact which the discovery of America had on Europe include J. H. Elliott, *The Old World and the New, 1492–1650* (1970; Cambridge, UK: Cambridge University Press, 1992), and Roger Schlesinger, *In the Wake of Columbus: The Impact of the New World on Europe, 1492–1650* (Wheeling, IL: Harlan Davidson, 1996).

Of the vast literature on the Spanish Conquest, works noteworthy for their attention to comparative or ethnographic contexts include: J. H. Elliott, *Empires of the Atlantic World: Britain and Spain in America, 1492–1830* (New Haven, CT: Yale University Press, 2006); Matthew Restall, *Seven Myths of the Spanish Conquest* (New York: Oxford University Press, 2003); Anthony Pagden, *Lords of All the World: Ideologies of Empire in Spain, Britain, and France, c. 1500–c. 1800* (New Haven, CT: Yale University Press, 1995); and Inga Clendinnen, *Ambivalent Conquests: Maya and Spaniard in Yucatan, 1517–1570* (Cambridge, UK: Cambridge University Press, 1987). For Spanish encounters in North America, see David J. Weber, *The Spanish Frontier in North America* (New Haven, CT: Yale University Press, 1992). Challenges to Spanish power in the Caribbean are discussed in Kris E. Lane, *Pillaging the Empire: Piracy in the Americas, 1500–1750* (Armonk, NY: Sharpe, 1998).

For England's encounter with America during the Elizabethan era, see Karen Ordahl Kupperman, *Roanoke: The Abandoned Colony*, 2nd ed. (Lanham, MD: Rowman & Littlefield, 2007); Michael Leroy Oberg, *The Head in Edward Nugent's Hand: Roanoke's Forgotten Indians* (Philadelphia: University of Pennsylvania Press, 2008); and Peter C. Mancall, *Hakluyt's Promise: An Elizabethan's Obsession for an English America* (New Haven, CT: Yale University Press, 2007). The Irish roots of English approaches to American colonization are discussed in Nicholas P. Canny, "The Ideology of English Colonization: From Ireland to America," *William and Mary Quarterly*, 3d ser., 30 (1973): 575–598.

CHAPTER 3

American Footholds

Planting Colonies, 1607–1732

In March 1638 Anne Hutchinson's long battle against the authorities in the Massachusetts Bay colony came to an end. As she listened to her sentence of excommunication from the Boston church, a flood of emotions must have washed over her: anger, resignation, regret, and perhaps even pride in having defended her beliefs against detractors far more powerful than she. Maybe she even paused to reflect on the circumstances that had brought her from her native England to this moment, the combination of political events and personal faith that had led her across the Atlantic and to this tiny settlement on the shores of a strange land. Another person in Hutchinson's shoes might have ascribed her misfortunes to bad luck, but she was a Puritan, and Puritans did not believe in luck, good or bad. Rather, they believed in divine providence, the inscrutable but undeniable will of God, which directed all human affairs. Hutchinson's faith in God had led her and her family to join other Puritans colonizing Massachusetts. Now she was being banished from the community of her co-believers. How hard it must have been for her to deal with the realization that her family's tribulations were not over, that God had more in store for them before they would know peace again.

Nothing in Hutchinson's background had indicated that this trouble would come her way. In England, she had been the model of a good wife: pious, industrious, and fertile (her church trial occurred during her fifteenth pregnancy). She could read and write, but so did many Puritan women, who cultivated their relationship with God by studying and talking about Scripture. She and her husband William were admitted to communion in the Boston church shortly after they arrived in America in 1634, and Anne took the message of one of its ministers, the Reverend John Cotton, to heart. Like other Puritan clergy, Cotton preached "justification by faith alone." That is, no good works or religious rituals could win a person salvation; only God, in his infinite mercy, could grant that. In prayer meetings she held in her home, chiefly for other women like her whose domestic responsibilities sometimes kept them away from weekly sermons, Hutchinson expounded on this creed.

The trouble started when men as well as women began attending these meetings. Like many other Protestant sects, Puritans had mixed feelings about lay preaching. While they did not believe that the clergy had a monopoly on interpreting Scripture, they also looked askance at women instructing men, which they believed violated St. Paul's proscription against women speaking in church. A woman helping other women cultivate their faith was acceptable, even laudable; a woman drawing large crowds of both sexes to hear her scriptural commentary was an affront to the natural order of things.

Hutchinson's growing reputation as a lay preacher emboldened her to speak out against members of the clergy she thought unfit for the pulpit. Along with John Cotton and her brother-in-law the Reverend John Wheelwright, she questioned whether some of the ministers who had come to Massachusetts were indeed saved. If not, they had no business acting as shepherds to the faithful. This was a touchy subject among clergy and laypeople alike. Ministers were respected leaders of the community. Many Puritans in Massachusetts were there because they had followed their ministers, who were being fined and jailed in England. Furthermore, a central doctrine of the Puritan faith was humankind's inability to fathom God's will. All humans, even those predestined for salvation by God, shared in original sin and were therefore imperfect creatures. No one could discern with absolute certainty God's grace in another, or even him- or herself. Too speak too confidently of your own salvation was to flirt with the heresy of antinomianism, the notion that God's grace washed away your sinful nature, freed you from biblical strictures meant to control it, and left you capable of passing judgment on the spiritual state of others.

As Hutchinson's pronouncements against some members of the clergy grew more direct and critical, the initially sympathetic Cotton withdrew his support from her. Wheelwright's open antagonism with other members of the clergy drew her into a brewing crisis in the political leadership of the colony. In November 1637 the colony's magistrates put her on trial for sedition. Her prosecutors, including Massachusetts governor John Winthrop, accused her of maligning the colony's ministers and "the weakning [sic] of the hands and hearts of the people towards them." Hutchinson defended herself ably by citing scriptural precedents for her actions and opinions, but she crossed a line when she claimed that God revealed his will to her "by an immediate revelation." Winthrop stated plainly, "I am persuaded that the revelation she brings forth is delusion." The majority of the court agreed, sentencing her to banishment from the colony. At her excommunication hearing, another one of her critics condemned her for having "stept out of your place, *you have rather bine a Husband than a Wife and a preacher than a Hearer; and a Magistrate than a Subject*."[1] With her family and a few stalwart followers, Hutchinson moved south to Narragansett Bay, where they founded the town of Portsmouth, Rhode Island. It was time to start over.

Anne Hutchinson's expulsion from Massachusetts is an often told tale, one as closely linked to the founding of New England as the first Thanksgiving. For many modern sympathizers, she has become an early American Eve, punished and exiled for acting independently of male authority. That approach to her story, however, also confines it to the specific regional and cultural context of the Puritan migration to New England. Like children in a grade school pageant, we tend to tell the story of seventeenth-century America as a series of parallel but discreet events, each with its own cast of characters, setting, and plot. The story of New England concerns religious exiles who struggled to balance liberty and orthodoxy. The founding of Virginia is a romantic adventure linking the beautiful and innocent Pocahontas with the swashbuckling Captain John Smith. New France and New Netherland were fur-trading colonies, more concerned with beaver pelts than people, and Florida and New Mexico were distant outposts of New Spain's conquistadors and missionaries. Divided into these distinct regions, each colony founded in the early seventeenth century had its own miniature epic to tell, its own heroes and villains to parade across the stage, its own romances and tragedies to unfold.

Fair enough. The colonies were founded at different times by different people, and for different reasons. Nevertheless, shared motives and experiences connected them. Hutchinson was a Puritan and a victim of that religion's particular form of zealotry, but her story can tell us much about the colonization of North America beyond New England's borders. What factors pushed colonists like Hutchinson out of their homes in the Old World and pulled them toward North America's unfamiliar climate, geography, and peoples? How did the grand designs launched by colonial promoters mesh with the individual ambitions of the migrants who implemented them? And why did the eastern seaboard of North America acquire an English character in its population, language, and institutions when other European powers also tried to plant colonies there?

Anne Hutchinson's American odyssey illustrates all these questions. Hers was a world in motion in the seventeenth century, and her decision to come to Massachusetts reflected the particular political and economic circumstances that drove English migration to North America at a time when other powers had great difficulty transplanting their countrymen there. Once in America, Hutchinson illustrated the tension between the motives of individual colonists and the plans of nations, corporations, and investors who tried to control them. Most importantly, Hutchinson's life illustrates how the law of unintended consequences applied to the colonization of America. No matter how well planned or how heavily capitalized, no colony ever managed to produce the outcome expected by its founders. It is in that distance between expectations and results that the most compelling and universal story of early American colonization lies, whether for those who hatched the plans in the Old World or those who implemented them in the New.

JAMESTOWN AND THE FOUNDATIONS OF THE CHESAPEAKE

In May 1607 three English ships weighed anchor at a marshy peninsula about fifty miles upriver from the Chesapeake Bay. The expedition's leaders named the river they were on the James after their king, and in a bit of redundant flattery, they christened their new settlement Jamestown. Back in London, King James I may have smiled on hearing this news, but within a few years he probably wished the brains behind Jamestown had attached someone else's name to the venture. In the annals of American corporate enterprise, few projects have gone so thoroughly and so quickly astray, at the cost of so many lives.

Roanoke had failed, but it did not deter the English from pursuing colonization in other regions of the New World. During the 1590s, Sir Walter Ralegh explored the northern coast of South America and wrote glowing accounts of Guiana. Other promoters organized schemes to colonize the West Indies and northern New England, but none of these efforts established a permanent English foothold in America. That "first" belonged to the Virginia Company of London, but in light of the tragedy that unfolded at Jamestown, it is a dubious distinction. Jamestown should have been abandoned. The fact that it was not is a tribute to human avarice and bullheadedness, not foresight or perseverance.

One of the lessons from Roanoke was that colonization was too risky to be undertaken by only a small group of backers. A great deal of money was needed to supply colonial expeditions and all could be lost if they met with pirates, foul weather, hostile natives, or foreign rivals. Initially, the Virginia Company followed Ralegh's model of relying on a coterie of wealthy investors for its capital, but in 1609 it started selling shares like a modern corporation, eventually attracting hundreds of investors who stood to profit according to the number of shares they owned. The crown granted charters to such joint-stock companies that allowed them to select their own leaders (the equivalent of a modern board of directors) and set their own rules and regulations, so long as they conformed to English laws. England's earliest colonies in North America were thus founded as business enterprises, and like all businesses, their primary objective was generating profit.

England was at peace with Spain when the Virginia Company was chartered in 1606, so the lure of privateering in the Caribbean was not nearly as strong as it had been during the 1580s. How then did investors in this enterprise expect to profit? The occupations of the earliest colonists in Jamestown offer some clues. About half of them were gentlemen, mostly sons or relatives of investors in the Virginia Company, and as such, they did not expect to engage in the hard labor of colonization. For that work they brought along a variety of tradesmen, laborers, and soldiers employed by the Virginia Company. The inclusion of such skilled workers as carpenters, bricklayers, and blacksmiths was practical enough—the erection of a stockade for defense and a storehouse to secure provisions were among the first orders of business—but the presence of goldsmiths, apothecaries, a jeweler, and a perfumer also indicated that the Company's directors were on a treasure hunt. Previous expeditions to the region had failed to turn up any precious metals or exotic spices, but that did not stop the Virginia Company from looking for exactly the same things, as well as searching for an inland passage to the Pacific Ocean. The results could have been predicted by anyone familiar with the Roanoke misadventure. Malnutrition, disease, and the psychological disorientation of finding themselves in a strange place weakened the Jamestown colonists' physical and mental health. About two-thirds of the first arrivals died within a year, their deaths attributed by one of their leaders to "Swellings, Flixes [fluxes, i.e. dysentery], Burning Fevers, and by warres... but for the most part they died of mere famine. There were never Englishmen left in a forreigne Countrey in such miserie as wee were in this new discovered Virginia."[2]

The consequences of this unraveling were far worse in Jamestown than they had been in Roanoke. The colonists' health problems were compounded by their location on a peninsula where tidal currents gave their drinking water a dangerously high salinity. Even if they had had plenty to eat, the colonists would have succumbed to salt poisoning so long as they relied on the river for their water supply. Also, they had settled in a region where neighboring Indians had already formed negative impressions of Europeans. During the 1570s, Spanish priests had failed in an attempt to establish a mission in the Chesapeake, leaving much ill will in their wake. The Jamestown colonists also heard reports that survivors of the lost Roanoke colony had migrated into the southern Chesapeake Bay and found refuge among native allies, but had then been wiped out by more powerful neighbors. The Chesapeake Bay Algonquians were more populous and united than any of the Indians the English had previously encountered. Not long before the founding of Jamestown, a powerful confederacy of thirty towns with a combined population of about twenty thousand emerged in the James River region under the authority of a paramount chief named Wahunsenacawh. Mistaking his title as chief for his name, the English came to know him as Powhatan, and they called the Indians he led the Powhatan confederacy.

At least one Jamestown colonist was already experienced in dealing with adversity in strange places. Neither a gentleman nor a laborer, Captain John Smith fit into a category all his own. Before signing on with the Virginia Company in 1606, he endured a remarkable four-year odyssey in Eastern Europe, Turkey, Russia, and North Africa. Hiring himself out as a mercenary, Smith fought with the Austrian army (the origin of his title as "Captain") against Muslim armies in Hungary, was captured by the Turks and sold as a slave in Istanbul, escaped into Russia, and sailed among pirates along the Barbary Coast. He returned to London just as the Virginia Company was recruiting for the Jamestown expedition. By temperament and experience, Smith was drawn to the venture, and in a rare bit of good judgment, the company's leaders must have thought that Smith's survival skills would come in handy in the new colony. Although Smith lacked genteel status, they appointed him one of the seven councilors who would oversee the settlement, a fact not revealed until the expedition had landed in America, perhaps out of concern for sowing rivalries among the councilors before they had even left England.

Smith did not get along with his fellow adventurers. For reasons that remain unclear, he was arrested during the Atlantic crossing and almost hanged, probably because rivals with greater social status feared that he would challenge their authority. After landing at Jamestown, Smith spent most of his time leading small exploratory parties in the Chesapeake Bay and extracting corn from neighboring Indians whether by trade, threat, or subterfuge. His refusal to stay in Jamestown for too long saved him from the disease and despair that wracked the settlement.

As a result of premature deaths and political intrigue, Smith eventually found himself the undisputed leader of the colony. He promulgated a new rule, "[he] who would not work must not eat," to force the colonists to spend four hours a day in such common labors as clearing and tending fields.[3] While hardly a taxing work regimen by modern standards, Smith's universal application and enforcement of it with military discipline shocked and angered his contemporaries. Elizabethan gentlemen did not work with their hands, period. Men of lower social status expected to work, but skilled tradesmen considered menial labor an insult to their status, and even soldiers and servants expected to have strenuous exertion balanced by frequent and leisurely breaks for food, drink, and conversation. Smith's dictatorial manner did not sit well with such men; he forced them to attend religious services and to participate in militia training. No doubt, many Jamestown colonists came to Virginia expecting to live in the style of Spanish conquistadors, surrounded by Indian slaves. Smith had little patience for such daydreams. He knew that without their own reliable food source, the colonists would never be able to negotiate from a position of strength with the Powhatans.

Maintaining that upper hand was the guiding principle behind Smith's Indian relations. He did not exhibit the same intellectual curiosity about Indians that Thomas Harriot and John White did in Roanoke, but neither did he blindly overreact when he felt aggrieved or threatened by them. Smith approached the Indians he encountered warily, even those who appeared welcoming. He refused to trade firearms with them, knowing that a monopoly on such weapons gave the English a psychological advantage that could compensate for their other weaknesses. He also insisted on keeping Indian visitors to Jamestown outside of its stockade, so that they would not be able to gauge with certainty the settlement's population or resources. When negotiating with Indians, Smith exchanged hostages at the outset as a way to discourage premeditated attacks. Previous experience had taught him that survival in a strange land depended on knowing the terrain and keeping potential enemies guessing about his strength.

In one typical episode, Smith's party came upon an Indian town with "large Cornefields" and inhabitants who indicated a desire to trade. The Indians entreated Smith to sail a little farther upriver, but Smith sensed a trap when several canoes of armed men appeared behind his party. Smith's men opened fire on the canoes, causing many of the warriors to swim ashore and seek refuge. Smith seized their abandoned canoes and began breaking them into pieces, which caused the Indians to "lay downe their bowes, making signs of peace." Smith told them he wanted "foure hundred baskets full of Corne, otherwise we would breake all their boats, and burne their houses and corn and all they had." They promptly capitulated and brought the corn. "So much as we could carry we tooke," Smith wrote, "and so departing good friends, we returned to James Towne."[4]

Incidents such as this one hardly seem calculated to create "good friends," but among his fellow colonists, Smith alone seemed capable of exhibiting strategic restraint during such confrontations. Contrast his conduct with another raid on an Indian town led by George Percy, who was trying to recover deserters who had run away from Jamestown. Percy and his men burned the town, cut down its corn fields, and killed more than a dozen of its residents. On their way back to Jamestown, they threw several children they had taken captive overboard and shot them in the water. They saved the mother of the murdered children so that they could burn her at the stake in Jamestown, but Percy decided instead to have her dispatched by the sword. Such self-defeating violence was exactly what Smith tried to avoid. He threatened, bullied, and bluffed, but he also knew that burning crops and murdering children would not feed Jamestown.

As Indians had done at Roanoke, the Powhatans could have doomed Jamestown simply by withdrawing their support, but they chose instead to approach the colonists with the same wariness that Smith showed them. Powhatan and his kinsman Opechancanough regarded the English as another community that might be incorporated into their confederacy. The strangers may have been hopelessly disoriented in their new home, but they controlled access to valuable trade goods and powerful weapons.

During a foray into the countryside in January 1608, Smith was taken captive by Opechancanough's warriors and carried to Werowocomoco, the seat of Powhatan's power on the Pamunkey River (renamed the York by the English). We know what happened next only from Smith's self-aggrandizing account published sixteen years later. Smith claimed he was brought before Powhatan, who was arrayed in a "great robe" of raccoon skins ("all the tayles hanging by"), surrounded by his multiple wives, and attended by two hundred "grim Courtiers" who "stood wondering at him, as he had beene a monster." After feasting and "a long consultation" with his audience, Powhatan ordered Smith dragged to "two great stones," where he was laid out and a battery of warriors stood ready with clubs "to beate out his braines." Suddenly, Pocahontas—ten years old and "the Kings dearest daughter"—dashed from the crowd, cradled Smith's head in her arms, and "laid her owne" on top of his "to save him from death." Moved by his daughter's display, Powhatan ordered Smith's life spared, so that "he should live to make him hatchets and her [Pocahontas] bells, beads, and copper."[5]

In his autobiographical writings, Smith fashioned himself into an Elizabethan James Bond who traveled to distant lands and outsmarted sinister enemies (see Figure 3.1). In these stories, Pocahontas was not the first exotic woman who became smitten with him and helped him out of a tight spot. In all likelihood, he embellished the details of his rescue at Werowocomoco and perhaps invented Pocahontas's role in it (Pocahontas did not appear in his published accounts of the story until after she had become famous in England). Nevertheless, the fact remains that Smith did survive his captivity there and Powhatan did send him back to Jamestown as his emissary. If Pocahontas interceded in these events, she was probably part of a mock execution and adoption ceremony meant to make Smith one of Powhatan's subordinate chiefs. Such ceremonial acts of submission occurred on both sides of the cultural divide. Not long after Smith's return from Werowocomoco, the English tried to "crown" Powhatan as a vassal of King James I. The Virginia Company provided a copper

Figure 3.1 ***C[apt]. Smith taketh the king of Pamunkee prisoner, 1608,*** **from John Smith,** ***The Generall historie of Virginia*** **(London: Michael Sparkes, 1624). Smith's penchant for depicting himself as a daring adventurer is evident in this illustration from one of the several autobiographical histories he wrote after returning to England from Jamestown. Grenville Kane Collection. Rare Books Division, Department of Rare Books and Special Collections, Princeton University Library. Courtesy of the Princeton University Library.**

crown, scarlet cloak, and trove of other presents, but Powhatan refused to visit Jamestown to receive them, insisting instead that the English come to him. Eventually, they did, but then Powhatan refused to kneel to receive the crown, despite the "many perswasions, examples, and instructions" offered by the English. The chief knew a gesture of submission when he saw it. With Powhatan unwilling to bend his knees, the English attendants resorted to "leaning hard on his shoulders" until he "stooped" far enough so that they could slide the crown on his head. Smith thought the whole affair a farce. Rather than making Powhatan more tractable, it led him to "so much overvalue himselfe, that he respected us as much as nothing at all."[6]

Smith's leadership brought some much needed discipline and common sense to the colony, but he was only one man, and an unpopular one at that. In October

1609 he was badly burned in an accidental gunpowder explosion. In need of a long convalescence, he sailed home, never to see Virginia again, although he followed the progress of the colony from London. Jamestown's greatest horrors followed in the wake of his departure. During the "starving time" in the winter of 1609–1610, colonists resorted to eating cats and rats and some even cannibalized the corpses of their dead companions. By the spring, only sixty remained alive, less than 10 percent of the seven hundred who had come to the colony after the first landing. Yet, the arrival of three hundred more in May 1610 ensured that this particular branch of hell would remain open.

Subsequent governors ruled in the spirit of Smith's policies, enforcing martial law, brutal punishments, and a regular work regimen on the colonists. In this manner, Jamestown limped along, although it remained dependent on neighboring Indians for food and new Virginia Company recruits to replenish its numbers. The colony also relied on Pocahontas, who became an important mediator between the newcomers and the Powhatans. She repeatedly visited Jamestown, and in 1613 the colony's leaders held her hostage as a way of pressuring Powhatan to negotiate with them. During her captivity, she became acculturated to English ways and converted to Christianity. John Rolfe, a prominent and recently widowed new arrival in the colony, received permission from the Virginia Company to marry her. Powhatan agreed to the union as well. In marriage, Pocahontas and Rolfe accomplished what Smith's mock execution and Powhatan's coronation had failed to do: create a bond of kinship between the Powhatans and English. The Virginia Company, anxious for some good news, sponsored a visit by Rolfe, Pocahontas, and a retinue of Powhatans to London in 1616. Having taken the Christian name Rebecca at her baptism, Pocahontas supposedly displayed the success of the Company's civilizing mission in America. In London, she had an unexpected reunion with Smith, who came to see her and to remind all who would listen that he was the first Englishman to befriend the now famous Indian.

Smith's description of the encounter provides the best glimpse we have behind the public mask Rolfe and the Virginia Company had created for Pocahontas. According to Smith, she initially "obscured her face" from him, "not seeming well contented." After some time alone, she "began to talke, and remembred mee well," addressing him as "father." When Smith balked at the title "because she was a Kings daughter," she insisted, "and you shall call mee childe, and so I will bee for ever and ever your Countrieman."[7] There was an obvious edge to her words. She told Smith that the Jamestown colonists had led her to believe that he was dead, but Powhatan had told her escorts to inquire after him anyway, "because your Countriemen will lie much." This matter-of-fact assertion made plain the element of distrust between Smith's people and her own that could not be erased by her conversion or marriage. Not long afterward, as her party prepared for the trip home, Pocahontas took ill and died. Rolfe buried her in a churchyard near the Thames.

English relations with the Powhatans deteriorated steadily thereafter. No other English leaders of the colony followed Rolfe's example and married into a high-ranking Indian family, thereby closing off an avenue for alliance-building that had obviously appealed to Powhatan. This failure is noteworthy, because it denied a tradition of diplomatic marriage already present in European as well as Native American cultures, and English men outnumbered English women in early Virginia by a ratio of 6 to 1. Whether by force or consent, the Jamestown colonists must have been taking native women as sexual partners, but they were unwilling to pursue such unions in a way that would have granted them legitimacy under English civil or religious law.

Rolfe was not able to save Jamestown by marrying Pocahontas, but he did help turn around the colony's fortunes in another way. Impressed by the profits the Spanish were making by exporting American tobacco to European markets, Rolfe experimented with the crop's cultivation in Virginia. Tobacco was indigenous to North America, but the type grown and smoked there by Indians tasted too harsh for Europeans, who preferred the sweeter flavor of tobacco from the Caribbean and Brazil. After some trial and error with seeds imported from the West Indies, Rolfe found a sweet-tasting variety that flourished in Virginia's soil and climate. At last, someone in the colony had struck gold.

Rolfe's discovery could not have come at a better time. Sixteenth-century writers had convinced wealthy Europeans that tobacco was a wonder drug. In his report from Roanoke, Thomas Harriot described how smoking purged "superfluous phlegm and other gross humours" from the body by opening all of its "pores and passages." No further proof of its efficacy was necessary than the Indians themselves, whose bodies "are notably preserved in health, and know not many of the grievous diseases, wherewith we in England are often times afflicted."[8] Some contrarians condemned tobacco as the "stinking weed," but their voices were drowned out by its popularity as a consumer good made affordable by plantation production in the Americas. Ironically, tobacco's chief detractor in England was King James I, whose namesake colonial settlement would have been lost without it. An observer in Jamestown in 1617 noted that the crop had taken over the settlement; colonists who had been reluctant to grow the food necessary to feed themselves devoted their days to it, planting it in every available space, right up to their dooryards. In 1620 the still struggling colony exported forty thousand pounds of the stuff. A decade later, that figure had increased to 1.5 million.

Tobacco saved Jamestown, but at a price. It was a crop that required constant labor at all stages of production, from sowing to weeding to harvesting to curing to packing. It was much more labor-intensive than the cereal crops English farmers were used to growing in their home country, but it also required little capital investment to get started. Anyone with a patch of land, a few tools, and seeds stood a chance of turning a tidy profit during the boom years before 1660. That opportunity worked as a magnet, drawing migrants out of England to Virginia despite the dire mortality rates and living conditions there. The Virginia Company encouraged this migration through its headright system, a grant of fifty acres of land to every individual who moved to the colony or paid for the transportation of someone else to do so. About 80 percent of the English men and women who came to seventeenth-century Virginia arrived as indentured servants, and thus did not receive such a land grant, but if they managed to survive their term of service (typically four to five years), their freedom dues included a headright that gave them the chance to cash in on the tobacco boom as well.

Tobacco brought new immigrants to the Chesapeake and powered their rapid dispersal, creating new colonies to the north and south of Virginia. Maryland was established on the shores of the northern Chesapeake Bay by a charter granted by King Charles I (son and successor of James I) to his political ally Cecil Calvert, the second Lord Baltimore in 1632. The Calvert family was Catholic and hoped that its colony would be populated by fellow believers seeking a refuge from religious persecution in Protestant England. Although Catholics were among the first colonists to arrive in Maryland in 1634, they quickly clashed with the more numerous Protestants who arrived in the region from England and neighboring Virginia. Maryland never became the safe haven Lord Baltimore intended, but it did cash in on the Atlantic tobacco market and shared many of the same social and economic characteristics as Virginia.

As land became scarcer along the James River, some freed servants unwilling to work as tenant farmers for their former masters moved southward, seeking their own land in the Albemarle Sound region of what eventually became North Carolina. Unlike tidewater Maryland and Virginia, this region lacked easy access to Atlantic markets. The Outer Banks could be difficult to navigate for ocean-going vessels, and there was no nearby deep-water port. Most of North Carolina's early colonists grew corn and raised livestock for local subsistence and trade; only after transportation improvements and integration into a wider international economy did North Carolina become the powerhouse of tobacco production that it remains to this day.

The tobacco boom in the seventeenth-century Chesapeake drew colonists to the region but also dispossessed Indians and discouraged self-sufficiency. On Good Friday in 1622, a coordinated surprise attack on the outlying plantations of Jamestown by the Powhatans killed close to one-quarter of the colony's inhabitants. This devastating loss reversed the gains the Virginia Company had managed to make in attracting investors and settlers. In 1624 James I revoked the company's charter and made Virginia a royal colony, governed directly by the Crown. Despite the success individual planters had found with tobacco, the company had never managed to return a dividend for its stockholders.

John Smith watched all this unfold from London. Like James I, he had little good to say about tobacco and described it as a "fumish foundation" on which to build a colony. He criticized the Virginia colonists for spending all their time "rooting in the ground about Tobacco like Swine" while relying on Indians, to whom they taught "the use of our armes," to hunt for them.[9] On this matter, the Virginia Company agreed. It ordered colonists to limit tobacco planting and raise more food crops and livestock, but planters ignored such restrictions. Criticism of the tobacco boom came from below as well as above. Richard Frethorne's parents had indentured him to the Virginia Company, no doubt intending to give him the opportunity to find his fortune in America. Instead, he labored on an isolated plantation known as Martin's Hundred, suffering from "the scurvie and the bloody flux," with only a "messe of water gruell, and a mouthfull of bread and beef" for his daily rations. "I have eaten more in day at home than I have allowed me here for a Weeke," he told his parents in a letter home, "If you love me you will redeeme me suddenlie."[10]

Frethorne's parents were not able to save him. His name was on a list of the dead at Martin's Hundred compiled not long after he wrote the letter. The odds had been against him from the start. Of approximately 7,000 migrants who came to Virginia before 1624, only 1,200 of them—about 20 percent—were alive when the Crown took over the colony. While that mortality rate declined over the course of the seventeenth century, coming to Virginia remained a gamble for anyone, high born or low. For people like Frethorne, Virginia was a nightmare made worse by the hopes and expectations with which they had left England. Yet, out of their suffering came the model on which England would build its Atlantic empire, one that relied on cash crops rather than gold and silver to turn a profit, that made use of imported workers rather than native laborers, and that concentrated wealth in the hands of the lucky few at the expense of the miserable many.

THE FUR TRADE IN NEW FRANCE AND NEW NETHERLAND

As the Virginia Company struggled to establish its foothold in the Chesapeake, French and Dutch adventurers launched their own colonial enterprises elsewhere along the eastern seaboard. New France and New Netherland had their origins in the search for the Northwest Passage (a northern sea route to the Pacific Ocean), but in each case, the fur trade provided reason enough for staying in North America rather than trying to get around it. Because they relied so heavily on Native American cooperation, New France and New Netherland also offered counterpoints to the models of colonization practiced by the English and Spanish. For French and Dutch colonists, the issue was not how to subdue native populations, but how to engage them as reliable allies and trading partners.

Jacques Cartier's attempt to colonize the St. Lawrence River Valley in the sixteenth century had failed, but that did not end French interest in North America. Annual fishing expeditions to Newfoundland and Labrador cultivated the fur trade with coastal Algonquian-speaking peoples, who exchanged beaver pelts for iron knives and hatchets, woven cloth, copper kettles, beads, and alcohol. Many of these goods were lighter, sharper, and more durable than their native counterparts, and so European-manufactured metal wares rapidly replaced Indian-manufactured stone tools and pottery. Other goods, however, became staples of the fur trade precisely because they resembled native goods. Glass beads from Venice shared many attributes in color, texture, and size with native beads made from marine shells, and Indians invested them with the same aesthetic and spiritual values. Indians also valued European goods for the ways in which they could be repurposed and adapted into their own material culture. When copper kettles became damaged or worn out, Indians cut them into pieces for making arrowheads, edged tools, and jewelry. Textiles could likewise be cut, sewn, and decorated in ways that reflected native dress rather than European fashions.

By 1600 French investors were once again interested in establishing a permanent presence in North America. The search for a Northwest Passage remained a priority, but now so too was protecting their Atlantic fishing industry and fur trade from European rivals. Some French colonists settled in Acadia, the coastal region along the Bay of Fundy in modern Nova Scotia, where they farmed, fished, and traded with the Micmac and Abenaki Indians. In 1608 the French explorer Samuel de Champlain returned to the site of Cartier's failed settlement in the St. Lawrence Valley and established Quebec, which became the base from which the French extended the coastal fur trade into the North American interior. From its beginnings, New France would be a colony of traders, not planters.

This was a vision adapted to the climate and geography of Canada, which was too far north to attract sustained migration from Europe. Some French families did settle in the St. Lawrence Valley as *habitants*, planting crops and tending livestock as tenants on seigneurial grants, feudal-style manors granted by the French Crown to prominent investors, religious orders, and military officers involved in the colonial enterprise. Crown policy, however, prohibited Protestants—who suffered considerable religious persecution at home and were therefore the French subjects most interested in emigrating abroad—from resettling in New France. Instead, Canada attracted *voyageurs*, young men from mercantile backgrounds who wanted to make their fortunes in the fur trade and then go home. Soldiers were another important part of Canada's early colonial population. Veterans of the *troupes de la marine* who served in Canada often stayed in the colony as craftsmen, farmers, or *coureurs de bois* ("runners of the woods"), unlicensed fur traders who skirted official restrictions on the trade by living among Indians in the interior.

New France's colonial population was overwhelmingly young, transient, and male. During the 1660s, the Crown subsidized the dowries of single women willing to move to the colony, but this policy had little impact on family formation and population growth. French soldiers and traders in New France were more likely to take native women as sexual partners and wives, and the offspring of such unions, known as *métis*, often became important mediators between the two cultures. French officials initially encouraged marriages between French men and Indian women, expecting that the wives in such couples would submit themselves to the patriarchal authority of their husbands and adopt European-style dress, family roles, and religious practices. Instead, French men were more likely to "go native" in such unions, because their Indian wives helped them negotiate trade and diplomacy in native communities. French traders did not balk at native marriage practices that allowed for polygamy and easy divorce, nor did they insist that their children be raised in European-modeled households. To a degree that few colonial officials were willing to endorse, interracial sex played an important role in facilitating the Canadian fur trade and blurred European and Indian family roles in interesting ways.

Missionaries were another important part of the French presence in Canada. Like Spain, France was a Catholic power and its American colonies became another front in the Counter-Reformation's attack on Protestantism. However, the Spanish model of conquest and forced conversions would not do in New France. Indian populations there were too dispersed and mobile to fall easy prey to military expeditions, a lesson learned by costly but inconclusive French invasions of Iroquois country south of Lake Ontario during the 1660s. Warfare also disrupted trade, and French merchants relied on Indian men and women to hunt, process, and transport the furs they exported home. The Jesuit missionaries of New France used perseverance and persuasion rather than force of arms to save souls. They learned native cultures and languages by traveling with Indians to their hunting and fishing camps, and they ingratiated themselves in Indian communities by giving gifts, sharing labor, and patiently enduring the manifold humiliations that any stranger in a new culture suffers. In many respects, the Jesuits were spiritual freelancers in the manner of the *coureurs de bois*, taking their business directly to their customers, but their vows of celibacy prevented them from acquiring the same degree of intimacy by marrying into Indian families and fathering children with Indian wives. Despite their mutual interest in peaceful Indian relations, missionaries and traders were often at loggerheads, the former describing the latter as agents of moral corruption who encouraged sexual promiscuity and drunkenness among their native partners.

Whether by means of missionaries or *coureurs de bois*, French influence extended along the interior waterways of Canada as more Indian nations were drawn into the fur trade. Established in 1642, Montreal became the hub for intercultural trade and diplomacy in New France. Each year, Indians from the Upper Great Lakes traveled there by way of the Ottawa River to trade and conduct diplomacy. French traders and soldiers established posts at key points throughout the Great Lakes watershed: Frontenac, on the passage from Lake Ontario to the St. Lawrence River; Michilimackinac, on the strait between Lakes Huron and Michigan; and Niagara, on the river connecting Lakes Ontario and Erie. French explorer Robert Cavelier de La Salle became the first European to navigate the Mississippi River, extending the French fur trade into modern Illinois and Arkansas. When La Salle reached the mouth of the Mississippi in 1682, there were barely ten thousand French subjects living in North America, but no other European power could claim such an extensive knowledge of the continent's interior or as many Indian allies.

The Dutch colony of New Netherland had similar origins to New France but developed along a different track. In 1609, the same year that Champlain explored the lake that bears his name, Henry Hudson approached the same region from the south, sailing up the river named after him. Although he was English, Hudson worked for the Dutch East India Company, looking for a passage to the Pacific. He failed in that venture, but encountered Indians anxious to trade. Shortly thereafter,

Dutch merchants established Fort Orange (modern Albany) near the juncture of the Mohawk and Hudson rivers, and in 1621 the Netherlands gave the newly formed West India Company a monopoly on Dutch trade in West Africa and the Americas.

The Dutch method of colonization owed much to precedents set by the Portuguese during the sixteenth century. They established coastal "factories"—fortified warehouses and merchant communities—in strategic locations around the globe, including West Africa, the Spice Islands of the Indian Ocean, Brazil, and the Caribbean. Acting on behalf of the West India Company in 1626, Peter Minuit purchased Manhattan Island from local Indians, making possible the growth of the company's factory there into the port city of New Amsterdam, the most important Dutch foothold in North America. It was blessed with the best harbor on the eastern seaboard, free from ice all year and accessible to ocean-going vessels. Dutch ships dominated the Atlantic "carrying trade," often crossing the ocean with cargoes purchased in other nation's colonies. New Amsterdam served not only as a depot for the fur trade, but also as part of the trans-Atlantic shipping routes for Dutch ships involved in the slave, tobacco, and sugar trades.

According to the West India Company, New Netherland extended from the Connecticut River to the Delaware River. Although the Dutch established trading posts on each of those waterways, they lacked the settler populations necessary to assert undisputed possession of them and faced challenges from Puritans in New England and Swedish and Finnish traders on the Delaware Bay. To stimulate migration to the colony, the West India Company gave land grants known as patroonships to its investors on the condition that they recruit and sponsor settlers for them, but few migrants wanted to come to the region so long as the company insisted on monopolizing the fur trade. The one patroonship that did succeed was Rensselaerswyck, which encompassed land on both sides of the upper Hudson and surrounded Fort Orange. The Rensselaer family was able to populate its land grant because it attracted *bushlopers*, the Dutch equivalent of Canada's *coureurs de bois*, unlicensed fur traders who conducted their own business with nearby Mahican and Mohawk Indians. Unlike the French, the Dutch showed little interest in converting Indians to Christianity, and they tended to keep the natives at arm's length when not engaged in business with them. Nor did they exhibit the same wanderlust as the French, preferring instead to remain within the stockades of their trading posts and have Indian customers come to them. The Mohawks described the Dutch as "those beere-bellies" at Fort Orange, a peculiar and insular breed.[11]

On Manhattan, life was a bit more cosmopolitan. The ethnic diversity and religious pluralism for which Amsterdam was famous in Europe were evident in its namesake in North America. The Dutch carrying trade brought a variety of people to New Amsterdam as merchants, sailors, traders, soldiers, servants, and slaves, although many proved to be just as transient as the *voyaguers* of New France. De facto toleration brought religious refugees of every stripe to the tiny colony, including Puritan dissenters and Quakers chased out of New England and

Catholics and Jews unlikely to find safe havens elsewhere in North America. When Governor Peter Stuyvesant tried to crack down on religious unorthodoxy in New Netherland, his West India Company bosses told him to desist because it was bad for business. The Dutch orientation remained eastward toward the Atlantic rather than westward toward the continent's interior. The stockade they built along the landed approach to New Amsterdam gave the city its most famous place name: Wall Street.

During the 1640s, the West India Company abandoned its monopoly on the fur trade in an effort to attract more settlers to the colony. This policy worked, but only to a point. The colony's population grew from 2,500 in 1644 to 9,000 twenty years later, but poor leadership, trading abuses, and land pressure led to warfare with Indians in the lower Hudson Valley. Like New France, New Netherland remained an underpopulated colony dependent on infusions of human and financial capital from home to keep afloat. Unfortunately for both colonies, European governments and investors were much more likely to turn their attention to the sugar industry developing in the Caribbean.

THE PLANTATION COMPLEX IN THE CARIBBEAN

While colonial enterprises struggled to turn a profit in North America, other ventures got under way in the Caribbean. During the sixteenth century, Spanish conquistadors occupied the Greater Antilles—Cuba, Hispaniola, Puerto Rico, and Jamaica—but their conquests in Mexico and Peru diverted their attention from the Lesser Antilles, an arc of small, volcanic islands that stretched from Puerto Rico to the coast of Venezuela (see Map 3.1). These islands became havens for pirates and footholds for the French, Dutch, and English in the American tropics. By the mid-seventeenth century, sugar had become the most valuable commodity of this region, and its cultivation transformed the landscape and its people. The plantation system that slowly took root in seventeenth-century Virginia flourished quickly in the Caribbean and created new extremities of wealth and human suffering.

The European taste for sugar was a by-product of the Islamic World's intercontinental trade. Arabic traders first brought it to Mediterranean markets from India, and during the Crusades, Italian merchants invested in sugar plantations on the islands of Cyprus and Crete. Arab merchants did the same in the Islamic kingdoms of North Africa and the Iberian Peninsula. By the time of Columbus's voyages, the Spanish and Portuguese were growing sugar in the eastern Atlantic on the Canary Islands and the Madeira Islands, respectively. By the 1560s, Portuguese sugar plantations in northeastern Brazil were Europe's chief supplier of this popular consumer good, and its production gradually spread into the Caribbean.

The first generation of English migrants to the Caribbean did not intend to plant sugar. Settling on the small islands of St. Christopher (known as St. Kitts today), Barbados, Nevis, Montserrat, and Antigua, they raised livestock and planted tobacco, cotton, and indigo. They came from the same pool of young, single males

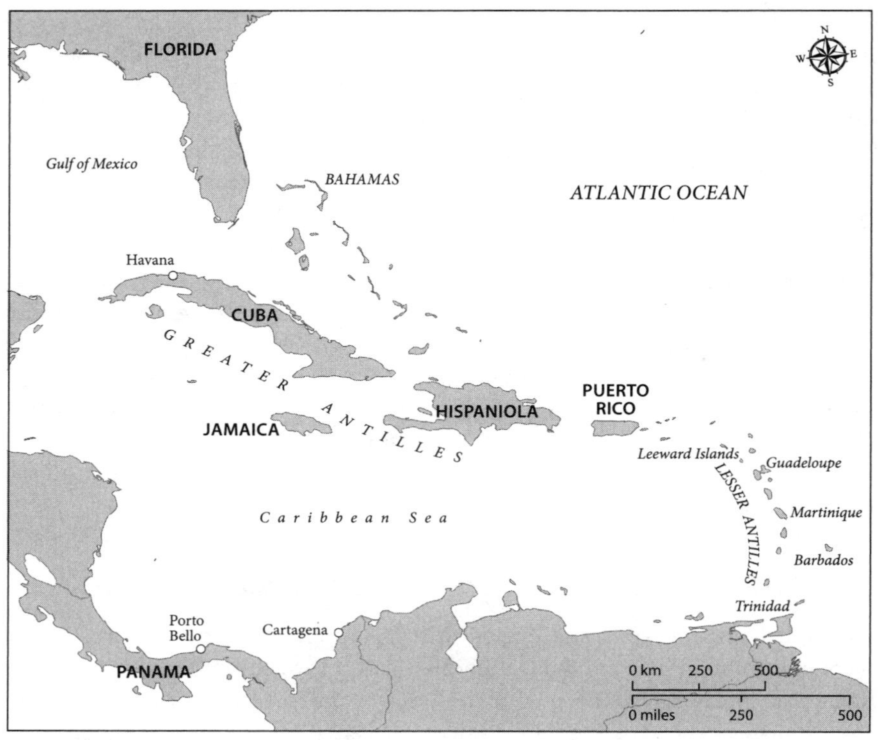

Map 3.1 The Caribbean, *c.* 1660.

who were going to the Chesapeake, and they encountered the same difficulties with hunger, disease, and exploitive labor. Despite its small size (only 166 square miles), Barbados emerged as the most significant colony in the Lesser Antilles. As the easternmost island in this chain, it was the usual first stop for ships sailing into the Caribbean from Europe or Africa. In 1655 about twenty-three thousand colonists lived there, a number equal to those living in New England and about double those living in Virginia at the same time. The English Civil Wars (1641–1649) and Oliver Cromwell's campaigns in Ireland and Scotland (1645–1653) produced a wave of political exiles, prisoners of war, and convicted rebels who either chose or were forced to migrate to the Caribbean, increasing competition for already limited land. At roughly the same time, London merchants began to invest in sugar production on the island, providing the necessary capital for equipment and labor. Slaves imported directly from Africa began supplanting white indentured servants and gave a competitive advantage to those planters wealthy enough to own them. Barbados became an important link in the Atlantic slave trade and the first public slave market in the English Atlantic.

The rise of sugar cultivation in the Caribbean put the squeeze on small, independent producers getting by on tobacco cultivation and subsistence agriculture. This transformation was evident in the shifting demographics of Barbados. The island's white population of 23,000 in 1655 declined to 19,568 in 1684; over the same period, its slave population increased from 20,000 to 46,602. Barbados became the first English colony in the New World to have a black majority, and by the early eighteenth century, slaves outnumbered whites there by 3 to 1. Sugar production in the Caribbean increased exponentially after England seized control of Jamaica from Spain in 1655. Jamaica had ten times more landmass than all the other English colonies in the West Indies put together. By 1713 it surpassed Barbados in sugar production and had a ratio of eight slaves to every white colonist in its population. Whether free or unfree, European or African, the life expectancy of any new arrival in the West Indies plummeted, chiefly because of exposure to new diseases and malnutrition. Planters imported thousands of slaves annually just to replace those who had died. According to one estimate, planters in Barbados imported eighty-five thousand slaves between 1708 and 1735, producing a net gain of only four thousand in the island's black population over the same period.[12]

Like tobacco in the Chesapeake, sugar production tended to consolidate economic and social power in the hands of wealthy landowners at the expense of propertyless and unfree laborers. In the Caribbean, the effects of this process were even more pronounced, because there was less available land for small producers and growing sugar required much more start-up capital than tobacco. On Barbados, the average sugar plantation had more than two hundred acres of land and more than one hundred slaves. Planters also had to maintain expensive equipment. Workers extracted the juice from sugar cane by crushing it in a three-roller mill. After collecting the juice in a cistern, workers transferred it to a series of vats known as coppers, where it was boiled down (see Figure 3.2). The crystallized sugar then needed to be dried in curing houses and packed for shipment. Molasses, a by-product of the refining process, could be distilled into rum or exported directly. Each stage required skilled labor and supervision, as well as careful maintenance of tools and machinery. With its high capital costs, specialized tasks, and regimented labor, a sugar plantation was like a factory, and as with other kinds of industry, economies of scale awarded the greatest profits to those who could produce in the greatest quantity.

Richard Ligon, a royalist exile from the English Civil Wars, lived in Barbados for a number of years and observed the sugar revolution firsthand. A man of genteel background himself, he expressed sympathy for the planters' exposure to the vagaries of broken equipment, diseased livestock, and bad weather (the English had never encountered weather systems as destructive as hurricanes before). He believed that the slaves on the island enjoyed better living conditions than the servants, because masters were mindful of their lifetime investment in a slave's labor. On the other hand, they tried to wring the maximum amount of work out of servants before their indentures expired. Whether black or white, workers received the same monotonous diet of plantains and sweet potatoes, worked the same dawn-until-dusk hours, and faced exposure to the same diseases. They also suffered the same brutal corporal punishment. "I have seen an

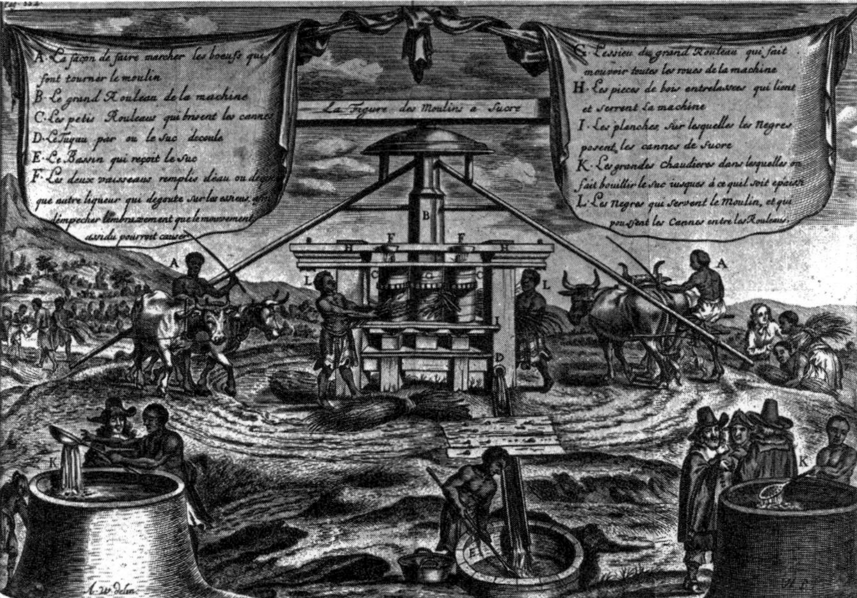

Figure 3.2 Slaves operating a three-roller sugar mill in the West Indies, from Charles de Rochefort, *Histoire naturelle et morale des Iles Antilles de l'Amerique* (Rotterdam: Chez Reinier Leers, [1681]). In this depiction of the sugar production process, African slaves work the sugar mill and boiling vats while white planters supervise them. Courtesy of the Library Company of Philadelphia.

Overseer beat a Servant with a cane about the head, till the blood has followed, for a fault that is not worth the speaking of," Ligon wrote, "Truly, I have seen such cruelty there done to Servants, as I did not think one Christian could have done to another."[13]

Ligon's Caribbean seethed with class resentment and racial tensions. It is no wonder then that many of the great planters preferred to return to England and live in a high style. Using their money and connections, they supported a "sugar interest" in Parliament that protected the slave trade and kept customs duties on West Indian sugar imports low. By 1700 close to twenty sugar planters had received titles of nobility from the English Crown; by contrast, only three North American colonists—Sir William Phips and Sir William Pepperrell of Massachusetts and Sir William Johnson of New York—ever received such an honor. As was the case with the English aristocracy's estates in Ireland, sugar planters treated their Caribbean plantations as cash cows whose day-to-day operations were best left in the hands of local managers or sons who needed to learn the family business. Although some planters did remain on their estates in the Caribbean, this region was slower than the Chesapeake or Spanish Mexico to develop a native-born ruling class that came to identify with the land and its people.

CITIES ON A HILL IN NEW ENGLAND

When the *Mayflower* dropped anchor off of Cape Cod in 1620, English mariners had already been coming to the northeastern coast of America for over a century. They engaged primarily in exploration, fishing, and fur trading, but some had also tried to plant colonies, all of which failed. During the 1610s, this region became the focus of John Smith's promotional efforts. He published an accurate and detailed map of the land he dubbed "New England," and urged would-be colonizers to turn their attention northward from the Caribbean and Chesapeake Bay. They might not be able to grow sugar or other tropical crops so far north, but Smith assured his countrymen that they would find a climate and soil similar to England's there, and the land and sea were teeming with nature's bounty.

Smith's advice appealed to religious dissidents who believed that the cause of the Protestant Reformation had stalled in England. The groups that we have come to identify as the Pilgrims and Puritans shared common origins in the Elizabethan era. When Elizabeth I came to the throne in 1558, she calmed religious tensions within her realm by refusing to settle definitively controversial matters of doctrine and liturgy. Like her father Henry VIII, who had broken ties with the Roman Catholic Church during the 1530s, Elizabeth was no theologian. In her own words, she did not desire "a window into men's souls," only their outward conformity. So long as the clergy and their flocks were willing to recognize her authority as the head of the Church of England, she was willing to grant them some latitude in personal belief and practice.

For a minority of Elizabeth's Protestant faithful, this settlement would not do. Swept up in the radical changes in personal piety and church governance that the Reformation had unleashed in Europe, these reformers believed that the Church of England had not gone far enough in purging itself of corrupt Catholic precedents in its hierarchy, liturgy, and devotional practices. True, England's faithful no longer answered to the pope in Rome, clergy no longer took vows of celibacy, and Scripture could be read in English rather than Latin, but England's churches still looked and sounded Catholic in many ways. Bishops and archbishops enforced orthodoxy and prosecuted dissenters in ecclesiastical courts. Worshippers kneeled at elaborate altars to receive communion from clergy dressed in special vestments. Church bells, stained glass, incense, and all manner of other sensory stimuli diverted attention from the preaching of Scripture during services. For critics of such "popish remnants," the problem with England's Reformation was that it had not gone far enough. Opponents of these agitators called them "Puritans," because their insistence on purifying the Church of England threatened the fragile peace that Elizabeth's deliberately fuzzy religious settlement had restored to the realm.

Although there were some prominent advocates of the Puritan cause in the high offices of church and state, it was at heart a grassroots movement inspired by the intense piety of men and women pursuing a more direct and personal relationship with God. By sweeping away all sorts of intercessory practices common in the Catholic faith—veneration of saints, pilgrimages and holy relics, the sacrament of confession, and the elaborate iconography and ritual of the mass—the Reformation brought the individual believer face-to-face with God. Only prayer and Scripture, whether studied personally or learned through sermons, offered a way to understanding God and the divine purposes behind creation. Puritanism took root among reform-minded ministers and their congregations when they rejected the formalism associated with Catholic worship in favor of renewed commitments to personal and communal piety. Puritan churches imposed stricter rules of conduct and higher standards for membership on their congregants. A person became a member of the Church of England simply by being born a subject of the queen, and only grave sin or heresy could break that tie. Puritans did not like the idea of so promiscuously admitting sinners into communion with the saved. To be a full member of a Puritan congregation, individuals had to present some positive evidence, usually in the form of personal testimony, of God's grace within them. In other words, good behavior and outward conformity—the only demands the Elizabethan Church made on its members—were not enough. Puritans expected a believer to engage in constant self-examination and to submit to the spiritual judgment of others.

After some agitation during the 1560s and 1570s, the Puritan movement quieted toward the end of Elizabeth's reign. Although individual clergy and congregations continued to embrace its message, it was overshadowed by the spirit of anti-Catholic nationalism that united the country against Spain. The hopes Puritan ministers had for reforming the Church of England revived when James I ascended to the throne in 1603. Before coming to London, the new king had been James VI of Scotland, a country that had already embraced a more thorough-going reform in its church structure. James, however, was of a different mind. In his foreign relations, he sought rapprochement with Spain and his family had close ties with France. Furthermore, having survived all manner of political intrigue and religious controversy on the Scottish throne—no easy task in the sixteenth century—James arrived in London intent on enjoying his newfound wealth and power. When pressed by Puritan leaders to take up their cause, he told them to cease their agitation or face exile.

Even without James's threat, some Puritans considered moving abroad a better option than remaining part of a corrupt church. In 1582 Robert Browne published *A Treatise of Reformation Without Tarrying for Any*, which inspired a movement among some clergy and congregations to disavow the Church of England entirely. These Separatists, or Brownists as they were also called, established independent churches, each congregation recognizing no spiritual authority higher than itself. Some moved to the Netherlands, where they could worship as they pleased without fearing persecution. The Pilgrims who established the Plymouth colony in 1620 were one such group, who after a number of years in the Dutch city of Leyden, decided to seek even greater autonomy in North America. The migration to Plymouth was small, and the colony soon found the obscurity it had sought, quietly going about its business far removed from the political and religious controversies engulfing England.

Plymouth was quickly overshadowed by the planting of a much larger colony on Massachusetts Bay. Unlike the Pilgrims, the leaders of this migration, which got under way in 1629, were not Separatists. Rather than renouncing their membership in the Church of England, they described themselves as its pure remnant, removed from the corrupt majority before the whole was irretrievably damaged. The Puritan migrants to Massachusetts Bay also differed from their Pilgrim neighbors in that they did not seek quiet obscurity. In the words of their first governor John Winthrop, they came to America intending to "be as a City upon a Hill," so that the world might witness their success and "men shall say of succeeding plantations: the lord make it like that of New England."[14] These words have been quoted ever since as evidence of America's divine mission and destiny in the world, but Winthrop's soaring rhetoric masked a diversity of motives that brought migrants to New England. Like the Pilgrims before them, Puritans traveled to America in their own congregational communities, joining their ministers, family members, neighbors, and friends in an effort to achieve the spiritual perfection they sought but knew they could not achieve in England. It was not so much a city on the hill they were after as many cities on many hills, each with the ability to govern and police its own membership.

More than eighty thousand migrants left England during the 1630s for destinations in Europe, Ireland, and the Americas. Of these, about thirteen thousand traveled to New England, while larger numbers went to the Caribbean and Chesapeake. The "Great Migration" to New England, as subsequent generations came to call it, was therefore a wheel turning within a much larger wheel, and its participants had much in common with migrants headed to those other destinations. All were feeling the pressure of England's unprecedented population growth, a 40 percent increase between 1550 and 1650, as well as the disruptions of its changing economy. The textile industry was in severe recession during the early seventeenth century. In rural areas, landowners displaced their tenants by enclosing common fields and converting them into sheep pasturage.

Despite these common circumstances, the New England migration was set apart by several characteristics evident in the passenger lists of ships that carried migrants to England's colonies. On ships bound for the Chesapeake or Caribbean, men outnumbered women by ratios of 6 to 1 and 9 to 1, respectively. On ships to New England, there were three males to every two females. The age distribution for passengers on these ships also differed significantly. Approximately two-thirds of migrants headed to the Caribbean or Chesapeake were young adults between the ages of fifteen and twenty-four; the remaining third ranged in age from twenty-five to sixty. Among the New England migrants, children from infancy to puberty made up approximately one-third of the passengers. As these numbers indicate, migrants to New England were likely to be traveling with family members, whereas those heading to the Caribbean or Chesapeake were typically unmarried and traveling alone. Adult males on the New England lists were also likely to be identified by their occupations: about two-thirds were farmers or artisans, about a quarter worked in the cloth trades, and a small percentage were professionals. Passenger lists rarely identified the occupations of migrants headed to the Caribbean or Chesapeake, in all likelihood because they possessed no training, education, or property associated with such status. Ships going to New England were not nearly as crowded as those going to other destinations. Passenger lists for the Caribbean and Chesapeake often contained over one hundred names; those for New England showed greater variance, some numbering below forty. One possible reason for this difference is that New England migrants crammed available room with more supplies and belongings, while those headed elsewhere went with little more than the clothes on their backs.

Data culled from passenger lists make plain that the New England migrants came from middling backgrounds, neither rich nor desperately poor, and tended to move as families. Indeed, analysis of place names indicates that these migrants moved together as neighbors as well as families, often organizing themselves into a group before arriving in London or another port city to leave for America. Although they did not formally identify themselves as religious dissidents on the lists, which would have endangered their freedom to emigrate, their Puritanism was evident in their communal identity and purpose, which mimicked the congregational foundation of their churches.

People of such middle-class backgrounds naturally had stronger safety nets during hard times than the poor and young servants crowding ships to the Caribbean and Chesapeake, so factors other than economic want must have played a role in their decisions to migrate. One of them was Charles I, who succeeded his father James I to the throne in 1625. Ironically, Charles lived his private life in much greater accordance with Puritan beliefs than his libertine father, but his public actions flew in the face of the Puritans' desire to continue the reformation of the English Church. In 1629 Charles dissolved Parliament and initiated an eleven-year "Personal Rule," effectively silencing the Puritans' voice in politics. Forgoing taxes raised by Parliament, he funded his government by reviving medieval customs and privileges that disregarded England's long tradition of representative government.

Most disheartening for Puritans, Charles exhibited Catholic sympathies in his foreign relations and religious policy. He married a French Catholic princess and continued his father's diplomatic rapprochement with Catholic powers. He also appointed William Laud the archbishop of Canterbury, the highest spiritual office in the Church of England. Laud's theology promoted the "covenant of works," the notion that a person's actions in this life affect his or her potential for salvation in the next. This doctrine flatly contradicted Puritan beliefs in predestination and smacked of Catholic rituals and practices designed to manipulate God's will. Puritan clergy who refused to preach Laud's theology faced fines and imprisonment. To them, Laud's rise to power indicated that the Reformation, merely stalled during James I's reign, was now sliding backward under Charles I.

That sense of the imminent undoing of the Reformation in England convinced many Puritans to leave. John Winthrop, the first governor of the Massachusetts Bay colony, described the decision to migrate in an essay titled "Reasons to be Considered, and Objections with Answers." Like many Puritans, he tried to discern

God's will in the events of the day. A gentleman lawyer, Winthrop led a comfortable life in England, but he believed fervently that worse times lay ahead. "This Land growes weary of her Inhabitantes," he warned, so much so that children were now burdens rather than blessings to their parents and it was "allmost impossible for a good and upright man to mainetayne his charge and live comfortablie." Misguided leaders like Charles I and Laud had corrupted the nation's "Fountaines of Learning and Religion," allowing the people to sink to intemperance and immorality for lack of proper instruction. Winthrop predicted that the nation's manifold sins would soon bring a "general calamity" of divine judgment, leaving the faithful "noe place lefte to flie into but the wildernesse." For those uncertain that migration to America was part of God's divine plan, Winthrop pointed to the signs. God had already sent "prophets among us who he hath stirred up to encourage his servantes to this Plantation." He had also sent "a great Plauge" to consume the Indian populations of New England so that there would be room for them there. As for those who believed that the tribulations of earlier colonies proved that God did not favor such ventures, Winthrop blamed those failures on promoters whose "mayne end was Carnall and not Religious," and who recruited "a multitude of rude and misgoverned persons, the very scumme of the Land" to undertake them.[15] New England, he knew, would be different.

And under the watchful eye of Winthrop and the other leaders of the Massachusetts Bay Company, it was different. Having learned the lessons of previous ventures, the Puritan migrants were generally better prepared for the hard work that lay ahead of them. More carefully recruited and better provisioned, they experienced a much lower mortality rate at sea than other migrants. Arriving with more even sex ratios and the second generation already in tow, they achieved a stable, self-sustaining population much more quickly. The New England climate protected them from many of the diseases that killed migrants to the Caribbean and Chesapeake. English men and women actually increased their life expectancy when they moved to New England, an outcome unique in the annals of New World colonization.

The communal purpose that united the New England migrants was evident in the way they settled the land. Rather than dispersing to the best lands and exploiting each other for labor, they gathered themselves into orderly communities with clear geographic and spiritual centers. The Massachusetts Bay Company briefly experimented with a headright system similar to that in the Chesapeake, but quickly opted to distribute land to towns rather than individuals. After landing and reshuffling a bit in America, migrants organized themselves into groups that petitioned the Massachusetts General Court, the company's governing body, for a land grant. Once they had received and surveyed the land, they signed town and church covenants with each other outlining how they would govern their political and religious affairs and pledging themselves to live peacefully together. When dividing the land, they replicated the social order they knew in England by granting more to those with higher social status, but they also made allowances for need by giving more to larger families, and they held undivided land in common for distribution to subsequent generations. Late arrivals, if judged spiritually and socially worthy, would be admitted to the town and given land, although their descendants were not likely to have a claim on future allotments. Approximately forty towns were founded in Massachusetts between 1630 and 1650 in this manner, each typically with homes clustered around a town commons and meeting house and ringed by fields, meadows, and pastures where the inhabitants tended cereal crops and livestock. In a significant departure from Old World precedent, New Englanders adopted a freehold system of land tenure, ensuring that most adult males owned the land they worked rather than laboring as tenants for an elite class of landlords.

Compared to the plantation colonies, early New England had little social conflict. Widespread land ownership created a compressed social order with a more equitable distribution of wealth than anywhere else in the English-speaking world at that time. Family labor predominated. Servants and slaves could be found in colonial New England, but they lived and worked alongside their masters, and for servants their unfree condition marked a passage in life, not a final destination. Like other migrants to the New World, Puritans came to America hoping to improve their material lives. Their religion taught them that success in one's worldly calling—the role God had predestined an individual to fill in society—was a sign of divine favor, and the fur trade and fisheries of New England offered plenty of opportunity for enterprise. Most New Englanders, however, described success not as riches but as "competency": the ability to live comfortably (but not extravagantly) off the fruits of one's labors and to pass that security along to the next generation. This sort of prosperity was exactly what Winthrop saw disappearing from England when he wrote that it had become "allmost impossible for a good and upright man to mainetayne his charge and live comfortablie." Remarkably, the Puritans found it in New England.

The chief threat to New England's stability came not from disease, hostile natives, or an exploited workforce, but from tensions within the Puritan creed between the individual and communal pursuit of salvation. Migration was an individual decision, and the calculus behind it varied from one person to the next. Yet, in the words of Winthrop, for the colony to succeed, "wee must be knitt together in this worke as one man."[16] Not all those who migrated to New England shared in Winthrop's vision or even his Puritan faith. Contemporaries often divided New England's colonial population into "saints" and "strangers," the former being church members living and worshipping in established towns and congregations, and the latter being the more transient types often drawn to colonial enterprises: servants, laborers, fur traders, disbanded soldiers, and similarly unattached adventurers. New England's proximity to the cod fisheries of the North Atlantic also gave it a significant population of fishermen drawn from a variety of religious and ethnic backgrounds. Neither complete religious conformity nor ethnic homogeneity characterized New England. "Strangers" were vital to the economic success of colonization there, if not Winthrop's city on a hill. Even more problematic were those migrants who proved to be *too* Puritan to stay in line behind Winthrop.

Taken to its logical conclusion, Puritanism made each man or woman a church of his or her own, responsible for cultivating a direct relationship with God through only Scripture and prayer. Anne Hutchinson was one of several upstarts whose criticism of the colony's leaders during the 1630s revealed how easily this elevation of individual conscience could fracture the unity sought by Winthrop. Authorities accused Hutchinson and her followers of the heresy of antinominanism, a too certain conviction in one's own salvation that rendered clerical guidance and church discipline unnecessary. Another threat came in the form of Separatism, the impulse to disavow association with the unsaved and corrupt. In England, the spirit of Separatism had led the Pilgrims and similar groups to disavow their membership in the Church of England, but in Massachusetts, it threatened to splinter Puritans apart from each other. During the 1630s, the charismatic minister Roger Williams advocated stricter rules for church membership and challenged the legitimacy of the Massachusetts Bay Company's claim to Indian land. He was a perfect example of the unrelenting challenge Puritanism presented to any church or state authority that attempted to enforce conformity to its laws. Such radicalism had suited Puritan clergy and politicians well in England, where they had lived as dissenters to the established order. But when they migrated to Massachusetts, they became the establishment. Williams's peers had little patience for a dissenter like him once they had their hands on the reins of power, and so they banished him.

The congregational organization of the Puritan colonial enterprise ultimately held it together. In each town, the social community and spiritual community reinforced each other. Membership in the church, rather than property ownership, marked a person's inclusion in the community. By agreeing to that membership, the individual also submitted to the surveillance and discipline of the whole. The congregational structure of Puritan church government provided latitude for each community to interpret and enforce the Puritan creed as it saw fit; no king or archbishop would impose orthodoxy from above. The Massachusetts General Court admitted representatives from each town into its general assembly and extended freemanship—that is, the right to vote and hold office in the colony's government—to all adult male church members. The simultaneous expansion of political liberties and reliance on each community to police its own kept the fragmentation threatened by antinomianism and Separatism at bay. Puritanism elevated individual conscience, but it also required the individual believer to belong to the group if he or she wanted to be judged eligible for salvation and the more earthly benefits that accrued with church membership.

The flip side of this inclusion, of course, was the exclusion of those judged unfit. The congregational model was resilient in this respect, too. Many Puritan migrants who found Massachusetts unsuitable simply moved on with other like-minded people. Those given a deliberate push, like Hutchinson and Williams, moved south to Narragansett Bay, where they established Rhode Island as a colony committed to religious toleration. Williams believed that governments had no business passing laws that would force the saved to worship alongside the unworthy. Rhode Island became a haven for nonconformists, not because Williams believed all faiths to be equal but because he considered it no business of his which path to hell the damned chose to take.

Other Puritans left Massachusetts voluntarily, in miniature continuations of the Atlantic migration. Following the same congregational model, they established towns along the coast and river valleys of Connecticut, along the southern Maine coast, on Long Island, and even in eastern New Jersey, each region taking on its own character. The Connecticut River towns that formed the colony of Connecticut in 1635 were nucleated around Hartford and adopted more liberal requirements for church membership than the churches in Massachusetts from which they had come. A few years later, other migrants from Massachusetts established the colony of New Haven, which outdid Massachusetts in enforcing strict standards of public behavior. One visitor from Boston commented disapprovingly that "their Lawes made Offenders" of those who engaged in "a harmless Kiss or Innocent merriment among Young people."[17] Meanwhile, Puritans who settled in more ethnically diverse regions such as Long Island and New Jersey endorsed religious toleration as a way of preserving their own peculiar beliefs and habits.

During the English Civil Wars of the 1640s, Puritans who had remained in England came to power, arresting and executing the hated Laud and Charles I. Those events led some New England Puritans to return home, but the vast majority remained in America and reacted disapprovingly as the Puritan regime in England split into opposing factions and spawned new, more radical religious sects. Migration to New England virtually ceased after 1640, and newcomers after that date did not always find a warm reception. Anabaptists and Quakers who crossed the Atlantic hoping to find converts to their antinomian ideas were expelled from Massachusetts but found a foothold in Rhode Island. Between 1659 and 1661, Massachusetts authorities executed four Quakers who returned to the colony in violation of their banishment. The most notorious among them was Mary Dyer, who thirty years earlier had been a supporter of Anne Hutchinson. In a 1647 pamphlet addressed to radicals who would challenge Puritan orthodoxy in Massachusetts, Nathaniel Ward made his colony's position on toleration painfully clear: "I dare take upon me... to proclaim to the world, in the name of our colony, that all Familists [a Dutch mystical sect], Antinomians, Anabaptists, and other enthusiasts shall have free liberty to keep away from us; and such as will come, to be gone as fast as they can, the sooner the better."[18] The freedom to worship in Massachusetts extended only so far as worshipping in the right way. Those seeking their own city on a hill were welcome to go build it somewhere else.

PROPRIETARY DESIGNS IN THE LOWER SOUTH

The Puritans were not alone in vesting their colonial enterprise with a purpose higher than simply making money. Whether to recruit migrants, investors, or royal patronage, all promoters of colonization made some altruistic objective part of their scheme. In the late sixteenth century, Sir Walter Raleigh wanted to save the Indians from Spanish thralldom and the Hakluyts wanted to provide opportunity to England's poor. As it raised capital to keep Jamestown afloat, the Virginia Company also solicited funds for a missionary school, although the plans were abandoned after the Indians' Good Friday attack in 1622. Often enough, the promoters used the language of philanthropy to sell their own quixotic vision of how the world should be, if only they were in charge. For those people wealthy and well connected enough to launch such ventures, colonization was a chance to clear the slate and build a new society from the ground up. The people they recruited to populate those ideal worlds, however, were not figments of their imagination. They were human beings who rarely saw eye-to-eye with the promoters and investors who claimed authority over them.

This tension between the grand plans of a few and the personal agendas of the many was especially evident in the spate of colony-making that occurred after the restoration of the English throne in 1660. Charles II rewarded friends who had remained loyal to the Stuart royal family during the Civil Wars by granting them colonial dominions in America, over which they held not only proprietary right to the land but to the government as well. In these so-called proprietary colonies, a family or group of families held, on paper at least, the unparalleled power to make a new society according to their own specifications. As was fitting for aristocrats who had just experienced prolonged civil war, religious division, and social upheaval, all these proprietors looked backward in concocting their colonial schemes and tried to transplant to America a feudal order of political deference and economic stability that was rapidly disappearing in their own world.

The proprietary model of colonization had been tried in the first half of the seventeenth century with mixed results. James I had given Nova Scotia to fellow Scot Sir William Alexander in 1621, but the colony failed to attract settlers willing to recognize Alexander's title to the land. Instead, French subjects settled in the region and called their colony Acadia. Farther south, in the Chesapeake Bay, Maryland was established as a proprietary colony owned by the Calvert family, but the Protestant colonists who settled there showed little sympathy toward or cooperation with the Calverts' efforts to turn the colony into a Catholic refuge. Despite such an undistinguished record of success, Charles II revived the proprietary model for colonization when he assumed the throne, perhaps because it was such a cost-effective way for him to settle his political and financial debts. After all, it cost almost nothing to draft a charter; the expenses of actually colonizing the land would be borne by the proprietor, not the Crown.

The eight aristocratic families that received the proprietary grant to the Carolinas in 1663 were not trying to solve any of England's intractable social and religious problems, but they still did not fare much better than the Calverts. The Carolina proprietors gave the task of formulating a government for their new American dominion to the political philosopher John Locke. Locke is most famous today for writing *The Second Treatise of Government*, which set forth the natural rights argument used by Thomas Jefferson in the Declaration of Independence. Locke's "Fundamental Constitutions of Carolina," however, looked backward to an idealized feudal past rather than forward to a world of human equality. In Locke's blueprint, the proprietors sat on top of a hierarchy of landowners, supported by an invented colonial nobility (Locke gave the fanciful names of "landgraves" and "caciques" to two hereditary classes), and followed by freemen, serfs, and slaves. As had become customary by that time, the Carolinas would have a representative assembly, but the minimum property requirement of five hundred acres for the right to vote would make sure that only substantial landowners were represented.

Locke's grand plan could not have been any less practical if he had scribbled it onto a cocktail napkin at 2:00 a.m. Colonists already settled in the Albemarle Sound region were economically and socially tied to Virginia. Generally poor and dependent on the subsistence crops and livestock for their livelihood, they paid little mind to the Carolina proprietors and even less of the taxes and customs duties they tried to impose on them. Likewise, the planters who came to the Carolinas in the late seventeenth century were interested in profits, not the fanciful aristocratic titles promised in Locke's Fundamental Constitutions. In the face of resistance to their authority, the Carolina proprietors tried to strengthen their influence first by dividing their grant into the colonies of North and South Carolina, and then in 1712 by appointing a separate governor for each colony. Such administrative moves had a negligible impact on the colonists themselves. The proprietors' efforts to collect quitrents—a feudal tax paid by a tenant annually to acknowledge his lord's right to the land—proved fruitless. Colonists did not like having their land encumbered with such antiquated obligations; they wanted to own it outright. Squatters ignored proprietary agents who tried to collect money from them for the land they occupied. The Carolina proprietors finally gave up in 1729 and sold their rights back to the Crown, at which point North Carolina and South Carolina became royal colonies, governed directly by Crown-appointed officials.

The Carolina proprietors may have hoped to populate the Carolinas with feudal tenants and serfs, but a different kind of economy developed in South Carolina, one much more influenced by the Caribbean model of colonization than anything dreamed up by John Locke. Warmed by subtropical temperatures and watered by several broad rivers, the Carolina lowlands were close enough in climate and distance to attract the attention of Caribbean planters. In 1670 an expedition of about two hundred Europeans and Africans established the city of Charles Town (rendered Charleston after the American Revolution) on the Ashley and Cooper rivers. Fifty percent of them were from Barbados. Caribbean sugar planters looked at South Carolina in the same way that some investors in the Virginia Company had looked at Jamestown, as a place to send heirs who had little chance of inheriting the family estate or fortune at home. The germ of South Carolina's planter class, known as the "Goose Creek men" because of where they located their plantations, was a group of such younger sons and relatives, and they brought their slaves with them from the Caribbean.

Initially, the plantation system failed to thrive in South Carolina. Sugar and tobacco were not well suited to the lowlands' swampy environment. Instead, early colonists raised livestock to export to the West Indies and traded for furs and slaves with the populous Indian nations of the Southeast. Some Indians taken in this slave trade ended up working for the Carolina colonists, but most were shipped to the Caribbean, where they labored alongside Africans in the cane fields. The first generation of Africans in South Carolina, on the other hand, worked as "pioneers," clearing land, cutting wood, tending livestock, hunting and fishing, and navigating boats along coastal rivers. Some white servants migrated to the colony, but political and economic stabilization in England after 1660 slowed this flow, leaving the Goose Creek men with unchallenged authority over the colony. After 1690 the character of South Carolina changed as its planter class adopted rice cultivation. Slaves from the Senegambia region of West Africa brought their knowledge of this crop with them to the New World. By constructing dikes that kept salt water out and irrigation systems that allowed fresh water in, slaves turned the lowlands into remarkably productive rice paddies. South Carolina exported 400,000 pounds of rice in 1700, 1.5 million in 1710, and 20 million in 1720. Along with sugar and tobacco, rice became one of the great cash crops of the Atlantic plantation complex.

South Carolina planters owned, on average, more slaves and more land than their peers in the Chesapeake, but they were not as wealthy as the Caribbean great planters they emulated. The slave code South Carolina adopted in 1696 borrowed wholesale from the one drafted in Barbados in 1661. South Carolina planters also imitated the sugar planters' absenteeism. During the summer season, they abandoned their plantation homes for Charles Town, which became colonial North America's only major urban center south of Philadelphia and the largest slave market on the eastern seaboard. By the time of the American Revolution, about fifty of South Carolina's richest families maintained homes in England. In its demographic profile, South Carolina also came to resemble the Caribbean. It was the only North American colony with a black majority population: blacks outnumbered whites there 2 to 1 by 1740, and in some parts of the lowlands, the ratio was as high as 9 to 1. Unlike in the Chesapeake region, slave language, architecture, work habits, and naming patterns in South Carolina continued to show pronounced African influences throughout the eighteenth century. As was the case in the Caribbean, high slave mortality rates meant that planters relied on the Atlantic slave trade rather than natural increase to supply their workforce, which kept African cultural influences alive within the colony.

South of the Carolinas, a different kind of proprietary scheme unfolded during the early eighteenth century. In 1732 James Oglethorpe, a military officer and philanthropist interested in helping England's debtors, orphans, and other unfortunates, led a group of twenty likeminded gentlemen in founding Georgia, a colony established in the contested borderland between South Carolina and Spanish Florida. The Crown endorsed their plan because it was concerned with defending the Southern colonies from the Spanish, but it also put an expiration date on the proprietorship: after twenty-one years, the colony would revert to royal control. In another innovation, the British Parliament contributed funds to this project, the first time that it did so for a colony in North America. During the 1740s, Parliament provided similar funding to reenergize the colonization of Nova

Scotia, intending for that colony to serve as a defensive bulwark against French Canada. From its start, then, Georgia had a hybrid character, one part looking backward to the grand proprietary schemes of the seventeenth century and one part looking forward to the government-funded militarization of British North America during the eighteenth century.

Oglethorpe's plans for Georgia combined a feudal emphasis on order and hierarchy with Enlightenment ideas about humanitarianism and self-improvement. He laid out the capital city of Savannah in a gridiron pattern, believing that regular and ordered physical spaces would encourage social order and cooperation. To encourage industry and sobriety among the two thousand migrants he culled from London's debtor prisons and workhouses, Oglethorpe outlawed slavery and alcohol. Anticipating armed conflict with the Spanish in Florida, he insisted that Georgia's colonists engage in regular militia service and settle in compact, easily defended communities, which he encouraged by limiting the amount of land a person could possess. Like other colonial proprietors, he expected Georgia's colonists to respond to his efforts with deference and gratitude. He got neither. The religious dissidents from Germany and Switzerland and adventurers from South Carolina who migrated to Georgia did not share in Oglethorpe's philanthropic vision nor appreciate his military bearing. They also complained that his social causes limited their economic opportunity. Coastal Georgia was similar in climate and geography to the Carolina lowlands, and so it attracted migrants anxious to grow rice with slave labor. They also wanted a piece of South Carolina's fur trade but knew that they could not compete in that market unless they had rum to sell to Indian customers. After facing continual opposition to the bans on slaves and alcohol, the Georgia proprietors threw up their hands and transferred the colony to royal control a year early in 1752. The Crown made no effort to check landholding, alcohol sales, or slave importations, opening the door for Georgia to develop a plantation economy similar to that in South Carolina.

PROPRIETARY DESIGNS IN THE MIDDLE COLONIES

In addition to rewarding his friends, Charles II used proprietary grants as a way of challenging England's imperial rivals in North America. The Carolinas grant, for example, was aimed at checking Spanish expansion north of Florida. In an even more provocative act, Charles granted to his brother James, duke of York, the same territory between the Hudson and Delaware rivers claimed by the Dutch. New Netherland was not well populated, but it drove a wedge between English colonial dominions in New England and the Chesapeake Bay and provided a safe harbor for Dutch ships trading illegally with English colonies. Starting with Oliver Cromwell during the 1650s, England's rulers fought a series of naval wars with the Dutch aimed at ending their supremacy in Atlantic shipping.

The moment of reckoning for New Netherland came in 1664, when three English warships appeared off the coast of Manhattan to make good on Charles II's proprietary grant to his brother. As any older brother knows, the best part of having a younger brother is getting him to do your dirty work for you. James was the admiral of the English Navy, and so had a bit more resources at his disposal than most younger siblings. The English force offered generous terms if New Amsterdam surrendered, including the security of the colonists' property. New Netherland's governor Peter Stuyvesant was an old soldier who had lost a leg fighting the Spanish in the Caribbean. He was not afraid to defy the invaders. His councilors, all two-legged and apparently anxious to keep it that way, were less sanguine, and the Puritan Long Islanders who made up a substantial portion of Stuyvesant's militia defected to the English. Stuyvesant had no choice but to capitulate, and New Netherland became New York, renamed for its new proprietor. New Amsterdam likewise became New York City, and Fort Orange Albany. The Dutch briefly reconquered the colony in 1673, but in a peace treaty signed a year later, they returned it permanently to the English.

New York was a proprietary colony until James succeeded his brother to the throne in 1685, at which point it became a royal colony. As a proprietor, James did not challenge the cultural and economic characteristics that had taken root during the Dutch era. New York remained ethnically diverse and religiously tolerant, an underpopulated colony dominated by mercantile families living at opposite ends of the Hudson River. The English conquest did diversify the colony's elite class by opening its administrative offices and fur trade to English and Scottish adventurers. Like other colonial proprietors, James also parceled out generous land grants to friends and associates who were supposed to recruit settlers and represent his interests within the colony. The only surviving patroonship from the Dutch era—Rensselaerwyck, which encompassed thousands of acres on both sides of the upper Hudson River—provided a model for manorial land grants by James to Dutch, English, and Scottish families in the lower Hudson Valley and Manhattan. In addition to engrossing about three-quarters of the colony's prime farmlands, manor lords enjoyed such feudal privileges as the right of first refusal when their tenants sold surplus crops, a monopoly right to the construction of grain mills on their estates, and the power to convene small-claims courts for cases involving their tenants. Of all the proprietary colonies, New York came closest to transplanting a feudal land system to America, but the power that manor lords had over their tenants was never absolute. A manor lord had to treat his tenants well, granting them long-term leases with minimal rents, or they would desert him for freeholds they could acquire elsewhere.

New Jersey originated as a proprietary subdivision of New York made by James to reward his political allies. Bordered by the Delaware River on the west and the Atlantic Ocean on the east, this region was already home to a small but ethnically diverse colonial population when it came under English control. The colony's new proprietors added to that mix by splitting their grant into two halves, East Jersey and West Jersey, and then recruiting settlers for them from new ethnic and religious groups. East Jersey was owned by a group known as the Scottish proprietors, and it included a number of towns near the Atlantic port of Perth Amboy. Some of these communities had been established by Dutch, Puritan, and Quaker settlers before the Scottish proprietors received their grant, and so they showed little cooperation with the proprietors' efforts to govern and collect rents in the colony. However, several hundred Scots migrated to East Jersey during the 1670s and 1680s, adding to its ethnic diversity and establishing Presbyterianism as an influential religion in the region. West Jersey centered around Burlington on the Delaware River, and it attracted Quaker migrants after investors associated with that sect took over its proprietorship in 1676. Befitting its split personality and factious politics, New Jersey was more commonly known as "the Jerseys," even after the proprietors gave up on their schemes to govern the colony and ceded it back to royal authority in 1702. A landowning class eventually emerged there, but one without the same political and social authority as the manor lords of New York. It faced opposition from tenants and small freeholders, who although divided by ethnic and religious differences, united in resisting quitrents and similar feudal obligations that outsiders tried to impose on them.

Pennsylvania was the last proprietary colony established by Charles II. Like other recipients of proprietary grants, William Penn came from a wealthy, well-connected family. But Penn was also a religious radical and visionary who intended to make a "Holy Experiment" of his colony. Penn first exhibited his penchant for nonconformity as a young man, when he was expelled from Oxford University and packed off to Ireland by his father to manage the family's plantations there. That experience should have drummed the idealism out of him, but instead young William converted to Quakerism and embraced its radical doctrines of pacifism, social equality, and religious toleration. Despite his prominent family background, he spent time during the 1660s and 1670s as a Quaker evangelist, occasionally finding himself in prison for expressing his inflammatory criticisms of the Church of England. He joined other Quaker investors in the West Jersey proprietorship, but his interest in American colonization took a new turn in 1681 when Charles II granted him a proprietary charter for a colony between Maryland and New York. It was a sweetheart deal, and historians have wondered ever since exactly why the king did it: perhaps to settle a debt owed Penn's father, perhaps to rid his realm of a troublesome religious sect, or perhaps his attention was diverted by one of his many mistresses. Regardless of motivation, William Penn—the Quaker malcontent and son of privilege—had suddenly become North America's single greatest landowner.

As a colonial promoter, Penn balanced his religious idealism with entrepreneurial practicality. He recruited settlers in the British Isles and Germany by making use of his Quaker connections and promising toleration to anyone recognizing the divinity of Christ, regardless of sectarian affiliation. Even non-Quakers found much to like about the Quaker principles that informed Penn's plans. His commitment to pacifism meant there was no compulsory military service in the colony, nor any taxes levied to pay for soldiers and their arms. His disavowal of a state church meant that no one would be prosecuted for heterodox beliefs, nor would anyone be compelled to attend or pay taxes to a church they did not support. Even among other antinomian faiths, Quakers were noteworthy for their progressive attitudes. They recognized no professional clergy. Believing that God's grace, or the "inner light," could inspire anyone, they even condoned female preaching. A remarkable variety of Protestant sects—Lutherans, Baptists, Presbyterians, Mennonites, Schwenkfelders, Dunkers, Amish, Moravians, and others—migrated to Pennsylvania, some sharing the same pacifist principles as the Quakers.

Penn's liberal approach to colonization helped his dominion grow quickly. He purchased the site for his capital city of Philadelphia from Swedes who had already begun clearing it, and he allowed the "three lower counties" populated by earlier Dutch, Swedish, and Finnish fur traders to form their own separate colony of Delaware under his proprietary authority. Penn also moved quickly to assert his interests against his neighbors. He disputed the southern boundary of his colony with Maryland (a conflict not resolved until royal surveyors mapped the Mason-Dixon Line during the 1750s), and he successfully challenged New York's claim to the Susquehanna Valley. By virtue of Penn's commitment to honest dealings and fair play with the land's indigenous inhabitants, the colony also avoided the Indian wars that had plagued other colonies.

In managing his colony, Penn planned to grow rich off land sales, but it was not to happen. Like other colonial proprietors, Penn thought his plan was foolproof: secure a colonial charter, recruit migrants, and sell them the land. The mid-Atlantic region seemed perfect for attracting settlers. Its climate was more temperate than New England's and its soil more fertile. Its growing season would not accommodate tobacco, rice, or sugar, but a farmer there could generate surplus grains and pork to export to the West Indies. Despite the rapid population and economic growth Pennsylvania experienced, Penn could never wring a return on his investment. As in other proprietary colonies, migrants had little interest in paying quitrents or any other form of rents to Penn, his agents, or the absentee landlords to whom he granted substantial estates. As progressive as he was in his religious opinions, Penn could be downright feudal in his expectations for controlling the colony's politics, an attitude that probably derived from his experiences as a young man managing his father's Irish plantations. Pennsylvania, however, was much farther away from England than Ireland, and when it came to dealing with recalcitrant people, Penn was no Oliver Cromwell.

A three-way political struggle emerged in the colony among Quaker grandees connected to Penn, a much larger number of Quakers at odds with the proprietary party, and an even larger number of non-Quakers who believed Penn's plan of government unduly favored that sect. Penn visited the colony twice, in 1682–1684 and again in 1700–1701, but on neither occasion was he able to contain the political fissures that undermined his authority. Back in England, he was briefly confined to debtors' prison and he died insolvent in 1718. His sons and heirs abandoned their father's Quaker faith and became Anglicans, joining the church that had persecuted their father during the 1660s and 1670s. In a final irony, eighteenth-century migrants called his colony "the best poor man's country" because of its cheap land, low taxes, and religious liberty. The Holy Experiment had prospered, just not for the Experimenter.

North America proved to be a graveyard for proprietary dreams, regardless of their origin or nature. Some, like Locke's plan for the Carolinas, looked backward to an idealized past of agrarian order and stability. Others, like Penn's Holy Experiment and Oglethorpe's Georgia, hoped to bring peace and prosperity to people who suffered because of religious belief or material want in the Old World. A cynic can easily dismiss such utopian blueprints as the pie-in-the-sky dreaming of aristocratic lords too far removed from the harsh realities of colonization to realize the impracticality of their plans, but those proprietors who wanted nothing more than cash from their American possessions were invariably disappointed too, unable to pry even small annual quitrents from their tenants. An optimist may look at the proprietary failures and choose to see the individual triumphs of the colonists: poor farmers who found a measure of material security, religious dissidents who found freedom of conscience, servants who became freeholders, squatters who thumbed their noses at distant lords and settled wherever they pleased. All the proprietary dreams ultimately foundered on the refusal of individual colonists to defer to them. A few grand plans were wrecked upon the backs of thousands of little ones. In that sense, all of colonial America was the best poor man's country (see Map 3.2).

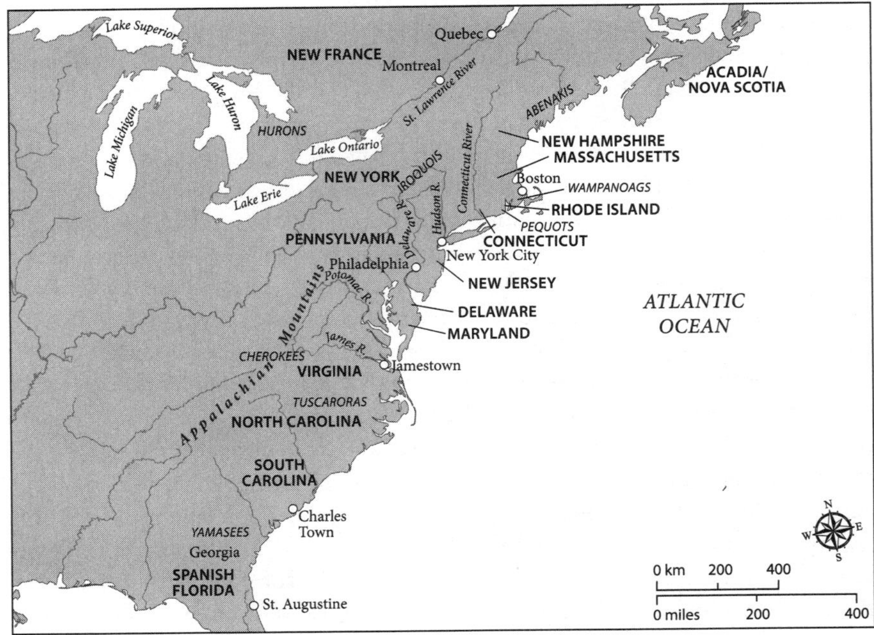

Map 3.2 Eastern North America.

FATE AND CHANCE

After her banishment from Massachusetts, Anne Hutchinson moved with her family and a few likeminded souls to Narragansett Bay, but her American odyssey did not end there. New divisions arose among those Puritans who settled the town of Portsmouth, Rhode Island, and after the death of Hutchinson's husband in 1642, she chose to move again, this time to New Netherland. With a number of her children, she settled in what is now Westchester County, near other English Puritan communities on Long Island and the Connecticut coast. Her life ended abruptly not long thereafter, when Indians provoked to war by the governor of New Netherland attacked her homestead and killed all its inhabitants except a young daughter.

To her Puritan detractors in Boston, Hutchinson's fate was a reminder that all unfolded according to God's plan. Hutchinson may have defied the clergy and magistrates of Massachusetts and dodged her opponents in Rhode Island, but she could not escape God's judgment. A violent death at the hands of Indians needed little in the way of interpretation: Hutchinson got what she had coming.

Modern observers are more likely to see cruel chance rather than a vengeful God at work in Hutchinson's death. Like so many seventeenth-century migrants to North America, Hutchinson found herself in the wrong place at the wrong time. Her sudden and violent end in a conflict she had not caused and could have barely understood is a reminder of how fragile life in colonial America was. For every migrant who achieved a better life, far more died in a strange place among strange people for reasons that defied their comprehension. The causes of death were apparent enough—disease, malnutrition, violence, accident, unending labor in an unforgiving environment—but whether in the flash of a tomahawk or the wasting slowness of a sickbed, too many colonists must have asked with their dying breath, "Why me?" Migration was a gamble against sobering odds. Time and place affected those odds, but there was a randomness about them from which no colonial design—no matter how small or grand—was immune.

CHRONOLOGY

1607	Jamestown is established by the Virginia Company of London.
1608	Samuel de Champlain founds Quebec on the St. Lawrence River.
1616	Pocahontas and John Rolfe visit London.
1620	Pilgrims establish the Plymouth colony.
1626	Dutch West India Company purchases Manhattan.
1629–1640	Puritans' "Great Migration" from England leads to founding of Massachusetts, Rhode Island, Connecticut, and New Haven.
1634	Calvert family sends the first colonists to Maryland.

1638	*Anne Hutchinson's trial and banishment in Massachusetts.*
1640s	Colonists begin growing sugar on Barbados, transforming the economy of the Caribbean colonies.
1643	*Hutchinson and her family are killed in Indian attack in New Netherland.*
1664	The English conquer New Netherland and rename it New York.
1670s	English and African colonists from Caribbean establish Charles Town (modern Charleston, South Carolina). East and West Jersey colonized by Scots and English Quakers, respectively.
1682	Pennsylvania founded by William Penn as the Quaker "Holy Experiment."
1732	James Oglethorpe leads the colonization of Georgia as a refuge for English debtors and orphans.

NOTES

1. The quoted passages are from David D. Hall, ed., *The Antinomian Controversy, 1636–1638: A Documentary History* (Middletown, CT: Wesleyan University Press, 1968), 326, 337, 343, 383.
2. George Percy, "Observations by Master George Percy" (1607), in Lyon Gardiner Tyler, *Narratives of Early Virginia, 1606–1625* (New York: Charles Scribner's Sons, 1907), 21.
3. Karen Ordahl Kupperman, ed., *Captain John Smith: A Select Edition of His Writings* (Chapel Hill: University of North Carolina Press, 1988), 118.
4. Kupperman, ed., *Captain John Smith*, 106–107.
5. Kupperman, ed., *Captain John Smith*, 64–65.
6. Kupperman, ed., *Captain John Smith*, 166–169.
7. Kupperman, ed., *Captain John Smith*, 72.
8. "Harriot's Brief and True Report of the New Found Land of Virginia," in Richard Hakluyt, *Voyages to the Virginia Colonies*, ed. A. L. Rowse (London: Century, 1986), 117–118.
9. Kupperman, ed., *Captain John Smith*, 82, 195.
10. Susan Kingsbury, ed., *The Records of the Virginia Company of London*, 4 vols. (Washington, DC: Government Printing Office, 1906–1935), Vol. 4, 58–62.
11. Narrative of Pierre Esprit Radisson in *In Mohawk Country: Early Narratives about a Native People*, ed. Dean R. Snow, Charles T. Gehring, and William A. Starna (Syracuse, NY: Syracuse University Press, 1996), 89.
12. Richard S. Dunn, *Sugar and Slaves: The Rise of the Planter Class in the English West Indies, 1624–1713* (Chapel Hill: University of North Carolina Press, 1972), 87, 314.
13. Richard Ligon, *A True & Exact History of the Island of Barbadoes*, 2nd ed. (London: Peter Parker and Thomas Guy, 1673), 44.
14. John Winthrop, "A Modell of Christian Charity," in *The Founding of Massachusetts: Historians and the Sources*, ed. Edmund S. Morgan (Indianapolis: Bobbs-Merrill, 1964), 203.

15. John Winthrop, "Reasons to be Considered, and Objections with Answers," in *The Founding of Massachusetts*, 175–182.
16. Winthrop, "A Modell of Christian Charity," 203.
17. "The Journal of Madam Knight," *Colonial American Travel Narratives*, ed. Wendy Martin (New York: Penguin, 1994), 63.
18. Nathaniel Ward, "The Simple Cobler of Aggawam" (1647), in *The American Puritans: Their Prose and Poetry*, ed. Perry Miller (Garden City, NY: Anchor Books, 1956), 96–97.

SUGGESTIONS FOR FURTHER READING

Of the raft of new books published to coincide with the 400th anniversary of the founding of Jamestown, Karen Ordahl Kupperman, *The Jamestown Project* (Cambridge, MA: Harvard University Press, 2007), is noteworthy for breathing new life into an old topic. Likewise, Camilla Townsend, *Pocahontas and the Powhatan Dilemma* (New York: Hill & Wang, 2004), and Lorri Glover and Daniel Blake Smith, *The Shipwreck That Saved Jamestown: The Sea Venture Castaways and the Fate of America* (New York: Holt, 2008), offer engaging retellings of the Jamestown story from the perspective of Native Americans and colonists, respectively. Still well worth reading are Edmund S. Morgan, *American Slavery, American Freedom: The Ordeal of Colonial Virginia* (New York: Norton, 1975), and Alden T. Vaughan, *American Genesis: Captain John Smith and the Founding of Virginia* (Boston: Little, Brown, 1975).

For the origins of New France, see David Hackett Fischer, *Champlain's Dream* (New York: Simon & Schuster, 2008), and W. J. Eccles, *France in America* (New York: Harper and Row, 1972). For the role of Indian women in the French fur trade, see Susan Sleeper-Smith, *Indian Women and French Men: Rethinking Cultural Encounter in the Western Great Lakes* (Amherst: University of Massachusetts Press, 2001). On New Netherland, see Oliver Rink, *Holland on the Hudson: An Economic and Social History of Dutch New York* (Ithaca, NY: Cornell University Press, 1986), and Jaap Jacobs, *The Colony of New Netherland: A Dutch Settlement in Seventeenth-Century America* (Ithaca, NY: Cornell University Press, 2009). The colonization of the Caribbean is described in Richard S. Dunn, *Sugar and Slaves: The Rise of the Planter Class in the English West Indies, 1624–1713* (Chapel Hill: University of North Carolina Press, 1972). The transformation of Barbados into a sugar colony is addressed in Russell R. Menard, *Sweet Negotiations: Sugar, Slavery, and Plantation Agriculture in Early Barbados* (Charlottesville: University of Virginia Press, 2006).

The Puritan colonization of New England has inspired a vast literature. Works that analyze the Puritan migration include Virginia DeJohn Anderson, *New England's Generation: The Great Migration and the Formation of Society and Culture in the Seventeenth Century* (Cambridge, UK: Cambridge University Press, 1991), and Alison Games, *Migration and the Origins of the English Atlantic World* (Cambridge, MA: Harvard University Press, 1999). Edmund Morgan's engaging biography *The Puritan Dilemma: The Story of John Winthrop* (New York: HarperCollins, 1958) remains one of the best introductions to early Massachusetts. For dissenters from the Puritan orthodoxy, see Morgan's *Roger Williams: The Church and the State* (New York: Harcourt, Brace, and World, 1967), and Philip F. Gura, *A Glimpse of Sion's Glory: Puritan Radicalism in New England, 1620–1660* (Middletown, CT: Wesleyan University Press, 1984). More recently, Joseph A. Conforti has provided an overview of New England's colonization in the context of Britain's Atlantic empire in *Saints and Strangers: New England in British North America* (Baltimore: Johns Hopkins University Press, 2006).

Peter Wood, *Black Majority: Negroes in Colonial South Carolina from 1670 through the Stono Rebellion* (New York: Norton, 1975), remains the authoritative treatment of early South Carolina, although S. Max Edelson weaves environmental history into the story in *Plantation Enterprise in Colonial South Carolina* (Cambridge, MA: Harvard University Press, 2006). For a succinct explanation of the Caribbean roots of colonization in the Carolinas, see Jack P. Greene, "Colonial South Carolina and the Caribbean Connection," *South Carolina Historical Magazine* 88 (1987): 192–210. Intercultural relations in early Georgia are the focus of Julie Anne Sweet, *Negotiating for Georgia: British-Creek Relations in the Trustee Era, 1733–1752* (Athens: University of Georgia Press, 2005), and John T. Juricek, *Colonial Georgia and the Creeks: Anglo-Indian Diplomacy on the Southern Frontier, 1733–1763* (Gainesville: University Press of Florida, 2010).

As is fitting of their varied origins and ethnic and religious diversity, the middle colonies have a disjointed historiography, although a good synthesis is provided in Ned C. Landsman, *Crossroads of Empire: The Middle Colonies in British North America* (Baltimore: Johns Hopkins University Press, 2010). Robert C. Ritchie, *The Duke's Province: A Study of New York Politics and Society, 1664–1691* (Chapel Hill: University of North Carolina Press, 1977), describes New Netherland's transition into New York. For the social and political development of New York, see Joyce D. Goodfriend, *Before the Melting Pot: Society and Culture in Colonial New York City, 1664–1730* (Princeton, NJ: Princeton University Press, 1992), and Patricia U. Bonomi, *A Factious People: Politics and Society in Colonial New York* (New York: Columbia University Press, 1971), respectively. Brendan McConville, *These Daring Disturbers of the Public Peace: The Struggle for Property and Power in Early New Jersey* (Ithaca, NY: Cornell University Press, 1999), examines the struggle between proprietors and colonists in New Jersey. John Smolenski's *Friends and Strangers: The Making of a Creole Culture in Colonial Pennsylvania* (Philadelphia: University of Pennsylvania Press, 2010) describes William Penn's Holy Experiment and the Quaker imprint on the colony's formative years. Two worthwhile essay collections on early Pennsylvania are Richard S. Dunn and Mary Maples Dunn, eds., *The World of William Penn* (Philadelphia: University of Pennsylvania Press, 1986), and Michael Zuckerman, ed., *Friends and Neighbors: Group Life in America's First Plural Society* (Philadelphia: Temple University Press, 1982).

CHAPTER 4

Remaking America

In August 1700 a young English gentleman named John Lawson arrived in Charles Town, South Carolina. According to Lawson, an associate in London had told him that "*Carolina* was the best Country I could go to," and so he immediately booked passage for America.[1] Not long after landing, he joined a small expedition into the Carolina backcountry. With several other colonists and four Indians, Lawson traveled for two months by canoe and on foot, visiting many Indian towns and scouting possible locations for colonial settlements. He kept notes as he moved through the landscape, describing its geography, climate, flora and fauna, and native inhabitants.

Like many other European travelers in America, Lawson was impressed by the bounty and diversity of its resources. The soil produced tremendous yields of maize, beans, wheat, rice, and other crops. Bays, inlets, and rivers teemed with fish of all varieties. The forests Lawson passed through could supply shipbuilders with unlimited timber and fur traders with an equally impressive source of pelts. Even the strange beasts Lawson encountered could be put to profitable use. Lawson did not find the meat of the Carolina panther pleasing, but its pelt "makes fine Womens Shoes, or Mens Gloves." He even speculated that the American buffalo might be interbred "with our tame Cattle," creating a hybrid that would "much better the Breed for Largeness and Milk."[2]

Lawson was no pipe-dreaming schemer. He had come to America to make his fortune, and with the knowledge he collected from his expedition, he set about doing exactly that. In 1705 he established Bath, the first incorporated town in North Carolina, on land he had purchased near the Pamlico River. Three years later he became the surveyor-general for North Carolina, an office that offered insider opportunity for land speculation and sales. He returned to England in 1709, where he published *A New Voyage to Carolina*, a book that detailed his explorations eight years earlier and promoted migration to America. While in London, he also recruited several hundred Swiss and Germans to move to land he located for them on the Neuse River. Their settlement, New Bern, became North Carolina's first capital.

When he returned to America with the New Bern migrants in 1710, Lawson must have felt a considerable sense of accomplishment. Within a decade he had managed to make a name for himself as an explorer, writer, surveyor, and colonial promoter. He had described North Carolina's landscape, plants, and animals, and counted and mapped its indigenous inhabitants. He had also exhibited mastery over the land by measuring it out and placing new towns on it, populating them with recruits from the Old World. No colonial proprietor in London, not William Penn, Lord Baltimore, or any other royal favorite, had ever been able to accomplish what Lawson seemed to be doing with apparent ease: remaking America according to his own design.

But Lawson was not entirely in control of the events he set in motion. His mere presence in North America was a good example of what scientists call the observer effect: the very act of observing something for the sake of measurement or classification changes it. Lawson, simply by collecting and publicizing information about the Carolina wilderness, was changing it irrevocably. His identification and description of various plant species turned them into valuable resources to be harvested for use in shipbuilding, medicine, textile production, or any number of other industries. Some of the animals he described, such as whitetail deer, became valuable as commodities in the trans-Atlantic fur trade, while others, such as rattlesnakes and wolves, became marked for extermination as vermin (see Figure 4.1). Newcomers such as Lawson also introduced invasive species to the land, sometimes purposely, such as when they brought Old World livestock and crops to their American farms, and sometimes inadvertently, such as when they introduced deadly microbes to Indian populations. Human beings, whether European migrants who came of their own accord or African slaves forcibly carried across the Atlantic, were an invasive species in their own right, transforming America in ways that would make it more familiar to them, right down to renaming the landscape so that it might evoke memories of the Old World. As a land speculator, Lawson knew that familiar names would encourage and comfort migrants who found themselves in a strange place. Thus, the first town he founded, Bath, was named after a famous English resort town, and the second, New Bern, after a capital city in Switzerland.

From Lawson's perspective, colonization was about remaking America from a strange New World into something that resembled the more familiar Old. The landscape had to be mapped and divided into farmland and towns, new plants and animals classified and turned into commodities, indigenous peoples rendered docile and useful. But the transformation was never as thorough as the colonizers would have liked. They hoped to see America and its native inhabitants assimilated into their world, but they did not anticipate the ways in which their own values and customs would be affected by this new environment. Colonization would be a process of acculturation on both sides, and the changes it wrought could occur with imperceptible slowness or with sudden violence, as Lawson himself would find out.

LAND USE, PROPERTY RIGHTS, AND ANIMALS

When John Lawson undertook his journey through Carolina in 1700–1701, the colonial population there was still small and mostly confined to the coast, but he found evidence of its presence everywhere. He saw fields planted with grains, rice,

Figure 4.1 Animals of the Carolinas, from John Lawson, [*A New Voyage to Carolina*] *The History of Carolina* ([London: T. Warner, 1718]). Lawson's narrative of his travels in the Carolinas included a careful description of the country's plants and animals. The page numbers included in this image tell the reader where to find descriptions of buffalo, terrapins, rattlesnakes, black snakes, squirrels, opossums, wildcats, bears, and raccoons in the narrative. Courtesy of the John Carter Brown Library at Brown University.

peas, and other Old World crops, and he marveled at how the colonists' livestock thrived in this new land. Indians who lived near colonial settlements had already altered their work patterns and material culture in response to their new neighbors, building corn cribs to store their surplus and incorporating an array of new goods into their daily lives, including guns, metal tools, copper kettles, rum, and cloth of all kinds. In ways grand and small, subtle and profound, colonization was remaking the countryside and all its living inhabitants.

Colonists were not eco-tourists. They came to America deliberately intending to alter its environment. Tapping into the new land's bounty required manipulating it: animals had to be killed and processed into furs and hides, forests cut into lumber, fields cleared and planted with crops. That impulse to convert natural resources into marketable commodities defined how Europeans saw the land and asserted their right of property in it. Almost a century before Lawson's travels in America, John Winthrop, the leader of the Puritan migration to Massachusetts Bay, summarized the argument colonists made for seizing land already occupied by Indians. Winthrop was well aware that the Indians were there first, that they built towns and cleared land on which they grew crops, and that they defended their territory from interlopers. But the Indians' claim to the land, he explained, was only a "naturall right" of prior occupation. They did not possess the superior "Civill Right" to it because they had failed to "improve" it: "they inclose noe Land, neither have any setled habytation, nor any tame Cattle to improve the Land by, and soe have noe other but a Naturall Right to those Countries.... [I]f we leave them sufficient for their use, we may lawfully take the rest, there being more than enough for them and us."[3]

Winthrop's distinction between a natural and civil right to the land illustrates the willful blindness Europeans exhibited toward Indian land use. Time and again, explorers and promoters like John Lawson visited Indian towns, admired the bounty of their fields, and explained how they used fire to manage their hunting lands, yet at the same time they described Indians as nomads who lived off the land rather than on it. Indian homes, built most commonly of bark and saplings, did not meet European standards of civilization because they lacked such permanent fixtures as chimneys. Colonial observers attributed the productivity of Indian horticulture to the fertility of the soil rather than the skill of the farmers, who they described as sloppy and half-hearted in their work because they planted their three primary crops—corn, beans, and squash—together rather than separately, used hoes rather than plows to break the earth, and built no fences around their fields. Most damning of all in European eyes was the Indians' failure to keep livestock. With no cattle, pigs, horses, or sheep to tend, Indians had no reason to build barns or pens, nor any motive for collecting animal manure to fertilize their fields. More than any other factor, the absence of domestic farm animals defined the Indians in European eyes as nomadic forest-dwellers whose right to any particular spot of ground ended the moment they vacated it.

Indians had a very different notion of property and its relationship to land use and occupation. Their mobility allowed them to take advantage of seasonal variations in resources. In the summer and fall, they stayed close to their fields, but in the spring, they moved to fishing camps to take advantage of spawning runs and, in the winter, to hunting grounds where they pursued fur-bearing animals when their pelts were at their thickest. Rather than wanderers, they were commuters, returning annually to sites they claimed individually or collectively for various uses. When Indians sold land to colonists, they did not conceive of the transfer as a one-time deal that permanently alienated them from the tract in question. On the contrary, they believed that even after they had allowed newcomers to build and farm in a particular spot, they retained the right to use it for other purposes such as fishing, hunting, gathering, or traveling through it, all of which constituted trespass in the eyes of Europeans.

Domestic farm animals were often at the center of conflicts arising from these divergent notions of property and land use. Drawing on the Old Testament stories of Adam and Noah, European colonists contended that God had granted humankind dominion over the beasts of the earth. Keeping animals for use as food, transportation, and muscle power was one of the ways in which societies climbed the ladder from savagery to civility. By taming, caring for, and breeding animals, a farmer acquired a property right to them, in the same manner that he did when he "improved" land by clearing, planting, fertilizing, and building on it. Brands and notched ears on livestock marked them as the property of their owners and set them apart from the wild creatures of the field and forest. Indians conceived of human–animal relations in more reciprocal terms. They observed a variety of ritual practices and taboos designed to honor and appease the spiritual "gamekeepers" of animals they took in the hunt. By defending their hunting and fishing territories from outsiders, Indians asserted collective ownership over animals, but they generally did not recognize a right of exclusive personal property to an animal until it was killed. Thus, when Indian travelers helped themselves to colonial farm animals along their route or killed those that had strayed from their owners, they did so in accordance with the rules that had long governed their own notions of land and animal use. Not surprisingly, their European neighbors saw such behavior as deliberate acts of trespass and theft.

Of the various domestic species the colonists brought to America, pigs and cattle had the most profound environmental impact. Sheep fell prey too easily to wolves to propagate quickly in America, and goats' omnivorous eating habits made them unwelcome among farmers planting orchards. Cattle, however, were indispensable for their versatility, providing muscle, meat, milk, and hides for colonists, and pigs were such prolific foragers that pork became the staple meat of colonial diets. Despite these advantages, each species also caused environmental problems. Grazing cattle threatened indigenous plants, caused erosion, and took forage from deer. Pigs invaded the Indians' unfenced fields and storage pits and competed with indigenous species for food. These problems were compounded by their owners' willingness to allow them to wander freely in a semi-feral state. Colonial farmers found it cheaper and more labor-efficient to let their cattle and pigs forage for themselves rather than confining them to pens and growing fodder crops to feed them. This free-range husbandry, practiced year-round in the southern colonies and during the warm weather seasons in the north, heightened tensions between colonists and Indians over access to and control of these animals. It facilitated the transmission of livestock diseases such as anthrax and brucellosis to American species and also sped soil exhaustion, because colonial farmers did not collect the manure of free-range animals to fertilize their fields.

Unlike epidemic diseases, which could empty the countryside of its human inhabitants with terrible speed, the transformations wrought in plant and animal life by colonization occurred more slowly and subtly. In European eyes, American forests, fish, and fur-bearing animals seemed endless in their supply, and the continent itself an Aladdin's cave of bottomless riches. Colonists felled old growth forests for fuel and building materials. The white pines of New England became a new source of masts for the king's navy, and royal officials promoted entrepreneurial schemes to turn the versatile resin of pitch pines into tar, turpentine, and other naval supplies. The insulating qualities of forests were lost as they were turned into lumber, making summers hotter, winters colder, and periods of drought more frequent. Likewise, the over-hunting of beaver for the fur trade altered the landscape as their dams were broken or went unbuilt, emptying ponds that provided habitats for other species. Elsewhere, colonists dammed rivers to provide power for mills, interfering with the spawning runs of fish and altering the habitats of other aquatic species. Lawson may have contemplated domesticating the American buffalo, but by the time he journeyed into the Carolina country, changing environmental conditions had already substantially reduced this animal's range east of the Mississippi.

Whether deliberately or unintentionally transplanted to America, Old World species from humble dandelions to herds of livestock upset local and regional ecosystems. In doing so, they also interrupted the Indians' traditional methods of subsistence and entangled them in a web of new market relations, some of which spanned the Atlantic. In our environmentally conscious age, it has become fashionable to romanticize Indians as resisters of this change, as people who refused to turn the land and its resources into commodities to be bought and sold, but that image overlooks their agency in this change, particularly their role as suppliers in the fur trade, their avid consumption of European goods, and in some regions, their successful adoption of European-style animal husbandry and farming. The environmental change put in motion by colonization caused conflict between Indians and Europeans, but in these instances it also illuminated their common humanity as they struggled to adjust to new environmental and economic realities.

What ultimately set Europeans' environmental attitudes and practices apart from those of the Indians was the former's utter conviction in their rightful lordship over the land. Indians regarded their relationship with nature as something that needed to be kept in constant balance, so that the spiritual forces governing it would remain beneficial rather than harmful to human enterprise. In contrast, European colonists acted with the certainty of divine sanction, as expressed in this series of votes from a Milford, Connecticut, town meeting in 1640:

> "Voted: that the earth is the Lord's and the fullness thereof;
> "Voted: that the earth is given to the Saints;
> "Voted: we are the Saints."[4]

The hubris in this statement was founded on the same logic as Winthrop's defense of the colonists' right to claim the land as their own. In the Old Testament, God made it clear that he expected humans to subdue and transform the earth, not merely occupy it. Indians, despite the evidence of the various ways in which they used the land, failed to meet this definition of stewardship because quite simply, they were heathen. They needed to be taught the arts of European farming and the tenets of the Christian faith. Colonists believed these two tasks would go hand in hand, and so by subduing the environment, they would also achieve dominion over its native inhabitants.

MAKING CONVERTS

Not long after beginning his journey through Carolina, John Lawson spent a night with some Santee Indians, whom he found to be a "well-humour'd and affable People." He also noted that "living near the *English*" had made them "very tractable." When it came to Indians, Lawson and his contemporaries automatically linked these qualities together. Human sociability would lead Indians to want to live near colonists, which in turn would make then want to live like colonists. Colonial promoters such as Lawson had no doubt that all Indians would eventually live under the European government, but the smart ones would realize it was in their best interests to do so without resistance. All colonial societies shared the bedrock assumption that Christian faith and disciplined labor would simultaneously raise the Indians' out of their savagery and cement their dependence on their new overlords. Colonists referred to this transformation as "reducing the Indians to civility." To make it happen, Indians needed to end their geographic mobility and fix themselves on a spot of ground, so that missionaries could oversee their cultural conversion to European modes of labor, gender and family relations, diet, and dress.

While all colonial ventures paid at least lip service to the notion of lifting the natives out of heathen darkness, the Catholic and Protestant powers exhibited sharply different levels of commitment to this task. Protestant clergy who migrated to North America during the seventeenth century, whether Dutch or English, came to minister to the spiritual needs of their fellow colonists. Only a handful learned the languages necessary to preach to Indians, and they did so with only their personal commitment and private donations to support them. Not until after 1700 would any Protestant churches dedicate substantial resources or exclusive manpower to converting Native Americans. In French and Spanish colonies, on the other hand, missionary orders were present from the beginning, and they received encouragement and support from state and church authorities in Europe. These contrasting approaches to missionary work were one expression of how the international rivalry unleashed in Europe by the Protestant Reformation was transplanted to North America. Generally speaking, Protestants came to America to build exclusive religious communities over which they could exercise tight control of membership, while Catholics, at least those tied to missionary orders, came to gather as many natives as possible within their fold.

The Spanish brought the mission system they had already established elsewhere in their New World colonies to Florida in 1565 and New Mexico in 1598. In both regions, missionaries from the Franciscan order moved with the aid of Spanish soldiers into native communities, where they established churches, catechized residents in the Catholic faith, and subjected them to tributary labor necessary to support Spanish rule. In Florida, these missions spread from St. Augustine on the Atlantic coast northward into modern Georgia and westward across the Florida panhandle, incorporating Indians from the Apalachee and Timucua peoples. Disease greatly reduced the population of these initially powerful groups, but the survivors became key players in maintaining Spain's tenuous hold on this region. Florida had no gold or silver to attract Spanish colonizers, but the Spanish Crown regarded it as vital to the security of its Caribbean shipping and possessions. Apalachee and Timucuan converts helped keep Spanish forts at St. Augustine and Pensacola provisioned and gave Spanish traders access to the Southeastern deerskin trade. The number of Indians in the Florida mission system peaked at about twenty thousand during the 1670s. Thereafter it declined, in large measure because of raids by English-allied Indians from the Carolinas, who attacked Spanish-allied converts, sold thousands of captives as slaves to the English, and dispersed survivors among Gulf Coast nations. By 1710 the once flourishing mission system in Florida had contracted to small satellite communities of St. Augustine.

In New Mexico, Spanish missionaries concentrated their efforts on the sedentary Pueblo peoples of the northern Rio Grande Valley. "Pueblo" referred to the distinctive multifamily dwellings built by these Indians, who comprised more than fifty distinct groups speaking a number of different languages. Already living in fixed locations with high population densities, they were natural targets for conquest and conversion by the Spanish. In each town they entered, missionaries appropriated the sacred *kivas*, circular subterranean rooms in which male spiritual societies performed rituals associated with bringing rain and fertility to the community, and built their churches on top of them. The missionaries were especially concerned with policing their converts' sexuality, and they used the lash to suppress polygamy and divorce and to enforce new dress codes in keeping with European standards of modesty. Not surprisingly, their intolerance encouraged much opposition, and tensions were exacerbated by the labor demands of the Spanish, who put the Pueblos to work on farms and ranches without compensation.

In 1680 a shaman named Popé inspired a widespread rebellion among the Pueblos that killed about a fifth of the Spanish colonists and forced the survivors to abandon the colony for over a decade. Called before a Spanish interrogator to explain why the rebellion had occurred, one elderly Pueblo man testified that the Indians resented the Spanish who "took away their idols and forbade their sorceries and idolatries; that they have inherited successively from their old men the things pertaining to their ancient customs; and that he has heard this resentment spoken of since he was of an age to understand."[5] As these words indicate, the Spanish missionary endeavor had been broad but not deep. Neither persuasion nor brute force had been able to eradicate native beliefs or guarantee conversions deeper than a fragile outward conformity to the new regime.

In Canada, the French pursued a different tack in their attempts to convert Indians to Christianity. During the 1630s and 1640s, missionaries there focused their work on the Hurons, a populous confederacy of Indians who lived in modern Ontario, astride the trade routes between the upper Great Lakes and Quebec. Jesuit priests who lived and traveled among the Hurons tried to win over leading families whose influence in this clan-based society would be indispensable. They challenged the spiritual authority of native shamans by using their ability to predict eclipses, to communicate via reading and writing, and to operate mechanical devices such as clocks as evidence of their god's superior power. They also used sacred material objects associated with Catholic piety—images of saints, religious medals, rosary beads—to present their message in the native context of gift-giving. Their words and actions impressed many Hurons, although in keeping with native ideas about manitou, some described the missionaries as demons whose spiritual powers could just as readily destroy the Indians as help them. Nowhere was this more evident than in the relationship between the priests and smallpox. The missionaries seemed to bring the disease with them, although they also ministered to the sick and grieving and seemed to possess the power to resist the disease themselves. Whether good or bad, these Black Robes, as the Indians called them, were clearly figures whose spiritual powers could not be ignored.

In the *Jesuit Relations*, annual reports printed in France to publicize their American missions, the Jesuits claimed to have converted sixteen thousand Indians in Canada in the years between 1632 and 1672. By their own admission, about one-third of these were baptisms administered to unknowing infants or dying adults. Nevertheless, they won enough healthy adult followers to make their presence a divisive force within Huron communities. The missionaries expected their converts to cease their participation in native practices they considered pagan and sinful, such as polygamy, dances, and the torture and execution of prisoners. In an effort to prevent backsliding, they encouraged the faithful to live apart from the unconverted and to avoid marriage partners who were not receptive to Christianity. After warfare with the Iroquois in the 1640s left many Huron towns shattered, the Jesuits withdrew with their surviving converts to new homes closer to Montreal and Quebec. These communities became the foundation of the *reserve* system in Canada, in which Christian Indians from different nations amalgamated into new autonomous communities that lived in symbiotic social and economic relations with the French. The Indians of the seven major *reserves* in Canada lived under the spiritual supervision of missionaries but never submitted themselves to the political authority of the colonial government. They continued to govern their internal affairs according to their clan system and to rely on a mixture of mobile hunting, fishing, and farming to sustain themselves. In effect, they became allies rather than vassals of the French.

In the English and Dutch colonies along the Atlantic coast, the greatest missionary effort during the seventeenth century occurred in Massachusetts, where a handful of Puritans committed themselves to seeking converts among the Algonquian-speaking peoples of that region. The Mayhews, an intergenerational family of ministers, won converts among the Wampanoag Indians of Martha's Vineyard, forging a spiritual partnership with them that endured through the colonial era. On the mainland, the Reverend John Eliot preached to remnant bands of coastal Algonquian Indians displaced by disease and the Puritan migration. He was the driving force behind the Puritans' establishment of "praying towns," in which Indian converts adopted European farming practices and standards of dress, diet, and gender relations, in addition to Puritan theology and devotional practices. At their peak in the early 1670s, about 2,300 Indians lived in Massachusetts' fourteen praying towns, of which approximately 1,000 were baptized Christians. The largest praying town and the primary focus of Eliot's labors was Natick.

Added together, the Indian converts won by the Mayhews and Eliot were only a fraction of New England's Indian population and a very poor showing when compared to the Catholic missions of the Spanish and French. Part of the problem was resources: the English simply were not as interested in evangelizing Indians as these other powers. But the Protestant missionary effort was also hindered by the cultural rigidity of its proponents. In particular, the Puritans expected a full-scale cultural transformation from their Indian converts; they had to become Englishmen before they could become Christians. Praying towns sought to make this transformation possible by fixing the Indians in communities where they could be subjected to English laws and forced to conform to English standards of conduct in their private and public lives. Unlike Catholic missionaries, Puritans did not have a panoply of material artifacts at their disposal with which to attract and catechize potential converts, only bibles that remained incomprehensible until Indians learned to read English or their own tongue, provided someone, as Eliot did, took on the laborious task of translating scripture into their native language. Furthermore, the Puritans tended to treat their converts as inveterate backsliders who needed to be quarantined and policed. Far from incorporating Christian Indians into colonial society, the praying towns had the opposite impact of segregating them, in the same manner that colonial authorities used pest houses to separate the physically ill from the healthy.

Regardless of the region or type of Christianity preached there, conversion offered Indians at best only second-class status in colonial society. It is fair to ask then what prompted Indians to convert and if those conversions were, in fact, genuine. As a survival strategy, conversion offered Indians suffering from the upheavals of war, disease, and dispossession some measure of security. The inhabitants of Spanish missions, Canadian *reserves*, and Puritan praying towns could make firmer claims to their land and property against grasping colonists than other native communities, and they also had greater success in extracting material support from colonial governments in times of need. Missionaries became valuable diplomatic go-betweens for these communities with colonial authorities, sympathetically conveying their grievances about land frauds, trading abuses, and similar points of friction with colonial neighbors. It is harder to fathom the more intangible motives of Indian converts, but many no doubt saw missionaries as spiritually potent figures whose god just might help them heal the sick, protect their families, and restore stability to a world gone dangerously out of balance. When Indian converts in New England related their conversion narratives, they emphasized sins they committed in dealing with other people rather than sins related to their relationship with God (as English Puritans were likely to do in their narratives). In other words, they saw in Christianity a creed that would help them govern their personal conduct in the here and now, and were less concerned with how it might guide them to salvation in the hereafter.

The cultural transformation that missionaries expected in their converts was never complete. Although it is true that Christian Indians did give up many of their native practices and adopt new European ways, these changes always took place along a spectrum and were never as simple as flipping an on/off switch. Christian Indian men, for example, may have given up participating in the ritual torture and execution of their enemies, but they still went to war to take captives and scalps. Some female converts embraced the value of chastity and insisted on marrying only fellow Christians, but they still dressed in a native style that missionaries bemoaned as immodest. The Wampanoags of Martha's Vineyard absorbed enough Calvinist theology to ask their Puritan neighbors about their sectarian differences with other Protestants, yet they continued to bury their dead according to traditional customs. The degree to which native peoples adopted Christian beliefs and practices differed by time and place, but overall, Indian converts exhibited a strong desire to have their children baptized and to participate in communal forms of worship, such as singing and praying. They were less enamored of Christian proscriptions regarding sexuality and were slow to abandon their traditional rules of marriage and kinship. Indian Christianity was a syncretic faith, blending new beliefs and customs with old ones in ways that no missionary could have anticipated. The European tendency to keep Christian Indians at arm's length, to cordon them off in separate communities, and to treat their spirituality as suspect and compromised, impeded the absorption of converts into colonial society but also allowed room for their spiritual autonomy to flourish.

TAKING CAPTIVES

Indians had their own method of affecting the cultural conversion of outsiders. Rather than relying on religion and labor to do the job, they employed warfare and captivity. Long before Europeans or Africans arrived in America, Indians had been using captivity as a means of converting strangers into members of their families and communities. Rather than territory or riches, they pursued human spoils when they went to war. Children and women taken as war captives were likely to be adopted into their captors' communities, but adult male captives often met a different fate involving ritualized torture and execution. Those colonists who witnessed this treatment of male captives were so shocked by the practice that they dismissed native warfare altogether as prima facie proof of the Indians' savagery. Nevertheless, as time passed and each side had its opportunity to pursue the cultural conversion of the other, some commentators could not help but marvel at how successfully Indians were able to turn their captives into members of their families and communities, while the efforts of Christian missionaries yielded only frustration, apostasy, and occasional martyrdom. These contrasting results challenged the optimism expressed by Lawson and others about the superiority of European civilization and the natural desire of Indians to adopt it.

The treatment and use of war captives varied by native group and region, but captive-taking was a universal practice among Native Americans, and Europeans encountered it wherever they went. Depending on the time and place where they were taken, European captives faced the possibility of adoption, enslavement, execution, or ransom. Regardless of their ultimate fate, captives found that their assimilation into native society began immediately. Warriors marched their captives home quickly, often over hundreds of miles, moving them away from familiar surroundings, people, and possessions. Among Iroquoian and Algonquian peoples in the Northeast, it was customary for the entire community to turn out when a war party returned and to greet captives by dividing into two narrow rows, so that they could strike and jeer at the captives as they "ran the gauntlet" into the town. More humiliations followed for the captives as they were stripped of their clothing and exposed to verbal and physical indignities from old and young alike. The heads of families decided what happened next. Those captives chosen for adoption—typically, women and children—were taken by their new kin, ritually washed and dressed in new clothes, and given new names to raise them up in place of deceased family members. So began the immersion process by which they learned a new language and assumed their place among people who identified themselves as brothers, sisters, mothers, fathers, and other extended relations.

Those captives who were not adopted in this manner faced a briefer but no less thorough incorporation into the community. This fate, generally reserved for adult males, unfolded as the captive was told to prepare for his death feast. At the appointed time, he was bound to a stake and slowly tortured to death by having his extremities burned and his skin flayed. A warrior was expected to endure such torments as long as he could, while recounting his feats of martial prowess and bravery in his death song and encouraging his captors to do their worst. When he finally expired, his tormentors took his scalp and dismembered the rest of his body for communal feasting, so that everyone might consume some portion of the fortitude and other virtues he had exhibited.

In the Southeast, the fate of captives also rested on whether or not they were adopted as family members, but the emergence of the Indian slave trade in the colonial era complicated the process. Among the Choctaws, Creeks, Cherokees, and other cultural descendants of the Mississippians, it was common to enslave captives by preserving their lives but not extending to them the kinship ties that would have incorporated them fully into the community. Such "owned persons" could be enemy Indians, or during the colonial era, European or African war captives. They were likely to be put to work as laborers or traded, or given as diplomatic gifts to allies. The colonization of South Carolina in the late seventeenth century created a commercial market for such Indian captives. Traders purchased them from their Indian captors in exchange for guns and other manufactured goods, creating a new impetus for warfare in the Southeast and a new use for captives. Approximately twenty-five thousand Indian slaves were exported from South Carolina between 1675 and 1715, most of them sold to sugar planters in the Caribbean. An equivalent number labored alongside European servants and African slaves on South Carolina's early plantations. Southeastern Indians also exchanged European and African war captives in the same manner. The result was a type of slavery in the colonial Southeast that was not racially exclusive; Europeans, Africans, and Indians were all exposed to it.

Europeans who witnessed the Indians' torture and execution of captives condemned them as savages but also marveled at the tenderness with which they treated those captives they adopted as new family members. Cadwallader Colden, an eighteenth-century New York official who wrote a history of the Iroquois peoples, explained that it was "a constant Maxim" among them to "save the Children and Young Men of the People they Conquer, to adopt them into their own Nation, and to educate them as their own Children, without Distinction." This method of adoption was so successful that "no Arguments, no Intreaties, nor Tears of their Friends and Relations" could persuade the captives "to leave their new Indian Friends" when given the opportunity to return home.[6] Colden's contemporary Benjamin Franklin echoed this sentiment when he contrasted the results of European and Indian attempts to assimilate each other into their respective cultures. Franklin observed that "when an Indian Child has been brought up among us, taught our language and habituated to our Customs, yet if he goes to see his relations and make one Indian Ramble with them, there is no perswading him ever to return." On the other hand, European children who had been ransomed out of Indian captivity invariably "become disgusted with our manner of life, and the care and pains that are necessary to support it, and take the first good Opportunity of escaping again into the Woods, from whence there is no reclaiming them."[7]

Colden and Franklin were observing an uncomfortable truth about cross-cultural adoptions that challenged European presumptions of cultural superiority. Indians were supposed to want to become more like Europeans, especially as they grew more familiar with Christian civilization. Instead, the Indians' response to missionaries ranged from polite indifference to outright hostility, while Europeans seemed predisposed to adopt the Indian way of life. Authorities were not willing to tolerate the latter sort of border-crossing. In every colonial society in North America, Indian converts were treated as second-class citizens and colonists who chose to live among Indians were suspected of cultural and moral degeneracy. On the other side of the cultural divide, Indians exhibited much greater toleration and flexibility. Membership in an Indian community did not depend on one's religious identity, place of origin, or skin color. Rather, it was a function of kinship: the creation of interpersonal bonds with others gave a person an identity within an Indian family and clan. Once achieving that status, an adoptee suffered no permanent disability or inequality because of prior condition or physical features; he or she became a fully enfranchised member of the community.

In the contest between native and colonial cultures in early America, neither side succeeded entirely in incorporating the other. The incorporation of

European captives did help replenish some native communities, but there simply were not enough to counter the devastating impact of disease on their numbers. Furthermore, colonial governments made commodities out of captives by offering ransoms for their return. As time passed, Indians became accustomed to returning captives in exchange for money and trade goods. Such transactions helped with their short-term material needs but altered the role captivity had traditionally played in sustaining their communities over the long run. Among Europeans, commitment to converting Indians waned as colonial populations became less reliant on Indians for survival. Unlike their native counterparts, colonists made no attempt to incorporate Indian war captives into their families and communities. Instead, they were most likely to export them as slaves to the sugar plantations of the Caribbean. In Florida and New Mexico, Spanish law prohibited enslaving converts, but hostile Indians taken as war captives were likely to be exported to labor on Caribbean plantations or in Mexican silver mines.

TRANSFORMATIVE IMPACT OF WAR

The pursuit of captives and converts in colonial America was part of a wider competition for resources that often culminated in armed conflict. Warfare challenged the military cultures of both sides. Europeans faced a new kind of enemy for whom they adapted a new set of rules about fighting. Indians encountered new technologies for fighting that changed their tactics and strategies. The result was a distinctly American way of war that left a bloody trail as it unfolded across the continent.

In 1609 Samuel de Champlain and two other Frenchmen from Quebec accompanied a party of about sixty Montagnais and Huron warriors traveling south into the Lake Champlain region. Champlain's Indian allies were entering the country of their traditional enemy, the five Iroquois nations (from east to west, the Mohawks, Oneidas, Onondagas, Cayugas, and Senecas). Near the southern end of the lake, they found what they were looking for: a group of about two hundred Mohawks, prepared for war. The two sides greeted each other, confirmed their intentions to fight, and then spent the night in their respective camps, preparing for battle with songs and ceremonies. In the morning, the two sides marched on each other in massed formations, using war clubs, stone hatchets, and bows and arrows for weapons. Some wore body armor made from woven bark, reeds, and leather. Champlain and his fellow Frenchmen marched behind their Indian allies, hiding their loaded muskets from the Mohawks. When they were within firing range, the Hurons and Montagnais parted and Champlain discharged his musket directly into the enemy's ranks. Three of the Mohawk leaders fell, and the rest of the Mohawks panicked. After one of Champlain's companions discharged a second musket, the battle turned into a rout and the Mohawks fled the field.

This brief encounter at the outset of the seventeenth century foreshadowed the impact European firearms had on Native American ways of making war. Before their immersion in the trans-Atlantic fur trade, Indians fought with traditional weapons and for traditional reasons. War was a highly ritualized affair knit into the fabric of their lives. It served as a rite of passage and source of social distinction for young men, as a means of channeling disruptive emotions and behaviors outside their communities, and as a source for captives who would augment their populations. As evidenced by Champlain's engagement with the Mohawks, Europeans and their technology upset the equilibrium in this type of warfare. Firearms had an immediate impact, but other, more subtle changes were put in motion by the Indians' contact with colonizers. Over the course of the seventeenth century, these changes produced what Europeans called the "skulking way of war," a collection of tactics and objectives they considered uniquely Native American for their violence and treachery.

At the time of European contact, Indian warfare in eastern North America followed the precedents of what anthropologists call the "mourning war complex." Within a native community, war was a means of dealing with the grief and related ill feelings stirred by the unexpected death of one of its members. If such emotions could not be assuaged through other avenues of mourning, survivors of the deceased agitated for going to war. Leading men recognized for their martial skills organized war parties, recruiting young men anxious for reputation, plunder, or vengeance. A successful war party brought back enemy captives while avoiding casualties of its own, and scalps and other war trophies taken by warriors offered tangible proof of their prowess in battle. Warriors might be goaded into joining a war party by their family members or friends, but no one ever compelled an individual to fight; it was a personal decision undertaken for personal reasons.

European firearms changed the methods of Indian warfare. Those Indians who acquired muskets from European allies gained a decisive advantage in battle over those who did not. Bows and arrows were more accurate and much quieter than muskets, but they were not as lethal nor did they convey the psychological advantage of the musket's noise and smoke. Trade with Europeans also brought other substitutes for traditional weapons—iron knives and hatchets in place of their stone and bone equivalents—that made the Indians' combat more deadly. Armor made from organic materials was of little use against such weapons, as were the tightly packed frontal assaults witnessed by Champlain. In keeping with the mourning war's objective of limited casualties, warriors employed surprise whenever possible, took cover when engaging the enemy, and retreated quickly in the face of superior forces. The skulking way of war, described by many colonists as a natural expression of the Indians' treachery, was in fact an adaptive response to their encounter with Europeans.

Other factors related to European colonization contributed to this transformation in Indian warfare. The staggering impact of epidemic diseases on Indian communities increased the demand for captives, and the fur trade sparked an arms race among Native Americans. Once the Dutch began supplying arms to the Iroquois at Fort Orange in the 1620s, French traders responded in kind with their allies in the St. Lawrence Valley, sharply intensifying the traditional enmity between the Iroquois and St. Lawrence Algonquian nations. The same pattern repeated itself in the Southeast, where English, French, and Spanish traders competed with each other for the Indians' deerskins. Indians anxious to acquire animal pelts and captives plundered each other's towns, contributing to a cycle of raid and reprisal that reverberated throughout Indian country. Other market forces introduced by Europeans changed the reasons why Indians fought. Scalps, traditionally valued by warriors as personal marks of distinction, became commodities that could be traded for cash when colonial governments offered bounties for them. Likewise, some Indians chose to sell war captives taken in intertribal conflicts to European slave traders rather than to adopt them into their own communities. Regardless of their national origin, missionaries generally decried the methods of Indian warfare, especially its use of torture and ritual cannibalism, yet they encouraged their converts to fight against enemies, whether native or colonial, they deemed a threat to their enterprise. Missionaries became some of the most effective recruiters of Indian auxiliaries for colonial forces.

Colonists in North America responded in different ways to the skulking way of war. In seventeenth-century Canada, whenever the French sent large armies of conquest into Iroquois country, they found that their quarry simply abandoned their towns and returned to fight another day. French militia and *troupes de la marine* learned to fight more effectively by adopting the methods of their Indian allies and joining them in surprise winter raids on frontier settlements in New York and New England. In Florida, the small number of Spanish soldiers available meant that colonial authorities had to rely on mission communities for their security. They learned quickly to allow their Indian allies broad latitude in how they prosecuted war against their common enemies. In the English colonies, a similar reliance on the methods of irregular warfare or *la petite guerre* emerged during the seventeenth century. Very few British regular troops were posted in North America before 1755, and they were spread thinly over extended borders with French Canada and Spanish Florida. In their stead, colonial militias did the bulk of the fighting against hostile Indians. The law compelled all free, able-bodied adult males to belong to the militia, and in times of crisis, the governor had the power to call them out for the colony's defense. In southern colonies, the militia also became an important means of policing the slave population and suppressing slave rebellions.

After 1660 a new code of warfare emerged among Europe's aristocracies in response to the wholesale plundering and slaughter of civilian populations that had occurred during the religious wars of the previous century. These new rules defined civilized warfare as battles fought between uniformed, professional troops and it strictly narrowed the legitimate uses of such terror tactics as torture, mutilation of corpses, and the murder of noncombatants. Seventeenth-century colonists were far removed, both physically and intellectually, from these changes. With little experience in professional military forces and even less interest in limiting their tactical options against Indians or rebellious slaves, colonial militias and other irregular forces made up their own rules of engagement and proved to be remarkably amenable to adopting methods they condemned as savage and barbaric when practiced by others.

In the Chesapeake, the Jamestown colonists exhibited little restraint when fighting the Indians of the Powhatan confederacy. The deadly surprise attack launched by the Powhatans against Jamestown in 1622 ended the hope for mutual coexistence that John Rolfe's marriage to Pocahontas had encouraged. Afterwards, extirpation became the goal of any military measures colonial Virginians took against neighboring Indians, culminating in 1646 with the murder of Powhatan leader Opechancanough while he was being held prisoner in Jamestown.

Although Indian relations were initially more peaceful in New England, the tenor of intercultural warfare there turned out to be much the same as it was in Virginia. The first major conflict occurred in 1636–1637, when militia forces accompanied by allied Mohegans and Narragansetts attacked the Pequot Indians of eastern Connecticut. The New Englanders launched a surprise assault on the Pequots' stronghold, a town of several hundred inhabitants on the Mystic River. The soldiers set fire to wigwams filled with sleeping Indians and then fired on men, women, and children alike as they tried to escape. Practically all the town's four hundred inhabitants were killed, either burned in the conflagration or shot down and cut to pieces as they fled (see Figure 4.2). Based on reports he heard from participants in the attack, Plymouth colony governor William Bradford described it as "a fearfull sight to see them [the Pequots] thus frying in the fire, and the streams

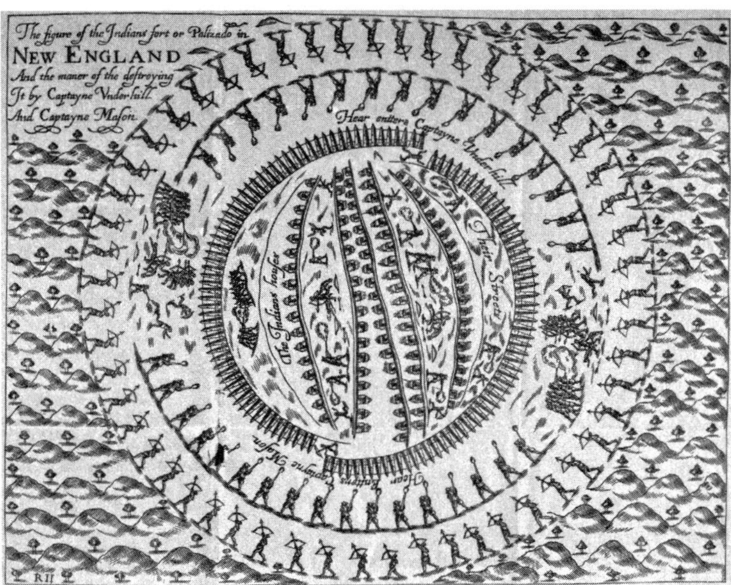

Figure 4.2 **"The Figure of the Indians fort or Palizado in New England And the Maner of the destroying It by Captayn Underhill and Captayne Mason," from *Newes from America by Captaine John Underhill, A.D. 1638; reproduced by David Harris Underhill... A.D. 1902* ([Brooklyn, NY?]: Underhill Society of America, [1902]). This image, originally published in 1638, depicts the English attack on the Pequot village on Mystic River in May 1637. The English (armed with muskets in the image) and their Indian allies (armed with bows and arrows) surrounded the village's stockade and shot or cut down the inhabitants as they fled their burning homes. Courtesy of the American Antiquarian Society.**

of blood quenching the same, and horrible was the stinck & scent thereof, but the victory seemed a sweete sacrifice, and they [the colonists] gave praise thereof to God, who had wrought so wonderfully for them, thus to inclose their enemies in their hands."[8] The stunned Mohegans and Narragansetts who witnessed the carnage said the English method of warfare killed too many. The colonists were pleased to have made such a strong impression.

In 1675–1676 New England experienced its most convulsive intercultural conflict, King Philip's War. Metacom, a Wampanoag chief known to the English as King Philip, knit together a loose confederacy among other New England Algonquians distressed by the colonists' increasingly high-handed approach to claiming Indian land and subjecting its inhabitants to English law. In the forty years following the Pequot War, the Indians had grown more accustomed to colonial society and its technology. Relying now on muskets as their primary weapon, they raided frontier towns, burned homes and fields, destroyed livestock, and took hundreds of captives. Initially, the colonial response was weak and unfocused. Militia forces had little success tracking raiding parties and complained of the Indians' refusal to fight them openly. The besieged New Englanders saw enemies everywhere. Suspecting that the praying towns were complicit in the attacks, they rounded up Indian converts and forced them to relocate to islands in Boston Harbor, where many died from hunger and exposure. The tide of war changed as Metacom and his allies ran out of gunpowder and other supplies necessary to sustain the war. Gradually, the Indians sued for peace and ransomed their captives. Metacom himself was killed by an Indian allied with the English, and his decapitated head was publicly displayed in Plymouth for many years.

As had been the case in Virginia, the Puritans used King Philip's War as a pretext for permanently weakening the Indians' hold on the land. Those Indians taken prisoner were sold into slavery in the West Indies. Survivors were either confined to small reservations or dispersed among Indians living along the Canadian-New England frontier. Even the praying Indians faced dispossession. Only four of their fourteen towns were reestablished after peace was restored. King Philip's War also produced a flood of printed reports, narratives, and sermons that explicitly gave divine sanction to purging New England of its native inhabitants. In this new rhetoric of war, Indians became pawns of God's design, sent to afflict Christians who had grown spiritually lax and proud. Mary Rowlandson, whose captivity narrative became a foundational text in American literature, marveled at "the wonderfull providence of God in preserving the heathen for farther affliction to our poor Countrey.... [H]ow to admiration did the Lord preserve them for his Holy ends, and the destruction of many still amongst the *English*!"[9] Rowlandson's equation of King Philip's War with divine providence had a lasting impact on the way Anglo-Americans came to regard Indians: they were an obstacle put in place by God, to be surmounted for the glory of His name.

In the Carolinas, intercultural war erupted during the second decade of the eighteenth century, as the pressures of colonial settlement, the deerskin trade, and the slave trade mounted for native populations. Initially, those Indian nations that allied with the English colonists benefited from increased access to trade goods, especially firearms that they used in slaving raids against Spanish mission Indians in Florida. Mounting debts to traders and spiraling intertribal violence, however, gradually turned those advantages into liabilities, even for the most powerful nations. In 1711 war erupted between North Carolina colonists and the Tuscaroras, a populous Iroquoian-speaking nation who resented new settlements being made on their land. Colonial militia aided by a substantial number of allied Indians burned Tuscarora towns and crops, enslaved captives, and prompted the survivors to abandon their homelands and move northward, where they became the sixth nation of the Iroquois confederacy. Several years later, a similar conflict broke out in South Carolina. The Yamasees had been consistent suppliers to the English of deerskins and Indian slaves, but this relationship soured after 1700 as English traders grew abusive and the Yamasees fell deeper into debt. In 1715 Yamasees rose up, killing or taking captive the English traders in their territory and raiding plantations that encroached on their lands. Authorities responded by raising an irregular army of colonists, African slaves, and allied Indians that burned Yamasee towns and forced the survivors into Spanish Florida.

After the Tuscarora and Yamasee wars, the permanence of European settlements in North America was never again in question. The Pueblo Revolt and King Philip's War had offered the most serious challenges to their survival, but the superiority of European firepower consistently outdid Indian efforts to push back the tide of colonization. From New England to the Carolinas, epidemic disease, environmental change, and the fur trade had conspired to weaken the autonomy of native groups, while settler populations acquired the footing necessary to sustain themselves independently of overseas governments or investors. In the contest for America's natural resources, colonists gained the upper hand by drawing Indians into dependent economic relationships, engrossing ever larger portions of their territory, and sparing no violence when war made it possible to push them aside. The French and Spanish colonies in North America never achieved the populations necessary to make living without the Indians possible. Native populations were too important as laborers, customers, converts, and allies to be eliminated entirely; without them, the French and Spanish colonial enterprises would have collapsed. The English colonies created a different kind of human landscape. The fur trade was important to their economies, but cash crops, fish, lumber, and a variety of other commodities figured just as prominently in their plans for the future. By 1720 in British North America, it was possible to envision a future in which Indians lived entirely apart, on an ever-shrinking frontier being pushed relentlessly westward by an expanding colonial world.

BORDERLAND VARIATIONS

The Atlantic seaboard experienced the most thorough-going transformation as a result of colonization, but Europeans and Africans found their way into North America by other approaches as well. As the French presence in Canada and the

Spanish presence in New Mexico indicated, colonization did not occur as a single east-to-west movement by which newcomers displaced natives from the Atlantic to the Pacific. On the contrary, colonial societies grew like ivy in tendrils and shoots, flourishing in some spots and withering and contracting in others. Waterways provided the most important avenues for this expansion, as was evident by the St. Lawrence, Hudson, Delaware, Potomac, James, Santee, and Savannah rivers on the east coast. But the Mississippi Valley watershed provided an equally appealing artery into the continent's interior from the Gulf of Mexico, as did the Rio Grande from northern Mexico. During the seventeenth and early eighteenth centuries, new colonial borderlands—places where neither colonists nor Indians held the upper hand over the other—developed in these regions. Unlike the Atlantic seaboard, colonial populations in these borderlands were not predominantly English-speaking, nor did they attract migrants who were trying to establish New World social or religious utopias. Instead, in these regions small and isolated colonial populations had to learn to work according to the rules of larger, more powerful native groups if they wished to acquire their trade and alliance. Intercultural violence and warfare were common in colonial borderlands, but in those places conversion and captivity helped to mediate differences as much as exacerbate them.

Twelve years after the Pueblo Revolt had forced the Spanish to abandon New Mexico, they returned to the northern Rio Grande Valley. The previous century of colonization among the Pueblo peoples had already altered the landscape and its human inhabitants in important ways. The Spanish had introduced horses, sheep, and other livestock to the Pueblos, as well as trade goods that attracted the attention of more mobile groups inhabiting the Southwestern Plains. Hunter-gatherers and sedentary groups had always had a symbiotic relationship in the Southwest. Plains Indians traveled great distances to annual trade fairs with the Pueblos, exchanging buffalo hides, furs, and dried meat for maize, fruits, and textiles. War captives were also a part of this exchange, given as part of the diplomatic gifts that were necessary to establish and renew peace among trading partners. The Spanish presence in New Mexico widened the orbit of this native economy, as horses made transportation over great distances easier, and Spanish metal tools and weapons became important acquisitions for native peoples. Those groups that adopted equestrian culture by purchasing, stealing, and breeding horses of their own acquired a military advantage over those that did not. Northwest of New Mexico, the Utes of modern Nevada and Utah muscled aside their Paiute and Shoshone neighbors and began trading directly with the Spanish by 1700. The Comanches, another horse-powered culture, did the same northeast of New Mexico, pushing the Apaches southward to gain easier access to Spanish and Pueblo traders.

The Spanish relied on religion to differentiate among the various Indian nations they encountered in this borderland. Indians who submitted to Spanish authority and religious instruction were incorporated into the colonial social order as *genízaros*, detribalized natives who worked as agricultural laborers, craftsmen, domestic servants, or auxiliary troops. Although clearly second-class citizens, they did have certain legal protections—most importantly, freedom from enslavement—while Christian baptism gave them the chance to be incorporated into Spanish kinship networks through the practice of god-parentage. Those Indians who lived beyond Spanish social and spiritual supervision were *indios bárbaros*. If taken captive or received as such in trade, they could be enslaved and exported to work in the silver mines of northern Mexico.

As the Spanish colonial order in New Mexico took deeper root, Indian captives came to play an important part in it, not only as laborers in its economy, but also as a means of increasing the population and negotiating with outsiders. The exchange of captives between the Spanish and their Indian trading partners became an Americanized version of the Iberian practice of *rescate*, an economy of raiding, ransom, and enslavement that had been used by Christian and Islamic peoples in the Mediterranean world to make both war and peace. *Indios bárbaros* wishing to trade with the Spanish offered captives as diplomatic gifts, or if seeking to make peace, each side repatriated captives as signs of good faith and renewed alliance. Spanish colonists were likely to sell adult male captives to work in Mexican mines, but they kept female and child captives for religious conversion, domestic labor, and sexual partnership. The Spanish also learned that female captives could play an important role in intercultural diplomacy. As Spanish missionaries and soldiers moved among the Apaches in the Sonora region (straddling northern Mexico and Arizona) and the Caddo peoples of southern Texas, they found it difficult to secure footholds if they arrived without women to offer as captives or marriage partners to their native counterparts. In many Southwest Indian cultures, women played the role of peacemakers and mediators; an all-male party of strangers signaled war, not peace and trade. Only when the Spanish learned to incorporate native women into their diplomacy were they able to negotiate successfully within this cultural system.

The French also had to learn a new set of rules for intercultural diplomacy when they ventured westward from the St. Lawrence Valley as traders and missionaries into the Great Lakes watershed. The French referred to this expansive region as the *pays d'en haut*. It stretched from Lake Superior in the north to the Illinois and Ohio rivers in the south and encompassed Indians from a number of different language and cultural groups. In such a culturally diverse area, bonds of fictive kinship formed by the exchange of gifts and captives became the means of securing trade and alliance. Early French explorers in the Great Lakes and Mississippi Valley learned the protocol of the calumet, a long-stemmed ceremonial pipe that was ritually displayed and smoked whenever native peoples in this region engaged in diplomatic negotiations. The French also learned that they could not conduct the fur trade without simultaneously engaging in rituals of hospitality and gift-giving. Indians of the *pays d'en haut* gave the French governor of Canada the ceremonial name Onontio, "the great father," expecting him to exhibit the same characteristics and conduct of a father in their own kin relations: generosity, patient mediation, and wise counsel, but not dictatorial coercion or compulsion.

As more Indian nations came into the orbit of the New France, captives came to play an important role in their diplomacy with Onontio. French colonists in

Canada had little use for enslaved Indian labor, but Indians from the *pays d'en haut* gave captives as gifts to the French in diplomatic councils, presenting them as proof of their prowess in war and their worth as allies. The French governor also learned that orchestrating captive exchanges among Indian nations was one of the ways in which native allies expected him to fulfill his role as Onontio. The exchange of captives helped "cover the graves" of those killed during war, and when incorporated into the families of former enemies, captives created bonds of kinship that cemented new alliances. By the early eighteenth century, Indian captives working as domestic servants and laborers could be found in the households of French colonists in Quebec and Montreal. Although never a large part of New France's workforce, these Indian slaves were evidence of how trade and diplomacy in the *pays d'en haut* reverberated throughout the colonial order of New France.

A similar process of accommodation unfolded as French traders took their business west of the Mississippi. Not long after La Salle's explorations in the 1680s, French traders were operating on the Missouri, Arkansas, and Red rivers, bringing their wares to Plains Indians in exchange for buffalo hides, deerskins, and beaver pelts. In a manner similar to the rise of the Comanches on the southern Plains, the Sioux adapted horses to their hunting and transportation, and over the course of the eighteenth century rose in power over more sedentary groups in the Missouri Valley. Further south, the Osage and Quapaw Indians dominated the region between the Missouri and Arkansas rivers, serving as middlemen between French traders and Plains groups stretching westward into modern Oklahoma and Texas. By 1750 these trading networks were bringing French traders and their goods into the Spanish Southwest, leading colonial authorities there to suspect French designs on New Mexico. Even more so than the *pays d'en haut*, the lower Mississippi Valley was a trading borderland in which French military or religious power counted for very little. French missionaries came to the Arkansas Valley but did not stay, driven out by the indifference of the souls they sought to save. The soldiers garrisoned in French Louisiana were too few to overawe the populous native groups of the lower Mississippi region. This was a borderland in which any pretense of colonial authority had to be accommodated to native rules of diplomacy and exchange.

Whether in the Southwest, Mississippi Valley, or Great Lakes, borderlands were distinguished by the comparatively even distribution of power among native and colonial peoples. Colonization in these places did not occur as a result of invasion, conquest, and subjugation. Instead, it came as a series of waves that slowly but profoundly transformed the landscape and its native inhabitants: new diseases, invasive plant and animal species, strange goods and technologies, and captives acquired from distant lands arrived in advance of missionaries and soldiers claiming to represent the sovereignty of unknown gods and kings. Some native groups prospered in these borderlands as they assimilated new technologies of hunting and warfare and extended their authority over key territory, but that was probably little comfort to other natives enslaved or dispossessed by these changes. In the profound physical and psychological dislocation suffered by a captive forced to live among strangers hundreds of miles from home, we can only begin to glimpse the collective trauma visited on native peoples by the process of colonization.

DEATH OF A DREAM

John Lawson's efforts to colonize North Carolina contributed to the outbreak of the Tuscarora War. When he returned to the Carolinas in 1710 with his Swiss and German migrants, the land he located for them on the Neuse River was in Tuscarora country. As Lawson was escorting the settlers' leader, Baron Christoph von Graffenreid, on a survey of the region, they were captured by the Tuscaroras and taken back to one of their towns, where a council of chiefs deliberated on their fate. Although new to the country, Graffenreid kept his composure and assured his captors that neither he nor his people were complicit in the land frauds and trading abuses that had caused them to take up the hatchet. Convinced of his sincerity and pleased with the prospect of ransoming the captives for trade goods, the assembled chiefs decided to release them with a message of warning for their fellow colonists. The next day, however, Lawson got into an argument with one of the chiefs, and to Graffenreid's horror, the council reconvened and decided this time to execute the prisoners. Graffenreid managed to get a reprieve, but Lawson's fate was sealed.

Graffenreid did not witness Lawson's death, but from other reports and Lawson's own field work among the Carolina Indians, we can surmise how it unfolded. In *A New Voyage to Carolina*, Lawson had described how Indians treated prisoners they marked for death. "They inflict on them Torments," he wrote, "wherein they prolong Life in that miserable state as long as they can, and never miss Skulping [scalping] of them, as they call it, which is to cut off the Skin from the Temples, and taking the whole Head of Hair along with it, as if it was a Night-cap." Sometimes, Indians split "Pitch-Pine into Splinters" and stuck them all over the prisoner's body: "Thus they light them, which burn like so many Torches, and in this manner they make him dance round a great Fire, everyone buffeting and deriding him, till he expires."[10]

So, if the Tuscaroras decided to execute Lawson in this manner, it could not have come as a surprise to him. It is impossible to recover what thoughts may have gone through Lawson's mind as the pine splinters were inserted under his skin and set alight. Did he accept his fate calmly, struck by the irony that if any of his Indian tormentors were unsure how to proceed, his own book could have served them as a how-to manual? Or, did he die angry and confused, explaining to deaf ears that in his book he had defended the Indians from aspersions of savagery and urged colonial authorities to treat them with fairness and justice?

What we do know is that Lawson's successful career as a colonial promoter came to a sudden end that day in Tuscarora country. Graffenreid gained his freedom after several more weeks of captivity, but his negotiation skills did not prevent attacks on his fellow migrants in New Bern. Ultimately, the Tuscarora War did open more of the Carolina frontier to colonization, but at considerable human cost on both sides. The colonial world Lawson had envisioned in *A New Voyage to Carolina*, a place where tractable Indians lived alongside European farmers and peacefully absorbed their religion, work habits, and values, would not come to pass. Instead, a far rougher hand transformed the American countryside and its inhabitants, tilting the balance irreversibly in favor of confrontation and expropriation rather than accommodation and assimilation.

CHRONOLOGY

1595	Spanish Franciscans initiate missionary work among the Apalachee, Timucua, and Guale peoples of northern Florida.
1598	Spanish establish colony of New Mexico in Rio Grande Valley among Pueblo peoples.
1609	Samuel de Champlain and allied Montagnais and Huron Indians engage in pitched battle with the Mohawks, introducing firearms to warfare in the Northeast.
1632–1672	French Jesuit missionaries in Canada establish *reserves* for their converts near Montreal and Quebec.
1636–1637	Pequot War in Connecticut.
1651–1675	"Praying towns" established in Massachusetts for Indian converts of John Eliot and other Puritan missionaries.
1675–1676	King Philip's War in New England
1675–1715	Approximately twenty-five thousand Indians exported from South Carolina to West Indies as a result of Southeastern Indian slave trade.
1680	Pueblo Revolt forces Spanish to abandon New Mexico temporarily.
1700–1709	*John Lawson's travels in the Carolina country.*
1710	*Lawson is captured and executed by the Tuscarora Indians.*
1711–1715	Tuscarora War in North Carolina.
1715–1716	Yamasee War in South Carolina.

NOTES

1. John Lawson, *A New Voyage to Carolina* (1709; Ann Arbor: University Microfilms, 1966), 1.
2. Lawson, *A New Voyage to Carolina*, 115, 118.
3. John Winthrop, "Reasons to be Considered, and Objections with Answers," in *The Founding of Massachusetts: Historians and the Sources*, ed. Edmund S. Morgan (Indianapolis: Bobbs-Merrill, 1964), 177–178.

4. Cited in Ian K. Steele, *Warpaths: Invasions of North America* (New York: Oxford University Press, 1994), 94.
5. Charles Wilson Hackett, *Revolt of the Pueblo Indians of New Mexico and Otermín's Attempted Reconquest, 1680–82*, trans. Charmion Clair Shelby, 2 vols. (Albuquerque: University of New Mexico Press, 1942), Vol. 1, 60–61.
6. Cadwallader Colden, *The History of the Five Indian Nations Depending on the Province of New York* (1727, 1747; Ithaca, NY: Cornell University Press, 1958), 8, 181.
7. *The Papers of Benjamin Franklin*, eds. Leonard W. Labaree, et al., 39 vols. (New Haven, CT: Yale University Press, 1959–), Vol. 4, 481–482.
8. William Bradford, *Of Plymouth Plantation*, ed. Harvey Wish (New York: Capricorn Books, 1962), 184.
9. Mary Rowlandson, *The Sovereignty and Goodness of God, with Related Documents*, ed. Neal Salisbury (Boston: Bedford/St. Martin's, 1997), 105.
10. John Lawson, *A New Voyage to Carolina*, 198.

SUGGESTIONS FOR FURTHER READING

For an excellent introduction to the environmental consequences of colonization, see Alfred W. Crosby, *The Columbian Exchange: Biological and Cultural Consequences of 1492* (1972; Westport, CT: Praeger, 2003). For a study that approaches many of the same questions from a Native American perspective, see Shepard Krech III, *The Ecological Indian: Myth and History* (New York: Norton, 1999). For more closely focused regional studies, see William Cronon, *Changes in the Land: Indians, Colonists, and the Ecology of New England* (New York: Hill & Wang, 1983); James D. Rice, *Nature and History in the Potomac Country: From Hunter-Gatherers to the Age of Jefferson* (Baltimore: Johns Hopkins University Press, 2009); and Timothy Silver, *A New Face on the Countryside: Indians, Colonists, and Slaves in South Atlantic Forests, 1500–1800* (Cambridge, UK: Cambridge University Press, 1990). Virginia DeJohn Anderson, *Creatures of Empire: How Domestic Animals Transformed Early America* (New York: Oxford University Press, 2004), examines the role Old World animals played in reshaping the American landscape and European-Indian relations.

Several general studies of the European-Indian encounter are noteworthy for their attention to the role of missionaries, converts, and captives. See Daniel K. Richter, *Facing East from Indian Country: A Native History of Early America* (Cambridge, MA: Harvard University Press, 2001); Colin G. Calloway, *New Worlds for All: Indians, Europeans, and the Remaking of Early America* (Baltimore: Johns Hopkins University Press, 1994); James Axtell, *Natives and Newcomers: The Cultural Origins of North America* (New York: Oxford University Press, 2001); and Francis Jennings, *The Invasion of America: Indians, Colonialism, and the Cant of Conquest* (Chapel Hill: University of North Carolina Press, 1975). For excellent case studies of the spiritual dimensions of the French-Indian encounter and the Puritan-Indian encounter, see Allan Greer, *Mohawk Saint: Catherine Tekakwitha and the Jesuits* (New York: Oxford University Press, 2005), and David J. Silverman, *Faith and Boundaries: Colonists, Christianity, and Community among the Wampanoag Indians of Martha's Vineyard, 1600–1871* (Cambridge, UK: Cambridge University Press, 2005), respectively. The course of the European-Indian encounter in the Southeast is admirably reconstructed in Christina Snyder, *Slavery in Indian Country: The Changing Face of Captivity in Early America* (Cambridge, MA: Harvard University Press, 2010); Alan Gallay, *The Indian Slave Trade: The Rise of the English Empire in the American South, 1670–1717* (New

Haven, CT: Yale University Press, 2002), and James H. Merrell, *The Indians' New World: The Catawbas and Their Neighbors from European Contact through the Era of Removal* (Chapel Hill: University of North Carolina Press, 1989).

For general studies of intercultural warfare in colonial America, see Ian K. Steele, *Warpaths: Invasions of North America* (New York: Oxford University Press, 1994); John Grenier, *The First Way of War: American War Making on the Frontier, 1607–1814* (Cambridge, UK: Cambridge University Press, 2005); and Armstrong Starkey, *European and Native American Warfare, 1675–1815* (Norman: University of Oklahoma Press, 1998). For studies focused on New England, see Guy Chet, *Conquering the American Wilderness: The Triumph of European Warfare in the Colonial Northeast* (Amherst: University of Massachusetts Press, 2003); Patrick M. Malone, *The Skulking Way of War: Technology and Tactics Among the New England Indians* (Lanham, MD: Madison Books, 1991); and Jill Lepore, *The Name of War: King Philip's War and the Origins of American Identity* (New York: Knopf, 1998).

Colonial borderlands have become the focus of much recent work in early American history. For the Spanish experience in New Mexico, see Ramón A. Gutiérrez, *When Jesus Came, the Corn Mothers Went Away: Marriage, Sexuality, and Power in New Mexico, 1500–1846* (Stanford, CA: Stanford University Press, 1991); James F. Brooks, *Captives and Cousins: Slavery, Kinship, and Community in the Southwest Borderlands* (Chapel Hill: University of North Carolina Press, 2002); and Ned Blackhawk, *Violence over the Land: Indians and Empires in the Early American West* (Cambridge, MA: Harvard University Press, 2006). For the Great Plains borderlands, see Kathleen DuVal, *The Native Ground: Indians and Colonists in the Heart of the Continent* (Philadelphia: University of Pennsylvania Press, 2006); Julianna Barr, *Peace Came in the Form of a Woman: Indians and Spaniards in the Texas Borderlands* (Chapel Hill: University of North Carolina Press, 2007); Pekka Hämäläinen, *The Comanche Empire* (New Haven, CT: Yale University Press, 2008); and Colin G. Calloway, *One Vast Winter Count: The Native American West before Lewis and Clark* (Lincoln: University of Nebraska Press, 2003). For the *pays d'en haut*, see Richard White, *The Middle Ground: Indians, Empires, and Republics in the Great Lakes Region, 1650–1815* (Cambridge, UK: Cambridge University Press, 1991); Brett Rushforth, *Bonds of Allegiance: Indigenous and Atlantic Slaveries in New France* (Chapel Hill: University of North Carolina Press, 2012); and Tracy Neal Leavelle, *The Catholic Calumet: Colonial Conversions in French and Indian North America* (Philadelphia: University of Pennsylvania Press, 2012).

CHAPTER 5

American Slavery

On Christmas Day, 1747, Briton Hammon left his home in Marshfield, Massachusetts, "with an Intention to go a Voyage to Sea." Hammon was a slave, but he was not running away. Rather, he had his master's permission to sign on as a crew member for a sloop sailing to the Caribbean. Such arrangements were not uncommon among New England slaves and their masters. For the slave, the voyage promised a chance to get away from a cold New England winter, to earn a sailor's wages, and perhaps even save money for the purchase of his freedom. The master gained by not having to feed, clothe, or shelter his slave during the winter months and by claiming a percentage of his wages on his return. Hammon's voyage in 1747 was not the kind we typically associate with North American slaves. Rather than being forced to endure the horrors of a slave ship, he came onboard voluntarily, perhaps anticipating adventure and opportunity, or at least a break from his work-a-day life on land. Nevertheless, sailors also faced confinement and bondage, as Hammon soon learned.

His ship made two stops in the Caribbean without incident, but on the way back to New England, it ran aground on a reef off the Florida coast. While trying to get ashore, the crew was besieged by a much larger force of Indians armed with muskets. Hammon remembered the ship's mate saying, "*My lads, we are all dead Men*" before their assailants opened fire. In the confusion that followed, Hammon jumped into the water, "chusing rather to be drowned, than to be kill'd by those barbarous and inhuman Savages." He did not get his wish. The Indians hauled him aboard one of their canoes, beat and bound him, and told him in broken English that they intended to "roast me alive." To Hammon's surprise, the Indians instead "us'd me pretty well." Several weeks later, a Spanish schooner passed by, and its captain surreptitiously carried Hammon to Cuba. A party of Indians followed and demanded that the Spanish governor in Havana return their captive. The governor refused and instead paid them ten dollars as compensation.

In all likelihood, the governor ransomed Hammon because Hammon was a fellow Christian; colonial officials commonly extended such aid to Indian captives, even those from foreign nations. That status, however, did not make Hammon a free man. He spent a year working as a servant for the governor, but when he resisted a press gang that tried to force him into service on a Spanish ship, he was imprisoned for four and a half years in "a close Dungeon" in Havana's fortress. A New England ship captain visiting Havana learned of Hammon's imprisonment and intervened on his behalf. He convinced the governor to release the prisoner, but Hammon remained the governor's property for almost three more years, gradually earning "my Liberty to walk about the City, and do Work for my self." Finally, Hammon escaped Havana by boarding an English ship moored in the harbor. When a Spanish patrol demanded that he be turned over, the ship's captain refused, telling Hammon, "He could not answer it, to deliver up any *Englishmen* under *English* Colours." The ship left Cuba without further incident and eventually carried Hammon to London, where a chance encounter reunited him with his New England master. He returned home to Massachusetts in 1760, thirteen years after he had left on his winter voyage to the Caribbean.

Hammon was not a typical North American slave, but the trials he endured and the ways in which he overcame them tell us much about the experiences of Africans and African Americans during the colonial era. Too often, the chains and shackles that are the dominant symbol of New World slavery serve as an all-encompassing metaphor for the slaves who wore them, locking them in place as anonymous laborers on sugar, tobacco, coffee, and rice plantations. But as Hammon's experience indicates, slaves were mobile. Movement and adaptation, not stasis, defined their lives. Africans were the largest group to cross the Atlantic during the colonial era, and they did so in numbers that dwarfed European migrations. Furthermore, they dispersed more widely than any other newcomers to the New World. Slaves could be found in every colonial society, and although the laws of such societies prohibited them from acquiring educations or entering into professions, they worked in a broad array of occupations essential to the development of those regions, as field hands, herdsmen, artisans, miners, river pilots, servants, soldiers, and sailors. They experienced the same exposure to disease, malnutrition, and other misfortunes that plagued free colonists and those trials were compounded by the labor discipline and physical abuse to which their masters subjected them. Yet, as Hammon's odyssey reveals, they retained their initiative and identity as individuals against remarkable odds. Within the confines of an institution that defined them as property, they carved out for themselves means of acquiring and expressing their autonomy as human beings, whether by seizing new opportunities (such as when Hammon signed onboard his winter voyage) or by resisting those who would impose their will on them (such as when Hammon refused the press gang in Havana).

Hammon also tells us something about the process by which Africans became African Americans. We know his story because it appeared as a short book in Boston in 1760, making it the first slave narrative published in the New World, the start of a genre that would leave a profound impact on African American identity and American literature.[1] In its pages, Hammon never states where he was born, but clues within the story indicate that it was most likely in America. In other words, he was descended from Africans carried across the Atlantic in the slave trade but was himself someone who considered himself a native New Englander. At key points in his narrative, his white contemporaries recognized a spiritual or social connection with him. The Spanish governor of Cuba freed him from his Indian captivity

Figure 5.1 John Singleton Copley, *Watson and the Shark* (1778). This painting is based on a 1749 shark attack on a British sailor that occurred in the harbor of Havana, Cuba. Note the African American sailor standing in the center of the boat. Like Briton Hammon, many African Americans, free and enslaved, worked in the maritime occupations of the Atlantic World. Courtesy of Museum of Fine Arts, Boston.

because he was a fellow Christian; a New England ship captain helped free him from a Havana dungeon perhaps out of sympathy born of their shared geographic roots; and another ship captain came to his aid because he looked upon Hammon as a fellow Englishman. Not one of these figures described Hammon as his equal, but in coming to his aid, they all recognized in him certain characteristics—his religion, his place of origin, the language he spoke—that defined him as something other than a piece of property to be used or ignored. To himself and those around him, Hammon was never just a slave: he was also a seafarer, a Christian, an Indian captive, a New Englander, even an Englishman (see Figure 5.1).

THE ATLANTIC SLAVE TRADE

Europe's Atlantic slave trade with West Africa predated the colonization of the Americas and continued well after the empires established there had either been destroyed or debilitated by revolutions and wars of independence. In other words, the Atlantic slave trade began earlier and endured longer than the colonial era itself. For almost four centuries, it served as a foundation for Europe's global expansion, and every nation that colonized the Americas participated in it. As the largest forced migration in human history, it left an indelible imprint on the modern world.

That said, it is no easy task to reconstruct the history of the Atlantic slave trade in its entirety. Documentary evidence is scattered in archives on four continents, and the vast majority of the people who were swept into its vortex remain anonymous to us. Most records concerning the slave trade's operation date to the late eighteenth century, when abolitionists undertook the first efforts to study it quantitatively. More recently, researchers working on the Trans-Atlantic Slave Trade Database have compiled data on nearly thirty-five thousand slaving voyages, providing the most complete statistical portrait of the trade available. By their estimates, more than 11 million Africans left their homeland on slave ships, and approximately 9.6 million arrived in the New World (making for a 13 percent mortality rate during the Middle Passage). Of those arrivals, approximately 45 percent landed in the Caribbean, 46 percent in Brazil, 5 percent in Spain's mainland colonies, and 4 percent in British North America (see Map 5.1).[2] As those numbers indicate, the slave trade's reach was wide but not uniform. Nine out of ten Africans brought to the Americas worked on a sugar plantation in the Caribbean

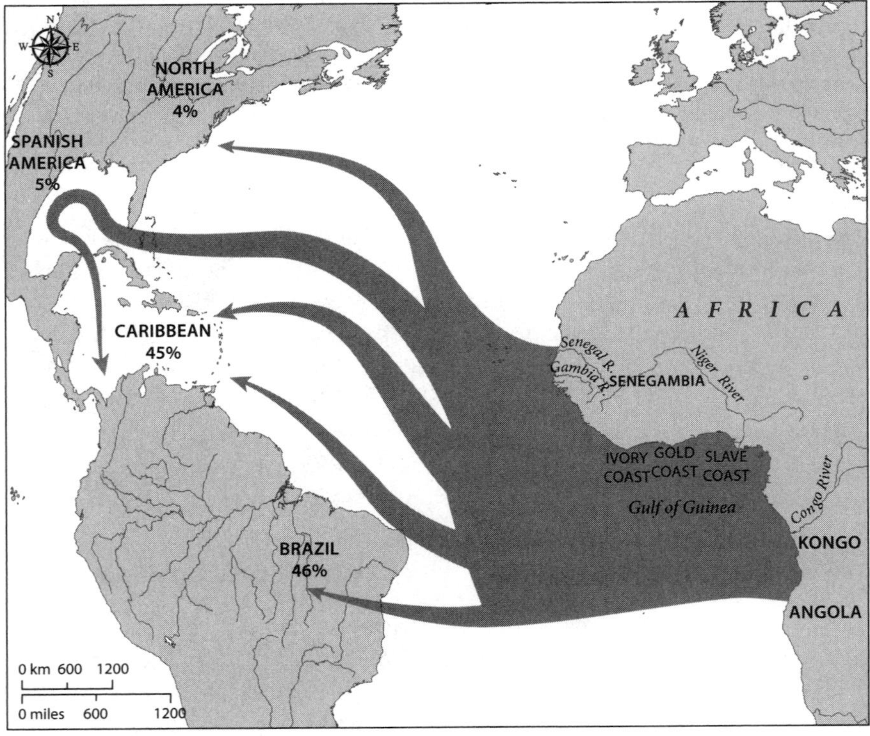

Map. 5.1 West Africa and the Atlantic Slave Trade.

or Brazil, but others ended up laboring in the mines of Peru, the workshops of Mexico City, the tobacco fields of the Chesapeake, and even like Briton Hammon, in the maritime trades of New England.

Numbers alone cannot tell the full story of the Atlantic slave trade. The physical and emotional trauma it inflicted on those Africans separated unwillingly from their homes and families is incalculable and perhaps the most difficult dimension of this historical experience to recover. Captivity and slavery were common features of West African society, but people who found themselves in those conditions still lived in a world of familiar surroundings, customs, and relationships. Transportation across the Atlantic severed those connections suddenly and irrevocably. The slave ship, therefore, marked more than just abrupt and involuntary departure; it was a place of profound disorientation and apprehension, where an individual's ability to anticipate and explain life suddenly faltered and time and place became unmoored. On the trans-Atlantic voyage, physical dangers of disease, confinement, and malnutrition were compounded by the psychological impact of despondency and loss.

The Atlantic slave trade began in the 1440s, a half-century before Columbus's first voyage to America, when Portuguese seafarers acquired the technology and expertise to sail between the Iberian Peninsula and West Africa. From their earliest contacts with Africans, these ships traded textiles and metal wares for gold, ivory, hides, pepper, beeswax, and slaves, engaging states and peoples from the Senegambia region in the north to Angola in the south. During the next four centuries, the geographic center of the trade shifted periodically as different European powers muscled their way into this business and African states chose to enter or withdraw from the trade. Portugal dominated the trade before 1630, drawing most of its slaves from the central African region surrounding the Congo River. During the mid-seventeenth century, the Dutch took the lead by purposefully supplanting the Portuguese in key regions, but they were superseded in turn by the British. During the seventeenth and eighteenth centuries, much of the Atlantic slave trade transpired north of the Congo basin along the Gulf of Guinea, and the names Europeans put on maps of this region tell the tale of their trade there: the Ivory Coast, the Slave Coast, the Gold Coast. To the north, the French slave trade flourished on the Senegal River and the British established themselves on the nearby Gambia River. By the late eighteenth century, the Congo region was again providing the majority of slaves to Atlantic markets, and it continued to do so until slavery was finally abolished in Cuba and Brazil in the 1880s.

Despite centuries of involvement in the slave trade, European powers did not acquire political or economic control over West Africa before 1800. In this regard, their experience differed sharply from that in the New World, where epidemic diseases and European firearms enabled colonizers to conquer native peoples with considerable speed. Europeans brought superior firepower and maritime technology with them to West Africa, but states there were strong enough in their political and military organization to keep would-be colonial invaders at bay. The disease environment in West Africa also reversed the epidemiological advantage

Europeans enjoyed in the Americas. European sailors, soldiers, and merchants living along the African coast succumbed in staggering numbers to malaria, yellow fever, and other diseases, and those mortality rates did not decline until the introduction of quinine, an anti-malarial agent, to European medicine in the mid-nineteenth century. It is a telling comparison that throughout the era of the slave trade, European posts in West Africa remained confined to the Atlantic coast, while by 1650 in North America, European fur traders and colonial officials had established themselves at such interior locations as Montreal on the St. Lawrence River, Albany on the Hudson, and Hartford on the Connecticut. In North America, trade with native populations opened the door quickly to colonization, and settler populations sprouted up along interior trading routes. In West Africa, European penetration and conquest would wait until the era of the railroad and machine gun.

The customs and rules that Europeans had to follow in order to acquire slaves gave further evidence of the control Africans maintained over this trade. After entering into treaties with local kings, chiefs, and merchants, slave-trading companies built posts they called "factories" where they could anchor ships, store goods, and collect slaves. They paid for this privilege in the form of taxes, duties, and diplomatic presents handed over to their African business partners. Along the Slave Coast during the eighteenth century, such payments were referred to as *comey*, and they included port duties, premiums paid to local rulers, and charges levied on each cargo of slaves. Africans also determined the type and quality of goods they received for slaves. Iron bars, which African blacksmiths worked into tools and weapons, became a standard unit for reckoning the value of slaves. African customers also valued European textiles, which they incorporated into their clothing as prestige goods and amassed as a form of bride wealth, the payment a groom made to his wife's family at the time of marriage. European guns acquired via the slave trade transformed African military tactics and powered the rise of new states. By the eighteenth century, West Africans were also thoroughly integrated in the Atlantic consumer markets for tobacco and rum.

Along the coast of West Africa, the Atlantic slave trade bore little resemblance to the piratical raiding and pillaging associated with the enslavement of Indians in America. On the contrary, it was organized and businesslike, involving diplomatic negotiation, capital investment, and managerial oversight. The letters of Paul Erdmann Isert, a surgeon posted at a Danish slave factory during the 1780s, give a sense of the scale and organization involved in the day-to-day operations of such a place. Isert's employer, the Baltic Guinea Company, maintained four forts and six smaller trading stations along the Gold Coast. A hierarchy of company officers supervised the merchants, artisans, soldiers, and clergy employed at these posts at the company's expense. The company also employed hundreds of free and enslaved Africans as interpreters, soldiers, and laborers. European and African cooperation was greased by what Isert described as "one of the most peculiar customs" of the slave trade, temporary marriages between European men and African women: "It is called *cassare*, a word which comes from the Portuguese and means to set up house."[3] Such sexual unions appealed to European traders for business and personal reasons, and the children produced by them became intercultural agents in much the same manner that the offspring of fur traders and native women helped lubricate the fur trade in North America. The most extensive intermarriage in West Africa occurred among the Portuguese and Africans, producing a biracial class of *lançados* who operated autonomously along the coast, describing themselves as Christians and loyal Portuguese subjects but doing business with whomever they pleased. They provided indispensable service to slave-trading companies as brokers, interpreters, and canoemen.

Of course, the business of slave trading looked very different from the perspective of the slave. European traders tapped into an internal market for slaves that already existed in West Africa, but their entry into this business changed how Africans experienced enslavement. War captives made up the bulk of the slaves traded to Europeans, but some Africans found their way into slavery as punishment for crimes or as a result of having been sold by themselves or their families to settle a debt. As demand in Atlantic slave markets peaked during the late eighteenth century, some Africans—especially children—were kidnapped for the sole purpose of selling them into slavery. The commodification of human flesh in these markets altered the practice of slavery within Africa. Adult male war captives were less likely to face ritual execution, but all slaves were more likely to face exportation abroad and, therefore, much greater social alienation and physical suffering than if they had remained within Africa. The Atlantic slave trade put people on the move in West Africa. By increasing the demand for captives, it acted as a human magnet, drawing people out of the interior in a widening arc of warfare and trade, until they arrived at the coast and encountered the greatest shock of all: the slave ship.

Olaudah Equiano, an eighteenth-century slave-turned-abolitionist, wrote the most famous account of this experience.[4] Recent scholarship has raised some doubts about whether Equiano, who worked as a slave for a British naval officer before acquiring his freedom, was actually born in Africa, but his time spent among other slaves, his extensive maritime travels in the Atlantic and Mediterranean, and his long association with controversies surrounding the slave trade give his story an air of authenticity. Equiano claimed to have been kidnapped at age eleven from his village. His captors carried him for several days through the countryside until selling him to the first of several masters he had while still in Africa. Each time he was sold, Equiano moved farther away from his home, yet initially enough was familiar to him to make sense of the people and places he encountered; his enslavement was an unfortunate but not incomprehensible experience. All that changed as he approached the coast. The people he encountered seemed foreign to him and their customs struck him as odd and offensive. Even before he laid eyes on Europeans, he encountered material evidence of the Atlantic slave trade in the iron pots, crossbows, and cutlasses used by these strangers.

More than six months after his kidnapping and after many days of travel by foot and canoe, Equiano reached the coast and was taken aboard a slave ship. As he was manhandled by the sailors, his sense of the familiar immediately abandoned him. "I was now persuaded," he wrote, "that I had gotten into a world of bad spirits and that they were going to kill me." The sailors' complexions, strange language, and violent manners convinced him of their evil intentions. Forced into the ship's hold, he encountered another shock, "Such a salutation in my nostrils as I had never experienced in my life." The stench and miserable cries of his fellow sufferers left Equiano so despondent that crew members resorted to force-feeding him. When his senses returned, he sought out his countrymen among the slaves in the ship's hold and peppered them with questions: Where did the ship come from and where was it taking them? Why did the crew have no women among them? Did they intend to eat or sacrifice him? Equiano's brief but vivid description covered the range of emotions that a slave ship must have aroused in its passengers, from abject horror to disgust to trepidation. Here was a new kind of slavery, one that put him at the mercy of strangers whose very humanity seemed doubtful, whose purposes for taking him to an unknown place could only be sinister and terrifying. This was an altogether different kind of bondage than what he had suffered in Africa, so much so that "I even wished for my former slavery in preference to my present situation."[5]

A slave ship combined the characteristics of a modern prison with those of a modern factory, relying on strict supervision and coordination of its occupants to ensure the profitable outcome of its voyage. It was crowded place, with every conceivable space designed to maximize its human cargo. Below deck, specially fitted platforms increased the carrying capacity of holds but forced manacled slaves to lie side by side in spaces so cramped that they could not sit up or turn over. As a rule, every slave ship left the African coast at full capacity because investors wanted to minimize their financial losses from the mortality that inevitably occurred at sea. A slave's confinement on board ship could be prolonged by the time a captain spent coasting from one West African port to another in order to acquire a full cargo, a process that took at the minimum several weeks and often several months. The crowding on slave ships was compounded by their large crews, typically twice the size as on other merchant vessels and necessary for controlling the slaves. The total number of people on a slaving voyage varied according to the size of the ship, but a common ratio was 1 crew member for every 8 slaves. A typical eighteenth-century slave ship might hold more than three hundred passengers during its Atlantic crossing, giving it a higher human density than any other contemporary ocean-going vessel, including ships that carried troops, European migrants, and convicts to American colonies. Not surprisingly, they also had the highest mortality rates. The 13 percent mortality rate for slaves during the Middle Passage was substantially more than the 8 percent for ships carrying European migrants and convicts. European sailors suffered higher mortality rates on slave ships as well, primarily because of their susceptibility to disease during their time spent coasting along West Africa.

As in any prison, order was maintained on a slave ship through surveillance and physical coercion. While at sea, adult male slaves spent most of their time shackled at the wrist and ankle. Women and children were likely to spend more time unshackled, but still under the watchful eye of the crew. In good weather, all slaves spent time on deck, where they experienced periods of forced exercise (called "dancing" by captain and crew). The despondency and withdrawal described by Equiano were common on slave ships; crew members had to be vigilant to prevent suicides. They outfitted their vessels with nets to keep slaves from throwing themselves overboard, and relied on the whip to compel obedience and firearms to put down any resistance.

Over the course of the Atlantic slave trade's operations, investors and ship captains tried to make it as efficient as possible, but such efficiency was aimed at increasing profits rather than alleviating human suffering. Thus, the capacity of slave ships grew larger not to afford the slaves more room, but to pack even more into a ship's hold. Likewise, the incorporation of more reliable firearms into a ship's arsenal allowed captains to reduce the number of crew members necessary to police the ship but did not make the brutality of the Middle Passage any less severe for the slaves. By the second half of the eighteenth century, investors were outfitting slave ships with copper sheathing to protect their hulls from sea worms, which also increased their sailing speed. This technological improvement shortened the Middle Passage, but it was motivated by a desire to lengthen the lives of wooden ships, not their human cargoes. The drive for efficiency on a slave ship meant that crew members themselves were subjected to the lash more often, as captains and their officers relied on corporal punishment to keep sailors in line. Equiano recalled in his narrative how shocked he was to witness a sailor being flogged to death. After seeing the corpse dumped over the side of the ship, Equiano feared "these people even more; and I expected nothing less than to be treated in the same manner."[6] Captains made slaves watch floggings and executions of recalcitrant or mutinous sailors for exactly this reason. Such displays of violence inspired a sense of helplessness among the slaves meant to sap their potential for resistance.

The Atlantic slave trade had a profound impact on Africa, but not always in ways that were apparent to its participants. Throughout the period of its operation, African rulers and merchants maintained their control over the trade and their political independence from Europeans. Although the slave trade carried almost ten million people to America, it did not cause a population collapse in West Africa, nor did the importation of European goods associated with the trade spell doom for African domestic production of cloth, iron wares, and other goods. Before 1700 slaves accounted only for a small part of the total value of African exports, and most slaves came from within fifty miles of the coast.

Nevertheless, the slave trade did involve some significant economic and social costs for Africa, especially between 1700 and 1820, when approximately 80 percent of the trade occurred. At the trade's peak during the 1780s, slave ships were carrying eighty thousand people a year out of Africa. This rate of exportation put pressure on local suppliers, encouraging warfare and raiding. The slave trade took prime workers from the African economy, healthy young men and women, and forced them to expend their productive and reproductive powers elsewhere in the service of others. The exportation of two male slaves for every female slave upset sex ratios and marriage patterns, further disrupting the social fabric of regions heavily affected by the trade. In essence, the Atlantic slave trade was an extraction industry that removed a precious resource (human labor) from local economies and concentrated the profits from its use in the hands of a distant few. When framed in this manner, the slave trade promoted the colonization of Africa because it took a natural resource and left economic dependency in its wake.

By serving as the primary engine of the Atlantic diaspora of Africans, the slave trade also had a global impact. It brought Africans to every colonial region in the Western Hemisphere and from there into even more distant corners of the globe. Although hardly typical, the travels of Briton Hammon and Olaudah Equiano depicted this uprooting in miniature. Both sailed throughout the Atlantic World in varying conditions of freedom and bondage, calling the Caribbean, North America, and England their homes at different times. The forced exile of so many Africans by the slave trade cut them loose from their homelands, but also encouraged them to cultivate a common identity and sympathy with each other, a pan-African identity that was a product of the shared experience of dislocation from family, home, and community.

FIRST GENERATIONS

African slaves lived and worked in every colonial society in the New World, but the institution of slavery developed in different ways in different regions. Any number of factors affected this evolution, such as the success or failure colonizers had in exploiting other forms of labor, the demographic mix between African and European peoples, and the nature of the colonial economy. Different colonial peoples also brought with them different legal and religious precedents for defining slavery as a social institution. In short, slaves were everywhere in colonial America, but there was no single kind of slavery. This reality was especially evident among the earliest Africans in America, who arrived in small numbers and followed a variety of avenues into colonial society. Their experiences laid the foundation of New World slavery, but also differed markedly from those of slaves who arrived during the height of the Atlantic slave trade in the eighteenth century.

The first Africans in America were participants in the Spanish Conquest. Some came as slaves, but others arrived as soldiers, servants, and free laborers. During Alvar Nuñez Cabeza de Vaca's eight-year odyssey along the Gulf Coast of North America (see Chapter 2), one of his companions and a fellow survivor of their doomed expedition was Esteban, a Moroccan-born slave. Both the Spanish and Portuguese had long experience with African slaves before the colonization of America. War and trade with the Islamic kingdoms of North Africa provided them their first contacts with sub-Saharan Africans. The Spanish and Portuguese built a social and legal system of slavery that borrowed from the ancient Roman, Islamic, and Christian traditions. These precedents justified the enslavement of war captives and heathens, but also held out the possibility of freedom to those slaves who converted to Christianity. Spanish and Portuguese slaveholders also put slaves to work in a number of occupations, such as artisans and soldiers, that provided avenues for self-purchase and social advancement. When Portuguese ships began trading directly with West Africa in the mid-fifteenth century, the number of African slaves living on the Iberian Peninsula increased considerably, and by 1550 the Iberian port cities of Lisbon and Seville had black populations of about ten thousand and six thousand, respectively.

The earliest slaves in Spanish and Portuguese America often came by way of the Iberian Peninsula and so exhibited a high degree of acculturation to European customs and manners. Although they may not have been willing partners in the colonial enterprise, they participated in it as more than brute labor. Along with their Spanish and Portuguese masters, they found sexual and marriage partners among native women and contributed to the formation of mixed-race populations (called *pardos* by the Portuguese and *castas* by the Spanish) that eventually made up the majority of the colonial societies they helped establish. By 1600 the slave population in Iberian America was changing, as increasing labor demand brought more slaves directly from Africa. Iberian captains took their slave cargoes from Angola and Kongo, regions of Africa already enmeshed in the Atlantic trade. Even if they had never set foot on the Iberian Peninsula, many of these slaves were already conversant in the Afro-Portuguese pidgin that had become the lingua franca of the slave trade and they had already been baptized in the Catholic faith. The work regimes they encountered on Brazilian sugar plantations and in Mexican or Peruvian mines were brutal and dangerous, but in language and religion, they at least had a measure of acculturation that helped them negotiate this strange new world. When Spain initiated its "second conquest" of the Americas during the 1760s—a fresh wave of expeditions and missions that included forays into Texas, Arizona, and California—free and enslaved Africans again played an important role as soldiers, laborers, and settlers who established and protected these outposts of Spanish power.

The first Africans to live and work in the English Atlantic came to these colonies by way of the Portuguese or Dutch Atlantic slave trade, and worked alongside free and indentured white laborers who shared their living conditions. Unlike the Portuguese and Spanish, the English did not have much experience with African slavery before colonizing America. Some Elizabethan navigators and pirates raided and traded along the West African coast and sold slaves on both sides of the Atlantic, but in England's domestic economy, slavery had not existed since the early medieval period. Although slaves were present in England's American colonies almost from the very beginning, it took much longer for the legal institution of slavery to evolve there. Put another way, the early English colonies had slaves before they had slavery.

Like other Christians, the English believed that the Bible condoned slavery (plentiful references are made to it in the Old and New Testaments), especially as a means of bringing non-Christians into the faith. They also shared the Roman legal precedent for enslaving war captives, although they usually stopped short of enslaving fellow Christians. During the sixteenth and seventeenth centuries, the English dealt quite severely with their Irish and Scottish enemies. They expropriated their lands, subjected some to summary executions, and sold others into long terms of servitude, but they did not enslave them for life or condemn their children to the same condition. Indentured servitude was a common form of labor in Elizabethan England, and people entered into it with varying degrees of consent. Apprentices signed multiyear contracts that committed their masters to teaching them their trades, and rural servants typically agreed to their service one year at a time. But some servants, such as convicted criminals, vagrants, and orphans, exercised much less choice about the length and nature of their bondage. Nevertheless, English common law defined servitude as a contractual relationship: no one could be born into such a condition nor confined to it for a lifetime.

Evidence suggests that the earliest Africans in Virginia lived and worked in circumstances suspended somewhere between indentured servitude and lifetime slavery. At the time of Jamestown's founding, the Dutch were supplanting the Portuguese as the chief carriers in the Atlantic slave trade. Most of the first Africans in Virginia arrived on Dutch ships by way of the Caribbean. They were sold, as white indentured servants were, to tobacco planters anxious to get their hands on any kind of labor, and they lived, worked, and slept alongside those servants, enduring the same harsh discipline, meager diet, and debilitating diseases. Court cases make clear that these Africans and white servants sought sexual companionship among each other and sometimes cooperated in running away and rebellion. Yet, the same records indicate that English masters and lawmakers set Africans apart from white servants. Courts accorded more protections and rights to Christian servants than non-Christians, and they punished white servants more severely for fornication and running away if they engaged in those activities with Africans partners. From the very start, Virginia's elites exhibited a religious and color prejudice against Africans as they imposed order on their labor force.

Yet, for several decades those prejudices were not institutionally strong enough to keep some Africans from gaining freedom and creating independent lives for themselves. Anthony Johnson first appeared in Virginia's records in 1621 as "Antonio a Negro," and a few years later he appeared again, listed as a "servant" who had married "Mary," another African. At some point over the next several years, Antonio became Anthony Johnson, a free man who along with his wife and children worked their own land on Virginia's Eastern Shore. There are no records of exactly how Antonio gained his freedom, but it is likely that he negotiated his self-purchase with his master, and his adoption of an anglicized name consciously marked his passage from a life of servitude to one of independence. He participated in the local economy of the Eastern Shore, amassing a landed estate of 250 acres, suing and being sued by neighbors in the county court, and even acquiring other servants to work for him.

Johnson's path from servant to property owner was rare in early Virginia, but it was not singular. Among his contemporaries were other Africans who followed similar routes to freedom. Like Johnson, these men arrived in the Chesapeake with names that indicated roots in the Portuguese Atlantic and acculturation to European society: "Francisco a Negroe," Anthony Longo, and Emanuel Driggus.

Perhaps they convinced authorities that they were Christians and therefore not eligible for lifetime enslavement, or perhaps their language and social skills were sophisticated enough for them to negotiate self-purchase with their masters. Regardless of how they achieved it, these free Africans illuminated the plasticity of race relations in the early Chesapeake. English prejudices were such that only Africans could be slaves, but those prejudices had not yet created a legal or social order that mandated that all Africans had to be slaves.

In the Caribbean, the shift from servitude to slavery was more accelerated. Indentured servants provided the majority of labor in Barbados during its first three decades. The Africans who arrived in the colony came by way of the Portuguese and Dutch Atlantic trade and lived and worked alongside free and indentured whites. After 1650 the experiences of black and white laborers diverged as racial slavery became the foundation of the colony's sugar production. By the early 1660s, the black population of Barbados exceeded that of the whites, and the colony's rulers formulated the first systematic code of slave law in the English Atlantic, defining slavery as a lifetime, hereditary condition and slaves as chattel property with no civil liberties or protections that masters were bound to observe. This slave code provided the model for those subsequently adopted in Jamaica and South Carolina.

Africans were a part of the founding colonial populations north of the Chesapeake Bay as well. In seventeenth-century New England, Africans worked in urban centers as household servants, craftsmen, and maritime laborers, and in the countryside on commercial farms and in mines and iron furnaces. Their numbers, however, were quite small, ranging from 2 percent of the population in Massachusetts to 5 percent in Rhode Island. These black New Englanders experienced a degree of familiarity with their white neighbors that facilitated their acculturation to the Puritan world. The Massachusetts Body of Liberties, adopted by that colony's government in 1641, recognized the legality of slavery but also the humanity of the slaves, allowing them access to the courts and requiring masters to provide for their spiritual instruction and physical well-being. New England's cold winters and rocky soil discouraged the year-round plantation production that made slavery so profitable in regions southward. Masters had to think creatively about how to use their slaves' labor profitably, and so sometimes hired them out temporarily or allowed them to pursue wage work on their own, as Briton Hammon did when he signed on for his winter voyage to the Caribbean. The success of such arrangements relied on a level of negotiation and trust between master and slave that would not have been possible without some degree of personal intimacy between them.

New Netherland, because of its close ties to the Dutch Atlantic, had the largest African population north of Maryland. The Dutch West India Company traded directly with West Africa, and although practically all the slaves it exported to the Americas ended up in Brazil or the Caribbean, the Company did employ some of them in New Amsterdam and the Hudson Valley as field hands, maritime laborers, servants, and soldiers. As with Africans in early New England

and the Chesapeake, slaves tended to come to New Netherland by way of the Caribbean, where they had already acquired language skills and religious affiliations that helped them negotiate colonial society. Some possessed names—such as Jan Guinea, Anthony Portuguese, and Francisco Cartagena—that testified to their well-traveled backgrounds. When New Netherland became New York, the Dutch West India Company exited the colony, but the Africans it had brought there remained. The sizable minority of blacks who obtained their freedom during the Dutch era remained at liberty, but as the English elaborated their own law and practice of slavery, the ranks of the free dwindled. During the early eighteenth century, New York had more slaves than any colony north of Maryland, both in numbers and as a percentage of total population, and African American bondage became a fixture in New York City, the Hudson Valley, and Long Island.

Whether in the Caribbean or North America, the distinguishing feature of the earliest Africans in the English colonies was their Atlantic origins. They were men and women of African ancestry who exhibited a remarkable degree of mobility and experience in the multi-ethnic and multiracial world being knit together by trans-Atlantic trade and colonization. Many arrived in English colonies already possessing Christian names as evidence of their baptism, and although they may not have arrived speaking English, they could communicate in the trading argot of West African and Caribbean ports. These characteristics proved advantageous as they negotiated their way in colonial societies that were still in the formative stages of their race relations. There is no doubt that they suffered prejudicial treatment in English America because of their skin color, but some—as many as one in five in some regions—managed to define their bondage as servitude and gain their freedom. As the plantation economy expanded, that window of opportunity closed, and the division between slavery and freedom became a stark contrast in black and white.

FROM SLAVES TO SLAVERY

Before 1680 Africans arrived in England's North American colonies in small numbers, usually as by-products of international trade, smuggling, or piracy. All that changed during the last two decades of the seventeenth century, as English merchants began trading for slaves directly with West Africa and the plantation system became a fixture of England's overseas expansion. The rising number of slaves imported from Africa altered the demographics and economics of plantation production, which in turn affected the institutional development of slavery. Although each colonial region experienced these changes in a different way, the same general pattern prevailed in the plantation colonies: enslaved Africans displaced white servants, small producers were squeezed out of markets for land and labor by great planters, and the gap between enslaved blacks and free whites grew wider.

In 1672 King Charles II chartered the Royal African Company and granted it a monopoly on the importation of slaves to England's American colonies. As with the joint-stock companies that had funded the establishment of Virginia and Massachusetts, the Royal African Company married private enterprise to the pursuit of state interests. In this case, opening the West African trade was just one part of a broader effort by Charles II to challenge the maritime supremacy of the Dutch, which he also pursued in a series of naval wars against them and by seizing the colony of New Netherland. By monopolizing the importation of slaves to England's colonies, the Royal African Company closed a profitable market for Dutch traders and helped channel the growing wealth of the colonies back to England.

After the Royal African Company established its own factories on the African coast, the number of slaves imported to England's colonies increased markedly. Political stabilization and economic growth in England after 1660 reduced the flow of indentured servants across the Atlantic, and the growing restiveness of former servants who lacked access to land encouraged planters to divert their capital to the purchase of slaves, who could be held in bondage for their lifetimes. In England's Caribbean colonies, imports from the Royal African Company sped a conversion from indentured to slave labor that had gotten under way during the 1650s. In 1660 the white and black populations of Barbados had been roughly equal, about twenty-seven thousand each. By 1700 blacks outnumbered whites there by a ratio of 3 to 1. In Jamaica, which became England's most productive sugar colony in the eighteenth century, blacks outnumbered whites by a ratio of 8 to 1. On mainland North America, a similar transformation occurred, although at a slower rate and without the same extremities in population redistribution. In Virginia, where Africans had accounted for only 5 percent of the population in 1670, they rose to 13 percent by 1700 and 40 percent by 1750. In South Carolina, where Africans were present in significant numbers from the start, slaves accounted for 60 percent of the colonial population by 1760. Unlike in the Caribbean, the slave population in North America expanded as a result of natural increase as well as increased importation from Africa. A generally healthier climate on the mainland enabled slaves to live longer there than in the West Indies, increasing the incentive for planters to invest their capital in more slave purchases.

At its height, the Royal African Company was importing five to ten thousand slaves per year to the colonies, but the planters' demand for labor was such that the company's monopoly was never secure. Colonists continued to engage in contraband trade with foreign slave ships, and the English government ended the Royal African Company's monopoly so that other English merchants could legitimately engage in the trade. Facing increased competition, the Royal African Company shifted its business in Africa toward other goods, and by the 1730s it was out of the slave trade entirely. By that time, however, other merchants in London, Liverpool, and Bristol had taken their place, and English ships dominated the Atlantic slave trade for the rest of the century.

The influx of so many Africans to the colonies (they were the largest immigrant group to British America between 1680 and 1807) altered the nature of slavery in those societies where it became the foundation of economic production. On Caribbean sugar islands, the wealthiest planters engrossed the arable land and amassed slave workforces numbering in the hundreds. Former servants—whether white or black—lacked the capital to compete, and so their economic independence diminished as sugar production increased. The great planters resorted to importing corn, grain, pork, and fish from the northern mainland colonies to feed themselves and their slaves. The character of the slave population changed as well. The earlier generations of slaves who arrived in dribs and drabs by way of Portuguese and Dutch traders gave way to wave after wave of Africans new to the Atlantic slave system. These "outlandish" or "saltwater" slaves, as planters called them, brought cultural practices and beliefs with them that became the foundation for a Caribbean slave culture deeply rooted in African traditions. Concerned about the presence of such a large alien population among them, planters passed slave codes that granted masters absolute authority over the lives and bodies of their slaves. By law, slaves could not assemble or absent themselves from their plantations without permission from their masters. They could not bear arms or use such traditional African means as drums and horns to communicate with each other. Masters even came to regard slave funerals, occasions for the expression of African musical traditions and spiritual beliefs, with suspicion. From the slaves' perspective, a sugar colony was a police state where surveillance was constant, punishment arbitrary, and personal liberty nonexistent.

English planters brought the institution of chattel slavery with them from the Caribbean to South Carolina, where it provided the foundation for a plantation society. After two decades of trial and error with different economic ventures, planters adopted rice as their cash crop in the Carolina lowlands and imported African slaves to work as its cultivators. Unlike sugar and tobacco, rice was a crop grown in West Africa before the advent of the Atlantic slave trade, particularly in the region between Senegambia and Sierra Leone known as the Upper Guinea Coast. Some of the slaves who arrived in South Carolina during the formative years of its plantation economy undoubtedly brought expertise in rice cultivation with them, although slave imports from the Upper Guinea Coast to North America peaked several decades later, between 1750 and 1775. Historians therefore debate the extent to which slaves influenced the decision to adopt rice as this region's cash crop—the planters' access to capital and their entrepreneurial willingness to experiment with new ventures mattered as well—but they agree that the methods used to sow and process rice in the Carolina lowlands had West African roots.

Climate also affected the development of a slave society in South Carolina. The English were not inclined to settle in the lowland swamps where rice grew best, for fear of succumbing to malaria or yellow fever. Wealthy slaveholders preferred to live in Charles Town and leave the management of their estates to overseers. The overwhelming black majority in the lowlands (as high as 9 to 1) made the constant white supervision of the labor force impossible. Instead, the task system evolved, in which foremen assigned slaves tasks to complete at their own pace, after which they had the balance of the day to themselves. Tending a quarter-acre of rice became the standard "task" on these Carolina plantations, and gradually the system expanded to include other types of labor. After they had completed their task, slaves typically engaged in other labor intended to supplement their livelihood, such as hunting, fishing, raising livestock, or cultivating garden crops. Slaves often sold the produce of these endeavors, sometimes to their own masters, giving them a degree of autonomy in their economic lives that would have been much more difficult to achieve under the gang-labor system used on Chesapeake tobacco plantations. However, slaves in the Carolina lowlands faced higher mortality rates than in the Chesapeake, and the methods of punishment and discipline used by their masters were reputed to be the most severe in North America.

In the Chesapeake region, the legal status of slavery developed gradually. Even after the entry of the Royal African Company into the slave trade, Virginia and Maryland remained distant after-thoughts of slave traders plying their business in the Caribbean. Neither colony had a city that could rival South Carolina's Charles Town, which became the eastern seaboard's leading slave market. Nevertheless, as the African population of the Chesapeake steadily grew, the institution of slavery emerged from a welter of legislation intended to control the region's changing labor force.

In keeping with the biblical and Roman precedents that justified slavery, Virginia's House of Burgesses initially used the terms "Christian" and "negro" to distinguish between Europeans and Africans in legislation regarding slavery. Hence, a 1662 law mandated that "christian servants" who ran away in the company of slaves would be forced to serve additional time beyond the usual penalty. But drawing a line between servant and slave based on religion raised another question: Did conversion to Christianity allow a slave to claim his or her freedom? The House of Burgesses answered that question with a definitive "no" in a 1667 act declaring that "the conferring of baptisme doth not alter the condition of the person as to his bondage or freedome." The legislature was also concerned with regulating interracial sexual relations and their offspring. A 1662 law made clear that slavery was a hereditary condition that passed from the mother to the child; the same law assessed a double fine on any "Christian" convicted of committing fornication with "a negro man or woman." Thirty years later, another act provided for the banishment from the colony of any free white man or woman who "shall intermarry with a negro, mulatto, or Indian man or woman."[7] This desire to prevent marriages or other sexual unions that might lead to the creation of a free, mixed-race population stood in stark contrast to the Portuguese and Spanish colonies, where *pardos* and *castas*, respectively, occupied a broad middle place on the spectrum between slavery and freedom. More so than their European contemporaries, the English were intent on compressing this spectrum into two absolute and opposite categories of slavery and freedom, recognizing no gradations of condition between them based on birth, rank, religion, or physical appearance.

By the time Virginia adopted a comprehensive slave code in 1705, the legal contours of slavery within the colony had been set. As opposed to servitude, which was contractual and of limited duration, slavery was a biological condition that children inherited from their mothers. Neither baptism nor marriage altered the slave's status. And even though any person taken as a captive in war was eligible for enslavement, in law and practice, Virginians limited that fate to only those people of African descent. This distinction was made evident in a 1670 act that subjected Indian war captives to terms of servitude of up to thirty years, but stated that all those "servants not being christians imported into this colony by shipping shall be slaves for their lives."[8] Such legislation made African descent the defining characteristic of slavery in the Chesapeake.

Within such a system, free blacks found it increasingly difficult to maintain their economic and social independence. A 1670 law prohibited them from owning white servants, placing them at a disadvantage in Virginia's competitive labor market. The House of Burgesses moved against the colony's free black population again in 1691 by requiring any masters who freed their slaves to provide for their transportation beyond Virginia's borders. Such legislation never eliminated free blacks entirely from within Virginia, but it did create a legal atmosphere hostile to their rights, liberties, and long-term security. The descendants of Anthony Johnson moved to Maryland's Eastern Shore toward the end of the seventeenth century and from there disappeared from historical records. The world their ancestor had known, in which a former slave could gain his freedom and take his place alongside other free men, had disappeared.

Along the Gulf Coast, slavery developed in an opposite manner than it did in the eastern seaboard colonies. The investors who funded the establishment of Louisiana in 1699 hoped to turn the lower Mississippi Valley into an extension of the plantation economy in the French Caribbean, but local circumstances initially conspired against them. The French inhabitants of the colony were mostly fur traders and soldiers, transient adventurers with little economic resources of their own. During the 1720s, the direct importation of thousands of slaves from West Africa by the French Compagnie des Indes changed the character of the colony. New Orleans became its capital city and plantations began producing tobacco and indigo for export to Atlantic markets. Very quickly, Louisiana acquired a black majority population (about 60 percent by 1730) and a wealthy planter class that dominated its economy. Just as abruptly, that changed in 1729, when the Natchez Indians rose up against the French because of grievances over land and trade. Disaffected plantation slaves, many of whom had intermarried with local Indians, joined in the two-year rebellion. When it was over, plantation society in the French colony had sustained an irreversible blow. Slave importations declined along with exports of tobacco and indigo. Africans and African Americans, however, remained in the majority of Louisiana's population, working in more diversified occupations as free and enslaved farmers, herders, maritime laborers, urban craftsmen, and domestic servants. Although officially prohibited, intermarriage among whites, blacks, and Indians in Louisiana was commonplace, and New Orleans developed a significant free mixed-race population. Plantation-style production and slave importations from Africa would not revive in the region until after the American Revolution.

PATTERNS OF RESISTANCE

In Briton Hammon's narrative of his Atlantic odyssey, only once does he describe an episode of outright resistance to those who tried to hold him against his will. While working for the Spanish governor in Havana, he refused to be pressed into service in the Spanish Navy. For taking this stand, he paid severely by being confined to prison for four years. Hammon's pride in refusing to serve on a Spanish ship is indicative of his geographic roots. New England sailors and fishermen were notorious for expressing similar sentiments whenever the British Navy tried to force them into service.

Hammon's stand against the Spanish press gang probably had as much to do with his identity as a New England mariner as it did with his life as an African American slave. It reminds us that slave resistance or rebellion in the colonies was never monolithic or uniform in character. Rather, it took on many different characteristics and expressions, depending on the particular circumstances of the slaves who engaged in it and the degree of their acculturation to colonial society. Resistance, whether in the form of subtle day-to-day encounters or violent armed confrontations, had its root in the slaves' perception of injustice, the notion that some boundary of acceptable conduct had been violated. As a slave, sailor, and Indian captive, Hammon experienced all sorts of limitations on his personal liberty, but for him, it was a press gang's insistence that he serve on a naval vessel that violated his sense of justice. For other Africans and African Americans caught in the maelstrom of New World slavery, factors specific to their time and place triggered their own acts of resistance.

Consistent with their character as floating prisons, slave ships were often sites of collective resistance by Africans against their enslavement. Approximately five hundred such incidents occurred between 1650 and 1860, including more than ninety attacks on slave ships from shore as they traded along the West African coast and almost four hundred incidents of rebellion by slaves already loaded onto ships. Such incidents were most likely to occur while a slave ship was still anchored along the African coast. In 1686 rebellious slaves onboard the *Charlton* killed the crew and ran the ship aground. In 1750 a similar incident occurred onboard the *Ann* when slaves slipped their irons, armed themselves with the crew's guns, and managed to get the ship to shore.

After a ship had sailed beyond sight of the African coast, the likelihood of shipboard rebellion decreased but never disappeared entirely. In fact, about one-third of such incidents occurred during the Middle Passage, and the potential for rebellion at this time increased if sickness or short rations weakened a ship's crew. The best available evidence indicates that about one in ten slaving voyages experienced some kind of collective violence undertaken by Africans. Although the vast majority of these rebellions were put down by crewmen using the onboard arsenals they carried for exactly that purpose, instances of successful mutiny, such as the *Amistad* case in 1839 in which slaves on a ship sailing out of Havana killed the captain and commandeered the vessel, made slave ship captains and crews constantly vigilant.

Acts of collective shipboard rebellion might appear to have been driven overwhelmingly by circumstance: slaves simply seized upon lapses in a ship's security to rebel, whenever and wherever they occurred. Analysis of the available evidence, however, indicates regional and chronological variations in such episodes that may be linked to circumstances other than a crew's supervision of its human cargo. For example, shipboard revolts in the Senegambia region surged during the second half of the eighteenth century as the coastal trade there intensified. The growing demand for slaves in this region's Atlantic trade placed pressure on its domestic slave system, and some slaves who would have been previously insulated from the Atlantic trade because of special skills or kinship ties now found themselves loaded onto ships for export. When they rose up against their handlers, they may have been motivated not because they objected to their enslavement per se, but because the nature of that enslavement had suddenly changed, facing them with the prospect of permanent exile in an unknown land. Even in opportunistic acts of collective resistance, slaves acted on grievances as various as their backgrounds.

Patterns of slave resistance in the New World exhibited the same variations based on time, place, and personal circumstances. All slaves had recourse to such day-to-day acts of resistance as feigning illness, purposefully completing slow or careless work, breaking tools and other equipment, and pilfering goods from their masters. Slave owners constantly worried about two acts of resistance in particular, arson and poisoning. Fires destroyed valuable property essential to a plantation's daily operations: barns and warehouses, curing houses for tobacco and refining equipment for sugar, even crops in the field. Urban colonial populations feared that rebellious slaves could torch an entire city. As for poisoning, it was difficult to prove that slaves deliberately employed this means of resistance, but that did not stop whites from making the accusation and dealing severely with suspects. Masters and overseers believed that poisoning was an element of African folk knowledge that slaves carried with them across the Atlantic and transmitted to subsequent generations. In court cases, a suspected poisoner was often described as a "Negro doctor" who used his or her skills to prepare herbal concoctions that could harm as well as heal. The extent to which slaves actually used poisoning against their masters is debatable, but their masters' paranoia about it is evidence of the tensions that arose from living among a population held against their will. Slaves attuned to such fears could obviously manipulate them to their advantage.

Slaves also ran away to find either temporary or permanent relief from their bondage. If apprehended, runaways faced disciplinary actions that ranged in severity. First-time offenders were likely to be whipped or forced to wear heavy irons. Chronic runaways might be branded or mutilated—a cropped ear or amputated toes—so that they could be more easily identified as a fugitive should they run again. A master could also "outlaw" a runaway slave whom he considered too dangerous or incorrigible to be worth retrieving; this act legally authorized others to kill the fugitive and paid a reward from public funds for doing so.

Despite the best efforts of slave owners and colonial governments to keep slaves from stealing themselves, runaways were a chronic problem in Atlantic slave societies. Unique motives and circumstances shaped each runaway's decision to flee, but this was not a random act. When incidents of running away are viewed in aggregate, patterns emerge that link the individual decision to wider trends in the development of New World slavery. In the British colonies in North America and the Caribbean, newspaper advertisements for fugitive slaves provide the best source for these data. Runaway advertisements typically described the physical features of a runaway or group of runaways, the circumstances under which they absconded, and the reward offered for their return. By providing this group portrait, the advertisements tell us what types of slaves were likely to run away, what motivated them to do so, and where they were likely to go.

Most runaways engaged in *petit-marronage*, that is, a temporary absence from their master's authority intended to gain them some sort of amelioration in their working or living conditions. Truant slave had many reasons for going AWOL. They did so as a way of protesting unreasonable demands or excessive cruelty from their overseers; unsuitable rations, clothing, or housing; or their potential sale or transfer to a different location. By far the most commonly reported reason for *petit-marronage* was a slave's desire to visit family or friends from whom he or she had been separated. Many runaway slaves left one plantation only to seek out another, where they were welcomed and protected by kin or other sympathetic slaves. In such instances, running away was not so much an attempt to sever the master–slave bond as it was to renegotiate it, a means by which the less powerful half of this equation tried to force a concession from the more powerful one.

Those runaways who sought permanent freedom from slavery engaged in *grand-marronage*. Acculturated slaves who possessed valuable occupational skills stole themselves so that they might become masters of their own labor. They were drawn especially to colonial towns and cities, where employers were not likely to inquire too closely into their workers' backgrounds if they possessed the necessary training and would accept the right wage. Seaports provided runaways with the quickest access to transportation away from their masters. Merchant marine vessels, naval ships, and army companies perpetually needed fresh recruits to fill their ranks. Although sailors and soldiers labored in conditions not much different from slaves (they too endured confinement, floggings, and the loneliness of a single-sex workforce), these occupations provided something plantation life did not: a great deal of geographic mobility and frequent opportunities for desertion.

Some slaves engaged in *grand-marronage* to escape colonial society entirely. They sought refuge among Native American communities or among maroon communities established by other runaway slaves. The reception such runaways received among Indian peoples varied. Indian nations who were suffering population losses from disease and warfare were likely to value runaways as potential adoptees and marriage partners, but they might also perpetuate the runaways' enslaved status according to their own customs. In a 1763 advertisement in the *Georgia Gazette*, one slaveholder suspected that his slave Primus "might have gone away with a gang of Creek Indians" who had been visiting in the area. In other regions, Indians were less welcoming to runaways and exchanged them with colonial authorities for bounties in cash or trade goods.

Maroon communities varied in size, strength, and longevity. They were most commonly found in the Caribbean, where it was possible for runaway slaves to establish independent towns in the remote, mountainous interiors of islands such as Hispaniola and Jamaica. Planters found it prohibitively expensive to raise the troops necessary to destroy these communities, and so they negotiated truces with them, periodically granting them firearms, gunpowder, and other manufactured goods in exchange for the maroons' promises to cease raiding their plantations and to return runaway slaves. In North America, maroon communities were rarer and not nearly as populous because it was easier for the majority white population to eradicate autonomous African populations. Runaway slaves from the Chesapeake region did establish fleeting maroon communities in the Great Dismal Swamp, an inaccessible border region between Virginia and North Carolina. Likewise, slaves from the coastal lowlands of South Carolina and Georgia formed maroon communities along the interior tributaries of the Savannah River and in northern Florida. The intermarriage of runaway slaves with Native Americans along the Florida-Carolina borderland contributed to the ethnogenesis of the Seminole Indians by the early nineteenth century.

In addition to the circumstances of their working lives, the cultural background of slaves influenced how they ran away. "Saltwater slaves"—those who arrived in America directly from Africa with little previous acculturation to European society—usually ran away in pairs or larger groups. Unfamiliar with the colonial world around them, they sought assistance and safety from others like themselves and expressed a desire to find "the Way back to their own Country." As slaves became more acculturated to colonial society, they were more inclined to run away individually, which increased their chances of passing as free. Whereas runaway advertisements for African-born slaves tended to describe their personalities as confrontational—for example, "impudent," "surly," and "bold,"—advertisements for slaves born in America emphasized their ability to get along and to blend in, calling them "artful," "cunning," and "sensible." Some runaway advertisements described slaves who possessed valuable occupational and social skills, such as the "Caulker and Ship-Carpenter" described in a 1762 Boston newspaper who "speaks good English, [and] can read and write." Others presented snapshots of slaves who must have felt like strangers in a strange land, such as the "YOUNG NEW NEGROE WENCH, named SIDNEY," who "talks no English" and could be identified by "her country marks on her breast and arms," a reference to ritual scarification she had experienced in Africa.

Although it was extremely rare for a runaway slave to return to Africa, maroon communities did reconstitute as much as possible the social and cultural milieu that their residents had known in Africa. The inhabitants of Palmares, a collection of maroon towns in Brazil, governed themselves according to a West African model of kingship. Described by colonial contemporaries as an independent African nation in the Brazilian interior, Palmares had a population that numbered in the thousands and successfully withstood military assaults by European armies throughout the seventeenth century. As in West Africa, its leading men practiced polygamy and established multigenerational aristocratic lineages. The Jamaican maroon communities, which established themselves during the transition from Spanish to English rule of the island in the 1650s, likewise endured by reviving strong, centralized leadership and a military culture they had known in West Africa. The modern descendants of these communities still regard the treaties their ancestors signed with colonial officials in the eighteenth century as diplomatic recognition of their unique political status within Jamaica. The largest maroon community in colonial North America was Gracia Real de Santa Teresa de Mose, a free black town two miles north of St. Augustine in Florida. The Spanish governor established it to encourage slaves to run away from coastal Georgia and South Carolina, thereby destabilizing the English planter regimes in those colonies and boosting the defensive strength of Spanish Florida. Although never numbering much more than one hundred people, Mose survived for a generation, and its residents immigrated en masse to Cuba when the Spanish ceded control of Florida to Britain in 1763.

Full-scale slave rebellions in colonial America were much rarer than incidents of running away and other acts of day-to-day resistance, but the violence they unleashed exposed the brutality at the heart of this labor system. As the number of slaves in the American colonies increased, slave owners became increasingly vigilant to prevent slaves from cooperating in resistance. Slave codes prohibited slaves from possessing firearms, from congregating without white supervision, and from communicating with each other over long distances. Sheriffs and other local government officials detained and interrogated slaves traveling at night or without written passes from their masters, and county militias acted as security forces to put down slave insurrections. When purchasing slaves imported from Africa, some masters purposefully mixed slaves from differing ethnic and regional backgrounds, so that it would be more difficult for them to communicate and cooperate with each other.

The largest slave rebellion in colonial North America took place south of Charles Town, South Carolina, near the Stono River in 1739. Before dawn on Sunday, September 9, a group of about twenty slaves broke into a storehouse and armed themselves with guns they found there. They plundered and burned a planter's home and killed his family, then marched on, sparing a white tavern keeper known for his kind treatment of slaves but destroying other homes and families in the vicinity. They continued southward, "calling out Liberty," playing drums, and flying their colors to attract more slaves to their cause. After traveling about ten miles, the rebels, now numbering between sixty and one hundred, stopped in a field "and set to dancing, Singing and beating Drums, to draw more Negroes to them." By this time, word of the insurrection had spread, and the lieutenant governor of South Carolina had raised a militia force to march against the rebels. In a pitched battle, the slaves "behaved boldly" but the militia prevailed, killing on the spot any prisoners they were able to take. Those slaves who escaped this initial confrontation were also executed when they were apprehended, their decapitated heads displayed as a warning to others. All told, this brief but bloody episode resulted in the deaths of about forty slaves and twenty whites.[9]

In the Northern colonies, New York City was convulsed by two slave rebellions, first in 1712 and then again in 1741. In the first of these episodes, a group of about twenty slaves set fires and then attacked whites who came out to extinguish them. Authorities investigating the conspiracy arrested scores of slaves and condemned twenty-five of them to die in gruesome public executions, including three who were burned at the stake and one whose bones were broken on a wheel. Memories of 1712 fed the fear of a slave insurrection that nearly paralyzed the city in 1741, when another series of suspicious fires broke out in homes, barns, and public buildings. Investigation soon focused on the family and associates of a white tavern keeper known for entertaining blacks and for purchasing stolen goods from them. Accusations and arrests spiraled quickly, eventually encompassing more than 150 suspects. Historians still debate whether this second episode was the result of a genuine slave conspiracy or white fears of one. The court relied heavily on questionable evidence from white witnesses and confessions extracted from accused slaves led to believe that their testimony would save their lives (it did not). Nevertheless, the New Yorkers' suspicions exacted a terrible toll on the city's black community: thirteen of their number burned at the stake, seventeen hanged, and more than eighty sold into exile in the West Indies.

In these instances of rebellion, the methods slaves chose for claiming their freedom reflected circumstances peculiar to their time and place. The tactics used by the slave rebels in South Carolina in 1739 were an outgrowth of their African roots. Judging from their familiarity with firearms and their military organization, the leaders of the Stono Rebellion were probably former soldiers from the Kongo region of central Africa, which meant they were also likely Christians, previously baptized by Portuguese missionaries. They headed south to seek sanctuary in Florida, where the Spanish governor offered them freedom in exchange for their military service and conversion to Catholicism, a faith many of them had perhaps already embraced. The New York slave conspiracies reflected the unease and paranoia that could arise among whites living in a crowded colonial seaport. With slaves comprising roughly 20 percent of its population, New York City had the highest concentration of slaves in an urban area north of Charles Town. These slaves spent a great deal of time out of sight and earshot of their masters, working in the city's docks and streets, patronizing its taverns after hours, and fencing stolen goods. Their mobility and autonomy incited fears of conspiracy among whites, as did acts of arson, a crime often associated with malcontent slaves.

Regardless of their time and location, slave rebellions invariably resulted in a retaliatory clampdown by whites. In the wake of the Stono Rebellion, white South Carolinians passed the Negro Act of 1740, a thorough reworking of the colony's slave code that made it harder for slaves to congregate or arm themselves and easier for whites to kill suspected malcontents. In New York, as in South Carolina, fears of slave insurrection aroused suspicions that Spanish agitators were acting as agents provocateurs among local slaves, which in turn led to crackdowns on Catholic foreigners and suspected infiltrators. Slave rebellions also provoked some of the most brutal displays of state power in the colonies, from the revival of medieval forms of torture and execution to the public display of the heads and rotting corpses of convicted rebels, intended to remind others of the high cost of resistance.

EMERGENCE OF AFRICAN AMERICAN CULTURES

In his brief narrative of his travels and misfortunes, Briton Hammon exhibited a startling range of identities—New Englander, slave, mariner, Christian, captive, even Englishman—but he did not call himself an African or an African American. This does not mean, of course, that he was unaware of or uninterested in his African heritage, but it does illustrate interesting questions about the cultural adaptation of African peoples to their lives in the New World. When and how did African slaves become "American" in the way they thought about themselves and others like them? When did they come to regard the plantations, farms, and towns where they worked and lived as their homelands, and to what degree were they able to preserve and pass on to subsequent generations the values, beliefs, and practices of their African ancestors? There are no simple or uniform answers to these questions. The formation of African American cultures in the crucible of slavery varied across time and place. The longevity of Atlantic slave trade and its universal impact on the formation of colonial societies meant that the slaves in different regions produced a range of responses and adaptations as they carved out lives for themselves within a repressive labor system.

The first generations of Africans in the New World arrived already with a fair degree of acculturation to European societies. These Atlantic creoles—free, servant, and slave—bore names, spoke languages, and espoused religious beliefs that made it far easier for them to negotiate their way in colonial society than subsequent generations that arrived in America during the peak years of the slave trade. Saltwater slaves faced the most significant culture shock of any New World migrants. The physical and psychological trials of the Middle Passage, compounded by the slave trade's tendency to randomize the distribution of slaves from different African backgrounds throughout American colonies, meant that these Africans faced an abrupt severing from the bonds of family and community. As the number of saltwater slaves in colonial societies increased, the African background of slave populations became more pronounced, widening the cultural gap between masters and slaves. By the mid-eighteenth century, improving sex ratios and health conditions in North America made it possible for slaves to achieve a positive rate of reproduction, creating a native-born or creole slave population that eventually outnumbered slaves arriving directly from Africa. To these American creoles, Africa was a distant place, the home of ancestors they may have never known and strangers whose manners and languages they may have found incomprehensible. In the Caribbean and other parts of Latin America where slave mortality rates remained very high throughout the eighteenth century, this transition from saltwater to creole populations took much longer, which kept Africa a vibrant and immediate influence on the formation of their slave culture.

The process of the slaves' acculturation to America began before they even landed there. In the dark claustrophobic ship holds of the Middle Passage, Africans from different backgrounds created the pidgin dialects and personal connections that helped them reconstitute social ties in the New World. Although slave ships often completed their cargoes by coasting from one West African anchorage to another and some masters deliberately mixed ethnicities when purchasing slaves, it is also true that slaves coming from within the same cultural zone in West Africa would have possessed enough in common to communicate with each other even if they were from different nations. Slaves caught up in the Atlantic trade were not likely to find themselves alongside Africans from entirely different backgrounds until after they had arrived in America, when the sale of slave cargoes in piecemeal fashion dispersed the newcomers over a large area. Thus, for all its horrors, the Middle Passage was also a time during which slaves formed important bonds. Some shipmates developed fictive kin relationships to replace parent–child and sibling relationships they had been torn away from in Africa. These reconstituted kinship ties were strong enough in some cases to lead to incest taboos barring sexual relations between people who had crossed the Atlantic on the same slave ship. Advertisements from colonial newspapers also indicate that shipmates cooperated in running away from their masters. In other instances, slaves ran away to find shipmates from whom they had been separated after arriving in America.

By their nature, shipmate bonds were transitory and fragile. The formation of more enduring kinship and community bonds depended on the ability of slaves to create and sustain families. Several demographic factors played important roles in this process. First, the sex ratio in slave populations needed to approach parity between males and females, something that the economics of the slave trade conspired against. In the Caribbean and Brazil, slave traders imported approximately three males for every female. In North America and other regions of Latin America, that ratio was closer to 2 to 1. Slave populations did not reach sexual parity until American-born slaves outnumbered those born in Africa. Two other demographic factors figured in that balance: slave mortality and fertility rates. A quarter to a third of newly arrived slaves did not survive their "seasoning," the first year during which they were exposed to the work regimen and disease climate of America. Poor nutrition and overwork also reduced the fertility of slave women and contributed to the high rate of infant mortality among their offspring. Masters claimed the children of their slaves as their property, but as long as the Atlantic slave trade flourished, it was more profitable to purchase new adult slaves whose labor could be exploited immediately than to invest in the healthy upbringing of slave children. The formation of slave families, therefore, owed much more to the slaves' determination to recreate intergenerational kinship ties than to their masters' desire for a native-born workforce.

American creole slave populations first took root in the Chesapeake region, where a more temperate climate, a better diet, and less debilitating work than in the Caribbean enabled African slaves to live longer and nurture a rising generation. American-born slaves outnumbered those who were from Africa by about 1740 in Virginia. This transition occurred approximately thirty years later in the Carolina and Georgia lowlands, in part because planters there had more access to saltwater slaves via importations to Charles Town and Savannah. It was slower still in the Caribbean and Brazil, where the supply of African-born slaves did not substantially decline until after Britain and the United States banned the Atlantic slave trade in 1807–1808.

Regardless of where or when it became possible for slave families to sustain themselves, they had a profound impact on the cultural development of slave societies. Slaves who married and had children preferred to live in nuclear households where they could carve out a measure of privacy and autonomy away from white supervision. For many slave couples in Anglo-American colonies, this remained a goal rather than a reality because the law provided no legal recognition of their union. Masters could sell away a spouse or children of a slave union with impunity. Slave families were also split up when a planter gave some portion of his workforce to an adult child or when his death led to the division of his estate among his heirs. Still, wherever slave families took root, no matter how fragile, they changed the complexion of plantation communities. The barracks-like atmosphere of heavily male plantation workforces gave way to "the quarters," a geographic and social zone where slaves worked at their domestic tasks, practiced their own rites of birth, marriage, and death, and managed their affairs as independently of white intrusion as possible (see Figure 5.2).

Even after slave populations achieved demographic stability, family formation varied according to regional circumstances. In New England and the middle colonies, slaves lived healthier and longer lives than their counterparts in the South, but their numbers remained small relative to the white population. In rural and urban areas, they were likely to live under the same roof as their masters and therefore experienced a greater degree of white supervision in their domestic lives. Puritan and Quaker slaveholders, however, were also more likely than Southern plantation owners to respect the familial bonds formed by their slaves. Puritan ministers officiated at slave weddings and emphasized the master's responsibility for the spiritual instruction and well-being of all his dependents, including servants and slaves. Quakers were likewise inclined to take a paternalistic approach to their slaves that tempered, although never entirely eliminated, the deleterious impact that law and custom had on the formation and preservation of slave families.

In the plantation societies of the Southern and Caribbean colonies, slave families had greater social autonomy but were also more exposed to the vagaries of the marketplace. In addition to the high mortality rates associated with cash crop production, slave families could also be torn asunder by a planter's bankruptcy, death, or migration. By the mid-eighteenth century in the Chesapeake, soil exhaustion and population growth were pushing tobacco planters westward from Virginia's tidewater into its piedmont, putting slaves, even those who were American-born, on the move as well. In the Carolina and Georgia lowlands, white absenteeism and

Figure 5.2 ***The Old Plantation, c.*** **1790–1800. This painting by an unknown artist offers a vibrant depiction of slave culture on an eighteenth-century plantation, most likely in Virginia or South Carolina. The musical instruments and dancing suggest ways in which Africans adapted their original forms of cultural expression in their American environment and passed them along to subsequent generations. Courtesy of Abby Aldrich Rockefeller Folk Art Museum, the Colonial Williamsburg Foundation. Gift of Abby Aldrich Rockefeller.**

the steady importation of saltwater slaves meant that slave families incorporated more African cultural influences than in the Chesapeake. Although unbalanced sex ratios prevented the transfer of marriage customs involving polygamy, lowland slaves were far more likely than those elsewhere in North America to give African names to their children and to incorporate African aesthetics into their domestic architecture and pottery-making. Some lowland slaves spoke Gullah, a creole language that combined English with African loanwords and grammar. The maroon communities of the Caribbean and Brazil exhibited the most pronounced African influences in their family structure and social relations. In Jamaica's maroon towns, elite men practiced polygamy, even though the supply of women in these communities was a constant problem.

The preservation of slave families against enormous demographic and legal obstacles made possible the intergenerational passage of cultural values and practices that combined African precedents with American adaptations. Even within their constrained material circumstances, slaves managed to pass on from one generation to the next distinctive patterns in language, dress, diet, and child-rearing that reflected their African roots. The same held true in their religious beliefs and the customs surrounding their communal observances of births, marriages, and deaths. African American Christianity is one example. Many West

African slaves, especially those from the Kongo region, arrived in the New World already familiar with Christian beliefs. For these slaves, the process by which they combined Christianity with such African religious practices as spirit possession and ancestor worship was already well under way before they reached America. In America, no professional or hereditary caste of African priests emerged, but individual practitioners carried on traditional arts in healing, magic, and fortune-telling, and Christian converts adapted African customs to their new situation by grafting them onto officially tolerated Catholic practices. Thus, Christian saints, feast days, and holy objects acquired distinctive African meanings among slave populations. The records of the Mexican and Brazilian Inquisitions, church bodies charged with ferreting out unorthodoxy, provide ample evidence of slaves and free blacks whose Africanized practices of Catholic belief and ritual caused concern among priests and bishops.

In colonial regions dominated by Protestant populations, church and government officials devoted far less resources to converting slaves. Slaveholders worried that slaves would use baptism as a pretext for claiming their freedom, and the demands that Protestant sects placed on catechumens to be literate made evangelization a slow and difficult process. In British North America and the Caribbean, the first Protestants to sponsor missionary work among slaves were from sects that placed heavy emphasis on the Holy Spirit and direct spiritual revelation. These sects—Moravians, Baptists, and Methodists—gained their foothold in the colonies during the Great Awakening of the mid-eighteenth century, and they sought converts among peoples ignored or spurned by the dominant churches, including slaves who were drawn to their emotionally charged preaching style and insistence on the spiritual equality of all souls.

Slaves in the Northern colonies also created their own festive culture by grafting African customs to the civic and religious calendars of colonial society. The civic holiday known as Election Day had its roots in seventeenth-century Puritan New England, but by the mid-eighteenth century, slaves and free blacks in Massachusetts, Rhode Island, and Connecticut were using it as a day to convene their own public celebrations of feasting, drinking, and dancing, which white observers dubbed "Negro Election Day." In New York and New Jersey, a similar African American day of celebration occurred on Pinkster, a Dutch holiday that had its roots in the observation of the Christian holy day of Pentecost. Masters and employers accommodated these holidays by giving their black workers the day off and by providing them with special clothing and small amounts of cash to use on the occasion. On these holidays, local communities of slaves and free blacks sometimes elected their own "governor" or "king" from among their number and had him lead a celebratory procession through the streets. Pinkster and Negro Election Day allowed African Americans to parody white society without fear of reprisal, but these holidays also shaped their participants' sense of communal identity and solidarity. Music and dance performed in African styles reinforced their common heritage, and the recognition and celebration of their own leaders asserted their autonomy within the larger society.

AFRICAN IDENTITY IN THE ATLANTIC WORLD

Briton Hammon's story was the first slave narrative published in North America. In the nineteenth century, this literary genre flourished, producing firsthand accounts of slavery and plantation life in the American South. The handful of slave narratives produced in the eighteenth century, however, followed more closely the model provided by Hammon. Like Hammon, their authors were seafarers who experienced multiple captivities and encountered strange people in strange lands on both sides of the Atlantic. They embraced Christianity as a way of asserting their personal worth and autonomy in a slave system that wanted to deny them both. Perhaps because of their mobility, they also expressed multifaceted identities. Hammon's sense of self as a Christian New Englander shaped his descriptions of his Indian captors in Florida and his Spanish masters in Cuba. When Olaudah Equiano posed for the portrait that served as the frontispiece of his narrative, he proudly displayed his civility and Christianity by dressing in the clothing of an English gentleman and holding an open Bible in his hand. In the caption beneath that portrait, he identified himself as "*Olaudah Equiano*, or Gustavus Vassa, *the African*."[10]

No slave held in irons aboard a slave ship crossing the Atlantic would have identified himself or herself as "the African." If given the opportunity to record their names for posterity, such slaves would have identified themselves according to the family, ethnic, or national names that held meaning in their homelands. Only by being forcibly removed from those ties and exiled to a distant land did those slaves begin to identify with each other as people sharing a common origin and common plight. In the fetid holds of slave ships and on the auction blocks of slave markets, in plantation quarters and work gangs, in the backrooms and garrets of colonial cities, slaves used their African heritage as a foundation on which to build new identities that also incorporated European languages, religions, and material culture. To be African in colonial America, in other words, was to participate in a process of cultural diaspora and reconfiguration that spanned the Atlantic. Equiano "the African" was also Equiano the Christian and Equiano the Englishman. Briton Hammon, author of the first African American slave narrative, was also Hammon the New Englander and Hammon the sailor. African identity in colonial America was not a collection of baggage brought by slaves across the Atlantic and gradually discarded as they adjusted to life in the New World. It was the slow and adaptive construction of a new identity by slaves and their descendants as they made lives for themselves that could not be reduced or perpetually confined by the institution of slavery.

CHRONOLOGY

1440s	Portuguese ships begin importing West African slaves to Europe.
1640–1660	Barbados becomes the first English colony to transition from white indentured servitude to African slavery as its primary labor force.

1672	Royal African Company founded in England.
1712	New York City slave rebellion.
1729	Natchez Rebellion disrupts the development of plantation-style slavery in Louisiana.
1738–1763	Gracia Real de Santa Teresa de Mose in Spanish Florida becomes the most significant free black maroon community in North America.
1739	Stono Rebellion in South Carolina.
1739–1740	British officials sign treaties with Jamaican maroon communities, recognizing their territorial and political autonomy.
1741	Rumors of a slave conspiracy in New York City result in mass arrests, executions, and deportations of slaves.
1747	*Briton Hammon's odyssey begins with a winter voyage to the Caribbean.*
1760	*After enduring captivity in Florida and Cuba, Hammon returns to New England by way of London and publishes the first African American slave narrative.*
1780s	Peak decade of Atlantic slave trade.
1789	Olaudah Equiano publishes his slave narrative in London.
1807–1808	Britain and the United States, respectively, ban Atlantic slave trade.

NOTES

1. Briton Hammon, *A Narrative of the Uncommon Sufferings and Surprizing Deliverance of Briton Hammon* (Boston: Green and Russell, 1760).
2. The Trans-Atlantic Slave Trade Database is available online at http://www.slavevoyages.org/tast/index.faces. The statistics quoted here are from an article summarizing the Database's conclusions; see David Eltis, "The Volume and Structure of the Transatlantic Slave Trade: A Reassessment," *William and Mary Quarterly*, 3d ser., 58 (2001): 17–46.
3. Paul Erdmann Isert, *Letters on West Africa and the Slave Trade: Paul Erdmann Isert's Journey to Guinea and the Caribbean Islands in Columbia, 1788*, ed. and trans. Selena Axelrod Winsnes (New York: Oxford University Press, 1992), 156.
4. Olaudah Equiano, *The Interesting Narrative of the Life of Olaudah Equiano, Written by Himself*, ed. Robert J. Allison, 2nd ed. (1789; Boston: Bedford/St. Martin's, 2007).
5. Equiano, *Interesting Narrative*, 64–66.
6. Equiano, *Interesting Narrative*, 66.
7. All references to Virginia's seventeenth-century slave laws are from Willie Lee Rose, ed., *A Documentary History of Slavery in North America* (New York: Oxford University Press, 1976), 16–22.
8. Rose, ed., *A Documentary History*, 19.

9. [James Oglethorpe?], "Account of the Negroe Insurrection in South Carolina," in Mark M. Smith, ed., *Stono: Documenting and Interpreting a Southern Slave Revolt* (Columbia: University of South Carolina Press, 2005), 13–15.
10. For most of his life, Equiano used the name "Gustavus Vassa" that had been given to him by one of his English masters. He adopted "Olaudah Equiano" when he became active in Britain's anti-slavery movement during the 1780s and 1790s. See Vincent Carretta, *Equiano, the African: Biography of Self-Made Man* (New York: Penguin, 2005), 293.

SUGGESTIONS FOR FURTHER READING

Two excellent overviews of the Atlantic slave trade are Herbert Klein, *The Atlantic Slave Trade* (Cambridge, UK: Cambridge University Press, 1999), and Kenneth Morgan, *Slavery and the British Empire: From Africa to America* (New York: Oxford University Press, 2007). For essays that highlight quantitative data from the Trans-Atlantic Slave Trade Database, see Barbara L. Solow, "The Transatlantic Slave Trade: A New Census," David Eltis, "The Volume and Structure of the Transatlantic Slave Trade: A Reassessment," David Richardson, "Shipboard Revolts, African Authority, and the Atlantic Slave Trade," and Herbert S. Klein, et al., "Transoceanic Mortality: The Slave Trade in Comparative Perspective," in *William and Mary Quarterly*, 3d ser., 58 (2001): 9–16, 17–46, 69–92, 93–117. Two recent studies of the Middle Passage are Stephanie E. Smallwood, *Saltwater Slavery: A Middle Passage from Africa to American Diaspora* (Cambridge, MA: Harvard University Press, 2007), and Marcus Rediker, *The Slave Ship: A Human History* (New York: Viking, 2007). For works that describe the slave trade's impact on Africa, see David Northrup, *Africa's Discovery of Europe, 1450–1850* (New York: Oxford University Press, 2002), and John Thornton, *Africa and Africans in the Making of the Atlantic World, 1400–1800*, 2nd ed. (Cambridge, UK: Cambridge University Press, 1998).

For the development of regional slave cultures in British America, see Ira Berlin, *Many Thousands Gone: The First Two Centuries of Slavery in North America* (Cambridge, MA: Harvard University Press, 1998); Philip D. Morgan, *Slave Counterpoint: Black Culture in the Eighteenth-Century Chespeake and Lowcountry* (Chapel Hill: University of North Carolina Press, 1998); Sidney W. Mintz and Richard Price, *An Anthropological Approach to the Afro-American Past: A Caribbean Perspective* (Philadelphia: Institute for the Study of Human Issues, 1976); and Betty Wood, *The Origins of American Slavery: Freedom and Bondage in the English Colonies* (New York: Hill & Wang, 1997). For studies more specific to time and place, see T. H. Breen and Stephen Innes, *"Myne Owne Ground": Race and Freedom on Virginia's Eastern Shore, 1640–1676* (New York: Oxford University Press, 1980); Anthony S. Parent, *Foul Means: The Formation of a Slave Society in Virginia, 1660–1740* (Chapel Hill: University of North Carolina Press, 2003); Peter Wood, *Black Majority: Negroes in Colonial South Carolina from 1670 through the Stono Rebellion* (New York: Norton, 1975); Robert Olwell, *Masters, Slaves, and Subjects: The Culture of Power in the South Carolina Low Country, 1740–1790* (Ithaca, NY: Cornell University Press, 1998); and Jane Landers, *Black Society in Spanish Florida* (Urbana: University of Illinois Press, 1999). The debate over the African origins of rice cultivation in South Carolina is described in David Eltis, Philip Morgan, and David Richardson, "Agency and Diaspora in Atlantic History: Reassessing the African Contribution to Rice Cultivation in the Americas," *American Historical Review* 112 (2007): 1329–1358, and the subsequent *AHR Exchange* on this controversial topic in *American Historical Review* 115 (2010): 125–171.

For studies concerning slave resistance and rebellion, see Gerald W. Mullin, *Flight and Rebellion: Slave Resistance in Eighteenth-Century Virginia* (New York: Oxford University Press, 1972); Jill Lepore, *New York Burning: Liberty, Slavery, and Conspiracy in Eighteenth-Century Manhattan* (New York: Knopf, 2005); Mark M. Smith, ed., *Stono: Documenting and Interpreting a Southern Slave Revolt* (Columbia: University of South Carolina Press, 2005); and Richard Price, ed., *Maroon Societies: Rebel Slave Communities in the Americas* (Garden City, NY: Anchor Press, 1973). Negro Election Day and Pinkster are described in Shane White, "'It Was a Proud Day': African Americans, Festivals, and Parades in the North, 1741–1834," *Journal of American History* 81 (1994): 13–50. The question of African identity formation in the Atlantic World is explored in Vincent Carretta, *Equiano, the African: Biography of a Self-Made Man* (New York: Penguin, 2005), and the role black mariners played in the Atlantic World is described in W. Jeffrey Bolster, *Black Jacks: African American Seamen in the Age of Sail* (Cambridge, MA: Harvard University Press, 1997).

CHAPTER 6

Gender, Family, and Sexuality

John Atkins of Warraskoyack, a minute English settlement on the James River in the Virginia colony, purchased Thomasine Hall from his neighbor John Tyos. Given the scarcity of women in the still rough and struggling colony, Atkins presumably coveted the opportunity to acquire the service of someone with household skills such as needlework. Hall, however, did not come to Atkins's home without baggage. In February 1628 a man named Thomas Hall had been convicted along with Tyos and his wife for receiving goods stolen from a neighbor. In this frontier society, colonists could hardly limit their business dealings to those without a legal blemish. And the sale of indentured servants was a perfectly normal transaction. No. What made the acquisition of the twenty-five-year-old Thomasine Hall potentially disruptive is that she arrived in Virginia as Thomas Hall, and that Hall's sexual status had already provoked public controversy. Hall had done little to quell this controversy by proclaiming publicly before a regional official an identity as "both man and woeman."

Hall's anatomy and Hall's personal history confirmed this claim of a dual identity, male and female. Born in northeastern England and moving to London when she was twelve, Hall grew up as a girl. In her early twenties, Thomasine followed her brother into military service, becoming Thomas by cutting her hair and putting on men's clothes. After enduring a brutal campaign in France, Hall came back to England, dressing, living, and working in the needle and lace trade as a woman in Plymouth. Unlike the Pilgrims who departed that port a few years before, Hall actually made it to Virginia, embarking from that port and traveling as a man. Precisely when Hall resumed a female identity is not clear, but Hall's identity quickly aroused suspicion and concern among his new Virginia neighbors.

Many of these neighbors looked to Hall's body not Hall's life story for a definitive answer. Having intimately inspected Hall themselves, three local women, Alice Longe, Dorothye Rodes, and Barbara Hall, judged Hall to be a man, based on their determination that Hall had male genitalia. Captain Nathaniel Basse, who questioned Hall publicly, proclaimed Hall a female and ordered Hall to dress like one. After Thomas Hall's sale to Atkins, the locals Longe, Rodes, and Hall examined him again, this time as he slept, and again concluded that he was a man. The harassment soon became more overt, with five women and Atkins demanding that Hall let them see his body; subsequently, one of the women's husbands seized Hall and viewed Hall's body himself. These anatomical investigations seemed to indicate that Hall was a man, but Hall's statements and behavior left the denizens of Warraskoyack unsatisfied. Hall had told Captain Basse that his male genitals did not function and that he urinated like a female. Meanwhile, a rumor, which Hall denied, that Hall "did ly with a maid... called *greate Besse*" raised further questions about Hall's sexuality.

All this sexual ambiguity proved too much to bear for Hall's neighbors. The matter wound up before the governor and council of the colony. Hall testified, and two of Hall's male neighbors offered sworn depositions reporting the previous events in Warraskoyack. Virginia's leading men reached a decision that simultaneously ratified Hall's mixed identity and stigmatized Hall permanently by denying this servant the freedom to continue to cross sexual boundaries at will. Pronouncing Hall "a man and a woeman" the court ordered that Hall "shall goe Clothed in mans apparell" with "his head to bee attired in a Coyfe... with an Apron before him." While the rest of Hall's American odyssey is lost to history, the stigma imposed by the court's ruling and the short life spans of so many English migrants to the Chesapeake in this era were not conducive to happy endings.[1]

Loose ends notwithstanding, Hall's story helps us to glean how colonial Americans understood gender, sexuality, and authority, as well as how central and yet potentially unstable the heterosexual family was as a social building block. The Virginia General Court's decision to require Hall to wear clothes denoting masculinity and femininity acknowledged that Hall's identity had a physiological and a cultural component, or put another way, that people's sex derived from anatomy, while their gender derived from the roles, customs, and work that culture prescribed to males and females. What confused matters in Hall's case was that Hall's gender—wearing a dress, doing women's work—seemed to define him as female, despite anatomical features that indicated otherwise. But Virginia's leading male officials were not attempting, nor were they being asked, to develop theoretically nuanced definitions of gender; rather, they were attempting, and were being asked, to impose order and to exercise authority in a society far removed from established institutions.

To a new world that left them ample room for social experimentation, European colonists brought assumptions about men and women, their appropriate social roles, and their relative places in the social hierarchy. As we have seen in Chapter 3 with the case of Anne Hutchinson, a powerful female voice could cause tremendous consternation for male authorities, religious and secular. But even a more modest figure like Thomasine Hall had, it seemed, to be put into place to secure order. Rather than banishment for apostasy, Hall fell victim to public shaming for transgression. The required mix of clothing, as one historian has noted, was akin to the scarlet letter worn by Hawthorne's fictional heroine Hester Prynne—a plot element Hawthorne modeled after actual practice in Puritan New England. Public shaming, which also took on more brutal physicality with whippings and even the branding of runaway servants and slaves, was a key component of colonial discipline. But to colonial Americans, gender boundaries were even more effectively patrolled through daily routine. The emphasis placed on the clothes Hall wore drew on the assumption that attire defined a person's social class, as well as his or her sexual identity, in rigid and publicly transparent ways. Ideas about sex were hardly locked in place during the colonial period. Nonetheless, the ability of male authorities inside and outside the family to impose their will played an ongoing role in how colonial Americans, men and women, experienced their own bodies, wore their clothes, and did their work.

Yet as striking as the exercise of formal male authority to define sex and gender in this case was, an equally important feature of the Hall case is the role that women themselves played in regulating the boundaries of gender and making claims on ostensibly more powerful males. In the Hall case, groups of women on more than one occasion took the lead role in compiling bodily evidence. These women, moreover, refused to accept quietly the decision of Captain Basse, the local political authority. They also pushed Hall's master to reconsider his own judgments about Hall's sexuality, and may have played a role in perpetuating the rumor that Hall slept with another female servant, the rumor that led the General Court to take up the matter of Hall's identity. While the balance of power in defining women's roles inside and outside the family household tilted decisively toward men, it is vital to observe the many ways in which colonial women exercised power over their own lives. The women of Warraskoyack, like women everywhere in colonial America, formed communities within communities, carved out areas of expertise, and even made demands on males in positions of authority that shaped what it meant to be a woman and to be a man.

The ability to establish and maintain colonial households varied markedly across space and time. Environment and the mix of migrants initially affected the types of families and households that colonial Americans formed, with the economic prospects and cultural precepts of various regions continuing to influence the trajectory of family life thereafter. But in every region, gender, family, and sexuality were not only biologically dependent on the presence of women, they also were influenced profoundly by the ways in which women and men constructed their relationships toward each other and toward authority.

This chapter focuses on the intimate spheres of colonial communities, households, and bodies—sites of production and reproduction where ordinary people built their mostly humble fortunes, established and perpetuated family lines, and expressed as well as repressed their desires. The subsequent two chapters will expand these themes by looking more explicitly at the male-dominated spheres of politics and print culture, where ideas about the body, home, and community would be projected onto society and onto the natural world. Although the facts of Thomasine Hall's life were unique, the ways in which household members and neighbors shaped it captures much about how the close quarters in which colonial Americans lived and worked affected the most intimate details of their lives.

DEMOGRAPHY AND FAMILY STRUCTURE

Like Thomasine Hall's neighbors, most English migrants to North America shared some basic presumptions about what a family was, how work should be divided in a household between men and women, and the relationship between sex and morality. The forced migrants from Africa who by the late seventeenth century started to arrive in great numbers also had ideas about family, work, and sex. But individual migrants, voluntary and forced, confronted conditions and came in groups that sometimes challenged or at least channeled family structures in particular directions. In other words, migrants made families, but not under conditions of their own choosing. In New England, patterns of migration, settlement, and belief quickly reinforced one another to create families centered on married men and women and multiple children. In the Southern mainland colonies and the Caribbean, high mortality rates combined with class and racial hierarchies to severely complicate the creation of stable households.

God and worship were the acknowledged core of New England Puritan culture, but a central tenet of Puritanism was to live in rather than apart from the world. Thus, the formation and maintenance of families embedded in orderly communities were a vital aim of Puritan society. In reality, there was plenty of conflict between and even within New England families, as well as transgressions against official sexual mores. Still, New England society proved remarkably successful in establishing families bustling with children who grew up under the watchful eyes of their parents and who perpetuated essentially the same family structure generation after generation. Such biological and social reproduction led to the multiplication of Puritan towns throughout New England, heightened the stress of Native American communities, and altered that landscape; in time, generations of large Puritan families also led to crowding, particularly in older towns, creating challenges for parents to ensure a standard of living comparable with their own. But overall, New England proved almost from the very beginning to be a hospitable environment for English migrants and their descendants to perpetuate marriage-centered households.

The high proportion of intact families and the near universality of marriage among adult New Englanders allowed the region's European population to take full advantage of what they found to be a healthy climate. Puritan couples were fecund. Women averaged seven births. Some families grew to be far larger than that. In seventeenth-century Andover, Massachusetts, a town north of Boston, approximately 60 percent of first- and second-generation American families contained seven or more children who lived past twenty-one. Such a town could not sustain these substantial birthrates throughout the colonial era, but did so for several decades. While far more single men than single women migrated to New England, the high rate of natural increase smoothed out sex ratios over time, making marriage and the almost inevitable string of children that followed the anticipated path for young Puritan men and women. By the mid-seventeenth century, New England's European population no longer needed migrants to sustain itself.

The average ages of marriage varied over time and social circumstance, one early effect of the Atlantic migration being that the average age of marriage for females fell, especially for those who migrated to New England as children. The average female married in her early twenties, a substantially younger age than in England and France. As the migration generation ran its course in the middle of the seventeenth century, the gap between the average age for men and women decreased from approximately six to four years, as the surplus of male migrants gradually eased. Initially, the sexual imbalance forced men to marry later and women earlier. Again drawing on Andover as a case study, very few men, but approximately a third of women married before the age of twenty-one. Through the generations in Andover, the overwhelming number of women married before thirty and men before thirty-five. For the region as a whole, eldest sons, on average, married at age twenty-five, a younger age than their brothers, perhaps reflecting a bias toward establishing the first son's independence or toward keeping younger children available longer into their parents' declining years.

Most New Englanders married one time for life, and these unions produced pregnancies about once every two years until the wife's late thirties. The absence of contraceptive technology can only partly explain this pattern. Religion and culture emphasized procreation as a major function of family life. Puritans viewed the sexual pleasure of wives and husbands as essential to conception, but also believed such fulfillment was one of the bases for a stable household. The cycle of nursing and weaning of infants played a role in regulating or at least regularizing the cycle of births. Since breast feeding lowers fertility, the timing of weaning influenced the intervals of births; some women may have undertaken journeys to visit family in other towns as a way of facilitating weaning. The fact that Native American pregnancies in New England spanned three- to four-year intervals and that Native American women nursed their children longer than their English counterparts indicates that culture rather than mere fate was a key variable. In any event, the European and Native American inhabitants of Puritan New England were fully cognizant of the physical rhythms of reproduction, its pleasures as well as its pains.

Childbirth was by no means without its risks to mothers while the first year of life was not without danger. Approximately a tenth of Euro-American infants died before age one, though this made infancy in New England healthier than in England and much healthier than France at the time. A similar percentage of women may have died in childbirth, most deaths among mothers occurring after they had given birth several times. Successful births and tragic ones alike took place within a community of women, who supervised the process and transmitted knowledge across generations (see Figure 6.1).

The Puritan preoccupation with death may have contributed to the continued persistence of large families, even after the English population in New England had clearly established itself. Puritan ministers stressed that death was not only inevitable but also could strike any time. Puritan divine Cotton Mather, in a sermon prompted by the death of a twenty-one-year-old woman, shared the sobering wisdom, "*If an old Man has Death before his Face, a Young Man has Death behind his Back*; The *Deadly Blow* may be as near to one, as it is t'other."[2] Puritan parents

Figure 6.1 Gravestone of Prudence Hammond, Watertown, Massachusetts, created by Joseph Lamson (1711). This New England goodwife lived to age seventy-four, a lengthy life span common to Puritan settlers in this region. The text of the gravestone is crowned by the winged image of death, an hourglass, Latin mottoes, and a crossbones, all signaling the inevitability and finality of death, while it is flanked by strikingly carved icons of female fertility. Thus, the stone encapsulates key features of the Puritan life cycle, gender, and sexuality. Photograph from the Farber Gravestone Collection. Courtesy, American Antiquarian Society.

did not feel secure that their families were large enough to produce and sustain the material, as well as emotional, benefits required in a society where the most important source of wealth and security besides land itself was the labor of one's children. Evidence from the mid-Atlantic in the middle of the eighteenth century indicates the language of motherhood in colonial America valorized large families; men and women alike used agricultural metaphors such as "teeming," "flourishing," "breeding," "fruitful," "prolific," and "lusty" to describe the pregnant body. Such language put women's bodies and fertility at the nexus of economic production and biological reproduction (see Figure 6.2).

The most salient contrasts between New England and the Chesapeake were a sex ratio more heavily skewed toward men and a miserable mortality rate for immigrants of both sexes; these trends persisted for most of the seventeenth century. For much of Virginia's first century, a variety of obstacles and complications compromised the ability of its white and black inhabitants to form lasting families. In the colonial Chesapeake, wealth flowed from the aggressive pursuit of land and

Figure 6.2 John Hesselius, *Rebecca Holdsworth Young (Mrs. Richard Young) and her Granddaughter, Rebecca Woodward* (*c.*1763). This portrait from Maryland projects women's fertility in agricultural terms while conveying generational continuity. Both grandmother and grandchild cradle fruit at their waists. The child's hand on the grandmother's leg and the grandmother's embrace with her right arm emphasize stability, including gender roles, across the decades. White birth rates in English mainland colonies approached their all-time high in the mid-eighteenth century. Courtesy, Winterthur Museum, Painting, Rebecca Holdsworth Young (Mrs. Richard Young) and her granddaughter Rebecca Woodward, Maker: John Hesselius, 1763-1765, Annapolis, MD, bequest of Henry Francis duPont, 1958.1986.

labor to produce tobacco. This pursuit led to population growth, but of a different sort than in New England. Virginia's planters eagerly sought laborers to cultivate tobacco, a cash crop that served as cash itself.

Compared to their Northern cousins, the Chesapeake colonies took much longer to achieve population growth through the natural increase of an American-born population. New England started to sustain itself by the mid-seventeenth century, or approximately a generation after a brief burst of founding immigration. The colony that grew from Jamestown, founded over two decades before Massachusetts Bay, did not see sustained natural increase until the late seventeenth century. And yet Virginia's non-Indian population climbed substantially over the course of that same century—due to a large English migration, supplemented by the importation of African slaves. Across the last three-quarters of the seventeenth century, as many as 100,000 arrived in Virginia. While the stunningly low early odds of survival of the first two decades improved, at first they did so only slightly: though approximately fifteen thousand new arrivals entered the colony between 1625 and 1640, the colony's population grew by a mere seven thousand. Death by disease, overwork, and poor nutrition took its toll decade after decade. The maturation of apple orchards planted earlier in the century added healthy vitamins to Virginians' diets and something to drink besides contaminated water, while many Virginians relocated closer to healthful water supplies. These improvements addressed some of these problems, but not all.

The stream of immigrants to Maryland and to Virginia was overwhelmingly male, which had all sorts of demographic and cultural consequences. Male-female ratios, 6 to 1 in the early years and falling gradually thereafter, were sustained at imbalanced levels by markedly male-heavy shiploads of new English migrants through much of the century. The absence of a large-scale, highly fecund family migration did not smooth out the sex imbalance nearly so quickly as in New England, even though female Virginians likely died of disease at lower rates than men. Meanwhile, masters expected female servants to delay pregnancy and marriage until they completed their indentures; a servant who became pregnant was punished by having additional time added to her service. Still, a substantial number of female servants did get pregnant. Sometimes a pregnant servant's prospective husband would purchase the balance of her contracted service, but the effect of servitude was to push the age of marriage for females into their mid-twenties. By contrast, non-servant women married, on average, at age twenty. The fertility rate of English migrants did improve over the course of the century, but women did not consistently reach levels of reproduction experienced during the formative decades of the New England colonies. In St. Mary's County, Maryland, a mere 12 out of 105 parental wills between 1660 and 1680 list more than 3 surviving children. Perhaps only half of children born in Maryland made it to twenty years old, suggesting that even the native-born Chesapeake population struggled to survive, despite having had some antibodies to local diseases passed onto them.

Early death affected fertility and the Chesapeake population's profile in a variety of ways. Put simply, Chesapeake colonists arrived young and died young. Immigrant servants, male and female, largely arrived in their late teens or early twenties. Numerically speaking, these migrants had arrived at middle age. Most died in their late thirties or early forties. Evidence from Maryland indicates that 70 percent of male immigrants passed away prior to turning fifty, with women's life expectancies likely shorter.

The consequences of early and frequent death in the Chesapeake for marital stability were profound. With migrants lucky to live until the age of forty, the average marriage was short—at mid-century approximately seven years—and the rate of remarriage high, especially for women, who could count on numerous suitors immediately on the heels of widowhood. By contrast, given the odds, men could not count on finding a new wife. While Puritan New England widows and widowers remarried as well, the necessity of doing so was considerably lessened by the longevity of their lives and, thus, their marriages.

A child in the seventeenth-century Chesapeake could not expect to live until adulthood with both biological parents still alive. Data drawn from Middlesex County, Virginia, settled in the second half of the seventeenth century, tell a grim tale: 25 percent of five-year-olds, 50 percent of thirteen-year-olds, and over 70 percent of children in total lost at least one parent before reaching adulthood. A child in this county had a one in three chance of becoming an orphan. The prevalence of parental death and rapid remarriage of the surviving partner meant not only that children were commonly raised in part by a stepparent, but often by two stepparents, as a child's remarried biological father might well die, leaving that child under the care of a stepmother and her new husband. The resulting tangle of families meant raising children from two or three different marriages under one roof. Under these roofs, stepsiblings likely developed emotional alliances as well as rivalries.

Orphaned children growing up in a world of death were at risk of abuse and deprivation. The selection of reliable godparents might shield orphaned children from unscrupulous guardians like Gerrard Slye. Slye's malevolence toward the three young sons of William Watts produced testimony that the three Watts boys "have noe manner of Cloathes but such Raggs and old Clouts that scarce would cover their nakedness" and that they "were sadly beaten and abused by the overseer as tyed up by the hands and whipt." The Maryland judge before whom their case came found that the boys "have not the Common Care . . . as is usual for planters to have of their meanest Serv[an]ts or Slaves." Two years later, the boys finally were transferred to their grandfather's care, having the rare good fortune of an elderly relative to look out for their interests.[3]

Virginia and Maryland authorities understood well that the prevalence of parental death imposed an obligation to monitor the ethical administration of property inherited by minors. County courts regularly convened special sessions known as orphans courts. Guardians had to account to these courts for how they had handled the property of the children for whom they were responsible. The jurisdiction of these inquiries extended to mothers whose husbands had died because the children's property could be siphoned off by unscrupulous stepfathers. Fathers also sought to look out for their children's economic interests by placing livestock in their children's names at their birth, and there is also evidence of attempts to accelerate the age at which children could exercise independent control of their property. By contrast, some fathers in New England, anticipating living into old age, delayed the distribution of property well into their sons' adulthood.

Taken as a whole, the demography of family life looked quite different in the Chesapeake than in New England. Nonetheless, there were parts of the Northeastern colonies that, especially at first, resembled Southern colonies in some ways. Commercial fishing ports such as Gloucester and Marblehead in Massachusetts housed large numbers of unattached male immigrants and a rowdy culture that was at once more egalitarian and tolerant than agrarian, closed, and pious villages like Dedham and Andover. Meanwhile, towns in the Connecticut River valley in the seventeenth century quickly developed a commercial orientation marked by pronounced economic hierarchy. This commercial frontier attracted the poor and landless in greater numbers, further reminding us that underneath the term "New England" lay a diversity of social experiences, varying across space and time.

Indeed, New England was home to two of colonial America's most significant cities, Boston and Newport, Rhode Island, which over time posed their own challenges to the maintenance of families and to the quality of women's lives. Evidence from the eighteenth century indicates that male casualties in wars against French Canada, disease, and the dangers of maritime professions skewed sex ratios in New England's seaports. Male deaths through military and maritime service tilted female-male sex ratios in Boston and Newport. Boston became a magnet for unmarried women, widows and those who never married, with a quarter of that city's households in the 1760s headed by women. Women were much more likely to fall into poverty in New England's urban ports and become dependent on public charity. Fifteen percent of Boston's female-headed households were too poor to pay any taxes according to data generated in the wake of Boston's Great Fire of 1760. Female poor were more likely than men to be warned out of New England towns—that is, denied public aid on the assumption that responsibility for the poor lay with a person's town of origin. This trend reflects the fact that upon marriage, women were more likely to relocate to their husband's hometown than vice versa and a fear among officials that they would be liable to support poor women's dependent children.

In both New England and the Chesapeake, the goal was to make families the location that absorbed as many social and material functions as possible, as well as to serve as the conduit through which public authority flowed. The stability of families in New England combined with a Puritan orientation allowed families to function as a school, a business, a provider of welfare, as well as a place of discipline and moral regulation. A marriage was a contract freely entered into by a woman and a man, but once acknowledged and consummated, the wife entered a "reverend subjection in all lawful things to her husband," any property she owned and any wealth she generated subsumed under his. Children, too, were subject to their parents, with the conventional wisdom in seventeenth-century New England that a child's natural willfulness should be stifled without compromise. The Plymouth minister John Robinson insisted that a child's "stubbornness . . . must, in the first place, be broke and beaten down; that so the foundation of their education being laid in humility and tractableness, other virtues may, in their time, be built thereon."[4] The Puritan father, moreover, was to function as a substitute parent to servants—both in terms of discipline and obligation. Thus, the home was supposed to be the essential place to teach literacy, religious devotion, and respect for the law. Living singly, outside the supervision of a properly constituted household, was a violation of the law in more than one New England colony; when heads of households failed to supervise adequately their servants, even for sexual transgressions, these men could be criticized or even fined by the courts.

Demographic conditions made it almost impossible for early Virginians to consistently maintain households of the kind envisioned by custom and enforced by law in New England. Two men sometimes set up households, other times two men and a woman would comprise a household. As a consequence, colonial authorities in the Chesapeake were far less willing to rely on household heads to act as a first line of moral defense. Meanwhile, women enjoyed considerable leverage within and between marriages due to their scarcity as well as the wealth they commanded as widows in possession of significant bequests from their deceased husbands. Within the context of demographic misery, women could choose among suitors and exercise considerable influence in complex and sometimes transitory households where their biological and emotional connection to the children often outstripped that of the male head of household. That said, males in the Chesapeake aspired to occupy a patriarchal role in their homes and society at large, shaping the law to assist them in their quest for wealth and authority. In a society where the command of labor generated wealth, the legal classification of black women but not white women as tithables—counted in calculating a household's taxes—served a dual purpose. This classification helped to identify a degraded class of workers, while at the same time white wives and daughters laboring in the field produced profits without imposing additional taxes on the household. Meanwhile, laws that attached the status of a black slave mother to her offspring ensured that the control of a black woman's labor would continue to pay her master dividends even after death.

The disastrous demography of the West Indies amplified and extended the difficulties experienced in the Chesapeake while also underscoring the special characteristics of New England's growth and stability. The basic math of Jamaica ensured that population growth and stable families for whites were a steep uphill struggle. As in the early Chesapeake, white adult males dramatically outnumbered females in the early years of English colonization on Jamaica. Deaths outpaced births by a 2 to 1 ratio. As in the early decades of the Chesapeake, white marriages lasted approximately seven years before one spouse died, with the prevalence of death-shortened marriages growing worse not better over time. These marriages produced few children, and those children suffered extremely high death rates. Couples bearing more than one surviving child were the exception not the rule; many marriages produced no children at all. As in the seventeenth-century Chesapeake, most children would not grow to adulthood with both their parents alive. The culprits for this awful record of family formation, family growth, and family continuity even among the privileged white minority included a major earthquake, exposure to French attacks, and the debilitating presence of malaria and yellow fever.

A robust migration to this remarkably unhealthy climate did little to shore up growth or create a social structure in which families served as effective institutions of moral supervision. The ratio of white migrants to population increase from 1700 to 1750 in Jamaica might have been as bad as 10 to 1, meaning for every ten people who arrived during that period the population only increased by one over the long haul. Constant exposure to death contributed to callous live-for-today and take-the-money-and-sail-back-to-England mentalities.

The incredible wealth generated by the sugar colonies undermined the possibility of natural population growth for whites and blacks. The rapid emergence of large plantations worked by an enslaved black majority doomed any prospect of a society based on small family farms. Brutal conditions of sugar production wreaked havoc on the slave population. White men frequently took advantage of their dominant status to sexually exploit women from the black majority. The prevalent enjoyment of concubines by white men further eroded white population growth and made the formation of a stable family structure for either race that much more difficult. The slave societies of the Chesapeake, and even more so South Carolina, featured some of these same attributes, but not to the same extremes. The mainland colonies, moreover, eventually emerged from their prolonged demographic instability in a way that eighteenth-century Jamaica never did. As we have seen, New England was not immune to pressure on families either. But the social problems born of urbanization and land scarcity in certain long-settled regions were a product of their demographic advantages rather than their shortcomings. English colonization produced a range of demographic patterns and outcomes set in part by patterns of migration and values, but as much or more by varied economic and ecological conditions in the Americas.

GENDERED DIVISIONS WITHIN THE HOUSEHOLD

For colonial women and men, the boundaries between home and work were porous. Just as a kitchen or sitting room often also served as a bedroom, and just as sexual activities were subject to legal regulation, where a person's work life ended and family life began would have been difficult to determine for free people and for many of the people held in bondage as well. For the god-fearing and churchgoing, Sunday's Sabbath routine of church attendance marked a time apart within the week. But on other days, the relentless duties of sustaining the households and, to varying degrees, producing a surplus for exchange occupied the lives of all but the very youngest European and African colonists.

In the tobacco colonies, particularly in the formative decades prior to the take-off of slavery, the distinction between male and female work was often modest. The preference for and prevalence of male labor meant that men dominated tobacco production, but the demanding plant and the attraction of riches created incentives for male household heads to send female indentured servants, wives, and daughters into the field as well.

As a stable gentry class emerged whose wealth was girded by slave labor, elite white women withdrew from the fields entirely, while elite white men's work roles became supervisory—either directly over slaves or over overseers hired to manage the slaves. The plantation mistress, and her husband as well, shifted their focus to consumption and hospitality. Even in white households with few or no slaves, white women sought to withdraw from the fields and to define themselves in terms of domestic chores and talents rather than agricultural ones. A white woman who could cook, sew, churn butter, and press cider brought great value to the household, while the less time she spent in the tobacco field the less she would be associated with the degradations of slavery.

What it meant to mother, as well as what it meant to work, marked the boundaries of race and class in the Southern colonies. For the wealthy plantation mistress, nursing the children could be outsourced to slave wet-nurses, but cruelly, black mothers working in the field could not expect their masters to allow them time to nurse their own infants. Perhaps as part of an ongoing effort to distinguish their own society from that of the slaves among whom they lived, gentry families emphasized child-rearing and education, with the warm, affectionate mother leavening the colder, more authoritarian father.

For white people of all classes in the Chesapeake, education was a means of preparing boys and girls for the status they hoped to attain or retain. Thus, though there would be some overlap between male and female education in terms of basic literacy skills, girls were apprenticed to gain household skills like spinning, while poorer boys' apprenticeships emphasized a future trade like cooper and also included some basic mathematical skills thought unnecessary for girls. White parents who lacked substantial landholdings apprenticed their children to learn trades, so that their offspring would not be reduced to becoming agricultural laborers. The wealthier the family, the more elaborate the sons' education was likely to be, sometimes in preparation for overseas education or a career in law. A daughter's education, even in elite homes, was not likely to be as intense or to extend to as many academic subjects.

Slaves were overwhelmingly agricultural workers, male and female. That said, in South Carolina, where slaves comprised a majority of the population, an artisanal class of slaves developed earlier and more extensively than in the Chesapeake. Much higher percentages of men than women entered the skilled workforce, as some slave men developed expertise as carpenters, blacksmiths, and rivermen operating boats on the Southern colonies' many navigable waterways. Although from the 1740s forward, more black artisans appeared in Virginia, the presence of white workers in the Chesapeake made skilled black workers less dominant. The concentration of male and female slaves in menial and field work was a further way in which gender, race, and social class hierarchies reinforced each other in the colonial South.

Although less oriented toward staple commodity production and less dependent on slave labor, Northern households had distinctive ways of dividing household labor and economic roles, as well as providing formal and informal education to their children. A certain amount of continuity defined the New England household, but there, too, subtle changes developed over time. Prior to 1670, when the economy in subsistence-oriented agricultural towns was relatively simple, women and men were more likely to work together in the fields. The patriarchal structure of the New England family, with its emphasis on male economic authority and female reproduction, offered the flexibility to accommodate female production and initiative in certain circumstances. A wife was quite literally a *deputy husband*, prepared to conduct the family's business should her husband be absent for any reason and to contribute to the overall economic stability of the household in as many different ways as possible.

The most conventional division of labor between men and women was between farm fields and the area immediately surrounding the home. With a steady string of children to look after and to nurse, a married woman's mobility was limited. This necessity was also a virtue—as the immediate household environs contained many essential jobs. In our own kitchens, we take for granted that with a touch of a button or the turn of a dial we can generate the heat necessary to cook our food and warm our homes. Tending the open hearth fires used to cook food and heat homes was an essential and ongoing task. So, too, was keeping toddlers from entering these same fireplaces. Other tasks in and around the house included laundering, sewing, and ironing. Moving into the yard, there was gardening and, at the appropriate times of year, making cider and slaughtering smaller animals, as well as making butter and cheese from the cows women milked themselves. Since every household did not produce every possible food ingredient, women who lived in towns, especially coastal ones such as Salem, might spend a certain amount of time trading for sugar or spices, cheese or eggs. Bartering required knowing the value of things, knowing who had what, and maintaining good relationships. Women on the frontier gathered fruits and fish to maintain the family's nutrition.

A combination of physical strength and gendered custom separated male and female work. The use of oxen in plowing, clearing, and hauling made this work for adult men, while the use of heavy scythes for mowing also helped restrict this sort of work to men. But the corn harvest brought together men and women for picking and husking. Women joined male youths in these tasks as well as weeding and hoeing. Yet males reserved certain tasks such as leatherworking and shoemaking for themselves, as well as various house-building responsibilities and the transporting of grain. Women were expected to be in and around the home, their work vital to sustaining the household. Perhaps that is why one business enterprise in which it was not uncommon to find women in New England and the Chesapeake was tavern-keeping. In such a capacity, business came to women as opposed to women going abroad to transact business. Midwives constituted a dramatic exception. From the early years of colonial settlement, men and women recognized the essential expertise of midwives to the birthing process, compensated midwives for their services, and assumed that these women were ready to travel to see their clients.

As New England's economy developed, women's economic roles became more elaborate as well. Husbands who traveled—fishermen, sea captains, politicians, merchants, and the like—or who operated shops or engaged in long-distance trade needed to be able to count on their wives to pay bills, collect debts, and keep business and the farm functioning. Widows sometimes took over their deceased husbands' retail shops. Women also developed their own wage-earning and profit-generating home skills as New England moved past its initial phase of colonial settlement and growth.

The changing distribution of those quintessential tools of home production—the spinning wheel and the loom—underscores the shifting nature of household economic strategies. Spinning wheels were fairly common in New England households by 1700; in coastal Essex County, Massachusetts, about half the families may have owned spinning wheels, while in western Hampshire County, Massachusetts, over 60 percent did. Spinning wheels allowed families to turn flax or wool into thread. To turn thread into clothing, however, required a loom. And those were in short supply in homes at the beginning of the eighteenth century, meaning that households had to bring their thread to male weavers in order to produce finished cloth. Though there would continue to be far more spinning wheels than looms, an increasing number of families over the course of the eighteenth century appear to have acquired looms as well. In other words, increasing numbers of daughters and wives were now producing their own clothes. Families who deployed female labor in this way were not trying to cut down on the amount of money they spent on manufactured goods, but rather sought to save money for the ever-widening array of purchases that they could make as British imports began to pour into the colonies, not least among them sugar and tea. While women's presence in the wage-labor force of New England during the colonial era would only belatedly surpass 10 percent, some women did weave for cash or even learn tailoring. And at any rate, the entry of women into weaving suggests the flexibility within the gendered organization of labor, while underscoring the critical role of women in shaping and reshaping household strategies of production and consumption.

The structure of formal education also reflected the gendered nature of opportunity and the limitations on sexual equality. Women opened local schools, known as *dame schools*, to teach young children, emphasizing basic literacy skills and collecting much lower fees than the male schoolmasters who taught older children. Learning to read was essential to Puritans, whose devotional practices centered on reading the Bible and other religious texts. Yet, as in the Chesapeake, female education often stopped well short of male education; girls in New England learned to read, but not always to write. A 1647 Massachusetts law required the funding of teachers in towns of at least fifty families; towns of one hundred families had to have schools for boys who might go to Harvard. None of colonial America's nine colleges admitted females, ensuring that ministers, advanced teachers, and other professionals would continue to be men.

While only the tiniest minority of children in New England, male as well as female, experienced a college education, virtually all of them learned what it meant to work very early on in life. Household labor meant just that—everyone except the youngest was employed in some household or farm task. Farm families depended on their children as workers to help weed gardens, drive away crows, round up pigs, milk, and churn. As such, children who remained at home literally and figuratively followed in their parents' footsteps. Other children were apprenticed as young as six or seven.

Rather than recruiting large numbers of indentured servants from England or purchasing large numbers of slaves from Africa, New Englanders employed their considerable population of sons and daughters in wage work. Teenage girls frequently served stints in or performed chores for neighboring families, while boys hired themselves out for agricultural work such as hoeing and fence-making. Whether serving a wealthy master for a long period of time or a more ordinary farming family for a shorter period, servant girls supplemented their families' incomes and advanced their knowledge of housewifery. Beyond that, such service further inculcated the lessons of respectful subordination and the duty to serve that were part of female life in colonial New England. And throughout the colonial period, the vast majority of women worked within the home rather than for wages, even when wars against the French and their Indian allies called more and more men away to military service.

Precisely how a woman served her family, her community, or even her colony could be dramatically flexible—as the case of Hannah Duston demonstrates. A week after giving birth to her eighth child in March 1697, Indians descended on Duston's Haverhill, Massachusetts, home. Her husband managed to lead the older children to safety, but Duston, her attendant Mary Neff, and her baby were not so fortunate. The Indians took the two women captive, but, as Cotton Mather recounted the story, they "dash'd out the Brains of the *Infant*, against a Tree. . . ." Other English captives suffered similar fates as they, Duston, and Neff marched deeper into the wilderness. Several weeks and many miles later, Duston seized her opportunity for freedom—and for revenge. Shortly before dawn, she realized that the Indian family into whose custody she had fallen, two men, three women, and seven children, were all asleep. With the help of Neff and another English captive, Duston slaughtered ten of the Indians with hatchets; only one of the Indian women and one of the children escaped with their lives. Before departing, Duston and her accomplices scalped the dead. The Massachusetts legislature rewarded them with £50. They were further honored with a sermon preached by Cotton Mather, in which he exhorted the heroes to embrace the Lord, or "*Unhumbled* . . . you will be the Slaves of *Devils*" rather than the Indians.[5] Meanwhile, their fame spread at least as far as Maryland, whose governor "sent 'em a very generous token of his favour," according to Mather.[6]

Her fellow colonists did not denounce Duston's conduct as unwomanly; what she did was unusual but not transgressive. In acting as she did, she not only summoned her strength, she also registered her understanding of the racial and economic codes of her people. Thus, she scalped her dead former captors—who, she reported, had further debased themselves by praying in the manner of French Catholics—as proof of her deeds and in anticipation of a reward. And still, since she had not sought formal membership in the Puritan church, Mather, in celebrating her, reminded Duston of her personal failings. Those failings did not stem from her use of violence to seek manly retribution, but from the precarious state of her unconverted soul. Hannah Duston, mother of eight, was a hero, but not yet a saint.

There is even more to Duston's remarkable saga. Duston's sister Elizabeth Emerson had been convicted in 1693 of murdering her own infant twins, born out of wedlock. Of the very small number of people executed for murder in Massachusetts from 1630 to 1692, three others had been mothers convicted of infanticide. A woman who refused to be a mother, and was willing to kill, shattered the confines of gender and humanity. A woman who slaughtered and scalped the children of her captors did neither. Violence could be heroic or it could be deviant. As with love and desire, to determine the meaning of Hannah and her sister's violence, context was the key.

DESIRES AND DEVIANCE

Puritan poet Anne Bradstreet wrote of her husband Simon:

> My love is such that rivers cannot quench,
> Nor ought but love from thee, give recompense.

In another poem addressed to Simon, absent on business, Anne rhymed:

> My chilled limbs now numbed lie forlorn;
> Return, return, sweet Sol, from Capricorn;
> In this dead time, alas, what can I more
> Than view those fruits which through thy heat I bore?[7]

Bradstreet, one of the Massachusetts Bay colony's early English settlers, was exceptional for her literary gifts; but she surely was not alone in incorporating sexual desire into her self-understanding. Her children, she noted, were the product of sexual heat provided by a husband, whom she likened to the sun itself, in whose absence she became listlessly chilled. Puritans, like other Englishmen, believed women to be deeply passionate and even excessively vulnerable to desire; Puritans, in particular, also believed that excessive passion might tempt women (and men also) away from the godly path. Yet, within the confines of colonial societies organized, however precariously, around the heterosexual household, there were far more complicated and more socially threatening expressions of earthly physical desire than a woman's intense attraction to her own husband.

In matters of sex as in so many other areas of life, there is a tendency to assume facilely that our own progressive freedoms (or our own moral laxity) separate us distinctly from the past. But just as a variety of sexual desire is hardly new to our own times, the translation of some of those desires into action aroused controversy and provoked legal intervention in the colonial era. A willingness to be flexible sometimes jockeyed with the impulse to police what was deemed unhealthy and immoral sexual behavior, especially when men and women sought sexual satisfaction outside the marital bed. The assumption of humanity's carnal nature and the close quarters in which men and women lived made supervision of sexuality particularly necessary in the eyes of Puritans and other colonists. Sexual transgression, whether consensual or coerced, peppered colonial court records.

Sexual intercourse outside the boundaries of marriage carried with it both moral and material danger, but not all such transgressions were equal, nor sanctions against them equally applied. Fornication—sex between two unmarried people—might provoke public whipping, but adultery—sex between a married woman and someone other than her husband—was a capital offense in New England. Rape, too, was a capital offense, though viewed to be a much greater offense against a married woman than a single woman or a child. The allegedly strong sexual impulses of women made courts wary of reaching rape convictions even when a girl had not reached adolescence. Meanwhile, the aggressive masculinity of the Chesapeake gentry practically endorsed the notion that women, particularly lower-class whites and black slaves, who allowed themselves to be in the presence of men alone were making themselves sexually available. William Byrd II, the wealthy Virginia planter who recorded his surveying party's experience along the dividing line with North Carolina, indicates that this group of white men took liberties with black, Indian, and white women they encountered along the way. In any event, one of the clear aims of laws supervising sexual behavior was to preserve the exclusive sexual rights of husbands, who were in some sense, treated as the real victims of sexual crimes involving their wives. Even so, actual convictions for adultery were quite rare, lesser charges that did not precipitate the death penalty being easier to prove and less unsettling to enforce. If husbands had an interest in exclusive sexual access to wives, the community more generally had an interest in children not being born out of wedlock and becoming a public burden. Hence premarital sex, though hardly encouraged, was leniently regarded by authorities so long as the couples in question married.

Laws supervising sexuality tended to be enforced more harshly against women than against men, reflecting societal prejudices and power structures, but there were also distinctive regional patterns to enforcement. The Chesapeake's judges and lawmakers showed themselves to be much more committed to punishing crimes against property than actions deemed at odds with the moral, religious, and sexual norms of society. The Chesapeake colonies in their formative decades could not count on stable households as a bulwark of morality and authority; the New England colonies were predicated on the existence and perpetuation of just such households. Theft by unruly servants cut to the heart of the Chesapeake enterprise, lapses in personal moral conduct did so in New England. Not surprisingly, New Englanders not actually party to a violation such as fornication were more likely than Southerners to report such a crime. In the Chesapeake, crime victims themselves sued to receive justice for what the alleged perpetrator had taken from or done to them.

Attitudes toward transgressions not involving consensual sex between a man and a woman expressed a mix of severe punishment and pragmatism. The only sex-related execution in the history of the Plymouth colony was of a seventeen-year-old who repeatedly had sex with barnyard animals; in this case, the Pilgrim colony's authorities followed the biblical prescription of capital punishment. In a later case, a man convicted of attempting to have sex with a mare found himself branded with a "P" for "pollution" and exiled from the colony.

Homosexuality, while not embraced as acceptable, was also not prosecuted to the full extent of the law. In early Plymouth, one man was whipped and another whipped and branded for sodomy. Plymouth's lack of a royal charter made officials there extremely cautious about implementing the death penalty, while, as we have seen with adultery, authorities sometimes preferred to prosecute attempted rather than consummated violations, as the former did not lead to the death sentence. Moreover, because capital crimes required two witnesses for each purported incident, it was much easier to produce a conviction for attempted rather than actual sodomy. Thus, there were as few as two or three executions for sodomy in the entire history of colonial New England.

Beyond the difficulty of proof, the case of Nicholas Sension of Windsor, Connecticut, suggests that even if religious and secular authorities viewed sex between men as a serious religious and legal violation, communities might be more tolerant in certain situations. Sension, who arrived in Windsor in the 1640s, acquired a reputation for making sexual overtures to other men long before he faced the province's General Court for alleged sodomy in 1677. Even when finally convicted of attempted sodomy, Sension's punishment did not bring a whipping or a fine on this well-to-do man, but rather a promise of future good behavior secured by a bond on his estate. In the mid-eighteenth century, New London, Connecticut, Baptist minister Stephen Gorton's long history of acting on his attraction to men eventually led to a temporary suspension from his pulpit, but not a permanent ban. In the very few identified cases of authorities in New England prosecuting lesbianism, the accused were not brought up on charges of sodomy, but rather for lewd conduct that carried far less grave penalties. Even if the Virginia case of Thomasine Hall was provoked by the hint of a sexual relationship with a neighboring woman, Hall's ultimate punishment of a mixed dress code had little to do with sexual transgression as such. While none of this is evidence of unencumbered tolerance, these cases indicate some distance between official pronouncements against homosexuality and how actual communities responded to such conduct.

While New England's ministers inveighed against sodomy in their sermons, other colonial regions showed little appetite for either denouncing or prosecuting the practice. Living in a busy, cosmopolitan seaport, Philadelphians were aware of homoerotic subcultures in Europe as well as the increased legal crackdown against sodomy in Europe. Yet Philadelphia did not follow the European lead, and homoerotic literature imported from Europe was widely available there. The Quaker province's religious toleration, lack of a state church, and tremendous diversity may have protected homosexuals from burdensome scrutiny, let alone prosecution.

The meaning of sexual deviance in colonial America was neither uniform across space nor fixed across time, reflecting the prevailing power arrangements as well as the structure of religious authority. In the Southern colonies, even before African slavery became a pervasive institution, property interests shaped definitions of transgression and churches had difficulty extending their authority as fast and as far as colonial populations dispersed. Colonists often defined marriage on their own terms. Since servants could not marry without their masters' assent, sexual relations among many young adults ended up being illegal by definition. In the Carolinas and the Chesapeake, couples often did not rely on secular or religious authorities to sanction officially their marriages or divorces, making many relationships technically fornication or adultery and many births illegitimate. Clergymen and courts in many places played a game of catch-up, sanctioning unions already formed according to popular custom. In New England, where marriage was a civil rather than religious act, the lattice of town governments and church congregations was in a much better position both to back up and shape popular conceptions of sexual probity.

Yet even in the heart of New England, the manner in which sexual transgressions were handled by authorities and understood by ordinary people underwent changes by the eighteenth century. Authorities substituted monetary fines for public whipping. Meanwhile, male fornication increasingly went unprosecuted, women bearing the brunt of the law's force. Since the primary evidence of fornication was the child born out of wedlock, the law could easily identify women's culpability. Although these mothers were often pressed to name the father, courts could accept the accused father's denial sometimes based on the counter-accusation of the mother's reputation for loose morals. As a stunning case from Pomfret, Connecticut, in the mid-1740s revealed, women were far more likely to suffer the negative consequences of illicit sex than men. Sarah Grosvenor, age nineteen, became pregnant by Amasa Sessions, age twenty-seven. At the prompting of Amasa, Sarah began taking a powder that they believed would terminate the pregnancy. Amasa had obtained the abortifacient from John Hallowell, who had cultivated a reputation as a medical doctor, though he had no real training. The medicine failing to achieve its purpose, Hallowell performed an operation that induced a miscarriage, but also led to complications causing Sarah's death. Covered up by Sarah's peers for years, the events eventually did lead to a trial and conviction of Hallowell, who fled to Rhode Island before receiving a sentence that was to include twenty-nine lashes, but Sessions was acquitted of any wrong-doing. Married to another woman between the time of Grosvenor's death and the trial, he lived out his life as a respected member of the community; the price he paid for his sexual transgression and its tragic aftermath was incomparable to that paid by his one-time lover Sarah Grosvenor.

If white women were vulnerable to sexual double standards, then enslaved and racially stigmatized women of African descent were that much more so. Wherever ethnic or racial groups have lived at close quarters with one another in American history, men and women have sought sexual partners outside their own group—and where there is sex, there are children. Such cross-racial expressions of desire were deviant because the law made them so—with the law and, in at least some cases, the sex reflecting profound inequalities of power. Indeed, in the Chesapeake's evolution toward becoming a slave society, the ways in which lawmakers coded some sexual relationships as punishable and some not played a critical role in cementing race and gender as cornerstones of power. Thus, a body of law developed in Virginia that criminalized sex between black men and white women and deemed the offspring of black women, slave or free, as illegitimate. The same 1662 law declaring that the condition of slavery passed from mother to child also mandated that those guilty of fornication by a white person and a black person would pay twice the fine as those guilty of fornication between two white people. The most likely people to be punished by such a provision were white women who gave birth to darker-skinned children; a child born to a slave impregnated by her master would not likely come to the attention of colonial authorities. Almost thirty years later, as the importation of slaves surged, lawmakers upped the ante against interracial sex, expelling from the colony any white person who married a black, mulatto, or Indian, while imposing a period of thirty years of servitude on the nominally free non-white bastard offspring of any white woman. This law produced an upsurge of prosecutions of white female servants for interracial sexual transgressions. By defining such sex as deviant, white men granted themselves a legal monopoly over white women.

Such definitions of sexual deviance thus enhanced white male power, largely succeeding in constructing a society in which racial identity organized the legal, political, and economic hierarchy. Anyone identifiable as being even of partially African descent was presumed to be a slave, permanently affixed to the broad base of the social pyramid. Anyone who could claim exclusively European ancestry was presumed free and sharing at least some interests with all other whites, no matter how lowly or exalted. But these statutes never eliminated sex across the color line, or the efforts of mothers of free black children to protect their offspring from the ever-present danger of slipping into slavery during the punitively long period in which illegitimate mixed-race children were bound out for service. Free black women whose children were apprenticed attempted to ensure that local authorities understood that such indentures were not permanent.

The struggling French colony of Louisiana, which included the Mississippi River valley from New Orleans all the way north to present-day Illinois, wrestled with defining and enforcing rules for sexual behavior. Like the English Chesapeake and West Indies, single men dominated the European population. To the chagrin of Catholic missionaries, French men took advantage of the trade in female Indian slaves to keep concubines. Sometimes these relationships evolved into formal marriages. Based on the experience in Canada, French officials also hoped that sexual exchange and marriage between French traders and native women might cement fur trading relationships with neighboring Indian nations. But only certain nations, notably the Illinois, showed an interest in intermarriage as a means to facilitate commerce. In time, French secular and religious officials worried that French-Indian marriage, as well as sex, might undermine rather than extend French culture. Authorities took steps in 1728 to limit the property rights and control over the children's education of Indian women widowed by the death of French husbands.

Efforts to import females from France to stabilize the colony's social structure produced mixed results at best. Nuns successfully established a school for girls in New Orleans in 1727, contributing to the effort to introduce European mores through the refining influence of women. Still, imbalanced sex ratios, ingrained patterns of sexual promiscuity, continued exploitation of non-European women, and a Catholic clergy that commanded little respect made imposing sexual and moral order on the French population difficult.

In contrast to the ambivalence over intermarriage with Indians, French authorities quickly moved against black-white sexual relations. Slave importations in the early seventeenth century led the black population to surpass the white population by the mid-1720s. The 1724 Code Noir, adapted from the slave code in the French Caribbean colony of Sainte-Domingue, prohibited any white settler from marrying a black person, whether slave or free. A master who had children with a slave mistress was to be fined and to lose the services of the slave and her children, though they would not receive their freedom. The desire to draw clear racial lines between laboring, subordinate black slaves and a master caste of whites led the French to define interracial sex in lower Louisiana along West Indian rather than Canadian lines. Despite such provisions, a mulatto population emerged in this French outpost as it did elsewhere in colonial North America, physical attraction and the desire to take sexual advantage of inequality trumping the law.

In the English colonies of the North, all of which developed slave codes to police their small but not insignificant slave populations, sexual taboos and interracial transgressions coexisted. Court records contain a variety of cases of black women punished for delivering bastards. In 1742 a Connecticut man won a divorce based on his wife giving birth to a black child. Massachusetts in the early eighteenth century passed legislation designed to forestall "spurious and mix't issue"—threatening public whipping for black men and their white female sexual partners, with the black man "sold out of the province" thereafter. The same law also outlawed sex between white men and black women, with whipping for both parties and transportation out of the colony for the women.[8]

A particularly dramatic example of the public safety concerns swirling around interracial sex in the North came from New York. The sexual relationship between Caesar and Irish prostitute Margaret Kerry, who had a child by Caesar, symbolized for New York City authorities the interracial disorder that gave rise to the alleged

Great Negro Plot of 1741 hatched in John Hughson's Manhattan tavern. The most lurid versions of the conspiracy narrative that emerged from the investigation told of the black plotters slashing the throats of their white masters and taking their victims' wives for themselves. The thin line between actual interracial sex and the projection of a sexually violent race war was clearly not an anxiety unique to the colonial South. Meanwhile, the peculiar logic of racial slavery ensured that acts of sexual desire involving at least one black party would be classified as deviant and dangerous, when it served white authorities to do so.

OPPORTUNITIES AND LIMITS FOR WOMEN

Like slaves, white women in the colonies lived in a world bounded by custom and law, though it cannot be said that, like free blacks, they clung to the margins of society, or like slaves, that white women formed a vast class at the base of the social pyramid. But like slaves, white women contested and negotiated their status in ways that helped define the very nature of colonial society, seizing opportunities for informal power and seeking out spaces where women held sway. Negotiations over gender took place between women and men of every class and in every colony, within households, in communities, and even in the courtroom. Amid the diversity of these negotiations, one would be hard pressed to draw a uniform picture of progress from oppression to liberation or the reverse.

While the dominant patterns for assigning legal and moral authority in the colonial setting were adapted from mainstream English patriarchal models, some colonists forged crucial alternatives. In Dutch New Netherland, married women's property rights and ability to do business on their own account stood out in sharp distinction from English practice. Thus, the history of New Amsterdam contains striking examples of female economic autonomy. Dutch women kept their own last names at marriage, did business under their own names, and wrote wills with their husbands that made husband and wife joint owners of property so that should the husband die first, the widow controlled all the couple's property. Margaret Hardenbroeck, a Dutch émigré to New Netherland in the late 1650s, amassed a shipping fortune with successive husbands. When the English seized control of Manhattan and transformed the Dutch colony into New York, English law and custom eroded the tradition of egalitarian Dutch approaches to female property. As English law replaced Dutch law and Dutch elites married into English families and Anglicized their cultural practices, Dutch-style marital property arrangements became a fading memory.

The emergence of strong Quaker communities, particularly in the mid-Atlantic colonies, demonstrated the efficacy of alternative structures of gendered power in colonial America. In particular, the Quakers' separate female worship meetings allowed Quaker women to develop their own tradition of female preaching and speaking out on matters of faith. Unlike most other Christians, Quakers did not impose the notion of Eve's original sin on women, carving out more space for a positive female identity. Such a worldview had a secular impact as well;

female Quakers exercised their own authority over certain aspects of communal welfare, such as the approval of marriage partners and the distribution of relief to needy members of the community. Spinsterhood also was burdened with less prejudice in Quaker communities. More broadly, the priority of Quaker communities placed on marrying within the sect, their provision of land grants to young couples who did so, and their emphasis on nurturing Quaker beliefs in children gave women important responsibilities in sustaining the Friends' distinctive sense of community.

While the Dutch and Quaker example may appear to be exceptions that proved the rule, women in other parts of English North America found ways to exercise authority in particular spheres and even to push back against formal structures of male authority. The most thoroughly feminized sphere in colonial society was childbirth. Female midwives delivered the overwhelming number of babies; male doctors were few and far between and only rarely attempted to exercise their dubious expertise in the matter of bringing new life successfully into the world. Instead, local women of acknowledged skill and reputation presided over in-home births. In the town-based communities of New England, the excruciating pain of delivery was hardly a solitary affair, and a woman giving birth for the first time would be familiar with the process. Female relatives and neighbors gathered to lend material and moral support during these frequent scenes. The midwife herself likely was a person well known to the women in attendance, whose technical expertise was an important part of her rapport with her clients.

Midwives also served as a contact point between spheres of formal male authority and informal female authority. In cases of unwed mothers, midwives were in a unique position to extract confessions of paternity, a crucial part of not only enforcing moral sanctions against bastardry but also ensuring that fathers assumed financial responsibility for newborns. Legal authorities assigned midwives and other women the grim task of investigating charges of infanticide, questioning suspects and detecting signs of trauma to the dead infants' bodies. Thus, as was initially the case with Thomasine Hall, men conceded that there were certain bodily intimate matters in which a government of men had an interest but in which women were more capable, appropriate, and authoritative.

As the case of Alice Tilly reveals, the reliance of birthing mothers on a trusted midwife could even provoke women to challenge male legal authorities. In 1649 midwife Tilly found herself imprisoned in Boston in order to stand trial, charged with being responsible for the deaths of newborns and mothers. Both prior to and following Tilly's conviction, the Massachusetts General Court received written petitions on the midwife's behalf. Two hundred and seventeen women, many of whom signed more than one petition, questioned the charges and sought to persuade the authorities to allow Tilly to deliver children. Most of the women were of childbearing age. One petition labeled her "a woeman of singular use... and wee bless the Lord for her life and for the experience wee have had of her...." while another referred to "the present need tht some of us have of her" and a desire not "to putt our selves into the hands of any besides our midwife tht wee haue had experience of. . . ."[9] Despite displeasure expressed by the General Court at this encroachment on their legal prerogatives, it appears that they relented to these requests. The Tilly case is in many respects exceptional, but nonetheless illustrates the significance of particular midwives in women's lives as well as the existence of a sphere of experience in which women's authority was presumptive.

Another sphere in which women exercised significant power was through gossip. In communities where most of the members were known to each other and in which houses were not designed to promote privacy, reputations could be made or broken by what others said about you. While men as well as women were certainly capable of using what they had observed against one another, colonial women, largely deprived of any political or ecclesiastic power, had to rely on gossip as a means of protecting themselves and exercising power. The spreading of news about sexual irregularities, unwanted advances, fornication, and adultery—and the fear of being implicated in the spreading of such news—was a way of safeguarding women's reputations in the face of potentially predatory male sexual behavior. Crimes against property also might attract the attention of neighbors. A 1655 Kent County, Maryland, hog-stealing case began when Margaret Winchester shared her doubts with others about neighbors who offered her meat even though the family did not own any pigs. Word made its way to a local justice's wife, and the case eventually went to court.

In New England, the fact that women comprised a clear majority of most congregations underscores the centrality of women to the maintenance of Puritan culture while exposing the limits of female power. The Puritans believed in the spiritual equality of the sexes, but literally domesticated the potential radicalism of this belief by channeling women into the role of junior partners within marriage. The same could be said of Puritan churches, where women functioned as a silent majority, subordinated not only to male ministers, but also to the male lay leaders of the congregation. Still, without women serving as exemplars to their children and male relatives, replenishing the church's flock would have been far more difficult. Women influenced the structure of the church in other ways. Outlying precincts of New England towns split off to form new towns organized around new congregations, in part, because women's never-ending responsibility for young children made it difficult to trek too great a distance. Female displeasure with a minister might prove his undoing. When the town of Rowley, Massachusetts, declined to retain Minister Jeremiah Shepard in the early 1670s, he knew whom to blame. By their talk, Goody Elithorp and other townswomen undermined him.

The institution of marriage itself embodied the nature of women's opportunities to exert power over their own lives and the profound limitations of those opportunities. The choice of a marriage partner was in some sense the peak moment of a woman's power. Although marriage was almost inevitable, which man a woman married was not. Thus, the decision to encourage a male suitor or to accept a marriage proposal gave young women significant, if temporary power, while the consequences of that decision for future happiness (or lack thereof) were enormous.

The demographic conditions of New England and the Chesapeake help us to understand further the changing nature of female power. As we have seen, women in Puritan New England almost universally married, a trend that persisted into the eighteenth century. Given the extreme rarity of divorce, the death of one spouse or another was the only likely means of dissolving a marriage. Within marriage, the assumption was that husbands and wives would provide for one another's pleasure, but within a framework of presumed obedience of the wife to her husband. Indeed, a husband's sexual impotence was one of the few grounds for terminating a marriage. Failure to procreate was only part of the reason impotence justified divorce; husbandly duties included the "due benevolence" of sexual pleasure; without such benevolence the household itself might not be stable, with the wife more likely to seek fulfillment outside of marriage. But authority was hardly stacked in favor of women. Violent physical assaults of one spouse on the other were outlawed in Massachusetts, and subsequently in Rhode Island and Plymouth as well. In reality, only extreme cases of abuse were likely to be reported; the male head of household was supposed to be able to regulate everyone under his roof, including his wife, and only when his failure to do so attracted the attention of neighbors and the authorities was the law likely to intervene.

Husbands and wives in New England as well as the Chesapeake did seek to dissolve their marriages, sometimes with success. The Newport, Rhode Island, case of Herodias Long, which played out over two decades in the mid-seventeenth century, illustrates the potential complexities of family life. Herodias's first husband John Hicks abandoned her after being fined for physically abusing her, leaving Herodias destitute. He fled to New Netherland. A decade later governor Peter Stuyvesant granted Hicks's petition for divorce after Hicks presented evidence that his former wife had since taken up with George Gardiner and borne children by him. Herodias, in seeking to dissolve her bonds with Gardiner, explained to authorities that she had come to him originally in desperate straits. Growing unhappy with their arrangement, which was never a legally sanctioned marriage, she sought control of her house and property as well as child support. The Rhode Island Assembly fined both Herodias and Gardiner, a modest punishment given that in the Assembly's words "she had lived all this time in that abominable lust of fornication. . . . " At the same time that Herodias and Gardiner were thus separated, the Assembly also dissolved the bonds between John Porter and his wife Margaret whom he had already abandoned, after John agreed to a financial settlement. Not long afterward, John Porter legally married Herodias.[10] In Virginia, the decision of an unhappy wife to abandon her husband might prompt the posting of a declaration that he would not honor any commercial transaction or credit request made by the estranged spouse in her husband's name. Clearly, law enforcement and morality had ragged edges when it came to love and marriage in the colonial era.

When a woman's marriage ended as a result of the death of her husband, her access to property depended on her husband's will and legal custom. In the seventeenth century, men tended to leave their wives more property and with fewer encumbrances than men did in the eighteenth century. The widow's thirds, a legal requirement that a widow receive at least one-third of her husband's possessions and the use and profit from one-third of his land, was a floor, not a ceiling to what a husband might leave his spouse. New England courts that oversaw the disposition of property when the husband did not leave a will had the power to evaluate the surviving wife's conduct during the marriage when determining her inheritance; in contrast, Chesapeake laws granted no such authority to the courts. Nonetheless, early New England husbands expressed an impressive degree of trust in their wives when writing their wills, especially since three-quarters of women still of childbearing age would remarry, thereby passing control of their first husband's property to a second husband. Such remarrying couples sometimes drafted prenuptial agreements, designed to preserve the property interests of the children from the first marriage. In the eighteenth century, husbands grew far less willing to allow their wives such flexibility, inserting language in wills terminating their wives' right to their widow's thirds upon remarriage to another man. Accounting for this change is difficult. Certainly, the commercial economy of New England grew more complex in the eighteenth century, perhaps creating greater hesitancy to trust women. Meanwhile, more sentimental ideas about love, marriage, and women began to emerge which drew sharper distinctions between male and female personalities that emphasized the emotional side of mothering and deemphasized the ability of female "deputy husbands" to step into male roles as needed.

Free women in the seventeenth-century Chesapeake enjoyed much greater choice, leverage, and economic autonomy than they would in the eighteenth century. The highly imbalanced sex ratios enabled a relatively small number of women to select spouses from a large pool of unmarried or widowed men. Moreover, as we have seen, the high death rates meant that seventeenth-century Chesapeake English women were likely to find themselves widowed and eligible for remarriage with some frequency. While these high death rates surely produced wrenching physical and emotional suffering, it also created a number of property-holding adult women. Husbands in the seventeenth-century Chesapeake tended to provide a more generous inheritance to wives than the minimal requirement of the widow's thirds. Widows not only received additional grants of land, animals, and servants, but also commonly were selected by their husbands to act as the legal executor of the deceased husbands' will. Thus, it fell to surviving wives to oversee their former husbands' assets. Endowed with such responsibility and property, wealthier widows became even more attractive to unmarried men and remarried within a very short time. To protect their property, women sometimes made sure that the property interests of their children were protected prior to remarrying. On the flipside, a woman whose second or third husband died might find herself amassing control over ever more property.

Once again, data from Jamaica help to highlight distinctive mainland patterns. For despite unbalanced sex ratios and demographic instability in the white population, husbands showed far less inclination in their wills than in the Chesapeake to give their widowed wives control over property. Nor did white Jamaican men rush to remarry upon the death of their wives. The Chesapeake widow who controlled her own property might make for an attractive match; the Jamaican widow whose control over property was limited by provisions in her deceased husband's will was less so. Moreover, white Jamaican men, married or single, had ready, unembarrassed sexual access to slave women from the island's majority population. The large sugar plantation economy had from early on carved out little room for white women to make economic contributions to the family and, thus, demographic instability there produced fewer of the opportunities characteristic of the seventeenth-century Chesapeake or even New England.

The emergence of demographic stability and a class hierarchy in the eighteenth-century Chesapeake weakened many women's leverage over property and personal choice, while elite male aspirations for gentility pushed white women closer to the margins of economic production. At the higher reaches of planter society, marriage continued to be a strategy to consolidate wealth and advance social status. Thus, Virginia's wealthiest families wished to create alliances via marriage, with sons of the gentry seeking suitable matches in similarly wealthy families whose daughters would bring with them substantial dowries and social connections. Among Virginia's elite families, a young woman's ability to be flirtatious enough to be pleasing but not to the point of losing her reputation, let alone her virginity, was vital. Still, a young woman's power reached a momentary zenith during courtship, the ability to make or break a young man's ambitions resting in her hands. Once a couple agreed to marry, power rapidly tilted away from the female spouse toward her husband, who by the laws of coverture acquired control of any property she brought to the marriage. Meanwhile, Virginia jurists moved to adhere more strictly to the legal principle that women could not act independently of their husbands in court, restricting the independence of women up and down the social hierarchy.

Chesapeake women found their status slipping in another way—as widowhood less often represented a period of enhanced power. As in New England, the tendency of husbands to leave additional property beyond the required third and to appoint a wife as executor dramatically abated. The presumption of fast remarriage also faded. In a society organized around the egos and the interests of male patriarchs, empowering women at any stage of life was hardly a priority. A 1748 Virginia law that enacted a procedure for widows to reject their husbands' disposition of the estate may have indicated some sympathy for women whose deceased spouses did not entrust them with sufficient property. For enslaved women, any such disputes over the transfer of wealth treated them as property to be fought over, any attachments made to other slaves or even to white mistresses secondary to laws governing slaves and chattels. Slave marriages remained unrecognized by the law and their property rights even to their own bodies were obliterated by the very laws and courts designed to protect the transfer of property from one generation to another.

Women in colonial America were not cloistered, or hidden from public view. Still, William Byrd II's chilling comment in his commonplace book, "A woman shoud not appear out of her house, til she is old enough for people to enquire whose mother she is, and not so young as to have it askt, whose wife she is, or whose daughter," expresses the limited parameters and limited options in which colonial women operated.[11] A woman was a man's wife, a child's mother, a father's daughter, and these roles circumscribed to a profound degree her economic identity while completely denying her a political identity. She might be a good wife, admired for her piety, chastity, generosity, or hospitality, but she was nonetheless a wife, unless she was still living under her father's roof and protection. Few women ever went to the lengths that Hannah Duston did to protect herself, but a woman who went out in public without clearly establishing her ties to male authority was at risk, not from hostile Indians but the negative judgments or even the unrepressed desires of her male peers. Although marriage potentially offered many joys and satisfactions to colonial women, its intimacies were also its travails.

BIRTH, DEATH, AND CULTURE

In July 1766 planter Robert Wormeley Carter, a member of one of Virginia's wealthiest and most well-connected families, recorded these entries in his daybook:

> 7*th*. This day my Wife was delivered of a dead Child, a fine full grown Boy. What occasioned it's [sic] death I can't conceive.
>
> 15*th*. This day I have been married ten years. I have now living two Sons & a Daughter. My Wife has miscarried five times; brought a dead Child, & lost a fine little Boy about 18 months old.

He did not elaborate on the feelings of, or his feelings for, his wife Winifred Travers Beale Carter amid his tally of economic transactions. But the relentless cycle of pregnancies and miscarriages surely must have taken a heavy emotional and physical toll on Winifred Carter. Her seemingly fortuitous marriage hardly could have prepared her for this fate, just as her wealth, status, and privilege could not protect her from its results. Robert Wormeley, who was obviously not an innocent bystander in the conception of these children, could not "conceive" of the cause of such a calamitous sequence of events. Were he a Puritan perhaps, he would have wondered if God were passing some sort of judgment on him and his family, who otherwise lived so grandly, served and sustained by numerous slaves, and, through various marriages, burrowed deeply into the colony's network of powerful planter families. Perhaps he or Winifred wondered just that, but in any case, she could hardly have regarded herself as the mistress of her own fate or even her own body.

For Robert Wormeley Carter, a different, more explicable threat to his family's well-being provoked a more thorough disruption of his terse daybook entries the next month. Conflict between Robert and his father Landon, with whom he frequently argued, threatened to undermine the full enjoyment of his privileged position. Landon apparently looked askance at Robert's gambling habits and the two disagreed over management of the plantation; he even blamed Robert for "his Negroes running away." But Robert resolved to bite his tongue, for his father still controlled the purse strings in the present and through his will. He might even "take away the maids that tended my Children." As much as it pained him, Robert acknowledged to himself, "he is still my Father" and, therefore, he had no choice but to check himself from further antagonisms. While hardly as powerless as his wife, let alone his slaves, Robert was all too keenly aware of all that lay beyond his control.[12]

The colonial worlds of Virginians Thomasine Hall and Robert Wormeley Carter were separated by a vast gulf of time, status, and culture. Their experiences of sexuality, gender, and family life were in many senses profoundly different as well. The solution imposed on Hall by the General Court was the improvisational work of a frontier society where households were inherently unstable, with networks of authority and sociability informal and attenuated. Life, moreover, was short, and the cruelties imposed on the servant Hall may not have seemed too harsh by the standards of that time. A person who did not know his place sexually, morally, or socially had to be marked. The fashion of that marking—the bonnet and apron atop men's clothing—expressed ideas of sex and gender that foreshadowed aspects of the culture that would unfold over the many decades to come. A man incapable of producing offspring, of founding and heading his own household, was far short of a man, even in a world as manifestly unconducive to the stable formation of families as the early Chesapeake. The formation of male-directed households, indeed the perpetuation of male lines, remained a centerpiece of gendered identity for Virginians and many other white Americans throughout the colonial period.

Materially, of course, the plantation society of mid-century Virginia had profoundly transformed itself since Thomasine Hall's day. Life spans had lengthened, a genteel, self-perpetuating elite culture sat atop a well-established social and political hierarchy; even the slave population, despite all the cruelties physical and otherwise of their condition, had achieved the ability to reproduce their own numbers on American soil. And physically, unlike Hall, Carter's masculine sexual potency was manifest through his wife's multiple pregnancies, while his gambling, his access to slave labor, and his planter status were cultural markers of a man making his way through the topmost stratum of a well-established gentry culture. Winifred Carter's sexuality, her gendered role, and her familial status were also clearly established, following a well-worn, taxing path. Yet none of these three Virginians, let alone the Carter family slaves, experienced a mastery of their own fates—biology and culture combining to chart a set of complex roles that defined and confined them.

CHRONOLOGY

c. *1603*	*Thomasine Hall born in northeastern England.*
1607	Virginia colony founded at Jamestown.
1620	Plymouth colony founded.
c. *1627*	*Thomasine Hall emigrates from Plymouth, England, to Virginia.*
1628	*Thomas Hall convicted of receiving stolen goods.*
1629	*Virginia Governor's Council declares Thomasine Hall "a man and a woeman."*
1630	"Great Migration" to Massachusetts Bay colony begins.
1647	Massachusetts requires towns to fund teachers and schools.
1655	England seizes Jamaica from Spain.
1662	Virginia law determines that the condition of slavery passes from mother to child.
1724	Louisiana Code Noir bans sex between whites and blacks.
1741	"Great Negro Plot" in New York City.
1748	Virginia law provides widows with recourse to challenge deceased husbands' wills.

NOTES

1. *Minutes of the Council and General Court of Colonial Virginia, 1622–1632, 1670–1676*, ed. H. R. McIlwaine (Richmond: Virginia State Library, 1924), 194–195.
2. Cotton Mather, *Life swiftly passing and quickly ending. A very short sermon, on the shortness of humane [sic] life. Preached after the death of Mrs. Mehetable Gerrish....* (Boston: T. Fleet and T. Crump, 1715–1716), 16.
3. Quoted in Lorena S. Walsh, "'Till Death Us Do Part': Marriage and Family in Seventeenth-Century Maryland," in *The Chesapeake in the Seventeenth Century: Essays on Anglo-American Society & Politics*, ed. Thad W. Tate and David L. Ammerman (Chapel Hill: University of North Carolina Press, 1979), 145–146.
4. John Robinson, *The Works of John Robinson: Pastor of the Pilgrim Fathers*, ed. Robert Ashton (London: John Snow, 1851), Vol. 1, 240, 246.
5. Cotton Mather, *Humiliations follow'd with deliverances* (Boston: B. Green & J. Allen, 1697), 43, 49.
6. Cotton Mather, *Magnalia Christi Americana* (1702; Hartford, CT: Silas Andrus, 1820), 552.
7. Anne Bradstreet, *The Works of Anne Bradstreet*, ed. Jeannine Hensley (Cambridge, MA: Harvard University Press, 1967), 225, 226.
8. Quote from Lorenzo Johnson Greene, *The Negro in Colonial New England, 1620–1776* (New York: Columbia University Press, 1942), 208.

9. Petitions transcribed by Mary Beth Norton "'The Ablest Midwife that Wee Knowe in the Land': Mistress Alice Tilly and the Women of Boston and Dorchester, 1649–1650," *William and Mary Quarterly*, 3d ser., 55 (1998): 124, 125.
10. Gloria L. Main, *Peoples of a Spacious Land: Families and Cultures in Colonial New England* (Cambridge, MA: Harvard University Press, 2001), 89–91.
11. Byrd, quoted in Kathleen M. Brown, *Good Wives, Nasty Wenches & Anxious Patriarchs: Gender, Race, and Power in Colonial Virginia* (Chapel Hill: University of North Carolina Press, 1996), 281.
12. Robert Wormeley Carter, "The Daybook of Robert Wormeley Carter of Sabine Hall, 1766," ed. Louis Morton, in *The Virginia Magazines of History and Biography* 68 (July 1960): 312, 313.

SUGGESTIONS FOR FURTHER READING

For a detailed comparative appraisal of beliefs and legal practices in the Chesapeake and New England, which includes an analysis of the Thomasine Hall case, see Mary Beth Norton, *Founding Mothers & Fathers: Gendered Power and the Forming of American Society* (New York: Knopf, 1996). Carol Berkin, *First Generations: Women in Colonial America* (New York: Hill & Wang, 1996), provides an insightful overview of the colonial era.

A remarkably rich literature analyzes demographic conditions, family life, and women's experiences in New England. Classic accounts of the New England town include Philip J. Greven, Jr., *Four Generations: Population, Land and Family in Colonial Andover, Massachusetts* (Ithaca, NY: Cornell University Press, 1970); John Demos, *A Little Commonwealth: Family Life in Plymouth Colony*, 2nd ed. (New York: Oxford University Press, 2000); and Stephen Innes, *Labor in a New Land: Economy and Society in Seventeenth-Century Springfield* (Princeton, NJ: Princeton University Press, 1983). Richard Archer, "A New England Mosaic: A Demographic Analysis for the Seventeenth Century," *William and Mary Quarterly*, 3d ser., 47 (1990): 477–502, provides a wealth of valuable data, while Gloria T. Main, *Peoples of a Spacious Land: Families and Cultures in Colonial New England* (Cambridge, MA: Harvard University Press, 2001), covers a wide variety of issues with humanity and insight.

The difficult demographic conditions of early Virginia and Maryland and their implication for family life are charted in Lorena S. Walsh, "'Till Death Us Do Part': Marriage and Family in Seventeenth-Century Maryland," and Darrett B. and Anita H. Rutman, "'Now Wives and Sons-in-Law': Parental Death in a Seventeenth-Century Virginia County," both in *The Chesapeake in the Seventeenth Century: Essays on Anglo-American Society & Politics*, ed. Thad W. Tate and David L. Ammerman (Chapel Hill: University of North Carolina Press, 1979), 126–182, and Lois G. Carr and Lorena S. Walsh, "The Planter's Wife: The Experience of White Women in Seventeenth-Century Maryland," *William and Mary Quarterly*, 3d ser., 34 (1977): 542–571. Edmund S. Morgan, *American Slavery, American Freedom: The Ordeal of Colonial Virginia* (New York: Norton, 1975), continues to offer valuable insights. Trevor Burnard has written a series of articles, including "A Failed Settler Society: Marriage and Demographic Failure in Early Jamaica," *Journal of Social History* 28 (1994): 63–82, which facilitate comparisons between the West Indies and the mainland. Jennifer M. Spear, "Colonial Intimacies: Legislating Sex in French Louisiana," *William and Mary Quarterly*, 3d ser., 60 (2003): 75–98; and Carl A. Brasseaux, "The Moral Climate of French Colonial Louisiana, 1699–1763," *Louisiana History* 27 (1986): 27–41, chart erstwhile efforts to regulate sexual morality by French authorities.

The roles of women in New England society, which provides vivid accounts of the limits and opportunities that bounded their experience, are described in Laurel Thatcher Ulrich, *Good Wives: Image and Reality in the Lives of Women in Northern New England, 1650–1750* (New York: Vintage, 1980). See also, Jane Kamensky, *Governing the Tongue: The Politics of Speech in Early New England* (New York: Oxford University Press, 1997). Kathleen M. Brown, *Good Wives, Nasty Wenches, & Anxious Patriarchs: Gender, Race, and Power in Colonial Virginia* (Chapel Hill: University of North Carolina Press, 1996), covers the changing nature of women's positions in Chesapeake society. Martha Saxton, *Being Good: Women's Moral Values in Early America* (New York: Hill & Wang, 2003), facilitates comparisons of Puritan and Chesapeake societies. Gloria L. Main, "Gender, Work, and Wages in Colonial New England," *William and Mary Quarterly* 3d ser., 51 (1994): 39–66, and Laurel Thatcher Ulrich, "Wheels, Looms, and the Gender Division of Labor in Eighteenth-Century New England," *William and Mary Quarterly*, 3d ser., 55 (1998): 3–38, offer valuable data. Susan E. Klepp, *Revolutionary Conceptions: Women, Fertility, & Family Limitations in America, 1760–1820* (Chapel Hill: University of North Carolina Press, 2009), provides a broadly comparative perspective. C. Dallett Hemphill, *Siblings: Brothers and Sisters in American History* (New York: Oxford University Press, 2011), adds an important dimension to the study of families.

In addition to the works above, sexuality and deviance are investigated in Richard Godbeer, *Sexual Revolution in Early America* (Baltimore: Johns Hopkins University Press, 2002); Thomas A. Foster, "Deficient Husbands: Manhood, Sexual Incapacity, and Male Marital Sexuality in Seventeenth-Century New England," *William and Mary Quarterly*, 3d ser., 56 (1999): 723–744; James Deetz and Patricia Scott Deetz, *The Time of Their Lives: Life, Love, and Death in Plymouth Colony* (New York: Anchor, 2000); Cornelia Hughes Dayton, "Taking the Trade: Abortion and Gender Relations in an Eighteenth-Century New England Village," *William and Mary Quarterly*, 3d ser., 48 (1991): 19–49; and Clare A. Lyons, "Mapping an Atlantic Sexual Culture: Homoeroticism in Eighteenth-Century Philadelphia," *William and Mary Quarterly*, 3d ser., 60 (2003): 119–154.

CHAPTER 7

Patriarchy, Politics, and Government

Colonial Virginia was a great place to be in 1726. Some advantages were natural—mild summers, clean air, "and a Serene Sky." Some were social—in the absence of crime, property was secure. Others political—the legislature checked any tyrannical impulses of the royal governors dispatched from England. To paint this picture of his dominion, William Byrd II hearkened back to the Old Testament: "Like one of the Patriarchs, I have my Flocks and my Herds, my Bond-men and Bond-women.... I live in a kind of Independence on every one but Providence." He played a central role in ensuring that harmony reigned: "[T]his Soart of Life... is attended with a great deal of trouble. I must take care to keep all my people to their Duty, to set all the Springs in motion and to make every one draw his equal Share to carry the Machine forward." The fifty-two-year-old Byrd did not want this last remark to sound like a complaint. So he immediately added, " 'Tis an amusement in this silent Country and a continual exercise of our Patience and Economy" to supervise a plantation.[1]

Byrd had material and cultural advantages that few colonists of his era experienced, securing him resources and habits that fit him to rule. His father, a member of the governor's council in Virginia, sent his young heir to England to receive a classical education and, subsequently, training in the law. After absorbing English culture for almost twenty-five years, the younger Byrd returned to Virginia to assume control of Westover, his deceased father's James River plantation. A few years later, he secured an appointment to his father's seat on the governor's council.

Another lengthy stay in England to promote his political ambitions coming to naught, Byrd described his well-ordered world in a letter to his aristocratic English friend Charles Boyle, the earl of Orrery. The Virginia planter conveyed to the English aristocrat that contentment and authority could be achieved by an untitled though wealthy colonial. Byrd's presentation of his world offered a picture of fully functioning, successful patriarchal social order. He was ensconced on his plantation but engaged at the highest level of public service. As a father, he commanded respect from and exercised authority, directly or indirectly, over family, neighbors of lesser means, and slaves alike. As a master, he exhibited great acuity and an even temperament.

Figure 7.1 Hans Hyssing, *William Byrd II* (early eighteenth century). Wealthy planter, slaveholder, member of the governor's council, and diarist, this prominent Virginian devoted himself to projecting an image of confident, patriarchal self-control. Such composure masked a turbulent inner life, stifled ambition, and difficult family relationships. A ship in the background suggests the cultural, commercial, and personal connections to England so important to his life story and self-image. Courtesy of the Virginia Historical Society (1973.6).

In constructing images of Virginia and of himself, Byrd self-servingly exaggerated, and he left much unsaid. Byrd's actual experience complicates his image of confident mastery (see Figure 7.1). Byrd's longest-lasting and most important correspondent was himself. Byrd's diary, written in cypher, recorded his self-conscious effort to govern his temperament and his surroundings with the composure and confidence of an English gentleman. He woke up at 6 a.m.; he read regularly in Hebrew and Greek; he performed his daily calisthenics ("danced my dance" as he put it); he said his prayers. He looked after the health of his slaves; he visited with neighbors; he walked with his wife. But as his diary and the events of his life reveal, Byrd's desire to regulate his intense emotions did not always go smoothly. He did not get along well with his first wife, Lucy, who died in 1716 of smallpox after joining her husband in England during one of his periodic quests for office and influence. Keeping Lucy from reading his diary may have motivated the encryption of his diary. Byrd's children lived vexed lives. He threatened to cut ties to his teenage daughter Evelyn when she entertained a suitor of whom he did not approve; she never married. Though occurring decades after William II's death, his son and namesake William III ultimately committed suicide. Obsessed, even compulsive, about sex, over the course of his diaries Byrd recorded "flourish [es]" with his wife, pursued female servants and, later in life, female slaves. Although he imagined himself a friend and protector of his bondspeople, he once made his young house slave Eugene who had a bed-wetting problem "drink a pint of piss" as punishment.[2] The apparent ease of patriarchal governance never was, nor could be, as straightforward as Byrd indicated to the earl of Orrery, even or perhaps especially for a self-conscious practitioner like Byrd.

Nonetheless, Byrd's letter to Orrery and his life evoke important truths about the exercise of social and political power in the Atlantic colonies. In different ways and to varying degrees, each colony gave rise to a stable hierarchical order in which a few governed the many, using political power to preserve social authority and personal privilege. This order emerged at the intersection of local contests for authority, English dynastic politics, and imperial policy. Byrd and his fellow colonists, ordinary people as well as elites, received frequent reminders that the American provinces served a larger empire whose politicians, merchants, aristocrats, and designated representatives anticipated respect. Distance did not preclude feelings of familiarity between colonies and Crown. As English politics oscillated between reform and regime change, politically attuned colonists adjusted their goals and expectations. Byrd's life and family history were shaped by these larger forces and speak to how the appearance of tranquility had to be wrestled from less well-placed members of society who possessed their own ideas about justice and order.

THE FAMILIAL MODEL OF GOVERNMENT

"Honor thy father and thy mother: that thy dayes may bee long vpon the land, which the Lord thy God giueth thee."[3] This biblical commandment, the fifth of the famous ten, carried with it the implicit reward of long-term landholding security, one that generations of colonists wished to enjoy. And while this succinct expression of the primacy of parents was hardly the only word that the Bible contained on law and government, the divine directive contained within it an essential kernel of how colonists understood the nature of legitimate authority. The distribution of power in colonial societies had many sources and explanations, but the analogy between good government and properly ruled families carried an intuitive and customary logic backed up by the force of law.

According to the reigning sensibility, the governance of society just as the governance of families entailed maintaining orderly hierarchies, with power flowing from the top down. Those lower down on the hierarchy depended on those above them, not vice versa, in a chain that extended from God to kings, to magistrates, to heads of households, down to the lowliest children and servants. In the family, as in the state, the rulers reserved the right to discipline those subordinates who showed recalcitrance or strayed from rules of morality and obedience. Thus, the patriarchal model elevated the notion of fatherhood to a master metaphor. God-the-father authorized the power of a king, who exercised power as the father of his subjects, many of whom were fathers, whose grasp on power within the home secured the well-being and morality of its household members.

The centrality of households to this familial model of government was clearly more than just theoretical and, in terms of gender, was anything but even-handed. A good government should, like a well-governed household, have a male head who managed his resources and his family, servants as well as wife and children. The biblical injunction to "honor thy father and thy mother" notwithstanding, the chain of command followed a distinctly male line. To be sure, circumstance placed queens (Queen Elizabeth at the outset of England's colonial adventures, Queen Anne in the early eighteenth century) in the role of sovereign monarch. But the production of a line of male Protestant heirs effected the smooth transmission of dynastic authority. In ordinary society, as we saw in the previous chapter, women exercised certain types of authority over children and servants and, in the temporary absence of husbands, women made decisions about property and the household. Under normal conditions women were subordinated to the male heads of household. Moreover, women existed outside the political chain of command by which male heads of household voted, held office, and publicly communicated grievances.

Geographically removed from England and its elaborate set of social and political hierarchies, household governance in the colonies took on acute importance to order and harmony. Society could not hope to be well ordered, let alone prosperous, unless households themselves were well and properly governed. In an election sermon preached before Connecticut's legislature, minister James Lockwood explained how the proper exercise of parental authority both resembled and benefited general government. Lockwood noted that it was incumbent on parents to "form" children "to Holiness and practical Religion." The connections between family and government were seamless: "As the *Civil State*... is furnish'd with Members from private Families: if the Governors of these little Communities, were faithful to the great Trust reposed in them... the Civil State, would prosper and flourish from Generation to Generation." With religion "diffusing itself, among all Ranks & Orders," the "People" would experience "Peace as a River, and their Tranquility as the Waves of the Sea." The elected officials who Lockwood addressed as "Honoured Fathers" thus shared with fathers throughout the province the responsibility of buoying the morality and well-being of their children, real and metaphorical.[4]

The familial model of government required obedience throughout the social structure, but the government needed lots of help to succeed. In the household, fathers oversaw not only biological children, wives, and stepchildren, but also servants, apprentices, and slaves under their authority. To these dependents, fathers were expected to provide food, shelter, and education, which included religious and moral instruction. Public officials reserved the right to punish fathers who demonstrably failed to fulfill their duties. The law, meanwhile, underscored the kingly position of fathers by considering the murder of fathers and husbands by children and wives to be *petit treason*. Thus, overthrowing the father was analogous to rebelling against the government or king, meriting harsher punishment, such as bodily torture and mutilation, than ordinary murder. Family governance was thus a microcosm of the state. At the same time, rulers relied on householders to ensure public safety against domestic or foreign enemies, be they rebellious slaves or servants, hostile Indians, or invading Europeans. Fathers sometimes found the human instinct for liberty at odds with their authority. When slaves, servants, children, and wives asserted their will, the patriarch had to be prepared to respond forcefully. And where fathers failed, colonial laws sanctioning public whippings, brandings, hangings, and even dismemberment might succeed. The goal, however, was to delegate correction to households rather than governments that had only modest resources at their disposal.

The punitive, coercive edge of the family model of governance was unmistakable, but cultural and political forces could and did soften that edge particularly as the eighteenth century progressed. Gendered hierarchy within families did not exclude emotional and physical joy as a cohesive element of marriage. The educational and psychological theories of philosopher John Locke redefined the governing stewardship of children, emphasizing the cultivation of feeling and rationality as alternatives to dictates and physical correction. Affection for parents who cultivated sympathy and the development of good moral choices would, to those who followed Locke's lead, encourage emotional bonds between parents and children, as well as between subjects and rulers.

In the eighteenth century, aspects of this softer version of patriarchy influenced the way some Americans discussed and experienced royal rule. England's eighteenth-century monarchs were portrayed as deserving love and affection as rulers who did not infringe on their subjects' liberty, in juxtaposition to Catholic monarchs who allegedly drew power and liberty away from the people through a church and state that claimed absolute authority. The practice of subjects kissing the hand of the king and other members of the royal family symbolized a consensual submission to patriarchal power. For American colonists separated by an ocean from the monarch, a royal governor's provision of food, drink, fireworks, and processions for royal birthdays was a more common way to acknowledge their submission to the king and to receive the marks of his affection. This softer patriarchal model of familial and monarchical rule even penetrated the inherently coercive, at times violent slave plantation household, masters imagining themselves as protectors of and providers for their slaves, tempering punishment with mercy.

EMERGENCE OF A SOUTHERN PATRIARCHAL ORDER

The stable hierarchical world presided over by men of William Byrd II's standing reached fruition only in his own lifetime, his analogy to biblical patriarchs a mere façade of timelessness. Byrd's 1674 birth barely preceded a violent upheaval that threatened, redefined, and ultimately solidified Virginia's social structure for decades to come. When the well-connected Nathaniel Bacon arrived in Virginia in 1674, he might have taken his place peaceably alongside the younger sons of the English elite who had started to emerge as the ruling class in the tobacco colony. A previous generation of Virginians had scratched their way to wealth by controlling enough land and labor to supply Europe's growing taste for smoking. But new immigrants, including William Byrd's father, who inherited previously established land claims, reaped greater financial and political rewards than their predecessors, some of whom married into these newer families. Virginia's new elite occupied seats on the governor's council and used their positions, connections, and capital to enlarge their land claims. Bacon, who had ties to Governor William Berkeley, quickly gained a seat on the council himself. But Bacon, with whom William Byrd I would form an alliance, was not content to accept the status quo, and his opportunistic grievances shook the colony to the core.

Bacon had little respect for Virginia's leadership and grasped that their self-serving land policies gave him a chance to rally poorer, less fortunate Virginians in protest. Well-connected planters claimed so much land that servants released from their indentures were forced toward the frontier lest they end up laborers and tenants of their former masters. Predictably, smallholders on the frontier came into conflict with Indians. At the same time, Governor Berkeley and his cronies monopolized the fur trade at the expense of white frontiersmen. The administration's policy of building forts and seeking diplomatic accommodation appeared to be just another way in which the interests of the wealthy and well-connected took priority. Marginal men, as well as the still relatively small number of black slaves in the colony, provided Bacon with the support and leverage he needed to vault himself to greater power and prominence. His first instinct was to lead disaffected frontiersmen against the Indians. Berkeley tried to appease Bacon, but then turned against the upstart, accusing him of treason.

Bacon's demands were blunt and his methods violent, terrorizing Indians and seizing property from the plantations of whites who objected to his provocative defiance of the governor. Bacon and his hundreds of followers preferred to hunt down Indians, but Berkeley's attempts alternately to placate and to subdue the colonial rebels ultimately served to inflame rather than soothe their leader and his supporters. Bacon's July 1676 Declaration of the People denounced Berkeley's policies and favoritism, claiming that the governor had bargained with the Indians at the expense of white Virginians and then restrained white forces when he should have unleashed them. The governor proved to be no match politically or militarily for Bacon, who set Jamestown aflame two months later. Although Virginia had become a healthier place for immigrants than in its earliest years, Bacon himself soon died of dysentery or some similar affliction. Eventually, the Crown dispatched a small fleet of ships to help stamp out the rebellion, the last of the holdouts being some eighty black slaves and twenty white servants. Unlike these stalwarts forced back into servitude, William Byrd I had the wherewithal to switch sides, curry favor with Berkeley, and rise to further prominence.

William Byrd II grew up in a society that managed to either submerge or redirect the popular discontent, racial hatred, and elite divisions that Bacon and his allies, including Byrd's father, temporarily exploited. Tobacco planting remained paramount, with the more land and labor that a planter could control translating into greater wealth and prestige. But Virginia's local and provincial patriarchs increasingly assembled their labor force from the human cargo of the African slave trade. To secure power, the planter elite developed laws that dramatically distinguished between temporary white servitude and permanent black bondage—replete with incentives to discourage ordinary whites and black slaves from trading, sleeping, or rebelling together. Trade and sex between white and black proved impossible to eliminate, but banishing interracial political alliances was more readily achieved. White colonists had room for more than one set of prejudices; driving Indians from their land and subduing the African labor force complemented one another. Moreover, as the percentage of African slaves in Virginia's population grew to 40 percent, free whites, whether they owned slaves or not, developed a common interest in minimizing the potential for a servile rebellion. A Virginia planter was expected to keep his slaves in line; if a patriarch used humiliation or torture to do so, then that was his business and his prerogative.

At the upper levels of Virginia's hierarchy, elites learned to consolidate social, cultural, and political power rather than fragment it. As always in the Chesapeake, real estate had something to do with it. The great planters built their increasingly impressive homes on plantations that lay beside Virginia's tidewater rivers, making the transportation of their tobacco to overseas markets much easier, and providing visual cues to their elevated status. Smaller planters built humbler homes alongside creeks. Elite planter families expanded and intermarried across the years, creating an interlocking group of politically powerful cousins and in-laws who looked after each other's political interests in county and colony government. While there were a limited number of seats on the governor's council, where William Byrd II sat, the lower chamber, the House of Burgesses, offered opportunities to serve the colony and protect the landholders' interest, as did seats on county courts reserved almost exclusively for wealthy planters. Virginia's gentry families did not limit themselves or their labor force to a single location, but rather sought to place sons and move slaves across an expanding landscape. Seven Lee family cousins served in the lower house of the legislature in the 1750s, representing five counties. Securing legacies in this patriarchal order made the results of courtship vital; marriage between elite families widened and strengthened the circle of connections that perpetuated a family's wealth and power in the next generation.

Virginia's patriarchs competed with one another constantly, but within certain well-marked boundaries. The privileges and pleasures of intense competition in Chesapeake society were not open equally to all both by custom and because this competition required significant resources. Male planters pitted their reputations for courage and physical prowess against one another through horse racing. The spectacle of thundering steeds kicking up dirt while riding neck and neck in a quarter-mile sprint drew audiences from all levels of society. But the men who owned and mounted these beasts came from the gentry, and races visibly displayed their mastery and control, over themselves and nature. Only great men had the honor of racing great horses and the wealth to place wagers in amounts that ordinary planters could never risk. They also gambled on cockfights and, more privately, at cards and dice. In settings not exclusive to men, the Virginia elite also prized dancing ability and hospitality. The gentry tested themselves against one another in ways that set them apart and did not risk the sort of fundamental contest over legitimacy that Bacon aroused.

The gentry's patriarchal authority found many institutional expressions as well, notably in militia musters and courthouses. By calling together the local militia and marching lesser men through their paces, the commissioned officers selected from the gentry literally displayed that they were in command, while indicating to potentially rebellious slaves and the poor that collective force could be arrayed against them. Only a man of wealth could treat his militia men to strong drink after leading them in drill. Members of the gentry also were supposed to help equip the militias. A traveler's account captured the vanity of the Southern gentry, but also the importance that members of this class placed on public acknowledgment of their leadership when commenting: "Wherever you travel in Maryland (as also in Virginia and Carolina) your Ears are constantly astonished at the Number of Colonels, Majors, and Captains that you hear mentioned: In short, the whole Country seems at first to you a Retreat of Heroes...."[5]

The power exercised by the gentry as justices of the county courts went well beyond the symbolic. Wearing formal wigs like their English counterparts, the judges oversaw proceedings filled with official oaths and the reading aloud of court documents to crowds containing many illiterates. The decisions rendered, whether to postpone or execute the collection of a debt, whether to grant a license to operate a mill or a tavern, whom to offer a contract to build a bridge, deeply affected the livelihoods of the ordinary white folk who came before the esteemed body. And for slaves on trial for capital crimes, these courts had the power of life and death. The Chesapeake that William Byrd II described as "this Silent Country" dispersed its population widely across the countryside. But when Virginians congregated, formally or informally, reminders of their various places in the patriarchal order came with them.

In South Carolina, society was even more intensely invested in slavery for wealth, prestige, and power. Low-country rice plantations concentrated even larger numbers of slaves under the ownership of individual masters. Not surprisingly, the patriarchs of South Carolina were just as committed to the political and social privileges of their position as their counterparts in the Chesapeake. Like Byrd of Virginia, South Carolina planters imagined themselves as exercising regal powers over the slaves whose work actually generated their wealth. White planters knew that their status within the hierarchy of government, law, and lay leadership in the Anglican Church depended on their ability to manage their slaves to maximize profits in the rice and indigo trades, just as Virginia planters had to produce as much tobacco as they could for market. But for practical as well as psychological reasons, planters preferred to think of themselves as governing rather than exploiting their people, supporting their slaves through the distribution of food and clothing, as well as proffering favors in the form of food and drink for Christmas holidays and for personal occasions such as births and marriages. Masters regarded slaves' gardens and the trading of provisions for additional clothing as a benevolently granted privilege, even though slaves were supplementing their diet and wardrobes by performing work on their own behalf.

The logic of patriarchy attempted to mask and to justify slavery's manifold cruelties. Masters exacted physical punishment for acts that they saw as disloyalty or ingratitude, such as running away, stealing, or insubordination. A master always had the option of selling a slave away from his or her family, but by not exercising that option could think of himself as benignly protecting the slave family. Of course, masters did split up families, and adding insult to injury, punished slaves who ran away in attempts to maintain family ties. Thus, in 1740 a planter named Robert Pringle shipped a female slave to Portugal because she kept running away to see her parents on another one of Pringle's plantations.

By law and to ensure that profit-generating work on the plantation got done, masters of more than ten slaves employed overseers. While overseers occupied a position between masters and slaves in the social hierarchy, masters and slaves alike viewed overseers as outsiders to the patriarchal order; the master might intervene to mitigate an overseer's cruelty. Overseers hired on to the plantation sooner or later departed, while the master, in theory, had a permanent, ongoing relationship with the slaves there. Slaves surely understood the considerable, inequitable advantages their masters extracted from the plantation system. But because they wanted and needed tangible benefits—food, clothing, personal time, family integrity—they had to engage in what one historian has labeled a "tug of war" over how much work could be expected within the task system and what sorts of rewards might be forthcoming.[6]

Given their own wants—power, prestige, luxury, safety—the patriarchs of a slave society such as South Carolina had to work together to limit the choices and options of their putative black wards. The vast majority of low-country white households owned at least a small number of slaves, ensuring a widely diffused white identification with slaveholding interests. A system of laws and slave courts, as well as patrols and militias, dealt with extraordinary resistance such as murder or plots for rebellion. As much as possible, slaves could not be permitted to think, as had happened in the Stono Rebellion of 1739, that by working in concert, they might overpower their white masters.

The comfort and desires of South Carolina slaveholders also contributed to the paradoxical nature of patriarchy. The great planters maintained not only manor houses on their plantations, but also grand residences in Charles Town, the province's capital and a major Atlantic port. Thus, for reasons of commerce, climate, safety, and sociability, masters often lived at some remove from most of their slaves, though still in a world that catered to their class. In Charles Town, elite South Carolinians had black household servants, personal retainers, and sexual partners.

To a degree that vexed lower-status whites, Charles Town also hosted a large number of black craftsmen, such as carpenters and shoemakers, as well as waterfront workers and hawkers of meat and fish. Some masters allowed their slaves to hire themselves out for wages to be remitted in part to masters, while Charles Town attracted many runaways seeking anonymity and autonomy. Thus, the port city served the needs of the colony's slaveholding patriarchs, while also creating opportunities for some slaves to exercise greater control over their own lives.

The staple-producing slave societies of the South had more than a little in common with the British West Indies, but by comparison Chesapeake and South Carolina elites were less wealthy and more rooted in their colonial setting than the plantocracy of the British island colonies. William Byrd II's English education and lengthy English stays were far more typical of the West Indian plantation owners, whose children attended the elite English schools in numbers that dwarfed their North American counterparts. They could not pretend, like Byrd, that the islands were a "Silent Country," when English planters died so frequently of tropical diseases and when they knew that African slave majorities far in excess of South Carolina could revolt or form threatening maroon communities. The West Indian plantation version of patriarchy was in some ways both more aristocratic and more an impersonal business than the mainland variation. The great planters who dominated the island economy frequently absented themselves, using their wealth to ensconce themselves in the upper reaches of English society. These absentees hired managers and overseers to run their plantation operations. Those who remained or returned controlled island political institutions and offices. To preserve this steeply hierarchical society and the economic benefits of large-scale operations, West Indian planters sought to keep their massive landholdings in one piece by favoring a single heir.

North Carolina lacked the geographic or social conditions to produce the social structure and cultural characteristics that defined its sister colonies to the south and to the north, let alone the West Indies. Without a staple crop or a major port, a large slaveholding elite did not develop, let alone coalesce around an urban center and an accepted set of genteel standards of sophistication and comportment. A stable hierarchy thus emerged slowly. Slavery did develop a strong foothold in North Carolina. Approximately one in five North Carolinians was black by 1755, a significant percentage by New England or even mid-Atlantic standards, but a paltry percentage when measured against the West Indies, South Carolina, or the Chesapeake. Significantly, large slaveholders did not dominate the ranks of North Carolina legislators. As late as 1765, a French traveler to North Carolina remarked that the province was "a fine Country for poor people, but not for the rich."[7]

GREAT AND SMALL IN THE MIDDLE COLONIES

In contrast, New York was a fine country for the rich, the social hierarchy dominated by families with vast landholdings or extensive Atlantic mercantile connections. Moreover, like South Carolina and Virginia, New York's elite, and its economy in general, benefited greatly from the development of New World plantation societies. But despite the largest concentration of slaves north of Maryland, New York did not become a slave society. The organization and expression of social power rested much more on a combination of land, commerce, marriage, ethnic acculturation, and metropolitan connections. The great families of New York, their wealth, land, tenants, and slaves notwithstanding, began their precipitous climbs through the actions and opportunism of relatively humble men—men of a variety of ethnic extractions. The seventeenth-century roots of the family trees of leading New Yorkers included such occupations as minister, sea captain, craftsman, and soldier. Their progeny's Dutch, Scottish, English, and French surnames populated New York's intertwined economic and political elite for generations after their family's American founders established themselves by acquiring land, trade, and political connections.

Massive land grants to a select number of families skewed the social hierarchy in the Hudson River valley. Following a precedent set by the Dutch, English governors of New York transferred blocks of land to prominent colonists, some grants accompanied with privileges comparable to English feudal manors, in acreages that dwarfed the plantations of the Southern colonies. The goal was to delegate responsibility for settling the colony and to shore up New York's land claims against neighboring colonies. The Van Rensselaer family's holdings, a stunning 850,000 acres surrounding Albany, made the massive 160,000-acre Livingston Manor seem small. The great landed families enjoyed tremendous power and influence, both over the colony and the people who settled in their midst.

The great landlords extended their wealth and exhibited their superiority through a variety of contractual arrangements. Leases ranged from at the will of the landlord to a set term of years, to the lifetime of the leaseholder, to covering the lives of one or even two generations of the original tenant's heirs. Shorter leases gave landlords the flexibility to raise rents and to threaten eviction. The lords of Rensselaesrwyck, to the north, actually favored granting leases in perpetuity. Lifetime leases held advantages for landlords, serving as an incentive for prospective settlers, who would be more willing to make improvements on lands that they could occupy at length. More permanent leases also qualified the tenants as voters, ideally, from the landlord's perspective, increasing his political power.

Tenants of all kinds found themselves directly and indirectly obligated to landlords on unequal terms. Some tenants paid rent by ceding a portion of their produce to the landlord; tenants paid the property taxes and colonial quit-rents that their landlords otherwise would have to pay. Beyond paying rent, tenancy sometimes carried with it the obligation to provide labor, often building and maintaining local roads. Some tenants had to provide chickens to their landlords. Some landlords excused certain tenants from such obligations or accepted alternate payment, but leniency still underscored the difference between being great and ordinary. Even though rents were often low and not always collected, landlords who offered nonperpetual leases could command a hefty transfer fee—meaning that even those tenants who had purchased a lease without an annual rent owed the landlord as much as a third of the value of the land when conveying the lease to someone else. A son's inheritance of his father's leased farm came at a price, as did moving on. Similarly, a landlord who had cut a tenant slack for years by not collecting rent was in a stronger position to demand payment of all debts once a tenant sold his lease.

Some landlords sought to maximize the commercial advantage of their positions. They looked for ways to channel the wheat their tenants grew into their own hands by building gristmills and obligating their tenants to exclusively use them. Landlords also tried to demand that they get first claim on the exportable wheat grown on their lands. Landlords set up sawmills and general stores to further corner the market on their tenants' business.

As elsewhere in the colonies, the control of economic resources and political power went hand in hand in New York. Wealthy landholders, along with their rivals among the emerging class of wealthy New York City merchants, understood office holding as an expression of power as well as a way to protect their interests and prerogatives. Members of the landed families served on the local courts and as militia officers. Three New York manors came with seats in New York's provincial assembly, seats to which family members were duly elected. Although the mercantile elite ran their operations from Manhattan and Albany, families like the Van Cortlandts and the Phillipses also garnered wealth and prestige from their country estates.

Despite the limits to the great landlords' political and economic authority over their tenants, the manorial system came at a cost to New York's development. For all their privilege, New York's manorial system did not reproduce medieval feudalism: manorial courts were never established and the lands fell under town and county governmental jurisdiction. Landlords calculated lease terms and the degree to which they enforced those terms with an eye toward attracting and retaining people. Tenants could leave; they were not bound to the land like European serfs. Some tenants improved their leased lands enough to make the handsome profits necessary to strike out on their own. Farms owned outright by families that worked for themselves, sometimes with the help of a slave or two, were also quite common in New York, especially west of the Hudson River. Still, taking so much land off the market artificially slowed New York's population growth, as many migrants preferred to seek their fortunes where less land was encumbered.

New Jersey's history, like North Carolina's, was shadowed by its more commercially connected neighbor. Wealthy, well-positioned New Yorkers such as the Morris family looked to East Jersey to further their political and economic ambitions. Clashing land claims and ethnic cultures undermined the ability of proprietors to establish a stable hierarchy, a landed gentry commanding the respect of tenants while reaping the benefits of farms, forests, and mines. Within their own communities, transplanted New England Puritans and Dutch New Yorkers respected patriarchal norms, for instance, seating families in church according to the wealth and respect that they enjoyed locally. Outsiders, including a group of largely Scottish proprietors, commanded no such respect. Perpetually sharpening the edge to conflict in New Jersey were the overlapping, mutually exclusive land claims of settlers and gentry, creating disputes over several hundred thousand acres of valuable land. Whether purchased from Indians, granted by the governor of New York, or occupied by squatters, East Jersey farmers found themselves bumping up against vast royal grants of land to those who hoped the province would yield them wealth and aristocratic dominance. The emerging commercial potential of this land hardly dampened the willingness of settlers to sue, take up arms, or ignore demands of proprietors. A stable patriarchal order proved impossible to achieve, as ordinary people resorted to violence when necessary to assert their own land claims and cultural prerogatives against their would-be superiors.

Elsewhere, egalitarian religious and political ideas did not guarantee social equality, let alone perfect harmony. Their religious sensibility notwithstanding, Pennsylvania's successful Quaker merchants amassed impressive wealth, leveraging connections to relatives and co-religionists in the Atlantic World to good effect and taking their place atop the social hierarchy. Rural Quaker parents strived to achieve sufficiently large holdings that they could pass on to their offspring, whom they expected to marry other Friends. The attraction of Pennsylvania's backcountry and the ascendant port city of Philadelphia drew many immigrants, some of whom populated the lower reaches of the social hierarchy, while others took advantage of available lands to secure their autonomy and forge a respectable living.

SOCIAL ORDERING IN NEW ENGLAND

Compared to New York and New Jersey, let alone Virginia and South Carolina, the patriarchal structure in New England can seem at first blush far less deeply etched and predicated on less dramatic disparities of wealth and power. Nonetheless, New Englanders brought over with them ideas about authority that combined with conditions across several generations in North America to produce relatively stable social hierarchies. These hierarchies defined the contours of society every bit as much as in the middle and Southern colonies. That said, the closer one looks—and legions of historians have looked very closely—the more variegated the patterns of social hierarchy in New England turn out to have been.

After the founding generations grew old and began to die, many denizens of New England's towns retained some of the original zeal to protect the local exercise of authority on behalf of communities committed to shared religious values and a stable social order. In such places, the congregational model, in which every family attended a single Puritan church funded by local taxes that paid the salary of the town's minister, also applied to secular affairs. Certain founding families with property holdings larger than most in the town tended to comprise the slate of candidates for selectmen, the board of town officials who oversaw governance and tried to maintain an atmosphere of consensus. In church, where attendance was mandatory, seating reflected social status, the best families placed at the front. Church fathers and town fathers, church authority and town authority, though not identical, overlapped considerably. The training of ministers and other leading citizens at Harvard and Yale reinforced the notion that only certain men were qualified to speak to and for the community and that others should listen.

Despite acknowledged gradations of social status in the subsistence-oriented towns scattered across the New England landscape, the differences of wealth in these communities could be plotted on a very gradual slope that did not rise particularly high. Virtually everyone harvested the same crops and tended the same farm animals in the same fashion. Most of the labor, in the fields and in the home, came from within the immediate family. Still, original land distributions had not been equal, reflecting the standing of the migrants at the time of the founding, and a certain stature adhered to a town's founding families. Thus, authority accrued based on continuity and wealth, as well as reputation, forged across time in towns where families remained for generations.

Both within the family and the town, the distribution of land over time reinforced patriarchy. Through wills and gifts of land while still alive, a father had power over the most important resource for shaping the future of his sons. The sons' habits of respect and patience were almost a natural consequence of this reality, with the custom of providing land for every son—partible inheritance—diffusing this feature of patriarchy. Because towns reserved much of the land within their extensive original boundaries to be distributed over time to member households, a town's leaders had considerable leverage over its households to behave respectfully, sustaining rather than challenging political and moral authority.

The tensions of geography, population growth, and finite quantities of family and town land posed a challenge to patriarchal stability, but ironically also reinforced aspects of the patriarchal quality of the subsistence town. Land distributions pushed many farm families away from the original villages where church services and town meetings were held and school conducted. As a result, in both the seventeenth and eighteenth centuries, new clusters of farm families petitioned the provincial legislatures for the right to form their own towns, centered on their own churches, meetinghouses, and schools. The burdens of travel grew disproportionate to the benefit of maintaining old ties. Selecting ministers for a nearby church rather than paying taxes to sustain a distant one had more appeal. To the degree that those original villages sometimes looked unfavorably on such fission, this process threatened patriarchal arrangements, and yet such demands also honored the original impulse of setting up a new, more immediate, socially cohesive locus of religious and secular authority. Even increasing poverty reinforced patriarchal localism. New England towns were obligated to support their own poor, but free to "warn out"—in other words, to send back to the town of origin—any indigent person who could not claim legitimate roots in the town.

This highly localized, village version of patriarchy was never the only model of social authority in New England, and broke down more quickly in some places than others over the course of the seventeenth and eighteenth centuries. The Connecticut River valley of Massachusetts sustained from the beginning more dramatic economic inequality and a much more pronounced set of hierarchal arrangements. In the seventeenth century, the Pynchons, and in the eighteenth century the Stoddards and Williamses, established themselves as preeminent families, leveraging wealth and political connections to occupy a place comparable to the likes of the Carters and Lees of Virginia or the Livingstons and Morrises of New York. Centered in Springfield, Massachusetts, the Pynchons, first William and then John, leveraged wealth originally accrued in the Indian fur trade to dominate the economy of their town. Moving from furs to the export of grain and meat to the West Indies secured their economic future. Meanwhile, the Pynchons also became the major political connection between the colony's government in Boston and the vast western county of Hampshire. They loaned money to craftsmen wanting to start businesses, rented portions of their landholdings to tenants, invested in projects like mills, and employed as servants people down on their luck. Their economic centrality made the Pynchons patrons who dominated local politics rather than town fathers enforcing moral conformity. Like their Virginia counterparts, an array of public positions, in town meetings, county courts, and the militia, both cemented and symbolized this status. While they could be generous and forgiving, the power of the Pynchons lay in economic rather than moral authority. Exercised deftly and flexibly, that power sustained the family for decades, until late-seventeenth-century political turmoil curtailed, but did not eliminate, their influence.

In the eighteenth century, the names changed, but the pattern remained. The so-called River Gods of western Massachusetts continued the pattern of leveraging political connections with colonial authorities in the east to amass land, prestige, office, and authority. As the role of county government expanded, over and above the New England town, men such as Israel Williams and John Stoddard found ways to favor themselves, relatives, and friends in the awarding of militia commissions, contracts, and positions on the county courts. The ability of these families to control offices and patronage created a pattern of power that members of the Southern gentry might have admired, even though the lack of plantation slavery and the continued primacy of the Puritan Congregationalism would have seemed alien to the Chesapeake grandees.

The Connecticut Valley was not the only place in New England where resentment born of social and economic inequality had to be kept at bay. Just as the Connecticut River valley's connection to fur trading tied that region's fortune early and obviously to a wider world of trade, the coastal towns, first Boston and then Salem, produced more marked inequalities of status and wealth. Home to merchant investors, shipbuilders, sailors, dockworkers, craftsmen of all kinds, shopkeepers, widows, orphans, personal servants, Boston quickly grew beyond the boundaries of intimate agriculture-based society to a variegated urban one. The presence of the Puritan province's preeminent ministers set the moral tone for many, but could not stop the emergence of religious diversity or marked economic inequality. In Salem, the growth of successful commercial ventures promoted social division that likely fanned the flames of the infamous witchcraft hysteria. But the eighteenth century also saw the emergence in the coastal ports north of Boston of a commercially successful gentry class with the resources to sponsor churches and other institutions that brought greater stability and structure to waterfront communities.

In every colonial region, the emergence of social hierarchies reflected and was shaped by the interaction of values and economic opportunities. Wealth inevitably defined social rank, but the gentry explained their positions in terms of protection, patronage, and leadership. Patriarchy in all regions was about the exercise of power. And that fact drew patriarchs and would-be patriarchs into competition with each other; political competition and striving exposed the strengths and vulnerabilities of patriarchalism. The achievement of stability came through considerable effort, while the gentry ignored the potential for volatility at their peril.

REFORM AND REBELLION IN AN EMERGING EMPIRE

For much of the seventeenth century, England proved to be neither an example of nor a source of political stability for the colonies. The politics of religion and the Stuart monarchs' attempts at centralizing authority touched off resistance at home while often promoting distrust and defiance in the colonies. Even though England's rulers sometimes drove each other forcibly from power, conflicting regimes shared the idea that reorganizing colonial administration would advance the imperial project. Thus, the Puritan-dominated Parliament that ruled England in the wake of Charles I's beheading in 1649 initiated an approach to colonial trade that royal successors sought to continue. Believing that the colonies ought not to trade with England's rivals and enemies, the 1651 Navigation Act mandated that American outposts should trade exclusively with or at least through the mother country. Oliver Cromwell, the Puritan general who ascended to power in 1653, saw in the West Indies an opportunity to extend the power of Protestant England. Under his Western Design, England seized Jamaica from the Spanish, a presumptuous first step toward the broader goal of chasing the Spanish from the Americas. The presence of the English navy raised the possibility that the new trade law would be enforced, though actual enforcement remained quite limited. Despite the egalitarian visions that the destruction of the monarchy inspired in England and America, Cromwell's Protectorate pinned its New World hopes on large-scale enslavement. In addition to increased trade in African slaves, especially to Barbados, the Parliamentary and Cromwell regimes sought to stock the plantations with political enemies and the poor. Scottish rebels, Irish Catholics, English royalists, as well as felons and impoverished people, wound up in Barbados and other colonial destinations, sold for their labor. The revolutionary governments that ruled England between 1649 and 1660 articulated the idea of a commercially and politically cohesive empire, but did not intervene significantly in the internal politics of the mainland colonies. The inconsistent set of political arrangements of their royal predecessors remained. Much work lay ahead to reform colonial governance and to refine the English commercial navigation system that had been put on a new footing during the interregnum between Charles I and Charles II.

The restoration of the Stuart monarchy in 1660 initially only hinted at a new, more interventionist approach to colonial regulation and governance. New Navigation Acts passed in the early 1660s expanded the regulation of colonial trade to muscle the Dutch aside as Europe's leading commercial carriers. Valuable colonial exports, including tobacco, were singled out to travel only from the colonies to other English ports before being sold anywhere, while all goods imported by the colonies were to be funneled through England first. In the 1660s, imports of colonial products to England surged. The English government saw import duties as an attractive source of revenue.

Capturing the full benefits of colonial trade and taxes required more effective enforcement of these commercial laws. Thus, the Navigation Act of 1673 dispatched colonial customs agents across the Atlantic to make sure that royal revenues were collected in colonial ports. The 1673 Act also levied duties on the intercolonial trade in which New England's merchants specialized. The law carefully described the duties and methods that the new customs agents were to employ, signaling that the English government wished to leave little to chance.

Navigation laws alone, however, could not win complete colonial obedience, let alone colonial satisfaction. English officials who desired a unified, coherent set of governing principles would have to intervene politically as well as economically in the colonies to achieve their goals. The king loved the revenues that tobacco from the Chesapeake generated, but Virginians high and low wanted more not less free trade, while some wondered whether addiction to the production of the smokable plant actually hindered economic development. England's trade monopoly artificially lowered the price planters could charge for their staple. Only wealthy planters could bear the burden of taxes, whether from Parliament or their own House of Burgesses, without hardship. Massachusetts, meanwhile, blithely ignored the spirit and the letter of the Navigation Acts. The port of Boston gave berth to non-English ships and even the occasional pirate. The Bay colony had little economic incentive to limit its trade, since the West Indies welcomed its surplus grains and meats, and the lack of plantation staples meant that the colony made its money through transport itself. Indeed, New England merchants sailing to Virginia and the Carolinas regarded the navigation duty imposed as a mere toll, the payment of which gave them license to sail to whatever destination, English or non-English, that stood them a profit.

Officials in England took increasing notice of the gulf between their desire for order in the colonies and actual events. In 1675 Charles II established the Lords of Trade as a high-level advisory panel charged with tracking conditions in the colonies and communicating the Crown's wishes to colonial governors. Bacon's Rebellion in Virginia not only drew royal attention to the unsettled state of that colony by disrupting the king's tobacco revenues, it also prompted the dispatch of English troops to the Chesapeake to restore order. The evasion of the Navigation Acts in New England made royal authority appear weak. Meanwhile, Charles II granted to his friends and supporters proprietary charters for new colonies in the Carolinas, Pennsylvania, and New York. These arrangements that placed vast responsibilities for administrative policy in private hands increased the number and diversity of colonial governing structures in English North America. Conditions seemed ripe for an overarching reform and rationalization of the way England oversaw its colonial possessions.

Reordering the status quo required English and American officials to confront the fact that the empire was assembled piecemeal and under a variety of arrangements and conflicting assumptions. Ordinary English colonists believed that their rights as Englishmen, including the right to representative government as the legitimate source of laws and taxation, extended to the Americas. Meanwhile, proprietors, like Lord Baltimore in Maryland, assumed that a grant of colonial authority created powers that trumped the demands of the sometimes unruly settlers in their colonies. The charters held by Massachusetts and Connecticut seemed to imply a right to self-governance. None of these assumptions jibed with an emerging view among royal officials that no one in the colonies, from proprietors to slaves, had rights beyond what the king granted or tolerated. What the king as sovereign patriarch had given in colonial charters he could take away.

The debate about the theory of empire carried earthy consequences, as custom's collector Christopher Rousby discovered in 1684. Rousby had made himself a reviled figure with Lord Baltimore through the determination to collect tobacco duties in Maryland, thus asserting the primacy of royal over proprietary power. Baltimore's aide Colonel George Talbot provoked a shipboard brawl with Rousby, calling the custom's collector a "Sone of a whore." Rousby ended up fatally impaled on Talbot's knife. Legal maneuvers on two continents eventually produced a guilty verdict in Virginia against Talbot for the murder of royal official Rousby on Maryland's waters, though newly crowned King James II stayed the hanging. The king's power was very real, but jurisdiction and respect for authority were muddled.

During the 1680s, Charles II and his brother and successor James II moved aggressively to apply their French-inspired absolutism to colonial administration. Thus, the Stuart kings targeted the charters of English colonies and their representative assemblies. When Virginia received a new royal charter in 1676, the Crown refused to recognize the assembly's lawmaking and taxing authority as legitimate powers independent of Crown authority. Though the king did not dissolve or completely neuter representative government in Virginia, the House of Burgesses functioned at his pleasure, not by right. This downgrade was a mild precursor of what was to come. As the Stuarts' plans evolved, other colonies would not find themselves even that fortunate.

Royal officials regarded the commercial and political independence of Massachusetts Bay as increasingly intolerable. Secular and religious leaders in the Puritan colony dug in their heels on their rights, claiming that the Navigation Acts only applied if their own legislature approved. In 1684 the Crown revoked the Massachusetts charter and subsequently lumped the colony together with New Hampshire, Plymouth, Connecticut, and Rhode Island into the Dominion of New England. Far more than pride or individual autonomy was at stake here. In the

Dominion of New England, a royally appointed governor and council ruled, but without any kind of representative assembly. The powers of town meetings were likewise proscribed, and landholders had to register their land for a fee with royal officials. Edmund Andros, appointed governor of the Dominion of New England by James II, committed himself to make the Navigation Acts finally stick.

For Puritans, the legal and symbolic basis of their authority dissolved. Oaths had to be sworn on the Bible, a practice that Puritans viewed as a profanation of God's words. Quakers gained toleration and Andros's government took decisive measures to expand the presence of the Anglican Church while denying tax support to the Puritan clergy. Until a suitable church was built in Boston, Andros insisted that the Puritan's South Meeting House be used by the Church of England faithful.

James II had far more in mind than humbling Massachusetts when he consolidated colonial governments into the Dominion of New England. He also yanked the charter he had previously granted to New York allowing a representative assembly; along with New Jersey, James added New York to the Dominion of New England, thus creating a sort of super-colony that consolidated all English territory from New Jersey to Maine under a single royal governor (see Map 7.1). While the Catholic monarch showed a liberal touch in expanding religious toleration at home and in the colonies, the broader message sent by these measures

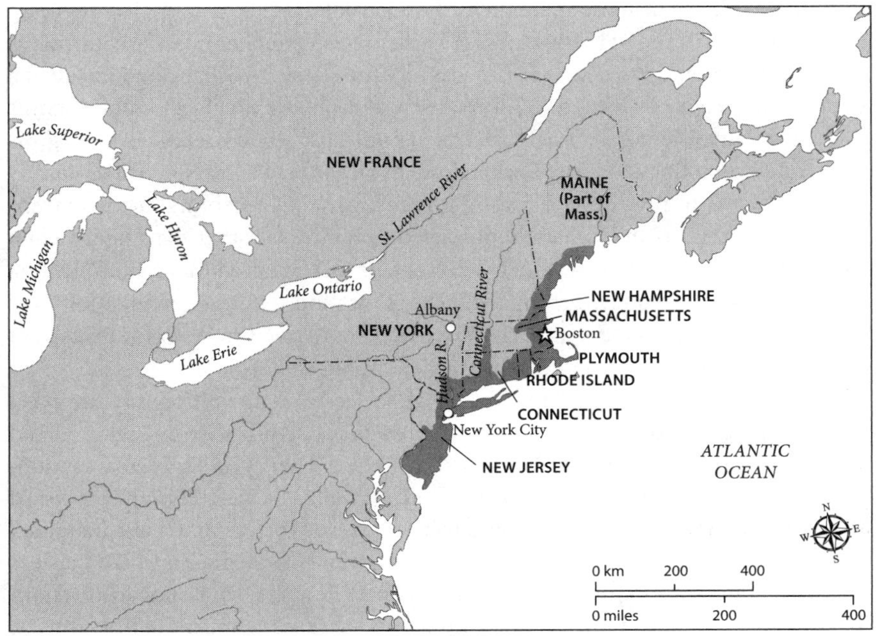

Map 7.1 The Dominion of New England, 1688.

and his blunt governor Andros was that political authority belonged in fewer hands and needed to be responsive to the king rather than to the people. A more rigidly patriarchal vision of governance had arrived in the Northern mainland colonies.

In 1688 the Glorious Revolution in England chased James II from the throne and replaced him with the Dutch prince William and his English wife Mary, daughter of King James. News of this Parliament-engineered regime change reached the colonies and placed Governor Andros and the Dominion of New England in great jeopardy. Over one thousand armed colonists gathered in the streets of Boston, the Dominion's headquarters, on April 18, 1689. Having denounced the government of the Anglican Andros as part of a Catholic conspiracy, the rebels secured the governor's surrender and placed him in chains, subsequently deporting him to England. The colonies bound together as the northern half of the Dominion, Massachusetts, Plymouth, Rhode Island, and Connecticut, quickly separated. Without knowing the will of the new monarchs, restoring former arrangements seemed the best bet, certainly better than allowing the Dominion to insinuate itself further into the political landscape.

In New York, the mercurial figure of Jacob Leisler threw himself into the political storm. The atmosphere of paranoia fueled by ethnic, religious, class, and regional divisions precluded either a holding pattern or restoration of the pre-Dominion status quo during the Glorious Revolution. Leisler, the German-born son of a Protestant minister, gained firsthand knowledge of the ravages of religious warfare in Europe. Making his way as a young military man to the Netherlands and then to New Amsterdam, he thrived under both Dutch and English regimes. His own good fortune notwithstanding, Leisler sensed sinister international forces at work. When the future King James was still the duke of York, he had installed a Catholic governor of New York. More alarming to Leisler, in 1685 France's Louis XIV ended the toleration of Protestants, sending frightened refugees fleeing his realm and suggesting to Leisler a spreading threat. In May 1689 New York's prickly lieutenant governor Francis Nicholson procrastinated in accepting the royal transition from James II to William and Mary despite the fact that the English coup had become common knowledge. Nicholson's delay prompted Manhattan's militia to seize power, ultimately turning the island's fort and then the colony itself over to Leisler. Once he became acting governor, Leisler saw himself as a Protestant avenger in an international struggle against Catholicism.

Leisler's supporters and detractors came to see him quite differently. Simmering resentments among ordinary Dutch colonists over their political, cultural, and economic displacement under English rule made Leisler, who was a zealous supporter of orthodox Dutch Calvinism, a hero to them. Despite Leisler's professed loyalty to the new English king and queen, these supporters may have imagined that Leisler would spearhead a Dutch restoration of New Netherland. To Leisler's political lieutenant and future son-in-law Jacob Milbourne, who came from a family of English religious radicals, the coup may have represented an opportunity to create a more egalitarian society.

In contrast, wealthy English and Dutch merchants viewed Leisler's rise with dismay. Many of these men had received substantial favors from the previous regime and, although Protestant, had a more tolerant, less puritanical view of religion. Leisler threatened stability and therefore their economic and political dominance. Leisler encouraged these fears through his bullying manner toward opponents, whom he branded as Catholic sympathizers and sometimes jailed. He also raised taxes and broke up commercial monopolies. Thus, Leisler's rebellion was an elixir to some, but a bitter pill to others.

Leisler himself seemed uncertain as to what political principles should guide his rule. He did not articulate a vision for the role that representative government would play in the colony's future, and only briefly permitted an elected assembly before dismissing it for scrutinizing his heavy-handed methods. Though a singular figure in many ways, Leisler, like many subsequent colonial governors, failed to master the appropriate balance between the legislature and the executive.

Leisler's religious certainty, on the other hand, ultimately determined his fate. The arrival of English Major Richard Ingoldsby and his soldiers to take over Manhattan's fort ahead of royally appointed Governor Henry Sloughter provoked Leisler's ire instead of his acquiescence. The acting governor accused Ingoldsby of "encourage[ing] and protect[ing] avowed Papists" and emboldening the deposed King James's allies "in divers parts of the Province to strengthen and prosecute their Godless designs." Upon his arrival, Sloughter quickly became convinced that Leisler himself was the true threat. The governor saw to it that Leisler and his son-in-law Jacob Milbourne were convicted of high treason and that they would die brutal public deaths as a cure for "the disease and troubles of this Government."[8]

Thus, Leisler turned out to be the wrong man for the right job of ushering out the Stuart monarchy. As the condemned man addressed the throngs who had come to watch him hang on a rainy Manhattan Saturday in May 1691, perhaps he took solace from those in the crowd who had supported and sustained him during his year-and-a-half as acting governor of New York. Leisler expressed a martyr's satisfaction in the superiority of his cause. He regarded his fate as a perversion of justice, asserting from the gallows, "I am a dying man & do declare before god & the world that what I have done was for king William & Queen Mary, for the defence of the protestant religion & the Good of the Country...."[9]

Leisler's Rebellion was the product of New York's volatile multiculturalism, but even in colonies outside the erstwhile Dominion of New England, the Glorious Revolution resonated. In Maryland, resentment swirled against the regime of Lord Baltimore, the Catholic proprietor, whose confrontational approach to that colony's assembly fueled the determination of Protestants there to seize power in July 1689. John Coode's rebellion in that province eased the path for the Crown to terminate Baltimore's proprietorship and create a second royal colony in the Chesapeake. In the process, Catholics lost the right to vote in their former refuge, though they retained the right to worship freely. In frontier Virginia where conflict with the Indians had set off Bacon's Rebellion only a little over a decade before, political instability stoked class antagonism and renewed fears of Indian attacks. To settle a deteriorating situation, Virginia's leaders apprehended the most militant frontiersmen. Subsequently, Francis Nicholson, the lieutenant governor that Leisler chased out of New York, managed to explain himself in London well enough to become royal lieutenant governor of Virginia and, a few years later royal governor of Maryland.

The Glorious Revolution did not sound the death knell for government through private individuals designated as proprietors. The Calvert family retained extensive land rights in Maryland and, in 1715, the heir to the family dynasty, a converted Protestant, successfully won the Crown's approval to take back the reins as the Chesapeake colony's proprietor. For William Penn, the Glorious Revolution had ambiguous implications. Penn had been personally close to James II, whose vision of religious toleration appealed to the prominent Quaker. The ascension of William and Mary for a time weakened Penn's influence in England and in his colony. The possibility that the Penn family might have to sell the proprietorship to the Crown remained real for years to come. On the other hand, the disintegration of the Dominion of New England lessened the likelihood that a Southern version, lumping the Carolina proprietorship with royal Virginia, would emerge. The Carolina proprietors held onto their claims for another three decades. When anti-proprietary South Carolinians framed their request in 1719 to become a royal colony, they did so in imitation of the Glorious Revolution Parliament, the colonists advancing their desire to replace arbitrary and unjust government with one that safeguarded English rights through royal rule. After a decade of provisional royal government, the Crown bought out all but one of the eight Carolina proprietors, and both South Carolina and North Carolina became royal colonies.

Massachusetts, the colony whose independent attitude was a target of James II's Dominion plan, discovered much more quickly than the Carolinas that previous arrangements would not survive. From the perspective of those English officials most interested in colonial administration, the Stuart template of more consistency in governance and enforcement of commercial laws had much to recommend it. Puritan colonists accustomed to ignoring or denying their subordinate role within the empire therefore had much to lose as royal officials evaluated colonial policy. In the wake of the coup that placed William and Mary on the throne, leading Puritan minister Increase Mather, already in London to make the case against the Dominion, worked to get the best deal he could for his beloved colony. That deal, enshrined in a new colonial charter granted in 1691, included a variety of provisions that profoundly altered the colony's future. Easy enough to swallow was the incorporation of Plymouth colony into the province. Much less palatable, however, was religious toleration. Massachusetts authorities, who had in the seventeenth century defiantly rejected Anglicanism, who had hounded religious radicals such as Anne Hutchison from the province, and who had even executed Quakers, could no longer deny the rights of other Protestants to establish their own churches. Moreover, church membership could no longer be linked to voter eligibility. Under its new charter, Massachusetts was a royal colony, with a royally appointed governor with the power to veto legislation. The first occupant of that office, Sir William Phips, was a native son of the colony, but the colony's identity as an autonomous people responsible only to God had taken a severe blow. Even so, Puritan Congregationalism remained dominant, with towns able to collect taxes to support local ministers. Town meetings also persisted as a pillar of governance, while the royal governor's effectiveness rested in no small part on his ability to cultivate allies in the legislature's lower house.

Structural changes were less jarring in other parts of the short-lived Dominion. Rhode Island and Connecticut resumed their self-governing charter colony status. In the aftermath of the Leisler debacle, the royal colony of New York finally attained on a lasting basis the Anglo-American colonial norm of a bicameral legislature with an elected lower house. New Jersey's proprietary government survived the Glorious Revolution, but turn-of-the-century violence against the courts in that colony helped prompt London to convert that colony to royal status as well.

The Glorious Revolution notwithstanding, the era of the latter Stuarts and their replacements marked an English attempt to place the colonies in a coherent imperial structure, as Spain had done with its colonies well over a century-and-a-half before. The outlines of a new imperial order undeniably took shape. Hopes for centralized oversight, of course, were tempered significantly by distance, tradition, and colonial conditions. The practice of representing the body politic through elected assemblies recovered and flourished, even though the Crown rebuffed every colony but Massachusetts that sought to declare an elected assembly as a right. In 1696 the Crown established the Board of Trade as the successor to the Lords of Trade. The Board's responsibilities in colonial administration included nominating candidates to the colonial councils, writing instructions to new governors, and evaluating colonial laws. More informally, the Board became the object of lobbying by mercantile and religious interests for decades to come. The system created to regulate colonial trade was strengthened by the passage of a new Navigation Act in 1696, expressly aimed at "preventing frauds, and regulating abuses in the plantation trade." The imperial commercial system applied to all colonies, not just royal ones. The formal union of England and Scotland in 1707 under one monarch and one Parliament made the colonies part of a British Empire placed on increasingly secure footing. However slack it might feel at times in the colonies, the tether of trans-Atlantic empire not only remained attached at the beginning of the eighteenth century, it also had been strengthened in terms of trade. Political and economic calculations in the colonies reflected this—up to the 1760s and beyond.

THE MEANING OF MONARCHY IN PUBLIC LIFE

An irony of the Glorious Revolution in America was that the monarchy became more—not less—central to colonial self-understanding, to the exercise of power, and even to social experience as the threat of Stuart absolutism receded. The installation of William and Mary, and, after Queen Anne failed to produce an heir, the importation from Germany of the Hanover line of kings starting with George

I in 1714, cemented the Protestant monarchy in the British nation. Eighteenth-century Britain was ethnically diverse and geographically dispersed, but a shared commitment to Protestantism increasingly bound together the lion's share of its free people. The monarchs personified this commitment and their history and lineage melded with that of the nation as a whole. American colonists did not need to travel to Britain, and very few of them did, to experience the perceived benefits of its monarchy. Instead, public events, images, and stories celebrating the Protestant monarchy made their way west across the Atlantic.

Reminders of the glories of the British monarchy proliferated in the eighteenth century. Indeed, colonial Americans learned to mark their calendars by the monarchy. Royal birthdays, the death of one monarch, and the coronation of another, the celebration of the arrival of new royal governors—each occasion called for public rituals, mostly joyous. Both elites and ordinary people found meaning in celebration. Speeches, marches, cannonades, formal balls—such ceremonies marked the power of the empire and served the elites who preserved hierarchy and order in the empire's name. Meanwhile, drinking, toasting, bonfires, and fireworks brought ordinary people directly into the action, while giving the wealthy people who provisioned the rituals a chance to show off their generosity. Colonists also celebrated the patron saint days of England, Ireland, Scotland, and Wales, underscoring the inclusion of multiple ethnicities into the empire along the same lines that ethnically themed parades and street festivals still do in the contemporary United States.

One of the oldest and most rowdy royalist celebrations, Pope's Day, underscored the belligerently Protestant character of colonial royalism. This November 5 commemoration of the failure of Guy Fawkes's 1605 plot to detonate Parliament became increasingly popular and elaborate in the decades following the Glorious Revolution. In Boston, rival neighborhood mobs marched their pope effigies and fought one another in the Boston Common. Effigies of the Catholic Stuart family's claimant to the English throne also became part of the Pope's Day celebration, giving more concrete political meaning to popular anti-Catholicism. The port cities that doubled as colonial capitals experienced such events more often and more intensely than towns in the hinterland, but royally inspired commemorations did filter inland. According to one historian's tally, forty years into the eighteenth century, the colonies' biggest cities saw six or more imperial celebrations a year with twenty additional days associated with royalty. These events, which eventually penetrated to the Georgia frontier, wove their way into the fabric of colonial life. Whether in the backcountry or a port, the king's colonial subjects could drink, sometimes to excess, in honor of the father of the empire.

Printed materials encouraged colonists to think of their history as intertwined with British and Protestant history. Almanacs recorded the dates of the various royal-related rituals and, along with minister's sermons, reminded colonists of major events of Protestant martyrdom such as the revocation of the Edict of Nantes, ending toleration of Protestants in France. Colonists who wanted to develop greater historical expertise could read dynastic histories and royal genealogies that traced

Figure 7.2 **Stoneware jug (mid-eighteenth century). The "GR" placed in the middle of a radiating sun stands for "George Rex" (King George) and celebrates the symbolic centrality of monarchy in colonial life. Tokens of the royal presence in the lives of English colonists were pervasive in the eighteenth century, from common objects like this one to public holidays celebrating royal birthdays. Jugs like this were exported to Britain and the British colonies from the German-speaking region of Westerwald and thus also betoken a burgeoning trans-Atlantic consumer culture. Courtesy, Winterthur Museum, Jug 1727–1760, Westerwald, Germany, gift of Thomas A. Gray, 1974.35.**

the history of Britain through monarchical timelines. For some members of the colonial elite, identification with royal lineages stoked their desire to see their own positions atop the social hierarchy as part of a firmly rooted lineage. Printed images of royalty, sometimes in books for children, as well as mugs and ceramics with royal symbols, were available for purchase (see Figure 7.2). Colonists could not mistake the royal origin of authority when royal portraits hung in public buildings and court proceedings began with the exhortation "God Save the King."

Yet for all royalism's penetration of American consciousness, the habits of English political thought and the working out of institutional details in the colonies ensured the continuance of a vein of skepticism and resistance toward certain forms of royal authority. The monarchy might occupy the central place in the colonists' conception of the political universe, and even Puritans might preach that the stability of the Hanoverian line indicated divine favor. In practice, however, politics involved clashing interests and ideas that royalism struggled to reconcile.

Individual colonies sought to influence imperial policy at its source, employing lobbyists in London. These agents were more often Englishmen than colonists dispatched across the ocean. Their job was to use their connections and knowledge of the various parts of the British bureaucracy—the Board of Trade, the Privy Council, the secretary of state, the Treasury—with responsibility for colonial oversight to advance their employer's agenda, as outlined by the elected assemblies. Colonies wished to see that their own laws were approved by the Board of Trade, intercolonial boundary disputes were resolved in their favor, and imperial trade policy was sensitive to their economic needs. In the 1750s, agents cooperated to facilitate transmission of military subsidies from the British government to the colonies during the war with France. Previously, the agents had not usually coordinated their efforts, sometimes because they did not have the same goals. The plantations of the British West Indies reaped a windfall from the Molasses Act, which granted these islands an exclusive right to sell sugar within the empire, much to the chagrin of mainland colonists who preferred to have legal access to cheaper sugar from the French islands. In general, the mainland colonies and their agents could not match the access to power and privilege enjoyed by the British West Indies, whose wealthy absentee plantation owners oversaw the English end of slave- and sugar-trading operations. The most successful absentees settled onto vast English estates, occupied seats in Parliament, and even garnered aristocratic titles. Still, the mainland colonial leaders understood that persuasiveness, contacts, and even bribery could manipulate British officials in their favor. North American politicians were under no illusion that the British state would automatically look out for each colony's interests or understand colonial perspectives.

Mixed, if not muddled, priorities and structures undermined the ability of the British state to render its rule more consistent or forceful in America. Domestic political calculations guided the British officials best positioned to influence colonial policy, most notably Treasury minister Robert Walpole and the duke of Newcastle, who served as secretary of state from 1724 to 1748. Proposals from the Board of Trade to regularize and tighten colonial governance often were shunted aside, as Walpole sought to minimize the cost of colonial administration and to conduct government with as little interference of Parliament as he could manage. Parliament could be induced to support particular economic interests, passing bills such as the Molasses Act (1733) that prohibitively taxed the colonists' importation of foreign sugar and the Hat Act (1732) that protected domestic hat-makers from colonial competition. Yet Parliament did not insist on asserting its own or Crown supremacy in the colonies.

The colonists' enthusiasm for the monarchy did not easily translate into the more consistent or effective exercise of royal power in America. The symbols and celebrations of English royal history and benign Hanoverian rule proved easier to disseminate than the concrete benefits of government patronage. Royal governorships sometimes went to particularly well-connected American-born men, but more often the king's leading emissaries to his colonial subjects emerged from Britain's own aristocratic and military patronage networks, as did the relatively small handful of other royally appointed offices in the colonies. The governor's council, which functioned as a sort of upper legislative chamber and advisory cabinet, had only a small number of seats to offer leading members of the provincial elite. At the local level, opportunities for the prestige of political office remained relatively static, as imperial officials hesitated to expand the number of counties listed on colonial maps in the early years.

The scarcity of offices and thus the limited reach of royal patronage in America would have mattered less had not the colonies experienced such rapid population growth and economic expansion during the eighteenth century. The amount of room at or near the top of local and provincial hierarchies was finite; the potential demand for access to places toward the top of those hierarchies, meanwhile, was growing. Love for the monarchy could not change this imbalance.

In any event, colonials proved adept at distinguishing between the distant, benevolent monarchy and the monarchy's representatives in their midst. Careful research has debunked the once accepted libel that Lord Cornbury, the governor of New York and New Jersey from 1702 to 1708, dressed in women's clothes to embody the authority of Queen Anne more vividly. But that three New Yorkers conveyed this scurrilous story reveals something about the contempt that leading colonists could muster for their governors. The pattern of bitter factional rivalry that Jacob Leisler's rise and fall left behind in New York made that province a rough place for royal governors to earn the benefits of the patronage that landed them in Manhattan in the first place. And *earn* is the right word. Colonial royal governors depended on the provincial assemblies for their salaries. The assemblies thus enjoyed leverage over their royally appointed executives, a leverage that weakened when it did not torment the governors.

Royal governors, and therefore royal government itself, occupied a peculiar institutional position. The Board of Trade at home and the assemblies abroad pinched from the governors some of the patronage positions that might have enhanced their authority. Still, the governors had significant powers beyond patronage—such as the ability to veto legislation, to dissolve the legislative assembly for extended periods, to remove judges, and to create courts. These powers actually exceeded those the British monarchs could exercise on the home island. But giving a person this sort of power only made colonists wary and untrusting. The New Jersey Assembly pointedly noted to their new governor Robert Hunter that "the most violent and imprudent Stretches of Arbitrary Power were stampt with the great Name of the Queens Prerogative Royal" by previous governor Lord Cornbury, who ruled, they alleged, through "Bribery, Extortion, and a Contempt of Laws. . . ."[10]

For those colonists well read in English popular political theory, as well as those steeped in the history of the usurpatious Stuart kings, unchecked executive power led to corruption and the destruction of liberty. Such fears of gubernatorial corruption may make us want to label some educated colonials as paranoid, hypocritical, or both. Colonial elites, as we have seen, had no problem sitting atop gendered and racial hierarchies, hoarding the benefits of liberty for themselves. Be that as it may, an embrace of royal histories and imagery did not prevent colonial political elites from contesting royal policies and challenging royal appointees.

Colonial elites liked to believe that the king intended for them to exercise a free hand politically, even against his rotating emissaries in the governor's office. Thus, colonial assemblies refused to view the governors' instructions as binding on them. As one newspaper essayist in Pennsylvania explained, neither reflexive imitation of English constitutional models nor the enhancement of the governor's power would produce desirable change. Indeed, such changes would not be "consistent with our liberties." For those who believed that a strong colonial executive was necessary "to curb the contentions of jarring parties," the essayist answered, "There can be no liberty without faction; for the latter cannot be suppressed, without introducing slavery in the place of the former."[11] Free white colonists assumed that their benevolent monarchs would not ask them to make such a trade. They also knew how to play the game. Pennsylvania, though a proprietary colony, still had to send its laws for royal review every five years. Passing laws of a shorter duration, sending several laws all at once, and re-passing vetoed laws provided alternatives to submitting to the will of distant authority.

While the Glorious Revolution helped to settle certain aspects of Britain's unwritten constitution and to integrate the American colonies more fully into a Protestant empire, ambiguities were a part of the new imperial order. In particular, the meaning of representative government in and for the colonies remained a puzzle. In Britain, Parliament confirmed its supremacy over the monarchy by seizing control of the royal succession twice within a generation, first to install William and Mary and later the House of Hanover. But from a colonial point of view, the logic of the Glorious Revolution also seemed to make their legislative assemblies the legitimate locus of political power—a mini-Parliament for each colony. It was not only Catholic leanings, but also the impulse to strip away local power that had made the Stuarts so objectionable in England and in the colonies. For the first several decades of the eighteenth century, few people on either side of the Atlantic had obvious incentives to clear up the role of the British Parliament in American political life. In colonial politics, ambiguity could sometimes be more useful than certainty or clarity.

DEFERENCE OR DEMOCRACY: THE NATURE OF COLONIAL GOVERNMENT

One way to participate in colonial governance was to win an election. That was the plan in 1738 of Edmund Scarburgh of Accomack County on Virginia's Eastern Shore, who sought the seat of a recently deceased member of the House of Burgesses. Accordingly, Scarburgh generously provided "strong Liquors" at a horse race and at a militia muster. On election day, he supplied drink from a cart "near the Court-house Door, where many People drank thereof." The question before Virginia's legislative assembly, to which Scarburgh had been elected, was whether anything improper occurred, as it seemed clear enough that Scarburgh had distributed all this liquor to facilitate his election. The body, after debating the matter, resolved Scarburgh to be "duly elected." If Scarburgh had stepped too close to the line of acceptable campaigning, he did not cross it. In reality, though, Scarburgh acted in accordance with Virginia's political customs. Providing ample liquid refreshments to potential voters such as those attending militia muster, or having a network of prominent political allies do so, demonstrated the sort of liberality Virginia voters expected from their leaders.

There were multiple centers of government power in the colonies, but the eventual presence of elected assemblies in every colony and the lack of titled lords with inherited access to office encouraged democratic dynamism. The results were slanted, the contestants for power hardly drawn from a universal pool of colonial talent. Still, competitiveness among elites, jockeying between royal and representative institutions, and strikingly large pools of voters accustomed to being courted moved the political culture beyond mere deference to anointed leaders. Scarburgh obviously did not take the chance that his election was a foregone conclusion, his desire for office motivating him to invest significant resources. His votes, a majority of his new colleagues in the Virginia Assembly concluded, were well earned, and no doubt the assemblymen regarded their own votes the same way.[12]

Structurally, colonial politics rested on offices controlled by the Crown as well as those that required the endorsement of colonial voters. On the mainland and in the British West Indies, a council, typically of twelve, served as an upper legislative chamber, as an advisory panel to the governor, and as a court of appeals. Royal governors as well as other people with access to the Board of Trade recommended potential members of these governor's councils. The Board then made life appointments to the council. (The charters of Connecticut and Rhode Island allowed for the election of council members to serve alongside the elected governor.) Membership conferred additional stature, influence, and access to royal patronage on a small number of men. The governor did not require the council's approval to exercise his considerable prerogatives, such as the irreversible veto of legislation.

The political action increasingly occurred in the elected lower legislative houses. Well-to-do and long-established men found their way into provincewide office far more frequently than more middling neighbors. Candidates frequently ran unopposed. Nonetheless, elites, as Scarburgh understood, could not always expect that voters would validate their particular ambitions. As a consequence, popular influence flavored political systems designed by colonial elites and overseen by imperial authorities.

Property ownership both opened up and limited the scope of participatory politics in the colonies. The freehold, possession of a piece of land for life, was the essential qualification to vote. Some colonies defined the necessary amount of land a potential voter had to own by acreage, others by the land's monetary value. In New England, local elections sometimes had less stringent property standards than voting for assemblymen. The assumption brought over from England continued that land ownership signified a person's ability, character, and commitment to independently make judgments about the best interest of society. Several colonies determined that paying taxes sufficed. Colonial cities also granted citizenship rights to skilled tradesmen or even poorer people deemed worthy. In any event, compared to England, the relative availability of land to European settlers led to the enfranchisement of over half of adult white men in the eighteenth century. Depending on the colony, these voters either cast their ballot verbally before official recorders or by secret paper ballot. New York, New Jersey, and the Chesapeake colonies fell in the former category; Pennsylvania, South Carolina, and the New England colonies in the latter.

Property standards left a lot of men sidelined from colonial politics, while other laws and customs further whittled down the electorate. Men under twenty-one, even if receiving an early inheritance, could not expect to vote in most instances. The combination of the principal of coverture, assumptions about gender differences, the use of the male pronoun *he*, and more explicit prohibitions in voting laws generally denied women access to the ballot and kept them out of public office. Because property ownership was not a perfect filter against social outsiders, some colonies barred Catholic, Jews, or both from voting. Some Southern colonies also explicitly denied free blacks and Indians the franchise. Clearly, within the colonial context we must not conflate the terms *democratic* or *popular* with *universal*. At the same time, a candidate for office, no matter how well heeled and no matter how circumscribed the electorate, had to take into consideration how to win over his neighbors. Sooner or later in most colonies, ambitions collided, factions formed, or public controversies arose to turn out voters and to remind incumbent officeholders in local and provincewide positions not to take votes for granted.

Both democracy and deference can be found in the pursuit of local authority in the New England countryside, although scruples and customs perhaps made the recruitment of supporters more subtle than in Virginia. The tendency during the seventeenth century to return the same elite men to town office year after year diminished over time. The maelstrom of the Glorious Revolution swept officeholders from their places in local and provincial government. The unpopularity of the Dominion of New England even temporarily overturned elite rule in western Massachusetts, where the uncontested dominance of Hampshire County, Massachusetts, by John Pynchon came to an end. Even his ability to lead the local militia was compromised. There were also long-term causes of more frequent office rotation. Easing property requirements enlarged the electorate. Evidence from Dedham, Massachusetts, suggests that the assumption the wealthier members of the community made the most suitable officeholders did not change. Rather, voters had a larger group of wealthier men from the community from which to choose. Thus, officeholders rotated more frequently, allowing newer faces to enter the ranks of leadership. Perhaps too, as fears of Indian raids and social disorder eased in some regions, less risk was perceived in political competition. In Dedham, just west of Boston, the more open town meeting became increasingly reluctant to cede authority to the much smaller group of elected selectmen.

In Boston and New York City, the desire to prevent royal officials and their local favorites from dominating local politics fueled political innovation and partisanship. Even as Boston's population surged past fifteen thousand, the city clung to town meetings. Throngs of eligible participants had a voice in the port city's affairs. Under the skillful leadership of Elisha Cooke, Jr., Bostonians checked attempts by royal officials and powerful merchants to take power out of the hands of the town meeting, which elected over two hundred officers, from tax assessors to town criers. Lax collection of local taxes was just one of the techniques used by local politicians to retain control of a place that, in terms of population, prominence, and commercial volume, was in every other respect a city rather than a small town. In New York City, factions battled for the political upper hand, though the governors exercised more direct influence over city governance in Manhattan than in Boston.

The seeds of New York's volatile politics were sewn long before Jacob Leisler's brief and controversial rule, ultimately providing democratic seasoning to the elite-dominated political mix. Until 1683 the province lacked an elected assembly, an institution of representative government found in other colonies, and was ruled only by the governor and his appointed council. The imperial turmoil of the 1680s that led to Leisler's rise and fall further truncated the province's experience negotiating conflict with the help of a legislature. For almost twenty years after Leisler's death, those who had opposed and those who had supported his cause continued to struggle against one another, the factions contending for the support of each new royal governor. Other factions emerged to divide New York's elite political class, specifically who should bear more of the burden of taxation, merchants or landholders. Each time a new governor arrived, the rival interest groups sensed the opportunity to rebalance political scales, the ire of whoever found themselves on the outside newly piqued. With a mere twenty-four representatives, three of which—or one-eighth—coming from the manors and with a few plumb appointments like chief justice and mayor of New York City at stake, political competition directly rewarded a relative and often already privileged few. Still, endemic political rivalry was not conducive to deferential behavior—toward the royal administration or one's rivals. When it suited political leaders at particular moments, they or their allies could call up the language of the rights of free people to combat executive tyranny, as Lewis Morris and his allies did in their battle against Governor William Cosby in the 1730s. In such an environment, courting public opinion became a part of politically competitive, indeed combustible, political culture.

Pennsylvanians in the early years of the eighteenth century did not defer to authority either. Quaker David Lloyd sought to rally popular support through the colony's assembly to clip the power of the Penn proprietorship. Lloyd and his allies maneuvered William Penn into approving a Charter of Privileges that did not provide for an upper house checking the assembly. The popular legislature sought to take advantage of the opportunity to expand its powers over the colony's finances. In the mid-eighteenth century, resentments about the Penn family's land policies as well as the challenges of frontier defenses led English-speaking politicians to draw German-speaking immigrants into the electoral fray. Through much of the century, Quaker politicians built a party that adroitly dominated the assembly and out-maneuvered the Penn proprietorship. In the middle colonies, the clash between English liberty and English executive prerogative undermined a consistently deferential political culture. Whenever imperial or proprietary authority seemed weak or the rules governing the empire underwent revision, the potential for political resistance intensified. But even in more ordinary times, colonists remained alert to the ways in which popular politics could advance their interests within the imperial system. Deference and democracy were stamped on the same coin with the king's visage.

DREAMS AND VISIONS

William Byrd II slowly came around to the idea that popularly elected officials could be used against the royally appointed governor. Yet Byrd simultaneously clung to his own dreams of basking in royal favor, becoming governor—or even something grander. Thus, Byrd, though a member of the governor's council, assisted opponents of Governor Alexander Spotswood in elections for the Virginia Assembly. For the patriarchy-minded Byrd, however, democracy might be a tool, but deference to wealth and power was the grand transport, one that ironically made him feel both large and small. A mere two days after his electioneering efforts, Byrd "dreamed the King's daughter was in love with me." Three months later, his unconscious royal imaginings became even more grandiose, if less romantic, as he recorded in his diary "dream[ing] I was very dear to the King and he made me Secretary of State...."[13] For much of his adult life, William Byrd II believed he should be governor, spending many years in London trying to make the right combination of connections, fruitlessly pursuing marriage with women above his station, while indulging in the pleasures of the flesh with those beneath him. Byrd gradually came to realize that a place at the very top of the Chesapeake's political and social hierarchy would elude him. He adapted his political focus and tactics accordingly. But as these diary entries betray, his desire for approval and patronage from the king of England as father figure persisted. We dismiss such visions as mere nocturnal fancies at our own peril.

However unrealistic these particular dreams were, William Byrd II had long believed that for better and for worse, unconscious visions were sometimes prescient. Byrd used his daily entries to chart his efforts to maintain his mental and physical health—his regular reading in Hebrew and Greek, his exercises, and his prayers. Yet sprinkled among recorded routines were omens projected through his dreams and in the heavens. He took heed because "sometimes dreams have been true," as when "my sloop" made it home safely from the West Indies. He also took heed because he lived in an environment where bad weather, debilitating illness, miscarriages, and death threatened to disrupt the peace and harmony of his carefully constructed world. Having dreamt illness of "several of my negroes," he noted "now it came exactly to pass." The dream of "a flaming star," he worried, "portends some judgment to this country or at least to myself." Once, in the midst of a winter rife with difficulties, Byrd even "had my father's grave opened to see him"—finding, however, that "he was so wasted there was not anything to be distinguished."[14] The dutiful child whose father had dispatched him to England in preparation for greatness still wanted answers about his own fate even after becoming a plantation owner, husband, and father. This particular plumbing of life's mysteries was unusually ghoulish, but Byrd's desire to dig beneath the surface of reality, to anticipate the future even if potentially disastrous, is familiar. In colonial America, neither patriarchs nor ordinary people subject to local as well distant imperial governance could resist the urge to read the signs—divine and natural, good and evil, ordering and disordering. The limits of their own earthly powers were all too plain.

CHRONOLOGY

1642–1649	English Civil War.
1649	Charles I executed; Commonwealth established.
1651	Parliament enacts Navigation Act.
1653–1658	Oliver Cromwell rules as lord protector.
1660	Stuart monarchy restored under Charles II.
1674	*Birth of William Byrd II.*
1675	Bacon's Rebellion breaks out in Virginia.
1681	*Byrd begins his study in England.*
1684	Massachusetts charter revoked.
1685	James II becomes king of England. Dominion of New England initiated.
1688	Glorious Revolution.
1691	Massachusetts receives a new royal charter. Jacob Leisler executed.
1696	Board of Trade established.
1705	*Byrd takes over his deceased father's Westover Plantation.*
1707	Act of Union unites England and Scotland.
1709	*Byrd becomes a member of Virginia governor's council; commences keeping a diary.*

1714	George I becomes king of Great Britain, establishing the Hanover line.
1729	South Carolina and North Carolina become permanent royal colonies.
1732	Hat Act.
1733	Molasses Act.
1744	*Death of William Byrd II.*
1760	George III begins reign.

NOTES

1. William Byrd II, "Virginia Council Journals, 1726–1753," *The Virginia Magazine of History and Biography* 32 (1924): 26–27.
2. William Byrd II, *The Secret Diary of William Byrd of Westover, 1709–1712*, ed. Louis B. Wright and Marion Tinling (Richmond, VA: Dietz Press, 1941), 113.
3. Exodus 20:12, *King James Bible* (1611), http://www.kingjamesbibleonline.org/1611-Bible/book.php?book=Exodus&chapter=20&verse=12.
4. James Lockwood, *Religion the highest interest of a civil community, and the surest means of its prosperity. A sermon preached before the General Assembly of the colony of Connecticut, at Hartford, on the day of the anniversary election, May 9th, 1754* (New London, CT: Timothy Green, 1754), 33–34, 40.
5. "Observations in Several Voyages and Travels in America," *The London Magazine*, July 1746, reprinted in *William and Mary Quarterly*, 1st ser., 15 (1907): 5.
6. Robert Olwell, *Masters, Slaves, and Subjects: The Culture of Power in the South Carolina Low Country, 1740–1790* (Ithaca, NY: Cornell University Press, 1998), 7.
7. "Journal of a French Traveller in the Colonies, 1765, I" *American Historical Review* 26 (1921): 738.
8. *The Documentary History of New-York*, ed. E. B. O'Callaghan (Albany, NY: Weed, Parsons, 1849), Vol. 2, 342, 380.
9. *Documentary History of New-York*, Vol. 2, 379.
10. *The humble representation of the General Assembly of Her Majestys province of New-Jersey, to His Excellency Robert Hunter, Esq; captain general and governour in chief of the provinces of New-Jersey & New-York in America, and vice-admiral of the same, &c.* (New York: William Bradford, 1710), 1.
11. *Pennsylvania Gazette*, March 21–March 30, 1737/1738.
12. *Journals of the House of Burgesses of Virginia, 1727–1734, 1736–1740*, ed. H. R. McIlwaine (Richmond, 1910), 370.
13. William Byrd of Virginia, *The London Diary (1717–1721) and Other Writings*, ed. Louis B. Wright and Marion Tinling (New York: Oxford University Press, 1958), 444, 494.
14. Byrd II, *Secret Diary*, 126, 207, 194, 133.

SUGGESTIONS FOR FURTHER READING

Kenneth A. Lockridge, *The Diary, and Life, of William Byrd II, of Virginia, 1674–1744* (Chapel Hill: University of North Carolina Press, 1987), provide valuable insights into the inner and outer life of a prominent and paradigmatic eighteenth-century Chesapeake patriarch. Kathleen M. Brown, *Good Wives, Nasty Wenches & Anxious Patriarchs: Gender, Race, and Power in Colonial Virginia* (Chapel Hill: University of North Carolina Press, 1996), offers an analysis of the social world constructed by, as well as challenging to, Byrd and men of his ilk.

Works helpful for conceptualizing the familial model of government and patriarchy include: Gordon S. Wood, *The Radicalism of the American Revolution* (New York: Knopf, 1992); Mary Beth Norton, *Founding Mothers & Fathers: Gendered Power and the Forming of American Society* (New York: Knopf, 1996); and Jay Fliegelman, *Prodigals & Pilgrims: The American Revolution against Patriarchal Authority, 1750–1800* (Cambridge, UK: Cambridge University Press, 1982).

Philip D. Morgan, *Slave Counterpoint: Black Culture in the Eighteenth-Century Chesapeake & Lowcountry* (Chapel Hill: University of North Carolina Press, 1998), applies the concept of patriarchy to slavery in two crucial regions. Rhys Isaac, *The Transformation of Virginia, 1740–1790* (Chapel Hill: University of North Carolina Press, 1982); Bernard Bailyn, "Politics and Social Structure in Virginia," in *Seventeenth Century America*, ed. J. M. Smith (Chapel Hill: University of North Carolina Press, 1959), 90–115; T. H. Breen, *Puritans and Adventurers: Change and Persistence in Early America* (New York: Oxford University Press, 1980); and Trevor Burnard, "A Tangled Cousinry? Associational Networks of the Maryland Elite, 1691–1776," *Journal of Southern History* 61 (1995): 17–44, offer insights on the development and cultural articulation of patriarchy in the Chesapeake.

There are plethora of studies of social structure, authority, and politics in New England. Richard L. Bushman, *From Puritan to Yankee: Character and the Social Order in Connecticut, 1690–1765* (Cambridge, MA: Harvard University Press, 1967); Kenneth A. Lockridge, *A New England Town: The First Hundred Years*, expanded ed. (New York: Norton, 1985); Stephen Innes, *Labor in a New Land: Economy and Society in Seventeenth-Century Springfield* (Princeton, NJ: Princeton University Press, 1983); Gregory H. Nobles, *Divisions Throughout the Whole: Politics and Society in Hampshire County, Massachusetts, 1740–1775* (Cambridge, UK: Cambridge University Press, 1983); John Frederick Martin, *Profits in the Wilderness: Entrepreneurship and the Founding of New England Towns in the Seventeenth Century* (Chapel Hill: University of North Carolina Press, 1991); and Christopher Grasso, *The Speaking Aristocracy: Transforming Public Discourse in Eighteenth-Century Connecticut* (Chapel Hill: University of North Carolina Press, 1999), are among the most important. On urban society and politics, see G.B. Warden, *Boston, 1689–1776* (Boston: Little Brown, 1970); and Gary B. Nash, *The Urban Crucible: Social Change, Political Consciousness, and the Origins of the American Revolution* (Cambridge, MA: Harvard University Press, 1979).

Valuable studies of society and politics in particular colonies also include: Robert Olwell, *Masters, Slaves, and Subjects: The Culture of Power in the South Carolina Low Country, 1740–1790* (Ithaca, NY: Cornell University Press, 1998); A. Roger Ekrich, *"Poor Carolina": Politics and Society in Colonial North Carolina, 1729–1776* (Chapel Hill: University of North Carolina Press, 1981); Patricia U. Bonomi, *A Fractious People: Politics and Society in Colonial New York* (New York: Columbia University Press, 1971) and *The Lord Cornbury Scandal: The Politics of Reputation in British America* (Chapel Hill: University of North Carolina Press, 1998); Sung Bok Kim, *Landlord and Tenant in Colonial New York: Manorial Society, 1664–1775* (Chapel Hill: University of North Carolina Press, 1978); Brendan McConville, *These Daring Disturbers of the Public Peace: The Struggle for Property and Power in Early New Jersey* (Ithaca, NY: Cornell University Press, 1999); and Joseph E. Illick, *Colonial Pennsylvania: A History* (New York: Scribner's, 1976). For analysis of Jacob Leisler and the complexities of his rebellion, see David William Vorhees, "The 'Fervent Zeale' of Jacob Leisler," *William and Mary Quarterly*, 3d ser., 51 (1994): 447–472. Andrew Jackson O'Shaugnessy, *An Empire Divide: The American Revolution and the British Caribbean* (Philadelphia: University of Pennsylvania Press, 2000), facilitates comparisons between the West Indies and the North American mainland.

Carla Gardina Pestana, *The English Atlantic in the Age of Revolution, 1640–1661* (Cambridge, MA: Harvard University Press, 2004), investigates a period of transition for politics and the acquisition of labor. On the policies and politics of the Stuarts that touched off a revolution of sorts on both sides of the Atlantic, see David S. Lovejoy, *The Glorious Revolution in America* (New York: Harper & Row, 1972); and Alison Gilbert Olson, *Anglo-American Politics 1660–1775: The Relationship between Parties in England and Colonial America* (New York: Oxford University Press, 1973).

Brendan McConville, *The King's Three Faces: The Rise and Fall of Royal America, 1688–1776* (Chapel Hill: University of North Carolina Press, 2006); Jack P. Greene, *Peripheries and Centers: Constitutional Development in the Extended Polity of the British Empire and the United States, 1607–1788* (Athens: University of Georgia Press, 1986); and Bernard Bailyn, *The Origins of American Politics* (New York: Vintage, 1967), provide contrasting perspectives on the political culture of empire in the eighteenth century and its implications for colonial governance. Robert J. Dinkin, *Voting in Provincial America: A Study of Elections in the Thirteen Colonies, 1689–1776* (Westport, CT: Greenwood, 1977), offers a comprehensive review of voting laws and practices. James Henretta, *"Salutary Neglect": Colonial Administration under the Duke of Newcastle* (Princeton, NJ: Princeton University Press, 1972), details the development of British colonial policy. Michael G. Kammen, *A Rope of Sand: The Colonial Agents, British Politics, and the American Revolution* (Ithaca, NY: Cornell University Press, 1968), investigates the men and the means deployed to influence that policy.

CHAPTER 8

The Natural and Supernatural Worlds

As autumn gave way to winter in 1671, Elizabeth Knapp continued to confound her master, minister Samuel Willard, with hateful verbal outbursts and bizarre physical displays. On Sunday, December 17, the servant girl's shocking and erratic indications of diabolical possession reached a climax: the devil, it seemed, drew Elizabeth's tongue from her mouth "most frightfully to an extraordinary length and greatness" while her body contorted. When Willard returned from church, "a grum, low, yet audible voice" spoke from inside Knapp, taunting the minister, "Oh! you are a great rogue." Steeled by his faith, Willard examined Knapp to see whether the event was "counterfeit." Knapp appeared to be in a trance. Willard and the diabolical voice emanating from the girl then engaged in a dialogue, the voice accusing Willard of telling "the people a company of lies." When the minister denounced Satan, whom he presumed to be speaking through Knapp, as a "liar," the voice jeered elusively, "I am not Satan, I am a pretty black boy, this is my pretty girl. . . ." Worrying that engaging the devil in such a conversation would do "little good," Willard instead decided to lead those with him in the room in prayer. This tack temporarily stilled the voice inside Knapp, but once the prayers concluded, the voice returned, threatening to carry away Knapp and claiming, "I am stronger than God. . . ."

The sixteen-year-old Knapp forced leading men of Groton, Massachusetts, including her own father, as well as a local doctor, and Willard himself, to make some difficult judgments about cause and effect and, more deeply, about the relationship between the observable natural world and the more inscrutable supernatural world. Neither Elizabeth nor her examiners lacked guidance in trying to make sense of her afflictions. Indeed, they had medical treatises, popular knowledge, religious teachings, and the Scripture itself on which to draw as they puzzled over Elizabeth's condition. Unfortunately, none of these sources offered a surefire explanation for what was happening, why it was happening, and what should be done about it. Willard proceeded cautiously, not wishing to jump to conclusions.

Knapp, who first showed signs of acute distress in October, offered various accounts over the course of her tribulations as to what drove her to speak and act in such threatening ways. Initially, she attempted to play down her "sudden shrieks," but then would "burst forth into immoderate and extravagant laughter." Soon, however, there was no denying the seriousness of her condition; on October

30, she cried out as a pain rapidly worked its way up her body, and she claimed to be strangled. On succeeding days she fell into "violent fit[s]." Knapp's first explanation took the form of a witchcraft accusation against a woman in the neighborhood. Having backed off of the charge, Knapp detailed her encounters over the previous three years with the devil, who sought to draw Knapp into league with him by offering her, in Willard's recounting, "such things as suited her youthful fancy, money, silks, fine clothes, ease from labor to show her the whole world." The devil subsequently grew more persistent in his pursuit of Knapp, showing her a book of covenants penned in blood that other people had made with him; he also grew more macabre, trying to convince Knapp to kill her parents, Willard's children, and Willard himself. Knapp several times over the course of her affliction insisted that she resisted entering into the devil's covenant, but her story continued to evolve. She claimed the devil assumed the form of a black dog who hounded her to sign the covenant. She again leveled witchcraft accusations against a neighbor. Meanwhile, her intense fits continued, even causing her to emit dog barks and calf bleats. The tormented girl finally confessed to signing the devil's covenant in her own blood, Satan, this time in the guise of an old man, guiding her hand since she did not know how to write. Two days later she recanted this admission of a blood oath, while continuing to tell stories of satanic encounters.

As Willard understood, Knapp's descriptions of her travails, like her physical suffering, were deeply troubling, but they were neither unique nor to be taken at face value. In New England, as in Old, community members did from time to time accuse one another of witchcraft. Puritan New Englanders, moreover, knew all about covenants. Puritans understood society as a series of covenants—between husbands and wives, masters and servants, ministers and congregations. Each new church congregation represented a covenant among its founders. Puritans viewed their place in America as a covenanted relationship between themselves and God directly akin to that between the Lord and the Israelites in the Old Testament. Satan's attempts to lure Christians off the righteous path by soliciting an oath sealed in blood were a perverse mockery of the sacred covenants that bound together Puritan society.

But as Samuel Willard and at least some of his neighbors also understood, not every accusation of witchcraft or satanic malfeasance was true. Moreover, as Willard frankly acknowledged in his account of Knapp's ordeal, such suffering often had more commonplace physical explanations. Thus, not long after his servant's initial confession, Willard had a doctor examine Knapp, "who judged the main part of her distemper to be natural," explaining that "the foulness of her stomach and corruptions of her blood" caused "fumes in her brain," leading to "strange fantasies." The medicine the doctor prescribed showed some initial signs of working, before Knapp began to backslide. That the doctor's explanation stemmed from theories of the body that would not constitute medical science in our own time should not detract from the fact that Willard sought and the doctor initially rendered a physiological explanation for her afflictions. Confronted with Knapp's continued derangement, the doctor conceded that the cause was in fact "diabolical," recommended fasting, and then divorced himself from the case, leaving the girl in the hands of the ministers. Natural and supernatural explanations were alternatives, but belief in one clearly did not preclude belief in the other.[1]

Like modern Americans, colonial Americans were scientific and superstitious. They identified themselves with one or another religious denomination and practiced various forms of folk magic. They learned by book and word-of-mouth wisdom. They contemplated the marvels of the American landscape and consumed the latest scientific thinking from Europe. They viewed physical disease as God's will yet pursued medical advances. They accused one another of witchcraft and tested those accusations in the courtroom according to the rules of law. The executions associated with the infamous Salem Witch Trials of 1692 tend to obscure the complexity and even subtlety of how colonists understood their own relationship to natural and supernatural forces that, they believed, shaped their fortunes. Meanwhile, the backlash against the fatal Salem prosecutions tends to shroud the changes and the continuities in how colonists viewed their physical environment and its place in a God-centered universe.

The transition from the seventeenth century is not a simple one from trembling superstition to confidently secular enlightenment, or from a hodgepodge of magical beliefs to a systemized set of scientific ones. Nonetheless, an emerging emphasis, particularly in learned circles, on observation-based approaches to nature challenged and began to tame the impulse to assign divine meaning to discrete natural events. The natural did not vanquish the supernatural, but the supernatural did have to share more of the road, especially in matters of law and letters.

Although this chapter has more to do with how people thought than what they did, the Knapp-Willard episode indicates how a crisis of presumed supernatural origin reveals something about power and social conflict in colonial society. But then again, as this chapter will demonstrate, the scientific interpretation of nature also reflected and was forged by power relations and social inequities of the era. Knapp's taunting denunciations of her minister-master, the fantasies of violence she expressed toward Willard and her own parents, the transfer of her allegiance to the devil as her new master—all suggest deep feelings of unresolved anger and resentment by a young woman who had limited control over her own circumstances, future as well as present. Social rank and gender had carved out a place of female subordination against which she had almost no socially acceptable recourse to protest, save, perhaps, possession itself. Alternatively, we might assign Knapp's suffering to a chemical imbalance or condition such as schizophrenia. From this distance, we cannot diagnose precisely what caused Elizabeth Knapp and her neighbors to endure her prolonged trial. Still, historians have drawn on this event and others like it to interpret some of the underlying tensions and contradictions of the society in which she lived. In feeling the tug of anger at her gender-determined fate, the seemingly helpless Elizabeth Knapp was certainly not alone.

Such insights notwithstanding, we also should conclude from this event that, like all people, colonial Americans groped toward an understanding of the world around them by using the materials and assumptions they had at hand. For them, those materials and assumptions included a set of theologically sanctioned beliefs about God and Satan, a literature that recorded wonders, miracles, and "remarkable providences," and a mélange of centuries-old folk beliefs about magic, fortune-telling, and witchcraft. To satisfy their curiosity about the natural world, they also studied scientists, philosophers, and medical practitioners extending backward to the ancient Greeks and forward to their own times. It is useful to understand their conflicts and discoveries using our own medical, scientific, and psychological knowledge, but it is more essential that we understand the natural and supernatural worlds of colonial America on the colonists' terms.

PROVIDENTIALISM AND THE LORE OF WONDERS

As awful and disorienting as Elizabeth Knapp's torments were, it seemed to Willard that God had intervened at key moments to protect her. Thus, Willard recorded that Knapp almost threw herself into a well, but "God's providence prevented" her from doing so. Knapp also explained to Willard that at one point she almost signed the devil's covenant, "but . . . by God's goodness she had been prevented from doing that, which she of herself had been ready enough to assent to. . . ."[2] Providence—God's direct participation in and control over human affairs and God's ongoing attempt to convey, however obscurely, his purposes—was an article of faith for many Christian believers. Providentialism provided an almost irresistible way for the faithful, ministers and ordinary people alike, to interpret their observations of the everyday world. In other words, God not only controlled the sweep of history and the role of human communities in the unfolding of a divine plan, but God's will also was indicated through all sorts of signs, wonders, and natural events. Such events were as immediate and earthy as the death of livestock and as remote and heavenly as a comet streaking across the night sky. Ordinary events, as well as Knapp's extraordinary behavior, prompted colonists to see the operation of Providence in their own lives, in ways that while sometimes comforting to them, often produced tremendous anxiety.

Puritan migrants to New England and their offspring had both religious and historical reasons to think in providential terms. The Calvinist doctrines at the core of their belief system emphasized an all-powerful God. Human beings did not have the power to manipulate God's will or to affect their own divinely prescribed fates. This stern rejection of claims the Catholic Church made to having intercessory powers that could assist the faithful in securing their salvation as well as centuries of occult practices by ordinary people helped fuel the purifying zeal of certain English Protestants. Puritans believed the Anglican Church did not sufficiently commit itself to rooting out such beliefs and practices, whether Catholic or pagan in origin. Puritans did believe that one could pray to God for forgiveness or the gift of saving grace, but the results were entirely beyond the agency of humans. The Puritans' very presence in the American landscape expressed God's Providence. The Lord had chosen the Puritans to establish a godly order and literally cleared the path for his people by sending plagues to empty New England of its native inhabitants.

God's power superseded the established laws of nature and could punish individuals, whole communities, or even entire colonies or peoples, in the manner and timing of God's own choosing. Thus, New Englanders believed any sin from murder to Sabbath-breaking was liable to provoke, sooner or later, God's wrath. In the later decades of the seventeenth century, Puritan ministers warned their congregations with increased intensity to expect providential punishment because of the people's laxity in their faith. The stunning attack by Metacom and his Indian allies known as King Philip's War provided dramatic proof of God's fateful, reproving hand, while the ultimate defeat of Metacom's forces displayed God's providential deliverance.

The ministerial emphasis on Providence fed the inclination of clergymen and ordinary inhabitants of New England to detect all sorts of signs and portents. God was all-powerful, and God's will was unknowable. But that did not prevent people from wanting to detect from whatever intermediate sources available the connections between what they could see and what remained hidden. The world was suffused with wonders, remarkable occurrences—in the heavens, in the weather, in the cycles of birth and death. The very shape of the clouds in the sky might indicate something beyond the likelihood of rain; eclipses, unaccountable noises, earthquakes, and stillbirths were signs of punishment for past transgressions or dark hints of suffering still to come. Thus, New Englanders lived in what one historian described as an "enchanted universe" in which supernatural forces shaped nature in obscure, yet meaningful ways.[3]

New Englanders did not have to know precisely what a wonder meant to find it remarkable enough to record and puzzle over. Joseph Beacon, lying in bed in Boston, purportedly had a conversation with a mutilated apparition of his brother in London, who reported that he had been "most barbarously and injuriously Butchered, by a Debauched Drunken Fellow." Over a month later, Beacon received word from England that his brother had died the very day of the original apparition, having been attacked by a man wielding a fireplace tool snatched from a tavern.[4] Dreams might be prophetic, as when Boston minister John Wilson related to Massachusetts Bay colony founder John Winthrop, "Before he was resolved to come into this country, he dreamed he was here, and that he saw a church arise out of the earth, which grew up and became a marvellous goodly church." Those who witnessed the healing of the fatally injured or who survived rough sea voyages had wondrous tales to tell. But almost by their very nature, the meaning of wonders was not transparent. Harvard student Edward Taylor recorded a story from the college president of a seven-month-old baby who allegedly told his nurse, "This is an hard world."[5]

Increase Mather, Massachusetts' leading minister, admitted the gulf between observance and understanding. He commented in 1684: "One providence seems to look this way, another providence seems to look that way, quite contrary to one another. Hence these works are marveilous."[6] So much of the world's operation was hidden from sight that those shards of the supernatural that revealed themselves were that much more irresistible and therefore remarkable.

Rather than challenge the lore of wonders, the information directly and indirectly available to this highly literate population only encouraged people to look for and believe in miraculous phenomena. When it came to the lore of wonders, there was no obvious line to be drawn between the literate and the illiterate, the sophisticated and the plain. Traditions long predating the Protestant Reformation attuned New Englanders to supernatural signs. The Bible itself, which Puritans were enjoined to read, contained ample examples of miracles and prophecies. Colonists brought knowledge of wonders with them, as the London printers kept alive a tradition going back to the Middle Ages, with such titles as *The Doome warning all men to Judgemente: Wherein are contayned for the most parte all the straunge Prodigies hapned in the Worlde.* Printed collections drew on evidence going back to Roman times. Extreme weather conditions, shooting stars, the movements of the planets, and unique specimens of deformation from the animal world—all were fodder for such volumes.

American colonists were not to be completely outdone by their English cousins and predecessors. Cotton Mather, Increase's son and a leading minister in his own right, set about collecting wondrous stories of "Illustrious Providences" for publication, as had Edward Johnson and Nathaniel Morton before him. The younger Mather enlisted the support of his clerical colleagues to gather materials for his book. For Puritans, a world of wonders, visible signs of otherwise invisible phenomenon, may well have had a particularly powerful resonance. Their theological model juxtaposed an invisible, true church of saints to the visible world of their own churches made up of members who believed they had been infused with God's saving grace. No one, however, could be sure to what extent the invisible, true church overlapped with the visible one. Such beliefs left everyone, including the most pious, suspended in uncertainty. The desire to know more—more about the fate of one's own soul and that of neighbors—helped keep the lore of wonders alive.

Men and women often did not content themselves to merely observe wonders or to accept their earthly fates. The ultimate status of their souls might be in God's hands, but the uncertainty of their physical circumstances, the suddenness with which they could experience material setbacks, personal catastrophes, or death made the appeal of magic powerful. Prayers placed the prayer at God's mercy; magic had the appeal of changing the course of events, or at the very least warding off unwanted evils. Similarly, if natural events such as comets and eclipses contained portents—in other words, if aspects of the future were at least conceivably knowable—then the presumed powers of astrology to read human implications into the movements of the stars and planets were very attractive to some colonists. The fortune-tellers and healers appealed to ordinary people for the same reason. To leave fate to its own devices or to submit to ailments for which doctors had no dependable cures bumped up against the desire for knowledge and help. Colonists wanted more specific answers than divine Providence for why bad things happened to otherwise seemingly good people.

As with the lore of wonders, popular magic drew on centuries of folk knowledge passed down through the generations and incorporated into medieval Christianity. While magical thinking did not constitute an organized and systematic alternative religion to Protestantism, the appeal of human beings able to predict and even control aspects of the future persisted. How-to guides and instruction manuals from England were surreptitiously passed around in New England. The use of common household objects—for instance, observing the motion of a sieve balanced on scissors while posing questions—made simple magic readily available. Ordinary people who engaged in magic or relied on the perceived powers of others did not see themselves as repudiating their Christianity, but supplementing it, taking into their own hands for their own practical purposes the power that ministers and other learned men claimed to have to make sense of wonders.

The Anglican Church in England paid lip service to combating the lore of magic and its practice, but never to the Puritans' satisfaction, which suggests that belief in magic, divination, and the efficacy of ritual crossed the Atlantic with immigrants to the Southern colonies as well. Rural English people viewed the hearth as a potential entranceway for witches that might be secured through witchposts and carvings. Virginia planter William Byrd II, as we saw seen, put considerable stock in dreams and portents.

For their part, the West Africans who began to arrive on the North American mainland in great numbers in the late seventeenth century brought a diversity of spiritual ideas and customs that fed the stream of American supernaturalism. Belief in divination was common among Africans, while Africans and Europeans shared the notion of witchcraft as a malevolent art. Instead of harnessing the power of the devil, as Europeans understood witchcraft, Africans believed witches harnessed the power of particular deities in African cosmology. Even the use of urine in certain witchcraft-related rituals echoes across the cultures of masters and slaves. Superstition, like so much colonial American culture, involved a process of adaptation; archaeological excavation from George Washington's Mount Vernon turned up the penis bone of a raccoon that may have been worn as a fertility charm.[7] The anticipation of a spiritual return to Africa upon death of those that survived the Middle Passage illustrated the poignancy and even the psychological necessity of trans-Atlantic supernaturalism. A slave committing suicide near a body of water was attempting to affect the spirit's return to Africa. While scholars are still working out the meaning of funerary symbols and customs unearthed in lower Manhattan's black burial ground, here, too, the idea of a return journey is in evidence.

Conflict between community members helped sustain the use of popular magic. The ideals of communal harmony in New England ran up against the realities of jealousy, misfortune, and personal incompatibility among neighbors. When things went wrong, when a cow died, when a child got sick, when a person experienced unaccountable pains or disturbing fantasies, community members sometimes looked for another person to blame, a proximate cause for misery, a tangible source for the unseen and the unforeseen. The widespread belief in magic combined with tensions between community members to provoke the suspicion that a person who wished you ill actually had done you ill. Hence, people deployed countermagic against one another. Countermagic could be passive: the placement of a horseshoe above the doorway to keep a suspected witch out of the house. But countermagic also could take more active and vengeful forms. Driving the spell from a sick animal might necessitate burning part of the animal's body or delivering some other wound to the animal. Urine of the suspected malefactor might be boiled with pins in it to inflict painful revenge from a remote location. That some misfortune might strike after a conflict with a neighbor only heightened some people's suspicion that magic had been used against them. By no means were the colonies a Harry–Potter-like realm marked by an arms race of charms and countercharms. But magic persisted amidst more orthodox practices of prayer and faith—in no small part because magic addressed some of the same concerns as did complicated Puritan doctrines about wonders, sin, community, and the struggle between satanic evil and divine goodness.

Ministers inveighed against the evils of folk magic and its "cunning" practitioners. In the latter part of the seventeenth century, ministerial concern that New Englanders were falling away from their responsibility as a chosen people intensified denunciations of popular magic. Clergymen were not inclined to acknowledge that their own endorsement of the lore of wonders, the dangers of the devil's temptations, and even their own emphasis on the power of Providence in some sense stoked the desire of the laity to peer into the supernatural world to address practical and psychological needs. But ministers like Cotton Mather had other grave concerns as well. There was, of course, the implicit challenge to religious authority when ordinary people, especially women, claimed for themselves not only supernatural knowledge but also supernatural power. More importantly, people who regarded themselves as Christians might think they meant no ill by dabbling in the occult. But, to put the ministers' fears in a more modern idiom, magic might function as a gateway drug. By such logic, experimenting with magic or putting one's faith in fortune-tellers prepared people to allow the devil himself into their lives. Satan's much grander promises imperiled not only individual souls but also entire communities. Many colonists, especially New Englanders, suspected as much. For it was ordinary people who cried, "Witch!" when they could neither endure nor explain their troubles in other ways.

THE TRIALS AND TRIBULATIONS OF WITCHCRAFT

Elizabeth Knapp, in a quest for answers, and perhaps relief from her suffering, twice tried to lay blame on neighboring women for practicing witchcraft against her. Her accusations, Samuel Willard indicated, were investigated, but not ultimately prosecuted. In leveling such charges, Knapp was not breaking new ground and, in dismissing them, Groton's leaders were not expressing skepticism at the possibility of bewitchment but rather at the specific charge. Indeed, in one instance Willard indicated his relief that "God was pleased to vindicate" the accused woman who was "a person (I doubt not) of sincere uprightness before God."[8] Willard, in other words, accepted the existence of witches; he just doubted whether this particular woman could have been a witch.

Colonial Americans brought their knowledge of witchcraft with them from the Old World. From the mid-fifteenth to mid-eighteenth century, an estimated ninety thousand people came to trial for witchcraft, with perhaps forty-five thousand executions.[9] While England was not in the forefront of such activity, authorities in this cradle of colonial emigration did pursue witches, usually though not exclusively women, who allegedly used magical means to harm their neighbors. Theologians believed witches acquired powers by entering into pacts with the devil, either individually or as part of a circle of witches. In proportion to total population, New England surpassed the Old World in its pursuit of witches, though the witch hunt in parts of continental Europe outpaced New England.

New England was the region of North America most deeply involved in detecting and combating witchcraft, but non-English cultures and non-English regions experienced comparable concerns with witches and contributed to witch-hunting culture. In the West Indies, West African beliefs about manipulating supernatural forces for good and for benign and harmful purposes entered a region where Arawak Indians believed in malicious shape-shifting spirits and in dreams that represented actual occurrences in parallel reality. The occult beliefs of slaves blended with those of their European masters. In New France, Jesuit missionaries and Indians beleaguered by new diseases each thought the other guilty of sorcery. Organized punishment of witches, however, was virtually nonexistent in Canada, as the French did not establish the sorts of closely woven communities that produced tensions leading to witch trials in the home country.

Spain's North American colonies produced distinct patterns of witchcraft accusations in different places and times. Spanish folk practices of magical, bewitching love spells had long existed, but witch hunts were far less prevalent in Spain than in northern Europe. In eighteenth-century Mexico, European women sometimes turned to Indian neighbors whose supernatural knowledge in the use of potions might help to discipline abusive and sexually wayward husbands. Women thus sought a means of exercising power in a world controlled by men. In a variation on Elizabeth Knapp's Satanic canine, one woman of mixed African and Indian heritage abandoned by her husband described in 1747 a twenty-year cooperation with the devil, who took the form of a friendly dog. The Inquisition, the church body charged with rooting out heresy in the Americas as well as Spain, tended in Mexico to dismiss the use of spells as expressions of ignorance that once confessed required no further official intervention, the process of confession restoring the gendered hierarchy. Earlier on the New Mexico frontier, by contrast, Spanish religious and secular officials battled suspected Indian sorcerers as part of the project to subject those they also sought to convert. The Spanish assumed that the devil inspired obstinate religious behavior, while in the face of implacable demands of Christian colonizers and deteriorating conditions Indians reasserted practices that the Spanish regarded as diabolical. A mass witchcraft trial in 1675 that led to three executions and other punishments preceded the 1680 Pueblo Revolt. In the English Caribbean, political uncertainty bred the sort of conflict that produced antiwitchcraft prosecutions. Fallout from the English Civil War's violent contest between parliamentary Puritans and royalist Anglicans touched off a series of witchcraft accusations in Bermuda, leading to five executions, in the early 1650s. As in New Mexico, political and religious upheaval heightened islanders' sensitivity to the possibility of neighbors practicing the dark arts on one another.

Puritan New Englanders' preoccupation with a world so deeply imbued with the special manifestations of Providence sustained a heightened sensitivity to the manipulation of supernatural powers that focused inward. The ideological stress placed on communal harmony based on religious devotion and observance of hierarchies of age, sex, and status meant that certain types of hostile behavior in small face-to-face communities would be construed as a sign of witchcraft. While there was a significant gap between popular and clerical interpretations of witchcraft, the prominence of the Puritan clergy in New England granted a theological legitimacy to ordinary people's suspicions that some of their neighbors crossed the line between benign magic and malevolent witchcraft. A belief that God's special attachment to New England made the region a particular target of the devil proved, in some sense, to be a self-fulfilling prophecy. Even so, witchcraft accusations were not completely unknown outside New England. In 1706 Grace Sherwood of Princess Anne County, Virginia, found herself on the wrong end of a witchcraft accusation. Her accusers subjected her to the dunking test—the process of submerging the accused in water to see whether she sank or floated as a means of detecting witches; though she floated, a sign that she was a witch, her punishment went no further than a brief jail sentence.

Witchcraft accusations in New England also centered on women, who made up a vastly disproportionate number of those accused (just shy of 80 percent), those tried, and those convicted of witchcraft. Men implicated as witches were often related to female witchcraft suspects. Historians have suggested a variety of related explanations for this gendered pattern. Particularly in the seventeenth century, male authorities viewed women as more susceptible to physical and then spiritual conquest by Satan, as women were conceived of as at once weaker than men and yet creatures of great passion and desire. Samuel Willard, who went onto a distinguished ministerial career in the years following the Knapp episode, wrote vividly of Eve's seduction by Satan in the Garden of Eden. Women's ongoing susceptibility to such satanic assaults constituted a particular threat to the social order because once in Satan's thrall female witches possessed powers that rivaled or surpassed those of male authority figures. Thus, female members of the community with a reputation as fortune-tellers or healers ran the risk of being turned on by community members and identified as witches.

The marked preponderance of females among the accused, as well as among those, like Elizabeth Knapp, who suffered diabolical possession, also indicates the particular strains and stresses that Puritan gender roles imposed on women and girls. Perceived transgressions of gender norms, in particular aggressive or anti-social behavior by women, sometimes signaled deeper or more profound transgressions for neighbors and judicial authorities. The psychological dynamics of witchcraft also placed certain categories of women in a vulnerable position. In a society in which child-bearing and child-rearing made up such a large and central component of female identity, post-menopausal women, particularly those with a reputation for antineighborly disputatiousness, could become vulnerable to witchcraft accusations. One of the pieces of evidence sought in witchcraft investigations was the presence of an extra teat or nipple, at which animals or demons allegedly might suckle. Here, the irregularities of aging flesh intersected with fantasies of aberrant mothering to fix upon certain women the stigma of consorting with the devil.

Of course, the vast majority of women, like the vast majority of men, never faced the charge of witchcraft, requiring further precision in describing what kinds of women in what types of circumstances were brought to trial for witchcraft. Not counting the Salem outbreak of 1692, there were upwards of sixty prosecuted cases of witchcraft in New England, with several more court cases involving people who sued others for defamation of character when they spread rumors of witchcraft. Although Widow Glover of Boston, who was executed in 1688 for allegedly tormenting her neighbor's children, was a Gaelic-speaking Irish Catholic, most of the accused were of English stock, ostensibly living within the orbit of the established town churches.

Women's vulnerability and their deviance from social norms could be exacerbated by several factors. Women with few or no children in famously fertile New England, women who had involved themselves in inheritance disputes, often precipitated by the lack of male heir, women with a reputation for thievery or a sharp tongue—all found themselves more likely to develop reputations as witches. Careful reconstruction of individual life histories of accused witches sometimes reveals years of conflict with their neighbors. A formal accusation and trial, in other words, might be the product of accumulated suspicion and a reputation forged over many years within intimate communities. For example, Eunice Cole of Hampton, Massachusetts (now in New Hampshire), was a poor but assertive woman who had been charged with slander and thievery before being accused of witchcraft in 1656.

New England's accused witches were often particularly vulnerable or marginal people, whose refusal to bear their difficulties quietly made them deviant. Speaking up for oneself was not considered a female virtue in New England. Nor was acknowledging the depth of one's dissatisfaction; the Connecticut servant Mary Johnson executed in 1648 reportedly admitted that "her first familiarity with the Devil, came through *discontent*... whereupon a devil appear'd unto her *tendring* her, what *services* might best *content* her."[10] Tellingly, it was not just sex, age, and economic status that might tip the balance against certain women, but the lack of male relatives. The odds of being accused, tried, convicted, and executed all increased absent the intervention of husbands, brothers, and sons. The absence of strong male ties marked women as deviant. Younger females' accusations of bewitchment might also have stemmed from the anxiety that certain cantankerous, unattached women provoked about their own futures.

When ordinary people accused their neighbors of witchcraft, they were much more likely to be concerned with harm done to their person or property than with the accused's potential theological transgressions. When someone used supernatural means to do harm, that person crossed the boundary from magic to witchcraft. The unexplained illness of a child, death of livestock, or disappearance of property were the kinds of evidence that neighbors brought against accused witches. Plaintiffs and other witnesses rarely mentioned the devil's involvement at all.

Evidence presented against witches thus did not dovetail with what ministers and judges considered to be the most convincing evidence of guilt: the accused's freely given confession of entering into a covenant with Satan. In English law, witchcraft was a capital offense and required testimony from two witnesses for conviction. Moreover, like their English counterparts, New England magistrates were highly suspicious of torture as a means of extracting information and confessions. For many judges, this bias against torture extended to the dunk-and-float test. Due to such guiding legal principles, prior to the Salem Witch Trials, obtaining an actual conviction was surprisingly difficult. According to one scholar's calculation, in pre-Salem witch trials, barely more than a quarter of people tried for witchcraft were convicted. In court, lay people emphasized their suffering at the hands of witches, but authorities wanted evidence of a diabolical pact. Either way, proof was not easy to generate for skeptical judges and juries.

Escaping conviction and preserving one's life in the face of a witchcraft trial could not, of course, erase the stigma of the public accusation and testimony. In 1683 Mary Webster of Hadley, Massachusetts, was attacked in her home by a group of men in the wake of her acquittal. The widowed Katherine Harrison of Connecticut repeatedly faced trial as a witch in the late 1660s, with neighbors testifying that their suspicions dated back several years. Harrison received at least one acquittal for witchcraft and had one conviction modified to mandated exile rather than the death sentence; after this last instance, she moved to New York. Her new community was not happy to have a person of such ill repute among them, though when her daughter married the son of one of her new detractors, her problems abated. John Godfrey, an unmarried man with almost no kin, was in continual litigation with his neighbors in Essex County, Massachusetts, and he faced multiple accusations of witchcraft. Yet he drifted about the same precincts for most of his life, suing and being sued, acquiring and selling property, living on society's margins but remaining very much a part of a small world.

THE SALEM CRISIS

The scale and scope of the 1692 witchcraft outbreak in Salem and elsewhere in Essex County surpassed any such proceedings before or after in colonial America. Salem and the surrounding communities, which combined to produce dozens of possessions and confessions and scores upon scores of accused witches, underlined key themes of New England witchcraft while also composing a unique chapter in its history. Two Salem Village girls, Betty Parris and Abigail Williams, the daughter and niece of Reverend Samuel Parris, fell into mysterious trances. The girls pinned their bewitchment on Tituba, an Amerindian slave woman whom Parris had brought with him from the West Indies. Two more girls endured fits, blaming their affliction on Tituba and two other women in the community. These accusations accelerated when Tituba's lengthy confession described a far-flung network of witches facilitated by magical transportation and working with various demonic animals. Her account, likely prompted by beatings from her master and recalling supernatural beliefs from the Caribbean, touched off a cycle of investigation, further accusations, and, ultimately, trials that preoccupied the colony's highest religious and legal figures for over a year. The communities surrounding Salem were drawn into the web of recrimination and confession, with no less than 144 people accused before this grim episode ran its stunning course.

Like firefighters to a burning building, Americans have been drawn to the story of this outbreak, never quite quenching the embers of uncertainty, no matter what angles are explored and techniques deployed. Like a number of New England communities, Salem had endured religious controversy prior to the witchcraft outbreak, involving both the personality and style of the minister and the location of the church. Key figures in Salem's story, the Reverend Samuel Parris and the Reverend George Burroughs, had their supporters and, perhaps more important, their detractors in and around Salem, with tensions and resentments continuing to linger. The connections between Quakers, still considered heretical by many in the Bay colony, and some of the accused suggest underlying religious and cultural instability. The desire by residents of the outlying Salem Village to have their own church, separate from that of Salem Town, fed the acrimonious climate. Historians have, with some success, correlated supporters and detractors of Parris with the accusers and accused in the witch trials. Salem was a community witnessing the challenges and opportunities of commercial transition, led by seaport Salem Town, to which the more modest village was joined. Winners, losers, and people with uncertain futures in Salem's commercial economy felt more than a little suspicious of one another and even of themselves.

Massachusetts was also a colony under great political stress. The Bay colony's days as a self-governing province had come to an end with the revocation of its charter in 1684, followed by several years of political turbulence that spread from England to North America. In 1692 the implementation of a new government charter was imminent, bringing not only a newly appointed royal governor, but also official toleration of non-Puritans such as Anglicans and Quakers. Puritan hegemony was upended. Given the providential mindset of many Puritans, satanic afflictions testing Puritan resolve were almost a logical corollary to these earthly events.

While many people in and around Salem surely did not have these broader concerns consciously in mind as the crisis broke, the state of political flux had practical consequences for the handling of the initial accusations. Magistrates conducted fact-finding hearings during the early months of 1692 but no actual trials until the new governor, William Phips, arrived in May. In past trials, ministers and legal authorities had usually urged caution and skepticism when evaluating evidence against accused witches, but in this case the clergy and magistrates fanned the flames of panic. In particular, the decision to conduct public inquisitions in which the accused and accusers were both present created a stage on which the afflicted girls could dramatize and generate additional accusations. Whether one takes all those who claimed to be afflicted as sincere, this public vetting no doubt stoked rather than tamped down popular fears that the devil was indeed afoot in their communities.

Matters only intensified when the trials commenced in May. The selection of nine prominent men as judges provided a powerful official endorsement of the view of various ministers insisting that satanic forces were at work in Salem. The court decided to accept spectral evidence—that is, evidence that an accused witch's image had tormented the accuser. Pre-trial investigations had relied, in part, on testimony regarding the words and actions of suspects' ethereal images. Judges in previous cases had exhibited great reluctance to admit such evidence because it skirted the two-witness rule. Drawing on, let alone admitting, any sort of spectral evidence helped seal the fate of particular defendants and led accusations to spiral. Detractors of the trials also charged that certain people had their confessions in which they admitted to being witches extracted through torture. Compounding Salem's deadly irregularities, the magistrates spared confessed witches, as they implicated others in the apparent satanic conspiracy. Perversely, protestations of innocence led to conviction, admission of guilt to official protection or clemency.

Another facet of colonial crisis—the ongoing collapse of Puritan settlements on the Maine frontier in the face of Abenaki Indian assaults—helps explain the special characteristics of the Salem crisis. Several key figures among the accusers, the accused, and the authorities had ties to the vexed fate of English colonists in Maine, who had endured repeated assaults by Abenaki warriors and their French Canadian allies. Some of Salem's afflicted girls, such as Mercy Short and Susannah Sheldon, had directly experienced the terrors of Indian warfare. Several refugees from Maine had resettled in Essex County. Significantly, former Salem minister George Burroughs, around whom a noose of suspicion gradually tightened, had been a prominent figure in the erstwhile Maine settlement and one suspected of betraying his fellow settlers to the Indians. Likewise, merchant John Alden, an otherwise unlikely target of a witchcraft accusation, had been involved in the collapsing fortunes of the Maine enterprise. Events in Maine had clearly demonstrated the inadequacy of the colony's leadership in protecting its people. Reading events this way, the Salem trials can be seen as both a projection of and a diversion from elite failures, sustained in part by very real traumas suffered by members of the Salem community.

Instead of a fire, we might think of the Salem crisis as a sort of "perfect storm" whereby existing assumptions about witchcraft and what kinds of people were witches mixed with deeply unsettling events to explode into a paroxysm of officially sanctioned violence. Notwithstanding some unusual variations such as the large numbers of confessions, Salem still reflected a deeply engrained belief in an invisible world shared by New Englanders at all levels of society. Indeed, the crisis in some sense represented mass public acknowledgment of private facts. Personal feelings of guilt and shame, seasoned by ideas about gender, by ideas about divine grace, by ideas about the source of evil and who was most susceptible to evil, were drawn to the surface, as the colony's battle against Satan was dramatically rejoined in 1692.

Yet as the death toll mounted and as accusations spread further into the countryside and up the social hierarchy, doubts began to accumulate. Proceedings ground to a halt in 1693 not because anyone had rethought the culturally engrained system of sexual inequality let alone basic concepts of good and evil, but rather because a belief system designed to promote social harmony and to sustain certain types of social hierarchy seemed to be producing the opposite results. The people of Massachusetts had, it seemed, unwittingly played into the devil's trap, viciously and uncontrollably turning against one another. The disorder would not reflect well in England on the new governor's leadership, as he himself came to realize. Some leading ministers and, more to the point, the provincial legislature itself came to recognize that the trial procedures had placed too much power in the wrong hands and did not give the accused a fair shot to defend themselves. Tituba, the Indian slave, was eventually released, once she was purchased by a new master who paid the expenses of her lengthy imprisonment. With the blood of nineteen executions and one death by torture on their hands, Salem's residents were allowed to wrestle with their consciences more privately once again.

SKEPTICISM, SCIENCE, AND THE NATURAL ORDER OF THINGS

Witchcraft accusations and trials declined precipitously in colonial America after 1692, a result of the Salem debacle as well as long-term developments in trans-Atlantic scientific and religious culture. The Salem outbreak itself was a late episode in the history of European witch hunts. No matter how autonomous New England Puritans thought they were or wished to be, they could not ignore intellectual and political currents less accommodating to their beliefs in Providence, wonders, and diabolical pacts. To begin with, English law had always been to some degree predicated on the structured skepticism of the courts. In the colonies, there had long been a considerable difference between believing that a neighbor was a witch and proving her guilty of that charge through the formal presentation of evidence.

With regard to the special messages of Providence, skepticism was bred not so much by God's inscrutability as by conflict; religious and political opponents too easily reached different or self-interested conclusions about the meaning of signs and wonders. Meanwhile, astrology, the interpretation of the movements of the stars and planets for their impact on human affairs, had hovered beyond the officially accepted pale of providentialism for much of the seventeenth century. But as New England clergymen began to lose their hold over what printers could publish and astrology made its way into New England almanacs, reading the movements of heavenly bodies gained at least some additional legitimacy while at the same time losing its capacity to shock as a form of dangerous heterodoxy imperiling the entire community (see Figure 8.1). Thus, the Salem controversy dramatically contradicted and, in its regrettable excesses, contributed to these broader trends.

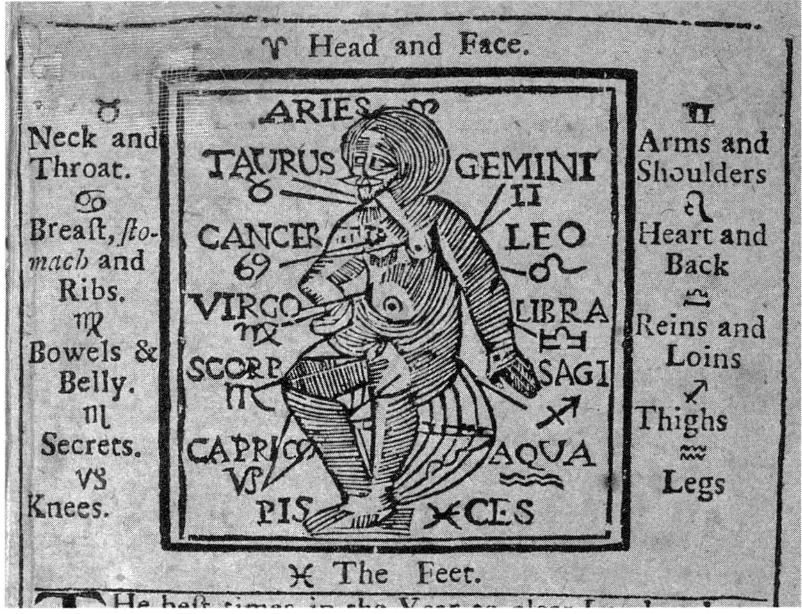

Figure 8.1 **"The Man of Signs," from Nathaniel Whittemore, *An almanack for the year of our Lord, 1721.... Calculated to the meridian of Boston in N. England, where the north pole is elevated 42 d. & 25. m. north, and 71 deg. wastward [sic] from London* (Boston: Printed by T. Fleet, 1721). Charts like this one, indicating how the zodiac governed different parts of the body, were featured in almanacs alongside projections of the weather, advice, and other astrological information. Even as wonder lore and Puritan orthodoxy weakened their grip on New England, the desire to read the future persisted, while the popular desire to understand the body and the heavens in systematic ways paralleled the same impulse among those in the Atlantic World engaged more formally in scientific inquiry. Courtesy, American Antiquarian Society.**

Subsequent to Salem, belief in the occult did not disappear from popular culture, but that belief lost substantial ground in its ability to marshal official sanction.

At the same time that dramatic shifts in how the colonies were governed began to occur, the tidal pull of Enlightenment thought undermined providentialism and the notion it sustained that one could read either God's or the Satan's intentions as discrete judgments or signs. With the restoration of the monarchy in 1660, Anglican Church leaders made a concerted effort to redirect religious understanding toward reason and moderation and away from so-called enthusiasm. Thus, Anglican thinkers stressed the overall reasonableness of Scripture rather than doctrinal disputes over particular passages. Similarly, the Anglican notion of Providence emphasized the *general* over the *special*, meaning that historical events and the fate of nations followed a divine trajectory but that God far less often communicated tightly focused, let alone individualized, messages. Indeed, since individuals would receive their punishment or reward after death, there was little point meting out earthly chastisement as a means of divine communication. Archbishop of Canterbury John Tillotson, whose writings became increasingly influential within the colonies in the final decades of the seventeenth century, criticized the notion of predestination as well as the notion that God or Satan directly intervened in a person's thoughts or actions. Although Puritan intellectuals like Cotton Mather did not surrender before such critiques, it was still dismaying for American Puritans, who believed that they had done their share to fight religious extremism in their midst, to find their understanding of providentialism falling in the scorned category of "enthusiasm."

The Anglican political agenda was designed to address England, but had considerable implications in America. The emphasis on reason undermined the radical democratic energy that allowed religious dissenters to declare the superiority of their own spiritual visions, instead reasserting the orderly supervision of religious and secular elites. Polite argumentation not blunt assertions of righteousness became the approved cultural style. In America, Anglicanism was already the established, if not well-staffed, church in Virginia; in New England, however, Anglicans, as well as Baptists and Quakers, were the dissenting sects. The Glorious Revolution confirmed the right of Anglicans and other Protestants to compete for hearts, minds, and souls, shattering the illusion of Massachusetts and the other Puritan colonies that they constituted a unified spiritual body sharing a unified fate. Providential thinking did not fare as well in such a context. As religious tolerance, however begrudged, became the norm in Massachusetts, fiery jeremiads warnings of supernatural punishments of the Lord's specially selected people became the province of a fading generation of older ministers.

Emerging trends in scientific thought supported the proposition that reason was the best means of comprehending God and nature, as well as organizing society. In particular, the work of Isaac Newton reshaped the understanding of the universe, with order and predictability replacing divine intervention as explanations for worldly and celestial events. In seeking to describe the physical mechanisms, such as gravity, that explained movements in the heavens and on earth, Newtonianism not only revealed nature, but also God. The miraculous was redefined. Isolated wonders had to share or even concede ground to the amazing manner in which nature in general operated according to discernible principles and natural laws. In the hands of the right theologians and writers, Providence then could be described as benign rather than threatening, the great wonder being the orderly design of the universe itself. The place to ponder miracles was not in the exceptions, but rather in the rules.

Once the presumption of God's orderly creation took root, then phenomena like the aurora borealis, which might be taken as a wondrous communication or sign from God, instead could be attributed to physical causes worthy of uncovering scientifically rather than interpreting divinely. Puritans could and did debate just such questions. But in doing so, old-style providentialists played on a new scientific and religious field. When reason and reasonableness became an acknowledged standard for judging even religious texts, the language and the underlying belief in the meaning of wonders, signs, and judgments shifted.

Indeed, influential men like Cotton Mather and influential institutions like Harvard wished to participate in the sophisticated scientific and religious conversations, not to eschew them. Mather, a prolific writer who engaged in trans-Atlantic discourses, regarded himself as a man of science. He was a member of the Royal Society, England's premier scientific body. He also admired the concept of gravity, which in his view confirmed God's greatness. Yet in shaping his correspondence with the Royal Society, Mather played down his still active interest in the world of wonders, a tacit acknowledgment that his more skeptical interlocutors held the upper hand in the interpretation of nature.

And yet a 1734 Massachusetts court case involving a haunted house demonstrated that at a popular level the tension between skepticism and the lore of wonders achieved only an uneasy truce, even as witch-hunting passed deeper into history. Plymouth, Massachusetts, landlord Josiah Cotton fought an unsuccessful legal battle against former tenants who claimed the house that they had once occupied was haunted. Word of specters, mysterious lights, and unexplained noises emanating from the house, allegedly ghostly reminders of the tragic deaths of a Captain Thompson Phillips and his wife, made the property unrentable. Cotton's slander suit, in which he accused his tenants of creating false tales, did not bring Cotton the satisfaction he sought. The jury acquitted the tenants. Cotton appealed, but again the defendants won, their attorney convincing the jury that his clients responded sincerely to what might plausibly have been supernatural occurrences. Wonder lore bested Josiah Cotton's legal onslaught.

For Jonathan Edwards, born forty years after Cotton Mather, integrating the new natural sciences into Puritan theology was a worthy goal rather than a threat to be accommodated. Edwards, who would enjoy fame as a western Massachusetts revivalist minister, read from a young age the works of Newton and viewed inventions like the telescope as signs that the world was moving closer to a millennium when all God's glory would be revealed to his faithful followers. He deployed metaphors from nature to describe theological concepts and believed that God signaled through nature aspects of divine grace and redemption. Edwards likened the light of the moon and stars to the partial illumination of the Old Testament, which gave way to the sunshine of the New Testament. The sun itself, Edwards wrote, communicated the story of redemption: "The rising and setting of the sun is a type of the death and resurrection of Christ."[11] Putting his own stamp on the emerging vocabulary of physics at a young age, the precocious Edwards understood atoms as irreducible and thus divine proof that "there is no proper substance but God himself."[12] His understanding of a term from the Hebrew Scripture as *gravity* underscored the divine as the binding force in nature that, more importantly, drew together the faithful with their God. Still, inspiring faith more broadly required something less subtle than scientific erudition. Ministers in the Connecticut River valley took a 1727 earthquake as a sign to launch a religious revival. A culture of divine messages and supernatural marvels persisted despite significant changes in the culture of learned inquiry.

FLORA, FAUNA, AND LANDSCAPE

Almost from the moment word of Columbus's discoveries reached Europe, the Americas constituted a world of wonders unto itself that challenged existing knowledge about nature. The new people, animals, and landscapes encountered in America proved that neither classical nor Christian texts provided a comprehensive view of creation. The colonies helped generate boundless curiosity. English naturalists, in conversation with other Europeans, began to detail the world in new ways, with a new and expanded scientific vocabulary. The two-way intellectual exchange between Europe and the colonies fueled scientific knowledge, while at the same time forging new identities, voluntarily and involuntarily, for the diverse peoples of the Atlantic basin. In the process, religion and the concept of wonder were not replaced, but rather placed on new foundations, based in no small part of the desire to comprehend the New World's seemingly infinite novelties.

Take the case of the opossum. To us, this common creature's instinct for playing dead is amusing and its ability to sniff out unsecured garbage bags, not so much. But to Europeans, the opossum was deeply strange—a monstrosity of sorts. Scientists there had never contemplated a marsupial before. From head to tail, the opossum seemed to be an assembly of parts from a variety of different animals, while the pouch in which the female opossum carried its barely developed progeny appeared to be truly something new under the sun. Yet the impulse to recoil from the perversion of expected animal forms gave way to a desire to comprehend. Virginia's William Byrd II presented the Royal Society with an opossum in 1697. Curious scientists set about uncovering nature's secrets through careful anatomical analysis (see Figure 8.2). God, not the devil, it would seem, lay in the details of this remarkable creature. Indeed, the marsupial's special capacities for effective mothering, its ability to protect its young from harm by offering its pouch for safety, suggested how God provided for reproduction and protection in ingenious

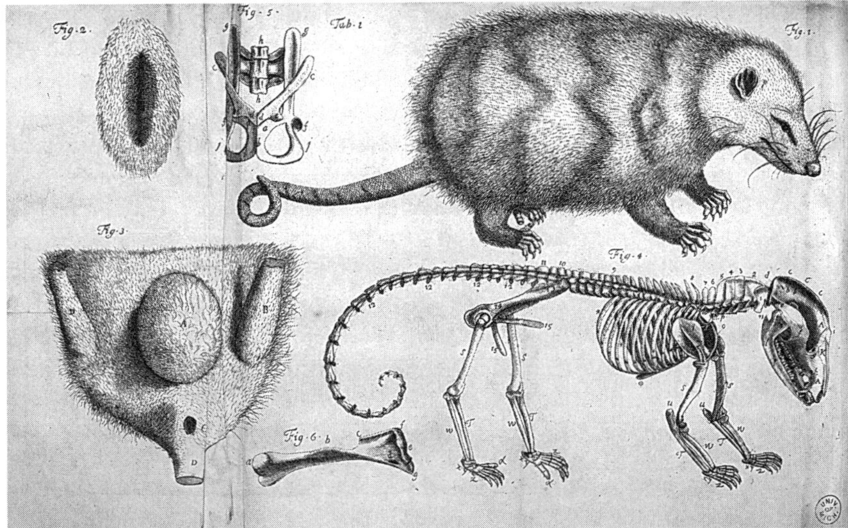

Figure 8.2 **Edward Tyson, "Cariegueya, Seu Marsupiale Americanum; or, The Anatomy of an Opossum, Dissected at Gresham-College, originally published in the Royal Society of London, *Philosophical Transactions* 20 (1698): 105–164. Animals not found in Europe, such as the opossum, fueled European study of the natural world. These drawings published in the annals of England's premier scientific organization rendered the physiology of this marsupial's method of birthing and raising newborns. The female opossum also sparked commentary on the nature of motherhood. Special Collections Library, University of Michigan.**

ways. Because the development process of incipient opossums could be viewed much more easily than in nonmarsupials, scientists and moralizers could take this at first seemingly outlandish animal to be an object lesson in the centrality of mothering to female mammals generally. Nature's monstrous emanations had, in earlier times, signified divine warnings to wayward members of the human flock; in the eighteenth century, a former monster could serve as a role model to define and shape gendered human norms.

From a broader perspective, it was not isolated social allegories that naturalists sought in American nature, but rather raw materials for the allegory of enlightenment itself. The new scientific enterprise required two things for understanding nature—data collected from nature in the form of specimens and a system for classifying all those specimens in a logical way. Europeans, most prominently the Swedish naturalist Carolus Linnaeus, provided the classification. Groups such as the Royal Society could spread discoveries through publications. And inventions like the microscope could literally and figuratively magnify curiosity by exposing more to the human eye. People on the ground in the American colonies, however, provided the specimens. Without the plants, the birds, the bugs, and the opossums, without the detailed description of American climate and topography, European curiosity could not be sustained, let alone converted into a system of knowledge. English naturalists could not simply issue orders because they could not know precisely what they wanted. Travelers sometimes crossed the Atlantic to gather their own information and to burnish their scientific credentials. Hans Sloane, who would serve as an officer of the Royal Society for decades, composed a lavishly illustrated, path-breaking natural history of Jamaica, based on his brief service as doctor to the island's governor. But it was much more efficacious to make use of people with local expertise, including white planters, slaves, and Indians; Sloane himself had relied on all three during his sojourn. Americans, native or transplanted, had direct familiarity with their environs and their knowledge and discoveries could be channeled across the Atlantic as special New World commodities.

The rise of trans-Atlantic naturalist networks transformed the self-understanding that some colonists had of themselves as much as it did their understanding of nature. One of the fears that plagued early generations of English colonists was that the American environment would lead to mental, physical, and cultural degeneration. If, as received wisdom of humor theory had it, climatic factors such as humidity and temperature shaped mental and physical health, then perhaps America could not sustain the level of civilization allegedly achieved in Europe. The growth of scientific curiosity, while not completely assuaging these fears, validated the essential role of sophisticated, even if self-taught, American naturalists in generating knowledge and exercising their discernment. Such colonists sometimes expressed provincial insecurity or contrived to sound falsely modest in their correspondence with their English colleagues, but they knew, nevertheless, that they played a critical role in an ongoing scientific exchange. The identification of plants accelerated dramatically after 1730, in part because of the labors of Pennsylvanian John Bartram, who alone informed his British associates of approximately three hundred new species.

Trans-Atlantic curiosity contributed to subtle but not inconsequential shifts in the regional balance of colonial American life. European naturalists found most interesting those parts of America that had less in common climatically with their home country. The ecology southward of New England, extending all the way to the Caribbean, seemed more likely to produce natural marvels than the Puritan heartland. Thus, key participants in the naturalists' exchange included New York Lieutenant Governor Cadwallader Colden, Bartram of Pennsylvania, William Byrd II of Virginia, and Scottish immigrant to South Carolina Alexander Garden. Because planters like Byrd and Robert Beverley had the time and the economic wherewithal to pursue their naturalist inclinations, these men of leisure were well suited to join the naturalist fraternity.

One did not have to be a Southern planter, of course, to provide a vital link in the chain of scientific knowledge, as the career of John Bartram proved. He was a farmer holding no special rank. While the Pennsylvania Quaker had attended school as a youth, he did not have college training and his modest knowledge of

Latin, the ostensible language of learning and science, was self-taught. Bartram's *Observations on the Inhabitants, Climate, Soil, Rivers, Productions, Animals... in His Travels from Pensilvania to Onondago, Oswego, and the Lake Ontario* (1751) acquired an international reputation. Linnaeus himself called Bartram the world's premier botanist and the Royal Society published his letters in its *Transactions*. In 1765 he received recognition from George III, who appointed Bartram as a royal botanist for North America. Bartram's extraordinary career was thus symbolic of the ways in which naturalist networks and scientific hierarchies could not afford to overplay the distinction between metropolis and provinces, or commoner and aristocrat.

Bartram also illustrates the ways in which natural science could prompt modifications in religious perception. In Bartram's case, the results were explicit and even dramatic. His observations of nature convinced him of the profound unity of life and made him suspicious of overly sharp distinctions between animals and plants. For Bartram, much could be learned about the life-sustaining structures of each category if one thought about circulatory systems and sexual reproduction as analogous in plants and animals. Similarly, he believed the study of nature could inform an understanding of the Bible, with observations of nature offering a more valuable guide to understanding God than clerical training. While such an attitude might not disturb his fellow Quakers, his insistence that divinity was a singular phenomenon encompassed by and expressed in nature led him to reject the divinity of Christ. For that, the Quakers excommunicated him. Bartram did not make nature into a god. Rather, he admired "the wonderful order and balance that is maintained between the vegetable and animal economy, that the animal should not be too numerous to be supported by the vegetable, nor the vegetable production be lost for want of gathering by the animal." This divine moderation was enhanced by the divine intelligence invested by God in nature, "such as the surprising tribes of the sensitive plants and the petals of many flowers shutting close up in rainy weather or in the evening until the female part is fully impregnated."[13] Curiosity disciplined by data thus tilled the soil for Deism, an understanding of the universe in which understanding God's creation did not depend on organized religious observance.

Bartram, however, did not seek to make his mark as a philosopher or religious rebel, but as an expert observer, quantifier, measurer, and evaluator. Like John Lawson before him, he was capable of assessing the future productive value of natural landscapes. And he had no qualms at all about supplementing his wealth by operating a mail order business selling the seeds and plants he discovered. Entrepreneurship, knowledge, and empire were as interwoven as American and English naturalists. As a result of circumstance and pride, Bartram and his American colleagues imitated, cooperated, and competed with their English colleagues. English naturalists imagined themselves to be part of a culture especially suited to cultivate and synthesize scientific knowledge. American naturalists imagined themselves to be even better situated, occupying a middle ground between urban distraction and uncivilized frontier.

The polite trans-Atlantic exchange of naturalists was dominated by white men, and yet the nature of gaining access to new specimens created space for nonwhite and nonmale participation in the empirical project. The net for specimens had to be cast widely and, necessarily, by many hands. Some white women entered the trans-Atlantic naturalist exchange, making productive use of connections to male relatives. South Carolina's Eliza Lucas conducted her own agricultural experiments, including the cultivation of indigo and, traveling to England with her prominent husband Charles Pickney, brought a bird and Carolina silk to the dowager princess of England. Cadwallader Colden's daughter Jane developed an international reputation as a botanist. London naturalist James Petiver conducted correspondence with a number of female collectors in America. Women could use female stereotypes to legitimize their interest in science, claiming, for example, that a supposedly natural inclination in their sex for observing and appreciating tiny detail made them well suited to botanical observation.

The integration of Native Americans and African Americans into naturalist networks was necessary, yet fraught with anxieties and prejudices. Colonists observed Indian displays of natural knowledge through the use of plants and herbs to heal or poison, as well as effective hunting and trapping techniques. Indians also had access to the interior of the continent, and hence the curiosities that might become specimens waiting to be classified. To take full advantage of what Indians knew, white colonists had to move away from the notion of Indians as satanic, their knowledge indicative of their witting or unwitting league with the devil; the supernatural, in other words, had to give way to the natural. Yet in general, whites did not place Indians on an equal plane with European naturalists. Instead, white students of nature stressed the distinctions between the Indian's instinctual or practical knowledge and European scientific understanding. White naturalists thus could conceive of themselves as necessary mediators in the trans-Atlantic intellectual exchange.

Africans in the Americas played a similar role to Indians in the generation of natural knowledge, although the growth of slavery sometimes made African expertise even more menacing to whites than Indian expertise. Slaves sometimes did the actual physical work of acquiring specimens for their master. English collector James Petiver understood the American labor system clearly enough to suggest to his plantation-owning correspondents such as Hannah English Williams that they use their slaves "for an hour or two once or twice in a weeke... to goe into the fields and woods to bring home whatever they shall meet with...."[14] Yet as whites knew well, Africans possessed plenty of their own insights into medicine, flora, and fauna, knowledge that sometimes arrived with the slaves themselves from Africa and that sometimes derived from their experiences in new surroundings. Southern newspapers reported on the medical skills of black slaves. Sometimes masters even freed those who made a particularly valuable medical contribution. Still, whites felt more than a little menaced by black pharmacological insights, as the enslaved who healed them might also poison them. Prosecutions for poisoning in the slave societies of Virginia and South Carolina were not uncommon.

Slaveowners' intimate dependence on their slaves made black knowledge disconcerting to the very white people who exploited their own power and knowledge to place peoples of African descent in a profoundly subordinate position. Even as witchcraft beliefs moved closer to the margins of legal and popular thought, the fear of individual and collective use of magic or magiclike knowledge by blacks grew. As the alleged plot against Manhattan in 1741, as well as rebellions in New York in 1712 and South Carolina in 1739 proved, the line between what slaves revealed and what they concealed could be difficult to detect and dangerous to ignore.

That being said, neither white authorities nor white naturalists crouched in a defensive posture when it came to evaluating black or Native American bodies. Indeed, the Enlightenment impulse to gather and classify information contributed to more explicit articulation of allegedly natural distinctions between races and between sexes. Just as the science of curiosity had its roots in the appraisal of marvels and wonders, the classification and evaluation of human bodies had its roots in the tri-cultural encounter of Indians, Africans, and Europeans that initiated the colonial era. The lower rank that white naturalists assigned to their Indian and African contemporaries in the accumulation of specimens suggested the broader direction in which the new naturalism moved.

MEDICINE, HUMAN BODIES, AND RACE

Science was not more immune than providentialism to the potential disfigurement of prejudice, as illustrated by a controversy that erupted in Boston in 1721–1722 over smallpox inoculation. In response to a smallpox outbreak, Cotton Mather advocated inoculation, a procedure by which a person was deliberately infected with smallpox in order to develop immunity to it. At Mather's urging, a Boston doctor, Zabdiel Boylston, initiated an inoculation program, starting with the successful inoculation of the doctor's own child and two of his black slaves. Mather's conversation with his own slave, Onesimus, on smallpox inoculation in Africa had inspired Mather's enthusiasm for the practice. The minister was challenged, indeed mocked, by Dr. William Douglass, for relying on an African informant to proceed with a medical experiment. Douglass, who had received medical training in various European universities before moving to New England, based his critique of Mather on both his belief in black inferiority and his insistence on sound empirical investigation. Other New Englanders, such as the 1730 anti-inoculation rioters of Marblehead, Massachusetts, had their own reasons for being skeptical of immunization. Not only was there something counterintuitive and personally risky about exposing oneself willingly to a disease, but common folk also worried that rich people who underwent inoculation could spread the disease to others if not properly quarantined, a concern that was not without foundation. In any event, the politics, elite and popular, of science in the colonies was almost as complex as the natural phenomenon (including disease and skin color) that science sought to comprehend.

The formal acquisition and transmission of medical knowledge developed slowly in the colonies. Like William Douglass, those with academic training in medicine either emigrated from Europe or traveled to Europe to study there before practicing medicine in America. Men without European training titled themselves as doctors, often though not always after apprenticing with older practitioners. Whether schooled in university or experience, these male doctors lacked the medicines, therapies, and technologies that we have come to associate with the ability to diagnose and cure illness. As the cases of afflicted girls in Groton and Salem indicate, doctors in early New England did not even possess a vocabulary, let alone a cure, to address either the physical or the mental trauma of certain disorders. Of course, there is still much that the medical science of our own day does not fully comprehend about sickness and health. The doctors of colonial America knew far less.

That is not to say that the benefits or lessons of natural science totally eluded colonial doctors. Faced with clear evidence that smallpox inoculation actually did protect people, Douglass changed his position on its value. Douglass also published his own important study on the outbreak of scarlet fever in Boston. Several of the most prominent academically trained physicians were also leading correspondents in the trans-Atlantic naturalist networks described already, their identity as medical practitioners in some ways subordinate to their identity as part of a scientifically informed intellectual elite. Indeed, in an environment where doctors encountered competition from traditional practitioners for prestige, and their own medical successes were not necessarily any more impressive, engaging in botanical investigations was a means for doctors to compile otherwise scant evidence of their own attainments. The first lectures on anatomy did not occur in the colonies until the 1750s and it was not until 1765 that the first school of medicine opened.

Colonial Americans were not limited to the purging and bleeding prescribed by university or apprentice-trained doctors, whose treatments still operated on humoral theories that dated to ancient Greece and viewed illness as an imbalance of various bodily fluids. A certain amount of self-education occurred through the importation of European books, as well as publications for the lay reader, most notably Virginia native John Tennant's *Every Man His Own Doctor: Or, the Poor Planter's Physician*. Colonial communities relied on a variety of sources for crucial knowledge about the body and the maintenance and recovery of health. Well-read clergymen, as the example of Cotton Mather indicates, offered medical insights to their parishioners. Some slaves developed followings among whites and blacks for their healing prowess; and American botanists sought out the plants and herbs that Native Americans seemed to deploy effectively.

Midwives also played an essential role in the maintenance of community health. Beyond their central role in the childbirth, midwives took the lead in the care of women and children. The knowledge of midwives did not differ greatly from that of most doctors, grounded in the same notions of bodily humors. Like doctors and various folk healers, familiarity with healing plants and herbs comprised an important facet of a midwife's expertise. Unlike the more ambitious and, one might say, pretentious doctors, colonial midwives did not preoccupy themselves with establishing a trans-Atlantic fraternity of science; nor did midwives seek to persuade lawmakers to regulate the practice of medicine. Nonetheless, midwives remained an indispensable part of a network of female caregivers. Meanwhile, a male medical establishment based on allegedly more systematic accumulation of biological knowledge had barely emerged from its embryonic stages by the mid-eighteenth century.

If medical knowledge blended the practical and the philosophical, so too did emerging theories about skin color meld naked self-interest and science-inspired theorizing. During the initial two centuries of the encounter between Europeans, Native Americans, and Africans, a series of transitions took place in European perceptions of difference. Early accounts often focused on the appearance and reproductive capacities of nonwhite women, alleging qualities both monstrous and marvelous such as the ability to deliver children painlessly or suckle babies over the shoulder. While certainly not incapable of admiring the bodies of non-Europeans, suspicions about European degeneration in alien-inhabited climes survived for a remarkably long time among European thinkers. In the eighteenth century, the discourse of natural history and the shifting ethnic composition of increasingly settled colonial societies prompted whites to wrestle inconclusively with what to make of the varieties of man, the undeniable humanity of blacks and Indians jangling against self-serving hunches that meaningful differences existed beneath the skin.

The language of blood illustrates how New World conceptions of race and older European notions combined in unstable and paradoxical ways in Spanish and English contexts. Prior to 1492, Iberians had grown accustomed through both the Muslim and Christian use of African slaves to associating dark skin with subordination. The fear that large-scale conversion of Jews and Muslims had not produced truly authentic Christians fueled a preoccupation with *limpieza de sangre* (purity of blood) that enhanced the status of those who could claim Old Christian lineage. Spanish colonists applied an analogous logic to Africans in the Americas, dark skin marking them as outsiders and as slaves. The large numbers of African-descended people who attained their freedom in the Spanish colonies, especially in comparison to English mainland North America, still bore the stain of impurity centuries after their initial arrival in the Americas.

Indians no more than Africans could escape European judgment, as the Age of Discovery shaded into the Age of Enlightenment science. Indeed, even after more than two centuries of contact, the nature of human biology in the Americas generated a great deal of theorizing. From the time of contact, that Native Americans had darker skin than Castilians and the Europeans who followed them was something of which the newcomers were well aware. For European Enlightenment figures, the problem transcended mere color, encompassing the American environment's total effect on human development. The notion of degeneration posited that the Americas produced weaker bodies along with wayward morals and benighted culture. Thus, Indians did not suffer from impure blood, but required protection and isolation, even as they were subordinated politically and economically.

On the ground in the Spanish colonies, race mixing threatened to undermine the powers of color-coded rank and privilege, creating a distinctive American impurity problem, especially given relatively large Indian populations in Spanish colonies beyond the Caribbean. As widespread sexual intermixing of European, African, and Indian populations went forward over the centuries of Spanish rule, a complicated set of distinctions emerged, attempting to account for sixteen, or even as many as fifty-two genealogical categories. By contrast, English colonists noted the existence of mulattoes mostly for the purpose of ensuring that mixed-race inhabitants suffered the same legal and social disabilities of slave society as people of exclusively African descent, although "passing" from black to white did occur. For the substantial numbers of mixed-race free people in the Spanish colonies, racial identities inevitably became untraceable, confused, and therefore malleable. Individuals and families sought to advance status in societies that valued a higher proportion of white heritage. People could register new racial identities at the time of baptism or marriage. The catch-all legal category of *castas* ultimately emerged to distinguish all blacks and mixed-race people from whites and Indians.

In Spanish America, the contest between the Spanish born (peninsulars) who monopolized official political power and American-born colonists who could claim Spanish descent (creoles) reinforced notions of European civilization's primacy. Jesuit missionaries in the Spanish colonies stood up for the Indians' ability to advance spiritually and intellectually, in keeping with the commitment to the transformative powers of Christian secular and religious education. Most creoles were more concerned with making their own case for superiority. They asserted their purity of blood to claim the same racial privileges as Spanish-born colonists and administrators. Chomping at the bit of discrimination, creoles rejected the notion that they degenerated in the American environment, asserting instead that they thrived. Indeed, creoles claimed they had outstripped Spain in artistic and intellectual achievement, measuring themselves favorably by the standards of the European Enlightenment, such as the founding of great universities and the publishing of lively journals.

English colonists developed a language of superiority as well. By the late seventeenth century, the English fixed on the Indians' demographic implosion in the face of disease and the robust growth of European populations to make the empirical case for inherent physical differences between old and new American populations. Yet concrete signs that Indians would not fade away, particularly on the frontier, prompted a visceral fury on the part of American colonists. In the 1670s, Bacon's Rebellion was rooted in part in Indian hatred, and King Philip's War devolved into something approaching genocidal revenge. In the eighteenth century, the persistence of Indian cultural and political integrity produced condescension as well as violence. For example, the enduring strength of the Iroquois confederacy led New Yorker Cadwallader Colden to cast Indians dismissively in the role of noble savages holding onto their particular stage of civilization, which presumably was bound to pass. Although not immune from dismissive European notions about the American environment, English colonists, as we have seen, found a variety of outlets for their scientific as well as political expression during the first several decades of the eighteenth century. This included sharpening racial boundaries.

The standards and language of science played an ambiguous, albeit biased role, in reinforcing racial divisions. The impulse to classify and order the world's plants and animals also applied to the classification of human beings. The great botanist Linnaeus identified various types of men, among them Native Americans, Europeans, Africans, and Asians. It seemed relatively straightforward, and consistent with the naturalist agenda of the day, to use physical characteristics along with region of origin to create categories. Science's emphasis on the observation of physical evidence almost inevitably attracted attention to physical distinctions. Explaining the cause of different traits, however, was a murky business, while ranking people by type presented a host of conceptual challenges. Speculations about skin color drew on Newton's work on the nature of light and color and prompted an elusive search for a subcutaneous fluid. Some identified whiteness as the original skin color, with blackness regarded as a degenerative condition. Yet cultural theories continued to militate against absolute distinctions. What did it mean to rank categories of man? If the differences between men resulted from historical stages of cultural development—from savage hunter-gatherers, through the pastoral and agricultural, all the way to commercial society—then could men from any particular category be permanently and inherently attached to a stage of development? Didn't the stages imply fluidity rather than fixed status?

The European scientific consensus was never complete. Virginia physician John Mitchell noted, "However different, and opposite to one another, these two Colours of Black and White may appear to be to the Unskillful, yet they will be found to differ from one another only in Degree" and suspected that at first all men were a tawny shade, which is to say an intermediate color neither black nor white.[15] Harvard professor John Winthrop IV reached the same conclusion. Ultimately, to make the leap to permanent racial hierarchy, the skin had to signify some cognitive or mental difference between various types of humans. Some Enlightenment thinkers, such as the Scottish philosopher David Hume, perpetuated claims of permanently inscribed differences in mental capacity. And yet, blacks, Indians, and others could not readily be ushered out of the family of man. This was, in part, because the evidence of the humanity of nonwhites—from cross-color sexual relations to the threat of organized revolts—was undeniable. Moreover, in this Christian culture, the belief that God only created humans once as told in Genesis attested to universal humanity. Indeed, clergymen asserted that Africans in their midst could be converted to Christianity—meaning that the most important attribute of nonwhites was their ability to receive God's grace.

Anglo-Americans did not take the leading role in scientific speculations on race, but colonial laws and social practices were predicated on the notion that distinctions of color mattered. Laws designed to discourage sexual reproduction involving black men and white women applied color to biological acts. The language used to describe interracial reproduction—the mixing of blood with which the Spanish had been concerned for centuries—suggested that real biological lines between groups were being crossed.

Whether subtle or blunt, negotiable or absolute, racial thought in English as well as Spanish colonial zones interpreted the descent categories in self-interested ways. The quest to organize and categorize nature, to understand the human body in accordance with newer scientific methods, and the desire to maintain order and rank in colonial societies were of a piece. The European colonists' desire for social control, labor, and frontier lands supported the articulation of distinctions among whites, blacks, and Indians. Still, the desire for medical breakthroughs as well as older biblical notions of creation sometimes led them to blur such distinctions. For their part, slaves, Indians, and even humble white servant girls did not always inhabit the inferior roles prescribed to them. Thus, passion and reason, interest and detachment jockeyed with one another on what threatened to become a more level playing field.

REASON AND FAITH

Though steeped in a world of wonders and providential assumptions, Samuel Willard was determined that reason not fear would dictate his responses to Elizabeth Knapp's alarming ordeal. Seeking to draw methodical and humane conclusions, Willard was fairly confident in his observation-based judgment that Knapp did not fake her ailments--and that she had fallen victim to the devil's afflictions not nature's. Had her condition been a medical one, he decided that her body would have shown more tangible signs of wear and wasting than it did. Similarly, he argued that the devil himself had spoken through Knapp, taking careful note that she had remained motionless during the climactic event of his conversation with the devil and that certain sounds were almost impossible to make if she did not use her lips. The swelling that Willard observed in Knapp's throat also seemed to indicate an intrusive presence. Moreover, Willard took seriously Knapp's admission that the devil appeared to her. On the other hand, the minister could not reach a clear conclusion as to whether Knapp ever signed a covenant with Satan; her own account was hopelessly inconsistent on this score.

In making sense of Knapp's experience as a whole, Willard counseled not anger, persecution, or hysteria, but rather "pity" and compassion, calling her "a subject of hope" whose "recovery" should be actively facilitated. Her accusations of witchcraft had already been deflected and discredited. Thus, the community did not experience a divisive crisis, while Knapp ultimately was able to reconstruct her life. She went on to raise a family, with history recording no outward or permanent stigma from her ordeal, while the community of Groton did not tear itself apart, unlike Salem two decades later.

Willard's equanimity and observation-driven approach notwithstanding, Knapp's ordeal signaled to the minister larger lessons about the universe in which he and his flock lived: Knapp was "a monument of divine severity; and the Lord grant that all that see or hear, may fear and tremble."[16] No matter how orderly the universe might be, no matter how much might be understood of that universe through careful observation, no matter how much compassion one human should feel for another, God exercised ultimate control over the natural and the supernatural, producing wonders and judgments that humans ignored—or imagined they could control—at their own peril. The eighteenth century delivered colonists alternatives to a severe view of Providence—with emphasis laid on recordable, measurable rhythms of nature and orderly manifestations of the divine. The days of the witchcraft trial ended and the regular passing of supernatural judgments did for some recede, while even in the most committed regions of Puritan orthodoxy, the emergence of religious diversity provided colonists with alternative ways to experience and interpret the world around them. Nonetheless, colonial Americans would continue to interpret many of their individual experiences and collective histories through the prism of what the Lord gave and what the Lord took away.

CHRONOLOGY

c. 1450–1750	European witch craze.
1651–1655	Twelve executions for witchcraft in Bermuda.
1671 (October)	*Elizabeth Knapp's fits begin.*
1672 (January)	*Knapp's fits subside.*
1674	*Knapp marries Samuel Scripture.*
1689	Cotton Mather publishes *Memorable Providences, Relating to Witchcrafts and Possessions.*
1692–1693	Salem Witch outbreak and trials.
1700	*Knapp gives birth to final, likely sixth, child.*
1711	Massachusetts passes law voiding Salem witch convictions.
1721–1722	Boston smallpox inoculation controversy.
1735	Swedish botanist Carolus Linnaeus (1707–1778) publishes the first edition of *Systema Naturae*, first of his many important works of biological classification.
1751	American naturalist John Bartram publishes *Observations on the Inhabitants, Climate, Soil, Rivers, Productions, Animals... in His Travels from Pensilvania to Onondago, Oswego, and the Lake Ontario*.
1765	First medical school in colonies established in Philadelphia.

NOTES

1. Samuel Willard, "A Brief Account of a Strange and Unusual Providence of God Befallen Elizabeth Knapp of Groton," in *Witch-Hunting in Seventeenth-Century New England: A Documentary History, 1638–1692*, ed. David D. Hall (Boston: Northeastern University Press, 1991), 198–212.
2. Willard, "A Brief Account," 200, 204.
3. David D. Hall, *Worlds of Wonder, Days of Judgment: Popular Religious Belief in Early New England* (New York: Knopf, 1989), 71.
4. Richard Godbeer, *The Devil's Dominion: Magic and Religion in Early New England* (Cambridge, UK: Cambridge University Press, 1992), 55.
5. Winthrop and Taylor, quoted in Hall, *Worlds of Wonder*, 87, 83.
6. Increase Mather, quoted in Hall, *Worlds of Wonder*, 94.
7. Denis J. Pogue and Esther C. White, "Summary Report on the 'House for Families' Slave Quarter Site (44FX762/40–47), Mount Vernon Plantation, Mount Vernon, Virginia," *Quarterly Bulletin of the Archaeological Society of Virginia* 46 (1991): 204.
8. Willard, "A Brief Account," 199.
9. Brian P. Levack, *The Witch-Hunt in Early Modern Europe*, 3rd ed. (New York: Pearson Longman, 2006), 21, 23.
10. Cotton Mather, *Magnalia Christi Americana, or the Ecclesiastical History of New England* (1702; Hartford, CT: Silas Andrus, 1820), Vol. 2, 396.
11. Jonathan Edwards, quoted in Janice Knight, "Learning the Language of God: Jonathan Edwards and the Typology of Nature," *William and Mary Quarterly*, 3d ser., 48 (1991): 541.
12. Jonathan Edwards, quoted in Wallace E. Anderson, "Immaterialism in Jonathan Edwards' Early Philosophical Notes," *Journal of the History of Ideas* 25 (1964): 189.
13. John Bartram, quoted in Thomas P. Slaughter, *The Natures of John and William Bartram* (New York: Knopf, 1996), 62, 65–66.
14. James Petiver, quoted in Susan Scott Parrish, *American Curiosity: Cultures of Natural History in the Colonial British Atlantic World* (Chapel Hill: University of North Carolina Press, 2006), 272.
15. John Mitchell, quoted in Winthrop Jordan, *White Over Black: American Attitudes toward the Negro, 1550–1812* (New York: Norton, 1968), 247.
16. Willard, "A Brief Account," 211–212.

SUGGESTIONS FOR FURTHER READING

Providential thinking, wonders, and magic in New England are impressively analyzed in David D. Hall, *Worlds of Wonder, Days of Judgment: Popular Religion in Early New England* (New York: Knopf, 1989); and Richard Godbeer, *The Devil's Dominion: Magic and Religion in Early New England* (Cambridge, UK: Cambridge University Press, 1992). Michael Winship, *Seers of God: Puritan Providentialism in the Restoration and the Enlightenment* (Baltimore: Johns Hopkins University Press, 1996), offers particular insight into the changing trans-Atlantic intellectual landscape that challenged crucial pillars of New England thought. Christine Leigh Hyerman, *Commerce and Culture: The Maritime Communities of Colonial Massachusetts, 1690–1750* (New York: Norton, 1984), integrates insights on religion into her social history of port towns. Mechal Sobel, *The World They Made Together: Black and White Values in Eighteenth-Century Virginia* (Princeton, NJ: Princeton University Press,

1987), provides a valuable glimpse into thinking about and experiences of the supernatural outside of New England.

The literature of witchcraft, which overlaps to some extent with the literature of wonders, includes such groundbreaking books as John Putnam Demos, *Entertaining Satan: Witchcraft and the Culture of Early New England* (New York: Oxford University Press, 1982), and Carol F. Karlsen, *The Devil in the Shape of a Woman: Witchcraft in Colonial New England* (New York: Vintage, 1987). Paul Boyer and Stephen Nissenbaum, *Salem Possessed: The Social Origins of Witchcraft* (Cambridge, MA: Harvard University Press, 1974), remains at the center of the study of Salem. Mary Beth Norton, *In the Devil's Snare: The Salem Witchcraft Crisis of 1692* (New York: Vintage, 2002), revisits the Salem controversy with an emphasis on the connection of the crisis to the Indian wars on the Maine frontier. For additional insights on gender and race, see Elaine G. Breslaw, *Tituba, Reluctant Witch of Salem: Devilish Indians and Puritan Fantasies* (New York: New York University Press, 1997); and Elizabeth Reis, *Damned Women: Sinners and Witches in Puritan New England* (Ithaca, NY: Cornell University Press, 1999). Alison Games, *Witchcraft in Early North America* (Lanham, MD: Rowman & Littlefield Publishers, 2010), offers a comparative approach that encompasses New Mexico and New France as well as the English colonies. Ruth Behar, "Sex and Sin, Witchcraft and the Devil in Late-Colonial Mexico," *American Ethnologist* 14 (1987): 34–54, describes a much more lax official attitude toward witchcraft accusations than found in New England. On the persistence of superstition in New England, see Douglas L. Winiarski, "'Pale Blewish Lights' and a Dead Man's Groans: Tales of the Supernatural from Eighteenth-Century Plymouth," *William and Mary Quarterly*, 3d ser., 55 (1998): 497–530.

Emerging ideas and networks that fueled the empirically oriented practice of science receive careful consideration in Susan Scott Parrish, *American Curiosity: Cultures of Natural History in the Colonial Atlantic World* (Chapel Hill: University of North Carolina Press, 2006). Thomas P. Slaughter, *The Natures of John and William Bartram* (New York: Knopf, 1996), offers a psychologically rich portrait of a family both emblematic of and influential in the construction of eighteenth-century natural history. Kay Diaz Kriz, "Curiosities, Commodities, and Transplanted Bodies in Hans Sloane's 'Natural History of Jamaica,'" *William and Mary Quarterly*, 3d ser., 57 (2000): 35–78, provides a case study for understanding the trans-Atlantic production of scientific knowledge. William J. Scheik, "The Grand Design: Jonathan Edwards' History of the Work of Redemption," *Eighteenth-Century Studies* 8 (1975): 300–314, elegantly engages the thought of an influential colonial minister. Ned C. Landsman, *From Colonials to Provincials: American Thought and Culture, 1680–1760* (New York: Twayne, 1997), places intellectual developments in their broad context.

Winthrop D. Jordan, *White over Black: American Attitudes toward the Negro, 1550–1812* (Chapel Hill: University of North Carolina Press, 1968), remains an invaluable exploration of the dynamic relationship between Enlightenment science and concepts of race. Joyce E. Chaplin, *Subject Matter: Technology, the Body, and Science on the Anglo-American Frontier, 1500–1676* (Cambridge, MA: Harvard University Press, 2001); Jennifer L. Morgan, *Laboring Women: Reproduction and Gender in New World Slavery* (Philadelphia: University of Pennsylvania Press, 2004); María Elena Martinez, "The Black Blood of New Spain: *Limpieza de Sangre*, Racial Violence, and Gendered Power in Early Colonial Mexico," *William and Mary Quarterly*, 3d ser., 61 (2004), 479–520; and Shawn William Miller, *An Environmental History of Latin America* (New York: Cambridge University Press, 2007), facilitate comparative inquiries into colonial-era ideas about race.

On medicine, see James H. Cassedy, *Medicine in America: A Short History* (Baltimore: Johns Hopkins University Press, 1991). Margot Minardi, "The Boston Inoculation

Controversy of 1721–1722: An Incident in the History of Race," *William and Mary Quarterly*, 3d ser., 61 (2004): 47–76, provides fresh insights. Although telling a story from a later period, Laurel Thatcher Ulrich, *A Midwives' Tale: The Life of Martha Ballard, Based on Her Diary, 1785–1812* (New York: Vintage, 1990), offers invaluable insights into the relationship between midwifery and the practice of medicine in early America.

CHAPTER 9

Unsettling America

Eighteenth-Century European Migrations

The city fathers of Aberdeen, Scotland, found out the hard way that Peter Williamson had a story to tell and intended to stick to it. Williamson's book *French and Indian Cruelty; Exemplified in the Life and various vicissitudes of Fortune, of Peter Williamson, A Disbanded Soldier* (1757) upset Aberdeen's magistrates because in it he claimed that he had been kidnapped as a boy in that city and dispatched to North America, where after surviving a shipwreck, he was sold into indentured servitude. Williamson's tale of woe in America also included being taken captive by Indians and falling into the hands of the French as a prisoner of war. But Aberdeen's magistrates could barely get past the opening pages. This son of Scotland had touched a nerve by indicting the city's merchants for their complicity in the business of "stealing young Children from their Parents and selling them as Slaves in the Plantations abroad."[1] The magistrates acted forcefully against these charges—going after Williamson rather than the merchants. They had him arrested and seized unsold copies of his narrative. Calling him an imposter and liar, they ripped the scandalous pages out of his books and had them burned. Then they banished Williamson from Aberdeen. Williamson, however, fought back. He hired a lawyer and sued the Aberdeen merchants and magistrates he considered responsible for his misfortune. Over the next several years, he collected enough evidence to prove his identity in court and win damages against his persecutors.

Despite the vindication he won regarding his kidnapping, not every aspect of Williamson's story would have stood up so well in a court of law. It is very likely that he embellished elements of his American adventure, particularly his Indian captivity. But his story did tap into the landscapes, experiences, and anxieties that defined the eighteenth-century immigrant experience. In his narrative, Williamson claimed to have survived an Atlantic crossing and a shipwreck, to have been sold in a public market to a kind-hearted Scottish master, and to have gained his freedom and established a frontier homestead. Whether truth or fiction, this tale of a perilous sea voyage, of exploitive servitude and ethnic solidarity, and of economic and geographic mobility would have rung true with many of his contemporaries who migrated to North America as indentured servants.

As his story moved toward the frontier, Williamson's darkening fate acquired the flavor of a tragic romance that has proven difficult to corroborate. The joys of his purported marriage to the daughter of a wealthy planter ended abruptly when Indians stormed his home and took him captive. Tortured and tormented himself, Williamson allegedly witnessed a series of savage cruelties wreaked on other white frontier families; he did not spare his reader the horrifying details, including the fate of Jacob Snider's family, with the husband, wife, and five children all scalped and left to die in their burning home. Williamson's original kidnapping by his Scottish countrymen paled in comparison to what he claimed to have seen in the American backcountry, including the prolonged execution of an elderly Indian deemed too weak to remain among his own people. Williamson's daring escape might have been a moment of triumph, if not for the discovery that his wife died while he was in captivity.

The twists and turns of the narrative after Williamson enlisted in the British army probably hewed closer to the truth. He may well have seen action on the New York frontier during the Seven Years' War, including the fall of Fort Oswego on Lake Ontario, where he became a prisoner of war. Williamson's American odyssey ended when he was placed aboard a ship loaded with other prisoners of war and sent back to Britain. Discharged from military service in Plymouth, England, he walked back to Aberdeen with little more than his story to tell.

The migrations that remade British America in the eighteenth century rarely if ever completed such an illustrious circuit as the one Williamson achieved, but his story contained elements that many other highly mobile people—even African American slaves—would have recognized. He repeatedly traversed the boundary between freedom and bondage; in a culturally diverse landscape, he enjoyed the benefit of a countryman's sympathy; he recounted a backcountry that lured people of various European origins with the promise of cheap and fertile land but generated hostilities between them and the land's native owners. As his confrontation with the Aberdeen authorities revealed, Williamson was willing to contest authority to protect his interests, while, also like other voluntary and forced migrants, his movements in the Atlantic World were shaped by currents of war and trade well beyond the control of ordinary people. A diverse set of men and women carried with them to colonial America identities forged on one side of the Atlantic that were reinvented, reconfigured, and absorbed in a variety of new and unpredictable ways on the other side of the ocean. The outcome of these personal and communal transformations depended as much on timing and geography as it did on individual intentions.

THE NEW EMIGRANTS: GERMANS, ULSTER SCOTS, AND OTHERS

Peter Williamson's kidnappers understood that there was a market for servants into which they could tap. Thus, his story does not fit into the seemingly simple but nonetheless valuable categories—*push* versus *pull*—that immigration

Map 9.1 Sources of Eighteenth-Century European Immigration.

historians use to explain what puts people in motion from one country to another. He had not chosen to travel to the Americas on his own, attracted by prospects of land, wealth, or freedom, so he was not exactly pulled by American conditions. Nor was Williamson pushed from Scotland, fleeing conditions of crushing poverty or religious persecution. But his assailants knew that the demand for bound labor existed to produce a profit for their efforts. And they adopted a business model that made their role in exploiting labor a trans-Atlantic one. In truth, the line between push and pull factors is always a bit blurry—the choices of emigrants, even when they move of their own volition, often are conditioned and constrained by factors beyond their control. To understand why non-English groups—Germans, Ulster Scots, Huguenots, and Jews among them—in the late seventeenth and eighteenth centuries turned to the English colonies is to reckon with what made old homelands less tenable and new ones across the Atlantic increasingly appealing (see Map 9.1).

Of approximately 300,000 European migrants to British North America between 1700 and 1775, emigrants from the German-speaking states, principalities, and duchies of the Holy Roman Empire made up the largest portion. Almost eighty thousand German-speakers arrived in that period, following on the heels of smaller numbers who came in the late seventeenth century. German-speakers established themselves in every British colony except those in New England, but as both entry point and final destination, Pennsylvania by far received the largest number. These migrants were identifiable to each other and to non-Germans by their persistent use of their own language, and their tendency to form communities apart from other European groups. Notwithstanding this distinctiveness, the German-speaking migrations included people of diverse experiences and religious backgrounds, a diversity manifested both before and after the Atlantic crossing.

Prolonged political instability and economic pressures prompted many women and men in German-speaking provinces along the Rhine River, including the Palatinate and the Kraichgau, to consider emigration. Religious diversity—Lutherans, Calvinists, Catholics, and a number of radical religious reformers known as Pietists—created conditions for religious discrimination and persecution. But the challenge for many peasants was more material than spiritual. These regions had been ravaged during Europe's seventeenth-century wars. With the restoration of peace, the population of these German-speaking lands grew rapidly, so much so that land became increasingly scarce in the eighteenth century. The political side of the reconstruction process imposed additional strains, as nobles and governments sought to rebuild their wealth and influence through increased demands for dues and taxes. Meanwhile, the expansion of commercial agriculture made some peasants wealthier, but left others struggling on less profitable holdings that had to be divided among heirs. A majority of the region's people were serfs, who by law owed obligations of military or labor service to their lords and could not leave his land without permission. Adding insult to injury, the territorial ruler could impose a manumission fee on those wishing to leave.

Such hardships increased the determination of many German-speakers to depart the region entirely, but America was not the obvious destination. Indeed, other areas of Europe to the east such as Russia and the Habsburg Empire drew far more emigrating German-speakers than did the English colonies of North America. The English colonies did not welcome Catholics, which reduced the pool of potential immigrants significantly. In the eighteenth century overall, fewer than 15 percent of German emigrants made the trip to British North America.

Germans who wished to migrate, whether free to go, paying manumission fees, or departing illegally, had to evaluate what prospective new homes had to offer. Word that some German-speakers had found a measure of success across the ocean was essential; so too was an affordable and reasonably efficient means of making the trans-Atlantic passage. Pennsylvania's reputation for cheap land, lack of required military service, and religious toleration made that colony particularly attractive.

Small initial bursts of German immigration eventually yielded to a more financially and socially sustainable model. Pietists, Protestants who emphasized personal religious devotion and early Christian simplicity, fled religious persecution to join German Quakers recruited by William Penn for his colony in the 1680s. The affinity between Quakers and Pietist sects grew from a shared commitment to pacifism, a refusal to support state churches, an emphasis on spiritual experience instead of elaborate ritual, and the formation of tightly knit religious communities. A group of over two thousand Germans fleeing agricultural crisis came to New York's Hudson Valley in the 1710s as part of a Crown-sponsored attempt to resettle Protestant religious refugees in England in the American colonies. These immigrants quickly cast off the role of laborers producing naval supplies, moving westward to the Mohawk Valley where they set up their own German-speaking communities.

A system of servant redemption developed that facilitated the large and steady migration. Those who could not pay for their travel from Rotterdam, the Netherlands port of departure from the Rhine River, agreed to become indentured servants to people on the other end of their journey who would purchase their contracts. On arrival, they had two weeks to locate a master rather than being auctioned off. This system allowed German-speaking migrants to locate relatives or otherwise favorably disposed fellow Germans to redeem the debt rather than being placed at the mercy of the servant market. The many German-speakers who emigrated in family units also sometimes financed their passage by having some of their children enter indentured servitude upon arrival in America.

The redemption model helped forge New World identities without severing European connections. Through the Philadelphia gateway, Germans poured into not only the Pennsylvania countryside, but also western Maryland, Virginia, and North Carolina (see Figure 9.1). Among the key features of German immigration was the clustering together of German-speakers. Thus, while groups of German emigrants from a particular village might disperse, German-speakers settled near one another, although with more land available, not in the tightly packed villages of their home country. This pattern of settlement facilitated the persistence of the German language among emigrants and their children, which in turn encouraged the emergence of a German ethnic identity in America.

Even as they established roots in America, German migrants maintained ties to their home communities. Word of success in America reached home villages, helping to prompt the next wave of migrants. German immigrants, moreover, had no intention of foregoing their inheritances from back home, even decades after their departure for America. Some emigrants employed agents to see that their

Figure 9.1 Jonathan Hager House. Subsequent to his 1736 arrival in Philadelphia, German immigrant Jonathan Hager moved to the Maryland backcountry and began building this substantial stone house in 1739. Hager married another German, Elizabeth Kershner, the next year. Approximately eighty thousand Germans migrated to English North America between 1700 and 1775, many settling on the frontier and maintaining their linguistic and ethnic identity. The house continues to stand in Hagerstown, Maryland. By permission of the City of Hagerstown.

portion of a deceased family member's estate was recovered; others returned in person to do the job, thereby becoming walking advertisements for migration to America as they shared firsthand accounts of their experience.

Religious identity played a distinctive role in German immigration, contributing to its diversity and, indeed, its divisions. Lutherans and Calvinists made up the lion's share of German immigrants, with the churches of these denominations serving as focal points for many German communities in the colonies. These Lutheran and Reformed churches were another distinguishing feature around which German ethnic identity formed. Indeed, the existence of a church helped draw additional German-speaking immigrants to a community.

German Pietists introduced new streams of religious dissent and even utopian dreams to the American landscape. Less than 10 percent of the total German migration, they nonetheless made their presence felt among Germans and non-German populations. Groups such as Moravians, Mennonites, Amish, and Schwenkfelders challenged the dominant Christian denominations by seeking a less worldly, less ritualized faith, one that could be practiced through shared labor and communal worship. They emphasized the purified commitment of a community of believers rather than church and state hierarchies, and often organized themselves around leaders whom they regarded as divinely inspired mystics. As so often happens with religious movements that explicitly challenge established churches, Pietist sects suffered persecution and legal disabilities, including taxes imposed on them because their pacifist principles led them to refuse military service. Under the sponsorship of Count Nicholas Ludwig von Zinzendorf, the Moravians became especially committed to missionary work, spreading their message among fellow Germans and ultimately Native Americans and African Americans.

Migration to America offered such groups the hope that they would leave the history of persecution in Europe behind, but Pietists managed to alienate their fellow German-speakers and others with their seemingly extreme views. Moravian views on sex and gender particularly challenged conventional German mores. Moravians hymns and pictorial imagery included sexual content, while their views of the Holy Trinity included the unorthodox idea that the Holy Spirit was feminine and that even Christ himself had both feminine and masculine attributes. As if these ideas were not threatening enough to the conventional patriarchy, the Moravians allowed women to preach and hold church offices. Despite much larger populations, mainstream German colonists had a relatively small number of clergy to see to their spiritual needs; they felt deeply threatened by the Moravians. The Moravians' inhospitable reception among other Pennsylvania Germans ultimately prompted them to move to the North Carolina frontier. As in the previous century, the colonial landscape was big, but not big enough for all Protestant migrants to live together in harmony, whether or not they spoke the same language. Meanwhile, the pacifist commitments of German Pietists who remained in Pennsylvania contributed to and complicated the contentious politics of frontier defense in that colony.

Other non-English European migrant groups exhibited their own variations on the themes evident in the German experience. The Huguenots, French Protestants who fled France after the toleration granted them under the Edict of Nantes was revoked in 1685, represent an object lesson in assimilation in the years after their arrival on American shores. Historians can trace the fortunes, often quite impressive, of Huguenot-descended families—the Laurens, the Jays, and the Reveres—in colonies such as South Carolina, New York, and Massachusetts. But evidence of sustained Huguenot community-building or the coalescence of a French Protestant ethnic identity is more difficult to find. Only 2,000 of the 200,000 Huguenot refugees who fled France made their way to the American colonies, mostly after first relocating to England. Dispersing to such ports as Charles Town, Manhattan, and Boston, Huguenots experienced little resistance to or resentment of their entrance. In South Carolina, Huguenots became slaveholders, forging a common racial and class identity with other whites in this slave society. The Huguenots in New York entered a colony defined by ethnic diversity as well as stark racial inequality. Although Huguenots did establish French Protestant churches in Manhattan and Boston, religion did not end up serving as the basis for ethnic identity—as immigrants and their offspring married non-Huguenots and affiliated with other Protestant churches. In New York as in South Carolina, slaveholding became a means of upward economic and social mobility. While Huguenot merchants in America sometimes did draw on ties to Huguenot relatives across the Atlantic, these mercantile networks did not prove to be exclusive, or the basis of lasting ethno-religious identity. The Huguenot communities of New Rochelle and New Paltz, both in New York's Hudson Valley, managed to retain their cultural distinctiveness longer than in urban or Southern environments, suggesting that some conditions were more hospitable than others to maintaining cultural and linguistic distinctiveness. Nonetheless, small numbers, white skin, and a broadly defined Protestant identity made the Huguenot story one of merger and absorption rather than persistence and separation.

For non-Protestant white immigrants, matters of cultural survival were somewhat trickier. Dating back to the seventeenth century, Jews, arriving via a variety of circuitous routes through Europe and the Americas, formed tiny communities in the port cities of New Amsterdam, Newport, Rhode Island, and Charles Town, South Carolina. The opportunity to worship freely and to conduct business was sometimes, but not always, matched by the granting of political rights on an equal footing with Protestant Christians. In 1697 Charles Town's Jews joined local Huguenots in successfully requesting that the governor and legislature grant them citizenship. Despite a long history in Newport, Jews who petitioned the Rhode Island government for full political rights in the mid-eighteenth century were denied. Jews exercised political rights in New York City, though prejudice did rear its head at times in that diverse and factious city. Individual Jews left the faith through intermarriage, but Jews adapted various customs to their new surroundings and persisted in an overwhelmingly Protestant British North America.

Anti-Catholicism constituted a much more consequential set of prejudices, making it difficult for Catholics to maintain their religious identity, let alone to construct a lasting ethnic identity. Several thousand Irish Catholics made their way to the mainland colonies in the eighteenth century, comprising as much as a quarter of the total migration from Ireland during this period. The poverty and dispossession that Irish Catholics faced under English subjugation in their homeland far outweighed the difficulties that non-Catholic Irish migrants sought to escape. So, in theory *push* factors might have generated much larger waves of Irish Catholic migration. However, the travails of the large numbers of Irish indentured servants shipped to the Chesapeake and the West Indies in the seventeenth century attached a stigma to American migration. A commitment to family, locality, and the Irish language also created barriers to emigration. Thus, Irish Catholic migrants tended to be those whose social and cultural ties had been most disrupted in regions most effected by the market economy and the penetration of the English language. Rather than family or chain migration, by which social ties were reestablished on the other side of the Atlantic, Irish Catholic immigrants were more likely to make their way in the New World as individuals than other migrant groups. The fragmented nature of Irish Catholic migration, along with strong anti-Catholic colonial laws and practices, made it all the more likely that these migrants would marry non-Irish and non-Catholics, their identities ultimately merging with the Protestant majority.

Catholic immigrants most often made their way to Pennsylvania, New York, and Maryland. But even Pennsylvania, a colony founded on the premise of religious toleration, buckled under English insistence that the colony adopt an anti-Catholic Test Act designed to prevent Catholics from holding office, while the miniscule number of Catholics, many of them German, living there did not dampen the impulse toward anti-Papist political rhetoric in the colony. Paranoia about Catholic strangers, aroused by periodic wars pitting Britain against France and Spain, could turn deadly. During the 1741 New York slave plot, immigrant John Ury, who identified himself as an Anglican, was suspected by the New York authorities of being an undercover Catholic priest and hanged like many of the suspected slave rebels. In certain circumstances in the English colonies, to be a migrant without a protective community was to be vulnerable indeed.

The thousands of French Catholics, known as Acadians, who the British forcibly removed from Nova Scotia in 1755 and deposited in various Eastern ports, were not greeted as a welcome addition to the colonial ethnic stew. The British governor deemed mass expulsion necessary as war loomed with neighboring French Canada, but displaced the fears of a French Catholic enemy southward to Britain's other colonies. Edward Lloyd, a Maryland planter, greeted the arrival of nine hundred Acadians in his colony with concern; he noted, "As Enemies they came here, and as such must certainly remain, because they are all rigid Roman Catholicks. . . . " Although contributing money to "save them from starving," Lloyd feared that these unwanted newcomers would produce "a great deal of Danger by their corrupting mine & other Negroe Slaves," who regarded themselves as fellow Catholics.[2] Massachusetts responded to the presence of one thousand Acadians with apprehensions. Authorities thought to spread the cost and the risk of the Acadian presence by distributing the exiles across many towns. The longstanding law barring Catholic clergy from entering Massachusetts expressed the province's wariness of Catholic observance. Nonetheless, Acadians did conduct services on their own and there is a record of one Acadian priest entering the colony. Pennsylvanians showed a similar impulse to disperse these forced migrants. A mob unsuccessfully targeted Philadelphia's one long-standing Catholic church, but Lancaster's church was not so lucky, suffering destruction in 1760. It is not surprising that so many Acadians did not view the English colonies as a suitable new home and found their way to French-speaking areas of the continent, most notably Louisiana.

As a young Peter Williamson was relieved to discover upon his arrival in Philadelphia, his situation was not utterly forlorn, as other Scots had preceded him to the middle colonies. There, his countrymen had forged settlement patterns, religious institutions, and an ethnic identity distinct from their English and other neighbors. East New Jersey began as a Scottish proprietary colony. Although it did not last long before conversion to an English royal colony, the Scottish proprietors along with the Scottish tenants and servants who traveled to East Jersey formed the core of an area of significant Scottish settlement that extended to New York and Pennsylvania.

The steady trickle of thirty thousand Scots who arrived on the eastern seaboard of North America between 1700 and 1760 came from a country that had a long tradition of out-migration to other parts of Europe. In the eighteenth century, Scotland underwent a process of rapid transformation from a strikingly poor country to an increasingly dynamic region fortuitously close to the core of an expanding British Empire. The character of Scottish migration to North America reflected the traditions of Scotland's past, as well as the effects of its ongoing transformation.

Most of the pre-1760 Scottish migrants came from the lowlands, where the preeminent position of Scottish lairds meant that many ordinary Scots had little experience with land ownership, ties to specific plots of land, or even village life. Tenants served the lairds but seldom held long-term leases and felt little incentive to invest efforts in building substantial homes. Mobility within a parish, where one might expect to find various relatives, was common. The Scots' relationship with their English neighbors was a fraught one. In the border regions closest to England, Scots were particularly determined to distinguish their own history, folk culture, and religious affiliations from the English. As a reaction against English domination, Presbyterianism became the state religion of Scotland, even though England and Scotland united under a single parliament in 1707. Still, the influence of the more powerful nation to the south was hard for some Scots to resist. Indeed, particularly in northeast Scotland, the urge to modernize took hold, with lairds experiencing mixed results in their attempt to have their tenants adopt more modern agricultural techniques, including enclosure and crop rotation. The Scottish proprietary experiment in East New Jersey, which lasted from 1683 to 1702, was an extension of the modernizing ambitions among some Scottish elites.

The patterns of landownership, mobility, and community formation in the Scottish lowlands framed settlement in America. Large landowners sought out Scottish immigrants and occupied prominent positions in New Jersey politics. In colonies whose hallmark was cultural diversity, ordinary Scottish migrants sought out each other. These migrants in imitation of their homeland experience tended to settle in small clusters, with quite a bit of movement among them. By following this approach, Scots formed regional rather than town-based webs of community, mutual assistance, and kinship. Their tradition of dividing inheritances equally among male heirs extended the web of Scottish community, as did the inclusion of married daughters in the family circle even when they married non-Scots.

A key feature of Scottish migration was the coalescence of Scots from a variety of regions into a unified and self-conscience group in America. In this sense, Scottish and German migrations were similar. Like the German migrants, Scottish migration included a diversity of religious affiliations, Quakers and Anglicans as well as Presbyterians. Over time, Scottish immigrants gravitated increasingly to the Presbyterian Church, where Scottish identity in America became affirmed and ingrained.

Trade and accomplishment magnified the significance of Scottish immigration, while paving the way for large waves of Scottish immigration after 1760 from the lowlands and the highlands. Scottish merchants developed a significant presence in the Americas in the eighteenth century, taking full advantage of the commercial opportunities that union with Britain provided. In New York, the Scottish Morrises and Livingstons quickly became two of the most prominent families in the colony, using their mercantile connections to acquire great landed estates. The most famous Scottish trading enterprises connected Scotland to Chesapeake tobacco growers, helping to fuel the rise of Glasgow as a major British port. Scottish merchants established connections to port cities up and down the Atlantic coast, as well as the West Indies. These traders became adept at making the most of ethnic connections to maintain effective networks not only across the Atlantic but also among colonies such as New York, New Jersey, and Pennsylvania. The development of Scottish universities also made education a Scottish export to the colonies, with such accomplished figures of medicine and science as Cadwallader Colden and William Douglass hailing from Scotland. Indeed, the vast majority of formally educated American doctors received their training in Scotland, as did many notable ministers, teachers, and professors. Ambitious Scots also worked their way into the Crown's administration of the colonies, and several served as colonial governors in North America and the West Indies.

The waves of migrants from Northern Ireland who landed in North American during the eighteenth century were, in part, a product of the broader Scottish history of mobility and out-migration, but they experienced these phenomena in distinct ways. Scottish Presbyterians migrated across the Irish Sea to the northern counties of Ireland—collectively known as Ulster—during the seventeenth century. There, they forged an identity separate from Ireland's Catholic majority and its English overlords. Beginning with James I in 1603, the Stuart royal family, which originated in Scotland, supported Scottish migration to Ulster because they believed it would cement their rule there. Troops from Scotland also assisted in the suppression of Catholic uprisings and, during the Glorious Revolution, the Ulster Scots helped undermine efforts by the deposed James II to use Ireland as a launching pad for his restoration.

In Ireland, the Scots migrants learned that the rewards of loyalty and a shared Protestant heritage with those who ruled the land had distinct limits. While their Scottish cousins established Presbyterianism as the official church in Scotland, in this new home the Church of Ireland, a subsidiary of the Church of England, held sway. This made the Ulster Scots dissenters, as they, like the Puritans, were Calvinists. The Test Act in 1704 confirmed this subordinate status. The Ulster Scots had to pay a church tax, or tithe, to the Church of Ireland, while they also found themselves barred from holding public office. Participation in formal political life became difficult. Although historians debate how much hardship such measures actually entailed, the stigma and the insult were not something easily forgotten or ignored. As one historian succinctly put the matter, the Ulster Scots were subject to "second-class status in a second-class kingdom."[3]

Discrimination by Anglo-Irish elites and disdain for Irish Catholics may have marked out the cultural and political boundaries for Ulster Scots, but their shifting economic fortunes provided a more direct motive for migration to America. The Ulster Scots had invested themselves heavily in the production of linen, which is a cloth spun from flax. Economic dependence on export markets for linen made the Ulster Scots vulnerable to declines in demand, as occurred in the 1710s and 1720s. Compounding instability in the linen trade were deteriorating conditions in Ireland, including a major agricultural crisis starting in 1717. Rising rents and rising Church of Ireland tithes stretched the Ulster Scots' resources. Such difficulties, experienced against a background of discrimination and divisive disputes over doctrine among Ulster Presbyterians themselves, created a push to leave Ireland.

Ulster migrants did not choose migration to America out of pure desperation nor did this solution come by random chance. During the initial burst of eighteenth-century emigration to America, four-fifths of travelers paid their own way, only one-fifth entering the trade in indentured servants. Presbyterian spinners and weavers from Ulster parlayed money made in the linen trade along with land sales and the subletting of rented property to purchase tickets to what they hoped would be a land of greater opportunity. Ties to Pennsylvania and New England only grew stronger when the Linen Act of 1705 gave Ulster the privilege of trading directly with the North American colonies rather than channeling their exports through England. Meanwhile, Ulster Scots believed that their Calvinist creed, which stigmatized them in Ireland, would make them welcome in America. Their fellow Calvinists, the Puritans, still dominated New England, while the only American presbytery, the affiliated form of church governance that the Ulster Scots practiced, was in Philadelphia. Thus, Ulster Scots sailed to Boston and, in far greater numbers, to Pennsylvania and Delaware ports. The immigrants followed the same route on the same ships as the linen that Ulster produced.

As migrants left Ulster for North America, paying ministers' salaries and tending to the Irish Presbyterian communities' poor became increasingly difficult. Meanwhile, word from America made it back to Ulster along the established trade-and-migration route. The initial prospects of a warm welcome from their fellow Calvinists in New England quickly soured, as clashes in theology, culture, and institutional organization emerged, but the middle colonies became an enticing destination. Recruitment agents promoted the more heavily trafficked route to Pennsylvania by offering inexpensive passage and stories of cheap land and low taxes. Although shipboard travel conditions could be quite difficult, news from the colonies ignited the desire of Ulster's dissenting Protestants to leave behind their hardships in Ireland for greener pastures. A pamphlet by an Irish landlord decrying the 1720s migration described letters from America to Ireland "in which... they set forth and recommend the fruitfulness and commodities of the country, they tell them, that if they will but carry over a little money with them, they may for a small sum purchase considerable tracts of land...." Such letters claimed "that any industrious man [in America], may in a very little time procure to himself a good and comfortable settlement, free from all those oppressions and impositions which they are subject to here." The author of the pamphlet called this urge to move a "strange humour," but it was clear that the attraction of relocating from Ireland to America, as their forebears had relocated from Scotland to Ireland, was strong indeed.[4]

Place names signaled that the new colonists quickly established a prominent place in the American landscape as well as their attachment to their former Ulster homes. Hence, communities such as Donegal, Derry, Londonderry, and Tyrone dotted the colonial map—just as Manheim, Heidelberg, and Germantown denoted the presence of German migrants. While language marked immigrants from the Holy Roman Empire as Germans, the Ulster-accented English of the Irish immigrants may have heightened the sense of difference between them and other English-speakers in the colonies. Other colonists stereotyped the Ulster Scots as prone to drinking and violence. In 1729 a mob formed in Boston to prevent ships from Ulster from unloading their human cargo. That same year, Benjamin Franklin confessed in his newspaper the *Pennsylvania Gazette* that he sympathized with his fellow colonists who felt a "Disrespect and Aversion to" the Irish immigrants.[5]

While Franklin and Anglo-Americans found it distressing to observe the increasing numbers of German and Irish immigrants in their midst, the strength the migrant communities themselves derived from their relatively large numbers had its limits. Huguenots, Jews, and Scots worked out their identities in different ways, assimilation and adaptation, as well as the creation of linguistic and religious niches where their identities might persevere for varying lengths of time. As we have seen, through language and religion Germans synthesized an ethnic identity out of diversity, though certain sharp religious rivalries continued to sustain diversity and produce tensions.

The Ulster Scots struggled to make their Old World experiences serve them well in their New World surroundings. For a time, a renewed commitment to the Presbyterian articles of faith established in Scotland served as a force for cohesion. This response to frontier conditions, in which the church was often the only institution capable of imposing social discipline on the community, could only last for so long. As many migrants to port cities and the rapidly expanding backcountry found out, relative freedom and diversity created opportunities to experiment with new ways, as well as jarring challenges to old ways. Economic circumstances, political rivalry, and religious tensions pushed many migrants toward America. The lure of prosperity in the backcountry pulled many migrants farther west, in the process reshaping their material prospects, political affiliations, and religious sensibilities.

TRANSFORMING THE BACKCOUNTRY

Whether Peter Williamson actually experienced Indian captivity, his narrative captured a basic truth, that the backcountry was contested ground. Native Americans, settlers, wealthy Eastern landowners, colonial governments, and imperial powers all staked claims to the lands west of the well-established strip of settlement along the Atlantic coast. Life in the backcountry reflected these overlapping claims and ambitions. Migrants to the backcountry, many of them recently arrived from Europe, achieved an impressive, albeit often modest, level of prosperity, while spreading the zone of European settlements westward and hundreds of miles north and south along the mountainous spine of the seaboard-based colonies. The backcountry excited an appetite for land speculation among Eastern elites while occasionally challenging their political hegemony. Meanwhile, the move into the backcountry prompted a new cycle of cultural cooperation and cultural rivalry between European and Native American peoples, with violent confrontation only one of a range of responses that also included trade and cultural cross-pollination (see Map 9.2).

The mountains and valleys beyond the coastal zone of seventeenth-century European settlement underwent a continuous series of upheavals during the eighteenth century. Native Americans attempted to meet European demand and their own desire for European trade goods by intensifying the hunt for beaver pelts and deer skins. But these trading relationships caused ecological, epidemiological, and military crises that not only pitted colonists versus Indians, but also Indians against one another, in ways that provoked Native American internal migrations and opened up more space for European settlement. As happened earlier in New

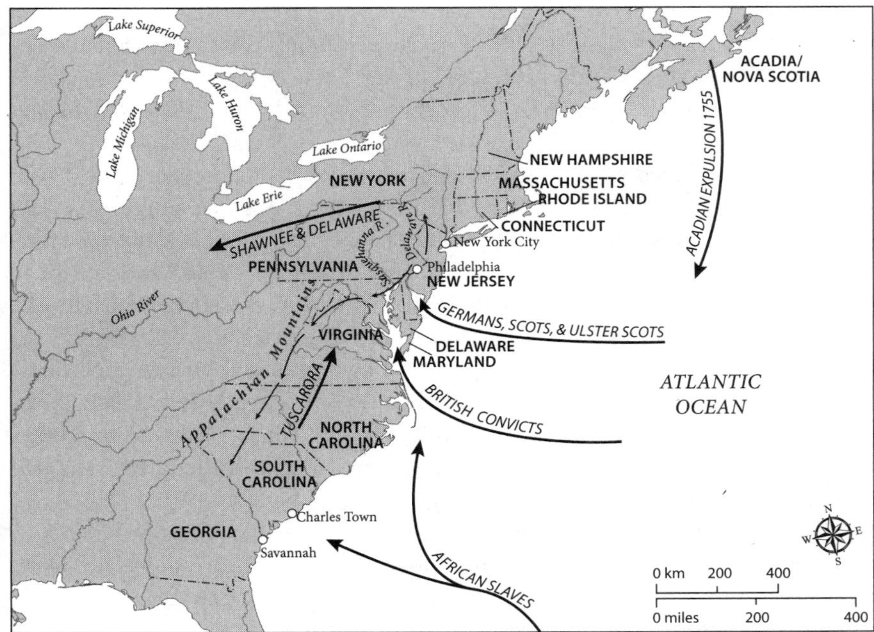

Map 9.2 Eighteenth-Century Migrations.

England, the beaver population of the mid-Atlantic backcountry collapsed, while European diseases eroded Indian populations—even as the desire for guns, metal pots, textiles, and alcohol remained strong. The construction of gristmills and dams undermined Indian access to fish and European livestock trampled Indian corn fields.

After 1680 Indian migrations along the Susquehanna Valley, which connected Iroquois homelands south of Lake Ontario to the Chesapeake Bay, reshaped the mid-Atlantic backcountry. The Tuscarora migrated northward from North Carolina, along this route in the 1710s, joining the Iroquois confederation. The Shawnees' quest for more secure homelands led them to the Susquehanna, where they were later joined by Delawares from eastern Pennsylvania, who had been defrauded of much of their original land. These latter two groups, rivals of the Iroquois, also moved along westward tributaries of the Susquehanna River into the Ohio Valley in the late 1720s. As colonial traders, land speculators, and squatters familiarized themselves with these regions, they increasingly launched plans for their settlement, despite the opposition of Indians who regarded the same territory as a refuge and homeland.

Backcountry interaction between colonists and Indians did not follow a single pattern or trajectory. Moravian missionaries learned the Delaware language and established new communities of Indian converts, while traders and hunters forged diplomatic and kinship ties with their cross-cultural counterparts. Native converts learned European languages, such as the Mahican woman Towaneem, who discussed her religious beliefs in German and her native language with missionaries and Indians in the Pennsylvania backcountry. On the other hand, Indians also acquired the ability to curse, or at least to curse in English: as captive Jean Lowry observed, "These poor Pagans cannot Swear nor Curse in their own Language; all the Profanations of that sort, ever I heard among them, being in *English*, which (I suppose) they learned of our Traders. . . ."[6]

While undoubtedly white–Indian backcountry interaction was often driven by expedience and self-interest, it could also lead to more meaningful ties. The Palatinate German settlements in the Mohawk Valley, for example, developed intimate connections with neighboring Oneida and Mohawk Indians. Intermarriage appears to have been more common in this part of New York than in Pennsylvania, while economic relationships and cultural exchange grew deep roots, with Indians consuming imported tea and Europeans using traditional Indian medicines. German colonists leased and purchased land directly from their Indian neighbors, upsetting colonial authorities in New York City and Albany. Indians engaged in occasional wage labor for their colonial neighbors and slowly adopted European livestock and housing into their own domestic economies.

One of the great ironies of the eighteenth-century backcountry was that both Iroquois and colonial leaders imagined the backcountry as a buffer. Of course, who was being buffered from whom was an object of contention and controversy, as well as a source of opportunity. The Iroquois welcomed Indians dispossessed in various British colonies to resettle along their borders with European powers. The

Iroquois described these new groups as "props" to their confederacy, subordinate partners in its diplomacy and trade with outsiders. Sometimes these communities emerged from the remnants of Indian nations decimated by wars and epidemics, and they became known by names that reflected the geography of their new homes, such as the "River Indians" of the upper Hudson Valley or the "Conestoga" Indians of Lancaster, Pennsylvania, whose name derived from a tributary creek of the Susquehanna. In other instances, these newcomers to Iroquoia retained their distinctive cultural identities, as was the case with the inhabitants of Conoy Indian Town on the Juniata River, refugees from the Chesapeake Bay. The Iroquois preferred the presence of these groups along their flanks to that of colonists because they knew the Indian newcomers would not encroach as much on Iroquois lands. They also made more reliable allies in times of war, and Iroquois warriors could have free passage through their territory when traveling southward to attack more enemies, such as Cherokee and Catawba along the Virginia and Carolina frontiers.

Material ambition, demographic opportunity, and ongoing imperial designs made settling the backcountry with whites an increasingly important component of colonial policy. Officials in London conceived of frontier threats in military terms, suggesting a series of forts and potentially coordinating the supervision of colonial militia. Colonial governors, most notably in Virginia, favored policies through which a human web of backcountry settlements would secure the seaboard colonies from Indian and French enemies. In the early decades of the eighteenth century, Virginia's leaders decided that making land available to a growing pool of non-English Protestant migrants in the Shenandoah Valley would serve a variety of useful purposes, not the least of which was ensuring that the Chesapeake did not develop a mountainous maroon hinterland of runaway slaves, as happened in Jamaica. As early as 1700, the Virginia government allowed French Huguenots to settle west of the fall line, the border marking where rivers ceased to be navigable for ocean-going vessels and therefore the unofficial marker between Virginia's tidewater region and backcountry. Virginia Governor William Gooch used the incentive of land ownership to attract migrant families to fill in the backcountry. The land hunger of Virginia's elites would not indefinitely take a back seat to settling Ulster-Scot and German migrants, but the efforts of the 1730s and early 1740s lasted long enough for new cultural and landholding patterns to emerge in the colony once largely confined to the east.

South Carolina's Governor Robert Johnson hoped to draw inhabitants of the Pennsylvania, Virginia, and North Carolina backcountry southward to play a similar role in his colony. During the 1740s and 1750s, thousands of migrants made their way to the western edges of South Carolina, drawn in part by a headright system that granted free acres of land for each member of a household, including any slaves. By the 1760s, slaves made up a small but growing percentage of South Carolina's backcountry inhabitants—approximately 7 percent in 1764. For Pennsylvanians and Virginians seeking new economic prospects, the South Carolina backcountry proved to be an enticing destination. The fact that North

Carolina's backcountry did not feed into a port like Charles Town made South Carolina more attractive than its northern neighbor.

Settlers in the backcountry did not view themselves as pawns serving the purposes of empire nor did they come west to isolate themselves from one another. Rather, the opening up of the backcountry created social, economic, and political opportunities that settlers could have only dreamed of in their European homelands. The fertility and availability of land and the potential of the fur trade drew migrants into regions of the backcountry where authorities did not want them to go. Much to the chagrin of Pennsylvania officials, some backcountry migrants rented lands directly from Indians. In 1750 the Penn family sent agents to evict squatters who, they said, were illegally occupying proprietary land. The squatters insisted that they had a property right in any improvements—such as cleared fields, fences, barns, or homes—they had made on the land. The proprietors' agents would have none of it, and they set the humble log cabins of the squatters ablaze.

Such measures, however, were only temporary setbacks for families intent on living in the backcountry. Pushed out of one locale, they resettled in another or returned to their old homesteads once the danger had passed. Migrants who found Pennsylvania unwelcoming also had the option of following the Great Wagon Road south from the Susquehanna Valley into Virginia's Shenandoah Valley and the Carolina backcountry. Towns sprang up along this interior route to serve their needs. Indeed, growth was so intense between 1745 and 1763 that the biggest of the mushrooming Southern backcountry towns surpassed the population of their Eastern counterparts. These towns, such as Hagerstown, Maryland, Winchester, Virginia, and Salisbury, North Carolina, were often spaced by a day's journey along the Great Wagon Road. They collected together skilled artisans such as carpenters, potters, millwrights, and blacksmiths, as well as service providers such as innkeepers and the attorneys necessary to conduct land purchases. The North Carolina backcountry showed more economic dynamism than the colony's coastal regions. These towns suggest the robustness of the backcountry economy in this era of rapid growth. Nonetheless, backcountry inhabitants neither thought of themselves nor desired to be part of a region separated from coastal areas, for economic as well as political reasons. Backcountry inhabitants thought of themselves as settler-citizens who expected to be incorporated into the colonial commercial and political order as a means of advancing their own self-interests.

The backcountry was also a place where identities were formed, tested, and sometimes fractured. The Ulster Scots immersed themselves in the diverse world of the backcountry, scrambling individually for opportunities and advancement. Thus, even as they played a crucial role in settling and extending the backcountry, the Ulster Scots found it hard to sustain a unified ethnic identity. In Pennsylvania, they fought with Indians, with whom they also traded and drank. In these early years, civil authority in the form of courts was hard to find along the Pennsylvania frontier. Not content with their isolation, backcountry settlers agitated for more representatives in the legislature, county government, roads, and fortifications.

Political and economic improvements that would link them more closely to the port city of Philadelphia promised to give them access to markets and opportunity.

The backcountry's changing connection to Philadelphia and the Atlantic economy facilitated the accumulation of wealth while heightening social distinctions. Cash transactions took place alongside barter. As land values increased, the gap between successful and poorer migrants grew, with the wealthier members of the community not only purchasing luxury goods such as wigs, furniture, and petticoats, but also acquiring servants and even slaves. In the 1740s, a new wave of Ulster migrants to the frontier was much more likely to come as servants than their predecessors. To more established migrants to the backcountry, these new arrivals presented an opportunity to advance their own wealth and comfort, as well as a new threat of disorder, with newcomers running away, fornicating, and committing violent crimes. Meanwhile, a wave of religious revivals that rocked the region from the late 1730s onward exposed contrasting spiritual sensibilities and class divisions. For many Ulster Scots, these revivals would sunder ties to their old congregations and even dissolve affiliations with the Presbyterianism that they brought from the British Isles.

Language facilitated German ethnic identity in the backcountry, but their material interests required this community to participate in provincial politics. Indeed, Germans made up an identifiable voting bloc in Pennsylvania for which politicians contended. For several years, Germans found themselves at odds with proprietor Thomas Penn, who sought to enforce land claims and quitrents against settlers and to keep land prices high. Germans viewed the conflict with the proprietor as an extension of the encroachment of state and noble officials on village life in the Palatinate and the Kraichgau. As a result, in the 1740s and early 1750s, Germans allied with the dominant Quaker faction of the Pennsylvania legislature. For only the Pietist minority of German immigrants, however, was this alliance rooted in an affinity for Quaker pacifism. For the rest, the crucial calculation was who would be most likely to protect and facilitate land claims, the basis of German wealth and stability. Thus, when a new war with the French and their Indian allies broke out in 1750s, German backcountry voters faced a dilemma. Having borne, along with Ulster Scots, the brunt of frontier attacks, an alliance with pacifist Quakers became far less compelling, even though resentment toward the proprietary government persisted. In November 1755 hundreds of Germans marched to Philadelphia bearing the copses of victims of an Indian attack. This attempt to light a fire under the governor and the assembly bore fruit, a defense requisition bill becoming law almost immediately after this demonstration.

Military crisis in the backcountry placed Mennonites, Moravians, Schwenkfelders, and other Pietist sects further at odds with the Calvinist and Lutheran German majority who in wartime more readily embraced an anti-Indian white solidarity. Some German Pietists abandoned pacifism to join local militias. But many others became more firmly committed to an alliance with Quakers, even as many Friends in the provincial legislature caved to demands to invest tax collections in forts and troops. German pacifists resolutely swam against the tide.

They rejected the blanket condemnation of Indians and joined efforts to establish a permanent Delaware Indian presence in Pennsylvania's fertile Wyoming Valley. Meanwhile, most Germans closed ranks around war and broadened hostility to Indians. As a result of such division, German pacifists became a lightning rod for the resentments of English-speaking colonists. While for most German-speakers frontier warfare did not act as a solvent for ethnic identity, it helped nest that identity more deeply in a broader provincial and imperial politics.

Race and ethnicity played a crucial role in defining the backcountry from the beginning. Provincial officials who sponsored backcountry development saw white settlers as more reliable than Indian allies in safeguarding the English colonies. These same officials found the conflicting interests and identities of various Indians nations to be a source of frontier instability even as they sought to exploit Indian diversity and benefit from Indian trade. The stakes in the backcountry could not have been higher for the Conestogas, Delawares, Shawnees, Cherokees, Iroquois, and others as European migrants of various origins turned Native American homelands into the colonial backcountry. Along with religious, ethnic, and political identities, migrants to the backcountry negotiated and defined racial identities, especially in the crucible of a war their rapidly increasing presence provoked.

CONVICTS AND SOLDIERS

Sharing white skin hardly guaranteed peaceful racial solidarity, as a series of crime reports in the May 9, 1751, *Pennsylvania Gazette* made clear. In Maryland, a gang on horseback rode about on a crime spree, while elsewhere in that province the master and mate of a schooner lay dead, their throats slashed. In Virginia a store was robbed. Closer to home, Philadelphia merchants Levy and Frank caught a forger red-handed. The *Gazette*'s publisher, Benjamin Franklin, had a pretty good fix on who was to blame for all this disorder—British convicts shipped to the colonies as part of the mother country's official penal policy. Writing under the pseudonym Americanus, Franklin also offered a novel solution: rattlesnakes. Colonists were in the habit of exterminating "these venomous Reptiles" but instead they might be "*transported* to Britain" to be spread about, especially in the "Gardens" of that nation's leading officials. It was a fair exchange for the convicts shipped to America, where these miscreants practiced "*Housebreaking*" and "*Highway Robbing*", "*corrupted* and *hang'd*" sons, "*debauch'd* and *pox'd*" daughters, while gruesomely murdering husbands, wives, and children. The British would be getting the better of the trade, concluded Franklin, as "the *Rattle-Snake* gives Warning before he attempts his Mischief... the Convict does not."[7]

Franklin was correct that it was longstanding British policy to transport convicts to the colonies; but his righteous, albeit humorous anger dramatically overstated the social ills that traveled with these forced migrants to the Americas. Between 1715 and 1775, authorities from England, Ireland, and Scotland shipped some fifty thousand convicts to North America. Convicts accounted for almost one in four British migrants to eighteenth-century North American colonies, but because they landed mainly in the Chesapeake, their impact on colonial society was concentrated in that region. Their experience on both sides of the Atlantic was unfairly, indeed slanderously, characterized by Franklin's extended metaphor of dangerous snakes lunging fatally at the heels of vulnerable colonists.

The transportation of convicts offered a systematic solution to an old but evolving problem—how to respond to endemic crime in a society characterized by marked material inequalities and relatively modest resources devoted to law enforcement. The growth of Britain's population, especially in its cities, increased the difficulty of the poor struggling to survive amidst the plenty of a rapidly commercializing society, while also providing a cover of anonymity for criminals. The economy and employment raced and sputtered, as Britain mobilized for wars against European rivals and then signed peace treaties that brought soldiers and sailors home, swelling the ranks of the unemployed. When Peter Williamson was discharged from the army in 1757, he became one such figure, and his self-identification as a "disbanded soldier" in his narrative's title was shorthand for his poverty and desperation. Law and tradition offered limited options for dealing with crime. Britons celebrated their liberties and looked askance at the notion of maintaining a standing army to keep the peace. No systems of prisons existed; a dizzying array of crimes against people and property were punishable by death. In the wake of a failed rebellion on behalf of the heirs of James II and the conclusion of war with France, Parliament embarked upon a plan in 1718 that would make large numbers of convicts go away.

The Transportation Act privatized a key aspect of criminal justice—punishment—by exporting convicted felons to the colonies as servants. The terms of banishment were seven, and sometimes fourteen, years. British authorities paid ship-owners a set fee for each person taken to the colonies, while allowing these merchants to sell the labor of the men and women they carried across the Atlantic, thus publicly subsidizing a private trade in the involuntary servitude of British subjects. As a result of the act, banishment became a regular part of court business rather than a special act of mercy. The availability of transportation gave judges and juries more leeway. Rather than convict some people of capital crimes, juries could return verdicts for lesser crimes, knowing that the convict would be transported instead of killed. Before a judge handed down a sentence of transportation for noncapital and capital offenses, he made a judgment as to the severity of the crime, the crime's circumstance, the likelihood of rehabilitation, and the accused's criminal record. Grand larceny was the most common crime triggering transportation. The worst criminals were still publicly executed, but others found their sentences reduced. Meanwhile, community sentiment did not support transportation for minor crimes, such as small-time thefts or prostitution. The system thus allowed its supporters to imagine themselves as deterring serious crime and providing an avenue for rehabilitation without incurring the expenses of maintaining prisons or the unwanted spectacle of thousands of public executions. Merchants made their profits while convicts left behind the only homes and families they knew.

The objections of Franklin and others notwithstanding, transported convicts represented more of an opportunity than a problem for those who purchased them. The convict population was overwhelmingly, though not exclusively, male, commonly in their twenties. Most came with few skills; some had been part of organized criminal gangs, but most were not. They were a more desperate, less hopeful group than indentured servants, who were more likely to have artisan skills and faced shorter periods of service. By the time they arrived, convicts had spent considerable time in crowded and unsanitary jails and ships. Still, they met a demand for labor in the Chesapeake, where more than 90 percent of them wound up. Despite all the slaves deployed in and around the tobacco fields of Virginia and Maryland, the demand for labor remained high enough to absorb bound convicts, too, especially on medium-sized plantations. Convicts cost considerably less than slaves, while serving longer than indentured servants; at certain times, the law did not even require freedom dues for convict-laborers. Though some female convicts wound up as domestic servants and some men found their way into skilled work, most labored in the same fields as slaves growing tobacco, as well as wheat and corn.

The proximity of convicts and African Americans helped to reinforce the degraded status of each group. As a doggerel rhyme penned in Maryland put it: "*Old Transgressors* [will] cease to Sin/As well may *Ethiopian* Slaves, Wash out the Darkness of their Skin."[8] The degradation of sin and skin were each, it seemed, indelible. The odds were higher for convicts than slaves to transcend their lot, either through the expiration of their service, adopting a new identity, or finding a return trip home. Nonetheless, transported felons constituted a despised and abused group in a world with a deeply engrained tradition of brutal exploitation of labor.

There is little evidence that Britain's convicts plagued the colonies with a wave of crime. Court records from sample Chesapeake counties turn up very few instances implicating these forced migrants. Convicts neither made common cause with the slaves whose stigmatized identity marked them so permanently, nor did they find their new surroundings conducive to a life of crime. Compared to Britain's growing cities, there was much less opportunity in the rural Chesapeake for the types of property crimes these criminals had been convicted of in Britain: pick-pocketing, fencing stolen goods, larceny, and theft. Conversely, colonial success stories for British convicts were also few and far between. Some convicts amassed the financial resources to buy themselves out of servitude; others married well. But by and large, convicts disappeared from view.

To the degree that recidivism can be associated with America's imported convicts, it lay in the decision of some servants to run away and others to return illegally to Britain. By making their way home, convicts risked capital punishment, but whether a convict returned to a life of crime or not, these men and women rarely suffered that fate. Returnees to England benefited from a rudimentary law enforcement structure and bad record keeping. As Franklin eagerly pointed out, the Transportation Act was a highly insulting gesture of the mother country's regard for her colonies, but it was the convicts themselves, not other colonists, who suffered the consequences and risks of this policy.

The number of convicts transported plunged in the mid-1750s, as Britain mobilized men for war. Warfare thus became another way in which state policy forged a controversial link between the people of Britain and the colonies. Like convict transportation, dispatching of soldiers to America could be regarded as advancing the interests of the empire and colonial subjects, with the British state providing military protection rather than cheap coerced laborers. The results were similarly mixed. Once enlisted in the British army, soldiers had to fulfill their obligations under conditions of someone else's choosing and control. Sometimes these soldiers took on new and productive lives in the colonies, but colonists did not uniformly find the presence of British redcoats desirable even if they contributed to colonial security and the economy.

Soldiers deployed by European powers to their American colonies had long been a part of the stream of colonial immigration. In the fifteenth and sixteenth centuries, some Spanish men used the guise of soldiering to circumvent government-imposed limits on emigration to the Americas. In the eighteenth century, several thousand of the soldiers the Spanish government sent to the Americas permanently settled there. In New France, famously ineffective at retaining new arrivals for the long haul, French soldiers who settled there represented a major contribution to Canadian immigration. Marriage in New France seems to have proved decisive in prompting French soldiers to remain rather than return to the homeland, as so many of their colleagues and French indentured servants did.

In comparison to Spain and France, Britain stationed very few regular troops in North America before 1755. Three independent companies of soldiers, totaling anywhere from two hundred to three hundred men, were maintained in South Carolina, where they nominally protected Charles Town from Spanish attack, and in New York, four similar companies garrisoned a string of posts extending from Manhattan to Fort Oswego on Lake Ontario. When their enlistments expired, some of these soldiers found settling in the colonies more attractive than returning to the British Isles. Some of colonial Albany's leading artisanal families were founded by soldiers who elected to stay there, working as civilians in the shadow of the fort they had once billeted. Their connections to the region's military commanders helped these former soldiers get off to profitable starts as bakers, weavers, hatters, and brewers.

The British military presence in the colonies expanded dramatically during the Seven Years' War (1756–1763). The arrival of well over twenty thousand British regulars strongly influenced the colonies' politics and economy. British recruiting officers targeted the poor and transient with cash bounties and regular wages. Parliamentary acts in 1756 and 1757 also authorized pressing unemployed men into military service. The British recruited a multi-ethnic force in Europe for their

American campaigns, drawing on Irish, Germans, Dutch, and Swiss mercenaries. Large numbers of Highland Scots, disarmed in Britain as a result of their failed rebellion in 1745, joined Britain's American campaigns, presaging a heavy tide of Highlander immigration to the colonies after the war ended. Officers responded to soldiers who tried to desert with edifying brutality. Hangings and firing squads, along with last-minute clemency, were designed to discourage what surely had to be a strong temptation of soldiers to melt into the American landscape rather than continue to face the violence and deprivation of wartime service.

After the Seven Years' War, some British troops remained in America, either by choice or because the army did not pay the price of their return. Only those who were recommended as "genuine invalids," in the words of British commander General Lord Jeffrey Amherst, had their transportation and postwar care covered. Amherst thought it best that former soldiers remain "in this country as I think they may get their Livelihoods by Working much easier here than at Home."[9] Had he not been shipped home with a cargo of other prisoners of war, Peter Williamson may very well have spent the remainder of his life in America. A royal proclamation in 1763 encouraged the permanent settlement of British war veterans in America by offering land grants to them, ranging from five thousand acres for field officers to fifty for privates. That this same proclamation also declared the newly acquired lands west of the Atlantic watershed off limits to further settlement was far more troubling to American colonists than His Majesty's generosity to this particular group of new migrants.

The presence of British soldiers and sailors in the colonies during the mid-eighteenth century occasionally touched off conflicts with civilians. In 1747 British Captain Charles Knowles seized forty-six men in Boston for impressment into British naval service. His actions brought thousands of colonists into the streets in protest. The mob seized some of Knowles's officers, marched on the provincial council chambers, and pulled a barge out of the harbor and burned it. Governor William Shirley could not put down the riot with the city's militia because those same men had joined the mob. Impressment riots did not quell the British Crown's demand for colonial labor in this era of imperial war. In 1757 hundreds of colonists in Manhattan were swept up in Lord Loudoun's dragnet designed to collect men for the impending attack on the French fortress at Louisbourg. Masters of indentured servants complained that British recruiters were using alcohol and bounties to lure their human property into military service. Of course, many servants needed no prodding, as they jumped at the opportunity to escape their contracts for the geographic mobility, cash wages, and adventure promised by the army. Disputes that erupted in the 1750s over the quartering of British troops in colonial towns also anticipated one of the most contentious issues of the Anglo-American crisis leading to the War for Independence.

The mobs that attacked British recruiters represented a cross section of colonial communities, their members hardly restricted to the bottom rung. The response to British soldiers, like Franklin's response to convict laborers, did not indicate an all-encompassing cross-class solidarity among colonists. Colonists in a position to do so were fully ready, willing, and able to exploit convicts, slaves, indentured servants, and others clustered at the bottom of the social hierarchy. They also appreciated the importance of the king's soldiers and sailors in securing the colonies from their foreign enemies. But in taking advantage of the opportunities that being a part of the empire made available, some colonists also developed an awareness of their own collective subordination to policies determined an ocean away.

SERVANTS AND SLAVES ON THE RUN

"I have been the Tennis-ball of Fortune," declared William Moraley late in his 1743 memoir of a five-year sojourn in North America as an indentured servant. Knocked back and forth between hope and despair, opportunity and failure, Moraley served out one indenture to a New Jersey watchmaker and then skipped out on another in Philadelphia before returning to his mother in England. Titling his book *The Infortunate* (1743), Moraley provided a jarringly inconsistent portrait of life and labor for newcomers to the mid-Atlantic colonies. In Moraley's world, black slaves and white indentured servants sometimes shared a similar social space, but faced strikingly different prospects. Evocatively, he recorded the night that "a Ghost, in White, with a black Face" entered his room "stared me in the Face, and beckened [sic] with its Hand." Sharing this story with his master's household, which included another white servant and a black slave, Moraley reported that they told him the apparition was that of "a Negro killed some Years since by her Master, and that they had often seen it."[10]

Slavery cast a shadow on Moraley's sunnier observations about New World. He juxtaposed the "Affluence and Plenty" of white landholders with the "very bad" situation of lifelong slaves. Yet there were some rough parallels between indentured servants and slaves. Servants and slaves frequently ran away; both groups, in his estimation, rarely succeeded. The penalty suffered by each group for defiance was harsh, but not commensurate. Slave runaways were "unmercifully whipped" and, he observed, there was "no Law against murdering them." By contrast, as he learned from painful experience, a servant could complain to a magistrate if his master did not fulfill terms of the indenture, but "it is ten to one" that the magistrate would side with the master and that "Licks" would follow for the servant. Yet masters could also exhibit kindheartedness. Moraley's first master came to his aid, testifying to Moraley's status as a free man, when in fact he was on the lam from a new master. Moraley at one point in his narrative proclaimed Pennsylvania "the best poor Man's Country in the World."[11] His inability to achieve a stable fortune reflected Moraley's personal shortcomings to be sure. Nevertheless, eking out a modest living, not wealth and status, was the most that former indentured servants even in the prosperous middle colonies where Moraley's sojourn played out could hope to achieve. Meanwhile, Moraley's return to his English homeland to tell his sad tale marked a further distinction between the life of the indentured and the enslaved. Moraley was beaten about by fate; slaves, in his account, were simply beaten.

Half of the estimated 300,000 European immigrants who arrived in the colonies between 1700 and 1775 came as indentured servants or convicts, while virtually all the 250,000 or more Africans who arrived during the same period came as slaves.[12] For those who toiled near or at the bottom of the social ladder, seeking to outrun fortune became an important, albeit imperfect survival strategy. Newspaper advertisements reveal that if conditions were sufficiently intolerable, escape and a new identity sometimes proved to be a much more appealing alternative than making the best of a bad situation. But as the mobile poor of early American often discovered, the fact that there was plenty of work to do in chronically labor-short America hardly meant that social mobility followed. Race and class identities made many Americans marked men and marked women. Efforts by servants and slaves to mask themselves revealed the harsh realities of colonial inequality in a world that beckoned so many with the prospect of opportunity.

For bound laborers who remained with their masters, particularly in the port cities, the threat of an early death was all too real. The population of Philadelphia, capital of the "best poor man's country," boomed not because it was a healthy place to live, but because high birthrates compensated for high, disease-driven death rates. Smallpox outbreaks repeatedly wracked the city in the eighteenth century. The intervals between these outbreaks actually made the disease more deadly, as large numbers of people experienced their first and most dangerous exposure. Immigrants were both part of this problem and victims of it. The overseas journey served as an incubator of pestilence, distress, and, quite often, death. German migrant Gottlieb Mittlelberger described a 1750 voyage characterized by "smells, fumes, horrors, vomiting... fever, dysentery, headaches, heat, constipation, boils, scurvy, cancer, mouth-rot, and similar afflictions" made all the worse by "hunger, thirst, frost, heat, dampness, fear, misery, vexation, and lamentation."[13] As early as 1700, Philadelphia authorities tried a combination of inspection and quarantine to prevent migrants from spreading disease. Nonetheless, contagions made it onto the mainland, as did a group of men and women whose voyages compromised their health just as they entered a new environment. High immigrant mortality under such conditions was inevitable.[14]

Available evidence indicates that slaves arriving in mid-Atlantic port cities faced even tougher medical odds. The climate of Philadelphia and New York differed dramatically from that of the West Indies, where many urban slaves had previously lived. Late fall and winter proved to be particularly dangerous times for black Philadelphians. Almost everything about their situation conspired against their health: vitamin D deficiency from lack of consistent sunlight, a diet inadequate not only in diversity but also total calories, the lowest-quality clothing, and the least desirable lodging. Unlike the white population, the black population's fertility was low while infant mortality was high, further reflecting the toll that the physical and social conditions wreaked on this portion of the bound-labor population. Archaeological evidence from Manhattan's slave burial site confirms this grim picture.

As Moraley reported, servants and slaves in the mid-Atlantic, like their compatriots in the North and the South, took to the road in hopes of changing their lots. Data from Pennsylvania indicate that rural indentured servants were more likely to run away than urban servants; in the countryside, servants were more likely to be unhappily isolated from one another, while urban servants had more opportunities to socialize with one another. An estimated one in ten servants, more often males than females, skipped out on their indentures in Pennsylvania, risking the imposition of extra time added to their service and physical punishment if apprehended. Servants, particularly those from rural areas, joined the British Army as a way of cutting short their obligations. Some of these would subsequently desert and live as free men. Unlike eighteenth-century Virginia slaves, Pennsylvania's unskilled indentured servants were more likely to run away than those with identifiable occupational expertise.

Colonial masters had more than threats of extended service and brutal punishment to deter their bondspeople from taking to the road. Colonial newspapers served as clearinghouses for slaves and servants, announcing auctions, brokering individual sales, and posting runaway announcements. One Boston newspaper listed approximately two thousand different slaves for sale between 1719 and 1781. The statistics for Benjamin Franklin's *Pennsylvania Gazette* are startling: advertisements involving either the sale or attempt to locate servants and slaves accounted for about one-fifth of all advertisements; in the 1750s, up to twelve runaway servant ads were listed per issue, a far greater number than printed for runaway slaves, reflecting Pennsylvania's comparative preference for and access to indentured immigrants. Printers like Franklin not only profited from these advertisements, they also played a role in the exchange of human property, serving as middlemen between buyer and seller, apprehenders of runaways and masters offering rewards.

Names and identities were much more important when masters sought to retrieve their missing servants and slaves than when they sought to sell them. As a result, runaway advertisements reveal what masters thought they knew about their subordinates, as well as what runaways thought they knew about the society in which they hoped to become free. Runaway servants and slaves were most typically male, and usually ran off in the summer, when demand for their labor among other potential employers would be high. They tried to pass as free by affecting greater cultivation in language and dressing above their actual status—stealing clothes from their masters to do so.

Masters revealed their own blindspots and biases through the levels of specificity they brought to the descriptions of their human property. A survey of ads between 1750 and 1800 indicates that male runaways prompted more detailed descriptions than females, and white males more detail than black males. This data may indicate not so much who was more valuable to masters than the relative degree to which they reduced some people to level of commodity as compared to others. Masters also focused more on the clothes their servants and slaves wore or took with them than on any other feature of the runaways, ironic given that a runaway could change clothes far more easily than altering his physical appearance. The clothes that runaways took with them provided an opportunity to express or redefine their own sense of identity and style, although masters viewed these same clothes as a way of distinguishing one absconding bondsperson from another.

It was the person more than the clothes that masters sought to recover, as bound laborers contributed significantly to their masters' livelihoods. And it was masters far more than their servants who got to describe the story of what had transpired between them. Thus, in 1762 New York City newspaper printer John Holt accused his runaway mulatto servant Charles Roberts of embezzlement, the unauthorized purchasing of items on his master's credit, forging freedom documents, and committing a string of robberies. But Roberts's relationship to his master was far more complicated than Holt indicated. Holt needed Roberts back, but he had hardly been truthful about how he came to own the mulatto or why his labor was so vital to him. While publisher of a Connecticut newspaper in 1757, Holt accused Roberts of stealing lottery tickets that Holt himself likely had stolen and, as punishment, arranged to add thirty-seven more years to what had been Roberts's dwindling term of service. Moreover, there is evidence that the mulatto servant's talents as a printer and writer exceeded his master's. Leaving Connecticut for New York with Roberts, now essentially his slave, Holt set up shop as a printer once again. But much to the white man's chagrin, Roberts had other plans, and he began living life as a free man. His claim to liberty was an assertion of self-possession more than it was a ruse. While the experiences of most colonial migrants and servants may not have been as public or peculiar as those of Roberts, Moraley, or Williamson, their movements across oceans, onto frontiers, and into new roles displayed a widespread impulse to test the status quo. Opportunities were not, in fact, boundless in the backcountry or in port cities. But the impulse to refashion an identity by moving on was widespread.

HYBRIDS

Peter Williamson's story of escape, far more completely than Charles Roberts's or William Moraley's, was one of enjoying the best revenge not only by living to tell the tale but also by living well. The same year that Williamson won his legal victory against the city fathers of Aberdeen, *French and Indian Cruelty* entered its fifth edition. He continued to milk his trans-Atlantic adventure for decades after his return to Scotland. Settling in Edinburgh, the capital of the Scottish Enlightenment, Williamson profited by flavoring this rapidly developing corner of the old country with his rendition of the American backcountry. He opened a coffeehouse he called "Indian Peter's" where Williamson sometimes dressed as an Indian and told his American stories and displayed Indian artifacts to his customers (see Figure 9.2).

Figure 9.2 **"Mr. Peter Williamson in the Dress of a Delaware Indian," in Peter Williamson, *French and Indian Cruelty: Exemplified in the Life, and various Vicissitudes of Fortune, of Peter Williamson* (London, 1759). Williamson turned the experience of migration and cultural boundary crossing into a profitable enterprise, the Scotsman dressing up as an Indian to share some of the intrigue of frontier life with his countrymen. While his story was unique—and partially fabricated—Williamson, like many thousands of Europeans and Africans, participated in a massive and diverse wave of migration across the Atlantic and into the backcountry, creating new blends of colonial culture in the eighteenth century. Courtesy of the John Carter Brown Library at Brown University.**

With his tongue in his cheek, Williamson exploited for profit and notoriety the hybrid identities that trans-Atlantic migration made possible—indeed, that it required. Even when he dressed up as an Indian, Williamson's American travels helped form him as a Briton as well as a Scot. For many of Williamson's Atlantic contemporaries coming to the colonies produced a new or expanded ethnic self-consciousness that embraced people from the Old World with whom they previously would not have recognized a kinship; for others, the colonial experience acted as a solvent, eroding distinctiveness or encouraging the merging of identities with the English-speaking population. Ensconced in Edinburgh, Scotland, Williamson could play up his connections to the wider world. The free migrants, servants, slaves, convicts, and soldiers who spread out through British North America likewise brought the Old World, or at least a larger portion of it than ever before, to the cities, plantations, farms, and backcountry of colonial America. Their unsettling experiences tested the flexibility and durability of the social, religious, and political orders that had been established during the seventeenth century.

CHRONOLOGY

1685	Revocation of Edict of Nantes leads to Huguenot exodus from France.
1704	Test Act limits the rights of non-Anglicans in Ireland.
1705	Linen Act gives Ulster producers direct access to the colonial market.
1710s	Experimental German settlement formed in the Hudson Valley.
1710s–1720s	Economic downturn in Ulster.
1718	Transportation Act spurs shipping of British convicts to the colonies.
1720s	Shawnee and Delaware migration up the Susquehanna Valley to Ohio country.
1722	Tuscaroras join the Iroquois Confederacy.
1730s–1740s	Virginia pursues a policy of settling non-English Protestants in its backcountry.
1747	Knowles Riot in Boston.
1750s	Migrants surge into South Carolina backcountry.
1754	The French and Indian War begins.
1755	The British expel Acadians from Nova Scotia.
1756	Parliament authorizes impressing British unemployed for military service in the colonies.
1757	*Peter Williamson publishes first of several editions of* French and Indian Cruelty.
1762	*Williamson wins lawsuit against Aberdeen magistrates.*
1799	*Peter Williamson dies.*

NOTES

1. Peter Williamson, *French and Indian Cruelty, 1757* (New York: Garland, 1978), 3.
2 Edward Lloyd, December 9, 1755, in William D. Hoyt, Jr., "A Contemporary View of the Acadian Arrival in Maryland, 1755," *William and Mary Quarterly*, 3d ser., 5 (1948): 571–575.
3. Patrick Griffin, *The People With No Name: Ireland's Ulster Scots, America's Scots Irish, and the Creation of a British Atlantic World, 1689–1764* (Princeton, NJ: Princeton University Press), 64.
4. "A Letter from a Gentleman in the *North* of *Ireland*, to a Person in an eminent Post under His Majesty; concerning the Transportation of great Numbers from that Part of the Kingdom to *America*," in E. R. R. Green, "The 'Strange Humors' That Drove the Scotch-Irish to America, 1729," *William and Mary Quarterly*, 3d ser., 12 (1955):118, 116.
5. Franklin, quoted in Griffin, *The People with No Name*, 102.
6. *A Journal of the Captivity of Jean Lowry and her Children, Giving an Account of her being taken by the Indians, the 1st of April 1756, from William McCord's, in Rocky-Spring Settlement in Pennsylvania...* (Philadelphia: William Bradford, 1760), 13.
7. *Pennsylvania Gazette*, May 9, 1751.
8. A. Roger Ekirch, *Bound for America: The Transportation of British Convicts to the Colonies, 1715–1775* (Oxford: Clarendon Press, 1987), 152.
9. Lord Jeffrey Amherst to Colonel Henry Boquet, August 7, 1763, quoted in Stephen Brumwell, *Redcoats: The British Soldier and War in the Americas, 1755–1763* (Cambridge, UK: Cambridge University Press, 2002), 297.
10. William Moraley, *The Infortunate: The Voyage and Adventures of William Moraley, an Indentured Servant*, ed. Susan E. Klepp and Billy G. Smith (University Park: Pennsylvania State University Press, 1992), 108, 83.
11. Moraley, *The Infortunate*, 93, 94, 96, 89.
12. Aaron S. Fogelman, "From Slaves, Convicts, and Servants to Free Passengers: The Transformation of Immigration in the Era of the American Revolution," *Journal of American History* 85 (1998): 70–71; David Eltis, "The Volume and Structure of the Transatlantic Slave Trade: A Reassessment," *William and Mary Quarterly*, 3d ser., 58 (2001): 45.
13. Gottlieb Mittleberger, *Journey to Pennsylvania*, ed. and trans. Oscar Handlin and John Clive (1756; Cambridge, MA: Belknap Press of Harvard University Press, 1960), 12.
14. Billy G. Smith, "Death and Life in a Colonial Immigrant City: A Demographic Analysis of Philadelphia," *Journal of Economic History* 37 (1977): 863–889.

SUGGESTIONS FOR FURTHER READING

For more on Peter Williamson's life and self-created legend, see Timothy J. Shannon, "King of the Indians: The Hard Fate and Curious Career of Peter Williamson," *William and Mary Quarterly*, 3d ser., 66 (2009): 3–44. A variety of excellent studies focus on the migration and American experiences of particular cultural groups. Among these are: Philip Otterness, *Becoming German: The 1709 Palatine Migration to New York* (Ithaca, NY: Cornell University Press, 2004); Aaron Spencer Fogleman, *Hopeful Journeys: German Immigration, Settlement, and Political Culture in Colonial America, 1717–1775* (Philadelphia: University of Pennsylvania Press, 1996), which also contains valuable statistical information on a variety of immigrant groups; A. G. Roeber, *Palatinates, Liberty, and Property: German Lutherans in Colonial British America* (Baltimore: Johns Hopkins University Press, 1993); Patrick Griffin, *The People with No Name: Ireland's Ulster Scots, America's Scots Irish, and the Creation of a British Atlantic World, 1689–1764* (Princeton, NJ: Princeton University Press, 2001); Ned C. Landsman, *Scotland and Its First American Colony, 1683–1765* (Princeton, NJ: Princeton University Press, 1985); Jon Butler, *The Huguenots in America: A Refugee People in New World Society* (Cambridge, MA: Harvard University Press, 1983); Kerby Miller, *Emigrants and Exiles: Ireland and the Irish Exodus to North America* (New York: Oxford University Press, 1985); William Pencak, *Jews & Gentiles in Early America, 1654–1800* (Ann Arbor: University of Michigan Press, 2005); and Geoffrey Plank, *An Unsettled Conquest: The British Campaign against the Peoples of Acadia* (Philadelphia: University of Pennsylvania Press, 2001).

Valuable collections of essays that contain briefer overviews of multiple strands of migration and provide more global perspectives include *Europeans on the Move: Studies on European Migration, 1500–1800*, ed. Nicholas Canny (Oxford: Clarendon Press, 1994); *"To Make America": European Emigration in the Early Modern Period*, ed. Ida Altman and James Horn (Berkeley: University of California Press, 1991); and *Strangers within the Realm: Cultural Margins of the First British Empire*, ed. Bernard Bailyn and Philip D. Morgan (Chapel Hill: University of North Carolina Press, 1991).

For overviews of the colonial backcountry, see Eric Hinderaker and Peter C. Mancall, *At the Edge of Empire: The Backcountry in British North America* (Baltimore: Johns Hopkins University Press, 2003); and Gregory H. Nobles, "Breaking Into the Backcountry: New Approaches to the Early American Frontier, 1750–1800," *William and Mary Quarterly*, 3d ser., 46 (1989): 641–670. For insight into the origins, opportunities, and conflicts that characterized particular regions of the colonial backcountry, see Peter C. Mancall, *Valley of Opportunity: Economic Culture along the Upper Susquehanna, 1700–1800* (Ithaca, NY: Cornell University Press, 1991); David L. Preston, *The Texture of Contact: European and Indian Settler Communities on the Frontier of Iroquoia, 1667–1783* (Lincoln: Universities of Nebraska, 2009); Warren R. Hofstra, "'The Extension of His Majesties Dominions': The Virginia Backcountry and the Reconfiguration of Imperial Frontiers," *Journal of American History* 85 (1998): 1281–1312; Marjoleine Kars, *Breaking Loose Together: The Regulator Rebellion in Pre-Revolutionary North Carolina* (Chapel Hill: University of North Carolina Press, 2002); Rachel N. Klein, *Unification of a Slave State: The Rise of the Planter Class in the South Carolina Backcountry, 1760–1808* (Chapel Hill: University of North Carolina Press, 1990); Jan Stievermann, "A 'Plain, Rejected Little Flock': The Politics of Martyrological Self-Fashioning Among Pennsylvania's German Peace Churches, 1739–1765," *William and Mary Quarterly*, 3d ser., 56 (2009): 287–324; Jane T. Merrit, *At the Crossroads: Indians and Empires on a Mid-Atlantic Frontier, 1700–1763* (Chapel Hill: University of North Carolina Press, 2003); and James H. Merrell, *Into the American Woods: Negotiators on the Pennsylvania Frontier* (New York: Norton, 1999). For further backcountry material, see also the relevant portions of the immigration literature listed above.

For a remarkably rich study of the convict experience, see A. Roger Ekirch, *Bound for America: The Transportation of British Convicts to the Colonies, 1715–1775* (Oxford: Clarendon Press, 1987). On British soldiers and their colonial sojourns, see Stephen Brumwell, *Redcoats: The British Soldier and War in the Americas, 1755–1763* (Cambridge, UK: Cambridge University Press, 2002). Sharon V. Salinger, *"To Serve Well and Faithfully": Labor and Indentured Servants in Pennsylvania, 1682–1800* (Cambridge, UK: Cambridge University Press, 1987), and Susan E. Klepp, "Seasoning and Society: Racial Differences in Mortality in Eighteenth-Century Philadelphia," *William and Mary Quarterly*, 3d ser., 51 (1994): 473–506, offer insights into and statistics on servitude in the eighteenth century. On the nexus between servitude, running away, and print culture, see Jonathan Prude, "To Look upon the 'Lower Sort': Runaway Ads and the Appearance of Unfree Laborers in America, 1750–1800," *Journal of American History* 78 (1991): 124–159; David Waldstreicher, "Reading the Runaways: Self-Fashioning, Print Culture, and Confidence in Slavery in the Eighteenth-Century Mid-Atlantic," *William and Mary Quarterly*, 3d ser., 56 (1999): 243–272; and Robert E. Desrochers, Jr., "Slave-For-Sale Advertisements and Slavery in Massachusetts, 1704–1781," *William and Mary Quarterly*, 3d ser., 59 (2002): 623–664.

CHAPTER 10

An Aspiring Society

Social and Religious Reordering

"[B]y what I have seen and observed in my Travels or Rambles, through the American Provinces, I have found the Magistrates of evr'y Town and City... Busily employ'd within themselves without wandring abroad amongst their Neighbours and Strangers for Business...." As a result of their parochialism, the colonies leading citizens enjoyed too little success "reform[ing] and correct[ing] the reigning Vices and Irregularities of the Times."[1] The man who shared this advice with the readers of the *New-York Evening Post* in 1749 was not a minister, a scholar, a doctor, or a mariner; he was not even the well-heeled son of a gentleman, although he had intimated at one time or another that he was each of these things. Rather, the man who offered this observation about the "reigning Vices" in the colonies was Tom Bell, a con man famous up and down the eastern seaboard for duping the unsuspecting out of their possessions.

The basic elements of Bell's scams were simple. He dressed and acted the part of a gentleman—often claiming connection to another recognized person of quality. In Barbados he posed as the son of the former governor of New York to take advantage of a Jewish merchant there; in Boston he pretended to be the associate of merchant James Bowdoin in an attempt to defraud members of New York's wealthy Livingston family; in New York he pretended to be the son of a wealthy gentleman from Long Island. Once Bell was in the good graces of his hosts, their clothes, their money, even their horses were not safe. His confident "Air and Deportment" convinced Charles Dingee to leave Bell, posing as a Mr. Lloyd, unattended aboard Dingee's ship, while it was docked in Philadelphia. Bell walked off with a cache of shirts, breeches, handkerchiefs, and stockings. Dingee realized he'd been had by the "FAMOUS INFAMOUS *TOM BELL*."[2] Five years earlier, Bell had audaciously posed as Reverend John Rowland, a traveling religious revivalist, robbing the unwitting New Jersey family hosting him just before he was to preach a Sunday sermon. Attempting such crimes required more than daring: Bell needed to know what names to drop and how to come off as a man of genuine breeding and education; he also needed to know who might be impressed by such an act. His background and training provided him with some of these necessaries; his keen perception of the cultural values of the time provided others.

As a youth, Tom appeared to be on a course to advance his social status through legitimate means. His father, a Boston sea captain, had pointed his son toward a college education at Harvard. But the captain's death made this future uncertain. The son did not thrive in college and was unpopular with students and teachers. He stole—personal letters, wine, chocolate cake—made up convoluted lies, and ignored his schoolwork. Life outside of Harvard was hardly any better. Even before he was expelled, Bell's taste for clothes he could not afford led to a lawsuit with a Boston tailor over an unpaid debt. Still, Bell did not depart his early years empty-handed. He had received enough of an education to teach school, a vocation he would pursue off and on for the rest of his life. More importantly, he had acquired a veneer of cultural refinement, as well as a sense of what dressing for success looked like in an era of increasing access to luxurious trade goods from England and beyond. Bell understood which names to drop in what company, though, as in college, people sometimes caught onto his act before he had slipped offstage.

If his fellow colonists were scandalized by his antics, they also were entertained. An estimated one hundred newspaper stories ran about Tom Bell between 1738 and 1755. This homegrown celebrity both mocked and mirrored his countrymen. His most fortunate contemporaries had, through a combination of hard work and cultivated image, worked their way up the colonial social ladder, none more famously than Benjamin Franklin, the runaway apprentice turned printer turned gentleman, philanthropist, and politician. Part of being a man of discernment and quality was recognizing those same qualities in others. Yet even Franklin could not always tell the difference between counterfeit and real gentility. Advertising in his own *Pennsylvania Gazette* in 1738, Franklin offered a reward for the capture of man who stole a treasure trove of clothes and accoutrements from his home. These items included "a fine Holland Shirt ruffled at the Hands and Bossom" and "a coarse Cambrick Handkerchief, mark'd with an F in red Silk," the latter's fine thread woven into tougher fabric an unintended metaphor for Franklin's own ongoing transformation from tradesmen to gentleman. The thief, Franklin noted, "pretends to understand Latin and Greek, and has been a School-Master," suggesting that Franklin had let the man, who may even have been Bell, into his house based on his misappraisal of the man's character.[3]

Bell—and Franklin—were just two of thousands of mid-eighteenth-century colonists who pulled against the bridle of social rank while also paying homage to it, seeking in a world of goods and ideas the elements to fashion new, more polished identities. Bell was a rolling stone, gathering just enough moss to fool his next victim. Franklin, by contrast, invested his entire being in charting an upward path, based, he asserted, on honesty, hard work, generosity, and insight. But Franklin himself could not resist the power of the façade—as a boy in Boston, he secretly wrote satirical essays for his brother's newspaper the *New England Courant* under the female pseudonym Silence Dogood. In his famous almanac, Franklin created an alter ego for himself known as Poor Richard. Franklin and Bell may have been playing somewhat different games, but their respective ascents to fame and to infamy were accomplished with a wink and a nod. Hence, Bell's ironic remarks to the *New-York Evening Post* about "the reigning Vices and Irregularities of the Times." As the eighteenth century moved forward, colonial newspapers tracked the vices and ambitions of their readers, detailing in their advertisements and their news stories the widening array of imported goods for sale to American consumers. Yesterday's luxuries, such as tea cups and imported textiles, became today's necessities.

Franklin's and Bell's pursuits emphasized secular markers of success and learning, but each of these two men was well aware that many of his fellow colonists thirsted for spiritual transformation as much as or more than material advancement. Such religious awakenings threatened the established boundaries of religious authority even more than economic ambition tested the boundaries of social class. Franklin never pretended to be a preacher, but he admired and even promoted the religious revivals spreading across the colonies, in part because word of them sold newspapers. Bell took a more audacious and dishonest approach when he posed in New Jersey as an itinerant minister arriving to deliver a rousing sermon and the promise of salvation before skipping town with his host family's belongings rather than the souls of converts.

Part of what fueled the aspirations of eighteenth-century Americans was a sense that new rules had emerged to challenge old orthodoxies and old hierarchies. A candle-maker's son might become a scientist, an English actor a tribune of faith, an ordinary farmer a worthy subject of a portrait, a goodwife a connoisseur of East Indian tea. Meanwhile, some slaves and Indians challenged the notion that only Europeans should pursue the Christian gospel and cultural refinement. Colonial elites came to realize that while they were in the best position to cultivate the habits of gracious consumption, their access to the burgeoning British Empire's goods and ideas was hardly exclusive, and their control over what ordinary people made of them was even less complete.

IMBIBING EQUALITY: DRINKING AND CULTURE

Like many a colonial traveler, Tom Bell found himself in a tavern in July 1743, predictably planning his next caper. But in this instance, he was found out before he got very far into his story and forced to make a hasty exit.[4] The public house in early America was a crossroads where colonists of various social classes rubbed elbows, sometimes as strangers, sometimes as friends. Taverns and other public gathering places where drinking occurred exposed the desires and limits of colonial elites to impose order on an unruly society.

The manner in which colonists consumed and regulated the consumption of alcohol reveals a great deal about the conflicting priorities of those who governed these societies. Colonists consumed enormous amounts of distilled high-alcohol-content liquor—perhaps four gallons annually per capita—as well as beer, wine, and, especially, hard cider. Uncertainty about the quality of water supplies and longstanding beliefs about the health benefits of distilled beverages made the consumption of alcohol a given. But questions of who drank how much and in what settings did concern authorities. Colonial governments recognized that without public houses, it would be impossible to travel, and travelers expected such accommodations to provide them with food and drink as well as a place to sleep. Thus, small towns and crossroad villages sought to license public houses and seaports contained many such places.

Taverns served local populations as much or more than travelers. Authorities had the power to limit their numbers and hours through the regulation of licenses; here, however, a mix of motives came into play—for the licensing of establishments serving strong drink also generated government revenue. Thus, the challenge for lawmakers was to ensure that taverns did not incubate crime, vice, and disorder. Wherever liquor touched the loosened tongues of people at the end of their workdays, ensuring order was easier said than done.

The tactics lawmakers employed to police alcohol consumption enjoyed little success, as demand for strong drink was higher than the political willpower to enforce laws and regulations governing it. Early in the eighteenth century, Massachusetts attempted unsuccessfully to ban the sale of rum in taverns. Legislation also limited the length of time a person could linger in a tavern and the amount of credit tavern-keepers could extend to patrons, a measure clearly designed to control the drinking habits of the lower orders. New York sometimes prosecuted houses patronized by servants and slaves, who in theory should not have been making purchases without a master's authorization. Authorities hoped to suppress the sort of criminal conspiracies that might foment an uprising, such as the plot allegedly hatched by rebellious slaves in a New York City tavern in 1741. When a tavern was known as a place for conducting illicit business like prostitution and the fencing of stolen goods, officials sometimes intervened.

Eighteenth-century tavern culture exposed the fault lines of social class. In port cities, laborers congregated at drinking establishments close to the waterfront, while elites patronized establishments of their own closer to the center of town. These preserves of conviviality for wealthier townsmen seldom came under the scrutiny of authorities. In New York City, where the tiny social elite broke into rival political fractions, taverns doubled as clubhouses where liquor and political talk flowed freely. Segregating themselves by class, elites conceded social space and a certain measure of control to a mix of society's less powerful, control that could not easily be seized back.

Taverns also paradoxically delineated space according to gender lines while serving as one of the best sources of income for widowed women. Public consumption of alcohol, as opposed to drinking in the home, was largely a male activity; drinking establishments where women were regularly present seemed almost by definition disorderly and carried the stigma of prostitution. And yet authorities licensed widows to sell alcohol, particularly in cities, with striking frequency, likely because a widow operating the tap was far less likely to tap into public funds for poor relief. Alice Guest, the Philadelphia woman who ran a tavern out of a riverside cave in late-seventeenth-century Philadelphia, had many colonial successors. Indeed, the percentage of female license-holders in eighteenth-century Boston hovered near 40 percent and a more modest 25 percent in Philadelphia. In Charles Town that percentage approached half, though there married women made up a much larger proportion of license-holders than in the North, reflecting more liberal laws for female property holding.

For some colonial observers, the type of mixing and carousing that tavern life encouraged represented the moral hazard of social lines drawn indistinctly. A Virginia clergyman in 1751 observed that public houses had been "perverted from their original Intention" of servicing travelers, instead "becom[ing] the common Receptacle... of the very Dreggs of the People" where such unworthy activities as "Cards, Dice, Horse-Racing, and Cock-fighting, together with Vices and Enormities of every other Kind" proliferated.[5] In 1760 twenty-five-year-old John Adams expressed distaste for a Massachusetts tavern where he encountered "fiddling and dancing of both sexes and all ages."[6]

If some viewed the behavior of Americans at leisure as expressing too much license, we might just as easily see such evidence as expressing the material and symbolic benefits of liberty. To the European eye, evidence that the bottom rungs of society were not so distant from the top could be tangible and striking. The German music teacher and organist Gottfried Mittelberger noted that in Pennsylvania even people who lived within easy walking distance of church rode horses to Sunday services, as well as to weddings and funerals. In that prosperous middle colony, Mittelberger found that meat of all kinds was inexpensive and thus the common diet quite impressive: "Even in the humblest and poorest houses, no meals are served without a meat course; and no one eats bread without butter or cheese.... I do not believe that any country consumes more meat than Pennsylvania."[7] Material well-being bred a level of social confidence in equality. Staying overnight at an inn often required sharing a bed with a total stranger. A high-status traveler such as the Scottish-born doctor Alexander Hamilton might have to put up with all sorts of questions about himself whether he wanted to answer them or not. And much to Hamilton's consternation, American tavern dwellers did not let their inferior social status prevent them from sharing their considerable knowledge about politics and religion with him. European markers of wealth and status did not carry the same weight in America, nor was deference automatically accorded social betters.

SOCIAL RANK AND ORDER: PLEBIAN AND PATRICIAN

Such scenes of familiarity and boundary crossing notwithstanding, social distinctions most assuredly did exist in eighteenth-century colonial America, with significant consequences for how people lived their lives and how they interacted with one another. As illustrated in the previous chapter, the combination of slaves, convicts, and indentured servants dwarfed the number of free arrivals in the thirteen colonies between 1700 and 1775. These immigrants entered societies in which political and economic elites had consolidated their power by the early decades of the eighteenth century. Thus, colonial society contained patrician families who commanded the labor of others and possessed the leisure time for intellectual pursuits and public service. A much greater portion of the population performed physical labor, whether for themselves or others, and depended on the gentry to dispense personal favors and to lead public institutions such as courts and churches.

Patronage fortified and stabilized hierarchical relationships. New York City's carters, the men responsible in no small part for ensuring that the commercial port kept humming by moving fuel, goods, and supplies around the city, enjoyed the protection of the city's government, but also depended on it. Cartmen had to be licensed to do their work legally and had to accept regulation of their fees (similar to a cab driver's today), especially for the sale of firewood. Meanwhile, the carters profited from the city's racial hierarchy. From 1677 onward, blacks were excluded from receiving cartmen licenses, though carters could have blacks work for them. The artificial barriers to entry into the ranks of cartmen allowed these laborers to enjoy long careers. Carters also often handed down their status from father to son, and many carters did work for and rented land from New York City's Trinity Church, thus forging connections with the city's Anglican elite.

Sometimes the needs of the port cities' working classes for support could be painfully acute, as their straitened circumstances left them vulnerable to impoverishment from a variety of causes—disease, harsh weather, fires, and economic slumps, to name a few. Widows were at particular risk in a patriarchal society that provided few economic opportunities for independent women. Boston's Great Fire of 1760 drove many people who had been living hardscrabble lives to begin with into even more dire poverty. In Philadelphia during the winter of 1761–1762, the Committee to Alleviate the Miseries of the Poor provided blankets, clothing, and fuel to six hundred families, or about one in five families in the city. Thus, even in this economically dynamic city, let alone Boston, whose relative position among North American ports had been slipping for decades, the gap between rich and poor was pronounced, with many urban dwellers living on the precipice of penury and dependence.

The prevalence of patronage relationships underscored the importance of social hierarchy despite countervailing expressions of material and social equality. Not long after he arrived in Philadelphia as a runaway printer's apprentice, young Benjamin Franklin sought and received the encouragement of Pennsylvania's governor William Keith to open a print shop. Keith's promises of assistance led Franklin to travel to London to acquire printing equipment, and although Keith failed to follow through on his behalf, Franklin continued throughout his career to seek the favor of more powerful men, right up to the king himself. Tom Bell's confidence games often operated on the false impression he created of his ties to the rich and powerful. For many other colonists, elite patronage was an essential part not of upward mobility but simply making a living.

Even absent a formally entitled aristocratic class with pretensions to ancient wealth and familial honor, an important distinction existed between the few who possessed wealth, power, and freedom and the many who in obscurity hoed, hammered, and traded for themselves and for others. The relatively ample sustenance enjoyed by many farmers in the "best poor man's country" could not make up for the fact that social rank put people in their places, from the king down to the slave. In rural and urban settings, some men and their families had wealth and commanded public power, while others did not. There were no legal or formally articulated criteria that made some people gentlemen, or patricians, and others ordinary, or plebian. But any colonist knew the difference between these two types of people.

John Adams, an aspiring lawyer with a Harvard education but the middling social origins of a farmer's son, made sense of the distinction between gentleman and others this way: the nongentleman had "ordinary Parents," could "scarcely write his Name," and did not hold any appointed offices.[8] While a person could not control who his or her parents were, one could acquire the knowledge and cultivate the manners of a gentle person: hence, the youthful George Washington wrote out a list of "Rules of Civility & Decent Behaviour in Company and Conversation" to help him master the comportment of a gentleman. Among those rules was this advice on knowing your place: "In Company of these of Higher Quality than yourself Speak not ti[ll] you are ask'd a Question then Stand upright put of[f] your Hat & Answer in few words."[9]

Adams and Washington were hardly alone in planning their social ascent. In Worcester County, Massachusetts, many miles inland from Boston, the features that distinguished the gentry from plainer folk included a college education and connections to Eastern elites. Working as a lawyer, which resulted from an apprenticeship not a degree, was a boon as well. Such connections and training led to appointments from the provincial capital as justices of the peace, with the accompanying fees and prestige of processing the county's legal documents and conducting its courts, as well as overseeing roads and granting licenses to, among others, tavern-keepers. Serving as militia officers also helped advance aspiring elites.

The resource most essential to distinguishing the elite from the ordinary was wealth—for with sufficient wealth a man could withdraw himself and his immediate family from the ordinary world of farm and workshop. With sufficient wealth a man also could patronize other, less fortunate members of society, further confirming his patrician status. Benjamin Franklin's signature act announcing his final transformation from tradesman to gentleman was his retirement from the daily management of his print shop at the age of forty-two. He did not sell his business, which now operated as an intercolonial network of partnerships, nor did he stop writing. But he was now defined by his wealth, which also included paper mills and real estate, not his craft and its requirement of physical labor. He bought additional slaves and relocated his home away from the printing office now managed by his partner David Hall. A gentleman built his reputation on the offices he held and public service he provided, not his commitment to hard work.

In a colonial society that lacked banks and where circulating cash was chronically short, gentlemen provided an essential source of credit (even if sometimes they were in debt to English and Scottish merchants themselves). Loaning money, of course, generated income, while the willingness to carry a poorer neighbor's debt without collection generated appreciation, power, and prestige for the lender. The eighteenth-century English and American definition of friendship entailed the ability to bestow personal favors. Thus, the tremendously wealthy Charles Carroll of Annapolis expressed the pleasures of his station: "How commendable it is for a gentleman of independent means...to be able to advise his friends, relations, and neighbors of all sorts."[10] Carroll's self-serving statement did not fully factor in the self-interest that made others seek his favor; nor did Carroll's satisfaction measure the private resentment he might incur or the downright oppression of the slave system that underwrote his "independent means." Still, social stratification shaped the lives of patrician and plebian alike, each in some sense depending on the other.

Wealth allowed patricians and would-be patricians to erect tangible symbols of their distinctiveness and superiority. Given the lack of legally sanctioned social distinctions, colonial elites in the eighteenth century needed such symbols to mark their status. Thus, from the 1720s onward, elites across a variety of colonial landscapes sought to impress each other and their social inferiors by building houses that projected a sense of grace and power. Brick or painted exteriors replaced unpainted, weather-worn clapboard. The new Georgian-style mansions featured two full stories plus an attic, and presented a symmetrical façade featuring large glass-sash windows instead of narrow openings. These homes had entrance hallways, with visible stairways to the upper floor, rather than entrances directly into a functional living space and the traditional enclosed stairwell running alongside the chimney. The homes of the wealthy benefited from new technological innovations, such as the Franklin stove that circulated heat around the house via ducts rather than relying on the open hearth used for both cooling and heating in simpler homes. But the drive toward creating the gracious home stemmed from social aspiration more than technology. The light that large glass windows let in shined on homes where hosts could entertain guests in parlors rather than bedrooms and kitchens and display their tasteful acquisitions of china, silver, and lace.

CONSUMERISM AND SELF-FASHIONING

The wealthy men and women whose impressive new homes began to dot the landscape represented the leading edge of a transformation in the way colonists lived their lives, one that eventually reached well down the social hierarchy. A rising tide of consumer goods reached the Atlantic seaboard as the eighteenth century progressed, circulating up rivers and down rutted wagon paths into people's modest farmsteads. Meanwhile, colonial artisans sought to recreate versions of English silver and woodworking. Through their purchases of everything from tea cups and forks to bed linens and blouses, colonists sought to satisfy wants that their parents and grandparents either did not have or could not have named. In the process, rich and ordinary people alike developed their taste for items that, rather than making life possible, made life look and feel good. People far more honest and far less peripatetic than Tom Bell hoped that the acquisition of finer clothes and better manners could transform how others perceived them, or at least how they perceived themselves.

Living in an empire shaped governmental structures and political identities, but for many access to the material fruits of Britain's global commerce defined the imperial experience more directly. One of the reasons American colonists did not chafe against the restrictions imposed by the Navigation Acts is that British ships so steadily supplied the colonies with manufactured items like ceramic plates along with spices and beverages such as tea, coffee, and wine (see Figure 10.1). The population of the colonies boomed during the eighteenth century, but imports boomed even louder, the per capita value of imports increasing by half from 1720 to 1770. The economies of colonies and mother country became more intensely connected, with exports from England to North America more than doubling from 1750 to 1773.[11]

Freeing up wealth to purchase imported or locally produced luxuries involved shifting the priorities of household production. If American households could produce for their own consumption or local exchange items like linens, milk, and cider, more money would be available to acquire goods for comfort and display. The household production of women and slaves therefore was an essential element of increasing consumption. While farmers in regions less conducive to producing exportable staples concentrated their energies on feeding themselves, the ongoing need to purchase land for future generations necessitated the production of some market surplus items such as potash, maple sugar, and hides, as well as the development of carpentry, smithing, and clothes-making skills. Some of this surplus wealth could be diverted to upgrading the quality of life—better beds, more pleasing table settings, tastier food, and more stimulating beverages. Thus, selective specialization by families and local trading contributed to, rather than detracted from, the broader colonial society eager to import paper, glass, clothes, and furniture from abroad.

In its earliest phases, American consumption involved a certain amount of catching up to the mother country, provincials feeling the breeze of prosperity that blew through Britain with increasing strength after 1689. There, food surpluses, growing wages, and an ample labor force created the demand for nonsubsistence consumer items and the means of increasing production even absent any major new technological innovations. Wealthy gentry and prosperous city dwellers in London established their social reputations on the ability to adorn their bodies and homes with products made by others, often in imitation of the style of French courtiers. American conceptions of gentility emerged from these European sources.

American emblems of success changed. For much of the seventeenth century, the difference between wealthy and poor farmers was largely displayed through

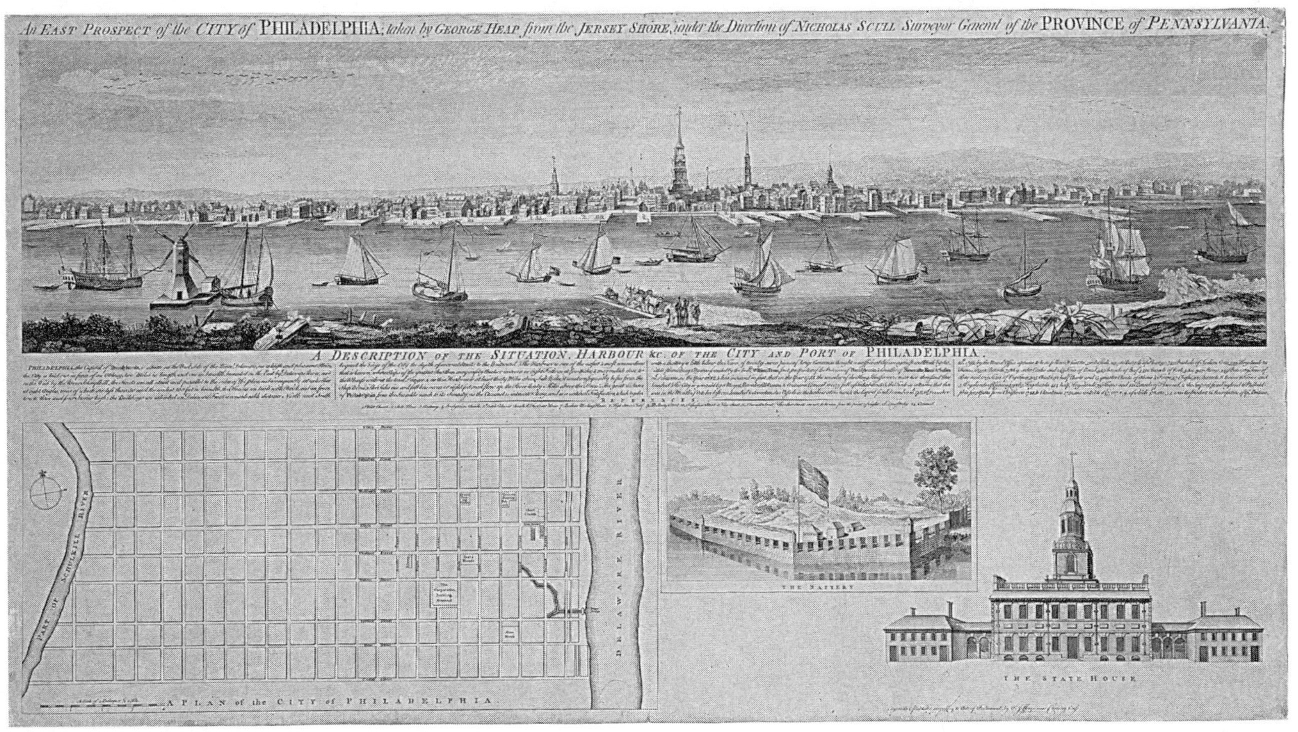

Figure 10.1 Nicholas Scull and George Heap, "An East Prospect of the City of Philadelphia" (1756). Philadelphia's waterfront burgeoned as this and other Eastern seaports such as Boston, New York, and Charles Town served as conduits for colonists' increasing consumption of imported goods. The Library Company of Philadelphia.

productive capacity—land, slaves, farm animals, barns—rather than by conspicuous displays of consumption. The mark of wealth was *more* rather than *better*. The eighteenth-century colonial gentry who fronted their estates with new homes and set their barns, stables, and servants' quarters back from the road or river identified themselves with English styles of refined living. The accoutrements of dining became more elaborate. Sets of matched chairs with stylized flourishes replaced a motley collection of stools and trunks. Matched plates and drinking glasses or cups became more prevalent. Banished to the past, or at least the lower orders, were communal stew pots into which hands reached or knives stabbed to acquire each diner's portion. The use of forks and spoons specialized for particular kinds of dishes enabled diners to display the quality of their individual manners. And the food courses themselves acquired their own specialized platters and serving bowls. When cleaned and put away, the equipment of genteel dining remained on display in corner cabinets. Home interiors subdivided to promote privacy also acquired particular furnishings. Rather than throwing clothes in a trunk on the floor, dearly bought garments found their place in dressers. Dressing tables, sometimes with looking glasses and small compartments for make-up, graced colonial bedrooms. At an even more intimate level, chamber pots replaced the need to tromp outside to relieve oneself of bodily waste.

Not all homes, not even wealthy homes, contained every single kind of item that marked the newly genteel form of living, and poorer homes might have relatively few. But forks, spoons, and cups by mid-century did start appearing in more modest homes. Even at the bottom of the social hierarchy, slaves sometimes dined off the castaway or perhaps stolen china of their masters. The variety of items imported from Britain encompassed many practical items—nails, guns, paint, and paper. Still, the desire and the ability to purchase such items from abroad made consumers of even ordinary colonists.

Tea lay at the very center of colonial consumer society—and its rapid spread down the social hierarchy and to the very edges of the hinterland—illustrates how luxuries could become necessities. As rich, middling, and poor drank imported tea from the East Indies, the need to acquire other imported items multiplied: West Indian sugar sweetened the hot drink brewed in kettles, served from pots, and poured into ceramic cups that rested on saucers. An ordinary family need not have every single imported item, let alone a matched set, to drink tea. But as tea drinking spread far and wide, the ties connecting colonial peddlers and shopkeepers to their customers deepened. The pathway to improved consumption became well marked.

As more goods flooded into the colonies, those who sold and distributed imports looked for ways to reinforce consumer demand. The wealthiest slaveholding planters established credit accounts and placed direct orders with English agents or through Scottish merchants. Encouraging consumption more widely, retail shops opened up, first in port cities but spreading into the hinterland as well. In inland Massachusetts, the greater the local agricultural production, the more likely there was a store to keep on hand the brass, ribbons, fabrics, and spices that local people might buy. In the Chesapeake, storekeepers, many of them Scottish, also opened up shop. In port towns big enough to sustain the growing number of newspapers, advertising also increased, describing more items for sale in increasing detail. Some advertisements used special borders or drawings to signal how plentiful their stock was. Where markets were smaller, peddlers gamely stepped in, traveling salesmen bringing the comforts, adornments, and conveniences of imported wares directly to the consumer. Similarly, for specialty items like painted portraits or services like shoe repair and tailoring, itinerants found their commercial niche.

For those with the means and the mind to do so, the experience of choosing from among a variety of options was itself transformative. The sheer number of items, broken down into ever more specialized categories—kinds of silk, lace, china, or paper rather than a generic category—meant that some colonial consumers became shoppers. The ability to make discriminating choices became part of the pleasure of acquisition and a way to express one's gentility or fashion. Storekeepers could cater to such feelings of power and discrimination, making their customers feel genteel by accommodating their particular tastes.

Colonists from different classes participated in this marketplace on unequal terms—which was at least part of the allure of consumption. In Philadelphia, urban merchants consumed markedly more than shopkeepers and artisans, perhaps five times as much. Thus, those at the top of the port city's social hierarchy enjoyed material comforts far in excess of those who occupied a middle position and lived in quarters that, according to one historian, "resembled those of the poor more closely than those of the rich."[12]

One of the motivating forces for a wealthy consumer to keep pace with changing fashions was to distinguish oneself from more ordinary neighbors. That the trappings of gentility could be purchased made advancements in status more widely attainable but also allowed, even compelled, men and women of wealth to demonstrate their superiority by always remaining a step ahead of those who aspired to be like them. This two-fold nature of consumption goaded the great planters of the Chesapeake to take on enormous debts to British creditors. In such a society, getting ahead and staying there were never ending games.

Colonial consumption, however, did not create a no-holds-barred acquisitiveness based solely on the crude amassing of material objects. Consumption also involved an element of performance or self-fashioning. As Bell and Franklin discovered in different ways, displays of polite manners and adherence to social rules helped colonists to take the measure of each other and to enforce a measure of social self-discipline. Thus, the tea table became the female-dominated counterpart to the male-dominated tavern and coffee house, where women not only could establish or undermine the reputations of others, including men, but also where standards of fashion itself could be discussed, negotiated, and established. Elites likewise played card games and, more publicly, attended balls, as a way to exhibit their mastery of manners. In their world, self-possession counted as much as possessions. The poems that well-placed men and women composed and shared in their social circles applied the logic of self-control and sophistication to the literary arts, while the portraits that elites commissioned of themselves reveal a desire to convey seriousness and mastery rather than material ease or gaudy abundance. Franklin's 1740s portrait shows hints at his wealth through his wig and ruffled cuffs, but his lack of adornment and upright bearing hardly suggest immodesty, indulgence, or unbridled arrogance (see Figure 10.2).

Colonial society, of course, generated other sorts of rules involving skin color that placed sharp limits on how far material acquisition and polite manners might carry a person. Still, the social significance and personal satisfactions derived from clothing hardly were confined to whites alone, with African Americans, including slaves, establishing their own codes and meanings. In his autobiography, the former slave Olaudah Equiano recorded his activities as a seaborne peddler, selling goods in ports like Charles Town and Philadelphia to accumulate cash to

Figure 10.2 Robert Feke, *Benjamin Franklin* (*c.* 1746). This portrait captures the transition that Benjamin Franklin made from wealthy tradesman to gentleman. The fine fabrics, ruffled cuffs, and wig signify a new status far removed from the print shop. Such markers of class, including the act of standing for a portrait, demonstrated the divisions in eighteenth-century colonial society, while also signifying the possibilities of mobility, as colonists sought to remake themselves through the objects they acquired and the ways they carried themselves. Harvard Art Museum/Fogg Museum, Harvard University Portrait Collection, Bequest of Dr. John Collins Warren, 1856, H47; Imaging Department © President and Fellows of Harvard College.

purchase his freedom. When on the island of Montserrat he finally attained his manumission, he records wearing his "Georgia superfine blue clothes" to dances that, he believed, "made no indifferent appearance."[13] The acquisition of clothing and the expression of personal style created a means by which slaves challenged their condition. Planters imported for distribution to their slaves clothing made from coarse fabrics, selected for durability not comfort or visual appeal. Law and, increasingly, custom aimed to outfit slaves plainly and predictably, a standard uniform marking their degraded standing.

Yet attempts to regulate slaves' material possessions and personal self-expression never completely succeeded. Illegal trading and the patching of clothes in deliberately colorful and lively patterns provided slaves with self-fashioning opportunities. Masters provided finer materials and distinctive clothing as a reward for slave loyalty and to distinguish slaves skilled in artisanal work or house service. Slaves' control over the length, arrangement, or partial shaving of hair provided a less costly, more direct means of self-fashioning. Clothing carried off by runaway slaves suggests another way in which marketplace goods created opportunities for self-assertion. The clothes stolen by runaway slaves may have indicated how some runaways pictured themselves living in freedom, or the runaways may have sold the clothes through black market exchanges as a way of funding bids for freedom. In some instances, consumer goods could serve as a means to fashion resistance.

As the experience of Native Americans indicates, the social significance of goods took on different meanings depending on who did the consuming. By way of the fur trade and presents distributed in treaty conferences, European products traveled into Indian country, where Native Americans used them for their own self-fashioning in the context of their material culture. For example, leading Indian chiefs often wore British regimental coats, ruffled shirts, and laced hats to diplomatic councils, where such outfits distinguished them from other Indians in attendance and put them on an equal level of sartorial splendor with their colonial counterparts. By using imported clothes to advertise their influence and importance, these chiefs then acquired more trade goods in the form of diplomatic presents that they redistributed among their followers. The Mohawk sachem Hendrick was known throughout the Northern colonies for his striking appearance as well as his oratory and political acumen, and in verbal descriptions, prints, and portraits he modeled the distinctive style colonists called the "Indian fashion."

Chiefs were not the only Indians to use European goods for sartorial self-expression. Indian women preferred to make their own clothes out of European textiles, rather than acquire garments finished according to European tastes. They used imported ribbon and lace to customize such clothing and refashioned the soft metal from copper trade kettles into jewelry. An inventory of presents that New York Indian agent William Johnson distributed at a 1755 treaty conference included such common trade items as guns, knives, kettles, and frying pans, as well as looking glasses, combs, gartering, hose, and shirts.[14] To be sure, the bestowal of consumer goods as part of diplomatic ritual enhanced the power and prestige of go-between figures like Hendrick and Johnson. These high-placed men, however, did not dictate the use or meaning that the ultimate recipients of these items, many being women and children, attached to them.

Each individual consumer in colonial American had his or her own reasons for wanting the best of what England had to offer, but collectively the weight of consumption and self-fashioning caused mid-century colonial culture to become more English than it had been in many decades. This process of what some scholars have labeled "Anglicization" had its limits. It was hardly necessary, let alone inevitable, that non-English colonists forsake their languages and cultures in order to tap into the material bounty of trans-Atlantic commerce. German immigrants could purchase goods that originally arrived in British hulls without ceasing to speak German or worship in Lutheran churches. Nonetheless, consumption highlighted the distinct advantages of the connection to such a mighty trading empire. And for the many colonists who took their fashion cues from Britain, the colonies had, indeed, reinvigorated the trans-Atlantic cultural ties that frayed during the tumultuous years of the seventeenth century. Anglicization, the slow but undeniable reattachment of colonial culture to the mother country's norms and standards, was a product of this taste for Britain's most appealing exports.

Attacks on consumerism in print and from pulpits did not turn the tide of consumer demand. Critics of spreading consumerism disparaged the mindless following of fashion and bemoaned the blurring of ranks in the social hierarchy. Even this criticism was in some sense imported, echoing British writers fearful about living in a world in which "pleasures of the pernicious kind are become, not the diversion or amusement, but the business of the high and low, rich and poor."[15] In a published sermon entitled *The Best Art of Dress*, one New England minister noted, "External beauty, great riches, and the like, may make us admired and revered by a croud [sic] of stupid, unthinking mortals, like ourselves; but will be far, very far, from rendring us glorious . . . in the eyes of God, or good men."[16] Women, in particular, became scapegoats for the detractors of consumption, who fretted that they would ignore their domestic responsibilities, and might, spoiled by choice, demand too much freedom, forsake marriage altogether, or drag their husbands and all of society into a state of effeminate, debilitating luxury. Such rhetoric may have chastened some Americans not to let material aspirations replace other moral, religious, and social commitments; and we cannot know for sure whether moralistic concerns acted as a drag on the escalating demand for imports. But such warnings did not cow colonial consumers, most of whom undoubtedly believed that they had come by their material pleasures honestly. Indeed, defenders of the American predilection for imports pointed out that heightened wants could inspire heightened industry.

Colonial consumption might even echo the logic of an orderly universe, as some Americans and Britons concluded as they attempted to make sense of imperial commerce. In 1760 Benjamin Franklin, who was then in London, explained that "a Manufacture is Part of a great System of Commerce. . . . A Part of such a System cannot support itself without the Whole, and before the Whole, can be obtained the Part perishes."[17] Neither Britain's European rivals nor the colonies could simply will themselves into becoming something they were not. Indeed, according to Franklin, skilled manufacturers who immigrated to America soon switched from the production to the distribution of consumer goods, a role more in keeping with the colonies' place in the imperial system. Commercial growth in the British Atlantic seemed to function according to an elegant logic, especially if one did not ask too many discomforting questions about the price some people paid for imperial prosperity.

Even colonists dissenting from certain aspects of British mercantile policy posited an underlying equilibrium between producing Britons and consuming Americans. A lengthy 1764 newspaper essay appearing in New York and Boston critiqued the rigidity of the Navigation Acts, while offering assurance that the colonial appetite for consumption meant that the colonists' wealth ultimately would flow to Britain. The colonial condition was such that "though we are not a rich people, we enjoy advantages equal to the richest and most opulent, having the necessities of life in great abundance. . . ." This economy almost fated Americans to spend their money overseas: "In order to procure one of the[se necessities] (*to wit*, Cloathing) and many conveniences, we are obliged to send abroad all the cash we acquire, and as fast as we acquire it. . . ." Even so, according to the writer, colonists gained a great deal. Britain "secures to us every thing else that is valuable in life," leaving "no reason to" complain.[18] One way or another, it seemed, consumption bound Britain and the colonies together, allowing both to thrive. Such detailed analysis and secular logic were an emblematic expression of the age.

THE ENLIGHTENMENT IN AMERICA: WORDS AND POWER

Time leapt eleven days forward in September 1752. From Maine to Georgia, September 14 came right on the heels of September 2. Mothers did not birth babies; death did not descend on the elderly and infirm; no court orders were executed either. This feat of colonial time travel was not, of course, an act of collective wizardry or a rupture in the time-space continuum. Rather, the colonies adjusted their calendars to accord with a 1751 Parliamentary law covering Britain and all its affiliated territories, putting the empire on the same calendar that various European states gradually adopted in the wake of Pope Gregory XIII's decree 170 years before. As another result, the new year would from that time forward begin in January instead of March. The older Julian calendar had failed to account precisely for the actual length in minutes of a year, so Britons were making up for lost time. Given how attached individuals and whole cultures can be to the annual rites and rhythms of the calendar—birthdays and the celebration of Christmas being among the cherished annual milestones—and given the still fierce anti-Catholicism of many colonists, Americans accepted the change with remarkable equanimity. The adjustment went off without a serious hitch.

The transition to the Gregorian calendar benefited from the development of particular institutions and sentiments more than the dissemination of sophisticated ideas about time and nature. Colonists need not fully grasp the mathematics of the matter to be aware that they were living in an age of burgeoning scientific discovery, that observation and logic revealed hidden truths about the natural world, or that more of the world was being mapped and plotted. Widespread literacy mattered, but so too did the increasing circulation of reading material such as almanacs and newspapers to get the word out.

The pluralism of American culture also weighed in favor of the change. Perhaps a fifth of white colonists, immigrants and their offspring from non-British European lands, already observed the newer calendar based on their prior customs. Conversely, the growing attraction that some colonists felt, starting with the provincial elites, for the mother country made obvious the need to fall in line with the British plan.

Even in this intensely religious age, the commercial logic of the move weighed heavily in the balance against cultural prejudice and force of habit. The expanding flow of goods across the Atlantic argued for as orderly a set of commercial arrangements as possible. Moreover, as Benjamin Franklin's popular *Poor Richard's Almanac* reminded readers in a variety of ways, time was money. Minding both carefully and consciously, as the avidly inquisitive Franklin knew, was the path to personal virtue and collective improvement. Looked at this way, the Enlightenment in America was not so much about ideas for their own sake as it was the application of new knowledge to improve self and society.

Nonetheless, ideas mattered—and they traveled across the Atlantic along the same routes as the imported goods Americans increasingly consumed. The insights of English scientists and philosophers, particularly Francis Bacon, Isaac Newton, and John Locke as well as their eighteenth-century successors, filtered into the colonies, sometimes directly and sometimes through more popular writers such as John Trenchard, Thomas Gordon, Joseph Addison, and Richard Steele. At the core of Enlightenment ideas and ideals was the replacement of arguments based on established, sometimes ancient, authority with empirical evidence observed and categorized to enable people to draw logical conclusions. Newton's discovery that certain laws governed the physical universe led to the compelling presumption that laws of human history, human nature, and human society could be deduced as well. Reason would claim priority over revelation and tradition as ways of knowing. As the eighteenth century wore on, Scottish "common sense" philosophers added potentially democratizing elements to Enlightenment thinking by emphasizing that truth was something regular people could derive from their perceptions of the world and that the inborn sympathy humans had for one another formed the basis of social order. An emphasis on reason inspired some colonists to embrace Deism, a philosophy that brushed aside a belief in miracles, biblical or contemporary, and divinely determined fate. These they regarded as superstitious obstacles to understanding God's creation through the study of nature and deriving moral understanding from logical observation.

For some colonists, new thinking and the spirit of participating in a conversation that, in theory, knew no borders played an even more profound role in reshaping their identities than clothes they wore and the tea they sipped. Books, newspapers, and colleges provided conduits for an Enlightenment sensibility that encouraged this trans-Atlantic reconsideration of the nature of man, morals, religion, politics, and the universe. Not surprisingly, the American Enlightenment also precipitated new social networks, as well as alternative institutions for conferring prestige beyond the narrow confines of church and state. The results registered not just among men in public life, but also among women and men alone, in pairs, and small circles contemplating their moral worth and the meaning of their lives. In the process, the Enlightenment at least implicitly challenged existing hierarchies in some ways, while reinforcing them in others.

As a young man in the 1750s, John Adams took great care to consider what the new learning of the age meant as he charted a path for himself. Adams, unlike Tom Bell, actually graduated from Harvard rather than getting kicked out, but like Bell, he sought to build on his collegiate experience, taking with him the substance and not just the style he had acquired. For Adams that meant finding a profession and a moral compass—in his case, one that directed intellectual forces quite differently than those that governed the thinking of his Puritan forebears. In college, to which his father dispatched the talented boy to prepare to become a minister, Adams encountered through Professor John Winthrop IV the scientific currents of the times, including Newton. Perhaps more important, Adams developed an appreciation for the scientific disposition to accumulate systematically bits of data to achieve larger insights. Adams determined not to enter the clergy, as that course "would involve me in endless Altercations... without any prospect of doing any good to my fellow Men."[19] For the time being, then, Adams became a teacher in Worcester, Massachusetts. There, Adams encountered philosophical free thinking that, while it did not shatter his religious faith, confirmed for him that the path to self-knowledge ran through study that placed man and nature at the forefront of inquiry rather than theological doctrine based on spiritual revelations. Reflecting his emerging evidence-based habits of mind as well as his temperament, Adams decided to become a lawyer.

For Adams, as for even less religiously orthodox thinkers than he, the late-seventeenth-century English philosopher John Locke provided the rock on which to ground new ways of thinking. Locke, like Adams, was a religious believer, but the Englishman's insights into psychology and education pointed in a different direction than the Calvinist doctrine of original sin and predestination. The philosopher maintained that knowledge was not inborn or, in our parlance, hard-wired into the brain. Rather, almost everything humans know they come to through the senses and experience. The acquisition of information ultimately becomes the evidence with which we reason and discover truth, religious and otherwise.

Against this philosophical backdrop, the extent of what could be known about the world and about humanity dramatically expanded. The study of history, of how nations progressed and declined, became all the more vital, as from such information could be gleaned lessons to design better laws and build more effective institutions to govern man, in imitation of the laws that God designed to govern nature. Adams marveled at what reason accomplished for the farmer "manuring the Land" as well as the scientist studying the heavens with a telescope or the earth with a microscope, and imagined what might be possible for society organized around reason.[20] Church and Scripture might help to spread new moral knowledge, but they would not be society's sole or even primary source for such improvements.

The ideas of the Enlightenment were hardly confined to the tiny percentage of young men who attended college or went into professions such as the law and medicine. As a young man in Philadelphia, Benjamin Franklin formed a circle of friends into a group that met to discuss books and debate ideas. In the "Junto," as Franklin called it, young artisans met weekly, taking turns to "produce one or more queries on any point of Morals, Politics, or Natural Philosophy, to be discuss'd by the company; and once in three months produce and read an essay of his own writing...." Even before this group, which included a surveyor, a shoemaker, a joiner, and a clerk, Franklin had gathered another group of young "lovers of reading" as a sort of literary society.[21] Franklin also joined the Freemasons, a group whose modern origins were in England in 1717 with the goal of spreading the virtues of the Enlightenment and serving mankind broadly rather than advancing particular religious creeds. By becoming a Mason, an artisan like Franklin was also securing himself access to a wealthier, more polished slice of Philadelphia society. As Franklin engaged the world of ideas, he also helped found institutions, including a lending library, a philosophical society, and the school that ultimately became the University of Pennsylvania.

Franklin turned his attentions to scientific discovery, becoming a generator as well as a transmitter of Enlightenment scientific knowledge. He grew fascinated with electricity, inventing a battery and coming up with a whole new vocabulary for describing how electricity functioned, including the notion of positive and negative charges. Famously, he ratified his hypothesis about the nature of lightning by attaching a metal key to the end of a line that he used to fly a silk kite in a thunderstorm. The transmission of the electric current demonstrated the pervasive presence of electromagnetic energy. His study of electricity also indicated that buildings could be protected from the ravages of lightning-sparked fires through the use of rods and wires conducting the heaven's energy harmlessly into the ground.

Essential to the spread of the Enlightenment culture in the colonies was an expansion in the amount and type of reading materials printed in the colonies. New England had from its early days generated a significant amount of printed material from a press in Cambridge, Massachusetts, designed to disseminate the sermons and religiously inspired wisdom of its influential and ambitious clergy. The notion that a local printer was a boon to the community or province was not widespread during the first century of English colonization, but in the eighteenth century printing gradually spread. In 1671 Governor William Berkeley celebrated the lack of a printing press in Virginia, sparing the colony unnecessary political and religious trouble. A press did not open for business in that colony until 1730. In New York, Governor Francis Lovelace had tried unsuccessfully to obtain a printing press for the province during his service between 1668 and 1673; it was not until 1693 that this goal was achieved.[22] But just as Britain was on the verge of expanding its appetite for regularly published, printed news, so too the colonies, or at least their port cities, were to feel that same hunger. The first successful newspaper, *The Boston News-Letter*, started printing under the auspices of a Scottish immigrant in 1704. By 1740 the colonies could boast thirteen newspapers published in seven different cities and towns. That number increased to twenty-two by 1760. The number of master printers in the colonies shot up from nine to forty-two between 1720 and 1760; by the latter year, two-thirds of these were concentrated in Boston, New York, and Philadelphia, with fourteen others scattered across nine other towns.

The spread of printers and newspapers connected colonists to the world and to each other in new ways. Accompanying the advertisements for imported goods, as well as runaway slaves and servants, were news stories from overseas. The emphasis on distant wars and dynasties made readers feel more cosmopolitan and more connected to their merchant and gentry counterparts in England. Local events might be more readily conveyed to the people who cared by word of mouth. The printers themselves were a peripatetic group, significant numbers coming from overseas and others moving from colony to colony. The emphasis on "foreign intelligences" in newspapers also seemed the safer path for many American printers. Incorporating news stories directly from British papers was an easy method of news gathering; it also spared printers from exposure to controversies that might be bad for a business that relied not only on sustaining a modest number of readers, but also the support of the authorities. With circulations usually under one thousand and subscriptions difficult to collect, newspapermen often counted on government contracts, such as the printing of laws and provincial assembly minutes—and of paper money—for their livelihood. Benjamin Franklin, for all his success and his partnerships with printers in other colonies, was no exception when it came to relying on public business to increase profitability.

In such a business and cultural climate, political contests represented a double-edged sword. Indeed, printers sometimes played up their artisanal identities and downplayed their intellectual identities so that they would not be blamed by one political faction or another for publishing material on local controversies. Neutrality, as one scholar has pointed out, was a business model, with the trick often being to be perceived as open to comment from all sides rather than as a partisan.

But the press and printers also occasionally served as irresistible tools for trying to shape disputes and rally support for political and religious purposes. The most prominent and significant intervention of a colonial newspaper into partisan political rivalry prior to 1763 occurred in New York, where opponents of Governor William Cosby set up German-born printer John Peter Zenger's *New-York Weekly*

Journal as a forum for airing their grievances against the government. Cosby came to New York in 1732 and immediately started making powerful enemies, including Lewis Morris, a judge who blocked a lawsuit by Cosby and who used Zenger's paper to publish his opinion. Cosby retaliated by removing Morris from the bench and promoting his allies within the court. In Zenger's paper, Morris and attorney James Alexander depicted Cosby as the embodiment of political corruption and patronage. Cosby, in turn, charged Zenger with libel and had him arrested. Morris and Alexander made the case for freedom of the press while Philadelphia lawyer Andrew Hamilton ably defended Zenger in court, arguing that publishing the truth could not be construed as libel and checked the power of the governor.

The Zenger case did not establish a precedent that other colonial courts followed, but it was a significant event in America's emerging print culture. The case demonstrated the possibility of a more expansive definition of freedom of the press, one that included the liberty to criticize authority. For most American printers before 1763, this freedom was unappealingly risky. Nonetheless, James Alexander, a man deeply immersed in Enlightenment thinking on a range of scientific, legal, and philosophical matters, had scored a victory for an embryonic version of our modern notion of freedom of the press.

But even in its more cautious form, the colonial press helped forge a public world for the exchange and discussion of news, political theory, and public controversies such as inoculation, paper currency, and religious revivalism. Those who read or composed newspaper articles and pamphlets subscribed to the notion that there was a place where judgments about quality, veracity, and virtue could be made not based on rank, power, or reputation, but rather on the strength and logic of the prose itself. Not everyone would agree with the public's verdict, just as Cosby and his allies did not agree with the jury's verdict, but anyone who published their views, quite often anonymously, in these public forums submitted to the scrutiny of the public sphere. Printers thus facilitated a crucial goal of Enlightenment culture—to test ideas through the ongoing application of human reason.

American readers did not limit themselves to news on current events and scientific discoveries. After 1740 English novels made up a small part of the colony's burgeoning trade, drawing women and men into new worlds of intimate contemplation. For some readers, the novel's implicit emphasis on exploring the development of individual identity and moral choice in a commercializing society hit home. Samuel Richardson's novels *Pamela* and *Clarissa* in particular spoke to female readers, as these stories traversed the perils of courtship and temptation. Like the heroine Clarissa, American readers could explore and express their feelings through letters to one another. And while novels had morals, they were not so didactic as sermons and other non-fiction, leaving ample leeway for readers to venture their own interpretations.

The cultivation of literarily informed friendship both complemented and transcended the face-to-face world of the tea table, which also drew together women of education and refinement. Novel reading and letter writing potentially deepened and widened such connections, as these activities became tools for moral self-betterment in the virtual social setting of writing whose deliberate qualities fostered contemplation and greater intimacy. Such literature-enhanced relationships modeled friendship not as an exchange of favors up and down the social hierarchy, but as a type of sympathetic bonding. This notion of friendship even had the potential to reshape views of marriage as less centered on utilitarian concerns about production and reproduction and more on emotional bonding.

Still, as some critics have noted, the trans-Atlantic print culture hardly established a level playing field and in some sense created new forms of hierarchy. Entry into the republic of letters, of course, required literacy, which was far more widespread in some regions, especially New England, than others, especially the Southern colonies. Slaves fought an uphill battle if they were to acquire literacy, women were sometimes taught to read but not to write, and lower-class whites in the South rarely had access to schools, let alone the tutors the gentry hired for their children. Printers might not verify the origin of every submission, but still were de facto gatekeepers for enlightened and not so enlightened publications. Thus, certain sectors of the emerging world of print, particularly newspapers, presumed and to at least some degree established a world of white male conversation to which others were expected to defer or at best to imitate.

The changing face of higher education, exclusively for men, in the colonies further reveals the blend of openness to change and elitism, as well as the mix of the secular and the religious that was characteristic of the American Enlightenment. The nine colleges founded before the American Revolution, six of them before 1763, had roots in specific churches. The earliest colleges, Harvard, founded in 1636 as a Puritan seat of learning in Massachusetts, and Yale, founded in 1701 by Connecticut Puritans who thought Harvard's doctrinal purity had eroded, stocked the ranks of the ministry. William and Mary, Virginia's Anglican college founded in 1693, had less luck attracting future clergy. Yet none of the colleges were seminaries, and from early on understood themselves to be producing men who would take up leading roles in society by joining the professions, by serving in government, and by being gentlemen of cultivated mind. And, as the case of John Adams illustrated, the secular subject matter of some college courses—science, math, as well as classical language and literature—could fire the imagination in ways that transcended genteel worldliness. Despite the religious foundations of the colleges, the need for students trumped any impulse to limit enrollment to members of a particular church. This ecumenical trend applied to the small wave of mid-eighteenth-century schools with church ties, including the Presbyterian college ultimately located in Princeton, New Jersey, and Baptist-founded Brown, in Rhode Island. The Anglicans encountered resistance to full control of colleges in Philadelphia and New York City that they took the lead in founding. Neither the market nor the public contribution that the colleges wished to make could sustain sectarian rigidity in higher education.

The founding of colleges expressed the moderate side of the Enlightenment and of the mid-eighteenth-century explosion of spiritual energy known as the Great Awakening. The Presbyterian founders of the College of New Jersey expected it to ensure that their church's future growth and development followed a smooth, intellectually constructive path. New Hampshire's Dartmouth College was an offspring of its founder's interest in the missionary education of Native Americans. Meanwhile, colleges in New York and Pennsylvania had early support from more culturally conservative Anglicans hoping to turn back the tide of evangelical revivalism. Still, as the founding and curriculum of early American colleges reveal, the pursuits of intellectual enlightenment and spiritual salvation in eighteenth-century America were not mutually exclusive.

PURSUITS OF SALVATION: THE GREAT AWAKENING

Jonathan Edwards, the third president of the College of New Jersey, may have been appointed to help promote the school's goal of a moderate, sustainable spiritual harvest, but the preaching that helped make his name two decades earlier was anything but moderate. Starting in 1734, the efforts of Edwards, a Northampton, Massachusetts, Congregational minister, and his colleagues spread the spirit of religious revival up and down the Connecticut River valley. Edwards had witnessed his preacher grandfather Solomon Stoddard lead local revivals. Focusing on youthful members of his community, Edwards decided to try his own hand at shaking the community out of spiritual complacency. Edwards also critiqued material greed in a region dominated by a network of elite merchant families. Reflecting on the path that members of his flock experienced on their way to the higher ground of salvation during the revival, Edwards noted, "Many... have scarcely been free from terror while they have been asleep, and they have awaked with fear, heaviness, and distress still abiding on their spirits." Hints of grace followed a "distress of conscience... turned into and humble, meek sense of... unworthiness before God...."[23]

Edwards drew damnation near. His famous 1740 sermon *Sinners in the Hands of an Angry God* illustrates his method. Edwards cited biblical chapter and verse, but his vivid imagery impressed upon his listeners the imminence of the Lord's wrath: "There is no fortress" including prayer itself "that is any defence against the power of God" who might be even more "angry" at some of Edward's audience "than he is with many of those that are now in the flames of hell." Edwards deployed terrifying images of vulnerability: God's hand lay on a "floodgate" holding back "fiery floods of... fierceness and wrath"; like an archer, "The bow of God's wrath is bent, and the arrow" pointed at the listener's heart; "God," he explained, "holds you over the pit of hell, much as one holds a spider, or some loathsome insect, over the fire...." Edwards shook his listeners from the self-satisfaction of merely being a good person or a regular churchgoer; to stave off eternal punishment, believers must be "born again" in the awareness of the Lord's absolute power over the fate of their souls.[24] Edwards's intense Calvinistic predestination had not stopped this Yale graduate from reading searchingly the scientific literature of the Enlightenment. Yet in his efforts to spread salvation in western Massachusetts, he refused to overvalue book knowledge or the relative ease of life in a colony well past its frontier phase. Faith alone was paramount. People in the Connecticut River valley came to feel the same way.

The 1734 revivals might have remained just another brief chapter in the complex religious history of New England had it not coalesced with similar stirrings in England. Boston minister Benjamin Colman coaxed Edwards to author a full account of the revival, *A Faithful Narrative of the Surprizing Work of God*, which he arranged to have published in London in 1737. English evangelicals took note of these remarkable Northampton events and sought to apply their own talents to the same end, soon drawing the mainland colonies and Great Britain into a broad and diverse awakening of the Christian spirit.

The paramount figure in making revivalism a mass, trans-Atlantic phenomenon was George Whitefield. Whitefield, the Oxford University–educated child of innkeepers, had shown an interest in stage acting. He fell under the tutelage of the great Anglican reformers Charles and John Wesley, whose intense approach to prayer and faith, with an emphasis on spiritual self-examination and charity, ultimately gave rise to a separate denomination known as Methodism. Whitefield developed a reputation for hugely successful outdoor sermons in England that received coverage in the American press in advance of his first American tour in 1739, during which he made sure to pay a visit to Edwards in Northampton. Whitefield's travels up and down the east coast of North America proved to be electrifying (see Map 10.1). Hundreds and even thousands of people turned out

Map 10.1 George Whitefield's Tour of the English Mainland Colonies, November 1739–January 1741.

to hear him, as he deployed his powerful oratory and stage presence in open-air sermons. Over the next thirty years, Whitefield would come to the colonies six more times to harvest souls and see to his charitable work.

Whitefield preferred to stress the open hand of salvation over the clenched fist of damnation. As he stated in a sermon delivered in Philadelphia, Christ "does not call you because you are already, but because he intends to *make you Saints*. No, it pities him to see you naked. He wants to cover you with his Righteousness." The same sermon concluded reassuringly: "He will sweetly guide you by his Wisdom on Earth, and afterwards take you up to partake of his Glory in Heaven."[25] Similarly, Whitefield downplayed the significance of his Anglican affiliation, recording a conversation in which he stated "that I saw regenerate Souls among the *Baptists*, among *Presbyterians*, among the *Independents*, and among the Church-Folks [his fellow Anglicans]: All Children of GOD, and yet all born again in a different Way of Worship; and who then can tell which is the most Evangelical?"[26] Thus, Whitefield generated a mass following by spreading a hopeful vision across regions and across denominational lines.

Whitefield also staked out a reputation for charity and established an orphanage in the nascent colony of Georgia. Benjamin Franklin recorded in his autobiography the experience of attending a Whitefield sermon, where he resolved ahead of time not to contribute a donation to what he believed was Whitefield's misguided orphanage project. Whitefield's powers of public persuasion, however, melted Franklin's determination, so that at the end of the preacher's remarks Franklin "empty'd my pocket wholly into the collector's dish, gold and all."[27] The Deistic devotee of the Enlightenment remained unconverted to Whitefield's spiritual vision, but was moved by the social benefits of his message.

Franklin and Whitefield both understood the power of publicity and marketing, two of the secular mainsprings that helped set the Great Awakening in motion. Franklin's *Pennsylvania Gazette* and his printing business benefited greatly from Whitefield's newsworthiness and his sophisticated understanding of self-promotion. One of the reasons Whitefield's audiences were so big was that he worked cooperatively with printers to spread word of his impending visits to colonial towns. The preacher and his agent, who had made his fortune as stock broker, made sure that advertisements and articles preceded the actual event. Meanwhile, Franklin and Whitefield collaborated on producing serialized versions of the preacher's *Journals*, which readers paid for by subscription and could have bound into book form. Franklin worked with his printing business partners in other colonies on ginning up subscribers to make a profit from the *Journals*. As big as Whitefield's crowds were, Franklin understood that there were many people who would only have access to him through the printed page.

The fact that Whitefield had many critics hardly detracted from the enterprise; indeed, the opposite was true. Newspaper coverage and publications by, for, and against Whitefield not only supplied Franklin with work—over half of his 1740 book catalogue concerned Whitefield—but also led to an upsurge in publishing throughout the colonies between 1739 and 1745. The winds of religious change filled the sails of literary commerce. For their part, neither Franklin nor Whitefield was the least bit embarrassed by their long-lasting friendship. They need not agree on everything to share the belief that doing well and doing good might be mutually supporting activities.

One charismatic English preacher cannot alone account for the spread of the Great Awakening and the controversies that surrounded it. Prior to the Awakening, most of the colonies had an established church. While colonial governments to different degrees tolerated other faiths, the legal and cultural advantages enjoyed by state-supported churches hardly made for a free religious marketplace. In some parts of the colonies, particularly the South and the backcountry, there was often a shortage of clergy and churches and exposure to religious services was sporadic at best. Meanwhile, in those regions with strong establishments, such as New England, local religious monopolies could result in complacency and indifference among clergy and laypeople alike. It was against this backsliding that Edwards inveighed with some early success. As Whitefield and the legion of itinerant ministers who followed him showed, these conditions made the colonies, each in their own way, ripe for something new.

Not everyone in New England found the winds of change refreshing. Revival undermined the prestige and authority of local ministers. It was bad enough to have to contend with the rising star of neighboring ministers like Edwards and visiting celebrities like Whitefield, but worse still, traveling preachers with dubious or nonexistent training swept into towns purveying passion rather than learning. Both on the basis of theological conviction and personal style so-called Old Light ministers condemned the New Lights for straying from orthodoxy and undermining the carefully wrought order of New England congregationalism. Disagreements over style and substance blended together. Whitefield himself had recorded in his published *Journals* that "the Reason why Congregations have been so dead, is, because they have had dead Men preaching to them."[28] Others, such as New Jersey itinerant James Davenport, charged that some ministers were themselves not properly converted, intruding on others' congregational turf to make such accusations. Critics of itinerant preachers noted that they enjoyed the advantage of being able to deliver the same sermon repeatedly before different audiences; established clergy had to inspire the same congregation week after week, while also attending to pastoral duties.

For some conservatives, the line between eroding respect for ministers and for authority more generally was a thin one. Indeed, Connecticut's provincial assembly sought to put a stop to rampant itinerancy through a 1742 licensing law. Not surprisingly, itinerant preachers refused to abide by such restrictions. In the western Massachusetts seedbed of the Awakening, it was not only Old Lights who lost their pulpits, but even Jonathan Edwards himself. In 1750 he found himself dismissed by his congregants after his attempt to enforce a stricter definition of who among them qualified as having been born again.

Resistance to the new revivalism originated from motives other than the clergy's self-interest and desire to preserve their job security. Spreading word of the "good book" without regard for traditional denominational guidance and restraint was one thing; claiming a direct knowledge of the Book of Life was another. To the alarm of even some of the Great Awakening's promoters, the spirit of revival induced some to report temporarily leaving the physical world altogether and meeting directly with Christ in his heavenly realm. In one vivid account from Lebanon, Connecticut, an unnamed parishioner "fainted" and "found my self at the bottum of a Grat mouenten" from which an angel ultimately led this fortunate soul to meet with Christ who "shewed me my name reten [written] in Letters of blood" as a sign of permanent salvation.[29] These and other such journeys violated not only Calvinist doctrine of unknowable predestination, but also seemed to leap beyond the bounds of Scripture—or at least to put certain believers in a realm of experience allegedly reserved for the age of the apostles. By contrast, believers in such spirit journeys imagined themselves living in apocalyptic times when miracles flowed from a deep and uncontrollable spiritual force.

Such instances of mystical transport put ministers like Edwards in a tough spot, as these stories seemed to validate the harshest allegations of emotional excess against the revivalists. Ministers sometimes sought to distinguish between the imagery that the converted used to describe their new birth and actual transportation to ethereal realms. Others accused conservative rivals of wrongly lumping a few rogue cases with the broadly successful harvesting of souls. For their part, conservatives viewed the specter of disorder as very real, as lay people—including women—shared their spiritual visions and preferences without deferring to the established ministry's learning or prestige. Clearly, the radical impulses that brought Anne Hutchison to loggerheads with John Winthrop a century before still existed, as the spiritual current of the Great Awakening inevitably overflowed its banks.

In the middle colonies, the combination of religious pluralism and ferment in the Presbyterian Church ensured that the Great Awakening would spur more than just the civic and charitable attitudes that Franklin lauded. As in New England, a tradition of revivalism had existed before Whitefield and others started connecting the dots across regions and across the Atlantic. In 1725 Minister William Tennent, Sr., founded a small school in Neshaminy, Pennsylvania, mocked as a "Log College," to prepare a new group of preachers who would emphasize spiritual rebirth above adherence to doctrine. His sons Gilbert, William Jr., and John took up the call to infuse their fellow Scottish Presbyterians in New Jersey with revived spirit. Whitefield's first tour of the colonies inspired the New Jersey revivalists to think in broader ethnic and regional terms. Gilbert Tennent traveled to New England to preach and also launched a frontal assault on the religious status quo. In the sermon *The Danger of an Unconverted Ministry*, delivered in Nottingham, Pennsylvania, and published by Benjamin Franklin, Tennent made blunt comparisons that men and women in this overwhelmingly rural world could readily appreciate. He described ministers insincere in their faith as a plague of "Caterpillars [who] labour to devour every green Thing." These men produced "Discourses" that were "cold and sapless, and as it were freeze between their Lips!"[30] Such deliberately inflammatory language illustrates why Presbyterians divided along Old

Side and New Side lines, much like their Calvinistic Congregationalist cousins to the north.

In the backcountry where many of the Ulster Scots had settled, the spread of revivals opened up a new set of options that would ultimately lead some out of the Presbyterian ranks altogether. Just as peddlers traveled down the newly opened roads to the backcountry, so too did itinerant ministers come through with their new spiritual wares. The results in Pennsylvania were divisive, with poorer areas inclined toward the New Side, while areas with more wealthy landholders and slaveholders were more likely to identify with the Old Side. Poorer folks perhaps felt less discomforted by a message of change. In the longer run, Presbyterian factions found ways to heal the intra-denominational wounds on the frontier, but in some ways it was too late. The revival message cut against sectarian identity; Christian conversion trumped denominational purity. As backcountry migrants moved south along the Great Wagon Road, many became Baptists, drawn to the anti-elitist message of that sect's autonomous congregations.

The social and religious character of the Southern colonies delayed and channeled the impact of the Awakening in particular ways. Whitefield toured the South and focused his philanthropy on his Georgia orphanage. The South's dispersed population made it harder for him to attract huge crowds there, but nonetheless his visits had, as usual, an impact. The Anglican planter elite generally looked askance at the revivals. For poorer whites, the preaching of New Side Presbyterian minister Samuel Davies and other itinerants presented an attractive alternative to establishment Anglican clergy who seemed geographically and culturally distant from them.

Revivalism associated with the Great Awakening threatened the hierarchical expressions of wealth and gentility in Southern planter societies. Evangelical Christians, first Presbyterians, then followed in order by Baptists and Methodists, presented an alternative view of religion and society that inverted the usual hierarchy. These dissenters against gentry-sponsored Anglicanism emphasized material modesty, spiritual sincerity, and equality within the community of believers. Revivalists and religious insurgents presented these traits as true Christian values in stark contrast to the dominant planter class's cultural mores. To their frustration, gentry efforts to quash the spread of these churches failed.

The prevalence of slavery—in Northern colonies as well as Southern ones—extended the impact of the Great Awakening and made it that much more threatening to the existing social order. Leading Northern revivalists like Edwards and Tennent, as well as Whitefield, welcomed African Americans to their revivals, while their opponents disparaged New Light revivalism for its noticeable appeal to slaves, free blacks, and other groups marginalized by traditional churches. The revivalist message that status, wealth, and church membership did not guarantee anyone salvation and, conversely, that salvation was available to all regardless of denomination or formal education had an appeal across racial, gender, and class boundaries. The extemporaneous style of itinerant preaching also broadened Christianity's appeal. African Americans responded to the Great Awakening in far greater numbers and intensity than they did to the long-standing efforts of Anglican missionaries from the Society for the Propagation of the Gospel in Foreign Parts to convert slaves. Even so, the earthly commitment of the awakened ministry to black equality was tepid at best. Whitefield was happy to convert slaves to Christianity, but he did not set out to free anyone. Indeed, he actively sought slave labor to sustain his Georgia orphanage, helped to undermine Georgia's initial ban on slavery, and thought of his preaching as steering slaves away from earthly rebellion in favor of heavenly rewards. Gilbert Tennent deployed the phrase "Moral Negroes" to denounce his allegedly unconverted rivals, suggesting that homely color prejudice and evangelical populism were hardly incompatible.[31]

Around the edges of Southern slave society, revivalism attracted active black involvement that helped to shape the Great Awakening's character. African Americans responded to and inserted into revivals expressions of emotional engagement and physical manifestations of spiritual transformation such as song, dance, and trance-like reverie and release. Such experiences corresponded to and flowed out of African religious traditions. Public expressions of spiritual transformation made personal rebirth a communal act forging new links among black and white believers, who gathered together in interracial baptism ceremonies and love feasts.

African Americans seized on their conversion to preach the gospel themselves. Slaveholders found a Christian awakening in the slave quarters troubling from the beginning of the movement; South Carolina authorities forced planters Hugh and Jonathan Bryan to apologize for converting large numbers of their slaves in the early 1740s, fearing this would provoke restive behavior. Blending of religious cultures did not necessarily produce Christian outcomes. African American New Yorkers appropriated the Dutch holiday of Pinkster, originally an occasion to celebrate the Pentecost, as a festival for enjoying African foodways, music, dance, and cultural self-assertion. While the overwhelming majority of slaves, especially those living and working on Southern plantations, experienced their spiritual lives quite apart from Christianity until the nineteenth century, the participation of some African Americans in the Great Awakening created an entering wedge for the Christianization of slave society.

Indeed, the embrace of gospel-inspired salvation for some African Americans, especially in the North, forged a deeper black connection to print culture, much as it did among white Christians. Jupiter Hammon, a slave from Long Island, New York, became the first black published poet in North American history with his "An Evening Thought: Salvation by Christ, with Penitential Cries," written on Christmas Day 1760. The poem asserted a universalistic, wholly inclusive message in its very first lines:

> Salvation comes by Jesus Christ alone,
> The only Son of God;
> Redemption now to every one,
> That loves his holy Word.[32]

The more famous Phillis Wheatley followed Hammon into print a decade later with her "On the Death of the Rev. Mr. George Whitefield" and authored other poems meditating on salvation. And although his path-breaking personal memoir did not appear in the United States until 1791, the former slave Olaudah Equiano prominently featured his passionate embrace of Christianity, with strong echoes of trans-Atlantic revivalism. Indeed, in his *Interesting Narrative*, Equiano reported hearing George Whitefield preach in Philadelphia. Hammon, Wheatley, and Equiano were exceptional figures, but they illustrated in their lives and writings the various ways that the victims of slavery, North and South, appropriated and leveraged Christianity to make claims about equality. Moreover, each derived spiritual satisfaction and personal meaning in a fashion that belied the notion that Christianity was the special property of people of one particular color or class.

As with African Americans, Native Americans responded to the Great Awakening in diverse ways, some finding in it more inviting access to Christianity than previous exposures, while others undertook efforts at spiritual renewal emphasizing their separate Indian identity. In Connecticut, Mohegan teenager Samson Occum was swept up in the evangelical fervor, which impelled him to seek salvation and a formal education. After more than four years of study with New Light minister Eleazar Wheelock, Occom undertook a mission to the Native Americans of eastern Long Island for several years, where his sponsors paid him a fraction of what they offered white missionaries. Occum later toured Britain, raising thousands of pounds for his mentor Wheelock, who ultimately diverted the funds from training Indians as missionaries to establish Dartmouth College in 1769, the clientele of which would be overwhelmingly white.

The crises that beset Native Americans in the Anglo-American colonies drew some Indians spiritually closer to their encroaching white Christian neighbors. On the Pennsylvania frontier, German Moravians enjoyed particular success, converting close to five hundred Mahicans and Delawares from 1742 to 1763. Complementing the emotional accessibility of revivalism was the willingness of Moravians to take seriously the spiritual significance of Indian dreams. Moravian religious imagery emphasizing Christ's wounds and bleeding may also have appealed to potential Indian converts who saw parallels to their own valorization of the ability to endure torture and suffering with equanimity. Family ties among Indians were another source of converts. Practical considerations surely were at work as well among Indian converts, who hoped that a religious alliance with white neighbors might stave off the loss of their land.

Other Indians experienced different visions and made different calculations—ones that sought salvation and protection by distancing themselves dramatically from white men and white ways. Neolin, an Ohio Delaware, experienced visions in which spirit guides told him that whites and Indians had to follow separate paths to earthly and otherworldly salvation. Neolin told his adherents to reject trade with Europeans, to stop drinking alcohol, to return to traditional practices and beliefs, and to embrace an Indian identity spanning beyond tribal divisions. Like religious awakenings among other colonial Americans, such revelations involved innovation as much as a return to old ways. Indians sometimes applied Christian moral standards to criticize white misdeeds and hypocrisy; they also borrowed

Christian imagery and concepts when talking about the torments of hell that awaited non-believers.

For whites, blacks, and Indians, the Great Awakening provoked conflict in large part because it inspired alternative forms and definitions of community. Native American and African American encounters with revivalism provoked an array of responses, from embrace, to selective borrowing, to renewed commitment to resistance. For white colonists, the lines between religious, cultural, and political responses blurred together as well. In New England, as in the Chesapeake, religious division combined with simmering secular conflicts to redefine the boundaries of community, to challenge traditional avenues of authority, and to force society to consider how to define religious toleration. In Concord, Massachusetts, where the people living miles from the meetinghouse resented having to travel to church on Sunday, controversy over the New Light minister facilitated defection to a newly formed neighboring town. Elsewhere, resistance to the notion that every townsperson owed allegiance and tax money to support a state-sanctioned church nudged some people to become Baptists. Similarly, Virginia's Anglican elites increasingly worried whether tolerating religious choice might undermine their place atop the social order.

Choice itself mattered—to consumers of religion as with consumers of tea and textiles. Gilbert Tennent used the idiom of the marketplace to defend New Lights who abandoned faithless clergymen and congregations in order to find new spiritual homes. "And if they should go a few Miles farther than ordinary, to enjoy those, which they profit most by; who do they wrong?" he asked. His rival ministers had to recognize the consequences of consumer choice, as well as the nature of religious supply and demand. "That we must make no Difference in our Choice... according to their different Gifts and Graces" made as much sense as saying "we must neither eat nor drink, or make any Choice in Drinks or Victuals.... " Tennent likened the denial of "Liberty of Choice" for believers to the imposition of Egyptian slavery.[33] In making his case for the Great Awakening, he articulated the ethics of a pluralistic world of religious competition that he was helping to create. That same logic applied to the secular realm of goods and ideas as well. The notion that colonists should fashion their lives around their aspirations—for gentility, comfort, salvation, enlightenment, or some combination of these—opened up new worlds of possibility for men and women up and down the social hierarchy. Sometimes when colonists appraised each other's progress, the saints and the scoundrels could be hard to tell apart.

CONFIDENCE

While fame, reputation, and wealth had distinct advantages for itinerant ministers like Whitefield and printers-turned-gentlemen like Franklin, for con man Tom Bell notoriety threatened to put him out of business. Indeed, for years newspapers warned readers that Bell was lurking about, "taking a Tour thro' the Colonies" up to his old tricks.[34] A 1749 report from New York claimed that Bell was so notorious that his ruses could only work on "innocent and unwary people," but it also bemoaned that "several honest persons have suffered at times, because they have been suspected to be like him. . . ."[35] In other words, Bell gave honest colonial travelers—like the Reverend Rowland whom he had once impersonated and other men of gentle deportment, good education, and impressive connections—a bad name. In a society where judgment was often based on appearance, a trickster like Bell made appearance an unreliable index of status or trustworthiness.

Bell's concern was not the reputation of others—let alone the reliability of self-representation—but his own reputation. Thus, soon after he was reported to be in Manhattan, Bell, or at least someone claiming to be Bell, defended himself at length in the pages of New York's *Evening Post.* He accused the editor of another New York paper of falsely attributing all manner of crimes to him, making Bell into a "*Dragon*, the Destroyer or the Devourer of the Lives and Properties of Mankind" when in reality, he was just a man who had served as a merchant, a soldier, a surveyor, and a teacher in his travels through the colonies. He had suffered "Imprisonments, Censures, and Reproaches" fit for "incorrigible Slaves and Offenders," whereas a man of his intellect would never become "a sincere Convert" through such punitive measures. Bell suggested that "a generous Pardon" and a fair examination of the actual facts would clear the air around them. In the meantime, he informed the newspaper's readers, he was ready to ship out as "an able and experienced Pilot or Sailor" to any other North American port.[36]

Although Bell had once posed as a revivalist minister, in claiming that he was both a changed and a misunderstood man, he elected not to describe his conversion in the language of saved souls and religious rebirths. Rather, Bell moved to Virginia and turned to a stable job suitable to his education and worldly experience—teaching. He also toyed with the idea of writing a memoir. If any potential readers accepted Bell's offer and took out a subscription on this autobiographical project, then they fell victim to yet another scam. No such book ever appeared. Instead, word from Antigua, in the West Indies, filtered back to the mainland that he had returned to the confidence game—posing as a doctor, his bearing, education, and daring once again in play. Bell's creative recidivism was no more typical of colonial American experience than Franklin's or Whitefield's amazing success. All three men pushed outward from their provincial beginnings to a wider world of contacts, ideas, and possessions, seeking threads that connected colonists beyond the narrow confines of a single colony or region. For those without the means or the desire to travel beyond their county or colony, the empire's customs and products found a way into their lives all the same. Growing ethnic diversity and religious pluralism notwithstanding, not only the "Vices . . . of the Times" but also the aspirations of the times for salvation, enlightenment, and prosperity ran the length and breadth of the colonies. Benjamin Franklin and George Whitefield counted on it, every bit as much as confidence man Tom Bell did.

CHRONOLOGY

1687	Isaac Newton publishes *Philosophiae Naturalis Principia Mathematica.*
1690	John Locke publishes *Essay on Human Understanding.*
1704	*Boston News-Letter* becomes first successful newspaper in English colonies.
1725	William Tennent, Sr., founds "Log College" in Neshaminy, Pennsylvania.
1733–1757	Benjamin Franklin's *Poor Richard's Almanack* appears in print.
1733	*Tom Bell expelled from Harvard.*
1734	Jonathan Edwards launches revival in Northampton, Massachusetts.
1735	The libel trial of John Peter Zenger in New York City.
1739	George Whitefield begins his first evangelical tour of the colonies.
1741	*Bell impersonates a revival minister in New Jersey.*
1742	Connecticut passes law against itinerant preaching.
1746	*Bell scams Charles Dingee in Philadelphia.*
1749	*Bell writes self-exculpatory letter to the* New-York Evening Post.
1752	Transition from Julian to Gregorian calendar.
	Bell seeks to raise money in Williamsburg for his autobiography.
1755	*Tom Bell in West Indies.*
1760	Jupiter Hammon composes first published poem by an African American.
1760–1761	Neolin, the Delaware prophet, experiences visions of Indian reform and revival.

NOTES

1. *New-York Evening Post*, September 4, 1749.
2. *Pennsylvania Gazette*, August 14, 1746.
3. *Pennsylvania Gazette*, February 15–February 22, 1738.
4. *Pennsylvania Gazette*, July 14, 1743.
5. *Virginia Gazette*, April 11, 1751.
6. John Adams, quoted in Sharon V. Salinger, *Taverns and Drinking in Early America* (Baltimore: Johns Hopkins University Press, 2002), 234.
7. Gottlieb Mittleberger, *Journey to Pennsylvania*, ed. and trans. Oscar Handlin and John Clive (1756; Cambridge, MA: Belknap Press of Harvard University Press, 1960), 43, 49.
8. John Adams, January 1761, *Diary and Autobiography of John Adams*, ed. L. H. Butterfield (Cambridge, MA: Belknap Press of Harvard University Press, 1961), Vol. 1, 198.

9. *George Washington's Rules of Civility and Decent Behaviour in Company and Conversation*, ed. Charles Moore (Boston: Houghton Mifflin, 1926), 17.
10. Charles Carroll, quoted in Gordon S. Wood, *The Radicalism of the American Revolution* (New York: Knopf, 1992), 71.
11. John J. McCusker and Russell R. Menard, *The Economy of British America, 1607–1789* (Chapel Hill: University of North Carolina Press, 1985), 279; Bernard Bailyn, "1776: A Year of Challenge—A World Transformed," *Journal of Law and Economics* 19 (1976): 447.
12. Stuart M. Blumin, *The Emergence of the Middle Class: Social Experience in the American City, 1760–1900* (Cambridge, UK: Cambridge University Press, 1989), 52–58.
13. Olaudah Equiano, *The Interesting Narrative of the Life of Olaudah Equiano. Written By Himself: With Related Documents*, 2nd ed., ed. Robert J. Allison (1789; Boston: Bedford/St. Martin's, 2007), 136.
14. Timothy J. Shannon, "Dressing for Success on the Mohawk Frontier: Hendrick, William Johnson, and Indian Fashion," *William and Mary Quarterly*, 3d ser., 53 (1996): 38.
15. *Boston News-Letter*, August 23, 1750.
16. Jonas Clarke, *The Best Art of Dress: or, Early Piety Most Amiable and Ornamental. A Sermon, Preached at Lexington, to a Religious Society of Young Men, on Lord's-Day Evening Sept. 13. 1761* (Boston: D. and J. Kneeland, 1762), 12.
17. *Boston News-Letter*, August 7, 1760.
18. *Boston Gazette*, September 10, 1764.
19. Adams, *Diary and Autobiography*, Vol. 3, 262.
20. Adams, May 16, 1756, *Diary and Autobiography*, Vol. 1, 27.
21. Benjamin Franklin, *The Autobiography of Benjamin Franklin* (Mineola, NY: Dover, 1996), 45, 28.
22. Michael Kammen, *Colonial New York: A History* (New York: Oxford University Press, 1975), 96.
23. Jonathan Edwards, *Edwards on Revival: Containing a Faithful Narrative of the Surprising Work of God in the Conversion of Many Hundred Souls in Northampton, Massachusetts...* (New York: Dunning & Spalding, 1832), 50, 71.
24. Jonathan Edwards, *The Works of President Edwards* (New York: Leavitt & Allen, 1852), Vol. 4, 314, 317–318, 321.
25. George Whitefield, *The Marriage of Cana. A Sermon Preached at Black-Heath and Philadelphia* (Philadelphia: W. Bradford, 1742), 34, 39–40.
26. George Whitefield, *A Continuation of the Reverend Mr. Whitefield's Journal from a Few Days after his Arrival at Savannah, June the Fourth, to His leaving Stanford, the Last Town in New-England, October 29, 1740* (Philadelphia: B. Franklin, 1741), 63.
27. Franklin, *Autobiography*, 83.
28. Whitefield, *A Continuation of the Reverend Mr. Whitefield's Journal*, 91.
29. Document reproduced in Douglas L. Winiarski, "Souls Filled with Ravishing Transport: Heavenly Visions and the Radical Awakening in New England," *William and Mary Quarterly*, 3d ser., 61 (2004): 43–46.
30. Gilbert Tennent, *The Danger of an Unconverted Ministry* (Philadelphia: B. Franklin, 1740), 3, 9.
31. Tennent, *Danger of an Unconverted Ministry*, 14.
32. Jupiter Hammon, *An Evening Thought. Salvation by Christ, with Penetential Cries: Composed by Jupiter Hammon, a Negro belonging to Mr. Lloyd, of Queen's-Village, on Long-Island, the 25th of December, 1760* (n.p., n.d).

33. Tennent, *Danger of an Unconverted Ministry*, 20, 26–7, 21.
34. *Pennsylvania Gazette*, June 16, 1743.
35. *Pennsylvania Gazette*, August 31, 1749.
36. *New-York Evening Post*, September 4, 1749.

SUGGESTIONS FOR FURTHER READING

Stephen C. Bullock, "A Mumper Among the Gentle: Tom Bell, Colonial Confidence Man," *William and Mary Quarterly*, 3d ser., 55 (1998): 231–258, provides a compelling portrait of Tom Bell and his times. Sharon V. Salinger, *Taverns and Drinking in Early America* (Baltimore: Johns Hopkins University Press, 2002), takes readers inside colonial taverns. Gordon S. Wood, *The Radicalism of the American Revolution* (New York: Knopf, 1992), offers a broad overview of the social structures and ideological assumptions that maintained the hierarchies defining colonial life. Richard Bushman, *The Refinement of America: Person, Houses, Cities* (New York: Vintage, 1992), describes the emergence of "gentility" and its material expressions. John Brooke, *The Heart of the Commonwealth: Society and Political Culture in Worcester, Massachusetts, 1713–1861* (Cambridge, UK: Cambridge University Press, 1989), highlights class formation in a rural setting. On poverty and patronage in urban settings, see William Pencak, "The Social Structure of Revolutionary Boston: Evidence from the Great Fire," *Journal of Interdisciplinary History* 10 (1979): 267–278; and Graham Russell Hodges, *New York City Cartmen, 1667–1750* (New York: New York University Press, 1986). Gary B. Nash, *Urban Crucible*, listed in Chapter 7, offers a broad overview of the urban landscape.

T. H. Breen, *The Marketplace of Revolution: How Consumer Politics Shaped American Independence* (New York: Oxford University Press, 2004), gives a powerful account of the growing role and nature of consumption in the eighteenth century. *Of Consuming Interest: The Style of Life in the Eighteenth Century*, ed. Cary Carson, Ronald Hoffman, and Peter J. Albert (Charlottesville: University Press of Virginia, 1994), collects several important essays and extended discussions of the topic in a single place: most noteworthy are essays by Lois Green Carr and Lorena S. Walsh, Richard L. Bushman, T. H. Breen, and Cary Carson. David S. Shields, *Civil Tongues & Polite Letters in British America* (Chapel Hill: University of North Carolina Press, 1997), provides extended insights into the cultural process of self-fashioning. On Native American self-fashioning, see Timothy J. Shannon, "Dressing for Success on the Mohawk Frontier: Hendrick, William Johnson, and Indian Fashion," *William and Mary Quarterly*, 3d ser., 53 (1996): 13–42.

Ned C. Landsman, *From Colonials to Provincials: American Thought and Culture, 1680–1760* (New York: Twayne, 1997), provides elegant interpretations of many facets of the American Enlightenment. The classic account of the general subject is Henry F. May, *The American Enlightenment* (New York: Oxford University Press, 1976). No single colonist is more closely associated with the Enlightenment than Benjamin Franklin; in addition to the *Autobiography of Benjamin Franklin*, available in many editions, see Gordon S. Wood, *The Americanization of Benjamin Franklin* (New York: Penguin, 2004). For a succinct discussion of another figure embodying the Enlightenment experience, see C. Bradley Thompson, "Young John Adams and the New Philosophical Rationalism," *William and Mary Quarterly*, 3d ser., 55 (1998): 259–280. On the transition to the Gregorian calendar and its implications, see Mark M. Smith, "Culture, Commerce, and Calendar Reform in Colonial America," *William and Mary Quarterly*, 3d ser., 55 (1998): 557–584. Stephen Botein, "'Meer

Mehcanics' and an Open Press: The Business and Political Strategies of Colonial American Printers," *Perspectives in American History* 9 (1975): 125–225, offers valuable information on a group of artisans crucial to spreading print culture. Michael Warner, *The Letters of the Republic: Publication and the Public Sphere in Eighteenth-Century America* (Cambridge, MA: Harvard University Press, 1990), provides a provocative account of the broader implications of that culture.

Frank Lambert draws explicit connections between the Great Awakening, the consumer revolution, and the Enlightenment; his works on the subjects include *"Pedlar in Divinity": George Whitefield and the Transatlantic Revivals, 1737–1770* (Princeton, NJ: Princeton University Press, 1993); *Inventing the "Great Awakening"* (Princeton, NJ: Princeton University Press, 1999); and *The Founding Father and the Place of Religion in America* (Princeton, NJ: Princeton University Press, 2003). Other key studies include: Patricia U. Bonomi, *Under the Cope of Heaven: Religion, Society, and Politics in Colonial America* (New York: Oxford University Press, 1986); Harry Stout, *The Divine Dramatist: George Whitefield and the Rise of Modern Evangelism* (Grand Rapids, MI: Eerdmans, 1991); and Jon Butler, *Awash in a Sea of Faith: Christianizing the American People* (Cambridge, MA: Harvard University Press, 1990). Putting the great Awakening into regional perspective are Gregory H. Nobles, *Divisions Throughout the Whole: Politics and Society in Hampshire County, Massachusetts, 1740–1775* (Cambridge, UK: Cambridge University Press, 1983); and Rhys Isaac, *The Transformation of Virginia, 1740–1790* (Chapel Hill: University of North Carolina Press, 1982). On slave religion and the Great Awakening, see Michael A. Gomez, *Exchanging Our Country Marks: The Transformation of African Identities in the Colonial and Antebellum South* (Chapel Hill: University of North Carolina Press, 1998); and Mechal Sobel, *The World They Made Together: Black and White Values in Eighteenth-Century Virginia* (Princeton, NJ: Princeton University Press, 1987); as well as the works by Philip Morgan and Ira Berlin listed at the end of Chapter 5. Jane T. Merritt, "Dreaming of the Savior's Blood: Moravians and the Indian Great Awakening in Pennsylvania," *William and Mary Quarterly*, 3d ser., 54 (1997): 723–746; and Gregory Evans Dowd, *A Spirited Resistance: The North American Indian Struggle for Unity, 1745–1815* (Baltimore: Johns Hopkins University Press, 1992), analyze Native American religious experience.

CHAPTER 11

Warfare and Empire

An unusual diplomatic embassy from North America visited London in 1762. It consisted of two American soldiers, Ensign Henry Timberlake and Sergeant Thomas Sumter, and three Cherokee Indians, Ostenaco, Cunne Shote, and Syacust Ukah. The group's translator, fur trader William Shorey, had died during their voyage, a misfortune that did not bode well for their venture.

Timberlake and Ostenaco were the leaders of this small party, and in some respects, each had crossed the ocean for the same reason. A native of Hanover County, Virginia, Timberlake was visiting Britain for the first time and hoping that the trip would land him a commission in the British Army. Like many ambitious Virginia gentlemen of his generation, Timberlake saw the British Army as an avenue to patronage and fortune, a way to rise above his provincial origins. As a Virginia militia officer in 1758, he had participated in a British campaign against the French post Fort Duquesne in the Ohio country, where he also encountered Cherokee warriors serving as British allies. Anglo-Cherokee relations soured not long after that, and the two sides waged war against each other for three years. Timberlake played an important role in ending that conflict when he volunteered to travel to the Cherokee Overhill towns (in modern eastern Tennessee) with the preliminary peace terms. He was also serving as a hostage, his presence helping to assure skeptical Cherokees that the British would keep the truce. During the several months he spent among the Cherokees, Timberlake met with many of their leaders and recorded notes about their population and military strength. By risking his neck in enemy country, he was acquiring knowledge and connections that would make him a valuable asset to his superiors back home.

The most important connection Timberlake made during his time in Cherokee country was Ostenaco. About sixty years of age, Ostenaco was an old and influential hand in the Cherokees' diplomacy with their colonial neighbors, but he also had rivals in this regard. Some of his fellow chiefs favored cultivating ties with French traders based in Louisiana, and others preferred dealing with merchants and officials in South Carolina. Ostenaco believed that the Overhill Cherokees would be best served by allying with Virginia. Among his own people, Ostenaco vied for influence with Attakullakulla (also known as Little Carpenter), a chief who favored the South Carolinians. Attakullakulla had visited London with a Cherokee embassy in 1730, where he helped initiate the Cherokees' alliance with the British Crown. Back home, Attakullakulla used his encounter with King George II to impress his countrymen and neighbors, such as when he told the governor of South Carolina in 1756 that he was the only living Cherokee to have met the king in person. Ostenaco may have befriended Timberlake because he saw in the Virginian soldier a chance to acquire that same kind of prestige.

And so, when it was time for Timberlake to leave the Overhill towns, Ostenaco and a party of Cherokees escorted him to Williamsburg. A local gentleman there invited them to dine at the College of William and Mary, where Ostenaco saw a portrait of the British monarch. "Long have I wishes to see the king my father," he told his hosts, "this is his resemblance, but I am determined to see himself; I am now near the sea, and never will depart from it till I have obtained my desires."[1] Knowing the risks and expenses involved in such a trip, the governor of Virginia tried to dissuade him, but Ostenaco prevailed and Timberlake agreed to join him.

Ostenaco and his two Cherokee companions were the latest American travelers to follow in the footsteps of Manteo and Wanchese, the Indians from coastal North Carolina who had visited England in 1584 (see Chapter 2). Back then, Sir Walter Ralegh had hoped that his sponsorship of Manteo and Wanchese would pay dividends for his Roanoke colony. In 1616 John Rolfe had brought Pocahontas and her entourage to London for much the same reason, and nearly a century later, New York colonial officials introduced three Mohawks and one Mahican to Queen Anne as "four Indian kings" from America. In Timberlake's and Ostenaco's lifetimes, Attakullakulla's Cherokee delegation had visited London in 1730, and James Oglethorpe had brought a delegation of Indians from Georgia to London in 1734 to meet the trustees of that recently established colony.

But Timberlake and Ostenaco's party was the first of these diplomatic ventures to occur in almost thirty years, and during that time, much had changed in the way Britain looked at North America and its native inhabitants. For all but six years between 1739 and 1763, Britain was at war with Spain or France, and these conflicts spilled into theaters in the Caribbean and North America. Powerful Indian peoples, such as the Cherokees and Iroquois, figured prominently in the imperial designs of these European powers. Furthermore, war in the colonies had made British officials and the British public much more discerning consumers of information about America in 1762 than they had been in 1730, 1710, or 1616. They knew Indians were important allies and trading partners, but they were also skeptical about the alleged authority of exotic foreigners presented to them as "Indian kings." Timberlake's embassy was fortunate to receive a favorable reception. A sympathetic official arranged for Ostenaco and his companions to meet King George III at St. James's Palace. Despite their lack of an interpreter, the meeting went well. Timberlake conveyed what he could of Ostenaco's speech to the king. As he would have in a diplomatic council back home, Ostenaco prepared his pipe and approached the king to "to smoak with his Majesty, according to the Indian custom of declaring friendship," but Timberlake intervened and convinced the chief to kiss the king's hand instead.[2]

When not negotiating such official business, Timberlake escorted Ostenaco and his companions around London, dining with local dignitaries and visiting such landmarks as St. Paul's Cathedral and the Royal Navy's shipyards. Curiosity-seekers crowded the Indians whenever they attended the city's theaters or other attractions. Artists painted portraits of the Cherokees and printers published engravings of them (see Figure 11.1). Timberlake was at once an instigator of the spectacle surrounding the chiefs—in his memoir, he defended himself from accusations that he was exhibiting the Indians for a profit—and a detractor of it, lamenting that his party was constantly indisposed by the "ungovernable curiosity of the people."[3] Matters came to a head one night at Vauxhall Gardens, an outdoor venue for drinking, dancing, and music. Plied with liquor by the curious onlookers, Ostenaco lost his composure, entered into an altercation with another patron, and had to be removed from the grounds. In the wake of that misadventure, the

Figure 11.1 *The Three Cherokees, came over the head of the River Savanna to London, 1762 /Their interpreter was poisoned* **(London, 1762). This image was one of several prints and ballads published about the Cherokees during Timberlake and Ostenaco's embassy to London. Ostenaco is the middle figure of the three Indians. The shadowy figure on the left is William Shorey, the party's interpreter, who died during their Atlantic crossing. The caption claims he was killed by poisoning, but in his memoirs, Timberlake attributed Shorey's death to an illness he contracted before their departure. Courtesy of Gilcrease Museum, Tulsa, Oklahoma.**

London press turned against the Cherokee embassy, questioning whether Ostenaco was, in fact, a king and comparing him unfavorably to Attakullakulla, who had exhibited much greater decorum during his London visit in 1730. Not long afterward, the Cherokees left for home, while Timberlake remained in London, trying to repair his damaged reputation.

Timberlake and Ostenaco's trip to London may have turned into a fiasco, but it illuminated imperial, provincial, and native perspectives on the British Empire at an important moment in its history. Warfare with France and Spain between 1689 and 1763 brought Britain a vastly expanded dominion in North America, one that stretched from Hudson Bay in the Arctic to the Florida peninsula and westward to the Mississippi River, not to mention increased trade in the Caribbean and undisputed naval supremacy in the Atlantic. During this same period, the colonial population of British North America surged past 1.5 million. Long ignored by Britain's rulers as a dumping ground for religious fanatics, political dissidents, and other undesirables, the American colonies now figured prominently in the future of Britain's designs for global power.

The same forces were bringing the colonial and native inhabitants of America into closer orbit around Great Britain. For most colonists at the turn of the eighteenth century, Europe was a far-off place, perhaps a home left behind and never to be seen again, or the birthplace of an earlier generation. The monarch's name was invoked in courts and churches (at least Anglican ones), but few colonists regularly encountered a living representative of royal authority, whether in the form of a soldier, customs agent, or governor. Likewise, Indians often heard colonial agents call the king a "father" to whom they all owed allegiance and submission, but for all those vague references, he might as well have been the Wizard of Oz.

By the time Timberlake and Ostenaco crossed the Atlantic, all that had changed. Britain's imperial wars with France and Spain brought royal power much closer to colonists and Indians. Royal officials collected data on the colonists' population, trade, and resources for their London superiors, and red-coated soldiers cut roads and built forts in the American wilderness. As evidenced by Timberlake's and Ostenaco's journey to London, the Crown now loomed large in the aspirations and struggles of Americans, whether colonial or native. True to its commercial roots, getting ahead in this empire still required entrepreneurial effort, but now, even in the backcountry of the Appalachian frontier, it was important for private ambition to harness itself to royal favor and protection.

EUROPE'S AMERICAN EMPIRES

For the first two centuries after Columbus, the struggle for a New World empire among European powers had little impact on colonists and Indians living in North America. The Spanish, English, and French engaged in some preemptive and retaliatory raiding against each other's early settlements there, but these were small, sporadic episodes compared to their predatory interactions in the Caribbean, where they fought over access to silver, sugar, and slaves. When North American colonists went to war in the seventeenth century, it was usually with their Indian neighbors or with each other in rebellions against their local rulers. That changed after 1689 when a series of disputed dynastic successions in Europe triggered wars that spread across the Atlantic. Colonists and Indians continued to fight each other during the eighteenth century, but their involvement in conflicts of European origin enmeshed them in a web of international rivalries that transformed the nature of warfare in North America.

When this new wave of imperial wars began in 1689, more than a century had passed since the first colonizers had arrived in eastern North America, and the balance of power among them had shifted considerably. The Spanish established an early foothold in Florida with the founding of St. Augustine in 1565, but their missions among the Apalachee and Timucua Indians had not flourished. By 1700 only about two thousand Spanish subjects lived in Florida, mostly soldiers, traders, slaves, and mission Indians living in or near St. Augustine. Spanish New Mexico was a distant and isolated borderland devastated by the Pueblo Revolt in 1680. In Europe, Spain's power declined throughout the seventeenth century, a victim of its own success abroad. American silver financed Spanish wars in the Netherlands, France, and Italy, but these conflicts left the government saddled with debts and an underdeveloped domestic economy. Such weakness at home prompted Spain's European rivals to cast envious eyes on Spanish colonies abroad. Spain had uncontested control over Peru and Mexico, but the Panamanian isthmus, important for its overland route to the Pacific, and various Caribbean islands were vulnerable to pirates and other opportunists.

The Netherlands was another European state whose power in the North Atlantic had contracted by 1680. During the first half of the seventeenth century, the Dutch built a global maritime empire in the footsteps of the Portuguese, establishing factories in the Indian Ocean, Africa, Brazil, and the Caribbean to trade in spices, slaves, sugar, and tobacco. Although their foothold in North America extended only to a handful of posts along the Delaware, Hudson, and Connecticut rivers, they profited handsomely from the "carrying trade" that ferried colonial exports across the Atlantic to European ports. The English Navigation Acts, which confined colonial trade to English ships with English crews, were aimed at eliminating the Dutch from the carrying trade. The English conquest of New Netherland in 1664 took more direct means to the same end by depriving the Dutch of their only North American colony. Although a great deal of smuggling persisted, Dutch migration to North America effectively ended after 1664.

Unlike the Spanish and the Dutch, the French had seen their influence in North America expand over the course of the seventeenth century, but in fits and starts that never seemed to guarantee their grip on the territory they claimed. From their bases in Montreal and Quebec, French fur traders and missionaries fanned out along the waterways of the interior, making new customers and converts among the Indian peoples of the *pays d'en haut*, a vast region encompassed by the Great Lakes, upper Mississippi Valley, and the Ohio River. At important portages along this network of rivers and lakes, the French built posts where they warehoused goods, arms, and troops. In this manner, the territorial boundaries of New France stretched from the Gulf of the St. Lawrence to the Mississippi, even though its colonial population, concentrated almost entirely in the middle third of the St. Lawrence Valley and the province of Acadia (modern Nova Scotia), barely numbered ten thousand souls (see Map 11.1). French migration to Canada, never large to begin with, ebbed for good after 1680. With its civilian population growth stalled, New France took on the character of a military colony. The French Crown appointed a series of military officers as its governor-general and sent over *troupes de la marine*, soldiers recruited in France for overseas service, to protect it from native and European enemies.

England may have been a late arrival in the scramble for empire, but by 1680 it had emerged as the most significant imperial power in North America. The tobacco boom cemented the English presence in the Chesapeake, and the New

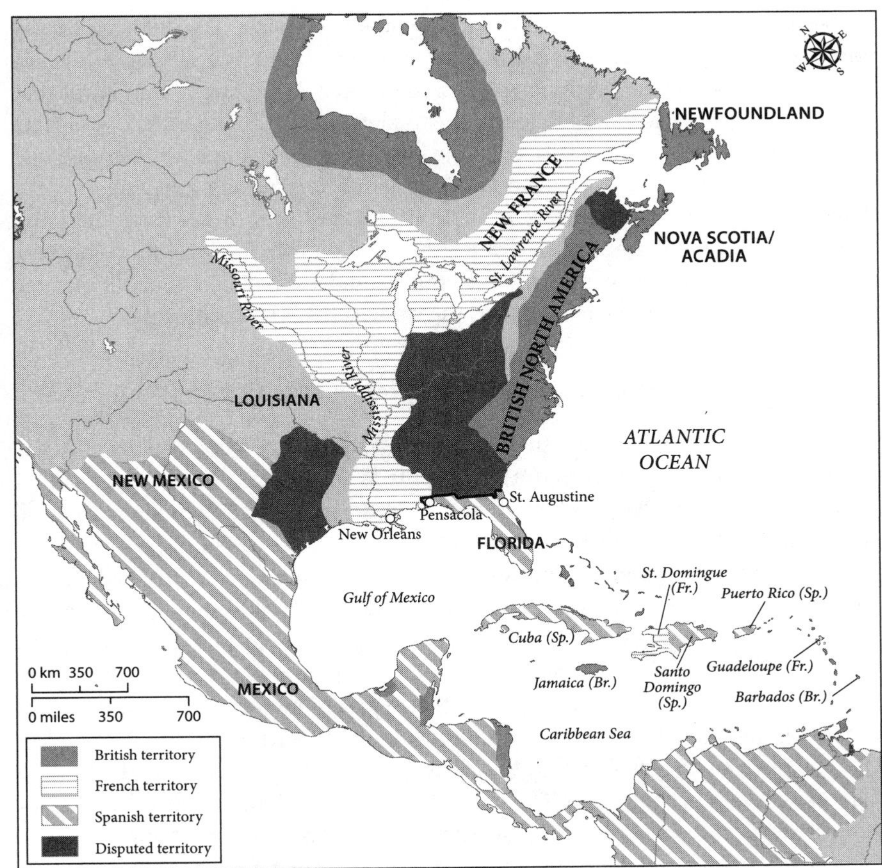

Map 11.1 Europe's American Empires, *c*. 1750.

England colonies prospered slowly if unspectacularly by tapping into the fur trade and North Atlantic fisheries. All this development occurred while England was embroiled in its own domestic troubles, especially during two decades of civil war and political instability that began in 1639. The restoration of the Stuart family to the throne in 1660 marked a new era not only in English politics, but also for the American colonies. By royal grant, Charles II established new proprietary colonies in New York, New Jersey, Pennsylvania, and the Carolinas, connecting the English colonies in North America into a single, contiguous band of settlement. By the turn of the eighteenth century, more than 200,000 English subjects were living in North America, far exceeding the aggregate colonial population of rival European powers there.

Despite these changes, it is important not to overstate North America's place in England's seventeenth-century conception of empire. When policy makers spoke of "empire," they meant trade, not people or territory. In its foreign relations, England advocated *mare liberum*, the freedom of the seas, a legal principle that allowed it to challenge the monopolies other European powers claimed on overseas trade. England's naval power grew after 1660 as it asserted that liberty for its mercantile class on a global scale. North American trade seemed miniscule compared to the profits waiting to be reaped in India, West Africa, the Caribbean, and the Mediterranean, and England expended its military and financial resources accordingly. As late as the 1740s, even the king's most well-informed advisers had only a foggy notion of the territorial boundaries and human geography of the American colonies. England's wars with its European rivals between 1689 and 1748 may be called "imperial" because they spilled over into colonial theaters, but no grand design for expanding the empire guided English strategists in these conflicts beyond their desire to extend the nation's overseas commerce.

THE IMPERIAL CONTEXT IN THE AMERICAS

England's Glorious Revolution in 1688, which chased the Catholic James II off the throne and replaced him with the Protestants William and Mary, had important consequences for the nation's foreign policy. Although they had fought three naval wars with the Netherlands between 1652 and 1674, the English did not object to placing a Dutch ruler and his English wife on their throne. In fact, they had already spent much of the seventeenth century modeling their banking and global trading companies after Dutch precedents and emulating Dutch tastes in painting, architecture, and gardening. The English economy and culture had been so thoroughly permeated by Dutch influences by 1688 that sending out for a Dutch king almost seemed redundant. But William's ascension to the throne embroiled England in the struggle of Europe's Protestant nations against the continent's most powerful Catholic monarch, King Louis XIV of France. When William and Mary's successor (and James's younger Protestant daughter) Queen Anne died without an heir in 1714, Parliament again called on a foreign prince to guarantee the Protestant succession. George I initiated the rule of the House of Hanover in Britain, yoking the nation's foreign affairs to a small German-speaking principality whose political and military fortunes were closely tied to Prussia, Austria, and Russia.

Keeping Britain's royal family Protestant, therefore, came at a price, exacted in a series of continental wars that followed the Glorious Revolution. For the most part, these conflicts originated in dynastic struggles within Europe and ended when the combatants had recalibrated the balance of power there or exhausted themselves trying. These were not "wars for empire" in the sense that they were undertaken specifically to expand dominions overseas, but they were "imperial" in that they involved the Atlantic colonies of these powers. Like pawns on a chess board, distant colonies were a way to strike at an enemy's weakness, to force it to divide and divert its military resources, and to make concessions in peace talks. Warfare in the Atlantic colonies was small and opportunistic compared to that in Europe, relying on the initiative of privateers and military adventurers seeking plunder and royal favor. From the perspective of Europe's royal courts and capital cities, the colonies were a side show, but they also contained resources that could be appropriated or traded away as necessary to pursue objectives closer to home.

The first of these wars was known in Europe as the War of the Grand Alliance (1689–1697). Led by William of Orange, the Grand Alliance united several Protestant powers to check Louis XIV's expansionist designs in the Rhineland, a border region between France and Germany. In North America, the war ignited hostilities between French and English colonists for the first time since a small English expedition from Virginia had attacked Quebec in 1628. King William's War, as it became known among English colonists, featured the kind of fighting that became the hallmark of frontier warfare in North America. War parties of Indians, *troupes de la marine*, and militia from Canada raided the isolated frontier settlements of New York and New England. Blending European and Native American weapons and tactics, these parties moved quickly along interior waterways and paths, often in the dead of winter, to launch surprise attacks on places like Schenectady, New York, and Wells, Maine. They killed civilians, plundered homesteads, slaughtered livestock, fired barns and houses, and took scores of captives, and then retreated home as rapidly as they had appeared. Such irregular methods of warfare, described in European military terms as *la petite guerre*, panicked New Yorkers and New Englanders, who responded by building frontier forts and calling out militia to pursue the enemy, but such efforts drained colonial treasuries without delivering effective deterrents or reprisals.

To counter the French, English colonists raised expeditionary forces to invade Canada by land and sea. On paper, such ideas always looked good. The English colonies had a clear population advantage over Canada, and their militias provided a ready pool of men who could be recruited for such campaigns. Furthermore, winter weather made it difficult for France to resupply Canada for long periods at a time, whereas England's most important American port, New York City, was navigable all year. Ambitious colonial leaders believed that with the proper blending of the colonies' manpower and the mother country's naval resources, the conquest of Canada would be a straightforward affair. Sir William Phips, a native-born New

Englander from humble origins who struck it rich salvaging a sunken Spanish treasure ship, excelled at the entrepreneurial war-making involved in such expeditions. In the spring of 1690, he led an army of seven hundred men in a seaborne attack on Port Royal, the chief French settlement in Acadia. The small French garrison in the town surrendered in the face of Phips's overwhelming numbers, and the victorious New Englanders returned home with loot and prisoners, not even bothering to leave a contingent of their force behind to hold the town.

Flush with his success, Phips orchestrated an intercolonial expedition against Canada a few months later. Funded primarily by New York and Massachusetts, this campaign adopted a land-sea strategy that became the blueprint used in many subsequent invasions of Canada. In New York, colonial adventurers gathered an army at Albany with plans to move northward via Lake Champlain toward Montreal, while a fleet of ships assembled in Boston to carry troops up the St. Lawrence River to Quebec. This time, Phips's good fortune abandoned him. The army in Albany fell victim to mismanagement and smallpox. Phips commanded the flotilla that sailed from Boston, but its late start gave the residents of Quebec plenty of time to prepare their defenses. After an ineffective siege, Phips abandoned the cause and headed home, this time with his ships full of sick soldiers instead of plunder.

Chastened by the loss of life and expense of the 1690 invasion, the English colonists did not mount another intercolonial expedition against Canada for the remainder of the war. The French governor-general, Louis de Buade, comte de Frontenac, continued to sponsor raids along the New England frontier, where the Maine settlements suffered severely at the hands of the Abenaki Indians, but he diverted most of his resources to punitive expeditions against the Iroquois nations who had allied themselves with the Dutch and English. When news of the Treaty of Ryswick arrived in North America in late 1697, it provided welcome relief for all the belligerents after eight years of sporadic but wasting warfare. As was common in European diplomacy of this era, the treaty restored the status quo *ante bellum* by returning wartime conquests and avoiding definitive settlement of contentious issues, such as the proper border between French Acadia and English Maine.

It was not long before another contested dynastic succession renewed war in Europe. After the death of Charles II of Spain in 1700, rival claimants jockeyed for the throne. Louis XIV threw his support behind his grandson, who was crowned Philip V, becoming the first Bourbon king of Spain and setting up the possibility of a joint French-Spanish monarch if Philip were to succeed his grandfather in France. The prospect of such a union between two powerful Catholic kingdoms was too much for Europe's Protestant powers to bear, and so the War of the Spanish Succession ensued (1702–1713). To the English colonists in North America, it was known as Queen Anne's War, named for William and Mary's successor and the last Stuart occupant of the British throne.

Hostilities in Queen Anne's War followed patterns established in King William's War, but this time the scope of the conflict expanded to include the Southern frontier. In 1699 France established the colony of Louisiana at the mouth of the

Mississippi River. French posts in Biloxi, Mobile Bay, and eventually New Orleans gave unwelcome competition to the English deerskin trade in the Southeast and raised the specter of France expanding its influence in the continent's interior. For the colonists of South Carolina, the more immediate threat was Spanish Florida, and the declaration of war in Europe gave them opportunity to act preemptively. South Carolina governor James Moore led an unsuccessful attack on St. Augustine in 1702; the following year, he led a smaller expedition made up mostly of Indian allies against the Apalachee mission communities allied with the Spanish. Moore's soldiers and their Indian allies sold approximately one thousand Apalachee captives into slavery, dealing a fatal blow to the Spanish mission system in Florida.

In the North, hostilities in Queen Anne's War followed the pattern of *la petite guerre*. The frontier towns of Maine, New Hampshire, and Massachusetts suffered disproportionately, in part because the Dutch inhabitants of Albany maintained an unofficial truce with their counterparts in Montreal. Like monasteries in Dark Ages that were raided repeatedly by Vikings, the isolated frontier settlements of New England suffered multiple Indian raids because they provided plenty of loot and captives. In 1709 Samuel Vetch, a Scottish-born colonial adventurer who had settled in New York, convinced Queen Anne's ministers to support an invasion of Canada. Vetch's ambitious plan called for the simultaneous deployment of colonial troops, British regulars, and British warships. Vetch and his partner Colonel Francis Nicholson organized an intercolonial force of several thousand men to again mount the two-pronged assault from Albany and Boston attempted by Phips in 1690. This time, the Crown failed to deliver the troops and ships it had promised, diverting them at the last minute to another theater of operations without any regard for the colonial resources already expended on the campaign.

Undaunted, Nicholson sailed for England to push for a renewal of the plan the following campaign season. The ministry responded positively to a scaled-down version aimed at Port Royal in Acadia. In that objective, Vetch and Nicholson succeeded, and unlike Phips in 1690, they did not merely plunder the town and leave. They renamed it Annapolis Royal after the Queen and garrisoned troops there to keep the local Acadians in line. Nicholson and Vetch raised colonial troops for another Canadian expedition in 1711. The stars seemed to have finally aligned in their favor when a fleet of sixty ships carrying an army of British regulars arrived in Boston. Augmented by colonial recruits, this force sailed for Quebec, but contrary weather and inept piloting impeded its progress until its British commanders decided to sail home.

Although its American engagements had been inconclusive, the peace that ended Queen Anne's War had important ramifications for the colonies. The Treaty of Utrecht (1713) strengthened Britain's hand in the North Atlantic vis-à-vis the French and Spanish. The French gave up their claims to two Caribbean islands, Hudson Bay, Newfoundland, and Acadia (called Nova Scotia by the British), although the precise border between this last province and French Canada remained undefined. To make up for the loss of Port Royal, the French built Louisbourg on Cape Breton Island, a fortress that guarded the approach to the St. Lawrence. By the Treaty of Utrecht, the British also received the *asiento*, a commercial monopoly on the importation of African slaves into Spain's American colonies. In addition, Spain surrendered to Britain two small but strategic islands in the eastern Mediterranean, Gibraltar and Minorca, which became important British naval bases. The Treaty of Utrecht initiated a twenty-six-year peace among the Atlantic powers, which enabled Britain to divert its warships into a decade-long effort to eradicate piracy in the Atlantic and Indian oceans. Its overseas empire may have originated in the piratical raids of Sir Walter Ralegh, Sir Francis Drake, and other Elizabethan sea dogs, but by 1725 the British flag represented the rule of law on the high seas.

British sea power figured prominently in the origins and prosecution of its next imperial conflict, known as the War of Jenkins's Ear (1739–1744). As the name suggests, this one did not start because of a contested succession, but rather what might politely be called involuntary cosmetic surgery. Captain Robert Jenkins commanded a British merchant ship sailing in the Caribbean in 1731. The captain of a Spanish coast guard vessel intercepted Jenkins's ship, accused him of smuggling, and cut off his ear as a warning to the English. Over the next several years, Anglo-Spanish relations deteriorated over similar clashes. At the behest of a pro-war party within the British government, Jenkins testified before Parliament in 1738, displaying his pickled severed ear as evidence of Spanish injustice. Britain declared war against Spain shortly thereafter.

This was officially a war to defend the doctrine of *mare liberum*, but the British also believed that Spain's weakness at home meant easy pickings among its colonial possessions in America. Since acquiring the *asiento* in 1713, Britain's trade in the Spanish Caribbean had expanded legally and illicitly. British buccaneers and colonizers had also ventured onto the Central American mainland, creating bases along the Honduran coast to cut logwood, trade for Indian slaves, and raid Spanish shipping. In North America, the founding of Georgia in 1732 reignited Anglo-Spanish tensions along the Carolina-Florida borderland. To Spain, Britain was the proverbial camel with its nose inside the tent, using the trading privileges granted by the *asiento* to creep its way into Spanish America.

There is no denying the predatory nature of Britain's operations against Spain in the Atlantic. The war began spectacularly when Vice Admiral Edward Vernon, commander of Britain's Caribbean fleet, captured Porto Bello, a city on the Panamanian isthmus that was as strategic to the Pacific trade as Gibraltar was to the Mediterranean. That victory led to plans for a much larger expedition against Cartagena, the Spanish fortress that guarded the Viceroyalty of New Granada (modern Venezuela, Columbia, Ecuador, and Panama). To attack Cartagena, Britain mobilized troops and ships on a scale unprecedented for an overseas operation. At his base in Jamaica, Vernon assembled nearly two hundred ships and more than twenty-five thousand soldiers and sailors. Included in that number were approximately thirty-six hundred men recruited by Virginia governor William Gooch and formed into the American Regiment. After much delay, the expedition got under way in the spring of 1741, only to face a humiliating defeat at the hands of the much smaller Spanish force defending the city. Meanwhile in North America, colonists in Georgia invaded Spanish Florida. In May 1740 Georgia governor James Oglethorpe led a force of about two thousand men against St. Augustine. An ineffective siege lasted for several weeks until Spanish reinforcements from Havana forced the British to withdraw. Oglethorpe turned back a retaliatory Spanish force sent against Savannah in 1742. The following spring, he led another attack on St. Augustine, but the fort proved impregnable without sufficient artillery.

As the War of Jenkins's Ear was being fought to a debilitating stalemate in the Caribbean and Lower South, another dynastic crisis prompted renewed warfare in Europe. The War of the Austrian Succession (1744–1748) once again pitted Britain and France against each other. British colonists called it King George's War. In New England, Massachusetts governor William Shirley organized an ambitious expedition against Louisbourg, the French fortress considered the key to Canada. The British force was composed of about three thousand colonial troops commanded by New Englander William Pepperrell and supported by a British naval squadron commanded by Peter Warren. A Cartagena-style disaster was certainly a possibility, but this time fortune favored the New Englanders. Although poorly trained, they were led by the well-matched Pepperrell and Warren. After a six-week siege, the French surrendered.

It was the single greatest British victory against the French in North America to date. From their pulpits and printing presses, New England clergy preached sermons of thanksgiving heralding the dawn of a new day, when Catholic France could no longer send its merciless Indian savages to terrorize God-fearing British subjects. Pepperrell and Warren feasted on the rewards of victory, taking French ships as prizes and receiving titles and favors from King George II. Denied the opportunity to plunder the town, the rank and file were less pleased. About one-third of those left to garrison the fort succumbed to disease during the winter of 1745–1746. Whether in defeat at Cartagena or victory at Louisbourg, colonial soldiers were learning that deployment in the service of the king was far more likely to produce slow death in a hospital bed than glory and riches on the battlefield.

The Treaty of Aix-la-Chapelle (1748) was more of a truce than a peace. It resolved nothing in the border wars between Britain, France, and Spain in America. British diplomats, however, wounded the pride of the New Englanders by giving Louisbourg back to France. To the disappointed Shirley, it was a reminder of how little attention the king's ministers paid to American affairs. To the clergy who had interpreted the fall of Louisbourg as an act of providential deliverance, its restoration was an abrupt contravention of God's plan to deliver North America from despotism and popery.

The four imperial wars fought in America between 1689 and 1748 yielded very little for their European belligerents. Britain's demographic advantage in North America had not dislodged the Spanish and French from their footholds there. In fact, the Spanish extended their grip on Florida by fortifying Pensacola Bay on the Gulf Coast, while the French established an important new base of operations in Louisiana. Further north, the French also built forts Niagara, Detroit,

Michilimackinac, and de Chartres at key points in the *pays d'en haut*. Warfare in North America experienced its own gradual transformation during these conflicts. Although *la petite guerre* remained the most typical kind of military engagement in North America, imperial wars expanded the geographic and human scale of conflict. The expeditionary forces raised by Phips in 1690, Vetch and Nicholson in 1709 and 1711, Gooch in 1741, and Pepperrell and Warren in 1745 brought thousands of colonial Americans into regular military service for the first time, with concomitant increases in the number of wartime casualties, albeit mostly from disease rather than battle.

Such forces, often raised out of the ranks of colonial militia, also made plain that there was a lagging military professionalism in America when compared to Europe. Even in the case of campaigns that were authorized by European governments, colonial warfare was still little more than adventurism, sponsored and led by elites who lured the rank and file into service with promises of plunder. European troops sent into the American theater, on the other hand, exhibited the hallmarks of eighteenth-century armies: heavily armed and professionally trained, they were the uniformed employees of their monarchs, portable and disposable, inured to the hardship and discipline that was their lot. In the Cartagena expedition, they endured battle, siege, and disease with a fatalism that shocked and impressed their colonial counterparts.

Thus, the scale of military conflict expanded in eighteenth-century America, but not enough to make the colonies anything more than a secondary theater in Europe's diplomacy and warfare. The priorities of monarchs and their ministers could be surmised from what they chose to attack or defend. Resources promised to the colonies were diverted to campaigns on the European continent without a second thought. All European powers considered protecting sugar exports from the Caribbean more important than the fur trade in North America. In peace negotiations, diplomats spent more time discussing fish than people, leaving colonial borders undefined but haggling over access to the fisheries of Newfoundland and the Grand Banks.

THE NATIVE PERSPECTIVE ON IMPERIAL WAR

The wave of imperial conflicts that spilled into America after 1689 did little to alter the methods or reasons that Indians had for making war. During the seventeenth century, Indian warriors had become adept at blending European technology with tactics of ambush and rapid retreat. They continued to go to war for traditional reasons—captives, personal reputation, plunder—but the escalating European rivalry in North America gave them additional opportunities to do so. Every European power tried to recruit Indians as military auxiliaries in their American campaigns, but none was able to compel native allies' service in the same way that they could commandeer the manpower and resources of their colonial subjects. Imperial warfare also altered the geopolitical landscape of native North America by making it possible for some Indian nations to emerge as powerbrokers between

European rivals. As had been the case during the first century of colonization, war with Europeans was not uniformly destructive for native peoples after 1689. Some even managed to prosper through their skillful manipulation of diplomacy and alliance.

Since their earliest arrivals in North America, European colonists had recruited Indians as allies to fight against other Indians, but after 1689 they also recruited Indians to fight other Europeans. The French had the greatest success in this regard, relying heavily on the residents of the *reserves* near Montreal and Quebec to augment the meager number of militia and *troupes de la marine* (anywhere from five hundred to one thousand were in New France at a time) in Canada. In every Anglo-French war after 1689, Indian warriors acting cooperatively with French soldiers and militia attacked New York and New England with devastating regularity. Small raiding parties burned isolated homesteads and settlements, but sometimes larger forces numbering between one hundred and five hundred men attacked towns that were supposedly well defended. These combined Indian and French forces were large enough to storm stockades and fortified houses, but small and light enough to move quickly through snow and difficult terrain because they carried no artillery or supply train. One such force sacked Deerfield, Massachusetts, in 1704 and took more than one hundred captives. In November 1745, Saratoga in the northern Hudson Valley endured a similar raid with similar losses.

The British had less success recruiting Indian allies and adapting their tactics. South Carolinians relied heavily on the Yamasees as allies when they attacked Spanish Florida in 1702 and 1703, but then lost that advantage when they turned on the Yamasees a decade later. During his campaigns against Florida in the 1740s, James Oglethorpe recruited Indians into his small force of regular troops and militia, but they were not enough to tilt the numbers in his favor against the Spanish. The British made their most sustained, and most frustrating, efforts to recruit Indian allies in the Northeast. For the projected invasions of Canada in 1690, 1709, and 1711, they recruited hundreds of Indians from among the Iroquois and the handful of New England praying towns repopulated after King Philip's War. Indians joined these expeditionary forces for the same reason their colonial neighbors did: in hopes of pay and plunder. They also died at a much greater rate, succumbing to smallpox, dysentery, and other diseases associated with military life. Indians serving as British auxiliaries learned quickly to avoid sieges and garrison duty because exposure to "camp fevers" was much deadlier to them than enemy fire.

The question remains, why would Indians choose to join a fight between rival European powers when an advantage might be gained by remaining neutral and letting them prey upon each other? Judging from the hedging responses that Indian leaders often gave to requests for military assistance, such watchful neutrality was, in fact, a strategy. However, the chiefs who led negotiations at treaty conferences could not compel the obedience of younger men who saw war as a means to acquire influence and reputation. Colonial agents enticed Indian warriors by supplying them with weapons, ammunition, and clothing; by promising them unhindered access to captives and plunder; and by paying them bounties for enemy scalps. Although the methods of Indian warfare may have stayed the same, alliance with Europeans created new incentives that challenged the authority of traditional chiefs.

Consider, for example, the changing nature of captivity. Indians still valued children and young women as potential adoptees, but among the Christian Indians of Canada and New England, the torture, execution, and consumption of captive adult males declined. Whether Catholic or Protestant, missionaries condemned ritual torture and cannibalism, and when possible, they interceded to save those marked for death in this manner. On both sides of the Canadian-New England border, colonial governments and private individuals offered ransoms to purchase back captives taken in enemy attacks. As the scale of frontier warfare expanded, so too did the number of Indian captives involved in prisoner exchanges between the French and British. In the summer of 1747, Boston received almost three hundred redeemed captives from Quebec and sent sixty-three back to Canada. The following year, 175 more captives were repatriated to Massachusetts.[4] In some cases, colonial officials may have asked Indian allies to target particular individuals for captivity, hoping to acquire valuable human bargaining chips. Such appears to have been the case with the Deerfield raid in 1704, when the town's most prominent citizen, the Reverend John Williams, was taken captive along with his family.

The balance of power shifted among native peoples along the Southern frontier during the first wave of imperial wars. The colonization of the Lower South in the seventeenth century had profoundly negative consequences for Indians living in coastal and tidewater regions, exposing them to disease and enslavement, but those groups living in the interior found new opportunities. As the Spanish and French extended their presence along the Gulf Coast after 1690, the Indian slave trade and the warfare associated with it intensified. Access to European trade and guns gave some formerly isolated Indian groups new advantages, while others displaced by disease and warfare resettled among other remnant groups and forged new cooperative diplomatic and military relations. These new confederacies became the native powers of the eighteenth-century Southeast.

The Creek confederacy emerged from Muskogean-speaking peoples who lived in the Chattahoochee, Tallapoosa, and Coosa river valleys of western Georgia and modern Alabama. They participated in South Carolina's slave raiding against the Apalachee Indians of Florida, but they cultivated ties with the Spanish and French, too, by trading with the former at their post at Pensacola and the latter at Fort Toulouse, established in the Alabama country in 1717. The Catawbas of the Carolina Piedmont region emerged from several distinct groups of Siouan-speaking Indians living near the confluence of the Catawba River and Sugar Creek. The populous but widely dispersed Cherokee peoples lived in the river valleys of lower Appalachia; their territory stretched from Virginia southward to Georgia and westward into modern Tennessee. They became prominent in colonial Indian relations after 1720 as a result of their role in the deerskin trade. Further west, the

Choctaws were trading partners and allies of the French in the lower Mississippi Valley, but they also cultivated relations with South Carolina traders, who supplied them with a greater variety of goods at lower prices.

A colonial governor in 1670 would not have placed the Creeks, Catawbas, Cherokees, or Choctaws on a map. In the case of the Creeks and Catawbas, these groups did not exist yet as political units; they were a product of human displacement set in motion by the colonization of the Carolinas and Gulf Coast. In the case of the Cherokees and Choctaws, these groups were too far removed from the coast to have much contact with early colonizers. By 1730 trade and imperial competition had changed that. Pack horse trains carrying deerskins, furs, and trade goods traveled hundreds of miles between the interior and coastal towns like Charles Town, Pensacola, Biloxi, and New Orleans. Confederacies like those of the Creeks and Cherokees formed, in part, to help culturally linked but politically autonomous native groups take advantage of their strategic position between rival European traders. As was the case in the Northeast, imperial powers built forts and trading posts in the interior to protect their access to the fur trade, but they remained guests in Indian country, tolerated only so long as they maintained a steady supply of goods at favorable prices.

The native peoples most successful in exploiting their position between rival European powers were the Iroquois nations inhabiting the region south of Lake Ontario. Judging from archaeological evidence and Iroquois oral tradition, the Iroquois League most likely originated before European contact, as a means of ending endemic war among five contiguous Iroquoian-speaking peoples: the Mohawks, Oneidas, Onondagas, Cayugas, and Senecas. During the early seventeenth century, Dutch and French colonizers brought the fur trade and its attendant diseases to the Five Nations. Though battered by smallpox and wars with French-allied Indians, the Iroquois managed to survive, in part because they controlled access to the Mohawk and Niagara rivers, important water routes by which furs from the *pays d'en haut* reached Atlantic ports. Their confederacy also survived, despite the migration of many Iroquois converted to Christianity by French Jesuits to the *reserves* around Montreal and Quebec.

In 1701 representatives from the Five Nations attended a treaty conference in Montreal that drew a total of thirteen hundred Indians from the St. Lawrence-Great Lakes region. Canada's governor-general Louis-Hector de Callière hoped to establish a peace between the Iroquois and their native enemies in Canada. After extensive negotiations over the return of captives, all parties finally came to terms. Meanwhile, in Albany, another Iroquois delegation negotiated with New York governor John Nanfan. The New Yorkers liked to think that the Iroquois owed an exclusive allegiance to the British. Yet, they were powerless to enforce such a policy, and their anemic military efforts against the French during King William's War convinced many Iroquois that an exclusive alliance with the British was the wrong bet to make. What they offered Nanfan instead was a cession that placed their western hunting grounds under the British Crown's protection. The boundaries of this territory were ill defined, but it included the Iroquois claims to a substantial portion of the *pays d'en haut* around the upper Great Lakes and Michigan peninsula, in essence, the same territory that Callière was trying to open to French trade with his negotiations in Montreal.

The deft diplomatic maneuvering of the Iroquois in 1701 has become known as the "Grand Settlement" because it initiated an era of Iroquois neutrality between the French and British that lasted for more than fifty years. It ended years of debilitating warfare with the French for the Iroquois and transferred the task of defending their territorial claims to the British. In the wake of the Grand Settlement, the Iroquois confederacy expanded to engage even more native and colonial partners in an alliance known as the Covenant Chain, which extended outward from the Five Nations in all directions. Britain made the Covenant Chain a foundation for its imperial pretensions in North America, claiming the Iroquois as British subjects. Such claims held little meaning to the Iroquois themselves, who still expected to be courted as allies. In 1710 Colonel Francis Nicholson, an English military officer and former governor of New York and Virginia, arranged for four Indians from the Albany region to visit London. The London public and press were impressed by these exotic strangers, styling them the "four Indian kings" of America, but in reality they were three Mohawks and one Mahican distinguished mostly for their willingness to undertake such a risky voyage. Nevertheless, their visit convinced the Crown to sponsor a missionary in Mohawk country and initiated a diplomatic relationship that has endured to this day.

Under the aegis of neutrality, the Iroquois continued to strengthen their diplomatic bond with the French. After the French established a fort at Niagara in 1720 to guard the portage between Lakes Ontario and Erie, the Senecas and Cayugas became important brokers in the western fur trade. Back in the St. Lawrence Valley, kinship ties between the Mohawks living on the Kahnawake *reserve* near Montreal and those still in the Mohawk Valley shaped relations between Montreal and Albany. Despite prohibitions against trading across the Canadian border issued by colonial authorities on both sides, the movement of Indian peoples between the Mohawk Valley and Kahnawake facilitated exchanges in gifts, goods, and captives. Compared to the continuing warfare between New Englanders and French-allied Abenakis, Indians and colonists living along the Hudson-Mohawk frontier enjoyed relative peace thanks to their hold on the Covenant Chain.

The Iroquois also extended their diplomacy southward after 1701 along the mid-Atlantic frontier. The Susquehanna River, which has its headwaters in Iroquois country and empties into the Chesapeake Bay, was a north-south highway of diplomacy and trade that the Iroquois dominated not by military force but by artful alliance with colonial governments and native peoples. After 1690 Indian peoples displaced from the Chesapeake and Delaware regions established new homelands in the Susquehanna Valley. Indian communities such as Conestoga, Conoy Indian Town, and Shamokin were polyglot settlements containing Delawares, Shawnees, Tuscaroras, Susquehannocks, Senecas, Tutelos, Nanticokes, Conoys, and others. The Iroquois absorbed them as "props" into their confederacy and oversaw their relations with colonial governments at treaty conferences.

This peaceful extension of Iroquois power peaked at a treaty conference convened in Lancaster, Pennsylvania, in 1744. Delegations from Pennsylvania, Maryland, and Virginia showered the Iroquois with presents and cash to settle trading disputes and secure land cessions in the Shenandoah, Potomac, and Ohio valleys. This treaty was also something of a diplomatic fiction: the Iroquois sold land they did not occupy to colonial agents who were well aware that Iroquois claims to the territory were questionable. Such shady deals would come back to haunt all parties involved, but the fact that the Iroquois could make them was testimony to how well they had used their strategic position between colonial powers to their advantage.

The rise of Iroquois power paralleled that of the Cherokees, Catawbas, Creeks, and Choctaws. Whether in the North or South, Indian peoples who formed confederacies were at a distinct advantage over those who did not. Although it was rare for an Indian confederacy to speak with single voice—power in Indian communities was too widely dispersed to accommodate such authority—nations that joined together for the purpose of dealing with outsiders projected power and solidarity that impressed their European counterparts. In a 1751 letter to a New York correspondent, Benjamin Franklin grudgingly complimented the Iroquois for exhibiting exactly the kind of union that the colonies lacked: "It would be a very strange Thing, if six Nations of ignorant Savages should be capable of forming a Scheme for such an Union, and be able to execute it in such a Manner, as that it has subsisted Ages, and appears indissoluble; and yet that a like Union should be impracticable for ten or a Dozen English Colonies."[5] When Iroquois and Cherokee delegations traveled to London, working in cahoots with colonial adventurers to impress British kings and queens, they projected this same power overseas, convincing ministers of state that imperial designs in North America rested on currying their favor. The credentials of such "Indian kings" may have been suspect, but illusory power was better than no power at all.

THE COLONIAL PERSPECTIVE ON IMPERIAL WAR

The imperial wars pulled colonial Americans closer into European affairs, but they did not disrupt colonial society with long-term military mobilizations. For most colonial Americans, the wars of 1689 to 1748 presented little in the way of direct threats to their persons or property. The exception, of course, was those colonists living in the borderlands of the Northeast and Southeast, where *la petite guerre* exposed them to chronic insecurity and occasion bursts of murderous violence. As was the case with Native Americans, it is hard to describe a single colonial perspective on the imperial wars because so much depended on time and place. Nevertheless, the imperial wars did generate some common experiences that made colonial Americans more aware of their connections to each other and the European empires to which they supposedly belonged.

The British expected their colonists to protect themselves rather than rely on professional soldiers sent from home. The British answer to the *troupes de la marine* in Canada was a small number of regular troops posted in New York and South Carolina. The four independent companies in New York arrived not long after the Dutch conquest. They numbered about two hundred men when at full strength and were distributed over a handful of posts that by the 1730s stretched from Manhattan to Lake Ontario. Too few to protect New York's border with Canada, their chief function seems to have been providing the New York governor with an appropriate retinue whenever he traveled to Albany to negotiate with the Iroquois. The three independent companies stationed in South Carolina were likewise too small in number to do much more than stare back at the Spanish troops stationed at St. Augustine in Florida.

Instead of uniformed soldiers in the pay of the king, the colonists depended on militias for their security. The colonial militias had their origins in the "trained bands" that provided domestic security in Elizabethan England. Every colony except Pennsylvania, founded by Quaker pacifists, had one. All able-bodied, property-holding adult white males were expected to serve; slaves, servants, transients, and free people of color were excluded. In peacetime, militia duty was more social than burdensome, usually involving training musters four to six times a year. In regions with significant slave populations, militias also provided the first line of defense against slave rebellions.

By their nature, militias were local and defensive. When colonial governments needed to recruit soldiers for the kinds of intercolonial military campaigns launched during the imperial wars, they offered bounties and other incentives to encourage short-term volunteer enlistments. Men with rudimentary militia training often joined such expeditionary forces, but their ranks were also filled by others typically excluded from the militia because of their unfree, propertyless status: slaves and servants, free blacks, Indians living in or near colonial populations, and the poor. If necessary, colonial governments filled their levies for an expeditionary force by conscripting "strollers," rootless transients with no discernible means of supporting themselves. Colonial military service, in other words, reflected the divide between middling-rank citizens, whose presence in the militia testified to their stake in society, and the lower sort, whose social and economic vulnerability brought them into expeditionary forces.

For most colonial Americans who served in arms during the imperial wars, fighting was not a professional occupation or a duty compelled by king or country. Instead, it was a voluntary interruption of their civilian life, undertaken with a concrete, short-term objective. The poor enlisted in expeditionary forces because they offered pay and provisions for the duration of their service. Runaway slaves and servants did the same because such service carried them quickly away from their pursuers. Even a young man from middling background might enlist out of a desire to leave home temporarily or to turn a cash enlistment bounty into a down payment on a farm or business. Everyone from commanding officers to the rank and file eyed plunder, whether at land or sea. Privateers engaged in licensed piracy, seizing enemy ships as prizes and distributing their dividends through a shares system. Soldiers also expected to have a free hand in looting conquered civilians, but this privilege could be denied by their commanding officers when they negotiated surrender with the enemy. Such terms were not extended to native populations, and colonial troops took Indian men, women, and children captive to sell as slaves or killed them for the bounties placed on their scalps by colonial governments.

Despite such incentives, military service was an uncertain path to material reward. Well-fortified cities like Cartagena and Quebec did not fall easily. Whether in the frigid North or tropical South, new climates and camp life meant exposure to new diseases. Casualty rates from disease could be astronomical. Only six hundred of the thirty-six hundred colonial Americans who shipped out of Virginia for the Cartagena expedition returned home, their compatriots carried away by yellow fever, dysentery, and other maladies. For British regulars, such mortality was an unfortunate but unavoidable fact of military life. The army compensated for it by recruiting in Ireland and the Scottish Highlands, where poverty made military service more attractive. In this manner, the empire expanded abroad on the backs of its most desperate people at home.

The same might be said of the colonists who served in the Cartagena campaign, but free colonial Americans enjoyed better prospects for improving their lot in life than poor Irish and Scots. They were much more likely to resist military service if it did not suit their expectations. Colonial soldiers deserted individually and en masse when they felt abused by their officers or that the terms of their enlistment had been violated. No American sailor would voluntarily serve on a British naval vessel when he could go to sea as a privateer. To most colonial Americans, the British Empire was a fine idea, so long as it did not involve any undue suffering or unrewarded risk on their part.

The costs and benefits of the imperial wars fell unevenly among colonial civilians. In colonial cities, the armies raised for expeditionary forces needed to be fed and clothed, creating economic opportunity for the mercantile class. The patriotic fervor exhibited by colonial elites during the campaigns against Cartagena in 1741 and Louisbourg in 1745 meshed easily with the self-interested pursuit of military contracts and commissions among colonial elites. On the other hand, residents of poorly defended frontier towns bore almost entirely the civilian casualties of these conflicts. The physical and psychic toll of *la petite guerre* was described in the multiple captivity narratives published in New England between 1676 and 1724. Best sellers of their day, these works were noteworthy for the voice they gave to women and families swept into the violence of war.

True to their Puritan roots, colonial New Englanders interpreted captivity as a spiritual as well as physical trial, inflicted on them by a loving but inscrutable God. In such narratives, "redemption" had a dual significance. It meant the captive's escape or ransom from bondage, but also the spiritual renewal that came from surviving such a test of faith. A representative example of the captivity genre from this era was the Reverend John Williams's *The Redeemed Captive, Returning to Zion*, published in 1707. It related the story of the Deerfield raid in 1704 and the trials of Williams's family and congregants in Canada. The Indians may have wielded tomahawks, but to Williams the greatest threat came from the French Jesuits ("Romish ravenous wolves") who pressed relentlessly on his captive flock to convert to Catholicism.[6] Although his daughter Eunice was adopted by an Indian family in Kahnawake and remained there the rest of her life, Williams expressed his greatest concern for his son Samuel, who temporarily renounced his Protestant faith while living under the tutelage of a Montreal schoolmaster.

The captivity tales told by Williams and others had an enduring impact on New England's regional identity. Captivity narratives made the violence that was visited so suddenly on these frontier towns comprehensible by interpreting it as part of God's providential design. From the perspective of London or Paris, the Canadian borderland was an insignificant theater of the imperial wars, but to New Englanders, it was the focus of God's attention. By remaining faithful to their covenant with God during their time of trial, these New England captives were keeping the forces of savagery and popery at bay in their new Jerusalem.

Not all colonists shared the New Englanders' providential outlook, but in ways subtle and obvious, the imperial wars spurred them to think about their place in the wider world. Attempts to foster intercolonial cooperation in military and Indian affairs were one example of this impulse. A newfound love for the British monarchy was another. Although the first two Hanoverian kings—George I and George II—were German-speaking strangers to their British subjects, colonial Americans celebrated them as benevolent, albeit distant, rulers. They toasted the king's health on public holidays and celebrated the royal family's birthdays and anniversaries. They printed the king's image on almanacs, cast it onto medals, and hung royal portraits in public buildings (remember, it was one such portrait that prompted Ostenaco's trip to London in 1762). All these public expressions of loyalty served an important purpose. In a land as ethnically and religiously diverse as British America, they reminded the colonists that they shared a common bond as subjects of the same crown.

Professions of love and loyalty to the king also asserted Americans' place within the empire. By venerating the monarchy, colonists reminded themselves and anyone else who would listen that they were entitled to a full and equal share in the liberties of their fellow subjects in the British Isles. By taking up arms against the king's enemies, they likewise claimed the right to partake in the fruits of imperial power. One of the earliest expressions of this growing American pride of place came from Benjamin Franklin. In his 1751 essay "Observations Concerning the Increase of Mankind," Franklin estimated that there were one million British subjects in North America, and that they were doubling in number every twenty-five years. By applying their industry to the natural bounty of the land, they were turning the colonies into a storehouse of resources for Britain, but even more importantly, they were creating an enormous export market for its manufactures. Franklin predicted that in another century, "The greatest Number of Englishmen will be on this Side the Water. What an Accession of Power to the British Empire by Sea as well as Land! What Increase of Trade and Navigation! What Numbers of Ships and Seamen!"[7] Such drum-beating was not unfounded. The value of British exports to America tripled during the first half of the eighteenth century. Most of Franklin's contemporaries in Britain still thought of the colonies as places to take things from—furs, fish, tobacco—but Franklin realized that they had become even more important for what they took in: sugar, tea, textiles, china, and a host of other goods.

A colonial soldier retching in the hull of a transport ship or an Indian captive trudging through February snows toward Montreal probably did not share Franklin's enthusiasm for empire. For colonial Americans of all stripes, life in the British Empire could be cruel and capricious, but the imperial wars also tied people to that empire in ways that could be deeply and sometimes surprisingly intimate. Virginian military officer Lawrence Washington returned from the Cartagena expedition in broken health, but he still thought highly enough of the British commander of that fiasco to name his estate on the Potomac River after him. When Lawrence died several years later, his younger half-brother George Washington inherited Mount Vernon. Susannah Johnson was taken captive by Abenaki Indians in New Hampshire and spent several years living among them. On the second day of her captivity, she gave birth to her third daughter. Mother and newborn slowed the raiding party as it headed north, but the lives of both were protected by Johnson's Indian master, who exhibited remarkable kindness to her along the way. Johnson named her baby girl Captive. Since their arrival on American shores, colonists had been naming things as a way of taking possession of them and rendering their new experiences intelligible. Lawrence Washington and Susannah Johnson used the same technique to make sense of their experiences in the imperial wars.

THE SEVEN YEARS' WAR IN NORTH AMERICA

Historians often describe the Seven Years' War (1756–1763) as the last of the imperial wars in North America, but placing it in that category can be problematic. In its origins and scale, it was a breed apart from those earlier conflicts. It did not begin because of a contested dynastic succession in Europe. Rather, hostilities broke out in a remote part of North America and continued for almost two years before a formal declaration of war in Europe. Although more commonly known today as the French and Indian War, some historians have called it the first world war because it involved a global deployment of resources to theaters of operations in the Caribbean, Africa, India, and the Philippines as well as Europe and North America. North American colonists experienced an unprecedented scale of mobilization that disrupted civilian life, challenged the autonomy of local elites, and reinvigorated royal power in their governments. When peace returned in 1763, the map of North America had been permanently reconfigured, and its native and colonial populations affected in ways no one could have anticipated when it began.

The War of the Austrian Succession ended in 1748 with little settled in regard to the Anglo-French rivalry in North America. With the ink barely dry on the

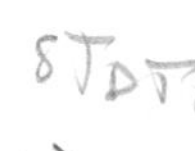

peace treaty, the French and British turned their attention to the region known as the Forks of the Ohio, where the Allegheny and Monongahela rivers meet to form the Ohio (modern Pittsburgh, Pennsylvania). The French eyed this region because the Ohio River offered a natural corridor for linking Canada and Louisiana. The latter colony's population numbered only a few thousand in 1748, but its temperate climate and access to the Caribbean promised to draw more French settlers to America than could be enticed to Quebec. If supplied more regularly by way of Louisiana, the French fur trade could also flourish in the Ohio country.

Fur traders in Pennsylvania had the same idea. Loaded with cheaper goods than their French competitors, they made their way into the Ohio country during the 1740s, where they built storehouses and established diplomatic ties with the local Indians. Traders from Virginia arrived, too, but they were also working as agents for the Ohio Company, a land-speculating venture launched by some of Virginia's most prominent planters and officeholders. Virginia claimed the Ohio country by right of its seventeenth-century "sea-to-sea" charter and its land purchase from the Iroquois at the Lancaster Treaty of 1744. Other than its shareholders, not many colonists supported the Ohio Company's plans, but neither did anyone in British North America wish to see the French in possession of the region.

The Ohio country's native inhabitants were stuck in the middle of these contending interests. During the 1720s and 1730s, many Indians dispossessed by war and colonization elsewhere had moved into the Ohio region, where they settled into multiethnic towns. From the north, Senecas migrated down the Allegheny River in search of better hunting to supply French traders at Fort Niagara. They mixed with Shawnees and Delawares from eastern Pennsylvania, as well as Miamis from further west in the Ohio Valley. Colonial traders and agents referred to these groups collectively as the Ohio Indians, describing them as a populous but fractious lot whose loyalties were as broadly dispersed as their population. The one point that the Ohio Indians agreed on was that the land was their own, and that no European power had the right to plant fortifications, soldiers, or settlers there without their consent.

The French uncharacteristically turned a deaf ear to such opinions. In 1749 the governor-general of Canada sent a military expedition into the Ohio country, where it buried lead plates asserting the French claim to the region. Captain Pierre-Joseph Céloron de Blainville expelled the British fur traders he met along his march, upsetting their native customers. Not surprisingly, when Céloron convened treaty councils with the local Indians, he found them unwelcoming and uncowed by his soldiers. Despite Céloron's cool reception, the French returned to the region in 1753 to build a string of forts along the passage from Lake Erie to the Allegheny River.

On learning of this, Virginia governor Robert Dinwiddie sent twenty-one-year-old militia officer George Washington to tell the French that they were trespassing on British territory. Dinwiddie and Washington were investors in the Ohio Company, which was about to build its own storehouse at the Forks of the Ohio, and so more than British patriotism inspired their confrontation with the French. Washington undertook a long journey in late 1753 to two French forts on the Allegheny River; in each case, the commanding officer received him civilly but made no effort to comply with Dinwiddie's order to withdraw. Washington then trudged home through winter snow and ice, the climate made even chillier by Indians exhibiting French inclinations. The entire episode calls to mind the hapless knights of *Monty Python and the Holy Grail*, marching up to French castles and making extravagant demands, backed by nothing more than coconut shells and a misguided conviction in the righteousness of their mission.

After hearing Washington's report, Dinwiddie resolved to do it right the next time. With approval from Virginia's House of Burgesses, he raised a force of two hundred militia troops, who marched under Washington's command back to the Ohio country in the spring of 1754. Workmen employed by the Ohio Company had already started building a storehouse at the Forks of the Ohio, but they were sent packing by a larger French force, which immediately started constructing a post they named Fort Duquesne. Washington decided to set up camp at Great Meadows, about sixty miles southeast of the French, a safe enough distance for scouting out his prospects against them.

In the early morning hours of May 28, a skirmish forced Washington's hand. Receiving word from his Indian scouts that a small French party was encamped in a nearby glen, Washington led a contingent of his troops in a surprise raid. In the exchange of fire, the French commander Ensign Joseph Coulon de Jumonville was wounded. He protested to Washington that the French mission was diplomatic, not hostile, but the conversation was cut short by Tanaghrisson, a prominent Ohio Seneca who buried his tomahawk in Jumonville's skull. Badly shaken by the affair, Washington put his troops to work at Great Meadows building a stockade that he christened Fort Necessity, a singular example of truth-in-advertising for eighteenth-century military nomenclature.

Jumonville's brother Sieur Coulon de Villiers commanded a detachment of several hundred soldiers and Indians from Fort Duquesne that marched on Washington's position. Pouring rain trapped Washington's men in their trenches while the French force used the cover of trees to keep them under a steady fire. At night, the militiamen inside Fort Necessity commandeered its rum supply, drinking themselves into a stupor in anticipation of being killed and scalped the next morning. Under a flag of truce, Washington signed articles of capitulation he could not read because they were in French, unwittingly admitting his responsibility for what the document called the assassination of Jumonville. The next day, July 4, he surrendered the post and marched his men back to Virginia, leaving the French in possession of the Forks of the Ohio.

The fiasco at Great Meadows made apparent what many colonial leaders already suspected: although the British colonies enjoyed population and resources far superior to those of New France, they were ill prepared to meet the challenge presented by the French supremacy in Indian relations and military organization. In a May 1754 edition of the *Pennsylvania Gazette*, Benjamin Franklin published his famous "Join, or Die" cartoon of a snake cut into several pieces, each representing a colony or group of colonies from Massachusetts to South Carolina. Although generations of Americans ever since have interpreted the "Join, or Die" cartoon as an early expression of American union, Franklin intended it to represent "the present disunited State of the British Colonies" in contrast to the French, who were "under one Direction, with one Council, and one Purse."[8]

A month later, Franklin traveled to Albany to attend an intercolonial treaty ordered by the British Crown to renew the Covenant Chain alliance with the Iroquois. Along with some likeminded delegates from New England, he seized the opportunity to draft a plan of union for the colonies that would place their military and Indian affairs under the management of an intercolonial assembly and royally appointed governor-general. Neither the colonial assemblies nor the British ministry endorsed the Albany Plan of Union, and it died a death mourned by no one except Franklin, who many years later wrote that it had offered a middle way in Anglo-American relations that might have forestalled the American Revolution.

In London, the king's ministers decided that British military intervention would deal with the French more effectively than a political union of the colonies. The king's prime minister, Thomas Pelham-Holmes, the duke of Newcastle, was concerned about the financial and political costs of another war with France, but neither did he want the French occupation of the Ohio country to go unanswered. On the advice of the nation's leading military figure, the duke of Cumberland, Newcastle ordered General Edward Braddock to take two regiments of regulars to America to accomplish what Dinwiddie and Washington had failed to do. Braddock arrived in Virginia in early 1755 and immediately began acting on the powers granted to him as commander in chief of British forces in North America. He recruited colonists to fill out the ranks of his two regiments and requisitioned provisions, horses, and wagons from the colonial governments. George Washington, anxious to redeem his reputation and to secure a powerful patron, volunteered to serve as Braddock's aide-de-camp.

Working in concert with Massachusetts governor William Shirley and New York Indian agent William Johnson, Braddock set in motion an ambitious campaign plan. He would march his army from Fort Cumberland on the Potomac River (modern Cumberland, Maryland) to the Forks of the Ohio, cutting a road wide enough for his artillery and supply train along the way. In the meantime, Shirley would collect an army of provincial troops at Fort Oswego on Lake Ontario for a projected attack on the French at Fort Niagara. Johnson would simultaneously lead another provincial army northward from Albany to take Fort St. Frédéric on Lake Champlain. In each of these instances, the British claimed to be acting defensively, seeking only to remove the French from territory that rightfully belonged to them. If successful, these coordinated attacks would not only push the French out of the Ohio country, but also cut off their access to the upper Great Lakes and push them all the way back into the St. Lawrence Valley.

Things seldom go as planned. Braddock's troops made painstaking progress over the steep mountains and hills of southwestern Pennsylvania, and the general won no support from the Ohio Indians when he refused to acknowledge their right to the contested territory. In late June, Braddock decided to speed his progress by moving half his army forward ahead of the slower-moving supply train. Two weeks later, this detachment had reached within ten miles of Fort Duquesne. After crossing the Monongahela River on July 9, it ran unexpectedly into a detachment sent out from the fort to determine the whereabouts of the British. In the confusion that followed, Braddock's force almost broke through the French line, but several hundred Indians seized the high ground and from the cover provided by brush and trees poured a withering fire into the British ranks. Confused and paralyzed, Braddock's army disintegrated. Approximately three-quarters of its officers were killed, leaving the survivors panicked and rudderless. Braddock himself was mortally wounded and died a few days later. Washington survived, despite finding bullet holes in his clothing.

The defeat was the most costly for British arms in North America to that date. It shocked the British so much that Braddock's second-in-command Colonel Thomas Dunbar made haste for Fort Cumberland, abandoning precious supplies and wagons along the way. His ignoble retreat confirmed the doubts the Ohio Indians had about the fighting spirit of the British and left the entire mid-Atlantic frontier exposed to attack.

The results of Shirley's and Johnson's expeditions in New York were only marginally better. Shirley had difficulty recruiting Indian allies and was therefore reluctant to move against Fort Niagara. Instead, he spent the 1755 campaign season building new fortifications at Oswego, the British fur-trading terminus on Lake Ontario. Johnson, who had lived in the Mohawk Valley since 1739 and forged commercial and familial ties with the natives there, drew away from Shirley any Indians willing to ally with the British. Many Mohawk warriors, led by the well-known chief Hendrick, joined Johnson's forces. Like Shirley, Johnson was a prominent officeholder but not a military man by training. He faced difficulties with desertion and insubordination among the colonial soldiers he commanded, especially after putting them to work building two forts to guard the portage between Lake George and the northern reaches of the Hudson River. Baron Dieskau, a German officer commanding French troops at Fort St. Frédéric on Lake Champlain, seized the opportunity to strike at Johnson first.

On September 8, 1755, his combined French and Indian force successfully ambushed an advance party from Johnson's camp but then pressed their advantage too far with a frontal assault on the rest of Johnson's army. Casualties on both sides were about equal, and both Dieskau and Johnson were wounded in the second engagement, but the French withdrew from the field first, allowing the British to claim the battle of Lake George as a victory. It was a costly one. Johnson's Mohawk allies had been at the head of the advance party and suffered heavy losses, including Hendrick. Disgruntled and shaken, the surviving Mohawks left for home and three years passed before a substantial number of Iroquois again accompanied the British into battle. Rather than press northward against Fort St. Frédéric as originally planned, Johnson decided to spend the rest of the season completing his fortifications on Lake George.

The British ministry's hope that it could find a quick answer to its troubles in the Ohio country died with Edward Braddock. Although a formal declaration of war would not come for several more months, by the end of 1755 it was clear that meeting the French threat would require far more military muscle than Britain had previously devoted to North America. Transporting armies large enough to lay siege to French posts in the interior would require cutting roads, building watercraft, and engaging in a new scale of military engineering in British North America. British regulars were well trained but lacked experience with *la petite guerre*; colonial soldiers were numerous but lacked discipline and effective leadership. Indians in the Ohio country and New York either defected to the French or remained neutral. Britain had enormous resources at its fingertips in America, but its institutions of colonial government were too fractured and weak to harness them.

In early 1756, King George II appointed the Scottish peer John Campbell, the earl of Loudoun, his new commander in chief for North America. Loudoun was a professional soldier used to having his orders obeyed. On arriving in America in July 1756, he clashed immediately with the colonial assemblies, who were accustomed to negotiating military matters with royal governors. Since the early seventeenth century, assemblies appropriated the funds that paid for fortifications, enlistment bounties, and soldiers' wages and provisions. In return, they expected to have a say in how royal governors deployed militia and provincial troops. When told by Loudoun to provide soldiers, money, and supplies for the British war effort, the assemblies attached strings to their appropriations, stipulating where and for what length of time their troops might serve. In light of such intransigency, Loudoun and his successors preferred to fight with British regulars whenever possible. Although suspect of provincial forces, they did recruit colonists into a new regiment of the regular army, the Royal Americans. Impressed by the exploits of Robert Rogers, a New Hampshire scout operating along the Lake Champlain borderland, they also formed independent companies of American Rangers, who were expected to scout and harass the enemy by employing the tactics of wilderness warfare.

Loudoun's difficulties with the assemblies were just one symptom of a wider clash in military cultures between the colonists and the British. For the first time, a significant number of colonists—mostly soldiers, but also civilian officeholders and merchants—were coming into direct contact with representatives of royal authority. Loudoun and his fellow army officers expected the Americans, soldiers and civilians alike, to support the British war effort unquestioningly. This assumption informed Loudoun's order that American officers in militia or provincial forces regardless of their rank or seniority were to be considered subordinate to any British officer at the rank of major or higher. Many colonial elites, such George Washington, who held military commissions from colonial governments, bristled at this insult to their rank and experience.

Nor did colonists at the other end of the social spectrum behave as Loudoun expected. Discipline and insubordination were major problems in provincial forces. Colonial soldiers went home when their enlistments expired, regardless of orders from their British commanders to stay put until relieved of duty. They regarded poor rations, hard labor, and corporal discipline as legitimate reasons for ending their service early. When faced with the kind of battle practiced by professional European armies—prolonged sieges that exposed them to artillery barrages and frontal assaults on entrenched positions—they failed to match the lockstep precision and steely resolve exhibited by the redcoats. One New England private summed up the colonists' opinion of this new kind of warfare when he wrote in his memoir, "[It] greatly surprised me, to think that I must stand still to be shot at."[9] New England soldiers also expressed shock at what they perceived to be the moral laxity of British regulars, who regarded drinking, cursing, and whoring as matters of professional pride. Long accustomed to interpreting warfare as a providential opportunity for moral and collective reformation, New Englanders took their ministers with them when they embarked on military expeditions. In contrast, Lord Loudoun and many other British officers prepared for their American service by taking their mistresses with them.

With Loudoun immobilized by the assemblies, the French seized the offensive. The French commander in chief Louis-Joseph, marquis de Montcalm, arrived in Canada in the spring of 1756 with more than one thousand troops to augment the *troupes de la marine* and Canadian militia. A few months later he took Oswego, which Shirley had invested so much time, money, and men in fortifying the previous year. Coming on the heels of Braddock's defeat, it was another heavy blow to British-Indian relations and frontier security. Montcalm also built Fort Carillon, more commonly known as Ticonderoga, at the passage between Lake Champlain and Lake George, where it could serve as a launching pad for an invasion of New York.

The French offensive in North America peaked the following year, when Montcalm led an attack on Fort William Henry, built by William Johnson in 1755 to guard the portage between Lake George and the Hudson River. Montcalm's force was a tableau of New France. In addition to six thousand soldiers, it contained two thousand Indians, including Christian converts from the *reserves* of the St. Lawrence Valley and warriors drawn from the far reaches of the *pays d'en haut*. Montcalm's force dwarfed the twenty-five hundred British regulars, American provincials, and civilians commanded by Lieutenant Colonel George Monro inside the fort's camp. Monro endured the siege for one week, hoping for reinforcements from nearby Fort Edward, but when he received word not to expect any, he negotiated surrender with Montcalm. The French commander, more impressed with Monro's defense of Fort William Henry than what he had seen at Oswego the previous year, offered generous terms, allowing the British to keep their regimental colors, firearms, and personal property in exchange for a promise not to engage in hostilities again for eighteen months.

Such "honors of war" were part of the professional code of conduct that governed eighteenth-century European armies, but they meant nothing to Montcalm's Indian allies, who had traveled great distances to take their own war honors in the form of captives, scalps, and plunder. As the garrison filed out of the fort on the morning of August 10, the French-allied Indians rushed in, killing and scalping the sick and wounded in the fort's hospital and then attacking the column of soldiers and civilians snaking down the road toward Fort Edward. According to eyewitness accounts, the Indians stripped soldiers and officers of their baggage and uniforms, took captives, and pursued those who fled for cover into the surrounding woods. Montcalm and his officers intervened, but their attempts to free captives led some Indian warriors to kill their human prizes on the spot so that they could at least take their scalps home. Judging from the available evidence, the Indians killed between seventy and two hundred people and took approximately three hundred captives, 90 percent of whom were redeemed by year's end. Thanks to James Fenimore Cooper's novel *The Last of the Mohicans* (1826), the Fort William Henry Massacre, as it became known, has become a fixture in American literature and film. The British blamed it on the treachery of the French, and the French on the savagery of the Indians. In hindsight, it is best attributed to the clash between two ways of war: the Native American *la petite guerre* and the new rules of engagement imported by European armies.

While Montcalm was humiliating British forces in New York, a different kind of war raged along the mid-Atlantic frontier. Before 1755 Pennsylvania colonists had enjoyed seventy-five years of peace with their Indian neighbors, a legacy of William Penn's commitment to peaceful coexistence and the pacifism of the colony's Quaker leaders. Penn's heirs, however, shared neither his faith nor idealism. They sought only to govern the colony as cheaply as possible and to profit from its land sales. Their refusal to pay taxes on their landholdings put them at odds with the Quaker-dominated assembly, and so the colony's defenses languished as war loomed in the Ohio country. The panicked retreat of Braddock's army after its defeat in 1755 left the Pennsylvania frontier exposed to the depredations of French and Indian war parties supplied out of Fort Duquesne. Unencumbered by baggage, supplies, or artillery, these parties fanned out in a broad arc from Pennsylvania's Lehigh Valley to Virginia's Shenandoah Valley, conducting surprise raids on widely dispersed settlements of German and Scots-Irish colonists. Many of these communities were only recently settled, made up of squatters who had no official recognition from the colonial governments. As such, they lacked the social cohesion and institutions necessary to mount an effective defense and relied instead on makeshift militias.

War parties terrorized the backcountry, burning homesteads, slaughtering livestock, and killing civilians. In the three years following Braddock's defeat, they took perhaps as many as two thousand captives. Refugees fled eastward with eyewitness accounts of cold-blooded murder and gruesome torture, sometimes parading mutilated corpses through the streets as visual evidence of their suffering. The war ignited a firestorm of anti-Indian rhetoric in newspapers and other public prints, much of it aimed at the Quaker merchants of Philadelphia whose critics accused them of supplying and protecting the colony's Indian enemies. The war exposed the fragility of Pennsylvania's social and political bonds. The colony's diversity of religious and ethnic identities, another legacy of Penn's beliefs, worked against a cooperative response to the crisis.

Virginia shared many of Pennsylvania's liabilities but fared comparatively better. Its backcountry population was also dispersed, ethnically divided, and ill governed; its militia was poorly trained and supplied. But at least it had a militia, which had been mobilized following Washington's misadventures in the Ohio country in 1754. Governor Robert Dinwiddie looked to the Cherokees, the colony's partners in the deerskin trade, for assistance. The Cherokees were receptive to his overtures, seizing the opportunity to cultivate a relationship that would provide them leverage in their diplomacy with South Carolina, but they also grew weary of the Virginians' inability to mount an effective counteroffensive against the French. In 1758 the slow progress of the British war effort in the Ohio country finally caused the Cherokees to defect entirely from it, setting in motion the events that brought Henry Timberlake and Ostenaco together in 1762.

Despite the ineptitude and disunion exhibited by the British in 1756 and 1757, several factors gave them important advantages over the French. William Pitt, who became the king's new prime minister in December 1756, redirected the government's resources away from the war's European theater to North America. Pitt knew that by taking the war to the colonies, he could reverse the advantages in population and military resources that France had in Europe. In America, the French were underpopulated and perennially undersupplied. If the British Navy blockaded the St. Lawrence, New France's miniscule civilian population would be unable to feed its soldiers or supply its Indian allies. The British colonies, on the other hand, had more than enough men and provisions to sustain the British war effort in North America, if given the proper incentives to do so. To ensure the Americans' cooperation, Pitt promised to reimburse the colonial assemblies for appropriations they made to feed and clothe the king's troops, and he declared that henceforth, American officers in provincial commands would rank alongside their peers among the regulars. Their egos and pocketbooks placated, the Americans found their patriotic spirit rejuvenated.

Pitt relieved Loudoun of his command in late 1757 and ordered General Jeffery Amherst to lead an amphibious expedition against Louisbourg, the French fortress at the mouth of the St. Lawrence. Pitt expanded the number of troops available for the king's service in America by simultaneously boosting the recruitment of provincials and sending more regulars across the Atlantic. Amherst sailed for Louisbourg in the summer of 1758 with an army of nine thousand regulars; approximately the same number were serving at the same time elsewhere in North America with approximately twenty thousand provincials; it was a commitment of British military resources to North America that would not be matched again until 1776.

As Pitt finally figured out how to tap the colonies' resources, the French faced the limits of what their colonial infrastructure could provide. Bad harvests in 1756 and 1757 made feeding their military and civilian populations difficult, especially as British warships intercepted supply convoys on the high seas. Many of the Indian allies who had served in the Fort William Henry campaign returned home embittered by its results and unwittingly carried smallpox with them. The subsequent spread of the disease in the *pays d'en haut* dampened the Indians' ardor for war. In 1758 Montcalm found himself on the defensive, facing the first well-coordinated British offensive operations since Braddock had arrived in America three years earlier.

The noose tightened unevenly around the neck of New France. Amherst's siege of Louisbourg was a dramatic victory that showcased the combined power of the British Army and Navy. After enduring a seven-week siege, the French fortress capitulated, opening Canada's front door to the British. Things did not go as well at the back door. In the northern Hudson Valley, General James Abercromby led a combined force of six thousand regulars and ten thousand provincials from Albany to the French position at Ticonderoga on Lake Champlain. Montcalm commanded a much smaller force at Ticonderoga, but his men had constructed an imposing abatis of sharpened logs and trees that guarded the approach to the fort by land. Hearing reports that the arrival of French reinforcements was imminent, Abercromby ordered a frontal attack, despite not having his artillery in place. The results were as devastating as they were predictable. From behind their fortifications, the French mowed down the advancing British. Not trusting in the provincials' resolve under fire, Abercromby sent his regulars repeatedly at the abatis, and the Scottish Highlanders of the 42nd Regiment, also known as the Black Watch, incurred especially heavy losses. The following day, despite the availability of his artillery and remaining troops, Abercromby folded his tent and headed back to Albany.

In the Ohio country, the progress of British arms was slower but steadier. At a series of treaty conferences convened in the Lehigh Valley town of Easton, Pennsylvania, the Pennsylvania government negotiated terms of peace with Indians in the Susquehanna Valley. At the same time, the Moravian missionary Christian Frederick Post and his Delaware partner Pisquetomen conducted behind-the-scenes diplomacy with the Ohio Indians, who agreed to lay down their arms if Pennsylvania renounced fraudulent land purchases made in the Allegheny region and if the British promised to keep settlers out of their homelands.

These terms, formalized in the 1758 Treaty of Easton, restored peace to the Pennsylvania frontier as a combined force of regulars and provincials marched westward toward Fort Duquesne. Nominally commanded by General John Forbes, who spent most of the campaign confined to his sickbed, the expedition was capably orchestrated by Colonel Henry Bouquet, a Swiss officer in the Royal American regiment. Instead of following Braddock's Road to the Forks of the Ohio, Forbes and Bouquet cut their own route westward from Carlisle, Pennsylvania, building forts along the way so that they would not be forced into the sort of all-out retreat that had sunk Braddock's mission. By September British troops were building Fort

Ligonier on Loyalhanna Creek, forty miles east of Fort Duquesne. The French position had become untenable; they could no longer maintain their Indian allies in the face of the Pennsylvanians' diplomacy, and the garrison at Duquesne lacked the provisions necessary to feed itself over the winter. As Forbes's army approached in late November, the French commander blew up Fort Duquesne and pulled his men back to Fort Venango on the Allegheny River. The Forks of the Ohio were finally in British hands.

The British offensive against New France continued in 1759. The British reoccupied Oswego on Lake Ontario in preparation for an assault on Fort Niagara. Aware that the winds of war had changed, the Iroquois became more receptive to William Johnson's diplomacy. In early July, an army of three thousand British regulars and one thousand Iroquois warriors departed for Niagara. The battle that followed was complicated by Native Americans involved on both sides. Shortly after the arrival of the British force, Senecas serving with Johnson expressed reservations about attacking the fort, whose defensive force included about one hundred of their kinfolk. A British commander unfamiliar with Native Americans may have dismissed such reluctance as treachery, but Johnson arranged with the French commander Captain Pierre Pouchot for a parley between the Senecas inside and outside of the fort. After consulting with each other, the two groups of Indians decided it was best to sit this one out, and they decamped upriver to a spot known as La Belle Famille. The British went to work building trenches that would enable them to place artillery within reach of the fort's defenses. Their commander General John Prideaux was killed accidentally by a mortar fired from one of these entrenchments, and William Johnson took his place. The slow progress of the siege continued, as Pouchot held out for reinforcements. Those troops, however, were ambushed by a combined force of redcoats and pro-British Iroquois as they approached the fort. His options exhausted, Pouchot surrendered the most important French post west of the St. Lawrence.

During that same summer, Amherst—now commander in chief of British forces in North America—gathered an army in Albany for an advance against Canada. In July he moved against Ticonderoga, but the French commander there withdrew northward and blew up the fort before it could fall into British hands. Not long afterward, the French continued their withdrawal from Lake Champlain by blowing up Fort St. Frédéric at Crown Point. The door was now open for a British invasion of Canada by way of the Champlain corridor, but the season was too far advanced for Amherst to press on.

Britain's 1759 campaign in North America was not over yet. James Wolfe, who had served under Amherst during the Louisbourg expedition, had been promoted to general and placed in charge of an ambitious plan to attack Quebec by way of the St. Lawrence. Pitt placed an army of nine thousand regulars and a fleet of warships at Wolfe's disposal. Their objective was the symbolic and political heart of New France, protected by natural and man-made defenses. Wolfe's fleet arrived within range of the city in early July. A prolonged game of cat-and-mouse followed, as Montcalm tried to anticipate where the British forces would land and

Wolfe probed for weaknesses in the French defenses. The civilian population suffered severely. Having already endured prolonged food shortages, they now had to deal with American Rangers who terrorized the countryside by burning and looting homes and farms. On the night of September 12, Wolfe landed approximately half of his men under cover of darkness and had them scale a cliff to the Plains of Abraham, high ground that commanded the city. As dawn arrived, Montcalm scrambled to redeploy troops to meet Wolfe's force. Not waiting for reinforcements that could have challenged the British from the rear, Montcalm hastily drew his troops into formation and marched on Wolfe. The British regulars ably dispersed the French force, and Montcalm and Wolfe received mortal wounds. Benjamin West's painting *The Death of Wolfe* (1771) lionized its subject as a martyr and became the most famous visual artifact of the war.

The fall of Quebec capped a remarkable year for British arms around the globe. Not only had France been brought to its knees in North America, but British land and sea power had also delivered blows to the French in Europe, India, and the Caribbean. The following summer, Amherst led a flotilla of ships carrying ten thousand troops from Oswego down the St. Lawrence toward Montreal, the last French stronghold in Canada. Accompanied by several hundred Iroquois warriors, Amherst arrived at Montreal with overwhelming numbers. The French governor-general surrendered in September 1760.

The conquest of Canada brought joyous celebrations on both sides of the British Atlantic. It also ignited a debate over whether or not Britain should return Canada to France in the peace negotiations. William Pitt led the charge for those who believed that restoring conquests abroad would only enhance France's power at home. Pitt's opponents believed that Canada was too big and too desolate to be governed effectively or profitably; they advocated instead returning it to France in exchange for sugar colonies in the Caribbean. The debate, carried out in British newspapers and pamphlets as well as the council chambers of government, testified to how the war had transformed Britain's view of America. Policy makers no longer regarded the colonies as a collection of backwater settlements. America had suddenly assumed great significance in British geopolitics.

Pitt resigned as prime minister in October 1761, displeased by the king's refusal to declare war against Spain, which had entered into an alliance with France. The following year, Britain declared war on Spain anyway, and in another wave of near-miraculous military campaigns, conquered Havana, the crown jewel of the Spanish Caribbean, and Manila, the key to the Philippines. These victories strengthened the British hand in the negotiations that produced the Peace of Paris in 1763. France surrendered all its possessions in North America east of the Mississippi to the British, except for New Orleans, which went to the Spanish, as did the vast Louisiana territory west of the Mississippi. In exchange for the return of Havana, the Spanish surrendered Florida to the British. Britain restored some but not all of the Caribbean islands it had seized from the French and likewise kept recent conquests from the French in India. The British also restored Manila to the Spanish and Gorée, a West African trading post, to the French. This reconfiguration of chess pieces among Europe's imperial powers committed Britain to governing dominions of continental dimensions in North America and India.

The first tests of British resolve in that regard arose in North America even before the peace treaty was signed. Along the Appalachian frontier, hostilities between the Southern colonies and the Cherokees continued despite the progress of British arms elsewhere. South Carolina governor William Henry Lyttelton exacerbated the situation by seizing Cherokee diplomats as hostages and holding them at Fort Prince George in the Carolina backcountry. When Cherokee warriors attacked the fort in early 1760, its defenders murdered the hostages, which prompted wider Cherokee reprisals against traders and settlers. Amherst dispatched regular troops to the region, who conducted a scorched earth campaign against several Cherokee towns. In July the Cherokees attacked Fort Loudoun, an isolated British post near modern Knoxville, Tennessee, and turned on the garrison after it surrendered, taking scalps and captives as vengeance for what had happened at Fort Prince George. Amherst ordered another campaign through Cherokee territory in 1761, which ended ultimately in the uneasy peace that brought together Timberlake and Ostenaco in their diplomatic mission.

Anglo-Indian hostilities also flared along the Great Lakes region after British soldiers occupied the former French trading posts in the *pays d'en haut*. William Johnson, appointed by the Crown as its superintendent of Indian affairs for the Northern colonies in 1756, convened a treaty conference in Detroit in 1761 with over five hundred Indians formerly allied with the French. He spoke eloquently of extending the Covenant Chain alliance and promised to exhibit the king's generosity as he stepped into the shoes of the French, but real grievances remained unaddressed. British forces had not withdrawn east of the mountains, as promised at the Treaty of Easton. Instead, they constructed the even bigger Fort Pitt where Fort Duquesne had stood. Furthermore, the wartime construction of Braddock's Road and Forbes's Road opened routes west into the Ohio country for squatters who cared little about Indian claims to the land. Nor did Amherst's actions as commander in chief inspire much regard for him and his fellow officers among Indians. As a cost-cutting measure, Amherst ordered Johnson to cease giving diplomatic presents to the Indians now that it was no longer necessary to woo them away from the French. He ordered traders to curtail the sale of gunpowder to Indians as well. The Indians of the *pays d'en haut* interpreted these measures as insults to their status as allies and threats to their livelihood.

In the spring of 1763, an Ottawa war chief named Pontiac led warriors from the Ottawa, Potawatomi, Ojibwa, and Wyandot nations in an attack on Fort Detroit. Throughout the *pays d'en haut*, other Indians followed suit, easily overcoming smaller posts and laying siege to the larger British garrisons at Niagara and Fort Pitt. At the same time, war parties launched new raids on the backcountry population, taking captives and creating another wave of panicked refugees. On both sides, this conflict was marked by an escalation in the language of separation and annihilation. Pontiac was inspired by the Delaware prophet Neolin, who claimed that during a trance-like vision, the Master of Life had told him to revive ancient rituals, abstain from the white man's liquor, and unite Indians in resistance to encroachments on their land. This spiritual message of keeping a cultural and physical distance from whites became a powerful unifying force among Indians of the trans-Appalachian frontier.

On the British side, the rhetoric of Indian-hating grew more extreme among British soldiers and colonial civilians. From the outset of hostilities, Amherst ordered his officers to retaliate without mercy and tacitly endorsed the execution of Indian prisoners. As Colonel Henry Bouquet led a relief column toward the besieged Fort Pitt in the summer of 1763, Amherst wrote to him inquiring about the potential use of germ warfare: "Could it not be contrived to Send the Small Pox among those Disaffected Tribes of Indians? We must, on this occasion, Use Every Stratagem in our power to Reduce them." Bouquet promised to investigate the possibility, but in fact, the commander of Fort Pitt had already taken such steps independently. During a parley he distributed blankets and handkerchiefs taken from smallpox sufferers in the fort's hospital to some Delaware chiefs. A fur trader inside the fort wrote of this exchange in his journal, "I hope it will have the desired effect."[10] Elsewhere in Pennsylvania, a group of Scots-Irish settlers from the Paxton region in the lower Susquehanna Valley murdered all the inhabitants of a small Indian community in Lancaster County. The cold-blooded nature of the Paxton Boys' attack on Conestoga Indian Town shocked many colonial observers. The town's twenty or so inhabitants were poor, peaceful, and isolated from other Indians, posing no threat to their white neighbors. But others defended the Paxton Boys' actions, describing all Indians as potentially treacherous enemies who deserved only exile or extermination.

Pontiac's War disrupted Britain's pacification of North America after the Seven Years' War, but the Indians lacked the firepower necessary to deliver a decisive blow to their new enemy. Without artillery, the Indians who laid siege to Detroit, Pitt, and Niagara could not breach the walls of those forts, and reinforcements were eventually able to reach them. With the fall hunting season approaching, Indian warriors deserted the fight and saved their dwindling ammunition to provide for their families. As Johnson worked his diplomatic network to restore peace, Bouquet marched an army of redcoats into the Ohio country in 1764 to force the repatriation of captives (see Figure 11.2). Meanwhile, the uncertain state of affairs in America convinced the British Crown of the need to assert a stronger hand there. In October 1763, the Crown issued a proclamation imposing a boundary line between colonial and Indian lands that ran north-to-south along the Appalachian Mountains (see Map 11.2). Colonists were prohibited from settling west of the line until royal agents negotiated land sales from the land's native owners. The Proclamation of 1763 displeased colonial elites such as George Washington who had invested in speculative ventures in the Ohio country, but it marked a new effort by the Crown to mediate between the native and colonial people it claimed as subjects in North America. It also committed the Crown to keeping an army of several thousand redcoats in North America to police a vast and hostile frontier.

Figure 11.2 Benjamin West, *Indians Delivering Up the English Prisoners to Colonel Bouquet* (London, 1766). During Pontiac's War, British commander Colonel Henry Bouquet marched an army into the Ohio country to dictate peace terms to the Delaware and Shawnee Indians. Bouquet insisted on the repatriation of all captives taken during the previous decade of war, even those unwilling to leave their adopted families. For a London publication, artist Benjamin West engraved this scene of the return of the captives, emphasizing the emotional bonds between captives and captors that were being severed by Bouquet's directive. Courtesy of the John Carter Brown Library at Brown University.

IMPERIAL AMBITIONS AND COLONIAL REALITIES

The expectations and disappointments that accompanied the end of the Seven Years' War in America were reflected in the careers of Henry Timberlake and Ostenaco after their embassy to London in 1762. Like many colonial Americans who served during the war, Timberlake had hitched his personal ambitions to the British Empire. His military service exposed him to many dangers but also opened many doors. In a year's time, he had gone from smoking peace pipes with Cherokee chiefs in the Virginia backcountry to persuading his Cherokee companion not to

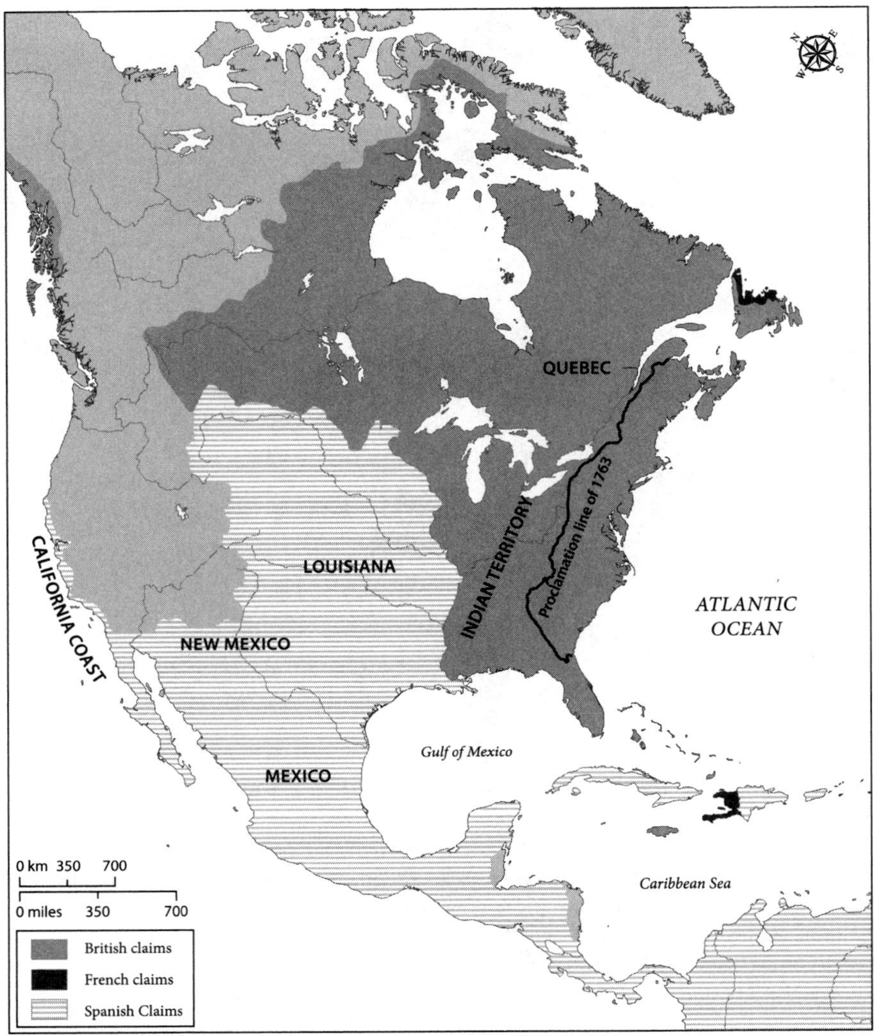

Map. 11.2 North America in 1763.

light one up at St. James's Palace in London. His efforts in guiding the Cherokee embassy of 1762 did bring him a lieutenant's commission in the British Army, a position that promised him a salary, pension, and potentially more patronage back in America. Unfortunately, upon reporting for duty in New York in 1763, he found out that his salary had been halved by budget cuts. In financial straits, he agreed to lead another Cherokee embassy to London in 1764. This time, two of the five Cherokee chiefs traveling with him died during the trip, and no government officials would receive the survivors as official guests of state. Apparently, neither the government nor the public had forgotten Ostenaco's embarrassment at Vauxhall Garden during Timberlake's previous visit. Unable to pay for the Cherokees' stay in London, Timberlake sent them home. Hoping to vindicate his conduct, he wrote *The Memoirs of Lieut. Henry Timberlake* but died shortly before the book was published in 1765.

Like Timberlake, many other colonial Americans found that the doors of opportunity opened for them by the Seven Years' War closed unexpectedly in its aftermath. Land speculators and squatters resented the Crown's attempts to proscribe western land sales and settlement. Nor did the traders and merchants involved in the fur trade appreciate new regulations on their business imposed by royal Indian superintendents. Merchants who had profited handsomely by trading illegally with their French and Spanish counterparts in the Caribbean during the Seven Years' War found themselves subject to prosecution in the navy's crackdown on smuggling after the war. The American colonists, who had expended far more blood and treasure in fighting the Seven Years' War than in all the previous imperial wars combined, felt pride and patriotism for their contribution to British victory. They were not prepared to be regarded as wayward children by military and civilian officials who believed they failed to exhibit proper subordination to royal power.

For Native Americans, the Seven Years' War also recalibrated the balance of power in North America. Compared to Timberlake, Ostenaco fared well after returning from his 1762 trip to Britain. His humiliation in London did not end his diplomatic career in America. He was one of the Cherokee delegates at the Treaty of Augusta in November 1763, which negotiated the boundary line between whites and Indians in the Southern colonies. Among the Cherokees, Ostenaco remained a strong advocate of the British, an alliance that would cost them dearly during the American Revolution. He died in 1780, as the empire his diplomacy had helped shape was once again collapsing into violence.

The demise of French power in North America made it impossible for native confederacies such as the Iroquois and Cherokees to play one European power off the other as they had after 1689. The Seven Years' War had eroded, if not entirely erased, the ground available for savvy neutrality and opportunistic alliance. In the decade following 1763, the focus of Anglo-Indian diplomacy shifted away from matters of trade and warfare toward land. As Indians struggled to stem the tide of settlers and squatters into their homelands, royal agents negotiated treaties and land purchases that pushed the boundary line farther west, slicing away portions of Indian territory in New York, Pennsylvania, Virginia, and the Carolinas. The intercultural diplomacy that had enabled Indian nations, colonial governments, and imperial powers to mediate their differences before 1754 became during the 1760s primarily a ritual of dispossession, a means of giving legitimacy to the kind of land-grabbing that had caused the Seven Years' War to erupt in the first place.

For France and Spain, 1763 marked an important turning point in their imperial designs in North America. With the cession of Canada to Britain and Louisiana to Spain, France abandoned its hopes of creating an interior American dominion that would have confined the British colonies to the Atlantic coast and made possible French expansion from the Appalachians to the Pacific. French colonial interests shifted entirely to the Caribbean sugar colonies of Sainte-Domingue, Martinique, and Guadeloupe. A generation later, Napoleon briefly revived French ambitions in North America, but his sale of Louisiana to the United States in 1803 settled the matter for good. Spain gambled and lost spectacularly when it entered the Seven Years' War, but its humiliations inspired initiatives and reforms in its colonial administration that led to a renaissance of sorts for its American empire. Convinced that the independence of the church and its missionaries had weakened royal power in Spanish colonies, the Crown expelled the Jesuits from Spanish America and sent a wave of new civilian officials to rationalize and strengthen government there. It loosened trade restrictions on colonial ports, which stimulated commerce and economic production. During the 1760s and 1770s, the Spanish also undertook new colonial ventures in California, Arizona, Texas, and the recently acquired Louisiana, expanding their defensive perimeter around New Mexico and Mexico. Although it remained much weaker than Britain, Spain had no intention of abandoning its North American empire, and in 1783 it won back Florida from the British in the peace that ended the American War for Independence.

Victory in war can sometimes be just as burdensome as defeat. In the decade after the Peace of Paris, Britain certainly found that to be true as it tried to reckon with the colonial and native inhabitants of North America. In their decision to retain Canada as a wartime conquest, British policy makers found that what had begun as a collection of privately funded and governed colonies had become a new continental dominion full of militant natives and independently minded colonists, all in need of stricter government and economic regulation. The responsibilities and costs of empire—of protecting it from foreign enemies, policing its trade, and keeping the peace among its component parts—skyrocketed with victory. After 1763 officeholders and policy makers on both sides of the Atlantic faced the unpleasant task of subjecting this unruly beast to some kind of coherent order.

CHRONOLOGY

1689–1697	War of the Grand Alliance (King William's War in America).
1701	"Grand Settlement" initiates Iroquois neutrality between the French and English.
1702–1713	War of the Spanish Succession (Queen Anne's War in America).
1739–1744	War of Jenkins's Ear between the Spanish and British in the Caribbean.
1741	Cartagena expedition proves disastrous for British forces.
1744–1748	War of the Austrian Succession (King George's War in America).
1745	New England forces are victorious in an expedition against the French fortress of Louisbourg on Cape Breton.

1749	Captain Pierre-Joseph Céloron de Blainville's expedition expels British traders from Ohio country.
1754	George Washington's surrender at Fort Necessity.
1755	July: General Edward Braddock's defeat on the Monongahela River. September: Battle of Lake George.
1756	French capture Fort Oswego.
1757	French capture Fort William Henry.
1758	July: French repulse British attack on Ticonderoga. July: Louisbourg falls to British siege. October: Treaty of Easton establishes peace between the Ohio Indians and the British. November: French abandon Fort Duquesne to advancing British forces.
1759	July: French surrender Fort Niagara to the British. September: General James Wolfe leads victorious attack on Quebec.
1759–1761	*Cherokee War brings Henry Timberlake and Ostenaco together in Overhill country (eastern Tennessee).*
1760	General Jeffrey Amherst takes Montreal; New France surrenders to the British.
1762	*Timberlake and Ostenaco travel to London and meet King George III.*
1763	February: Peace of Paris ends Seven Years' War. May: Pontiac's War erupts in *pays d'en haut*. October: Proclamation of 1763 prohibits colonial settlements and land purchases west of the Appalachian Mountains.

NOTES

1. Henry Timberlake, *The Memoirs of Lt. Henry Timberlake: The Story of a Soldier, Adventurer, and Emissary to the Cherokees, 1756–1765*, ed. Duane H. King (Cherokee, NC: Museum of the Cherokee Indian Press, 2007), 55.
2. Timberlake, *Memoirs of Lt. Henry Timberlake*, 72.
3. Timberlake, *Memoirs of Lt. Henry Timberlake*, 62.
4. Howard Peckham, *The Colonial Wars, 1689–1763* (Chicago: University of Chicago Press, 1964), 114, 116.
5. Benjamin Franklin to James Parker, March 20, 1751, *The Papers of Benjamin Franklin*, eds. Leonard W. Labaree, et al., 39 vols. (New Haven, CT: Yale University Press, 1959–), Vol. 4, 118–119.
6. John Williams, "The Redeemed Captive, Returning to Zion" (1707), in *Puritans Among the Indians: Accounts of Captivity and Redemption, 1676–1724*, eds. Alden T. Vaughan and Edward W. Clark (Cambridge, MA: Harvard University Press, 1981), 193.
7. *Papers of Benjamin Franklin*, Vol. 4, 233.

8. *Pennsylvania Gazette*, May 9, 1754.
9. Fred Anderson, *A People's Army: Massachusetts Soldiers and Society in the Seven Years' War* (New York: Norton, 1984), 77.
10. Colin G. Calloway, *A Scratch of the Pen: 1763 and the Transformation of North America* (New York: Oxford University Press, 2006), 73.

SUGGESTIONS FOR FURTHER READING

For the Cherokees' 1762 embassy to London, see Henry Timberlake, *The Memoirs of Lt. Henry Timberlake: The Story of a Soldier, Adventurer, and Emissary to the Cherokees, 1756–1765*, ed. Duane H. King (1765; Cherokee, NC: Museum of the Cherokee Indian Press, 2007). See also John Oliphant, *Peace and War on the Anglo-Cherokee Frontier, 1756–1763* (Baton Rouge: Louisiana State University Press, 2001), and Alden T. Vaughan, *Transatlantic Encounters: American Indians in Britain, 1500–1776* (Cambridge, UK: Cambridge University Press, 2006).

There are several good surveys of the imperial wars in North America, including Howard H. Peckham, *The Colonial Wars, 1689–1762* (Chicago: University of Chicago Press, 1964); Douglas Edward Leach, *Arms for Empire: A Military History of the British Colonies in North America, 1607–1763* (New York: Macmillan, 1973); and Ian K. Steele, *Warpaths: Invasions of North America* (New York: Oxford University Press, 1994). For the British perspective on these conflicts, see Lawrence Stone, ed., *An Imperial State at War: Britain from 1689 to 1815* (New York: Routledge, 1994), and Bruce Lenman, *Britain's Colonial Wars, 1688–1783* (Harlow, UK: Longman, 2001). For the French perspective, see W. J. Eccles, *The Canadian Frontier, 1534–1760*, rev. ed. (Albuquerque: University of New Mexico Press, 1983), and Guy Frégault, *Canada: The War of the Conquest*, trans. Margaret M. Cameron (Toronto: Oxford University Press, 1969). For the native perspective, see Richard White, *The Middle Ground: Indians, Empires, and Republics in the Great Lakes Region, 1650–1815* (Cambridge, UK: Cambridge University Press, 1991), and Daniel K. Richter, *Facing East from Indian Country: A Native History of Early America* (Cambridge, MA: Harvard University Press, 2001).

The methods and objectives of Native American warfare and diplomacy with imperial powers are described in Ian K. Steele, *Betrayals: Fort William Henry and the "Massacre"* (New York: Oxford University Press, 1990); Timothy J. Shannon, *Iroquois Diplomacy on the Early American Frontier* (New York: Penguin, 2008); and Eric Hinderaker, *The Two Hendricks: Unraveling a Mohawk Mystery* (Cambridge, MA: Harvard University Press, 2010). For colonial mobilization and participation in the imperial wars, see Alexander V. Campbell, *The Royal American Regiment: An Atlantic Microcosm, 1755–1772* (Norman: University of Oklahoma Press, 2010); Harold E. Selesky, *War and Society in Colonial Connecticut* (New Haven, CT: Yale University Press, 1990); and Fred Anderson, *A People's Army: Massachusetts Soldiers and Society in the Seven Years' War* (Chapel Hill: University of North Carolina Press, 1984). The experiences of Indian captives are described in John Demos, *The Unredeemed Captive: A Family Story from Early America* (New York: Knopf, 1994), and Evan Haefeli and Kevin Sweeney, *Captors and Captives: The 1704 French and Indian Raid on Deerfield* (Amherst: University of Massachusetts Press, 2003). The rising significance of the British Empire in colonial political culture is described in Brendan McConville, *The King's Three Faces: The Rise and Fall of Royal America, 1688–1776* (Chapel Hill: University of North Carolina Press, 2006).

The most comprehensive, one-volume study of the Seven Years' War is Fred Anderson, *Crucible of War: The Seven Years' War and the Fate of Empire in British North America, 1754–1766* (New York: Knopf, 2000). The war is examined from French, British, Anglo-American, and native perspectives in Warren R. Hofstra, ed., *Cultures in Conflict: The Seven Years' War in North America* (Lanham, MD: Rowman & Littlefield, 2007). For the war's impact on the backcountry, see Matthew C. Ward, *Breaking the Backcountry: The Seven Years' War in Virginia and Pennsylvania, 1754–1765* (Pittsburgh: University of Pittsburgh Press, 2003). For its impact on the Iroquois, see David L. Preston, *The Texture of Contact: European and Indian Settler Communities on the Frontiers of Iroquoia, 1667–1783* (Lincoln: University of Nebraska Press, 2009), and Gail D. MacLeitch, *Imperial Entanglements: Iroquois Change and Persistence on the Frontiers of Empire* (Philadelphia: University of Pennsylvania Press, 2011). The experiences of British regulars in North America are the subject of Michael N. McConnell, *Army and Empire: British Soldiers on the American Frontier, 1758–1775* (Lincoln: University of Nebraska Press, 2004), and Stephen Brumwell, *Redcoats: The British Soldier and War in the Americas, 1755–1763* (Cambridge, UK: Cambridge University Press, 2002).

The legacies of the Seven Years' War are described in Colin G. Calloway, *The Scratch of a Pen: 1763 and the Transformation of North America* (New York: Oxford, 2006); Gregory Evans Dowd, *War under Heaven: Pontiac, the Indian Nations, and the British Empire* (Baltimore: Johns Hopkins University Press, 2002); and John Shy, *Toward Lexington: The Role of the British Army in the Coming of the American Revolution* (Princeton, NJ: Princeton University Press, 1965). Two useful studies that examine the war's impact on Anglo-Indian relations are Kevin Kenny, *Peaceable Kingdom Lost: The Paxton Boys and the Destruction of William Penn's Holy Experiment* (New York: Oxford University Press, 2009), and Peter Silver, *Our Savage Neighbors: How Indian War Transformed Early America* (New York: Norton, 2008). For the war's impact on European empires in North America, see Paul W. Mapp, *The Elusive West and the Contest for Empire, 1713–1763* (Chapel Hill: University of North Carolina Press, 2011).

Epilogue

North America in 1764

Four years of college down the drain. That's the fate eighteen-year-old John Jay faced in April 1764, suspended for refusing to reveal the names of the culprits in a bit of student vandalism at New York City's King's College. Jay contended that nothing in the college's 1763 statutes, to which every student pledged to abide, required him to divulge who destroyed the table in question. But the faculty was unpersuaded by this argument. Mercifully, college president Myles Cooper reinstated young John prior to his May 22 graduation.[1]

Other people faced much bigger personal problems in May 1764. On April 22, twenty-five-year-old Harry, also known as Traso, decided he had had enough of his master, Samuel Cock, and enough of slavery itself (see Figure 12.1). Harry might go far. The Sussex County, New Jersey, master posted his runaway advertisement in the *New-York Mercury*, published dozens of miles away in Manhattan,

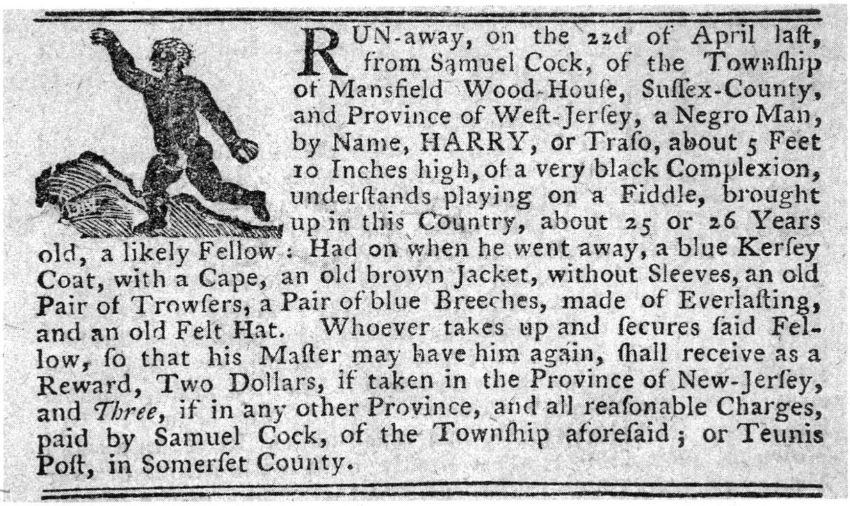

RUN-away, on the 22d of April laſt, from Samuel Cock, of the Townſhip of Mansfield Wood-Houſe, Suſſex-County, and Province of Weſt-Jerſey, a Negro Man, by Name, HARRY, or Traſo, about 5 Feet 10 Inches high, of a very black Complexion, underſtands playing on a Fiddle, brought up in this Country, about 25 or 26 Years old, a likely Fellow: Had on when he went away, a blue Kerſey Coat, with a Cape, an old brown Jacket, without Sleeves, an old Pair of Trowſers, a Pair of blue Breeches, made of Everlaſting, and an old Felt Hat. Whoever takes up and ſecures ſaid Fellow, ſo that his Maſter may have him again, ſhall receive as a Reward, Two Dollars, if taken in the Province of New-Jerſey, and *Three*, if in any other Province, and all reaſonable Charges, paid by Samuel Cock, of the Townſhip aforeſaid; or Teunis Poſt, in Somerſet County.

Figure 12.1 Newspaper advertisement, *New-York Mercury*, May 21, 1764. Harry, also known as Traso, ran away from his New Jersey slave master, who offered a reward for his return. Such advertisements provide concrete evidence of a common form of slave resistance, as well as details about the lives of individual slaves. Collection of the New York Historical Society, Digital ID #86594d.

on May 14 and then again on May 21, offering 50 percent more ($3 instead of $2) if Harry were caught outside of New Jersey. Harry may have only escaped with the clothes on his back and "an old Felt Hat," but he hardly was without resources, having been born in America and knowing how to play the fiddle. Although very few masters liberated their slaves in this era, a busy port city like New York, with ships clearing out to England, Canada, and the West Indies, might not have been a bad bet for seeking to start life anew. But even if Harry did manage to elude Cock, his prospects were infinitely worse than wealthy and well-educated John Jay, soon to begin his training as a lawyer and, as it turned out, an illustrious career of public service.

Simultaneously making, breaking, learning, and living by the rules, colonial Americans negotiated a world markedly different from the one their African, Indian, and European forebears had encountered over the previous two-and-a-half centuries. Some of these changes bore the impress of recent events, others occurred through the accretion of time and an almost infinite number of personal experiences.

The rules governing the relationship between the British Empire and colonial North America were simultaneously new and old in 1764. Europeans would continue to expect Indians to abide by boundaries drawn on European maps of North America and would seek acknowledgment of the British king's sovereign superiority. But Pontiac had proved that absent the French, the British would have to learn the intercultural rules necessary to negotiate and trade, rather than conquer, in the *pays d'en haut*. At the 1768 Treaty of Fort Stanwix, the Iroquois demonstrated that they played by rules of their own, ceding land that they did not control or occupy to Virginia and Pennsylvania. Meanwhile, the rumor that southern Indians might form new native alliances against the British convinced imperial officials that war would break out if colonial land speculators were allowed to lay claim to western territory. Ordinary white settlers, nonetheless, continued to move west as squatters into the prohibited regions, also making their own rules.

Even so, for Anglo-American colonists, the Empire loomed large. Indeed, there had been much in which to take pride about their British identity in the years just prior to 1764. Colonists could celebrate Prime Minister William Pitt's willingness to finance the colonies' role in ultimately defeating France, the ascent of new king George III to the throne, and the massive amount of North American territory added to the British realm through the Peace of Paris. Meanwhile, the basic outline of the Navigation Acts defining colonial trade had been in place for a century, with most of the details filled in for almost as long as anyone could remember. With a few notable outliers, the royalization of the colonies had also been completed decades before. If Benjamin Franklin and his allies were to have their way, Pennsylvania would soon be added to the royal fold. All the colonies were supposed to trade with and through the mother country. They also were expected to work with the colonial governors and customs officials the mother country rotated through the Americas.

Colonists had learned to treat rules and rulers as more flexible than the letter of imperial law might imply. Suspicion of royal governors and other imperial officeholders kept the property-holding electorate alert, adding volatility to the politics of what were, from the perspective of London, unsophisticated backwater provinces. Some American merchants and traders, meanwhile, observed a loose interpretation of Britain's trade monopoly—when they did not see fit to ignore those provisions entirely. British officials found it appalling that even in wartime, American traders did business with the French colonies. On the oceanic highway of the Atlantic, colonists used exits and entrances at their discretion, often ignoring the "do not enter" signs. But since Britain had access to the best goods and the most ships, the mercantilist regime still remained quite profitable.

Meanwhile, British authorities had decided that tightening the old rules and adding new rules were both in order, expecting compliance from the Crown's grateful and patriotic subjects. The twin blows of Pontiac's Rebellion and the Proclamation of 1763 drove home to the colonists that winning the west through war and diplomacy with France was not the same as the colonists themselves taking possession of the land and dispossessing its Indian inhabitants. A new initiative, crystallized in the Sugar Act of April 1764, aimed to eliminate illegal trade with the French Caribbean sugar islands, which the French had retained at the cost of Canada. The duty on foreign sugar was cut in half, but the English expected to collect it—bringing former smugglers out of the shadows. There was more at work than a new, by-the-book attitude. The Empire had placed itself on more expensive footing by financing its victory over France with deficit spending and by making the decision to keep 10,000 soldiers on active duty in America. In theory, a colonial population that had already surged well past 1.5 million could surely absorb the presence of a mere 10,000 with little stress. But postwar depression in America's port cities made the notion of competing with off-duty redcoats for jobs and paying additional taxes unsavory. Moreover, in a political culture that viewed standing armies with the utmost suspicion, the presence of so many troops could look downright sinister.

Many Americans paid little heed to the soldiers of the king, not because they were naïve or unsophisticated, but because they etched their big pictures on different landscapes. In 1760 birthrates for white colonists reached what would turn out to be a peak that would never again be exceeded, while black birthrates continued on an upward trajectory that persisted into the nineteenth century. While mapping these trends became a job for twentieth- and twenty-first-century social scientists, an astute eighteenth-century observer could tell that colonists had proven themselves extraordinarily successful at growing the size of their own families and of the colonial population at large. In 1751 Benjamin Franklin depicted in his "Observations Concerning the Increase of Mankind" a flourishing population doubling every two decades, a reasonably accurate assessment.

A rapidly growing population could be a double-edged sword. After a brief period of infancy and toddlerhood, children became workers, capable—with increasing skill, strength, and stamina—of sustaining farm, garden, and household.

Indeed, if children did their jobs right and if mothers and fathers supervised them effectively, over time children would contribute to the farm's surplus rather than draining it. Even in modestly productive regions, a surplus was essential, since few households actually produced everything needed for survival let alone comfort. But productivity was essential for still another reason. Male children would need resources to form their own families and female children would need to find partners who could do so. This meant that families had to produce enough wealth for the purchase of additional lands, or in the case of unusually well-placed or ambitious families, purchase or provide for the training of a profession, such as lawyer or minister. Those colonial fathers who commanded slave labor forces still faced the same challenge of providing land and gentility for their children to replicate the way of life that their own forebears had established. Land was not infinite, but the need to sustain and extend family well-being was a responsibility that colonial parents had to embrace, which meant locating markets in which to sell whatever surpluses they could generate.

In terms of population, colonists born in America could sustain themselves through natural means. That did not stop them, however, from importing thousands upon thousands of African slaves to grow the staples they would sell internationally. Established colonists also witnessed the arrival of assorted European immigrants, some indentured, others at liberty. In the same essay in which Franklin charted the colonies' demographic good fortune, he expressed his distaste for German immigration to what he thought should be an English land.

Clearly, pluralism generated its share of discontents. Whites could never be certain that black slaves were not plotting against them collectively and knew for sure that individuals such as the runaway Harry had other aspirations than lives of permanent servitude. Although notions of race remained inchoate, the daily distinctions made between black and white registered clearly enough on plantations and in homes, as well as being codified in laws drafted by generations of elected representatives with little guidance from the mother country. At the same time, frontier violence between settlers and natives drove home to new generations of white colonists what their forebears had concluded at various moments—that the interests of whites and Indians did not coincide and that, religious conversion or not, their identities did not overlap in any meaningful ways. If comfortably situated Eastern elites forgot this point, then frontier whites such as Pennsylvania's Paxton Boys stood ready to remind them. Whites of various ethnicities could forge common ground on such points even if Europeans of varying ethnicities did not always value each other's presence.

Ethnic homogeneity did not guarantee social peace, as Americans throughout the colonies in 1764 groped for ways to accommodate their differences. The Great Awakening's intense impact on New England was two decades in the past, but divisions and resentments lingered in some towns. The opportunities for dissenters, sometimes treated as heretics in the previous century, to establish their own churches continued to grow. Meanwhile, imported goods and fashions made their way into households great and humble across the colonies and into the interior of the continent. A hat or a tea cup did not make a poor man rich or a German woman English, or a slave a free man. But the rising power and appeal of British commerce provided new class markers and new ways to transcend class boundaries, new objects of desire that old ideals of work might help satisfy. Patriarchal rules, like imperial ones, privileged the authority of fathers, masters, ministers, and governors without completely binding the imagination of young people, women, and slaves.

The rules broken by the college student John Jay and the runaway slave Harry were, and they had every reason to believe would continue to be, colonial rules. They and their fellow Americans were provincial and cosmopolitan. The day before John Jay's graduation, in the same newspaper that again announced Sam Cock's claim on his runaway human property, Sidney Breese advertised an impressive array of textiles designed to dress up, indeed beautify, life and even death on the eastern edge of Britain's western empire: "Very rich Brocades... English Damask... rich Satttins... Velvets, Ribbonds, Mens Silk Hose, Mens and Womens thread... Irish Linnens, common and fine for Burials...." Drawing attention to this list, in much larger fonts, were "A great Variety of Looking-Glasses, Pictures and Looking-Glasses" (see Figure 12.2). The mirrors that Breese wished his customers to hold up to themselves on this spring day in 1764 were for personal vanity, not soul searching, let alone broad historical reflection.

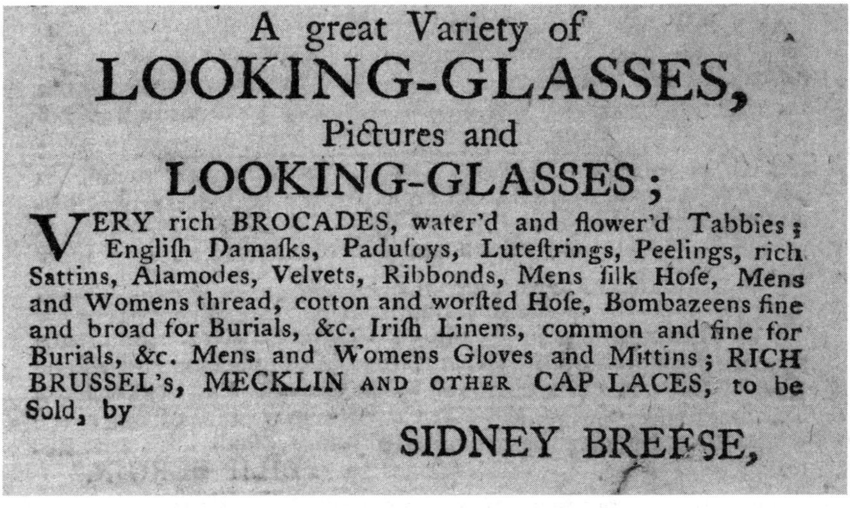

A great Variety of
LOOKING-GLASSES,
Pictures and
LOOKING-GLASSES;

VERY rich BROCADES, water'd and flower'd Tabbies; Engliſh Damaſks, Paduſoys, Luteſtrings, Peelings, rich Sattins, Alamodes, Velvets, Ribbonds, Mens ſilk Hoſe, Mens and Womens thread, cotton and worſted Hoſe, Bombazeens fine and broad for Burials, &c. Iriſh Linens, common and fine for Burials, &c. Mens and Womens Gloves and Mittins; RICH BRUSSEL's, MECKLIN AND OTHER CAP LACES, to be Sold, by

SIDNEY BREESE,

Figure 12.2 **Newspaper advertisement, *New-York Mercury*, May 21, 1764. Merchant Sidney Breese sought to attract customers with a variety of fabrics and clothes, highlighting the sale of mirrors in which they could examine their newly fashioned selves. Courtesy, American Antiquarian Society.**

If we hold up a mirror to colonial American society in 1764, we will not see our twenty-first century selves reflected, or even their more immediate revolutionary future. But if we look carefully, we can see a variety of pasts in Breese's looking-glasses—pasts lived in a set of diverse colonies stitched into the Atlantic World by trade and material ambition. A past full of choices and reinventions, made against the backdrop of intense conflict and sometimes even more intense private convictions. A past where the advancement of one person's or one ethnic group's definition of civilization or gentility was shadowed by violence, as well as the unpredictable certainty of death. In 1764, as at every stage of colonial history from 1492 to 1763, North America's inhabitants launched odysseys pregnant with possibilities on a continent both rich and raw with strife.

NOTE

1. Richard B. Morris, *John Jay: The Making of a Revolutionary: Unpublished Papers, 1745–1780* (New York: Harper & Row, 1975), 55–60.

SUGGESTIONS FOR FURTHER READING

For valuable vistas on colonial politics and society in the 1760s, see Collin G. Calloway, *The Scratch of a Pen: 1763 and the Transformation of North America* (New York: Oxford University Press, 2006); Woody Holton, *Forced Founders: Indians, Debtors, Slaves, & the Making of the American Revolution in Virginia* (Chapel Hill: University of North Carolina Press, 1999); Susan E. Klepp, *Revolutionary Conceptions: Women, Fertility, & Family Limitation in America, 1760–1820* (Chapel Hill: University of North Carolina Press, 2009); and Richard Lyman Bushman, "Markets and Composite Farms in Early America," *William and Mary Quarterly*, 3d ser., 55 (1998): 351–374.

INDEX